ISBN 978-0-332-48179-1
PIBN 11233591

Twenty-Ninth Annual Report

OF THE

Indiana State Board of Health

For the Fiscal and Board Year Ending
September 30, 1910

For the Statistical Year Ending
December 31, 1910

MEMBERS OF THE BOARD

To the Governor

INDIANAPOLIS:
WM B. BURFORD, CONTRACTOR FOR STATE PRINTING AND BINDING
1911

THE STATE OF INDIANA,
EXECUTIVE DEPARTMENT,
NOVEMBER 30, 1910.

Received by the Governor, examined and referred to the Auditor of State for verification of the financial statement.

OFFICE OF AUDITOR OF STATE,
INDIANAPOLIS, December 1, 1910.

The within report, so far as the same relates to moneys drawn from the State Treasury, has been examined and found correct.

W. H. O'BRIEN,
Auditor of State.

DECEMBER 1, 1910.

Returned by the Auditor of State, with above certificate, and transmitted to Secretary of State for publication, upon the order of the Board of Commissioners of Public Printing and Binding.

MARK THISTLETHWAITE,
Secretary to the Governor.

Filed in the office of the Secretary of State of the State of Indiana. December 1, 1910.

L. G. ELLINGHAM,
Secretary of State.

Received the within report and delivered to the printer, December 6. 1910.

A. E. BUTLER,
Clerk Printing Board.

LETTER OF TRANSMITTAL.

NOVEMBER 29, 1910.

HON. THOMAS R. MARSHALL, *Governor of Indiana:*

DEAR SIR—I have the honor to present herewith the thirty-ninth annual report of the Indiana State Board of Health, which, according to law, must be presented to the Governor by December 1st of each year. The report, according to the law's command, gives the transactions and expenditures for the fiscal year ending September 30, 1910, also complete report of the work of the two departments of the *State Laboratory of Hygiene,* which is under the control of the State Board. The statistical report, which according to law shall be for the fiscal year, cannot be compiled until after that date. We shall, therefore, send in said statistical report as soon after January 1st as it can be tabulated and analyzed; and with our present force and facilities it will take three, or perhaps four months, to do the work. We shall push this report with all practicable speed.

Very respectfully,

J. N. HURTY,
Secretary.

THIRTY-NINTH ANNUAL REPORT

OF THE

INDIANA STATE BOARD OF HEALTH.

HON. THOMAS R. MARSHALL, *Governor of Indiana:*

DEAR SIR—The Indiana State Board of Health, in accordance with the statutes, has the honor to present herewith its Thirty-ninth Annual Report.

ORGANIZATION.

The Board has organized under four departments, namely: Executive, Statistical, Bacteriology and Pathology, and Chemical. The first, as the name implies, executes the general policies and orders of the Board and directs the general work of all departments. The second looks after the collection of the vital statistics, their classification, tabulation and analysis, and is directed by the Superintendent of Vital Statistics. The third, attends to the execution of the "laboratory of hygiene law," making such bacteriological and pathological examinations and researches as are necessary in the combat against disease, and is under the direction of the Superintendent of the Laboratory of Hygiene. The fourth attends to the enforcement of the pure food and drug law, and the laws relating to water supplies, and the protection of the streams and lakes against pollution, and is under the direction of the State Food and Drug Inspector. Complete reports of all these departments are separately given in this report.

EMPLOYES.

The executive is the Secretary of the Board, and under the law has the title of "State Health Commissioner." At this time the position is filled by Dr. J. N. Hurty. The Assistant State Health Commissioner is Dr. Wm. F. King; chief clerk and bookkeeper, Capt. J. L. Anderson; stenographers, Mrs. Eva Case, Miss Louise Lingenfelter; mailing and correspondence clerk, Miss Ethel Hoffman.

STATISTICAL DEPARTMENT—Dr. Charles C. Carter, superintendent, assisted by Miss Fannie Stevenson, Miss Miriam Tull, Mrs. Eva Case.

BACTERIOLOGICAL AND PATHOLOGICAL DEPARTMENT—Dr. J. P. Simonds, superintendent; Dr. William Shimer, first assistant; Dr. Ada Schweitzer, second assistant; Miss Hervey Hooker, stenographer and record keeper; custodian and technical assistant, R. O. Johnson.

CHEMICAL DEPARTMENT—Mr. H. E. Barnard, B.S., superintendent, legal title, State Food and Drug Commissioner. First assistant, H. E. Bishop, B.S., food chemist; I. L. Miller, B.A., drug chemist; J. H. Brewster, water chemist; W. D. McAbee, assistant food chemist; A. W. Bruner, inspector; B. W. Cohn, inspector; F. W. Tucker, inspector; John Owens, inspector; Cullen Thomas, assistant in food laboratory; J. J. Hinman, Jr., assistant in water laboratory; J. P. VanWirt, assistant in water laboratory; Edith Hoffman, clerk; Goldine Grove, stenographer; Phillip Broadus, janitor.

CONTENTS OF REPORT.

This report, as the law commands, presents in full the "doings and investigations" of the Indiana State Board of Health for the fiscal year ending September 30, 1909; the Special Report of the State Health Commissioner, the Vital Statistics Report for the Calendar Year ending December 31, 1909, and the reports of the Departments of Bacteriology and Pathology and of Chemistry.

DOINGS AND INVESTIGATIONS.

Four regular and eight special meetings were held during the year, and the minutes fully set forth what was done. The quarterly reports of the Secretary, read at the regular quarterly meetings, give specific accounts of his office and field work. The special report of the State Health Commissioner reviews all work done by all departments, and comments upon the same.

VITAL STATISTICS.

Public health work is founded upon vital statistics. Their collection, classification, tabulation and analysis tell the progress of humanity. A civilized State which does not collect its vital statistics is a sorry example of defective government. Fortunately, Indiana has mortality statistics which approach closely to accuracy; but, unfortunately, her birth and morbidity statistics are very faulty. Two amendments to the Vital Statistics Law are necessary. The law, as it now stands, gives physicians and midwives twenty days in which to report births, and does not have an adequate penalty for not reporting. It should provide that births must be reported within two days, and failure to report be severely punished. The better class of physicians everywhere will favor such an amendment, for they already make reports of deaths, births and contagious diseases, without any law forcing them to do so, for they know it is their duty to their patients, to the State and to the Science of Medicine, which they practice. It is only the derelict for whom the law is needed.

SANITARY WORK.

A review of the quarterly reports of the Secretary to the Board as herein given, will show what sanitary work has been done. The State Board of Health has been active and has made strong efforts to awaken public interest in sanitary matters and has made strong effort to enforce the health statutes. The people surely appreciate these efforts, for the correspondence of the Board has steadily increased since our last report, and the demand for circulars and information is 20 per cent. greater than a year ago. Daily requests are received, asking that the Board pay visits to give advice on sanitary matters or solve sanitary problems which have arisen. The Secretary has answered these calls as far as he possibly could, but the majority of them must be answered by letter, simply saying—"We cannot come, inasmuch as the appropriation and force at our command will not permit." The members of the Board, also, with loss of time from their professional practice, have answered such calls. If the people's interest in public health work increases in the future as in the past, and it certainly will do so, as their enlightenment is bound to be increased, the time will come when the entire time of the Secretary will be required in the office, and no time then can be given to visits which are demanded by the people. There were 583 calls from the people in 1909 for personal visits. Of these only 54 were answered in person. The remaining 529 were put off by letters, explaining the situation as stated above. We are of the opinion it is not economy to so limit the efficiency of the State Board as these facts show it is limited. The question may be asked, "Why don't local health officers meet the demands of the people?" The answer is very simple. Very few physicians have studied that branch of medicine which is known as Hygiene and Sanitary Science. The elementary features of its practice they are equal to, but very many of the health officers are wholly at sea when they meet with an unusual epidemic, or when unusual and extraordinary conditions arise. Besides this, their salaries are so meager that they feel that they give annual services equal to twice what they are paid for. The laborer is worthy of his hire, and for life-saving work the people are certainly willing to pay what is reasonable and right. There would be little or no demand for State Board visits and advice if the law required that local health officers should be informed in Hygiene, and if the tenure of office and pay were such as to attract competent men. We recommend this change as being eminently practical and businesslike.

EPIDEMICS.

No very widespread epidemics have appeared in the State, except an epidemic of measles. This epidemic extended from about the middle of August until October. Measles was reported from every county as existing in epidemic form. The deaths from measles this year numbered 156. This disease should be better controlled because it so frequently leaves the victim with some imperfection or defect which follows them through life. Immediately succeeding measles, pneumonia is very prevalent, also acute kidney and liver troubles appear. Catarrh very frequently follows measles, so do various diseases of the ears and eyes. The disease is very destructive and, as said, should be better controlled, which control cannot be given until better machinery is supplied by the State. Smallpox has decreased as compared with the preceding year. In fact, it has almost disappeared. In the month of October just passed, there were only two cases reported. It is now to be considered that this disease has subsided, until a new generation, unprotected by vaccination is produced.

Tuberculosis has been endemic, as it always is. This is a reproach to our civilization, for as a very great author has said, "Tuberculosis is ignorance." We note a decrease of diphtheria deaths in 1909 when compared with 1908. The figures are—diphtheria deaths the first 9 months of 1909, 139. In the corresponding period of 1908, 147; decrease, 8. This decrease occurs with former years as follows: Diphtheria deaths 1900, 746; 1901, 554; 1902, 424; 1903, 462; 1904, 314; 1905, 366; 1906. 402; 1907, 336; 1908, 315; 1909, 338. This steady decrease in the mortality of diptheria is certainly due to the use of antitoxin, which we now know is a specific if applied in time. However, it is to be noted that the number of cases have not decreased. The mortality has greatly lessened, its prevalence is only slightly lessened. The free antitoxin law passed in 1907 has been the means of saving scores of lives.

We are sorry to have to record the appearance in the State of Indiana, of the terrible disease known as acute epidemic anterior poliomyelitis. It is known as infantile paralysis, because at first it was supposed to attack children only. It is now known that the disease attacks adults, but not so generally as children. The disease appeared in Massachusetts and other Eastern States in 1909, causing much destruction. Special investigations were made and reports issued. Very little is known of the origin of this disease, but it is known that it is transmissible. About 6 per cent. of exposures develop the disease as compared with 22 per cent. in the case of diphtheria. This slight transmissibility has led to the belief that it was not infectious or contagious.

The State Board of Health, at its regular meeting October 14, 1910, in accordance with the powers conferred by the statutes, passed a rule that this disease should be reported and should be quarantined, and efforts made for its control. Physicians all over the State approved this action of the Board. The statistics available in regard to the disease at this time are very imperfect, but from this time on, better statistics will be secured.

THE STATE LABORATORY OF HYGIENE.

There are two divisions in the State Laboratory of Hygiene, and both have done a great deal of excellent work. This fact will appear from a review of these departments as given in this volume. Hundreds of diphtheria examinations have been made in the Bacteriological Division of the laboratory. Also hundreds of typhoid tests, consumption tests, and examinations of tissues and pathological material. These examinations have been the means of stopping many epidemics, the preventing of much sickness and the saving of lives. The report of this department, showing the number of examinations made and the general work done, should be carefully reviewed by every person who is interested in the beneficence which follows from disease prevention.

The work of the Chemical Laboratory could be reviewed, but the report so splendidly sets forth its usefulness and its economical worth, that the same must be read for proper appreciation.

RECOMMENDATIONS.

In accordance with the law, which makes it the duty of the State Board of Health to make such recommendations concerning health laws as it may deem proper, we recommend as follows:

SANITARY SCHOOLHOUSES, MEDICAL EXAMINATION OF SCHOOL CHILDREN AND TEACHING HYGIENE IN THE PUBLIC SCHOOLS.

We suggest a statute requiring that all schoolhouses hereafter built shall conform to natural sanitary laws; also that the act should contain a clause requiring that hygiene be taught in the public schools, and that the medical inspection of school children be made compulsory. Not less than 10 per cent. of school moneys is now wasted on account of insanitary schoolhouses, in which start most of our epidemics and in which are laid the foundations in many instances for consumption and other diseases in after life. Massachusetts, Michigan and other States have statutes of the character we propose, and better health and progress among the school children has thus been secured, as well as better health in adult life. There is a great opportunity to strengthen the nation by building sanitary schoolhouses and in instructing the children in hygiene.

The medical examination of school children has become a necessity, and should not longer be delayed. In every primary schoolroom may be found defective and sick children. Many of the defectives may have their defects removed or ameliorated, and the sick ones should be immediately cared for. The British Board of Education says, in its report:

> "Medical inspection is founded on a recognition of the close connection which exists between the physical and mental condition of the children and the whole process of education. It seeks to secure ultimately for every child, normal or defective, conditions of life compatible with that full and effective development of its organic functions, its special senses, and its mental powers, which constitute a true education."

Medical inspection is a movement national in scope in England, France, Belgium, Sweden, Switzerland, Bulgaria, Japan, the Argentine Republic and Germany. In the United States, seventy cities outside of Massachusetts, and all cities and towns of the State, have systems of medical inspection.

Massachusetts has a compulsory medical inspection law. New Jersey has a permissive one, Vermont a law requiring the annual testing of the vision and hearing of all school children, and Connecticut one providing for such tests triennially. Japan has had medical inspection for ten years.

We heartily recommend such a law in Indiana. It is certain to come in time, and it will be an honor to the State when it does come. When we remember that fully 50 per cent. of all young school children are more or less defective or more or less ill, we at once must recognize it is not Christian to neglect or to refuse to give them relief.

POLLUTION OF STREAMS, WATER SUPPLIES AND SEWERS.

The legislature of 1909 passed a law referring to the controlling of pollution of streams, the protection of water supplies and the disposal of sewage. This law failed to meet expectations. "It is long and somewhat vague." In the efforts of the State Board of Health to enforce this law, many reverses have been experienced. At Princeton, gross pollution of an adjoining stream existed, and the orders of the Board issued under the antipollution law, which orders were directed by the attorney-general, were found inoperative, because of the indefiniteness of the law. This law should be revised or perhaps, replaced altogether by a simple, straightforward statute, covering the necessary points. That it is necessary to preserve our streams and lakes is apparent. They are valuable assets and should be zealously protected from pollution. They are sources of beauty, refreshment and health in the land. They are also sources of a valuable food supply, and the streams and lakes must eventually furnish public water supplies, for it is now known that the ground supply is rapidly diminishing and giving out. In August and September of 1909, the short water supply in various parts of the State became a very serious matter. In certain counties, notably Sullivan, Ripley, Monroe and Brown, many wells "went completely dry." Bloomington was compelled to haul water in tank cars from the White River at Gosport. The greatest economy in the use of water was practiced at Sullivan. Other instances could be mentioned. At Indianapolis the filtered supply from White River became perilously low. Had the drouth continued another two weeks, the command for great economy in the use of water would have gone forth. Cities and towns are continually making expensive mistakes in the matter of establishing public water supplies and building sewers and drains. It therefore, seems wise to adopt the successful method pursued in other States, to prevent such mistakes, with their consequent money loss and sanitary failure. The plans and specifications for public water supplies and sewers and drains should be submitted for the approval of the State Board of Health before the same may be considered. If this important, economical and sanitary work is to be done by the State Board of Health, it will be necessary to establish a sanitary engineering department and a proper antipollution law and create such a department in the State Board of Health. There should be a competent sanitary engineer appointed and a proper appropriation given for the enforcement of the act. A wise law of this character is absolutely necessary for the promotion of the welfare of the State and the preservation of the health of the people. This is a subject which certainly will not down, and the question about the matter is: "Shall the State attend to it now, or do so after disease, death and pecuniary loss compel action?"

PREVENTION OF BLINDNESS.

There are at the lowest estimate 2,400 blind people in the State of Indiana. It would have been an easy matter to have prevented 20 per cent. of this blindness. Investigation shows that 30 per cent. of all blindness is due to the disease known as ophthalmia neonatorum. This is an infection which occurs at birth from mothers who are infected with a transmissible disease. A law requiring that the eyes of the newborn shall be immediately attended to, would prevent, as said, not less than 20 per cent. of the blindness which exists. Other States have such laws and Indiana is behind the times in not putting forth efforts to prevent blindness which should never be. A law to prevent ophthalmia neonatorum will be presented to the legislature by a committee appointed by the State Medical Society, and the same is heartily supported by the State Board of Health. If this law is passed, it will certainly prevent much blindness and if the one prepared does not meet with too many amendments, we may depend upon it, that instead of increasing the capacity of the Blind Institute, future legislatures will be required to decide what shall be done with the excessive accommodations.

THE HEALTH LAW.

The health law, passed by the legislature of 1909, is faulty in several particulars. and these faults should be corrected in order to increase the efficiency of the health department and make it possible to give better service to the people. The said law creates the position of County Health Commissioner, and commands that his term of office shall be for four years, and that he shall be appointed by the County Commissioners. Also commands that he shall be a man informed and skilled in hygiene and preventive medicine. However, it does not give him the power to appoint deputies and properly compensate them. The lack of this authority brings many complications and failures. Each county in the State covers considerable area and it is obvious one man cannot be in two or three places at the same time. Again and again it has been reported by county health commissioners, that emergencies have arisen when they would be in one part of the county attending to epidemics or looking after health conditions, and the demand was made for their immediate appearance in a distant part. It is therefore, plain that we should have an amendment to the law, giving the power to employ deputies, to county health commissioners, otherwise much disease preventing and life-saving work must go undone. This is the only amendment to the health law which we recommend.

RABIES.

By reference to the report of the superintendent of the laboratory of hygiene, the conditions concerning rabies in the State will be discovered. This disease has caused the people a good deal of money, anxiety and sorrow. There have been several deaths from hydrophobia among human beings during the year, and probably one hundred thousand dollars' worth of livestock has been lost on account of it. This seems to us to demand proper amendment, and we therefore, recommend a law laying a tax upon the dogs to create a fund in the hands of the state treasurer, to be paid out by the State Board of Health for the free treatment of those bitten by rabid dogs. It is an occasional occurrence for father and mother to come into the office of the State Board of Health, leading a little child by the hand who has been bitten by a rabid dog. They generally are poor and unable to pay the expenses of the Pasteur treatment, and insure the preservation of the child's life. They are told that the State has made no provision, not even adequate provision, for the prevention of hydrophobia. not to speak of furnishing Pasteur treatment. We will say Pasteur treatment is furnished free by the governments of many States and by the government of Mexico. and many other governments of other States and Japan. The hydrophobia bill should contain sections in regard to the restraint of dogs at certain times and seasons. There is a law of this nature upon the books at the present time, but the enforcement of the same is given to the State Veterinarian. This law and enforcement should refer to the State Board of Health because it has health officers in every county, city and town. The State Veterinarian has no power for the enforcement of laws intended to control and prevent hydrophobia.

WEIGHTS AND MEASURES.

It is apparent from the reports of inspectors that gross fraud is practiced in the sale of foods by dealers who use short weights and measures, and who, ignoring the customary standards, sell by the cup, basket or package in such a way as to make it impossible for the customer to determine the true value of his purchase. The subjects of weights and measures is commanding wide attention and it is highly desirable that, anticipating the call for legislation along these lines, the work of the inspectors of the State Board of Health be so extended as to give them authority to seal weights and measures and prosecute those who fraudulently use them.

This can only be done by legislative act, and we therefore suggest the careful consideration of the subject, and the enactment of a statute covering the matter.

THE PURE FOOD AND DRUG LAW.

(1) Section 3 of the pure food law of 1907 has been declared invalid by the Supreme Court, and it is therefore impossible to convict proprietors who sell adulterated milk. This section should be amended by inserting in line 1 after the word *by* the word *himself*.

If this is not done it will be impossible, according to the ruling of the court, to convict any proprietor or owner of a dairy for selling adulterated milk, provided the same has been handled by an employe.

(2) It has been impossible under the provisions of the present food law to stop the traffic in rotten and decayed eggs, and this is because Section 4 of the pure food law was so amended at the time of its passage as to specifically regulate the sale of eggs and to declare unlawful the sale *knowingly* of eggs ufint for food. The insertion of the word "knowingly," invalidates the law because it is always impossible to prove that the offender knowingly sold bad eggs.

This section should be amended by striking out the sentence, "It shall be unlawful for any person, firm or corporation, to sell or offer for sale any eggs after the same have been placed in an incubator, or to sell or offer for sale, knowingly, eggs in a rotten, decayed or decaying condition to be used for food."

We most respectfully request that you give all of these recommendations your careful consideration, and we hope they will be supported and recommended for passage in your next message to the General Assembly.

Approved by the State Board of Health.

GEO. T. MCCOY, President.
WM. N. WISHARD, Vice-President.
T. HENRY DAVIS, Member.
FRED A. TUCKER, Member.
J. N. HURTY, Secretary.

FINANCIAL STATEMENT.

INDIANA STATE BOARD OF HEALTH.

For Fiscal Year October 1, 1909, to September 30, 1910.

1909			
Oct.	15.	To Dr. Geo. T. McCoy, board meetings...	$32 00
"	15.	To Dr. Wm. N. Wishard, board meetings..	22 00
"	15.	To Dr. T. Henry Davis, board meetings...	13 26
"	16.	To Dr. F. A. Tucker, board meetings....	19 05
"	31.	To Mrs. Eva Case, salary................	50 00
"	31.	To Mrs. Florence Vollrath, salary........	50 00
"	31.	To Ethel Hoffman, salary................	50 00
"	31.	To Louise Lingenfelter, salary...........	50 00
"	31	To Fannie Stevenson, salary.............	50 00
"	31.	To Miriam Tull, salary..................	40 00
"	31.	To J. L. Anderson, salary...............	125 00
"	31.	To Dr. J. N. Hurty, salary..............	250 00
Nov.	11.	To J. L. Anderson, expense..............	5 03
"	11	To Balke & Krauss, merchandise.........	1 50
"	11.	To Central Supply Co., merchandise.......	2 51
"	11.	To J. A. Downey, postal guide...........	3 50
"	11.	To Evans & Fulton, filing cases..........	148 30
"	11.	To Adams Express Co., services..........	3 89
"	11.	To American Express Co., services.......	5 53
"	11.	To United States Express Co., services...	5 03
"	11.	To Irving Fisher, M. D., books...........	7 50
"	11.	To Indiana Dental College, Med. Dicty...	4 50
"	11.	To Indianapolis Calcium Light Co., srvcs..	15 30
"	11.	To Indianapolis Telephone Co., services...	50
"	11.	To Central Union Telephone Co., services.	4 20
"	11.	To Dr. M. Knowlton, photo slides........	5 40
"	11.	To Geo. J. Mayer, merchandise..........	5 00
"	11.	To Multiplex Display Picture Co., mdse...	115 50
"	11.	To Neostyle Co., merchandise............	45 00
"	11.	To Smith Premier T. W. Co., merchandise	1 25
"	11.	To Stone & Forsythe, merchandise.......	10 00
"	11.	To Vonnegut Hardware Co., merchandise.	22
"	11.	To West Disinfecting Co., merchandise...	3 00
"	11.	To Western Union Telegraph Co., services	2 14
"	30.	To Mrs. Eva Case, salary................	50 00
"	30.	To Mrs. Florence Vollrath, salary........	50 00
"	30.	To Ethel Hoffman, salary................	50 00
"	30.	To Louise Lingenfelter, salary...........	50 00
"	30.	To Fannie Stevenson, salary.............	50 00
"	30.	To Miriam Tull, salary..................	40 00
"	30.	To Dr. J. N. Hurty, salary..............	250 00

Nov.	30.	To J. L. Anderson, salary................	$125 00	
Dec.	18.	To Aquos Distilled Water Co., merchandise	2 00	
"	18.	To Addressograph Co., merchandise.......	97	
"	18.	To Wm. B. Burford, print'g and stationery	164 66	
"	18.	To Evans & Fulton, merchandise.........	2 50	
"	18.	To Adams Express Co., services.........	3 03	
"	18.	To American Express Co., services.......	3 17	
"	18.	To U. S. Express Co., services...........	2 73	
"	18.	To Fertig & Kevers, merchandise.........	7 60	
"	18.	To Central Union Telephone Co., tolls....	3 20	
"	18.	To New Telephone Co., tolls.............	9 10	
"	18.	To Scofield-Pierson Co., books............	6 50	
"	18.	To Vonnegut Hardware Co., merchandise.	1 00	
"	18.	To J. L. Anderson, expense..............	24 93	
"	21.	To Mrs. Eva Case, salary................	50 00	
"	21.	To Mrs. Florence Vollrath, salary........	50 00	
"	21.	To Ethel Hoffman, salary................	50 00	
"	21.	To Louise Lingenfelter, salary...........	50 00	
"	21.	To Fannie Stevenson, salary..............	50 00	
"	21.	To Miriam I. Tull, salary................	40 00	
"	21.	To Dr. J. N. Hurty, salary..............	250 00	
"	21.	To J. L. Anderson, salary..............	125 00	
"	28.	To Dr. Geo. T. McCoy, H. O. Exams......	11 75	
"	28.	To Dr. Fred A. Tucker, H. O. Exams.....	10 96	
		Total first quarter..............................		$2,731 61
Jan.	14.	To American Medical Asso., Journal, 1910	$5 00	
"	14.	To American Toilet Supply Co., laundry..	3 75	
"	14.	To Wm. B. Burford, print'g and stationery	599 80	
"	14.	To Central Union Tel. Co., rents and tolls	23 90	
"	14.	To Indianapolis Tel. Co., rents and tolls..	24 20	
"	14.	To Adams Express Co., services..........	3 09	
"	14.	To American Express Co., services.......	2 54	
"	14.	To U. S. Express Co., services............	5 02	
"	14.	To Goder-Heimann Co., specimen.........	5 50	
"	14.	To G. M. Merrick, Agt., merchandise......	2 25	
"	14.	To The Henry Phipps Institute, report....	1 00	
"	14.	To Western Union Telegraph Co., services.	1 89	
"	14.	To Dr. J. N. Hurty, expense.............	135 90	
"	14.	To J. L. Anderson, expense..............	11 46	
"	3.	To Dr. Geo. T. McCoy, examination......	12 25	
"	3.	To Dr. F. A. Tucker, examination........	10 96	
"	14.	To Dr. Geo. T. McCoy, board meeting....	12 25	
"	14.	To Dr. T. Henry Davis, board meeting....	13 26	
"	14.	To Dr. F. A. Tucker, board meeting......	21 86	
"	15.	To Mrs. Florence Vollrath, salary.........	25 00	
"	31.	To Mrs. Eva Case, salary................	50 00	
"	31.	To Ethel Hoffman, salary................	50 00	
"	31.	To Louise Lingenfelter, salary...........	50 00	

Jan.	31.	To Fannie Stevenson, salary............	$50 00
"	31.	To Miriam Tull, salary..................	40 00
Feb.	2.	To Robt. H. Bryson, P. M., stamps.......	100 00
"	2.	To Dr. Geo. T. McCoy, Conf. Co. H. Com's.	13 25
"	2.	To Dr. Fred A. Tucker, Conf. Co. H. Com's	10 96
"	15.	To Aquos Distilled Water Co., mdse......	1 00
"	15.	To The Adder Machine Co., merchandise..	1 00
"	15.	To W. H. Bass Photo Co., merchandise...	3 50
"	15.	To Wm. B. Burford, print'g and stationery	163 16
"	15.	To The Druggists Circular, subs. 1910....	2 00
"	15.	To Adams Express Co., services..........	3 04
"	15.	To American Express Co., services........	4 19
"	15.	To United States Express Co., services....	1 67
"	15.	To L. E. Morrison Co., merchandise......	22 00
"	15.	To Sander & Recker Furniture Co., mdse..	42 00
"	15.	To Central Union Telephone Co., services.	7 05
"	15.	To Indianapolis Telephone Co., services...	2 95
"	15.	To J. L. Anderson, expense..............	3 21
"	28.	To Dr. C. A. Carter, salary..............	100 00
"	28.	To Mrs. Eva Case, salary................	50 00
"	28.	To Ethel Hoffman, salary................	50 00
"	28.	To Louise Lingenfelter, salary...........	50 00
"	28.	To Fannie Stevenson, salary............	50 00
"	28.	To Miriam I. Tull, salary................	40 00
"	28.	To Dr. J. N. Hurty, Jan. and Feb. salary.	500 00
"	28.	To J. L. Anderson, Jan. and Feb. salary..	250 00
Mar.	11.	To R. H. Bryson, P. M., postage.........	200 00
"	19.	To Aetna Cabinet Co., chair.............	9 00
"	19.	To Aquos Distilled Water Co., merchandise	1 50
"	19.	To Chas. F. Bretzman, photos............	3 00
"	19.	To Wm. B. Burford, print'g and stationery	156 09
"	19.	To Adams Express Co., services..........	4 43
"	19.	To American Express Co., services........	1 28
"	19.	To United States Express Co., services....	2 97
"	19.	To Indiana Seal Stamp-Stencil Co., mdse.	1 10
"	19.	To Indianapolis Calcium Light Co., expense	5 95
"	19.	To G. M. Merrick, Agt., merchandise......	1 50
"	19.	To Scofield-Pierson Co., text books.......	2 25
"	19.	To Central Union Telephone Co., tolls....	5 00
"	19.	To Western Union Telegraph Co., tolls....	1 88
"	19.	To McIntosh Stereopticon Co., merchandise	18 15
"	31.	To Dr. C. A. Carter, salary..............	100 00
"	31.	To Mrs. Eva Case, salary................	50 00
"	31.	To Ethel Hoffman, salary................	50 00
"	31.	To Louise Lingenfelter, salary...........	50 00
"	31.	To Fannie Stevenson, salary.............	50 00
"	31.	To Miriam I. Tull, salary................	50 00
"	31.	To Dr. J. N. Hurty, salary...............	250 00
"	31.	To J. L. Anderson, salary...............	125 00

Total second quarter.......................... $3,770 96

Apr.	8.	To The Addressograph Co., merchandise..	$5 19
"	8.	To American Toilet Supply Co., laundry..	3 75
"	8.	To Aquos Distilled Water Co., mdse......	1 50
"	8.	To W. H. Bass Photo Co., merchandise....	5 20
"	8.	To Wm. B. Burford, print'g and stationery	65 12
"	8.	To Dr. C. A. Carter, expense............	8 15
"	8.	To Adams Express Co., services..........	3 94
"	8.	To American Express Co., services.......	2 32
"	8.	To U. S. Express Co., services...........	4 26
"	8.	To Goder-Heimann Co., merchandise......	6 00
"	8.	To Indpls. Seal-Stamp-Stencil Co., mdse...	25
"	8.	To C. P. Lesh Paper Co., merchandise....	88 62
"	8.	To Geo. J. Mayer, merchandise...........	2 80
"	8.	To Central Union Tel. Co., rents and tolls.	21 70
"	8.	To Ind'polis Telephone Co., rents and tolls	25 20
"	8.	To Western Union Telegraph Co., tolls....	2 06
"	8.	To Dr. Geo. M. Sternberg, merchandise....	6 35
"	8.	To The Scofield-Pierson Co., merchandise.	3 50
"	8.	To J. L. Anderson, expense...............	8 09
"	8.	To Dr. J. N. Hurty, expense.............	148 07
"	8.	To Dr. Geo. T. McCoy, 2 board meetings.	24 00
"	8.	To Dr. Wm. N. Wishard, board meeting...	10 00
"	8.	To Dr. T. Henry Davis, board meeting...	13 26
"	8.	To Dr. Fred A. Tucker, 2 board meetings.	22 42
"	20.	To Dr. Geo. T. McCoy, meeting T. B. Hos.	16 25
"	20.	To Dr. Fred A. Tucker, meeting T. B. Hos.	14 51
"	30.	To Dr. C. A. Carter, salary..............	100 00
"	30.	To Mrs. Eva Case, salary................	50 00
"	30.	To Ethel Hoffman, salary................	50 00
"	30.	Louise Lingenfelter, salary..............	50 00
"	30.	To Fannie Stevenson, salary.............	50 00
"	30.	To Miriam I. Tull, salary................	50 00
"	30.	To J. L. Anderson, salary................	125 00
"	30.	To Dr. J. N. Hurty, salary..............	250 00
May	12.	To Aquos Dist. Water Co., merchandise...	2 00
"	12.	To W. H. Bass Photo Co., merchandise....	14 40
"	12.	To Wm. B. Burford, print'g and stationery	419 55
"	12.	To Adams Express Co., services..........	21
"	12.	To American Express Co., services........	1 98
"	12.	To U. S. Express Co., services...........	2 36
"	12.	To Goder-Heimann Co., merchandise......	9 50
"	12.	To Indiana Paper Co., merchandise.......	8 00
"	12.	To Indiana Seal-Stamp-Stencil Co., mdse..	1 65
"	12.	To C. P. Lesh Paper Co., merchandise....	52 50
"	12.	To Scofield-Pierson Co., books............	10 50
"	12.	To Stone & Forsythe, merchandise........	31 75
"	12.	To Central Union Telephone Co., tolls....	5 00
"	12.	To Indianapolis Telephone Co., tolls......	2 25
"	12.	To Western Union Telegraph Co., tolls....	1 55
"	12.	To Dr. Geo. T. McCoy, expense...........	51 98
"	12.	To J. L. Anderson, expense..............	6 04

May	24.	To Robt. H. Bryson, P. M., postage stamps	$100 00	
"	24.	To Dr. Geo. T. McCoy, bd. meeting & conf.	12 50	
"	24.	To Dr. T. Henry Davis, bd. meeting & con.	12 76	
"	24.	To Dr. Fred A. Tucker, bd. meeting & con.	10 96	
"	31.	To Dr. Chas. A. Carter, salary..........	100 00	
"	31.	To Mrs. Eva Case, salary..............	50 00	
"	31.	To Ethel Hoffman, salary...............	50 00	
"	31.	To Louise Lingenfelter, salary...........	50 00	
"	31.	To Fannie Stevenson, salary............	50 00	
"	31.	To Miriam I. Tull, salary..............	50 00	
"	31.	To J. L. Anderson, salary..............	125 00	
"	31.	To Dr. J. N. Hurty, salary..............	250 00	
June	2.	To Dr. Geo. Keiper, H. O. school.........	10 00	
"	2.	To Dr. Wm. F. King, H. O. school.......	10 00	
"	2.	To Dr. L. T. Rawles, H. O. school........	10 00	
"	2.	To Dr. H. S. Thurston, H. O. school......	10 00	
"	2.	To Claypool Hotel, room and board.......	4 50	
"	2.	To Dr. Geo. T. McCoy, exp. & bd. meeting	25 65	
"	2.	To Dr. Wm. N. Wishard, ex. & bd. meeting	20 00	
"	2.	To Dr. T. Henry Davis, exp. & bd. meeting	13 10	
"	2.	To Dr. Fred A. Tucker, exp. & bd. meeting	11 61	
"	15.	To J. L. Anderson, expense.............	7 48	
"	15.	To Aquos Distilled Water Co., merchandise	1 00	
"	15.	To Wm. B. Burford, print'g and stationery	442 02	
"	15.	To Dr. H. M. Bracken, Secy-Treas., dues..	15 00	
"	15.	To Adams Express Co., services.........	2 01	
"	15.	To American Express Co., services........	16	
"	15.	To U. S. Express Co., services...........	1 78	
"	15.	To The Fulton Evans Co., merchandise....	9 54	
"	15.	To Hogan Transfer Co., Frt. and drayage.	6 41	
"	15.	To Indianapolis Calcium Light Co., lantern	10 00	
"	15.	To G. M. Merrick, Agt., merchandise......	1 90	
"	15.	To W. K. Stewart Co., books............	3 25	
"	15.	To Central Union Telephone Co., tolls....	5 20	
"	15.	To Indianapolis Telephone Co., tolls......	2 60	
"	15.	To Western Union Telegraph Co., tolls....	2 56	
"	30.	To Dr. C. A. Carter, salary............	100 00	
"	30.	To Mrs. Eva Case, salary..............	50 00	
"	30.	To Ethel Hoffman, salary..............	50 00	
"	30.	To Louise Lingenfelter, salary...........	50 00	
"	30.	To Fannie Stevenson, salary............	50 00	
"	30.	To Miriam I. Tull, salary..............	50 00	
"	30.	To J. L. Anderson, salary..............	125 00	
"	30.	To Dr. J. N. Hurty, salary..............	250 00	
		Total third quarter...........................		$4,070 72
July	8.	To Dr. J. N. Hurty, expense............	$69 51	
"	8.	To Dr. T. Henry Davis, board meeting....	13 31	
"	8.	To Dr. Geo. T. McCoy, board meeting....	12 25	

July	8.	To Dr. Wm. N. Wishard, board meeting..	$10 00
"	8.	To Dr. Fred A. Tucker, expense..........	8 70
"	8.	To J. L. Anderson, expense.............	3 56
"	8.	To American Toilet Supply Co., laundry..	3 75
"	8.	To Aquos Distilled Water Co., merchandise	1 00
"	8.	To Wm. B. Burford, merchandise.........	100 42
"	8.	To Adams Express Co., services..........	2 43
"	8.	To American Express Co., services........	2 22
"	8.	To U. S. Express Co., services............	1 67
"	8.	To Dr. Millard Knowlton, lantern slides..	5 50
"	8.	To Dr. Geo. F. Keiper, express..........	3 75
"	8.	To Pettis Dry Goods Co., merchandise....	1 70
"	8.	To Central Union Tel. Co., rents and tolls.	22 25
"	8.	To Indianapolis Tel. Co., rents and tolls..	22 30
"	8.	To Dr. Geo. M. Sternberg, Treas., dues....	5 00
"	8.	To Miss C. C. Van Blarcom, Sec., photo, etc	5 50
"	8.	To Western Union Telegraph Co., services.	5 83
"	8.	To Mrs. Eva Case, work................	15 00
"	8.	To Indianapolis Calcium Light Co., services	24 50
"	31.	To Dr. C. A. Carter, salary.............	100 00
"	31.	To Mrs. Eva Case, salary...............	50 00
"	31.	To Ethel Hoffman, salary...............	50 00
"	31.	To Louise Lingenfelter, salary............	50 00
"	31.	To Fannie Stevenson, salary............	50 00
"	31.	To Miriam I. Tull, salary...............	50 00
"	31.	To Mrs. Florence Vollrath, salary.........	53 85
"	31.	To Dr. J. N. Hurty, salary.............	250 00
"	31.	To J. L. Anderson, salary...............	125 00
Aug.	16.	To Aquos Distilled Water Co., merchandise	2 00
"	16.	To Wm. B. Burford, merchandise........	56 00
"	16.	To Adams Express Co., services..........	13 03
"	16.	To American Express Co., services.......	11 94
"	16.	To U. S. Express Co., services...........	10 21
"	16.	To W. K. Stewart Co., merchandise......	10 14
"	16.	To Central Union Telephone Co., tolls....	2 25
"	16.	To Indianapolis Telephone Co., tolls......	1 30
"	16.	To J. L. Anderson, expense..............	24 51
"	31.	To Dr. C. A. Carter, salary.............	100 00
"	31.	To Mrs. Eva Case, salary...............	50 00
"	31.	To Ethel Hoffman, salary...............	50 00
"	31.	To Louise Lingenfelter, salary............	50 00
"	31.	To Fannie Stevenson, salary............	50 00
"	31.	To Miriam I. Tull, salary...............	50 00
"	31.	To Mrs. Florence Vollrath, salary........	16 65
"	31.	To J. L. Anderson, salary...............	125 00
"	31.	To Dr. J. N. Hurty, salary.............	250 00
Sept.	10.	To Aquos Distilled Water Co., merchandise	1 00
"	10.	To W. H. Bass Photo Co., merchandise....	3 14
"	10.	To H. Lieber Co., merchandise...........	75
"	10.	To J. E. Ewers, merchandise............	2 40

Sept. 10.	To Adams Express Co., services	$2 23	
" 10.	To American Express Co., services	71	
" 10.	To U. S. Express Co., services	3 25	
" 10.	To The Fulton Evans Co., merchandise	1 84	
" 10.	To Smith Premier T. W. Co., merchandise	1 75	
" 10.	To W. K. Stewart Co., merchandise	8 35	
" 10.	To Western Union Telegraph Co., tolls	1 91	
" 10.	To Central Union Telephone Co., tolls	6 10	
" 10.	To Dr. C. A. Carter, expense	19 95	
" 10.	To J. L. Anderson, expense	4 59	
" 28.	To Robt. H. Bryson, P. M., postage stamps	250 00	
" 28.	To American Toilet Supply Co., laundry	3 75	
" 28.	To Aquos Dist. Water Co., merchandise	1 00	
" 28.	To Wm. B. Burford, merchandise	592 41	
" 28.	To Adams Express Co., services	2 17	
" 28.	To American Express Co., services	4 21	
" 28.	To U. S. Express Co., service	1 00	
" 28	To Central Union Telephone Co., rents, etc.	20 65	
" 28.	To Indianapolis Telephone Co., rents, etc.	20 05	
" 28.	To Western Union Telegraph Co., tolls	1 33	
" 28.	To Dr. J. N. Hurty, expense	52 55	
" 28.	To J. L. Anderson, expense	2 35	
" 28.	To Dr. C. A. Carter, salary	100 00	
" 28.	To Mrs. Eva Case, salary	50 00	
" 28.	To Ethel Hoffman, salary	50 00	
" 28.	To Louise Lingenfelter, salary	50 00	
" 28.	To Fannie Stevenson, salary	50 00	
" 28.	To Miriam I. Tull, salary	50 00	
" 28.	To Dr. J. N. Hurty, salary	250 00	
" 28.	To J. L. Anderson, salary	125 00	
	Total fourth quarter		$3,735 49

RECAPITULATION.

Appropriations.

Appropriation, general	$10,000 00	
Secretary's salary, specific	3,000 00	
Chief clerk's salary, specific	1,500 00	
		$14,500 00

Expense.

1st quarter	$2,731 61	
2d quarter	3,770 96	
3d quarter	4,070 72	
4th quarter	3,735 49	
Reverting to general fund	191 22	
Total		$14,500 00

INDIANA STATE BOARD OF HEALTH—LABORATORY OF HYGIENE.

For Fiscal Year October 1, 1909, to September 30, 1910.

Oct.	25.	To Dr. Will Shimer, expense	$12 70
"	31.	To J. P. Simonds, salary	166 66
"	31.	To Will Shimer, salary	100 00
"	31.	To Ada Schweitzer, salary	100 00
"	31.	To Mabel J. Abraham, salary	50 00
"	31.	To Robt. P. Johnson, salary	75 00
Nov.	9.	To Aquos Distilled Water Co., merchandise	1 50
"	9.	To The Chemical Engineer, subscription	2 00
"	9.	To Druggists' Circular, subscription	2 00
"	9.	To Commercial Distilling Co., 1 bbl. alcohol	23 61
"	9.	To Adams Express Company, service	2 30
"	9.	To American Express Company, service	3 60
"	9.	To United States Express Co., service	90
"	9.	To Indianapolis Sanitary Co., service	12 50
"	9.	To Pittman-Myers Co., merchandise	312 30
"	9.	To G. E. Stechert & Co., books	3 50
"	9.	To Dr. J. P. Simonds, expense	30 28
"	9.	To Weber Drug Co., merchandise	25 00
"	19.	To Mabel J. Abraham, salary	28 12
"	19.	To Dr. Will Shimer, expense	17 33
"	29.	To Dr. J. P. Simonds, expense	7 70
"	30.	To Dr. J. P. Simonds, salary	166 67
"	30.	To Dr. Will Shimer, salary	100 00
"	30.	To Dr. Ada Schweitzer, salary	100 00
"	30.	To Miss Hervey M. Hooker, salary	26 88
"	30.	To Robt. P. Johnson	75 00
Dec.	18.	To Aquos Distilled Water Co., merchandise	1 50
"	18.	To Wm. B. Burford, print'g and stationery	13 07
"	18.	To Columbia School Supply Co., mdse	8 10
"	18.	To Adams Express Co., service	1 15
"	18.	To American Express Co., service	1 20
"	18.	To United States Express Co., service	3 17
"	18.	To Journal Medical Research, 2 vols	8 00
"	18.	To Dr. Will Shimer, expense	8 15
"	18.	To Wm. Schoenheit, Treas., merchandise	12 03
"	18.	To G. E. Stechert & Co., Journal, 1910	3 75
"	18.	To Weber Drug Co., merchandise	40 00
"	18.	To J. L. Anderson, expense	21 67
"	18.	To Dr. J. P. Simonds, expense	16 00
"	31.	To Dr. J. P. Simonds, salary	166 67
"	31.	To Dr. Will Shimer, salary	100 00
"	31.	To Dr. Ada Schweitzer, salary	100 00
"	31.	To Miss H. M. Hooker, salary	50 00
"	31.	To Robt. P. Johnson, salary	75 00

Total first quarter $2,070 01

1910.			
Jan.	15.	To Dr. J. P. Simonds, expense...........	$17 87
"	17.	To Dr. Will Shimer, expense............	7 25
"	14.	To American Toilet Supply Co., laundry..	18 62
"	14.	To Aquos Distilled Water Co., merchandise	1 00
"	14.	To Wm. B. Burford, print'g and stationery	178 31
"	14.	To Adams Express Co., services..........	60
"	14.	To American Express Co., services.......	3 04
"	14.	To United States Express Co., services...	1 10
"	14.	To The Francis Pharmacy Co., merchandise	5 05
"	14.	To Hogan Transfer Co., frt. and drayage..	3 97
"	14.	To Improved Mailing Case Co., mchndise..	34 82
"	14.	To The Johns Hopkins Press, subs., 1910..	2 00
"	14.	To Scofield-Pierson Co., text book........	2 50
"	14.	To G. E. Stechert & Co., text book........	3 75
"	14.	To Ward Bros. Drug Co., merchandise...	5 32
"	14.	To Weber Drug Co., merchandise.........	10 00
"	14.	To J. L. Anderson, expense..............	8 81
"	26.	To Dr. J. P. Simonds, expense	4 90
"	31.	To Dr. J. P. Simonds, salary	166 66
"	31.	To Dr. Will Shimer, salary..............	100 00
"	31.	To Dr. Ada Schweitzer, salary...........	100 00
"	31.	To Miss H. M. Hooker, salary...........	50 00
"	31.	To Robt. P. Johnson, salary..............	75 00
Feb.	11.	To Dr. J. P. Simonds, expense...........	21 75
"	15.	To J. L. Anderson, expense..............	13 30
"	15.	To Aquos Distilled Water Co., merchandise	1 00
"	15.	To Wm. B. Burford, stationery..........	4 00
"	15.	To Adams Express Co., services..........	40
"	15.	To American Express Co., services.......	1 80
"	15.	To United States Express Co., services....	1 19
"	15.	To The Francis Pharmacy Co., mrchndse.	1 50
"	15.	To The Pettis Dry Goods Co., merchandise	50
"	15.	To Pittman-Myers Co., merchandise......	9 90
"	15.	To Stewart-Carey Glass Co., merchandise.	2 00
"	15.	To Ward Bros. Drug Co., merchandise....	24 70
"	15.	To A. L. Barrow, M. M., merchandise....	2 00
"	15.	To Dr. J. P. Simonds, expense..........	6 50
"	15.	To G. E. Stechert & Co., text books......	36 00
"	25.	To Dr. Will Shimer, expense............	18 65
"	28.	To Dr. J. P. Simonds, salary.............	166 67
"	28.	To Dr. Will Shimer, salary..............	100 00
"	28.	To Dr. Ada Schweitzer, salary...........	100 00
"	28.	To Miss H. M. Hooker, salary...........	50 00
"	28.	To Robt. P. Johnson, salary.............	75 00
Mar.	19.	To Aquos Distilled Water Co., mdse......	1 50
"	19.	To Adams Express Co., services.........	1 35
"	19.	To American Express Co., services......	2 15
"	19.	To United States Express Co., services ...	1 75

Mar.	19.	To Pettis Dry Goods Co., merchandise....	$2 45	
"	19.	To Ward Bros. Drug Co., merchandise....	1 75	
"	19.	To Dr. J. P. Simonds, expense............	16 35	
"	19.	To Dr. Will Shimer, expense............	6 90	
"	19.	To J. L. Anderson, expense..............	12 69	
"	31.	To Dr. J. P. Simonds, salary............	166 67	
"	31.	To Dr. Will Shimer, salary..............	100 00	
"	31.	To Dr. Ada Schweitzer, salary...........	100 00	
"	31.	To Miss H. M. Hooker, salary............	50 00	
"	31.	To Robt. P. Johnson, salary............	75 00	
		Total for second quarter....................		$1,975 99
Apr.	8.	To Aquos Distilled Water Co., merchandise	$1 00	
"	8.	To American Toilet Co., laundry.........	20 70	
"	8.	To Adams Express Co., services.........	2 30	
"	8.	To American Express Co., services........	95	
"	8.	To United States Express Co., services....	1 00	
"	8.	To Francis Pharmacy Co., merchandise...	1 30	
"	8.	To Journal Medical Research, sub's......	4 00	
"	8.	To Dr. J. P. Simonds, expense............	7 25	
"	8.	To Vonnegut Hardware Co., merchandise..	3 30	
"	8.	To Weber Drug Co., merchandise.........	25 00	
"	27.	To Dr. J. P. Simonds, expense............	6 35	
"	27.	To Dr. Will Shimer, expense............	17 50	
"	30.	To Dr. J. P. Simonds, salary............	166 66	
"	30.	To Dr. Will Shimer, salary..............	100 00	
"	30.	To Dr. Ada Schweitzer	100 00	
"	30.	To Miss H. M. Hooker, salary............	50 00	
"	30.	To Robt. P. Johnson, salary............	75 00	
"	30.	To F. R. Bannon, salary................	9 50	
May	12.	To American Antiformin Co., merchandise.	80	
"	12.	To Aquos Distilled Water Co., merchandise	2 00	
"	12.	To Will Beach, merchandise.............	2 50	
"	12.	To Wm. B. Burford, merchandise........	20 51	
"	12.	To Adams Express Co., services...........	1 20	
"	12.	To American Express Co., services.......	2 08	
"	12.	To United States Express Co., services....	1 30	
"	12.	To The Francis Pharmacy Co., merchandise	1 00	
"	12.	To Ward Bros. Drug Co., merchandise...	2 00	
"	12.	To Weber Drug Co., merchandise........	1 50	
"	12.	To J. L. Anderson, expense.............	19 48	
"	18.	To Dr. J. P. Simonds, expense...........	12 95	
"	24.	To Robert H. Bryson, P. M., postage stamps	100 00	
"	31.	To Dr. J. P. Simonds, salary............	166 67	
"	31.	To Dr. Will Shimer, salary..............	100 00	
"	31.	To Dr. Ada Schweitzer, salary	100 00	
"	31.	To Miss H. M. Hooker, salary...........	50 00	
"	31.	To Robt. P. Johnson....................	75 00	
"	31.	To F. R. Bannon, salary...............	13 00	

June 15.	To J. L. Anderson, expense.............	$10 12	
" 15.	To Aquos Distilled Water Co., merchandise	1 00	
" 15.	To Adams Express Co., services..........	3 00	
" 15.	To American Express Co., services........	60	
" 15.	To United States Express Co., services....	80	
" 15.	To The Francis Pharmacy Co., merchandise	1 85	
" 15.	To Indianapolis Sanitary Co., work......	5 80	
" 15.	To Ward Bros. Drug Co., merchandise...	50 79	
" 15.	To Weber Drug Co., merchandise........	15 00	
" 15.	To Dr. J. P. Simonds, expense	38 40	
" 30.	To Dr. J. P. Simonds, salary	166 67	
" 30.	To Dr. Will Shimer, salary.............	100 00	
" 30.	To Dr. Ada Schweitzer, salary	100 00	
" 30.	To Miss H. M. Hooker, salary...........	50 00	
" 30.	To Robt. P. Johnson, salary............	75 00	
" 30.	To F. R. Bannon, salary...............	25 00	
	Total for third quarter........................		$1,907 83
July 12.	To American Toilet Supply Co., laundry..	$20 40	
" 12.	To Aquos Distilled Water Co., merchandise	2 00	
" 12.	To Wm. B. Burford, merchandise........	7 25	
" 12.	To Adams Express Co., services..........	4 63	
" 12.	To American Express Co., services.......	1 70	
" 12.	To United States Express Co., services....	90	
" 12.	To Hoover-Watson Printing Co., printing.	7 50	
" 12.	To Indiana Seal-Stamp-Stencil Co., mdse..	1 20	
" 12.	To Ind'polis Blue Print & Supply Co., mdse.	2 35	
" 12.	To Indianapolis Sanitary Co., labor.......	10 84	
" 12.	To Indianapolis. Tent & Awning Co., labor	50	
" 12.	To Pettis Dry Goods Co., merchandise....	3 00	
" 12.	To Jos. A. Arnold, ed., U. S. Dep. Ag., mdse	9 10	
" 12.	To Ward Bros. Drug Co., merchandise...	37 20	
" 12.	To G. E. Stechert & Co., Journal.........	3 75	
" 12.	To J. L. Anderson, expense.............	6 05	
" 12.	To Dr. J. P. Simonds, expense...........	1 75	
" 12.	To Weber Drug Co., merchandise.........	10 00	
" 31.	To Dr. J. P. Simonds, salary............	166 66	
" 31.	To Dr. Will Shimer, salary.............	125 00	
" 31.	To Dr. Ada Schweitzer, salary..........	125 00	
" 31.	To Miss H. M. Hooker, salary...........	50 00	
" 31.	To Robt. P. Johnson, salary.............	75 00	
" 31.	To F. R. Bannon, salary...............	25 00	
Aug. 16.	To Wm. B. Burford, merchandise........	257 49	
" 16.	To Adams Express Co., services..........	95	
" 16.	To American Express Co., services........	25	
" 16.	To United States Express Co., services....	1 25	
" 16.	To Indianapolis Sanitary Co., services....	10 84	
" 16.	To Dr. George F. Keiper, express........	5 00	
" 16.	To Ward Bros. Drug Co., merchandise....	10 85	

Aug.	16.	To J. L. Anderson, expense..............	$5 60
"	31.	To Dr. J. P. Simonds, salary.............	166 67
"	31.	To Dr. Will Shimer, salary..............	125 00
"	31.	To Dr. Ada Schweitzer, salary...........	125 00
"	31.	To Dr. W. F. King, salary...............	100 00
"	31.	To Miss H. M. Hooker, salary............	50 00
"	31.	To Robt. P. Johnson, salary..............	75 00
"	31.	To F. R. Bannon, salary.................	25 00
"	31.	To Mrs. Florence Vollrath, salary.........	16 67
"	31.	To Dr. W. F. King, expense..............	78 05
Sept.	10.	To Aquos Distilled Water Co., merchandise	3 00
"	10.	To Adams Express Co., services..........	1 10
"	10.	To United States Express Co., services....	75
"	10.	To B. H. Herman & Co., merchandise.....	1 25
"	10.	To Journal Med. Researhc, sub. 1911.....	4 00
"	10.	To Pettis Dry Goods Co., merchandise...	4 00
"	10.	To E. H. Sargent & Co., merchandise.....	1 82
"	10.	To Smith Premier T. W. Co., merchandise	75
"	10.	To Spencer Lens Co., merchandise........	14 40
"	10.	To W. K. Stewart Co., merchandise.......	42 75
"	10.	To Dr. J. P. Simonds, expense...........	58 15
"	10.	To Dr. Will Shimer, expense.............	7 45
"	10.	To Ward Bros. Drug Co., merchandise....	68 48
"	28.	To Robt. H. Bryson, P. M., postage stamps	200 00
"	28.	To American Toilet Supply Co., laundry..	21 30
"	28.	To Aquos Distilled Water Co., merchandise	2 00
"	28.	To Bausch & Lomb Optical Co., mdse.....	447 31
"	28.	To Wm. B. Burford, merchandise........	227 65
"	28.	To Wm. H. Armstrong Co., merchandise..	11 25
"	28.	To Adams Express Co., services..........	1 50
"	28.	To American Express Co., services........	65
"	28.	To Indpls. Sanitary Co., removing garbage	22 08
"	28.	To Miss Hattie Joplin, stenog. service....	10 00
"	28.	To Klee & Coleman, merchandise.........	2 50
"	28.	To Francis Pharmacy Co., merchandise...	51
"	28.	To Dr. W. F. King, expense.............	46 23
"	28.	To Joe Keedy, labor....................	10 00
"	28.	To Ernest Leitz, merchandise............	80 00
"	28.	To Pettis Dry Goods Co., merchandise....	2 41
"	28.	To Smith Premier T. W. Co., merchandise	75
"	28.	To E. G. Soltman, merchandise..........	22 25
"	28.	To G. E. Stechert & Co., books..........	8 76
"	28.	To W. K. Stewart Co., books............	48 40
"	28.	To Ward Bros. Drug Co., merchandise....	4 00
"	28.	To Vonnegut Hardware Co., merchandise.	3 25
"	28.	To Hogan Transfer Co., frt. and drayage.	3 59
"	28.	To J. L. Anderson, expense.............	7 65
"	28.	To E. H. Sargent & Co., merchandise.....	134 71
"	28.	To Dr. J. P. Simonds, salary............	166 67
"	28.	To Dr. Will Shimer, salary.............	125 00

Sept. 28.	To Dr. Ada Schweitzer, salary...........	$125 00	
" 28.	To Wm. F. King, salary................	100 00	
" 28.	To Miss H. M. Hooker, salary...........	50 00	
" 28.	To Robt. P. Johnson, salary.............	75 00	
" 28.	To F. R. Bannon, salary................	25 00	
" 30.	To American Express Co., services.......	3 10	
" 30.	To United States Express Co., services....	1 70	
" 30.	To Dr. Ada Schweitzer, expense..........	6 70	
	Total for fourth quarter........................		$3,955 22

Appropriation		$10.000 00
Expense first quarter............................	$2,070 01	
Expense second quarter..........................	1,975 99	
Expense third quarter............................	1,907 83	
Expense fourth quarter	3,955 22	
		$9,909 05
Balance reverting to General Fund........................		90 95
Total		$10,000 00

PURE FOOD AND DRUG LABORATORY.

For Fiscal year beginning October 1, 1909, and ending September 30, 1910.

Oct. 31.	To H. E. Barnard, expense.............	$42 70
" 31.	To B. W. Cohn, expense................	50 92
" 31.	To A. W. Bruner, expense..............	72 20
" 31.	To John Owens, expense................	109 25
" 31.	To F. W. Tucker, expense..............	82 42
" 31.	To H. E. Barnard, salary...............	208 33
" 31.	To H. E. Bishop, salary................	125 00
" 31.	To I. L. Miller, salary.................	116 67
" 31.	To W. D. McAbee, salary...............	60 00
" 31.	To Edith Hoffman, salary..............	50 00
" 31.	To Philip Brodus, salary................	50 00
" 31.	To A. W. Bruner, salary................	100 00
" 31.	To B. W. Cohn, salary..................	100 00
" 31.	To John Owens, salary..................	100 00
" 31.	To F. W. Tucker, salary................	100 00
Nov. 9.	To Adams Express Co., services..........	3 80
" 9.	To The H. Lieber Co., merchandise.......	6 73
" 9.	To Gr. Rapids Upholstering Co., repairs..	7 50
" 19.	To H. E. Barnard, expense..............	19 80
" 30.	To H. E. Barnard, salary...............	208 34
" 30.	To H. E. Bishop, salary................	125 00
" 30.	To I. L. Miller, salary.................	116 66
" 30.	To W. D. McAbee, salary...............	60 00
" 30.	To Edith Hoffman, salary..............	50 00
" 30.	To A. W. Bruner, salary................	100 00

Nov.	30.	To B. W. Cohn, salary..................	$100 00	
"	30.	To John Owens, salary..................	100 00	
"	30.	To F. W. Tucker, salary................	100 00	
"	30.	To A. W. Bruner, expense...............	62 10	
"	30.	To B. W. Cohn, expense.................	55 19	
"	30.	To John Owens, expense.................	60 46	
"	30.	To F. W. Tucker, expense...............	69 66	
Dec.	18.	To H. E. Bishop, expense...............	19 34	
"	18.	To Wm. B. Burford, stationery..........	3 95	
"	18.	To H. E. Barnard, expense..............	129 35	
"	18.	To Mrs. R. Loomis, transcripts.........	7 20	
"	18.	To Schnull & Co., merchandise..........	1 35	
"	31.	To H. E. Barnard, salary...............	208 33	
"	31.	To H. E. Bishop, salary................	125 00	
"	31.	To I. L. Miller, salary................	116 67	
"	31.	To W. D. McAbee, salary................	60 00	
"	31.	To Edith Hoffman, salary...............	50 00	
"	31.	To A. W. Bruner, salary................	100 00	
"	31.	To B. W. Cohn, salary..................	100 00	
"	31.	To John Owens, salary..................	100 00	
"	31.	To F. W. Tucker, salary................	100 00	
"	31.	To H. E. Barnard, expense..............	21 70	
"	31.	To A. W. Bruner, expense...............	56 55	
"	31.	To B. W. Cohn, expense.................	52 75	
"	31.	To John Owens, expense.................	73 03	
"	31.	To F. W. Tucker, expense...............	61 76	
		Total for first quarter........................		$3,999 71
Jan.	14.	To American Toilet Supply Co., laundry..	$18 75	
"	14.	To D. P. Blakiston's Son & Co., books....	2 50	
"	14.	To Adams Express Co., services..........	51	
"	14.	To American Express Co., services.......	3 74	
"	14.	To Frederick A. Stokes Co., text book....	3 22	
"	14.	To G. M. Merrick, agt., merchandise......	5 25	
"	14.	To Vonnegut Hardware Co., merchandise.	69	
"	31.	To H. E. Barnard, salary...............	208 33	
"	31.	To H. E. Bishop, salary................	125 00	
"	31.	To I. L. Miller, salary................	116 67	
"	31.	To W. D. McAbee, salary................	60 00	
"	31.	To Edith Hoffman, salary...............	50 00	
"	31.	To A. W. Bruner, salary................	100 00	
"	31.	To B. W. Cohn, salary..................	100 00	
"	31.	To John Owens, salary..................	100 00	
"	31.	To F. W. Tucker, salary................	100 00	
Feb.	1.	To H. E. Barnard, expense..............	9 95	
"	1.	To A. W. Bruner, expense...............	69 82	
"	1.	To B. W. Cohn, expense.................	22 90	
"	1.	To John Owens, expense.................	87 27	
"	1.	To F. W. Tucker, expense...............	68 84	

Feb.	15.	To Central Supply Co., merchandise......	$1 47	
"	15.	To James T. Daugherty, text book.......	2 00	
"	15.	To Adams Express Co., services..........	4 10	
"	15.	To American Express Co., services.......	1 76	
"	15.	To Pittman Myers Co., merchandise......	17 38	
"	15.	To E. H. Sargent & Co., merchandise.....	6 25	
"	28.	To H. E. Barnard, salary................	208 34	
"	28.	To H. E. Bishop, salary.................	125 00	
"	28.	To I. L. Miller, salary..................	116 66	
"	28.	To W. D. McAbee, salary................	60 00	
"	28.	To Edith Hoffman, salary................	50 00	
"	28.	To A. W. Bruner, salary.................	100 00	
"	28.	To B. W. Cohn, salary..................	100 00	
"	28.	To John Owens, salary..................	100 00	
"	28.	To F. W. Tucker, salary.................	100 00	
Mar.	2.	To H. E. Barnard, expense..............	7 75	
"	2.	To A. W. Bruner, expense...............	58 85	
"	2.	To B. W. Cohn, expense.................	36 40	
"	2.	To John Owens, expense.................	15 30	
"	2.	To F. W. Tucker, expense..............	66 28	
"	11.	To R. H. Bryson, P. M., stamps..........	100 00	
"	19.	To Wm. B. Burford, print'g and stationery	64 32	
"	19.	To Philadelphia Book Co., books.........	1 75	
"	31.	To H. E. Barnard, salary................	208 33	
"	31.	To H. E. Bishop, salary.................	125 00	
"	31.	To I. L. Miller, salary..................	116 67	
"	31.	To W. D. McAbee, salary................	60 00	
"	31.	To Edith Hoffman, salary................	50 00	
"	31.	To A. W. Bruner, salary.................	100 00	
"	31.	To B. W. Cohn, salary..................	100 00	
"	31.	To John Owens, salary..................	100 00	
"	31.	To F. W. Tucker, salary.................	100 00	
"	31.	To H. E. Barnard, expense..............	14 40	
"	31.	To A. W. Bruner, expense...............	67 05	
"	31.	To B. W. Cohn, expense.................	11 93	
"	31.	To John Owens, expense................	42 63	
"	31.	To F. W. Tucker, expense...............	87 81	
		Total for second quarter........................		$3,780 87
Apr.	30.	To H. E. Barnard, salary................	$208 33	
"	30.	To H. E. Bishop, salary.................	125 00	
"	30.	To I. L. Miller, salary..................	116 67	
"	30.	To W. D. McAbee, salary................	60 00	
"	30.	To Edith Hoffman, salary................	50 00	
"	30.	To A. W. Bruner, salary.................	100 00	
"	30.	To B. W. Cohn, salary..................	100 00	
"	30.	To John Owens, salary..................	100 00	
"	30.	To F. W. Tucker, salary.................	100 00	
May	2.	To H. E. Barnard, expense..............	12 00	

May	2.	To H. E. Bishop, expense	$30 50	
"	2.	To A. W. Bruner, expense	66 90	
"	2.	To B. W. Cohn, expense	53 91	
"	2.	To John Owens, expense	64 05	
"	2.	To F. W. Tucker, expense	82 17	
"	12.	To W. Gierke, book binding	1 50	
"	31.	To H. E. Barnard, salary	208 34	
"	31.	To H. E. Bishop, salary	125 00	
"	31.	To I. L. Miller, salary	116 66	
"	31.	To W. D. McAbee, salary	60 00	
"	31.	To Edith Hoffman, salary	50 00	
"	31.	To A. W. Bruner, salary	100 00	
"	31.	To B. W. Cohn, salary	100 00	
"	31.	To John Owens, salary	100 00	
"	31.	To F. W. Tucker, salary	100 00	
"	31.	To A. W. Bruner, expense	72 15	
"	31.	To B. W. Cohn, expense	41 53	
"	31.	To John Owens, expense	56 23	
"	31.	To F. W. Tucker, expense	71 05	
June	30.	To H. E. Barnard, salary	208 33	
"	30.	To H. E. Bishop, salary	125 00	
"	30.	To I. L. Miller, salary	116 67	
"	30.	To W. D. McAbee, salary	60 00	
"	30.	To Edith Hoffman, salary	50 00	
"	30.	To A. W. Bruner, salary	100 00	
"	30.	To B. W. Cohn, salary	100 00	
"	30.	To John Owens, salary	100 00	
"	30.	To F. W. Tucker, salary	100 00	
"	30.	To H. E. Barnard, expense	13 00	
"	30.	To A. W. Bruner, expense	62 17	
"	30.	To B. W. Cohn, expense	22 35	
"	30.	To John Owens, expense	59 85	
"	30.	To F. W. Tucker, expense	71 42	
		Total for third quarter		$3,660 78
July	12.	To American Toilet Supply Co., laundry	$3 75	
"	12.	To Adams Express Co., services	2 30	
"	12.	To American Express Co., services	2 10	
"	12.	To United States Express Co., services	1 70	
"	31.	To H. E. Barnard, salary	208 33	
"	31.	To H. E. Bishop, salary	125 00	
"	31.	To I. L. Miller, salary	116 67	
"	31.	To Edith Hoffman, salary	50 00	
"	31.	To A. W. Bruner, salary	100 00	
"	31.	To B. W. Cohn, salary	100 00	
"	31.	To John Owens, salary	100 00	
"	31.	To F. W. Tucker, salary	100 00	
"	31.	To A. W. Bruner, expense	73 25	
"	31.	To B. W. Cohn, expense	33 65	

July	31.	To F. W. Tucker, expense	$80 56	
"	31.	To John Owens, expense	54 55	
Aug.	31.	To H. E. Bishop, salary	125 00	
"	31.	To H. E. Barnard, salary	208 34	
"	31.	To I. L. Miller, salary	116 66	
"	31.	To Edith Hoffman, salary	50 00	
"	31.	To A. W. Bruner, salary	100 00	
"	31.	To B. W. Cohn, salary	100 00	
"	31.	To F. W. Tucker, salary	100 00	
"	31.	To John Owens, salary	100 00	
"	31.	To H. E. Barnard, expense	7 85	
"	31.	To A. W. Bruner, expense	47 55	
"	31.	To B. W. Cohn, expense	14 55	
"	31.	To F. W. Tucker, expense	48 29	
"	31.	To John Owens, expense	68 14	
Sept.	28.	To H. E. Barnard, expense	103 02	
"	28.	To A. W. Bruner, expense	68 10	
"	28.	To B. W. Cohn, expense	25 65	
"	28.	To F. W. Tucker, expense	51 20	
"	28.	To John Owens, expense	54 45	
"	28.	To Wm. B. Burford, merchandise	14 03	
"	28.	To Municipal Journal & Engr., sub. 1910	3 00	
"	28.	To Adams Express Co., services	4 75	
"	28.	To Badger Furniture Co., merchandise	23 00	
"	28.	To Pittman-Myers Co., merchandise	26 70	
"	28.	To H. E. Barnard, salary	208 33	
"	28.	To H. E. Bishop, salary	125 00	
"	28.	To I. L. Miller, salary	116 67	
"	28.	To Edith Hoffman, salary	50 00	
"	28.	To A. W. Bruner, salary	100 00	
"	28.	To B. W. Cohn, salary	100 00	
"	28.	To F. W. Tucker, salary	100 00	
"	28.	To John Owens, salary	100 00	
		Total for the fourth quarter		$3,558 64

RECAPITULATION.

Appropriation		$15,000 00

Expense.

First quarter	$3,999 71	
Second quarter	3,780 87	
Third quarter	3,660 78	
Fourth quarter	3,512 14	
Total		$14,953 50
Balance reverting to general fund		$46 50

INDIANA STATE BOARD OF HEALTH—WATER LABORATORY.

For fiscal year October 1, 1909, to September 30, 1910.

Appropriation				$5,000 00
1909.				
Oct.	31.	To H. E. Barnard, expense	$27 55	
"	31.	To J. H. Brewster, salary	116 67	
"	31.	To Goldine Grove, salary	50 00	
"	31.	To Cullen Thomas, salary	25 00	
"	31.	To J. J. Hinman, salary	30 00	
Nov.	8.	To J. H. Brewster, expense	14 00	
"	9.	To H. E. Barnard, water reports	25 00	
"	9.	To Adams Express Co., services	2 19	
"	9.	To American Express Co., services	4 90	
"	30.	To J. H. Brewster, salary	116 66	
"	30.	To Goldine Grove, salary	50 00	
"	30.	To J. J. Hinman, salary	30 00	
"	30.	To Cullen Thomas, salary	25 00	
"	30.	To Phillip Broadus, salary	50 00	
Dec.	18.	To Adams Express Co., service	5 40	
"	18.	To American Express Co., service	2 40	
"	18.	To United States Express Co., service	1 25	
"	18.	To Western Union Telegraph Co., service	1 73	
"	18.	To J. L. Anderson, expense	25	
"	18.	To Indianapolis Blue Print Co., mdse	2 35	
"	18.	To The H. Lieber Co., merchandise	6 73	
"	18.	To Pittman-Myers Co., merchandise	3 49	
"	31.	To J. H. Brewster, salary	116 67	
"	31.	To Goldine Grove, salary	50 00	
"	31.	To J. J. Hinman, salary	30 00	
"	31.	To Cullen Thomas, salary	25 00	
"	31.	To Philip Broadus, salary	50 00	
		Total first quarter		$862 24
1910.				
Jan.	14.	To J. H. Brewster, expense	$1 12	
"	14.	To Wm. B. Burford, print'g and stationery	27 05	
"	14.	To American Express Co., services	1 40	
"	14.	To Pittman-Myers Co., merchandise	3 90	
"	31.	To J. H. Brewster, salary	116 67	
"	31.	To Goldine Grove, salary	50 00	
"	31.	To J. J. Hinman, salary	30 00	
"	31.	To Cullen Thomas, salary	25 00	
"	31.	To Philip Broadus, salary	50 00	
Feb.	1.	To J. H. Brewster, expense	15 50	
"	15.	To J. H. Brewster, expense	9 00	
"	15.	To American Express Co., services	1 75	
"	15.	To United States Express Co., services	30	
"	28.	To J. H. Brewster, salary	116 66	

Feb.	28.	To Goldine Grove, salary	$50 00	
"	28.	To J. J. Hinman, salary	30 00	
"	28.	To Cullen Thomas, salary	25 00	
"	28.	To Philip Broadus, salary	50 00	
Mar.	19.	To J. H. Brewster, expense	32 36	
"	19.	To Adams Express Co., service	3 24	
"	19.	To American Express Co., service	4 99	
"	19.	To United States Express Co., service	40	
"	19.	To Pittman-Myers Co., merchandise	12 51	
"	19.	To R. L. Polk & Co., directory	6 00	
"	19.	To G. M. Merrick, agt., merchandise	3 50	
"	19.	To Standard Calorometer Co., merchandise	4 00	
"	19.	To G. E. Stechert & Co., books	18 85	
"	31.	To J. H. Brewster, salary	116 67	
"	31.	To Goldine Grove, salary	50 00	
"	31.	To J. J. Hinman, Jr., salary	30 00	
"	31.	To Cullen Thomas, salary	25 00	
"	31.	To Philip Broadus, salary	50 00	
		Total second quarter		$960 87
Apr.	4.	To H. E. Barnard, expense	$59 15	
"	8.	To American Toilet Supply Co., laundry	19 65	
"	8.	To Adams Express Co., service	45	
"	8.	To American Express Co., service	7 35	
"	8.	To United States Express Co., service	2 40	
"	8.	To F. H. Langsenkamp, merchandise	6 75	
"	8.	To E. H. Sargent & Co., merchandise	7 65	
"	22.	To J. H. Brewster, expense	42 00	
"	30.	To J. H. Brewster, salary	116 67	
"	30.	To Goldine Grove, salary	50 00	
"	30.	To J. J. Hinman, Jr., salary	30 00	
"	30.	To Cullen Thomas, salary	25 00	
"	30.	To Philip Broadus, salary	50 00	
May	2.	To J. H. Brewster, expense	46 36	
"	12.	To Arnold & Buttman, mdse. and copying	12 65	
"	12.	To Wm. B. Burford, print'g and stationery	17 94	
"	12.	To Central Supply Co., merchandise	15	
"	12.	To Adams Express Co., service	2 75	
"	12.	To American Express Co., service	5 05	
"	12.	To United States Express Co., service	3 80	
"	12.	To The H. Lieber Co., merchandise	5 91	
"	12.	To Pittman-Myers Co., merchandise	45 89	
"	26.	To Robt. H. Bryson, P. M., postage stamps	100 00	
"	31.	To J. H. Brewster, salary	116 66	
"	31.	To Goldine Grove, salary	50 00	
"	31.	To J. J. Hinman, Jr., salary	30 00	
"	31.	To Cullen Thomas, salary	25 00	
"	31.	To Philip Broadus, salary	50 00	
"	31.	To J. H. Brewster, expense	10 35	
"	31.	To H. E. Barnard, expense	27 68	

June	15.	To Wm. B. Burford, merchandise	$2 20	
"	15.	To American Express Co., services	2 05	
"	15.	To United States Express Co., services	2 10	
"	15.	To The H. Lieber Co., merchandise	90	
"	15.	To Schnull & Co., merchandise	3 00	
"	15.	To Central Union Telephone Co., tolls	1 60	
"	15.	To Postal Cable, Telegraph Co., tolls	1 23	
"	15.	To Vonnegut Hardware Co., merchandise	2 70	
"	15.	To J. H. Brewster, expense	19 70	
"	30.	To J. H. Brewster, salary	116 67	
"	30.	To Goldine Grove, salary	50 00	
"	30.	To J. J. Hinman, Jr., salary	30 00	
"	30.	To Cullen Thomas, salary	25 00	
"	30.	To Philip Broadus, salary	50 00	
"	30.	To J. P. Van Wirt, salary	25 00	
July	2.	To J. H. Brewster, expense	40 95	
"	2.	To G. W. Hunter, per J. H. B., launch	103 35	
"	5.	To J. H. Brewster, expense	25 40	
		Total third quarter		$1,469 11
July	12.	To American Toilet Supply Co., laundry	$13 20	
"	12.	To Wm. B. Burford, merchandise	12 94	
"	12.	To Adams Express Co., services	2 00	
"	12.	To American Express Co., services	4 63	
"	12.	To E. H. Sargent & Co., merchandise	12 02	
"	12.	To J. L. Anderson, expense	1 25	
"	31.	To J. H. Brewster, salary	116 67	
"	31.	To Goldine Grove, salary	50 00	
"	31.	To J. J. Hinman, Jr., salary	30 00	
"	31.	To Cullen Thomas, salary	25 00	
"	31.	To Philip Broadus, salary	50 00	
"	31.	To J. P. Van Wirt, salary	65 00	
Aug.	6.	To J. H. Brewster, expense	121 52	
"	16.	To Central Supply Co., merchandise	23	
"	16.	To Adams Express Co., services	2 55	
"	16.	To American Express Co., services	8 15	
"	16.	To United States Express Co., services	60	
"	16.	To J. L. Anderson, expense	35	
"	31.	To J. H. Brewster, expense	79 79	
"	31.	To J. H. Brewster, salary	116 66	
"	31.	To Goldine Grove, salary	50 00	
"	31.	To J. J. Hinman, Jr., salary	30 00	
"	31.	To Cullen Thomas, salary	25 00	
"	31.	To Philip Broadus, salary	50 00	
"	31.	To J. P. Van Wirt, salary	60 00	
Sept.	10.	To H. E. Barnard, expense	26 70	
"	10.	To A. Burdsal Co., merchandise	50	
"	10.	To Central Supply Co., merchandise	1 00	
"	10.	To Adams Express Co., services	8 06	
"	10.	To American Express Co., services	2 45	

Sept. 10.	To United States Express Co., services....	$1 90		
" 10.	To G. M. Merrick, merchandise..........	3 50		
" 10.	To E. H. Sargent & Co., merchandise.....	6 05		
" 10.	To The Star Store, merchandise..........	3 00		
" 10.	To J. P. Van Wirt, salary..............	15 00		
" 28.	To Robt. H. Bryson, P. M., postage stamps	100 00		
" 28.	To American Toilet Supply Co., laundry..	11 70		
" 28.	To J. L. Anderson, expense.............	25		
" 28.	To J. H. Brewster, expense.............	69 31		
" 28.	To American Express Co., service........	12 28		
" 28.	To Pittman-Myers Co., merchandise.......	92 23		
" 28.	To A. T. Sink, M. boat and equipment...	75 00		
" 28.	To J. H. Brewster, salary...............	116 67		
" 28.	To Goldine Grove, salary................	50 00		
" 28.	To J. J. Hinman, Jr., salary............	30 00		
" 28.	To Cullen Thomas, salary................	25 00		
" 28.	To Philip Broadus, salary..............	50 00		
	Total fourth quarter...........................		$1,628 16	

Appropriation		$5,000 00
Expense first quarter	$862 24	
Expense second quarter	960 87	
Expense third quarter	1,469 11	
Expense fourth quarter	1,628 16	
		$4,920 38
Balance		$79 62
Credit by cash received for boat.................		50 00
Total reverting to general fund.................		$129 62

ADJOURNED MEETING.

October 8, 1909.

The meeting was held at Terre Haute at the Terre Haute House, 12 m., October 8th.

Present: Drs. McCoy, Wishard, Tucker, Hurty.

President stated the meeting was called at Terre Haute, according to previous order of the Board, on account of the annual meeting of the Indiana State Medical Association at Terre Haute.

It was deemed advisable for the members of the Board to attend the medical meeting because matters pertaining to the Pure Food and Drug Law and the Health Law were to come up for discussion; besides, attendance would afford opportunity for the members to meet members of the medical profession, and so possibly help the health cause onward.

Dr. Wishard, being a member of the House of Delegates, reported the passage of the following resolution:

Whereas, The Indiana State Medical Association recognizes the great work that is being done in protecting the health of the people, and preventing the fraudulent sale of foods and drugs by the enforcement of the food and drug laws; and

Whereas, It is apparent that certain manufacturing interests are endeavoring to nullify such legislation and to harass and hinder the officials in the enforcement of the law. Therefore, be it

Resolved, That the Indiana State Medical Association expresses its confidence in the Indiana State Board of Health to resist any effort made by manufacturers or others which may in any way weaken the efficiency of the pure food and drug law, or restrict the scope of its operation.

. Resolved, That the Indiana State Medical Association does not accept the decision of the Referee Board appointed by Ex-President Roosevelt as final, and that we recommend to the President of the United States and the Secretary of Agriculture that further investigations conducted upon the broadest lines be continued, that the people and the food producer may know the value, the necessity or harmfulness of any or all food preservatives; and be it further

Resolved, That the Indiana State Medical Association recognizes and emphatically endorses the work of their fellow-citizen Dr. Harvey W. Wiley in his untiring efforts extending over many years to obtain for the people pure foods and pure food legislation, and that we express our appreciation of his work by sending him a copy of these resolutions.

Dr. Tucker, a member of the House of Delegates, reported the passage of a resolution directing that the president appoint a committee of three to consider and confer with other interested associations or individuals concerning the raising of funds with which to open and maintain the State Tuberculosis Hospital, which must remain closed and unoccupied when completed, unless ways and means could be found for its maintenance, as the legislature had failed to make provision.

Dr. Tucker further announced that Dr. W. N. Wishard, Dr. A. C. Kimberlin and Dr. Chas. H. McCully were appointed on said committee.

After discussion, it was

Ordered: That all health officers now in the health service shall make application upon blanks furnished, to the State Board, for a certificate of eligibility, the same based upon recent service, as provided.

REGULAR MEETING.

October 15, 1909

Called to order 2:30 p. m. by President McCoy.

Present: Drs. McCoy, Wishard, Davis, Hurty.

The president announced: This meeting is to consider and take action concerning the affairs of the quarter ending September 30, 1909, the last quarter of the fiscal year; also to consider the third quarter of the statistical year.

Minutes of the last regular meeting held July 6, 1909, and of the special meetings held July 16th, Sept. 7th, Sept. 24th, Sept. 30th, and Oct. 8th, were read and approved.

SECRETARY'S REPORT.

Report of Secretary for the quarter ending September 30, 1909, was read and ordered spread of record, as follows:

The routine work for the quarter was without event. The Secretary made only three visits—

July 10th, Sheridan, account of order of State Board of Health to reinspect schoolhouses Districts Nos. 11, 12, 13, Marion Township, Boone County.

July 14th, Ft. Wayne, account of lawsuit of local board and to inspect some schoolhouses with the county secretary.

July 20th, Evansville, account of schoolhouse inspection and consultation with city health officer.

Reports of these visits are appended:

Sheridan.—July 10th. In accordance with the order of the State Board of Health, I went to Sheridan, July 10th, and there met Mr. Howard, trustee of Marion Township, Boone County. With him I visited school districts Nos. 11, 12, 13. At the last meeting the Board authorized the second inspection in answer to a petition of the trustee and many patrons of the schools, to see whether or not the sanitary conditions were such as would warrant the extending of condemnation previously made. Authority was given to the Secretary to extend the same, if in his judgment, after inspection, it was thought best to do so. I now report I found the schoolhouses had been repaired, painted, papered and thoroughly cleaned. All sanitary conditions as ordered in the rules for the construction of sanitary schoolhouses were not complied with, nor could they be, yet on account of the neatness and cleanliness, and because the money was not at hand for constructing better buildings, the Secretary exercised his authority, and nullified the prior condemnation of the schoolhouses in Districts Nos. 11, 12, 13, of Marion Township, Boone County.

Ft. Wayne.—July 14th. I visited Ft. Wayne on account of urgent invitation of the City Board of Health, to join with them in abolishing a nuisance. The conditions were extraordinary. The local board had inspected the Eckart Packing House and found it unsanitary and unlawful. Orders had been issued, according to law, for the abolition of the unsanitary conditions, but the defendants had gone into court and secured a temporary injunction against the said board, forbidding it to enforce the law. The said board thereupon appealed to the county board and the state board, which were not under injunction, to abolish the illegal conditions.

Upon arrival at Fort Wayne I was met by the county health officer, Dr. Van Buskirk, and the City Board of Health. The situation was gone over and then in company with Dr. Van Buskirk, I inspected the Eckart Packing House. It seems unnecessary here to make a full report of the conditions discovered because the same have been set forth at full length in the records of the Ft. Wayne Board of Health. It will suffice here to say that the conditions of the law governing sanitary conditions of slaughterhouses were violated in almost all particulars.

After inspection was made, the prosecutor was consulted and arrangements were consummated for entering new prosecution. Within ten days afterwards, notice was received that all had been adjusted and a case in court was unnecessary.

Evansville.—July 20th. On July 20th I visited Evansville, for the school board and the City Board of Health had selected the state health officer as an arbiter in a dispute concerning certain sanitary conditions of an old schoolhouse. The difficulties were easily adjusted and the school board readily agreed to make the repairs and changes which I suggested.

Afterwards, I conferred with the county health officer, the city health officer, and the Committee on Health of the city council in regard to certain drainage plans. It seems unnecessary here to set forth in detail these entire plans and I will simply say that after thorough study of the said plans, certain suggestions were made which were adopted. The visit seemed to have been successful in all of its objects.

The following tables show the smallpox and typhoid fever status for the quarter:

SMALLPOX COMPARISON FOR THIRD QUARTER.

Date.	Number Cases Reported.	Number Deaths.	Number Counties Invaded.
July, 1908	65	0	13
July, 1909	61	2	8
August, 1908	45	0	7
August, 1909	29	0	2
September, 1908	32	0	8
September, 1909	51	0	9
Total, 1908	142	0	28
Total, 1909	141	2	19

TYPHOID FEVER COMPARISON FOR THIRD QUARTER.

Date	Number Cases Reported.	Number Deaths.	Number Counties Invaded.
July, 1908	207	58	53
July, 1909	267	78	60
August, 1908	478	81	69
August, 1909	464	106	69
September, 1908	446	118	76
September, 1909	757	132	81
Total, 1908	1,131	257	198
Total, 1909	1,488	316	210

The secretary presented several letters from physicians, asking the meaning of the term "recent experience" as it appears in the health law of 1909.

After discussion, and report of conversation by the secretary with Assistant Attorney-General White, the following rule was adopted.

RULE 24a.—Defining the term "Recent Experience" as used in Chapter 144, Acts of 1909, Section 10, and as used in the Rules of the State Board of Health governing the examination of applicants for certificates of eligibility to appointment to the office of county health commissioner, city health officer and town health officer, which rules were passed July 9, 1909.

RULE 24a.—The term "Recent Experience" as used in the health law approved March 6, 1909, and as used in the rules of the State Board of Health passed July 9, 1909, shall be held to mean: Actual experience as a regularly appointed health officer, or being a physician, experience as a member of a board of health, immediately prior to March 6, 1909, or for the year ending December 31, 1908.

RULE 24a was passed October 15, 1909, by the Indiana State Board of Health according to Chapter 144, Acts of 1909, as appears in the minutes of said board.

Attest: J. N. HURTY, Secretary.

ACTION ON EXAMINATION PAPERS.

The examination papers of applicants for certificate of eligibility to be appointed health officers were reviewed and the following persons were ordered certified. The grading was upon a basis of 1,000; required to pass, 750.

Name.	*Address.*	*Grade.* Per cent.
Joseph C. Alexander	219 Claypool Bldg., Indianapolis	86.8
A. C. Arnett	Lafayette	84.5
C. A. Ballard	Logansport	85.4
Emerson Barnum	Manilla, Rush County	90.1
Harry L. Bell	Knox, Starke County	77.5
J. W. Birchfield	2521 E. 10th St., Indianapolis	91.2
Charles S. Bosenbury	South Bend	93.
John C. Bradfield	Logansport	81.
E. H. Brubaker	Flora, Carroll County	79.
C. E. Canady	New Castle	81.
Charles A. Carter	Indianapolis	98.
Albert C. Clauser	Delphi	96.1
Walter J. Cluthe	Tell City	86.8
Ralph R. Coble	Spencer	90.
Charles N. Combs	Terre Haute	88.9
Claude C. Crum	Jeffersonville	94.
William Daniel	Corydon	92.5
Miles F. Daubenheyer	Butlerville	84.2
Albert T. Davis	Marion	86.
J. R. Dillinger	French Lick	98.
David B. Domb	632 Madison Ave., Indianapolis	90.
A. I. Donaldson	Washington	96.1
Edward J. Du Bois	1116 N. Capitol Ave., Indianapolis	94.8
R. B. Dugdale	South Bend	89.5
Thomas A. Dugdale	Liberty Mills, Wabash County	80.
George W. Eddingfield	Elwood	78.7
Harry Elliott	Brazil	78.9
John B. Fattic	Anderson	94.6
Gilbert R. Finch	Center Point, Clay County	78.9
J. D. Foor	Blackhawk, Vigo County	89.
Chas. E. Gillespie	Crothersville	80.5
Edmon A. Gilson	Hammond	93.
Clayton E. Goodrick	Peru	77.2
W. Q. Harper	Millersburg, Elkhart County	80.7

Name.	*Address.*	*Grade.* Per cent.
Harry S. Hatch, Madison		83.5
J. R. Hicks, Covington		94.
Paul Higbee, Sullivan		87.4
E. Hollingsworth, Washington		92.
E. S. Imel, Petersburg		84.7
Robert C. Johnson, Frankfort		76.7
John Glover Jones, Vincennes		78.3
Herman H. Kamman, Columbus		79.
George H. Kammon, Seymour		80.
Thomas A. Kearns, Flora, Carroll County		81.4
M. O. King, Rochester		79.
Millard Knowlton, Terre Haute		93.
H. M. Lamberson, Connersville		97.
John W. Little, 2635 E. 10th St., Indianapolis		85.5
Henry Lohrman, 427 Newton Claypool Bldg		81.
Harry S. Mackey, 1402 Union St., Indianapolis		87.
William J. Malloy, Muncie		83.
William R. Mattox, Terre Haute		86.2
F. R. Maxwell, Martinsville		77.3
Denis L. McAuliffe, North Vernon		82.2
Edgar H. Myers, South Bend		90.5
John P. Nicodemus, Logansport		79.4
Thomas W. Oberlin, Hammond		77.
Nettie B. Powell, Marion		97.
Ezra Prall, Henryville		85.7
J. H. S. Reiley, Shelbyville		76.
Joseph Shonkwiler, Rockville		78.
John W. Sluss, Indianapolis		91.6
James Albert Snapp, Goshen		81.
George E. Snearly, Roann		77.1
Clint Croasdale Sourwine, Brazil		80.2
Lewis A. E. Storch, 1357 S. Meridian St., Indianapolis		82.1
E. Trent Stout, Upland		83.5
Stephen W. Stuteville, Grandview, Spencer County		86.9
Thomas L. Sullivan, Jr., 503 N. Capitol Ave., Indianapolis		91.7
Thomas J. Swantz, South Bend		81.5
Frank A. Tabor, Terre Haute		89.5
J B. Thomas, 1021 N. Senate Ave., Indianapolis		98.5
A. W. Tobias, Elwood		82.
R. E. Troutman, Logansport		77.2
Earl P. Wagner, South Bend		86.9
James Y. Welborn, Evansville		92.
M. M. Wells, Fairland		80.9
George W. Willeford, Washington		90.5
John B. Berteling, South Bend		98.
Joseph L. Reeve, Edwardsport		80.
J. Lucius Gray, Laporte		95.

CONDEMNATION EXTENDED.

A petition signed by 18 patrons of the condemned schoolhouse, District No. 1, Hensley Township, Johnson County, was read, asking that the condemnation be extended from June 1st, 1909, to the same date in 1910, because of various unavoidable delays in securing a new site. After discussion it was

Ordered: That the condemnation of the said schoolhouse be extended as requested.

The Secretary announced he had appointed Dr. Chas. A. Carter a clerk in the office at a salary of $100 per month, and asked the confirmation of the Board.

Dr. Tucker moved the appointment be confirmed. Seconded by Dr. Davis.

Unanimously carried.

The Secretary asked permission to employ another man in the bacteriological and pathological laboratory, the increase in work demanding more help. After consideration it was

Ordered: The Secretary may employ one additional man in the bacteriological and pathological laboratory at $100 per month, and traveling expenses, his duties and work to be as directed by the Secretary.

LETTER FROM HAMMOND.

The following letter from Dr. Wm. D. Weis, Health Officer of Hammond, was read:

DECEMBER 22, 1909.

Dr. J. N Hurty, Indianapolis, Ind.:

Dear Doctor.—We believe the time has arrived when the Indiana State Board of Health should take action against those responsible for the polluted condition of the water supply of the cities of Indiana along the shore of Lake Michigan.

We, therefore, request that steps be taken by your board to prevent further pollution of the water supply of the city of Hammond.

We herewith extend to you our support in any manner that we may be of service to you or your officers.

Respectfully,

BOARD OF HEALTH AND CHARITIES,
Hammond, Indiana.

Per Wm. D. Weis, M. D., Secretary.

The Secretary reported this was an old matter, that the U. S. Maize Products Co., had long been polluting the lake near Hammond and much complaint from Hammond citizens had been received, that action had not been taken because the Hammond health authorities asked suspension of action until plea and persuasion had been exhausted. The letter was an announcement that the aid of the State Board of Health was now needed.

Dr. Tucker moved that the Secretary be instructed to have the matter fully investigated and, if he thought proper, to hand the matter over to the Attorney-General.

Measles.—President McCoy advocated that health officers be instructed to pay closer attention to the preventing of measles. In his experience the disease caused more fatalities than scarlet fever, and its sequela were to be feared. Accordingly, Dr. Davis offered the following:

Whereas, Measles causes a mortality greater than scarlet fever and as its sequela are dangerous and to be feared, therefore, it is

Ordered: That quarantine of cases of measles shall be absolute, and those who come in continued, close contact with infected persons, shall be quarantined, but the entire family need not be quarantined, according as the health officer may prescribe, he to allow liberty to only those who could not in his judgment, carry the infection.

Ordered: That a special conference of County Health Commissioners be held February 2, 1910, and that the Secretary shall make all arrangements for said conference.

SPECIAL MEETING STATE BOARD OF HEALTH.

DECEMBER 28, 1909.

Called to order by President McCoy, at 12 m.

Present: Drs. McCoy, Tucker, Hurty.

The President announced the special meeting was for the purpose of holding the *second regular examination* of those desiring to be eligible for appointment as health officers.

The Secretary reported there were 42 applicants present, although 60 applicants were on the list. He also reported the examinations had been in progress since 10 a. m. with Drs. McCoy, Tucker, and Hurty present.

Several incidents of the preceding examination were discussed and a course of procedure accepted.

There being no further business the Board adjourned.

SPECIAL MEETING STATE BOARD OF HEALTH.

JANUARY 1, 1910.

Called to order by President McCoy at 2 p. m.

Present: Drs. McCoy, Tucker, Hurty.

The President announced the object of the meeting was to consider the markings and take action as to who had passed the examination held as described in minutes of previous special meeting.

Dr. Tucker was appointed to select the examination papers and Dr. Hurty to open the sealed envelopes to determine the names of those examined.

After due investigation and study of the examination papers, the following persons were decided to have passed and that a certificate of eligibility be issued.

Name.	*Address.*	*Grade.* Per cent.
James R. Anthony	1607 College Ave., Indianapolis	90.06
H. L. Baker	Lebanon	87.5
Mahlon F. Baldwin	Marion	75.5
J. H. Barnfield	Logansport	86.
Joshua L. Blaize	Stendal	93.
R. M. Campbell	Lafayette	85.7
S. Roscoe Chancellor	Kokomo	90.7
Edward M. Corbin	Sullivan	80.2
Bruce Fleetwood	Linton	75.
R. F. Frost	Huntington	87.2
Edward M. Glaser	Brookville	93.7
Julian E. Hanna	Noblesville	85.8
James K. Hawes	Columbus	94.7
George B. Hoopingamer	Elkhart	92.
Frank H. Jett	Terre Haute	98.
W. W. Kneale	Anderson	82.2
John H. Lall	Anderson	79.
James A. Long	Anderson	85.
Will J. Martin	Kokomo	93.7
J. Creston Mast	Elkhart	85.
Carl W. McGaughey	Greenfield	86.5
J. H. Morrison	Hartsville	83.5
Luther A. Mott	Elwood	81.7
Charles W. Murphy	Salem	90.5
E. V. Nolt	Columbia City	80.
George G. Richardson	Van Buren	90.
Wilbur W. Ross	Laporte	80.5
Leslie C. Sammons	Shelbyville	87.

Name.	*Address.*	*Grade.* Per cent.
W. D. Schwartz,	Portland	80.4
Henry B. Shacklett,	New Albany	94.
T. J. Stephenson,	Lapel	75.
W. G. Swank,	Crawfordsville	97.5
A. S. Tilford,	Martinsville	85.5
Henry E. Vitou,	South Bend	81.5
John E. Yerling,	Peru	82.5

REGULAR MEETING STATE BOARD OF HEALTH.

JANUARY 14, 1910.

Called to order by President McCoy, at 2 p. m.

Present: Drs. McCoy, Davis, Tucker, Hurty.

President announced the meeting was to consider the affairs of the first fiscal quarter ending December 31, 1909, and the fourth calendar quarter ending December 31, 1909.

Minutes of last regular meeting held October 15, 1909, and of the special meetings held December 28, 1909, and January 1, 1910, were read and approved.

REPORT OF SECRETARY FOR THE QUARTER ENDING DEC. 31, 1909.

It may be truly said that the quarter ending December 31st has been extra strenous. Within that time two examinations of those desiring to become eligible to serve as health officers have been held. They were the first of said examinations under the new law. The difficulty of advertising them properly was felt in the beginning, but, not being provided with funds, the Board was compelled to depend upon the gratuitous service of newspapers to a very large degree. Notices of the examinations were sent to the newspapers in all counties with the request that the same be published as news matter. Probably, only in 50 per cent. of the instances were the notices published. Notices were also sent to health officers and to secretaries of county medical societies. It is to be hoped that another year proper paid notification of these examinations can be given.

EXAMINATION OF HEALTH OFFICERS.

The Indiana State Board of Health announces that the first examination of those wishing to become eligible for appointment to the position of County Health Commissioner, or City or Town Health Officer, will be held in the State House at Indianapolis, September 30, 1909. Licensed physicians intending to enter the examination, must make application upon official blanks by September 23d. Application blanks and rules governing the examination may be secured from the State Board. The Board announces the examination will cover generally, the fields of Hygiene and Sanitary Science, including food and drug inspection. A reasonable familiarity with the health statutes and the rules of the Board will be required, and the subject of vital statistics, the foundation of public health work, will be gone into thoroughly.

All applicants for admission to examination will be supplied with a pamphlet containing the health statutes and rules upon receipt of 4 cents in postage stamps. The edition of the pamphlet containing the statutes and rules is limited and cannot be generally distributed.

Application blanks and pamphlets of statutes and rules will be ready for distribution from and after August 10.

Mr. Editor: This item is a matter of general interest to the people because this examination marks the beginning of scientific and thorough disease prevention work in Indiana. A matter of the greatest economic importance.

J. N. Hurty,
Secretary.

Indianapolis, September 1, 1909.

The Board is already familiar with the facts connected with these examinations, and the minutes of previous meetings give full account of the same.

Epidemics.—In October, typhoid fever was the prevailing disease and there were several small epidemics of diphtheria and scarlet fever. Measles prevailed in many parts of the State quite unusually. There were 112 cases of smallpox, with no deaths. Compared with the corresponding month last year there was very little difference.

In November, tonsillitis was the most prevalent disease, pneumonia standing eighth in area of prevalence, although it may be said that November is a pneumonia month. Compared with the corresponding month last year, there is a slight decrease of this disease. There were a few epidemics of diphtheria, notably one in Cass County where there were 21 cases with 4 deaths. Marion County reported 37 cases, 3 deaths. Scarlet fever was quite prevalent in Allen County, and also in Brown, Clark, Clay, Elkhart, Laporte, Madison, Marion, Monroe, Putnam, St. Joseph, Tipton, Vanderburgh, Vigo and Wells. The disease seemed not to be virulent, for the deaths for the whole State for that month numbered 16. During the month 86 cases of smallpox occurred in Allen County, with 1 death. Smallpox also appeared in Grant County, 8 cases;

Delaware, 5; Daviess, 1; Carroll, 1; Marshall, 14; St. Joseph, 4; Steuben, 1; Marshall, 1; Wayne, 1.

A number of schools were closed during the month.

December.—Tonsillitis, as in the two preceding months, was reported as the most prevalent disease. Pneumonia stood sixth in area of prevalence. Following is the order of disease prevalence of the diseases named: Tonsillitis, bronchitis, rheumatism, scarlet fever, influenza, pneumonia, diphtheria, typhoid fever, measles, pleuritis, diarrhea. chickenpox, intermittent and remittent fever, erysipelas, whooping-cough, smallpox, inflammation of bowels, dysentery, puerperal fever, cerebro-spinal meningitis, cholera infantum, cholera morbus, typho-malaria fever.

VISITS BY THE SECRETARY.

The Secretary made 16 visits as follows:

October 4th, Pennville, account of condemnation of schoolhouse and complications.

October 6th, Terre Haute, account of meeting of State Board of Health in that city and account of meeting of State Medical Society.

October 14th, Newcastle, account of lecture under auspices of Henry County Medical Society, and to make sanitary inspection of the Maxwell-Briscoe Motor Works.

October 18th, Richmond, Va., account annual meeting of the American Public Health Association.

October 25th, Columbus, account of annual meeting of State Charities Association.

October 31st, Brazil, account of Teachers' Institute and to lecture upon school hygiene.

November 9th, Lebanon, account of Teachers' Institute, and to lecture upon "Medical Inspection of School Children."

November 11th, Ft. Wayne, to lecture upon Tuberculosis under the auspices of the Ft. Wayne Academy of Medicine and to help in demonstrating the tuberculosis exhibit.

November 21st, Lawrenceburg, account meeting with city council and mayor to consider municipal hygiene.

November 26th, Brazil, account of meeting of Clay County Medical Society, to read a paper before said society upon the work of the State Board of Health.

November 29th, Worthington, account of investigation of schoolhouse and to aid in public movement to secure a new building.

Also to lecture upon Municipal Hygiene before three men's and women's clubs of the town.

December 4th, Peru, account of meeting of Miami County Teachers' Institute, and to lecture before same upon School Hygiene.

December 7th, Westfield, to lecture upon Tuberculosis and to make sanitary survey of the Orphans' Home of the Indiana Society.

December 14th, Warsaw, account of public meeting called by the city council and citizens to consider municipal hygiene.

December 15th, Howe, on account of inspection of schoolhouse in accordance with petition from the people and recommendation of the Governor.

December 16th, Brazil, on account of inspection of creamery, also to confer with Dr. Williams, county health officer, in regard to schoolhouse conditions in two townships. Full accounts of these visits are appended.

Pennville.—This visit was made October 4th. The Pennville schoolhouse had been condemned by the State Board of Health two years ago, then for various reasons the condemnation had been extended. The differences between the various factions continued and the trustee had deliberately violated the condemnation of the State Board of Health. The people were not informed of my visit, but a large number of citizens gathered at the schoolhouse shortly after I arrived. The whole situation was discussed, the county superintendent fortunately being present. The trustee was not present. Inquiry developed the fact that the trustee had opened the schoolhouse and continued school in the face of the condemnation, upon the advice of ex-Judge Smith, attorney, at Portland. The judge argued there was no other place to hold school and that school must be held. He further argued that certain changes had been made for sanitary betterment. It was further shown that the trustee had made every endeavor to secure an appropriation and the same had been given, but he had been thwarted in his endeavor to secure a proper location. The schoolhouse at Pennville is situated right in the center of the town and the location is very bad. The location of the new schoolhouse should most certainly be outside of the business district, where more air and more ground can be secured. It was said that certain merchants resisted the change, and that the ground that was decided upon was held at too high a figure, and condemnation could not be instituted in time for holding the school. As there seemed to be a disposition to conform to the orders of the State Board of Health, and an honest belief that they could not be conformed to, and as there is evident intention to build a new schoolhouse, I therefore advised that no legal proceeding be taken, for, under the circumstances, to do so would be merely for the purpose of preserving the dignity of the Board. The sentiment at Pennville is with the Board, and the sentiment is for a new schoolhouse, but the retrogressive individuals have prevented a new building from being constructed.

Terre Haute.—At Terre Haute I attended a two days' meeting of the State Medical Society, and on October 7th attended the meeting of the State Board of Health, as previously ordered by the Board, and which was held in the Terre Haute House. The Secretary took part in several of the discussions which were before the Society, representing the State Board of Health. The meeting was very successful and a resolution was passed concerning the pure food and drug law, which has already been reported and recorded in the minutes of a special meeting.

Richmond, Va.—October 18th. According to the orders of the State Board of Health to appear as its representative I went to Richmond, Va., and attended the annual meeting of the American Public Health Association. It would be an easy matter to give a full review of the five days' session of this important association, but it is deemed unnecessary, as all that there occurred can be read at any time in the annual reports of the said association. I was called upon to occupy the chair upon two occasions and took part in numerous discussions and advised concerning sanitary questions. The reception of the society by the citizens of Richmond was more than cordial. I feel that my attendance was most profitable both to me and to the Board, imparting new enthusiasm and securing much new information. I was made a member of the committee of seven which controls the general affairs of the society, and also made a member of two other committees.

Columbus.—October 25th. On this date I went to Columbus to attend the Tuberculosis Symposium of the State Association of Charities in session there. I had the pleasure of attending but one meeting, which was held in the evening. There were a number of speakers, the most important address being given by Dr. Henry Moore, Chairman of the State Tuberculosis Commission. I was compelled to leave before the adjournment of the meeting in order to make train connections, and keep engagements next day. In doing this, I do not appear as taking part in the discussions.

Brazil.—October 31st. This visit to Brazil was to attend the Clay County Teachers' Association and deliver a lecture upon School Hygiene. On arrival I was cordially received by the county superintendent and teachers. A resolution of thanks was given for the lecture and a resolution also of support for the work of the State Board of Health.

Lebanon.—November 9th. This visit was made to attend the Boone County Teachers' Association. My lecture was upon Medical Inspection of School Children. Not only were teachers present, but also a large number of citizens. The general facts of medical inspection were presented and an appeal to the people to institute inspection was offered. A resolution of thanks was passed and also a resolution of confidence and commendation of the work of the State Board of Health. It is probable that in another year the authorities of Lebanon will institute medical inspection.

Ft. Wayne.—November 11th. This visit was made to deliver a lecture upon the Prevention and Cure of Tuberculosis, under the auspices of the Ft. Wayne Academy of Medicine. Our tuberculosis exhibit was taken along and Dr. Shimer of the laboratory of hygiene assisted me. The Academy of Medicine had advertised the matter very thoroughly and large crowds visited the exhibit which was displayed in the halls and corridors of the Carnegie library. In the afternoon I delivered my illustrated lecture to a large audience, and in the evening Dr. Frank Wynn of Indianapolis lectured before an equally large audience. This visit was undoubtedly attended with good results.

Lawrenceburg.—November 21st. Upon arrival at Lawrenceburg I met Dr. Fagaly, county health officer, and Dr. Jaquith, city health officer. Together we visited the courthouse and conferred with the county commissioners and afterwards met the Committee of Health of the city council. With said committee the subject of garbage collection and disposal was discussed and recommendations made. The question of a proper sewer system for Lawrenceburg was also discussed and recommendations offered. I hope this visit was attended with good results.

Brazil.—On November 26th, upon special invitation as a guest of honor, I went to Brazil to attend the meeting of the Clay County Medical Society. I met with a very cordial reception and read my paper entitled, "The Future Hygiene." The work of the State Board of Health was discussed, also the importance of vital statistics, and I believe the visit was attended with good results for the public health cause.

Worthington.—On November 29th, this visit was made together with Professor Bunnell of the State Educational Department. In the afternoon I inspected the schoolhouse. made an address to the pupils, also made a sanitary inspection of the town. I found that the health officer, Dr. Gray, had not kept records of births and deaths and had otherwise not fulfilled the duties of his office. We reported the matter to the City Board of Health and recommended his dismissal. His work was investigated and subsequently he was dismissed and Dr. J. B. Young appointed in his place. In the evening the opera house was filled with citizens to discuss the subject of a new schoolhouse; and the proper sewerage of the town. Professor Bunnell and myself both addressed the audience and afterwards some five or six citizens spoke upon municipal hygiene and improvement.

Peru.—On December 4th I adressed the Miami County Teachers' Institute. My subject was Medical Inspection of School Children. A vote of thanks was passed and the general work of the State Board of Health endorsed.

Westfield.—December 7th. The tuberculosis exhibit was displayed in the new school building at Westfield. The day was very stormy, but despite this fact over 100 citizens visited and studied the same. The high school pupils were instructed to study the exhibit and to present reports of the same. In the evening I gave my illustrated lecture, entitled The Prevention and Cure of Tuberculosis, in the Friends' meeting house. A resolution of thanks was offered.

Warsaw.—December 14th. In company with Dr. Henry Jameson, President of the Indianapolis Park Board, I went to Warsaw to take part in a public discussion concerning parks and municipal hygiene. Upon arrival we were met at the station by a committee of citizens, the city council being represented. In the afternoon, we took a ride and rode over the city, making a regular inspection. Later we conferred with the mayor and city council and in the evening, we addressed a large audience in the Warsaw opera house. A vote of thanks was offered for our attendance.

Howe.—December 15th. In reply to petition of citizens at Howe, and being at Warsaw, in the northern part of the State, I visited Howe upon December 15th. Upon arrival I went immediately to the schoolhouse and made an inspection of the same, and append it herewith, recommending that said schoolhouse be condemned.

Brazil.—December 16th. My third visit to Brazil was made on this date, to confer with the city authorities upon municipal sanitation. Garbage disposal and a sewer system for the whole city were discussed. It is hoped that good will come out of this visit.

The following tables show the status of smallpox and typhoid fever for the fourth quarter:

SMALLPOX COMPARISON FOR THE FOURTH QUARTER.

Date.	Number Cases Reported.	Number Deaths.	Number Counties Invaded.
October, 1908	54	0	10
October, 1909	56	0	10
November, 1908	185	1	13
November, 1909	128	2	23
December, 1908	112	0	10
December, 1909	92	0	14
Total, 1908	351	1	33
Total, 1909	376	2	47

TYPHOID FEVER COMPARISON FOR THE FOURTH QUARTER.

Date.	Number Cases Reported.	Number Deaths.	Number Counties Invaded.
October, 1908	464	129	72
October, 1909	478	155	75
November, 1908	441	113	70
November, 1909	301	104	71
December, 1908	242	76	53
December, 1909	131	52	50
Total, 1908	1,147	318	195
Total, 1909	910	311	196

JOINT MEETING OF THE OHIO RIVER SANITARY COMMISSION AT COLUMBUS, OHIO.

As a delegate from Indiana, appointed by Governor Marshall, I attended the joint meeting of the Ohio River Sanitary Commission December 1, 1909, and herewith present my report of said meeting:

REPORT.

The second joint meeting of the Ohio River Sanitary Commission was held at Columbus, Ohio, at the Neil House, December 1, 1909. Called to order at 2 p. m. by Mr. R. E. Vickers of West Virginia, who was chosen chairman. Dr. Chas. O. Probst, of Ohio, and secretary ex-officio of the Ohio River Sanitary Commission, fulfilled the duties of the position.

Those present were: Dr. Samuel C. Swartsel, Judge E. E. Corn, Mr. D. J. Sinclair, all of Ohio and composing the Ohio River Sanitary Commission; Mr. R. E. Vickers, West Virginia; Mr. C. W. Bente, West Virginia; Mr. Herbert Snow, Pennsylvania; Dr. M. K. Allen, Kentucky; Dr. J. N. Hurty, Indiana.

The engineer of the Ohio commission, Mr. T. Kimberley, was present and was called upon to read his sanitary survey of the Ohio River.

Summary of Survey.

The survey commenced at East Liverpool, Pa., near the Ohio line and stopped at the Indiana line. Population within area of survey 1,395,000; 800,000 drink Ohio River water. Forty-two cities, towns and villages were surveyed in their sanitary relation to the river; 88,000,000 gallons of water are used daily for domestic purposes from the Ohio in area mentioned; 37,000,000 used daily at Cincinnati, 100,000,000 used daily for industrial purposes. Total taken daily from the Ohio River, 188,000,000 gallons.

Pollution.

The total pollution not estimated. Pollution consists of the sewage from not less than 1,000,000 people, not counting Pittsburg; acid iron pickle from iron mills; sulphite liquors, spent bleach and raw paper stock from paper mills; spent dehairing liquors from tanneries; liquors from glue works; packing house wastes; canning factory wastes; spent dye liquors and wool scouring wastes from woolen mills, and waste from scores of small slaughterhouses.

At low water the percentage of pollution is very high, not less than 20 per cent. This constitutes an open sewer. United States laws forbid discharge of sewage and industrial wastes to a degree which would hinder navigation. No provisions against pollution for the protection of the public health. The typhoid fever rate on the river is 20 per cent. higher than in upper portion of Ohio.

The *spent pickle* from iron works each month deposited in the Ohio River, consists of 2,200 tons of sulphuric acid with some muriatic acid, and 1,200 tons of iron. *Spent pickle* is a concentrated solution of copperas, containing about 4 per cent. of free sulphuric acid.

Spent pickle kills fish, many tons being destroyed by it annually. It also unquestionably affects the health of those who drink the water. The fish are killed near the points where the *pickle* is discharged. Probably 80 per cent. of the *spent pickle* is discharged between East Liverpool, Pa., and Wheeling, W. Virginia. *Spent pickle* injures steam boilers, causing a loss of thousands of dollars annually. However, it tends to neutralize sewage.

At no point is the raw water of the Ohio River potable. It should never be used without being treated by subsidence, chemical treatment and filtration. The necessity for such treatment appears in the vital statistics of Cincinnati. In 1906, there were 239 typhoid deaths. In 1907 the filtration plant was in service and the typhoid deaths numbered 157. In 1908 there were 67, and in 1909, to December 1st, 33.

Between the points of the survey there are but two municipalities which do not get their drinking water from the Ohio River. These two obtain their supply from driven wells. Three cities, combined population 95,000, use the water direct and unpurified. Fourteen cities, combined population 211,000, use the water with no treatment other than reservoir storage (subsidence). Ten cities, combined population 415,000, drink the water after purification by subsidence, chemical treatment and filtration. This process is called "*mechanical filtration.*"

Twelve cities, combined population not given, get their water from wells driven in the bed of the river. About 12 per cent. of the people on the river use the water raw.

Mr. Herbert Snow, sanitary engineer for the Pennsylvania Health Department, made verbal report of the Alleghany and Monongehela Rivers and of the Ohio to the Ohio line. His story was of like character with Mr. Kimberley's. He presented numerous analyses, all proving the rivers named to be simply open sewers.

Dr. M. K. Allen presented a copy of a letter written thirty-five years ago by the then state geologist of Kentucky, which was a plea for the protection of the Ohio River against pollution. It accurately forecast the present conditions as given in Mr. Kimberley's report.

After discussion of the subject, the following resolution was adopted.

Whereas, It appears from the results of investigations made by engineers and health officers of the different States composing this Joint Commission that the water of the Ohio River is impure and unsafe for public use, and highly dangerous to the public health; therefore be it

Resolved, by the Joint Commission of the States of Pennsylvania, West Virginia, Kentucky, Indiana and Ohio for the purification of the Ohio River, now assembled, That we condemn the use of the water of the Ohio River in its present unhealthful condition as a source of public water supply, and that we recommend to the various municipalities along the Ohio River using the river as a source of water supply to take immediate measures to discontinue the discharge of unpurified sewage into the stream, and to purify the water taken therefrom and supplied for the use of their citizens.

RECOMMENDATIONS.

The sanitary conditions of the Ohio River are indeed bad, as shown by the Ohio report for that State, and most certainly they are as bad in Indiana. Indiana should also make a sanitary survey of the great river, for undoubtedly the health and lives of the people living on its shores are materially affected. Such survey would be the first step toward proper action.

The State Board of Health already has sufficient authority to make such survey, but it is not provided with the means. The antipollution law passed by the Sixty-Sixth General Assembly specially exempts all streams which form boundaries between Indiana and other States; and, therefore, if inspection of the Ohio is made possible by a proper appropriation, and if it is found necessary to protect it against pollution, statutory provision must be made therefor.

I call attention to the fact that the vital statistics show the average death rate for the last five years of the thirteen counties of Indiana bordering on the Ohio to be 14.6, while the same rate for the whole State was 13.5, difference of 1.1 in the thousand. The typhoid death rate in the same period for the thirteen counties was 34.9 per 100,000, and for the whole State, 33.9, a difference of 1. In other words, if the Ohio river counties had as low rates as the rest of the State, the lives of 1.1 persons in every 1,000 would be saved annually and there would be one fewer death in each 100,000 from typhoid each year.

Sanitary inspection of public school building at Howe, Indiana. Inspection made December 15, 1909.

SITE.—Area about three acres. Situated at north edge of town. Natural drainage good. Railroad passes about 500 feet away. Testimony of teachers was that trains did not disturb the school. From the present site, it would be difficult to carry away sewage because of the lay of the land and no stream being near. However, it would be possible to dispose of sewage by septic tank and filter beds.

BUILDING.—Built in 1874. Brick, and stone foundation, 3 stories. Contains 6 rooms and an assembly room in third story. Two halls, one on first floor and one on second. Stairway leading to second floor has twenty-six steps, 5-inch rise and 12-inch tread to each step. Two turns in the stairway. Assembly room in third story is difficult of access. There are five turns on a steep stairway. In case of fire only a few of the audience in the assembly room could possibly escape. All rooms are provided with slate blackboards which are satisfactory. The two halls are each 36 x 12 x 14. Heated by furnaces. There are no cloak rooms. Children are compelled to hang their cloaks and hats upon hooks inserted in the walls. Basement underneath the whole house. One room (Room No. 1) is used for the primary grade. In wet weather the walls are damp. The light is sufficient but it is introduced from three sides. Walls and foundation of building appeared upon superficial inspection to be sound.

HEATING AND VENTILATION.—The heating is accomplished by three furnaces in the basement. One furnace is directly under the stairway and a portion of the lower stairway, one corner, passes through the hot air chamber. The other two furnaces are in one of the west rooms of the basement. They receive their air from the outside, heat it and introduce it into the school rooms. No complaint to the effect that proper temperature is not maintained in cold weather. The furnaces are therefore, considered to be efficient, but the one under the stairway is certainly misplaced and constitutes a continual threat of fire. It is safe to say that if this schoolhouse would ever catch on fire from this furnace it would be impossible for children to make their escape by means of the stairway. The same is, therefore, most unfortunately located.

The ventilation is insufficient. The ventilating ducts do not work satisfactorily. The exit of the warm fresh air introduced by the furnaces after the same has become vitiated by breathing, is principally effected by windows. This is a wrong principle. The lower rooms immediately above the furnaces are continually filled with coal gas and the children and teachers complain of the same. This indicates that the joints of the furnace have probably drawn apart through warping owing to the heat, and coal gas and a little smoke find their way to the rooms immediately above. The second story rooms are affected very little in this way.

ROOM No. 1.—This is the primary room and is located in basement. 22 x 28 x 10 feet., a total space of 7,160 cubic feet. There is, therefore, space for 31 children. Enrollment 40, average attendance 39. This room is overcrowded and violates the health rule of the State Board of Health, which requires that each pupil shall have 225 cubic feet of space. Desks are non-adjustable. It was observed that several pupils could not put both feet on the floor, and some of the pupils were too big for their seats. These conditions always retard children in their progress and are liable to bring upon them deformity. The room is lighted from three sides and as above said the light is sufficient, but being lighted from three sides, it is wrongly lighted. Consequently, because of the wrong introduction of light, it was observed that many pupils held their bodies in bent and awkward positions, which is, of course, bad for growing children. The room is ventilated by one exit duct which is 6 x 18. This is closed by a register which fills fully one-half of the area of opening. I observed two children with flushed faces and drooping manner and both were evidently sick. This basement room opens into a little basement hall with low ceiling and very little light. The exit from this basement vestibule is by two turns and a short stairway upward to the level of the ground.

ROOM No. 2.—Is 26 x 29½ x 14, a total of 10,738 cubic feet. It, therefore, can contain 47 pupils. Enrollment 34, average attendance 33. The room is, therefore, not overcrowded. Lighted by 10 windows, 4 lights in each 20 x 40". The light is introduced from three sides and therefore wrongly introduced. On account of this wrong introduction, I observed a number of students sitting in queer postures with shoulders and backs bent in the endeavor to compensate for shadows and reflections. The quantity of light is sufficient. Gas from the furnace beneath and some smoke very noticeable. Ventilation of the room is known as the "Smead Method," but it does not work. The air was heavy with the odors due to vitiation by breathing.

ROOM No. 3.—Is 25 x 28 x14, a total of 9,800 cubic feet and therefore might contain 43 pupils. Enrollment 31, average attendance 29. This room was not overcrowded. Seats nonadjustable. I observed many children who did not fit in their seats and who, therefore, assumed distorted postures. I particularly noticed two girls who were so large that they were compelled to project their feet and legs into the aisle. It is wrong to force pupils into such small seats and thus run the risk of deforming their bodies. The room is lighted by 7 windows, 4 panes each 20 x 40. The light is sufficient, but is wrongly introduced. The remarks thereupon would be the same as for Room No. 2. Ventilation by "Smead Method," and it does not work. Furnace gas and little smoke easily detected by smell in the air. The air was heavy with the products of human respiration.

ROOM No. 4.—Is 25 x 28 x 14, a total of 9,800 cubic feet. Therefore cubic space for 43 pupils. Enrollment 25, average attendance 23. Room not overcrowded. Lighted by 7 windows, 4 panes each 20 x 40. Amount of light sufficient. Lighted from two sides and introduced from the right and rear. Light so introduced will certainly force eye strain upon certain children, hence such introduction is sanitarily wrong. I observed 10 children in this room who did not fit their seats and in consequence assumed bent and distorted postures. Ventilation by "Smead System," and it does not work. Gas and smoke easily noticeable. Air heavy with products of human respiration.

ROOM No. 5.—Is 25 x 28 x 14, a total of 9,800 cubic feet. Therefore space for 43 pupils. Enrollment 18, average attendance 17. Room not overcrowded. Lighted by windows on two sides, each one containing 2 panes, each 26 x 34. Light is sufficient. Light introduced over right shoulder and rear, hence wrongly introduced. Ventilation by "Smead System," which does not work.

ROOM No. 6, HIGH SCHOOL.—Is 25 x 28 x 14, a total of 9,800 cubic feet. Therefore space for 43 pupils. Enrollment 54, average attendance 52. Room is greatly overcrowded. Lighted by 9 windows containing two panes each 26 x 34. Light is therefore sufficient. Introduced from left and rear. Air was bad.

ROOM No. 7.—Is 25 x 28 x 14, a total of 9,800 cubic feet. Therefore could contain 43 pupils. Enrollment not given. Lighted by 10 windows containing two panes, each pane 25 x 34. Light sufficient, but wrongly introduced from the left right and rear. In this room I observed 7 boys who were too big for their seats and hence they occupied distorted positions. Ventilation by "Smead Method" and not good.

Outhouses.—The boy's outhouse was noisome and indescribable in its offensiveness. That for the girls was cleaner, but wrong in every particular.

Water Supply.—The water supply was from a driven well about 35 feet from the cesspools of the outhouses. If not polluted, it is liable to be polluted at any time.

SUMMARY AND REMARKS.—This is a very old schoolhouse, built without any knowledge of school sanitation in 1874. It is not provided with warm and ventilated cloakrooms. It is unsatisfactorily heated from the fact that gas and smoke are introduced into the lower rooms from the heating apparatus. It is insufficiently ventilated and every room is wrongly lighted, for modern sanitary requirements provide that schoolrooms shall be lighted from only one side and the light shall be caused to fall over the left shoulders of the pupils, as this will avoid shadows upon the work and permit the erect posture. When light is introduced from more than one side shadows fall upon the work of the pupil, causing him to bend his body in various directions and makes against the erect posture. It is also true that when light is introduced from more than one side, eye strain. astigmatism and myopia are produced.

The stairways are steep and winding and not easy of ascent. If the house were to catch on fire during school hours a large number of pupils would of necessity be roasted alive. The outhouses are insufficient and abominable. The water supply is in constant threat of being polluted if it is not already polluted. All in all the schoolhouse is insanitary and not fit for school purposes, the site only is unobjectionable.

I respectfully recommend to the State Board of Health that this schoolhouse be condemned as unfit for school purposes, the said condemnation to take effect June 1, 1910.

After consideration the following proclamation was adopted:

PROCLAMATION OF CONDEMNATION.

Whereas, It has been shown to the satisfaction of the State Board of Health that the schoolhouse at Howe, Lima Township, Lagrange County, Ind., is insanitary and consequently threatens the health and life of the pupils, and also interferes with their efficiency, and whereas, great danger exists from fire on account of the wrong position and construction of a furnace, therefore, be it

Ordered: That said schoolhouse at Howe, Lima Township, Lagrange County, Ind., is condemned for school purposes, and shall not be used for said school purposes after June 1, 1910, and if any school trustee, or trustees, any teacher or any person uses said schoolhouse for school purposes, or teaches therein, after the date above mentioned, he or she or they shall be prosecuted.

Any person mutilating or tearing down this proclamation shall be prosecuted.

Ordered by the State Board of Health, January 14, 1910.

Adjourned.

SPECIAL MEETING STATE BOARD OF HEALTH.

FEBRUARY 2, 1910.

Called to order at 12 m. by President McCoy.

Present: Drs. McCoy, Tucker, Hurty,

The President stated the object of the meeting was to attend the special conference of County Health Commissioners, with the State Board of Health and to attend to any other business which might be brought before the Board.

The Secretary reported the attendance at the conference was 86, all but six counties being represented. He also reported that a deep interest in the subjects discussed, was very evident.

The following program was being followed:

PROGRAM

CONFERENCE OF STATE BOARD OF HEALTH WITH COUNTY HEALTH COMMISSIONERS

OBJECT: To confer together concerning public health work. To discuss the best means—How to make good.

Palm Room, Claypool Hotel, Indianapolis, February 2, 1910, Called to Order 10 a. m.

Remarks....................................President George T. McCoy
Calling Roll.

SUBJECTS FOR DISCUSSION.

The New Law.
What are the Powers and Duties of County Health Commissioners?
What is a Nuisance?
How to abolish a Nuisance.
Special Monthly Report.
Collecting Vital Statistics.
Keeping Records.
How May the Co-operation of the Papers and the Public be secured?
Inspection of Schoolhouses.
What is a Sanitary Schoolhouse?
Inspection of School Children.
The Minute Book.
Paying Bills.
County Health Appropriations.
Conditions Which May Generate, Promote or Transmit Disease, and How to Abate.
Duties of Commissioners as Food Inspectors.
Attending Farmers' and Teachers' Institutes.
Quarantine. Expenses of Quarantine.
Disinfection. How? When?
Public Health Bulletins.
Conference of County Health Commissioners with Health Officers and Deputies in their Counties.
Slaughterhouse and Meat Markets.

There being no further business the Board adjourned.

SPECIAL MEETING.

February 25, 1910.

Called to order 12 m.

Present: Drs. McCoy, Tucker, Hurty.

President McCoy announced the object of the meeting to be to attend the third annual meeting of the Indiana Sanitary and Water Supply Association, which is in affiliation with the State Board of Health.

The Secretary reported that about 200 were in attendance, over 50 county health commissioners and city health officers being present. The program contained 15 papers, all upon sanitary, water and sewage problems.

Among prominent engineers present were Mr. George A. Johnson, New York; Mr. John W. Alvord, Chicago; Mr. Leonard Metcalf, Boston; Prof. Edward Bartow, Illinois State University; Prof. R. L. Sackett of Purdue University.

Upon petition, the Secretary had directed Dr. R. L. Hardwick, county health commissioner of Posey county, to make a sanitary survey of the public schoolhouse at Mt. Vernon and report upon the same. Following is the report of Dr. Hardwick:

February 25, 1910.

State Board of Health:

Gentlemen—In accordance with your request of recent date, I have the pleasure to report that I have followed your instructions and have made a careful sanitary survey of the central school building in this city.

First, as to Site.—The building is situated on a high, rolling piece of ground, having an area of approximately 296 feet, by 444 feet. The location is ideal. The premises are high and dry and well drained. The site is a most desirable one in every way.

Next, as to the Building.—The schoolhouse is built of brick. It was erected in 1867. Although the walls are seemingly in a very good shape, there are some moderate cracks, especially in the west wall. The building is two stories high, and contains eight rooms. The dimensions of the east and west rooms, both floors, are 23 feet 2 inches by 35 feet 3 inches. The north and south rooms, both floors, measure 23 feet 4 inches by 35 feet. The building is fairly lighted, ceilings high. The windows are placed on all sides. The east and west rooms, both floors, are lighted on all sides. The south rooms are lighted from south side and the north rooms are lighted from the north side. There are two sizes of windows. The uniform size of the larger windows is 3 feet 7 inches by 8 feet 4 inches. Each room has two tangent windows (see "A" in sketch enclosed herewith) whose dimensions are 2 feet 9 inches by 8 feet 4 inches. Each of the larger windows contains 24 panes 10 inches by 16 inches. Each of the "tangent" windows contains 18 panes, 10 inches by 16 inches. The windows show the effect of age—work poorly and fit loosely in the frames. The system of ventilation is not good. The only successful way to ventilate is to raise or lower the windows. The original plan in view seems to have been direct-indirect ventilation. The building is heated by steam heat. It has a No. 14 Acme firebox boiler. The draft is defective. The floors in the various rooms are mostly in a good condition. New floors have been put in from time to time during recent years. Most of the inside walls are in fairly good shape. All the rooms have metal ceilings, and these are in good condition. Noticed no particular dampness of walls. The building is poorly arranged from the standpoint of "fire possibilities." The facilities for vacating the building with dispatch are poor, and a fire might prove disastrous even with the present excellent system of fire drills. There are two halls in the building, each of which is 7 feet 8½ inches wide. In each hall there is a stairway 3½ feet wide. So it is evident that the stairways are too narrow, besides they are steep and difficult of ascent. The building is provided with two basements for boys' and girls' closets. The boys' basement has 12 urinals and 8 closets. The girls' basement has 12 closets. The basements are in a very good condition. I am enclosing herewith a rough plan of the building.

Now, as to the Recommendations: If this building is large enough to meet the demands, I do not consider its age and general condition such as to require its removal. The worst features I see about the building are the narrow stairways and halls. If it is necessary that much more room be had for the accommodation of the pupils, it is questionable as to whether the two buildings should be incorporated into one.

I hope what I have said, and the drawing or sketch enclosed will enable you to form a creditable conclusion, I am, Yours,

R. L. HARDWICK.

After full consideration of the report the following proclamation of condemnation was adopted:

PROCLAMATION OF CONDEMNATION.

Whereas, It has been shown to the satisfaction of the State Board of Health that the schoolhouse known as the Central School Building, at Mt. Vernon, Posey County, Ind., is insanitary and consequently threatens the health and life of the pupils and also interferes with their efficiency, therefore, it is

Ordered: That said schoolhouse at Mt. Vernon, Posey County, Ind., is condemned for school purposes, and shall not be used for said school purposes after July 1, 1910, and, if any school trustee, or trustees, any teacher or any person uses said schoolhouse for school purposes, or teaches therein, after the date above mentioned, he or she or they shall be prosecuted.

Any person mutilating or tearing down this proclamation shall be prosecuted.

Passed by the State Board of Health, February 25, 1910.

REGULAR QUARTERLY MEETING INDIANA STATE BOARD OF HEALTH.

APRIL 8, 1910.

Called to order by President McCoy at 2 p. m.

Present: Drs. McCoy, Wishard, Davis, Tucker, Hurty.

The President announced: "This meeting is to consider and take action concerning the affairs of the second fiscal quarter and the first calendar quarter of the year, both quarters ending March 31, 1910."

Minutes of the last regular meeting, held January 4, 1910, and the minutes of the special meetings, held February 2d and February 25th, were read and approved.

REPORT OF SECRETARY FOR QUARTER ENDING MARCH 31, 1910.

The work of the departments has gone forward without friction and without interruption. The monthly reports, as have appeared in the monthly bulletins, give the details of what has been done in the several departments.

Since the first of February and the installation of Dr. Chas. A. Carter, as statistician, much statistical work has been done which has heretofore been left undone. Dr. Carter has been active in securing accurate statements of causes of death, and he has also corresponded with many physicians in regard to the matter, securing their co-operation and aid.

The Secretary made twenty visits, as follows:

January 19th, Greenfield, to address a public audience upon "The Prevention and Cure of Tuberculosis."

January 21st, Topeka, on account of public address on "The Work of the State Board of Health."

January 24th, Evansville, to attend the Corn School of the State Farmers' Association and deliver addresses pertaining to the public health.

January 31st, Bloomington, to address the law class upon the health laws of Indiana.

February 5th, Burney, on account of condemned schoolhouse, to meet with trustee, advisory board and citizens.

February 6th, Crawfordsville, on account of address before the Women's Club.

February 14th, North Manchester, account of school inspection and to deliver address before the North Manchester Industrial Association.

February 16th, Brazil, account of address before Teachers' Association.

February 19th, Hammond, to confer with Board of Health in regard to sanitary conditions.

February 20th, Anderson, account of address to Parents' Club.

February 22d, Daleville, account of public meeting concerning schoolhouse sanitation.

February 24th, Laporte, on account of invitation of mayor to deliver public address upon "Municipal Sanitation."

March 6th, Tipton, on account of public address to Men's Club.

March 7th, Crawfordsville, account of inspection of high school building.

March 8th, Vincennes, on account of invitation of mayor and Board of Trade, to confer upon sewers and also account of inspections of schoolhouses at Decker, Monroe City, and Emison.

March 14th, Michigan City, on account of conference with Board of Health and to make public address on "Municipal Sanitation."

March 15th, Portland, on account of tuberculosis exhibit and to deliver a public address upon "The Prevention and Cure of Tuberculosis."

March 22d, Orleans, account of invitation of town authorities to address public meeting concerning school sanitation.

March 23d, Richmond, account of address upon "Dairy Sanitation."

March 28th, Covington, account of inspection of schoolhouse.

Full accounts and descriptions of these visits are appended:

Greenfield.—On January 19th I went to Greenfield. to take part in demonstrating the tuberculosis exhibit of the State Board and to deliver an illustrated lecture upon the "Prevention and Cure of Tuberculosis." The lecture was given in the Baptist church to a large crowd. I was told many were turned away. The lecture seemed to be appreciated, for resolutions of thanks and commendation were passed.

Topeka.—January 21st I went to Topeka upon invitation of the Sassafras Lecture Club, to deliver a public address upon the work of the State Board of Health. The meeting was held in the Carnegie Auditorium and a large audience was present. The lecture seemed to please theaudience, for a resolution of thanks and commendation was passed.

Evansville.—On January 24th, on account of invitation of the management, I went to Evansville to attend the Corn School of the State Farmers' Association. 2,000 farmers were in attendance. I delivered my address in Evans' Hall on the afternoon of January 30th, entitled, "Health Upon the Farm." In the evening in the same room, I gave my illustrated lecture entitled, "The Prevention and Cure of Tuberculosis." Large audiences were present both times, and resolutions of thanks and appreciation were unanimously passed.

Bloomington.—This visit was made on January 31st upon invitation of the Dean of the Law Department of the University, to lecture before the law students upon the health laws of Indiana. The entire class was present and also the entire law faculty. A resolution of thanks was passed.

Burney.—This town is situated in Decatur county, southwest of Greensburg. The visit was for the purpose of meeting with the trustee, the advisory board, and citizens, and Township School Teachers' Association, to consider the school sanitation. The meeting was certainly a success, for the authorities passed a resolution that a new schoolhouse should be built and that the same should be sanitary in every particular.

Crawfordsville.—This visit was made February 6th, the object being to address the Women's Club. The subject selected was "Hygiene vs. Social Plagues." Only adults were present. One hundred of our circulars were distributed and a reception was given to me at the end of the lecture. I believe this visit was attended with more than usual good results.

North Manchester.—This visit was made February 14th, account of invitation of the mayor and the officers of the North Manchester Industrial Association, also for the purpose of inspecting the schoolhouse and giving advice. Upon arrival, I was met at the station by a committee and every attention was shown to me. In the afternoon I visited the schoolhouse in conjunction with the school board and the city officials. No action of the State Board of Health is required, because the authorities are agreed upon what shall be done, and will do it. A new building will be constructed that is sanitary in every particular. In the evening I attended the annual dinner as special guest of the North Manchester Industrial Association, and afterward spoke upon "A Clean City." The address was received most kindly and resolutions of thanks were passed.

Brazil.—This visit was made February 16th, upon invitation of the county superintendent and the trustees of the county, to talk about school hygiene. I took a number of our envelope packages containing circulars upon infectious and contagious diseases, and made my talk along the lines of school sanitation. Every school trustee present promised to make the minor changes which are recommended in all schools under his supervision that needed the same. I believe a good impression was made and that the trustees were instructed to their advantage and to the advantage of the children.

Michigan City.—February 19th I made my second visit to Michigan City on account of the former conditions which were discussed on January 11th. Various complications had arisen and it was necessary to meet the authorities again. The second visit smoothed out the difficulties, and the sanitary recommendations made are now being carried out without friction.

Anderson.—February 20th (Sunday) I visited Anderson to speak to the Parents' Club at the Baptist church. The subject was "Hygiene vs. Sexual Plagues." The church was very comfortably filled and when I had finished my forty minutes address, a member arose and requested that the subject be continued. Various questions were asked and the meeting occupied over two hours. I believe it was one of the most profitable meetings I have ever attended, for the public health cause.

Daleville.—I visited Daleville upon invitation of the trustee and county health commissioner, February 22d, to discuss, with a public audience, the matter of school sanitation. The schoolhouse at Daleville is old, dilapidated and in every way unfit for school purposes. The public hall was well filled and well attended by business men. After my talk upon school sanitation, there were many questions asked, and we entered directly upon a discussion of the present situation. Finally they decided to build a new schoolhouse.

Laporte.—Upon invitation of the mayor and the public authorities, also upon invitation of the Medical Society, I visited Laporte on February 24th. We also took occasion to show the tuberculosis exhibit of the State Board, and Dr. Shimer, of the bacteriological laboratory, accompanied me. The exhibit remained at Laporte for two days and was largely attended, and the newspapers commented upon it most favorably. On the evening of February 24th I delivered my illustrated lecture on the "Prevention and Cure of Tuberculosis," in the Rink, which was provided for the occasion. A large audience was present. The lecture was received kindly, and resolutions of thanks were passed. The same evening I talked upon "Municipal Sanitation," laying particular stress upon the necessity of sewers. The sewer question is up at Laporte and it will not down until a complete sewer system is put in. I believe our visit to Laporte was attended with much profit in every way.

Tipton.—I visited Tipton March 6th (Sunday) to speak before the Men's Church Club upon hygiene and the social plagues. A large audience gathered in the Baptist Church. I was introduced by Dr. Horace G. Reed, ex-representative. He made some very complimentary remarks in regard to the State Board of Health. My lecture was well received and numerous questions asked. Afterwards a vote of thanks was passed.

Crawfordsville.—On March 7th I visited Crawfordsville, to make inspection of the high school building at that place, having been invited to do so by the school trustees. Accompanied by the superintendent and trustees I went over the building from basement to garret. It is an old structure and will be replaced by a new building. There is no necessity for action from the State Board of Health, because the local authorities are determined upon improvement, only desiring to consult with a representative of the Board upon the matter.

Vincennes.—I visited Vincennes, March 8th, upon invitation of the mayor, the Board of Trade and the county superintendent. Upon arrival I was met by a special committee from the council and taken to the hotel. In the evening I addressed the council upon "Municipal Sanitation," and especially upon the subject of sewers. The same evening I also addressed the Board of Trade upon "Municipal Sanitation." Both of these bodies passed resolutions of thanks and commendation for the work of the Board of Health. Later on the same evening, I read a paper upon the "Medical Inspection of School Children" before the Knox County Medical Society. The following day I made inspection of the schoolhouses at Decker, at Monroe City and at Emison. These surveys, in full are herewith presented.

Michigan City.—On March 14th I revisited Michigan City because of an outbreak of scarlet fever, and the appearance of a few cases of epidemic meningitis. Dr. Simonds accompanied me. Upon arrival we met Dr. V. V. Bacon, city health officer, and with him visited six cases of mild scarlet fever. These had all been disputed, and yet they certainly were true scarlet fever. All of them were desquamating around the finger nails, although each child appeared to be well and all right. The diagnosis made by Dr. Bacon was confirmed. Dr. Simonds visited the cases of supposed epidemic meningitis. He performed spinal puncture on one, but found it was tubercular. All of the cases he attended have been reported upon by himself. I think this visit was attended with good results, inasmuch as it settled the disputes among physicians and quieted the people, who were all torn up because of the difficulties.

Portland.—On March 15th I visited Portland with Dr. Simonds of the state laboratory, in order to place our tuberculosis exhibit before the public and in the evening to deliver a lecture upon "The Prevention and Cure of Tuberculosis." The exhibit was shown in a vacant room on the main street. We estimated that at least one thousand people visited the same. In the evening in the K. of P. Hall, a large audience gathered to listen to the illustrated lecture. Resolutions of thanks were passed.

Orleans.—On March 22d, in company with Professor Bunnell, assistant state superintendent, I went to Orleans, to confer with the citizens in regard to their new schoolhouse. This question has been in contemplation and discussion for four years. The schoolhouse was condemned four years ago, and then condemnation extended. Things have at last come to a head and all have agreed that a new schoolhouse shall be built and the question now is upon the selection of a site. A faction is determined to build the schoolhouse on the old site, which is right in the center of town, inefficient light, air, and in every way unfit. Professor Bunnell and myself took a stand against building a schoolhouse on the old site, and urged that they get a new site. We had a large audience in the opera house, and were kindly received. Resolutions of thanks were passed.

Richmond.—On March 23d I went to Richmond in company with Mr. Barnard to attend a public meeting to consider the public milk supply, dairy inspection and the tuberculin testing. A good audience listened to us in one of the churches. I spoke first upon "Dairy Hygiene" and Mr. Barnard followed with lantern illustrations, showing insanitary conditions found to exist in Indiana.

Miss Sickles, Secretary of the National Social Science Association, was in attendance and made proper remarks.

Covington.—I visited Covington on March 28th, on account of invitation of the school board and the health officer, to confer with them in regard to the new school building which they contemplate erecting. The school building in question is called "The Primary School." I present in this quarterly report a complete sanitary survey of this building, and recommend that it be condemned. The school board is in full accord with this, and all the members expressed their thanks for the aid which the State Board had given them.

The following tables show the smallpox and typhoid fever status for the quarter:

SMALLPOX COMPARISON FOR FIRST QUARTER, 1910.

Date.	Number Cases Reported.	Number Deaths.	Number Counties Invaded.
January, 1909	148	0	24
January, 1910	189	0	25
February, 1909	138	0	22
February, 1910	83	1	23
March, 1909	121	0	16
March, 1910	107	0	21
Total, 1909	407	0	62
Total, 1910	379	1	69

TYPHOID FEVER COMPARISON FOR FIRST QUARTER, 1910.

Date.	Number Cases Reported.	Number Deaths.	Number Counties Invaded.
January, 1909	194	36	39
January, 1910	131	47	40
February, 1909	68	19	30
February, 1910	110	34	36
March, 1909	68	31	30
March, 1910	71	33	30
Total, 1909	330	86	99
Total, 1910	312	114	106

STATE TUBERCULOSIS HOSPITAL.

Dr. Henry Moore, President of the State Tuberculosis Commission, appeared before the Board and extended an invitation to visit the hospital, now almost completed, at any date satisfactory to the Board. After consideration, it was

Ordered: That a special meeting be held at the State Tuberculosis Hospital at Rockville, April 13, 1910, and that the county health commissioner of Parke county be requested to call together the health officers and deputies of his county to meet with the Board.

OWEN BILL.

The bill introduced into the United States Senate, creating a department of public health, with a secretary in the Cabinet, was read and discussed and the president was appointed to frame a letter to the Senators of Indiana, and our Congressmen, asking them to support the said bill.

Ordered: The Secretary shall attend the meeting of the conference of State and Provincial Boards of Health of North America, at Washington, D. C., April 28-29-30, his expenses to be paid from the Board of Health fund.

Ordered: That Mr. Brewster should attend the meeting of the National Water Works Association at New Orleans, April 25th-30th, his expenses to be paid from the Water Laboratory Fund.

Ordered: That Drs. McCoy and Tucker should attend the annual meeting of the National Tuberculosis Association at Washington, D. C., June 2-5, their expenses to be paid from the Board of Health Fund.

BRUCE LAKE.

The Bruce Lake matter, which had been before the Board several times, was again discussed with much new matter presented, and the following resolution was adopted:

Whereas, it has been previously

Resolved, by the State Board of Health, That in its opinion the marshes and wet lands produced by the drainage of Bruce Lake in Fulton County with a small arm extending into Pulaski County, during certain seasons of the year are a menace to the public health of that locality and are declared to be a public nuisance; therefore, be it further

Resolved, That the Indiana State Board of Health reaffirms its former action and hereby directs the construction of a dam at Bruce Lake to abate this evil by restoring the waters of said lake to their former level as shown by surveys on file in the State Auditor's office, such dam to be constructed under the general supervision of Dr. J. J. Thomas, County Health Commissioner of Pulaski County, the cost to be paid out of the funds (to the amount of $200.00) voluntarily subscribed for that purpose by the citizens of Bruce Lake and vicinity.

MARKLE SCHOOLHOUSE.

The following letter was read:

MARKLE, IND., February 24, 1910.

The Indiana State Board of Health, Indianapolis, Ind.:

Gentlemen—We have been at a great expense in the last year, unexpected, and our financial condition is in such a shape that it would be positively impossible for us to build a new schoolhouse this year, for there is no way at all for us to get the necessary money.

It is our desire to as soon as possible build a new schoolhouse, one that will be of the proper kind and sanitary in every particular, and one that will meet the approval of the Indiana State Board of Health.

That in consideration of the above, we respectfully ask your honorable board to raise the condemnation now on our school building.

Very truly yours,

L. E. LAKEY. Secretary.

By order of the Markle School Board, Markle, Ind.

After consideration, it was

Ordered: The extension of date of condemnation of the schoolhouse at Markle, Indiana, shall be extended to June 1, 1911.

Ordered: The annual Health Officers' Conference shall be held May 24th, 1910, in Indianapolis. the Secretary to arrange program and to attend to all details.

SCHOOLS CONDEMNED.

Report of inspection of Schoolhouse No. 1, District No. 4, Wayne Township, Henry County, Indiana, by Mr. John Owens, January 26, 1910.

Site.—High, well drained, three miles north of Knightstown, Indiana. East side of road.

Building.—Brick, one story. Stone foundation, one to two feet from ground. Slate roof. Dimensions 40 feet by 27 feet, exclusive of cloakrooms and entrance vestibule. Walls in good condition. One-room building. Pupils enrolled, 18.

Lighting.—From two sides and rear. Each window admits 14 square feet of light and light area equals one-half of floor area. Cross-lights are everywhere and eyestrain is very pronounced.

Ventilation.—None whatever provided during school periods, and the air was very bad at the time of the inspection.

Method of Heating.—Two old stoves; one a box and the other a drum, were used.

Outhouses.—Both dilapidated; no screens, and very insanitary.

Interior.—Papered, black with soot—cobwebs in cloakrooms.

Front Door.—Lock split off; a padlock and loop used.

A gutter drain was leaking and spoiling a wall. Can easily be repaired.

It is recommended that the trustee be required (and he has expressed his willingness) to do the following:

1. To construct sanitary outhouses with suitable screens.

2. To scrape walls clean, and apply thereon some sanitary covering such as neutral colored paper or paint.

3. To provide at once adequate heating and ventilation. (A combined heater and ventilator is being used in other schools of the township with good results and the trustee expressed his willingness to install one in this building.)

4. To provide a good walk in front to the public road, to fix lock on front door and repair drain-pipe where broken.

5. To square broken corners of plaster in entry to cloakroom.

If the conditions are complied with at once, and the trustee gave me his promise that they would be, it is suggested that no formal order of condemnation be issued.

After consideration, the following proclamation of condemnation was adopted:

PROCLAMATION OF CONDEMNATION.

Whereas, It has been shown to the satisfaction of the State Board of Health that Schoolhouse No. 1, District No. 4, Wayne Township, Henry County, Ind., is insanitary and consequently threatens the health and life of the pupils and also interferes with their efficiency; therefore, it is

Ordered: That said schoolhouse No. 1, District No. 4, Wayne Township, Henry County, Ind., is condemned for school purposes, and shall not be used for said school purposes after June 1, 1910, and if any school trustee or trustees, any teacher or any person uses said schoolhouse for school purposes, or teaches therein, after the date above mentioned, he or she or they shall be prosecuted.

Any person mutilating or tearing down this proclamation shall be prosecuted.

Passed by the State Board of Health, April 8, 1910.

Sanitary survey of schoolhouse at Covington, Indiana, March 28th, by J. N. Hurty, State Health Commissioner.

This building is known as the Primary School.

Site.—One-half of a city block. Lower than the street on three sides. Of course, it could be filled. No drainage.

Building.—Brick, stone foundation, dilapidated, no basement. Walls are cracked on all sides. Built in 1886. Down-spouts are broken and bad and are washing the walls. The city water has been turned into the building for drinking purposes, and the overflow is turned right beneath the building, not being cared for in the slightest degree. The consequences are, there is a mudhole underneath the floor.

The building is two stories, four rooms with central hall. The stairway is wide and not steep. It has old floors which are badly sagged. Heated by stoves and no ventilating ducts.

All of the rooms are sufficiently lighted from three sides and are not crowded.

Outhouses.—Boys' outhouse is not screened and very foul. Girls' outhouse is screened and fairly clean. Cinder paths lead to them. Water is secured from public supply.

Remarks.—This is an old building, is insanitary on every count and is unfit for school purposes.

Recommendations.—I recommend this building be condemned, the condemnation to take effect June 1, 1910.

After consideration, the following proclamation of condemnation was adopted:

PROCLAMATION OF CONDEMNATION.

Whereas, It has been shown to the satisfaction of the State Board of Health that the schoolhouse at Covington, Fountain County, Ind., is insanitary, and consequently threatens the health and life of the pupils and also interferes with their efficiency; therefore it is

Ordered: That said schoolhouse at Covington, Fountain County, Ind., is condemned for school purposes, and shall not be used for said school purposes after June 1, 1910, and if any school trustee or trustees, any teacher or any person uses said schoolhouse for school purposes, or teaches therein, after the date above mentioned, he or she or they shall be prosecuted.

Any person mutilating or tearing down this proclamation shall be prosecuted.

Passed by the State Board of Health, April 8, 1910.

Sanitary survey of New Bethel Schoolhouse, Franklin Township, Marion County, by J. N. Hurty, State Health Commissioner, March 12th.

Site.—Low, wet site. At every point it is lower than the road. In wet weather many mudholes.

Building.—Brick, stone foundation, no basement. Four rooms; walls out of plumb. Baseboards drawing away from walls. Plaster off of ceiling in many places. No ventilating ducts. Heated by stoves. Floor sags in upper rooms. Stairs four feet wide, steep, and number of steps, 21. All the rooms are lighted on four sides, and not one of them having a sufficient quantity of light. Cloakrooms are in the halls, which are unheated. Outhouses are ordinary privies and very offensive and vile. Blackboards are painted on the walls, in all the rooms except the high school, which has slate blackboards. The water is supplied from a dug well.

Recommendations.—This schoolhouse is insanitary on every count. It is old, dilapidated and unfit for school purposes, and I therefore recommend its condemnation. Condemnation to take effect June 1, 1910.

After consideration, the following proclamation of condemnation was adopted:

PROCLAMATION OF CONDEMNATION.

Whereas, It has been shown to the satisfaction of the State Board of Health that the New Bethel schoolhouse, Franklin Township, Marion County, Ind., is insanitary and consequently threatens the health and life of the pupils and also interferes with their efficiency; therefore, it is

Ordered: That said schoolhouse, known as the New Bethel schoolhouse, Franklin Township, Marion County, Ind., is condemned for school purposes, and shall not be used for said school purposes after June 1, 1910, and if any school trustee or trustees, any teacher or any person uses said schoolhouse for school purposes, or teaches therein, after the date above mentioned, he or she or they shall be prosecuted.

Any person mutilating or tearing down this proclamation shall be prosecuted.

Passed by the State Board of Health, April 8, 1910.

Sanitary survey of schoolhouse at Emison, District No. 8, Busseron Township, Knox County, Ind., by J. N. Hurty, State Health Commissioner, March 9th.

Site.—Is a sand lot, 120 feet square, drainage bad.

Building.—Frame, two story, was originally one story, the second story being added in 1905. Three rooms in all, with upper and lower hall. Two narrow box stairways, with four turns to it. Halls not warmed. Basement is a mudhole, except at point where furnace is placed on concrete foundation. Water almost surrounded the furnace, which was reached from the stairway by a plank. Slate blackboards.

The Upper Room.—This room is over the entire building and is used for the sixth, seventh and eighth grades. It is 36 x 45 x 11. Enrollment 25, seats 25. Floor good, but settling badly; baseboards are drawing away from the walls, center of room sagging. Easily shaken by one man jumping up and down in middle of room. Walls shedding their paper. Light introduced from three sides.

First and Second Grades.—Room 36 x 22½ x 11. Enrollment 28, seats 30. Floor good Walls shedding their paper, light introduced from three sides and inefficient.

Grades 3, 4, 5.—Enrollment 22, seats 22. Walls shedding their paper, floor good, room lighted from three sides, but wrongly lighted.

Remarks.—The superintendent told me that in cold weather heating is inadequate and the school is practically broken up. One stove has been placed in the upper room, which is used for the sixth, seventh and eighth grades.

Opinion.—This schoolhouse is insanitary on every count and I recommend that it be condemned, the condemnation to take effect June 1, 1910.

After consideration, the following proclamation of condemnation was adopted:

PROCLAMATION OF CONDEMNATION.

Whereas, It has been shown to the satisfaction of the State Board of Health that the schoolhouse at Emison, District No. 8, Busseron Township, Knox County, Ind., is insanitary, and consequently threatens the health and life of the pupils and also interferes with their efficiency; therefore, it is

Ordered: That said schoolhouse at Emison, District No. 8, Busseron Township, Knox County, Ind., is condemned for school purposes, and shall not be used for said school purposes after June 1, 1910, and if any school trustee or trustees, any teacher or any person uses said schoolhouse for school purposes, or teaches therein, after the date above mentioned, he or she or they shall be prosecuted.

Any person mutilating or tearing down this proclamation shall be prosecuted.

Passed by the State Board of Health, April 8, 1910.

Sanitary survey of Schoolhouse No. 2, Decker Township, Knox County, by J. N. Hurty, State Health Commissioner, March 8, 1910.

Site.—High and dry with very sandy soil. Area, 1¼ acres. Drainage good.

Building.—Two-story frame, built in 1899. No basement, two rooms downstairs; one high school room and two recitation rooms upstairs. Stairway 3½ feet wide, very steep, 23 steps, three turns. Heated with stoves, no ventilating ducts.

High School Room.—This room is 60 x 24 x 12, 88 seats, 80 pupils; 10 windows, 8 lights to each window, each light 14 x 20 inches. The light is sufficient, but is not properly introduced, and therefore there are direct rays. The recitation rooms, adjoining the High school rooms, are small, heated with stoves and inconvenient.

Grades 2 and 3.—This is the east room on the first floor, 21 x 30 x 12; 45 seats, enrollment, 36; 7 windows, 8 lights to each, and each light 14 x 20. There is sufficient window area, but the windows are so placed as to leave dark areas in the room.

Primary and Grade.—This is the west room on the first floor, 12 x 33 x 21; 49 desks, enrollment, 49. This room has 8 windows. Each window contains 8 lights and each light is 14 x 20. The light is sufficient but wrongly introduced.

General Conditions.—Slate blackboards, floors generally good, desks good. All of the rooms are wainscoted and supplied with green curtains. The building is inadequate, has a leaky roof, and in every way insanitary. Outhouses are of the ordinary, offensive and repellent kind.

Recommendations.—I recommend that this building be condemned absolutely, the condemnation to take effect June 1, 1910.

After consideration, the following proclamation of condemnation was adopted:

PROCLAMATION OF CONDEMNATION.

Whereas, It has been shown to the satisfaction of the State Board of Health that the schoolhouse, District No. 2, Decker Township, Knox

County, Ind., is insanitary, and consequently threatens the health and life of the pupils and also interferes with their efficiency; therefore, it is

Ordered: That said schoolhouse, District No. 2, Decker Township, Knox County, Ind., is condemned for school purposes, and shall not be used for said school purposes after June 1, 1910, and if any school trustee or trustees, any teacher or any person uses said schoolhouse for school purposes, or teaches therein, after the date above mentioned, he or she or they shall be prosecuted.

Any person mutilating or tearing down this proclamation shall be prosecuted.

Passed by the State Board of Health, April 8, 1910.

Sanitary survey of schoolhouse at Monroe City, Harrison Township, Knox County, March 9, 1910, by Dr. J. N. Hurty, State Health Commissioner.

Site.—Area of site about one acre, in many places lower than the surrounding streets. Not easily drained and no drains. Grounds damp and in places wet. In wet weather the grounds are certainly very muddy for at the time I was there, this fact plainly appeared from the dried up puddles in various places.

Building.—Frame. Dilapidated and not in good repair. It is two stories, contains six rooms, with brick foundation and no basement. The old part of the building was built in 1880, four rooms. The new part built in 1899, 2 rooms. Heated by stoves, with slate blackboards. Floors are passable, roof is bad and leaky. The halls are not warmed and are used for the clothing of the children. No ventilating ducts.

High School and Eighth Grade.—Room, 30 x 22 x 11, 36 seats, enrollment, 38. Plaster off in places. Air was stuffy and bad. Room lighted from two sides.

Sixth and Seventh Grades.—Room, 32 x 22 x 11, 56 seats, enrollment, 55. Plaster off in one place on ceiling, paper peeling off; lighted from two sides.

Second and Third, High.—Room, 36 x 24 x 11, 44 seats, enrollment, 19. Walls shedding their paper, plastering off the ceiling in one place. Room lighted from two sides.

Second and Third, Low.—Room, 32 x 22 x 11, 54 seats, enrollment, 56. Walls shedding their paper, plaster off in places. Lighted from two sides.

Fourth and Fifth Grades.—Room, 32 x 22 x 11, 50 seats, enrollment, 49. Walls shedding their paper, plaster off in places. Lighted from two sides.

Primary and Grade 1.—Room, 36 x 24 x 14, 42 seats, enrollment, 36. Paper good. Room lighted from three sides.

Remarks.—The outhouses are of the very worst kind and in vile and bad condition. The schoolhouse and grounds are all insanitary.

Recommendations.—I recommend that this schoolhouse be condemned and the condemnation to take effect June 1st.

After consideration, the following proclamation of condemnation was adopted:

PROCLAMATION OF CONDEMNATION.

Whereas, It has been shown to the satisfaction of the State Board of Health that the schoolhouse at Monroe City, Harrison Township, Knox County, Ind., is insanitary and consequently threatens the health and life of the pupils and also interferes with their efficiency; therefore, it is

Ordered: That said schoolhouse at Monroe City, Harrison Township, Knox County, Indiana, is condemned for school purposes, and shall not be used for said school purposes after June 1, 1910, and if any school trustee or trustees, any teacher or any person uses said schoolhouse for school purposes, or teaches therein, after the date above mentioned, he or she or they shall be prosecuted.

Any person mutilating or tearing down this proclamation shall be prosecuted.

Passed by the State Board of Health, April 8, 1910.

Sanitary survey of School No. 15, Pipe Creek Township, Madison County, by Dr. T. J. Stephenson, County Health Commissioner.

To the State Board of Health:

Gentlemen—March 25, 1910, I visited School No. 15, Pipe Creek Township, Madison County, Ind., and inspected building.

I found building located on northwest quarter of block. Building facing north and east. The ground is high. Water runs in every direction from building except south. The building is one story, two rooms, brick and stone. Arches of doors and windows are stone. Foundation is stone, 24 inches high. Walls and foundation are good except a very few small cracks, two downspouts are off, water stains wall, slate roof.

Building consists of two rooms, east and west. East room is 23 x 38 feet, with 14-foot ceiling; 2 windows in south 2-8 x 8, 4 in east 2-8 x 8, and one window in north, 2-8 x 8. Circular bay window 8 feet in diameter, in northeast corner, has one window 1½ x 8 feet.

Anteroom or hall on north of room 9-4 x 6-9. Door from room into hall is 2-8 x 8. Door from hall to outside 2-8 x 7.

Double door in northwest corner of room, 5 x 8 and 1½ foot transom, leads into west room. Teacher's desk is in west side of room about middle way north and south. Heated by soft coal stove located in east part of room, opposite teacher's desk. Oiled floors, fairly good blackboards on west side of room. Room has been lately papered and is clean. Windows have drop wood blinds. Ventilated by raising and lowering windows.

West room is irregular shape, about 12½ x 33 feet; 14 foot ceiling. Has circular bay window in west side about center of room, north and south. Pump is in this circle, with good trough and drain. Two windows in west, one 2-8 x 8, and one in circle 1½ x 8. One arched window in north 6 x 8; door leading into east room 5 x 8 with ½ foot transom. One door leading out doors to west in northwest corner of room 5 x 8. This door leads into open arched hall 9-4 x 3 feet, with steps leading to ground. Teacher's desk in southwest corner of room. Stove near center of room. Oiled floors and room neatly papered.

There are no walks except a few cinders. Closets are brick, about

6 x 8. located on south side of school grounds, about 45 feet from school building. Closets are in fair condition. girls' clean, boys' fair only. coal shed about 12 x 20. on south side of ground between closet. Closets both have deep vaults and shields.

After consideration, the following proclamation of condemnation was adopted:

PROCLAMATION OF CONDEMNATION.

Whereas, It has been shown to the satisfaction of the State Board of Health that schoolhouse No. 15. Pipe Creek Township. Madison County. Ind., is insanitary and consequently threatens the health and life of the pupils and also interferes with their efficiency; therefore it is

Ordered: That said schoolhouse No. 15. Pipe Creek Township, Madison County. Ind., is condemned for school purposes, and shall not be used for said school purposes after June 1, 1910, and if any school trustee or trustees. any teacher or any person uses said schoolhouse for school purposes, or teaches therein. after the date above mentioned, he or she or they shall be prosecuted.

Any person mutilating or tearing down this proclamation shall be prosecuted.

Passed by the State Board of Health, April 8, 1910.

Sanitary survey of schoolhouse at Hortonville, Washington Township, District No. 2, Hamilton County, Ind., by L. J. Baldwin, Deputy State Health Commissioner.

State Board of Health:

Gentlemen—I herewith make my sanitary survey of schoolhouse and school grounds, situated at Hortonville, Ind., Washington Township, District No. 2, J. L. Furniss, Trustee; C. M. Hodson, Director.

1. The schoolhouse and grounds are situated on east side of the little town of Hortonville, on north side public highway, and about 700 feet east of nearest lot in the town. The grounds are surrounded on east, north and west by farm lands, and south by public highway and farm land. Size of grounds 273 feet by 165 feet, longest way extends east and west. (You will observe my rough drawing.) As to drainage, none except surface. On east and southeast, the end of grounds is often 2½ to 3 feet under water, grade from public highway is about 3½ feet higher than that part of grounds. Only small sewer tiling under grade. The nearest drain tile ditch is about 300 feet from northwest corner of grounds, and it has not capacity to carry water in wet weather. Observe in drawing I represent a ridge or raise in ground between drain tile ditch and where waste water flows from well. It is impossible for water to flow away from well at any time. The grounds are absolutely without drainage except surface, and that is bad. The well is situated 15 feet from public highway line, and about 15 feet from west property line, and about 11 feet from where eaves turn water off building and not any spouting on the building. Well is dug 23 feet deep, seep water, walled with brick, puncheon to cover top

of well. No drainage from well, nothing but public watering trough to convey water away.

2. The building is a two-story building, frame, made of pine and native lumber. The lower story has been built about 35 years, upper story about 23 years. Old and dilapidated, it is an unprepossessing appearing building from outside. Don't think there are two good whole boards in outside of building, paint scaling off *badly*. It has no basement. Has brick foundation, but badly in decay, brick falling out and crumbling to dust. One can kick brick out of foundation. The brick at first were second grade.

3. Three schoolrooms, two downstairs, one upstairs; an anteroom down and upstairs (see plans.) Rooms downstairs, 28 x 25 feet; upstairs, 28 x 50 feet. The west room, 12 feet to ceiling. Plastering falling off, much of plastering hanging 1 to 2 inches (sagging from laths.) West room, pupils face east, single desks. East room, pupils face west. Paper old, dingy and dirty. Single desks in all rooms, not fastened to floor. The floor in lower rooms, old, worn, cracks filled full dirt germs. Upstairs room, pupils face north. (See plan of rough drawing for windows and doors.)

4. The building heated with No. 20 cannon stoves, one to each room. (See plans No. 3, how stove is connected with flue.) Flue goes up and through both anterooms. Upstairs room stove is connected directly overhead with flue and it is resting on joists, making ceiling sag.

No walks to water-closets, only paths. No walk around building at all, gravel covers ground to some extent in front of building.

5. No ventilation except through broken panes or open door, or the open cracks in floor.

6. The windows are heavily and securely screened in with sheaving wire in rod-iron frame and securely fastened to building on outside, except one window where fire escape was put up. Said fire escape is made of light pine frame work, and was in state of decay and not safe for more than one person to be on it at a time. Size of platform of fire escape is 5 x 3 feet. Ladder does not reach within ten feet of ground.

7. Stairway.—I would draw plans, but I cannot. But, follow me. Enter anteroom from street through door that swings inward. Go north a few steps, turn east few steps, now turn south and begin going upstairs a few steps then turn west few steps up, then turn north a few steps and land in upper anteroom. Making a complete circuit and a half before you can get up or down stairs. Stairway is only 3½ feet wide. Imagine case of fire. Student trying to get down stairs and fire raging in anteroom below.

Mortar in both flues in attic is falling out badly. Roof leaks badly; water-closets in fair condition with cement vaults.

My opinion is that the building is insanitary, unsafe in case of fire or high winds. I think impossible to heat, as building is so pulled apart in joints, framage and poor workmanship. The well of water should be discontinued for use as drinking water.

My advice is for the State Board of Health to condemn the building, well and grounds, and not permit one piece of material to go into another school building. Further, act on this at once, so that the trustee can have ample time to erect another building. Also compel him, if possible, to submit his plans and specifications for your approval.

Will say that the grounds can be made in splendid condition by expenditure of small amount of money. And, remember, the well should be a tubular well and to secoud water.

Twenty-three pupils in upper room.

Twenty-six pupils in east lower room.

Twenty-nine pupils in west lower room.

P. S If I can be of any service in above matter, or if you want me to act in similar capacity on any other case, I am at your service.

After consideration, the following proclamation of condemnation was adopted:

PROCLAMATION OF CONDEMNATION.

Whereas, It has been shown to the satisfaction of the State Board of Health that the schoolhouse at Hortonville, District No. 2, Washington Township, Hamilton County, Ind., is insanitary, and consequently threatens the health and life of the pupils and also interferes with their efficiency; therefore it is

Ordered: That said schoolhouse at Hortonville, District No. 2, Washington Township, Hamilton County, Ind., is condemned for school purposes, and shall not be used for said school purposes after June 1, 1910, and if any school trustee or trustees, any teacher or any person uses said schoolhouse for school purposes, or teaches therein, after the date above mentioned, he or she or they shall be prosecuted.

Any person mutilating or tearing down this proclamation shall be prosecuted.

Passed by the State Board of Health, April 8, 1910.

Sanitary survey of schoolhouse at Urbana, Wabash County, by Dr. G. M. LaSalle, County Health Commissioner, March 26th.

To the State Board of Health:

Gentlemen—I made a survey of the Urbana school building today. The building is situated on the south part of the village on the west side of the street. The ground upon which the building is situated is about as high as in the neighborhood, but the west end of the school lot is low and drainage very poor, because no drainage is there. The size of the yard is plenty large enough if properly drained. The outhouses are very poor and insanitary. They are about 120 or 130 feet from school building. The school building is a brick structure of four rooms. The building on one half is old and very much in need of repair, the floors of the old part are very bad.

I have tried to draw a diagram of the first floor, and the second floor is the same.

I believe that the petitioners of Urbana are justified in stating that the building is old and dilapidated and unfit for school purposes, and ask that you visit same for your personal inspection.

After consideration, the following proclamation of condemnation was adopted:

PROCLAMATION OF CONDEMNATION.

Whereas, It has been shown to the satisfaction of the State Board of Health that the schoolhouse at Urbana, Wabash County, Ind., is insanitary and consequently threatens the health and life of the pupils and also interferes with their efficiency, therefore it is

Ordered: That said schoolhouse at Urbana, Wabash County, Ind., is condemned for school purposes, and shall not be used for said school purposes after June 1, 1910, and if any school trustee or trustees, any teacher or any person uses said schoolhouse for school purposes, or teaches therein, after the date above mentioned, he or she or they shall be prosecuted.

Any person mutilating or tearing down this proclamation shall be prosecuted.

Passed by the State Board of Health, April 8, 1910.

Sanitary inspection of District School No. 1, Jefferson Township, Jay County, March 17, 1910, by Dr. Will Shimer.

Indiana State Board of Health:

Dear Doctor—At the request of J. J. Jenkins I visited district school No. 1, of Jefferson Township, Jay County. This is the school about which you received a petition in January of this year.

The schoolhouse is situated on a triangular piece of ground of about one-half acre, formed by the intersection of three roads. The school yard is very low and not well drained. There is no gravel or any sort of walks about the school premises.

The schoolhouse is a low brick building, 22 x 26 feet inside, built in 1874 and now in bad repair. Long iron rods were put through the ends and sides of the building to keep the walls from falling apart. The floor is much higher in the center than at the sides. The walls are papered, not painted. There is only one room in this building, and that heated by a stove. The windows have no weights, only catches, discouraging the opening of windows.

There is no well and the water must be carried from a farmhouse one-fourth mile away. We advised the teacher to discontinue the use of the water bucket.

This school has an average attendance of 28 pupils with a capacity of 32. At the beginning of the school term there are usually 35 pupils in attendance.

The member of the advisory board most opposed to building a new schoolhouse is a breeder of fine stock. His fine, up-to-date barn has an open shed around the outside for the exercise of the stock. The floor of the shed is of concrete to keep the cattle out of the mud.

After consideration, the following proclamation of condemnation was adopted:

Proclamation of Condemnation.

Whereas, It has been shown to the satisfaction of the State Board of Health that the schoolhouse, District No. 1, Jefferson Township, Jay County, Indiana, is insanitary and consequently threatens the health and life of the pupils and also interferes with their efficiency, therefore it is

Ordered: That said schoolhouse, District No. 1, Jefferson Township, Jay County, Indiana, is condemned for school purposes, and shall not be used for said school purposes after June 1, 1910, and if any school trustee or trustees, any teacher or any person uses said schoolhouse for school purposes, or teaches therein, after the date above mentioned, he or she or they shall be prosecuted.

Any person mutilating or tearing down this proclamation shall be prosecuted.

Passed by the State Board of Health, April 8, 1910.

Sanitary inspection of schoolhouse, District No. 2, Jefferson Township, Putnam County, by Dr. J. M. King, County Health Commissioner.

This schoolhouse is situated off the main road in the town of Mt. Meridian, behind a block of dwellings, as per diagram. The schoolyard is a knoll sloping to the north. The north side being from ten to fifteen feet lower than the south side.

This lot is not level enough for a playground, it being too much on the hillside. However, the drainage is good. The lot faces to the north and is 120 feet east and west, by 156 feet north and south.

There are no gravel or board walks anywhere, and no indication that there ever has been, and there is nothing to protect the pupils from mud. The schoolhouse was erected in 1876. It is about the middle of the south half of the lot.

It is a one-story, frame structure. The weather boarding has been patched in several places. The building has not been painted for several years. The roof is of shingles and is apparently good.

The foundation is of stone and is not in good condition. It has some large openings for ventilation which makes the floor of schoolrooms cold The foundation is 30 inches above the ground on north side and 6 to 8 inches above the ground on the south side. There is no basement.

The well is situated about 23 feet northwest of the building. It is a drilled well about 100 feet deep. It has an iron pump, a cement platform, but no cover. There is one old tin cup which answers for all pupils.

There is a closet in each back corner of the lot. These closets when constructed were provided with screens, but have no paths leading to them. The boys' closet is about torn down. It has no floor, is filthy and dangerous because of the large vault, which is almost full. This closet is absolutely insanitary and could not possibly answer for any of the purposes of a privy. The girls' closet is slightly better.

The school building has two rooms and an entrance hall. The entrance hall is 9 feet 9 inches by 14 feet. Has two windows each 30 inches by 80 inches. This room has old shelving for dinner buckets and a few hooks and nails for hats and cloaks; also rubbish, coal buckets and a discarded stove. No heat is provided for this room. The floor is very bad. almost worn out and one panel is gone from the outside door. This hall has a door 31 inches by 8½ feet. including transoms. One transom is gone.

The west room (high school) is 25 feet by 17½ feet with 13½ feet ceiling, as per diagram. This room has one window in north end and two in south end. All windows are 30 inches by 80 inches; each section having six panes 10 x 20 inches. The window frames and casings are in good condition and all panes are in place. The plastering is good and is covered with a dark paper. The woodwork extends for 30 inches above the floor. A good blackboard extends the entire length of west side. This room is heated by a stove in the center of the east side of the room. There are 18 single seats and 5 double seats. The seats are old, dilapidated and too small for pupils of this grade.

East Room (Primary Room).—Inside measure 25 feet by 25 feet. Floor, pine, old and poor and has been oiled. Has three windows, one in north and two in south. The pupils face the east. Plastering good and covered with dark paper. This room is supposed to accommodate 45 pupils. It has 7 double seats and 25 single seats. Seats old, dilapidated and several are not stationary. Stove in center of west side of room. It would be impossible to properly heat this room by a stove. There is no provision for ventilation.

This building should be condemned because—

1. Of the location, it being situated behind a row of buildings, and having no approach except side street, and an insanitary alley. (The lot could be graded so as to make a good playground.)

2. Of the insanitary out-buildings.

3. No walks or gravel on the lot.

4. The anteroom is not sufficient to accommodate 68 pupils, boys and girls, no provision being made to heat it.

5. The shape of the schoolrooms is bad. The rooms are too small, the primary room (for 45 pupils and teacher) should contain 10,350 cubic feet of space, whereas it has only 8,437 feet.

6. Not properly lighted. Windows not properly located. In west room light equals one-tenth of floor space, in east room equals one-fifteenth of floor space.

7. Because of improper method of heating. It would be impossible to properly heat these rooms with stoves.

8. There are 80 to 90 pupils accessible to this school, but over twenty (20) are hauled to another district because of lack of room.

After consideration, the following proclamation of condemnation was adopted:

Proclamation of Condemnation.

Whereas, It has been shown to the satisfaction of the State Board of Health that the schoolhouse, District No. 2, Jefferson Township, Putnam County, Ind., is insanitary, and consequently threatens the health and life of the pupils and also interferes with their efficiency; therefore it is

Ordered: That said schoolhouse, District No. 2, Jefferson Township, Putnam County, Ind., is condemned for school purposes, and shall not be used for said school purposes after June 1, 1910, and if any school trustee or trustees, any teacher or any person uses said schoolhouse for school purposes, or teaches therein, after the date above mentioned, he or she or they shall be prosecuted.

Any person mutilating or tearing down this proclamation shall be prosecuted.

Passed by the State Board of Health, April 8, 1910.

Sanitary inspection of school building at Daleville, Delaware County, by J. L. Anderson, April 7, 1910.

State Board of Health:

Gentlemen—Upon April 6, 1910, I made a survey of the school building at Daleville, Delaware County, Ind., and beg to submit the following report:

Site.—South of the railways and on the west side of the main street running south from the depots. There is about an acre of ground in the lot, and there are a number of fine shade trees on the east half of the grounds. The lot is high, dry and an ideal location for a modern building, if not too close to the steam railroad, which is about 300 feet from the northwest corner of the lot. A good gravel walk leads to front door of the building, which faces the east. North of the building and about 30 feet away, is the coal house; a frame building about 15 x 20 with several wagon loads of ashes and cinders laying on the ground just west of it. The outhouses are west of the building, screened, and in fairly good condition, but need disinfecting. Gravel walks lead to each. The driven well is opposite and south of the southwest corner of the main building; about 20 feet from the building and about 50 feet from the boys' closet. There is a 10-foot wooden trough that carries the waste water to the slope so that it runs off down the hill.

South of the main building is a one-story frame building for the primary and first grade children. This is 24 x 41 feet outside measurement. The entrance hall is at the east end, 7½ x 23 feet, and has two windows in east end. The schoolroom is 23 x 33 feet 4 inches. The ceiling is 11 feet high with four windows in north side and two in west end. Windows are 2 feet 8 inches x 7 feet, and all have blinds. Walls are papered, slate blackboards on east and south walls, in good condition. Seats in good condition and suitable for the children. Floor, oiled and fairly good condition, but needs bracing at east end of room. Heated by a coal stove in northwest corner of room, which has a low sheet-iron screen around it. Ventilation by windows. Enrollment, 49; average attendance, 40.

Main Building.—Two story brick with slate roof and bell tower on center of building. Stone foundation; no basement. Walls in south end and west side beginning to crack and the northwest corner has settled enough to be plainly noticeable. Down-spouts in good condition and empty on ground. A good, covered cement porch at the entrance about 6 x 10 feet, and three steps above the ground. Cement steps at front and ends.

Large double doors opening outward lead into the vestibule, which is 16 x 21 feet in the clear. One window on each side of the door 3 feet 3 inches by 7 feet 4 inches. Two stairways lead to upper rooms, 3 feet 6 inches wide and making two turns; but the one on the south side is closed and the opening above floored over to give room for the office of the superintendent up stairs. A wooden handrail is fastened along the side of the wall, and the stairway is strong, but not wide enough. The cloakrooms are 4 x 16 feet and are entered from the vestibule by a 4-foot passage between the wall and stairways, also open into the schoolrooms, and have a window in each but no means of heating, nor is there any way of heating the vestibules.

Lower Floor, North Room.—This is the second and third primary grades, is 28 x 30 feet and 14-foot ceiling. There are 3 windows on the west, 2 on the north and 1 in east side, all curtained. Walls papered, wood wainscoted from floor to blackboards. Slate blackboards on north, east and south walls. Heated by stove in southwest corner. Has an opening into an outside ventilator shaft, but does not seem to get any air from there. Floors were badly worn, but oiled and clean. Wall paper grimy from coal smoke.

The teacher said she could not keep the children warm during the cold weather, and if the wind was strong from the northwest, the snow would blow into the room from around the windows. Enrollment in this room, 36; average attendance, 33.

South Room.—Fourth and fifth grades occupy this room. Same size and general conditions obtain as in the first room, with the exception that there is an outside air shaft opens under the stove, but the teacher says that she cannot leave it open as the room cannot be warmed when it is open. Enrollment, 27; average attendance, 27.

Upstairs Hall.—This hall is 12 x 16 feet. The south half is partitioned off for the principal's office and recitation room for high school pupils. This room is 14 x 16 feet, has a window in east and south sides. Heated by stove. Roof leaks and exhibited a coal scuttle one-fourth full of water caught that a. m. as proof. Plastering in this room and hall cracked and falling off. More would fall if not held in place by the wall paper.

North Room.—This is the sixth and seventh grade room, and is the same size and arrangement as the second and third grade rooms below it. The walls are in bad condition and paper dirty and discolored by water leaking into the room.

The teacher reported that he cannot keep the children warm in cold weather in this room. The janitor said that he has seen snow laying on the desks in this room last winter and he could not get the room warm enough to melt it. There was a bad odor in this room although the windows were up and ventilator open.

South Room.—This is the 8th grade and high school room and arranged the same as the one below it. The plastering is in bad shape and paper dirty and discolored from water and coal smoke. Ventilation better than in the north room. Same complaint about cold, and snow blowing into room.

The air shaft is built on the outside of the west side of the building and communicates with each of the school rooms. All windows are covered with coarse wire screens to prevent breakage. An iron rod is run through the main building to prevent spreading of walls to the north.

Recapitulation.—Site excellent, good drainage not over 200 yards away. May be a little close to the railroad (300 feet). Building both *unsafe* and *insanitary* and cannot be repaired. I would respectfully recommend that it be condemned.

Trustee, Frank McAllister, Daleville, not at home. Principal of school, William Graves. Five teachers employed. Dr. Kilgore accompanied me on the inspection.

After consideration, the following proclamation of condemnation was adopted:

PROCLAMATION OF CONDEMNATION.

Whereas, It has been shown to the satisfaction of the State Board of Health that the school building at Daleville, Delaware County, Ind., is insanitary and consequently threatens the health and life of the pupils and also interferes with their efficiency; therefore, it is

Ordered: That said schoolhouse at Daleville, Delaware County, Ind., is condemned for school purposes, and shall not be used for said school purposes after June 1st 1910, and if any school trustee or trustees, any teacher or any person uses said school house for school purposes, or teaches therein, after the date above mentioned, he or she or they shall be prosecuted.

Any person mutilating or tearing down this proclamation shall be prosecuted.

Passed by the State Board of Health, April 8, 1910.

Sanitary survey of Middlebury schoolhouse, Harrison Township, Clay County, Ind., April 5th, by Dr. C. C. Sourwine, County Health Commissioner.

Site—The school is located on a hill facing west, and is on a dirt road which gets in very bad condition. The playground is about one acre. No walks in front of building from road and no walk in the back yard to outbuildings, which are located down in the hollow. The building is poorly built and the walls in the old part are cracked in many places. The building is of soft brick on a stone foundation, which is not in very good shape, and they have holes in the foundation for ventilation under the floors. Tin roof. The old part of the building was built in 1884, and the new part in 1901. They have no sewer or well in the yard, so carry water from the houses close to the school. They use tin cups and buckets. Outbuildings in fair shape but vaults need cleaning.

On the inside of the building, the new part is in fair shape, but the old building is in bad condition. The walls are cracked and the ceiling has to be braced up by three wooden braces. The walls and floors in new building in fair shape, clean and papered. The floor in old building rough and uneven. The blackboards are not slate, but only painted on the walls; none are in very good condition. Ceiling very low, poor light, no ventilation but the windows, and the rooms are heated by stoves, which sit in the back part of the rooms.

Rooms are all the same size, 32 feet long, 28 feet wide and 10 feet ceilings.

First room has six windows, 2 feet by 6 feet, three to the north and three to the east. The children face the west. This room has 28 children.

Second room has seven windows, five 2 feet by 6 feet in the west and two windows 2 feet by 2½ feet in the east part of room. Very poor light. The children face the west. This room has 24 children in it.

Room 3, upstairs, has six windows, 2 feet by 6 feet, three in north and three in the east part. The children face the west. Thirty-one children in this room.

Room 4, upstairs, has 6 windows; four windows 2 feet by 6 feet in west, and 2 windows 2 feet by 2½ feet in east part of room. The children face the north. Very poor light. Twenty-four children in this room.

The building should be condemned and replaced by a modern building in a different location, where it is level, so the children can have a playground. The building should be ventilated and heated properly, with a better water supply and do away with the buckets and cups.

After consideration, the following proclamation of condemnation was adopted:

Proclamation of Condemnation.

Whereas, It has been shown to the satisfaction of the State Board of Health that the Middlebury Schoolhouse, Harrison Township, Clay County, Indiana, is insanitary and consequently threatens the health and life of the pupils and also interferes with their efficiency; therefore, it is

Ordered: That said schoolhouse, known as the Middlebury schoolhouse, Harrison Township, Clay County, Indiana, is condemned for school purposes, and shall not be used for said school purposes after June 1, 1910, and if any school trustee or trustees, any teacher or any person uses said schoolhouse for school purposes, or teaches therein, after the date above mentioned, he or she or they shall be prosecuted.

Any person mutilating or tearing down this proclamation shall be prosecuted.

Passed by the State Board of Health, April 8, 1910.

Sanitary inspection of Schoolhouse No. 4, Pierson Township, Vigo County, by J. D. Foor, M. D., Deputy State Health Commissioner, Blackhawk, Ind., April 5, 1910.

State Board of Health, Indianapolis, Ind.:

Gentlemen—I report as follows on the condition of above schoolhouse:

Site—One-half acre, located half mile south of the town of Blackhawk, in the southeast corner of Section 16, Township 10, north of Range 8, and lies at the foot of an eastern slope, and when it rains the water runs down from the hill above over the school ground.

Building is frame, 25 feet by 50 feet. Height of studding 12 feet. Foundation, stone pillars. Roof is pine shingles and leaks. Chimneys are brick. The mortar has shattered out so that smoke escapes into attic. Walls are papered and are smokey, some cracks in plaster. Weather-boarding cracked and split in places. Some holes in it where birds enter and build nests. Floor is in fair condition, but admits the passage of air, as there is insufficient protection around the foundation of the building.

Windows, 5 on each side, loose and improperly fit. The building faces the east and was built in one room about 40 years ago. In recent years, it was divided by a partition, one-third being set off as a room for lower grades and two-thirds for higher grades. There is not enough room to accommodate the pupils, and what room there is is very unhygienic and insanitary. Coal shed has tumbled down. Closets very loosely constructed, with no vaults or boxes, the deposit piled high as the seat.

The well is a dug well with brick wall. The platform is loose and waste water runs back into the well.

Recommendations—In regard to the disposition of above mentioned property, I recommend that the school building, closets and well be condemned as unfit for school purposes.

After consideration, the following proclamation of condemnation was adopted:

PROCLAMATION OF CONDEMNATION.

Whereas, It has been shown to the satisfaction of the State Board of Health that the schoolhouse known as District No. 4, Pierson Township, Vigo County, Indiana, is insanitary and consequently threatens the health and life of the pupils and also interferes with their efficiency; therefore, it is

Ordered: That said schoolhouse, known as District No. 4, Pierson Township, Vigo County, Indiana, is condemned for school purposes, and shall not be used for said school purposes after June 1, 1910, and if any school trustee or trustees, any teacher or any person uses said schoolhouse for school purposes, or teaches therein, after the date above mentioned, he or she or they shall be prosecuted.

Any person mutilating or tearing down this proclamation shall be prosecuted.

Passed by the State Board of Health, April 8, 1910.

Sanitary survey of schoolhouse, District No. 9, Center Township, Gibson County, Francisco, Ind., March 4, 1910, by A. L. Ziliak, County Health Commissioner.

Site.—The school building is situated in the extreme eastern part of the town on the summit of a rolling two-acre plot of ground. The building is high, dry, and well drained. Trees are numerous, but too small for shade. The well is situated in the most dependent part of the ground and is topped with an open wooden box arrangement. A galvanized iron bucket is used to draw the water. Drinking vessels consist of old and battered galvanized iron drinking cups, and are used in common.

The outhouses, especially that of the boys, are in a bad state of repair and are dirty, insanitary and have a surface drain. There are no walks leading to either of the outhouses.

Building.—The school building is a two-story frame, and L shaped. The main part was built 32 years ago, and the wing 9 years ago. It is in a fair state of repair. The foundation, built of brick, is bad in spite of repairs. It was repainted three years ago.

In the interior of the building, in the halls, new floors were laid and new staircases built, two years ago. The plastering in the rooms of the old part is rather interesting piece of patchwork, and is bad. The rooms in the wing have wall paper.

The only system of ventilation is through doors and windows. The building is heated by stoves.

In general, the building gives the impression of being old and unstable and I believe a building inspector would pronounce it unsafe.

After consideration, the following proclamation of condemnation was adopted:

PROCLAMATION OF CONDEMNATION.

Whereas, It has been shown to the satisfaction of the State Board of Health that the schoolhouse at Francisco, District No. 9, Cener Township, Gibson County, Indiana, is insanitary and consequently threatens the health and life of the pupils and also interferes with their efficiency: therefore, it is

Ordered: That said schoolhouse at Francisco, District No. 9, Center Township, Gibson County, Indiana, is condemned for school purposes, and shall not be used for said school purposes after June 1, 1910, and if any school trustee or trustees, any teacher or any person uses said schoolhouse for school purposes, or teaches therein, after the date above mentioned, he or she or they shall be prosecuted.

Any person mutilating or tearing down this proclamation shall be prosecuted.

Passed by the State Board of Health, April 8, 1910.

Sanitary survey of Green Hill Schoolhouse, Districts 1 and 2, Medina Township, Warren County, Ind., April 6th, by Dr. E. J. Yeager, Deputy State Health Commissioner.

Site.—Southwest part of town, area is approximately two and one-half acres. The campus is high, dry and well drained and contains 100 shade trees, and is well sodded for the amount of shade. It was formerly known as the U. B. Academy Campus.

Building.—Exterior.—Erected in the year 1872 by the U. B. Conference. The foundation is of stone, and superstructure of brick. Foundation rising 24 inches above ground, and of hewn stone. Height of brick structure to square, 26 feet, and gables of brick, with shingle roof. Four rooms and vestibule, with stairways and hall running entirely through center of the building. Town hall on second floor. Outer walls in good condition. Roof old and has been patched in numerous places. Heated by ordinary soft coal burners. Ventilation by windows only, by raising or lowering.

Outwardly the building is rather handsome for a structure of that date, having an old style cupola, with flagstaff. The interior consists of hallway 9 feet by 57 feet, and vestibule on either side at entrance 9 feet by 14 feet, each vestibule containing a stairway, with a closet under each stairway.

Four rooms, as follows:

1. Primary room, 14x22x12 feet, with 2 windows, 3 feet 4 inches by 8 feet 6 inches, and one door leading into hallway, and opening into school room. This room contains 27 children during term.

2. Intermediate, 14x22x12 feet, with 3 windows 3 feet 4 inches by 8 feet 6 inches, and one door leading into hallway and swinging into school room. This room seats 24 scholars during term.

3. Grammar or high school. 14x28x12 feet, with 5 windows 3 feet 4 inches by 8 feet 6 inches, and one door leading to hallway and swinging into school room. This room seats 13 students. Floors in all the rooms are in bad condition.

4. Cloak room, 14x15x12 feet, one window and one door. Size and condition as in other rooms. Inside walls are in good repair and are well painted.

There are three outhouses, a coal house 15 feet in rear of the school building and approached by a cement walk; 2 closets, each near 100 feet from building, on edge of bluff, and approached by dry paths. These three outbuildings are all constructed of wood.

I would recommend that the building be condemned and ordered remodeled before being used for school purposes again.

After consideration of the above, the following proclamation of condemnation was adopted:

Proclamation of Condemnation.

Whereas, It has been shown to the satisfaction of the State Board of Health that the schoolhouse at Green Hill, Districts 1 and 2, Medina Township, Warren County, Indiana, is insanitary, and consequently threatens the health and life of the pupils and also interferes with their efficiency; therefore, it is

Ordered: That said schoolhouse at Green Hill, Districts 1 and 2, Medina Township, Warren County, Indiana, is condemned for school purposes, and shall not be used for said school purposes after June 1, 1910, and if any school trustee or trustees, any teacher or any person, uses said schoolhouse for school purposes, or teaches therein, after the date above mentioned, he or she or they shall be prosecuted.

Any person mutilating or tearing down this proclamation shall be prosecuted.

Passed by the State Board of Health, April 8, 1910.

Sanitary survey of Prairie Creek schoolhouse, Vigo County, by F. W. Shaley, M. D., County Health Commissioner.

To the State Board of Health:

Gentlemen—I inspected the Prairie Creek schoolhouse Saturday, March 19, 1910, and herewith present the following report:

Prairie Creek school was built in 1870 and is situated on an elevated piece of ground which slopes too precipitately on all sides to make playground. By stepping off the ground, I find that it is approximately 285 feet long (north and south) by 235 feet deep (east and west). Through the southwest corner runs a swale, across which the boys have to go to reach their outhouse. Otherwise the ground is high and dry. A concrete walk extends from the entrance steps to the street in front. There are no other walks on the grounds. The building is of common brick, which are beginning, in numerous places, to crumble; is without basement and the foundation is composed of the same material as the superstructure. The first floor is sufficiently high to give good ventilation underneath.

The building comprises four rooms, an entrance hall and cloakrooms for each room. (See diagram and views.) The rooms are 21 by 36 feet and ceiling 14 feet high. The floors are old and the boards creak as you walk over them in all parts of the rooms. The windows are about worn out, leaving plenty of playroom in the casings, thereby affording a good chance for ventilation, but making it very uncomfortable in cold weather. I was told it was impossible to properly heat the rooms. The hall and cloakrooms are never heated. In rooms No. 1 and 3 the light enters from the back and right side of the pupil; in rooms No. 2 and 4 from the back and left. (See views Nos. 1, 2 and 3.) Room No. 4 I could not get because an examination for entrance to the high school was taking place there, but it is a duplicate of room No. 2, as No. 1 is of No. 3. Note that No. 1 and No. 3 are taken from opposite corners of the rooms. Note in view No. 1 the cold air duct that takes the air from the floor of room No. 3 passing it through the furnace to re-enter the schoolrooms. View No. 4 will give good idea of cloakrooms on first floor, together with beginning of stairway. The building was clean and as well kept as an old building could be. The floors are oiled, but the cracks in them are innumerable and of great extent. The building is heated by a small hot-air furnace which is placed in a hole dug out under room No. 1. This hole is surrounded with concrete walls and under the hall is a shallow cellar used as a coal bunker. The walls of the building have numerous cracks and the chimneys are ready, with a proper wind, to fall apart. Northeast from the building, about 15 or 20 feet, is an open well (see view No. 7) with an iron pump in it, which had formerly been used for drinking purposes, but at present is not used, the water supply being carried from neighboring houses. Girls' outhouse (view No. 6) is clean and in good condition. Boys' outhouse (view No. 5) contains no urinal and consequently seats and floor are in bad condition. The building is surmounted by a cupola, in which hangs a 400-pound bell.

I was informed by Professor McCarter, principal of the school, that the building was not adequate to accommodate the number of pupils and that the trustee was renting part of the first floor of a brick storeroom about a block away (the balance of said storeroom being used as a storeroom for farm implements) and using it as a school room.

Therefore, said Prairie Creek school building is—

1. Old and dilapidated and has outlived its usefulness.
2. In its present condition is a menace to the life, health and comfort of teacher and pupil alike.
3. Is not constructed of proper material, nor on lines which could be used in reconstructing or altering the same.
4. Is not large enough to accommodate the present number of pupils.

It is my unqualified opinion that said building should be condemned and not allowed to be used for school purposes.

After consideration of the above, the following proclamation of condemnation was adopted:

PROCLAMATION OF CONDEMNATION.

Whereas, It has been shown to the satisfaction of the State Board of Health that the schoolhouse at Prairie Creek, Prairie Creek Township, Vigo County, Indiana, is insanitary, and consequently threatens the health and life of the pupils and also interferes with their efficiency; therefore, it is

Ordered: That said schoolhouse at Prairie Creek, Prairie Creek Township, Vigo County, Indiana, is condemned for school purposes, and shall not be used for said school purposes after June 1, 1910, and if any school trustee or trustees, any teacher or any person uses said schoolhouse for school purposes, or teaches therein, after the date above mentioned, he or she or they shall be prosecuted.

Any person mutilating or tearing down this proclamation shall be prosecuted.

Passed by the State Board of Health, April 8, 1910.

Report on sanitation and safety of Crawfordsville high school, by J. N. Hurty, State Health Commissioner. Inspection made March 7, 1910.

Site.—Covers one city square, is high and well drained. Site is excellent in every way.

Building.—Erected in 1872. Three stories and a cellar. Brick with stone trimmings. Cellar, not a basement, is beneath entire building. Cellar is a labyrinth of passageways, dark rooms and black corners. The lighting and ventilation are insufficient even for a cellar.

Heating is by furnaces placed in the cellar. They take air from cold air rooms which have openings (windows) near the ground. In very cold weather and when wind is high and from certain directions, these furnaces cannot be efficient.

Ventilation is by ducts and floor pipes which are not efficient and so it is necessary to supplement with window ventilation.

Lighting.—Not a single room is properly and sufficiently lighted. In every room there are a number of desks so far from the light entrances, and necessarily so placed as to be dark and to cause eye strain to their occupants. With eye strain comes eye deformities, headaches, malnutrition and retardation.

Halls and Stairways.—The halls are wide and high but not sufficiently lighted. Their ventilation is not what it should be.

Stairways are narrow and winding. It is necessary to turn seven times in passing from the third floor to the ground. They are only three feet wide with banisters of only medium size and strength. In the event of a fire panic, these banisters would certainly be broken down and cause disaster.

Summary.—The high school building at Crawfordsville is wrongly constructed in almost every respect, from the dark labyrinthine cellar to the garret. The halls are not lighted and ventilated as they should be; the stairways are narrow and winding and not provided with sufficiently strong banisters; not one of the rooms is sufficiently and properly lighted, and the heating and ventilation are not up to the standard.

The rooms are overcrowded, pupils being compelled to carry a load of books when they pass from study to recitation rooms. The closet accommodations are small and are placed in poorly ventilated and poorly lighted cellar rooms.

A building of this size cannot be properly heated and ventilated by the gravity system; it must have a mechanical or force system.

Opinion.—This building should be condemned and a new structure erected. It cannot be economically remodeled. If remodeled it will still be a thing of shreds and patches, and will certainly be found inadequate in the near future. I say this from many experiences in remodeling. A remodeled school building, like a patched garment, does not meet the conditions and will not give the service desired.

I believe if we take care of the pennies, the dollars will take care of themselves; and, also, if we take care of the children the State will be safe. Therefore, the city of Crawfordsville cannot make a better business move, cannot make a higher economic move, than to erect a new sanitary schoolhouse of architectural beauty and of sufficient size to properly house her children.

After due consideration of the circumstances, the following proclamations of condemnation were adopted:

Proclamation of Condemnation.

Whereas, It has been shown to the satisfaction of the State Board of Health that the schoolhouse at Orleans, Orange County, Ind., is insanitary, and consequently threatens the health and life of the pupils, and also interferes with their efficiency; therefore, it is

Ordered: That said schoolhouse at Orleans, Orange County, Ind., is condemned for school purposes, and shall not be used for said school purposes after June 1, 1910, and if any school trustee, or trustees, any teacher or any person uses said schoolhouse for school purposes, or teaches therein, after the date above mentioned, he or she or they shall be prosecuted.

Any person mutilating or tearing down this proclamation shall be prosecuted.

Passed by the State Board of Health, April 8, 1910.

Proclamation of Condemnation.

Whereas, It has been shown to the satisfaction of the State Board of Health that the schoolhouse at Galveston, Cass County, Ind., is insanitary, and consequently threatens the health and life of the pupils, and also interferes with their efficiency; therefore, it is

Ordered: That said schoolhouse at Galveston, Cass County, Ind., is condemned for school purposes, and shall not be used for said school purposes after June 1, 1910, and if any school trustee, or trustees, any teacher or any person uses said schoolhouse for school purposes, or teaches therein after the date above mentioned, he or she or they shall be prosecuted.

Any person mutilating or tearing down this proclamation shall be prosecuted.

Passed by the State Board of Health, May 21, 1909.

The following notices to bakers and butchers were adopted:

NOTICE TO BAKERS.

The Pure Food Law of 1907 and the Sanitary Food Law of 1909 define insanitary conditions as they may exist in food producing and distributing establishments, and provide that all food in the process of manufacture, sale and distribution be securely protected from flies, dust and dirt.

Bread, pastries and other baker's goods which are not delivered to the consumer at the bakeshop, but which are carried unwrapped to grocery stores and other distributing stations in wagons, carts or similar conveyances, are not properly protected and the practice is in violation of law.

In order that the sale of bread, pastries and baker's goods may be conducted under sanitary conditions and in conformity with the laws of the State, bakers are hereby instructed that on and after July 1, 1910, all such goods, including bread, buns, rolls, biscuits, cakes, crackers, pies and other baker's products, must be properly protected while in transit or while displayed for sale.

For the guidance of bakers, it is ordered that bread shall be wrapped in suitable paper wrappers, or placed in suitable bags before being taken from the bakeshop, and that other goods shall be carried in tight, dust proof boxes or cartons.

This order shall not apply to baker's goods which are sold directly to the consumer at the bakeshop where they are made.

County, city and town health officers, state food inspectors, and all other officers whose duty it is to enforce the food law, will be governed by this notice in regulating the operation of bakeshops and the sale of bread and baker's products.

NOTICE TO BUTCHERS AND MEAT SHOP PROPRIETORS.

The Pure Food Law of 1907 and the Sanitary Food Law of 1909 define insanitary conditions as they may exist in food producing and distributing establishments, and provide that all food in the process of manufacture, sale and distribution be securely protected from flies, dust and dirt.

Meat and meat products which are piled on unprotected counters and meatblocks are not properly protected, and the display of fresh meats intended for sale as now practiced by butchers and dealers in meat is undoubtedly in violation of law.

In order that the sale of meats may be conducted under sanitary conditions and in conformity with the laws of the State, butchers and dealers in meat are hereby instructed that on and after May 15, 1910, carcasses and parts of carcasses, dressed for sale for food, fresh meat products of every description, such as hamburger steak, sausage, etc., poultry and game, fish and fish products, must at all times be kept in a refrigerator, cold storage room or ice box or, if displayed for sale, properly protected by glass, wood or metal cases. Dealers shall be permitted to keep on the meat block such parts of carcasses as may be necessary to the expeditious conduct of their business. This notice shall not apply to hams and bacons wrapped in paper, burlap or other impervious material, or to lard which is kept in covered containers. Whole carcasses of hogs, sheep or veal and quarters of beef, hams, bacon, smoked shoulders and other smoked meats or smoked meat products prepared in skins, may be hung outside the refrigerator or cold storage room only when protected from flies, dust, dirt and all other foreign or injurious contamination, by clean white curtains of cloth or other suitable material.

County, city and town health officers, state food inspectors and all other officers whose duty it is to enforce the food law, will be governed by this notice in regulating the operation of butcher and meatshops.

Report of survey of strawboard refuse in Wabash River at Terre Haute, by J. H. Brewster, Water Chemist, Indiana State Board of Health:

On February 9th, I visited the plant of the Terre Haute Paper Company, located at N. Nineteenth Street, Terre Haute, Indiana, to investigate the complaint made to the State Board of Health under date of January 27, 1910, by Dr. Bennett V. Caffee, 1333 Maple Avenue, Terre Haute, Indiana. Upon inspection of the plant, I found that the odor complained of was due to the gases which escaped from the rotaries when they are blown off, as is necessary in the course of their operation. This odor is very disagreeable, especially when the atmosphere is heavy, thus preventing the escaping steam from rapidly diffusing through the air.

The refuse from the plant passes through a settling basin 8 feet deep, 6 feet wide and 60 feet long and having a capacity of 21,600 gallons. This settling basin is under ground and no odor comes from it. The plant uses about 2½ millions gallons of water daily, all of which passes through this basin. Once each week the settlings are removed and deposited on land owned by the paper company. No appreciable odor is given off from the sediment. The refuse, after passing off through the settling basin, empties into the city sewer system and is carried to the Wabash River 2½ miles away. The sedimentation basin is admittedly too small to properly care for the waste, but as the refuse reaches the river as a part of the entire sewage of the city of Terre Haute, it is not clear how action can be brought against the paper company to compel them to discontinue the use of a city sewer to carry off their incompletely purified refuse until the city itself constructs a disposal plant to care for its own sewage. Since the odor complained of, which is the only feature of the operation of the plant which is held to be a nuisance, does not injure any water supply, it is evident that no remedy can be sought for the relief of the complainant under the Stream Pollution Law.

SPECIAL MEETING.

Held at Rockville, April 13, 1910.

Called to order by President McCoy.

Present: McCoy, Tucker, Hurty.

President McCoy announced the reason for holding the meeting at Rockville was for the purpose of inspecting the State Tuberculosis Hospital and to hold a conference with the health officers of Parke County.

Dr. Tucker presented the following resolution, which was passed and ordered spread of record:

Resolved, The State Board of Health, after careful inspection, approves with pleasure the plans and construction of the Indiana Hospital for Consumptives, and heartily congratulates the people and the Tuberculosis Commission. Special commendation is offered to Dr. Henry Moore, Chairman of the Commission, for his untiring devotion to the work of planning and constructing the institution.

The meeting with county health officials was not as successful as was wished for. This was due to a misunderstanding, the County Health Commissioner having notified all officers to attend at 3 p. m., and it was found the members of the Board would be compelled to leave at 2:50 in order to make R. R. connection. Consequently the only persons in attendance were Dr. C. C. Morris. County Health Commissioner, Dr. R. E. Swope, Health Officer of Rockville, and Dr. R. C. Peare, of Bellmore.

The various duties of the health officers were discussed and several minor sanitary problems presented were disposed of.

There being no further business and train time having arrived, the meeting adjourned.

SPECIAL MEETING.

May 24, 1910.

Called to order 12:15 p. m. by President McCoy.

Present: McCoy, Davis, Wishard, Tucker, Hurty.

President announced the object of the meeting was to attend the annual conference with the health officers of the State and to give a hearing to the bakers concerning the order made April 8th in regard to wrapping bread. Also to transact any other business which might come before the Board.

CONFERENCE WITH BAKERS.

The bakers of the State were represented by Attorney H. H. Hornbrook, who read his brief as below given. About fifty bakers from over the State were present. After hearing the brief, the Board appointed June 2d as the date for a second hearing. The second hearing being for the purpose of hearing Mr. Barnard in rebuttal of Mr. Hornbrook's argument, and also to secure time to make some investigations into the matter.

BRIEF OF MR. HORNBROOK, ATTORNEY FOR BAKERS.

May 24, 1910.

On behalf of a large number of bakers of the State, I want to thank the Board for granting this opportunity to present certain facts relating to the order of the Board, heretofore made, requiring all bread to be wrapped and all cakes, pastry, etc., to be protected from atmospheric contact on and after July 1st, next.

In the first place I want to say that I have full confidence that this Board will take up this matter with open minds. That you are all desirous of but one thing, and that is to do the right thing, that which is best for the people whom you serve.

I have the feeling that one of our public papers misquotes the Food and Drug Commissioner when it makes him say that if the bakers harbor a hope that the wrapping order may be modified, it is a forlorn hope that will not be realized, that the Health Board have taken a stand for this proposition and expect to stand by it.

I cannot believe that this statement correctly indicates the attitude of the Food and Drug Commissioner. I am morally certain that it does not correctly state the mental attitude of the members of the Board. I believe I am right in assuming that the attitude of the Board is that of absolute open mindedness, not only willing but eager to get at the true facts and then do the right thing, the fair thing. The law gives to this Board the right to make reasonable orders—*reasonableness* is the rule by which this order is to be tested, and we are alike interested in seeing that a proper application of the rule is made in this case.

Now I do not desire to weary the Board, but I do crave your attentive hearing of certain facts which I desire to lay before you, and I will be as brief as possible.

The order of the Board I need not stop to read.

I will address my remarks primarily to the bread proposition. In the nature of things this will mean the separate wrapping of every loaf of bread; and my statements and figures will be based upon this assumption.

Now the *ideal* thing *from a standpoint of cleanliness* undoubtedly is to have the bread wrapped after it is baked in a thoroughly sanitary room and passed on to the ultimate consumer without any exposure to the atmosphere. I say every one will admit this is the *ideal* thing from a *standpoint* of cleanliness, and so this order has a certain appealing force to people who are constantly striving for the ideal.

But ideals must be subjected to practical tests and limitations, and to my mind, and what is more important, to the minds of a large number of the bakers of the State, there are two practical factors which must be considered.

The first, of course, is the matter of cost.

The second, that of the effect upon the bread.

We are living in a day when the problem of the cost of living is a very pressing one. And when the problem involves one of the great staples, perhaps the primary staple of life, it is indeed, worthy of our serious consideration.

So I want if I can to get clearly before you as a concrete fact, what this order means if enforced, to the people of the State of Indiana. For obviously, the people must bear it. As I will show you in a little while, it can fall on no one else, and while others may suffer during the process of readjustment, the ultimate expense must be borne by the people.

One gross misconception exists in the minds of the average person considering this question; it did in mine when I first considered it. It had complete possession of the mind of the Food Commissioner some weeks ago, it has yet for aught I know. I have little doubt that it was the thought and belief of each member of the Board when this order was made.

That misconception is this: Bread as now sold is wrapped by the grocer. This order, it will be claimed, merely shifts the burden from the grocer to the baker, and that does not mean an added expense, but merely a shifting of expense, and the baker, if he relieves the grocer of this expense, can charge it to the grocer, and so the burden is in nowise a new or additional burden. I have even heard it said that there will be a saving, as the baker wrapping in large quantities can do it cheaper than the grocer. *We must clear up this misconception and get it absolutely out of the way before we can begin to consider this problem fairly.*

Will you believe me when I say that the expense to the baker will be about *seven* times what it is to the grocer? Yet, such is the fact. The grocer, almost without exception, wraps his bread in a cheap, coarse manila paper that can be bought for from 4 to 4½ cents per hundred sheets of the size required for a loaf of bread. This is a fact which any of you can verify in a few minutes by a call upon a paper house, and which I have had verified within the last three days. That represents the total expense to the grocer. He or his helper wraps the bread as it is sold, and the saving of wrapping to the grocer will not dispense with a single grocer's clerk in the State of Indiana. So the influence on the help problem to the grocer is absolutely *nil*, and 4 to 4½ cents per hundred loaves represents the total grocer's expense. Please get this clearly in your minds, not as a theory or hypothesis, but as a fixed fact.

What will it cost the baker? Dr. Barnard stated some time ago that he supposed thirty cents a hundred would represent a fair average cost to the baker of wrapping bread. I do not know what his present thought is, but I will show to the Board that his first estimate is approximately correct.

In the first place, the cheap manila paper used by the grocer cannot be used by the baker. The baker must wrap the bread, *first*, so it will look attractive. *Second*, so it will stay wrapped through all its handling. This absolutely requires a good grade of waxed paper costing from fifteen to seventeen and a half cents per hundred sheets. This is not a subject of debate, for bread is wrapped by bakers here and throughout the country, and the figures are absolutely correct. Since the order of the Board was made, representatives of the paper trust have been exceedingly busy soliciting orders for paper throughout the State, and they have been selling to some and offering to sell to all at these figures. So in paper alone the cost to the baker is four times that which the grocer bears.

And again: The cost of wrapping the bread will be from ten cents to twelve cents a hundred loaves. In the East, where a certain class of factory employes are secured at very low wages, bread is wrapped at ten cents a hundred loaves. Here it will cost probably twelve cents a hundred loaves. Mr. Bryce informs me that the actual cost to the Bryce Baking Company for labor is fifteen cents a hundred loaves.

Some idea of the added expense for the mere labor of wrapping can be gathered from the following facts:

The Taggart Baking Company alone bake about thirty thousand loaves of bread a day. A skillful employe can perhaps wrap from one hundred to one hundred fifty loaves an hour, and, in an eight-hour day, eight hundred to twelve hundred loaves. So that to wrap thirty thousand loaves a day will require the addition of twenty-four to thirty-six new employes.

So the cost of paper and labor in wrapping will be from twenty-seven to twenty-nine and one-half cents a hundred. In addition to this there are several elements of the increased cost of rehandling the bread at the bakery which I am assured will be not less than two to three cents a hundred loaves, making a total cost of the wrapping of bread of from thirty to thirty-two and one-half cents a hundred loaves.

Here is a wholly definite and fixed increase in cost of manufacture. There is another element which, while none the less certain, yet is somewhat conjectural as to the amount. I refer to the increased cost of delivery.

As bread is at present handled, a driver can load and unload his wagon with very considerable speed, but it would be quite otherwise when it comes to handling wrapped bread. From the very nature of the article it will have to be handled more as an individual loaf, and the time required in loading and unloading will be such as to require a considerable increase in the number of wagons necessary to deliver the product of a large bakery. There will be a very considerable increase of cost here which I will not attempt to put into dollars and cents, but leave it to you to consider in connection with the general situation.

Let us first get clearly in our minds that this is a *new and added cost*, and not a present expense shifted from the grocer to the baker. With this fact in mind, the whole aspect of this order as to its reasonableness is changed. You will readily see that this is a new cost, and if imposed must be borne somewhere, and, as I shall show later, by the ultimate consumer, either by paying a larger price or a smaller loaf.

But let us now see what this seemingly insignificant order means in dollars and cents.

The Taggart Baking Company are baking in excess of 220,000 loaves of bread a week. Taking thirty cents a hundred as probably the minimum cost of wrapping as above shown, and entirely omitting the added expense of delivery which I have referred to, this would mean an added expense of $660 a week, or $34,320 a year. I take it that it would be presumptuous to assume that the Taggarts sell 20 per cent. of the bread sold by bakers in the city of Indianapolis, when we consider that there are over 100 of them doing business, and not less than four doing an extensive business.

But let us assume that they do sell one-fifth of all the bakers' bread sold. This would then mean an added cost of $171,600 a year to the people of Indianapolis alone, growing out of this order. And when you consider that Indianapolis contains less than ten per cent. of the people of Indiana, who are the consumers of the bread which by this order is required to be wrapped, you will get some faint idea of the magnitude of the burden which the enforcement of the order will impose upon the people.

So when we ask, Is it a reasonable order to impose an added burden of over a million dollars a year on the people of the State of Indiana? who can hesitate in his answer.

For, gentlemen, it is the people who pay. The bakers would have to close their shops if they were required to bear the burden of this expense. There is no such profit in the business. And either the loaf must be reduced in size at the present price, or the price must be increased for the present sized loaf. And in either event the consumer pays more money for the same quantity of bread.

Do I hear some one ask at this point, Why then are the bakers so interested if they are to shift the added cost to the consumer?

The fact that this order adds an enormous amount to the cost of living ought to be the only fact necessary in determining the reasonableness of this order. But we are glad to answer this question.

Let no one be deceived at this point. While the people will pay the added expenses, the baker will also suffer greatly. The history of the baking business is this, that just in proportion as the baker is able to produce bread and sell it to the housewife at about the same price as the housewife can buy her flour and bake her own bread, so his business will increase. The demand responds with wonderful quickness to a larger loaf, and shrinks with the reduction in the loaf. It is a practical problem. If a family is getting and consuming each day three loaves of 18 ounces each, or 21 loaves a week weighing 378 ounces for $1.05 a week: and if by an order of this kind 2 ounces must be taken off the loaf, it will mean 23 2-3 loaves of bread must be bought to fill the want of that family, or an added expense of 13 cents. Now that 13 cents a week will determine many a housewife to do her own baking.

And out of the vast army fed each day, probably one-fourth to one-fifth would take to making their own bread if the size of the loaf were reduced one-tenth. This is true because the largest part of baker's bread is consumed by the laboring classes and those in moderate circumstances

This shrinkage inevitably means serious losses to the baker, for he not only loses the profit on the bread sales he loses, but he must pay the same fixed charges of his business on account of building and equipment, on the smaller output as the larger, and thereby he decreases his profits on the remaining business done.

I would like to put it another way before the Board, what this added expense of $175,000 a year to the living expenses of the people of this city means.

Probably most of you would be startled to learn that it is equivalent to more than doubling the wages of the employes engaged in the business of making bread. Yet such is the fact. In a modern bakery the cost of the labor of the manufacture of bread is from 21 to 24 cents a hundred loaves. Yet by this seemingly insignificant order to wrap bread you would be placing a burden *equivalent* to adding 130 per cent. to the wages of all employes engaged in the making of bread. Yet such is the fact. I have heretofore illustrated one phase of this by showing that it would require twenty-four to thirty-six additional employes at the Taggart Baking Company to wrap bread.

I have first discussed this aspect of the matter, because it is the one that is most tangible; it most appeals to our minds and becomes a definite, positive quantity for our consideration.

But from the bakers' standpoint there is another aspect quite as serious, and that is the effect of wrapping upon the character of the bread.

Here I am aware we are entering upon a debatable field, and yet there are I think, certain facts fairly well established.

In the first place the wrapping of bread while still in the experimental stage is yet no new experiment. It is being wrapped here today and in many other American cities. There is a kind of an appeal which can be made to *many* people through the wrapping of bread, which cannot be made in any other way. And yet the uniform experience is that the people *as a class* do not want wrapped bread. Why? Because it is wrapped? Of course not. Anybody would rather have wrapped bread than unwrapped bread, *all other things being equal.*

So it must be that other things are not equal. And they are not in two respects. The wrapped loaf of very necessity is not as large as the unwrapped, and the wrapped loaf to the notion of the average man, is not as good as the unwrapped loaf.

Why is it not as good? I will try to tell you. Of course in all baked bread there is a large amount of moisture, of water. This is inherent in the manufacture.

This moisture in the course of nature evaporates, and leaves the bread with a certain portion of its freshness, combined with crispness, which imparts the *flavor* which goes to make bread popular. Given that certain, yet indefinable flavor which we all want, and bread is altogether to our liking. Take it away, and it is quite otherwise.

Now bread wrapped at the bakery, so soon as it must be after the baking, a large part of that moisture still remains in the bread. Confined by the wrapper it settles in the crust of the bread and the crust loses its crispness and fine flavor. Let the bread get a little stale and the bread will become soggy and mouldy.

Nowhere is this effect of wrapping better seen than in two illustrations I will give you. What is known as Vienna bread, well known and liked by many of us, depends for its support upon the fine flavor of its *crust*. This is absolutely destroyed by wrapping. So that wherever bread has been wrapped it has been found impossible to make what is known as Vienna bread.

Again, one of the chief elements in the sweetness and flavor of bread is the milk that is used in its manufacture. If bread is wrapped, milk must be eliminated, for the experience of almost every baker who has wrapped bread has been, that bread in which milk was used when wrapped soon after baking, has a tendency to sour by the chemical changes in the milk. This simply means that water is generally substituted for milk in wrapped bread.

The effect of the wrapping of bread on public demand is interesting. The Taggart Baking Company began to wrap bread some years ago, advertised it extensively, and tried to push it on the market. People would buy it and use it a few times, but almost invariably of their own accord. would drift back to the unwrapped bread. And this in spite of the fact that the grocer had every motive to push the wrapped loaf. He made his one cent profit per loaf on that the same as upon the unwrapped, and in addition was saved the expense and annoyance of wrapping. And yet the fact is, that the total consumption of wrapped bread is less than 11,000 loaves a week, out of a total of 220,000.

The Bryce Bakery has been pushing a special campaign on wrapped bread during recent months, and have spent large amounts of money advertising. But in spite of that fact the sales of unwrapped bread have continued as large as before the campaign began.

In Washington, D. C., Korby Bros., the leading bakers there, carried on a tremendous campaign for wrapped bread, and for a time wrapped almost their entire output. But the people could not be satisfied with it, and they had to change or go out of business, and they were compelled to return to the unwrapped bread, and are now selling their entire output of bread unwrapped, although wholly against their wishes at the time, as they firmly believed in wrapped bread. When they found the change in public opinion they made extensive, scientific investigations, and found the reasons for the public taste in the elements I have cited.

In Detroit, the Morton Baking Co., and Wagner Baking Co., have a fine business in wrapped bread. Until a few years ago they had the cream of the trade. Then Gordon & Pagel entered the field and in only a few years have built up a trade on unwrapped bread, until they are the leading bakers in the city. All this in spite of the fact that they are giving no larger loaf than the wrapped bread. And so I might cite the experience in other cities.

Now these things mean something. They show there is some real, not fancied, relation between the wrapping of bread and the public taste, and if the people are forced to buy exclusively a wrapped oread, it will of necessity mean the return by hundreds and thousands of families to home-made bread. And we all know that not one housewife in many can bake bread at all equal to good bakers' bread.

Does it not have some significance, too, that no such order as this has ever before been made in any age, in any country, or in any State or city? So far as known, this is absolutely the first of its kind, the beginning of a new species. And does not that fact alone suggest the wisdom of caution and due deliberation.

Who is demanding wrapped bread? Not the people. They, as a class do not want it. Only a small per centage of the public can be persuaded into buying it.

So what is the supposed occasion for this order? Why to protect the bread from dust, flies and contamination from handling? We grant you that there is some opportunity for this, but can any one point to a single case, in all history, where any illness can be traced to such causes?

And will you bear in mind that there is probably more exposure to all of these things in the average kitchen after the bread is delivered than in the course of handling before it reaches the kitchen. Who does not breathe into his lungs each day many times the dust that can possibly come from bread? Will we next hear that all apples and other fruits must be wrapped and not exposed to atmospheric contamination? Where is this to stop?

I am trying to get before our minds clearly, the necessity, the occasion, the reasonableness of this order.

Now, gentlemen, do not misunderstand me. These bakers are not opposed to any reasonable or necessary order having a *real* relation to the health of the public, but imaginary and fanciful ills which bring upon the public enormous expense for their prevention, are a proper subject of inquiry and protest.

The bakers will gladly co-operate with you in every reasonable measure to make their shops more sanitary. And by several very simple devices practically the same result which you seek to accomplish by this order, can be obtained. If all wagons be made practically dust tight; if it be required that all bread be loaded into wagons apart from any place where horses are allowed to stand; if drivers be required to wear gloves and to remove them when handling bread, or visa versa; if the baskets in which bread is carried from the wagons into the grocery be required to be kept thoroughly cleaned and perhaps covered, these, with possibly some other minor changes, will accomplish practically the same result which will be accomplished by the wrapping of bread, at a comparatively small cost. They will, I say, be glad to take up these or other necessary and reasonable measures designed to fully protect the health of the people; and a committee of bakers here today will gladly meet with you and discuss measures of this kind to be adopted as a substitute for this order.

The bakers are reasonable men. They have made great changes from the old-fashioned way of making bread, and few people would recognize a modern bakeshop. You have made many regulations to aid in bringing about this change. If others are necessary, make them; but do not. I pray you, add a fixed and ever-continuing item to the cost of living. Whatever is required should be as a fixed initial expense.

I cannot forbear adding a word as to this whole modern tendency to sell goods in sealed packages, unexposed to the air. It is one of the most tremendous causes of the increase in the cost of living which we have.

We formerly bought things much more in bulk than we do now. We seem to require individual packages for each consumer. The wrapping of bread is but another phase of this same tendency. Next it will be desired in a closed carton.

Do you have any adequate idea of what this tendency has to do with the increased cost of living?

Let me give you a single illustration closely related to the subject matter of today's talk. I refer to soda crackers. All of you will remember when we all bought our soda crackers in bulk, and good crackers they were, too. Now most of us never see them in bulk, although of course large quantities are sold and sold every day at ten cents a pound. What has caused the change? Primarily Uneeda biscuits. Sold each year by the million of packages at five cents a package, containing from 5 1-3 to 5½ ounces to the package.

So to get soda crackers in the package we are adding 50 per cent. to the cost to the consumer.

Can a note of warning be sounded too loud against this tendency?

Is this talk of the increased cost of living a fact or is it a mere idle fancy? Do we simply hear of it remotely, indirectly, occasionally, or is it striking home to each and all of us directly, daily? Let each answer for himself.

I appeal to this Board that they reconsider their action. I do not believe that they understood the facts. I am satisfied that they were laboring under the popular delusion that they were merely shifting an existing item of expense from one account to another. Had they dreamed that they were adding $175.000 a year to the cost of living in Indianapolis, and from one to two million a year to the people of the State of Indiana, I do not believe for one minute that they would have made this order.

And I know they are all large enough, broad minded enough, public spirited enough, to modify this utterly unreasonable order, and if need be substitute for it other reasonable things which at a moderate cost will accomplish practically the same end, when they realize the real situation.

In the very nature of things the existence of this order requiring certain steps to be taken on July 1st, and which will require considerable time to make preparations for, if the order is enforced, is producing considerable unrest among the bakers of the State, and for this reason it is most respectfully urged that a prompt disposition of this matter be made.

The Secretary announced that the health officers' conference was successful in every particular, the attendance being 315, and the interest very good. Following is the program for the three sessions:

ANNUAL CONFERENCE OF STATE HEALTH OFFICERS, AUSPICES OF INDIANA STATE BOARD OF HEALTH.

Indianapolis, May 24, 1910. All sessions will be held in auditorium, 9th floor Hotel Claypool, Indianapolis.

PROGRAM.

First Session—10 a. m.

Called to Order....................................President McCoy
Welcome ....Governor Marshall
Laboratories in Public Health Work....................J. P. Simmonds
Superintendent Pathological and Bacteriological Laboratory.
Work of the Red Cross Society................F. A. Tucker, Noblesville
The Duty of the Health Officer in the Enforcement of the Pure Food and Sanitary Laws..........
H. E. Barnard, State Food and Drug Commissioner

Second Session—2 p. m.

A Predaceous Mite..............L. T. Rawles, Huntertown, Allen County
Preventive Medicine........................T. Henry Davis, Richmond
The Present Status of Serum Therapy...Dr. H. S. Thurston, Indianapolis
Malaria in Indiana..................................Ada Schweitzer
Assistant, Pathological and Bacteriological Laboratory.
Question Box—Statistics, Measles.

Third Session—8 p. m.

Prevention of Ophthalmia Neonatorum.........George Keiper, Lafayette
(Illustrated)
Consumption Sanitoria (Illustrated)..........J. N. Hurty, Indianapolis
Moving Pictures.

SCHOOLHOUSES CONDEMNED.

Inspection of high school building at Muncie, Indiana, by J. L. Anderson, Deputy State Health Officer, April 29, 1910.

Site.—High and dry, occupying one block, bounded by Adams Street on the north, Franklin on the west, Charles on the south and High Street on the east. There is plenty of shade and good walks from the north and south streets to the entrances.

The building is a three story and basement brick, with slate roof and a clock and bell tower over the north or main entrance. The basement is of stone, extending 5½ feet above ground. The building is about 75 x 100 feet on the outside, with extension of 15 x 30 feet at north and south entrances. The foundation, walls and stairways are in fine condition, but the roof leaks, as shown by condition of rooms on the third floor. Building erected in 1879. It is heated by steam heat from the city heating plant, and supplied with water from city water works. Drinking fountains are supplied in halls and main rooms on each floor. Entrance is obtained to the basement by outside doors at north and south sides and by 6-foot stairways from the main hall above. A main hall 20 feet wide extends the entire width of the building. The floor is cement, and has a 9-foot ceiling, except one room on west side, which is used for a recitation room and has a 9-foot 6-inch ceiling.

Basement divided into four large rooms, originally. The northeast room is used as a laboratory. It has a wooden floor, and is lighted by two windows on north and two on the east, and is about 37½ x 38¾ feet. The northwest room has been divided by a partition and only has one west window in the recitation room, this is about 18 x 38 x 9½ feet. The part cut off of this room is used as a storage room. The two south rooms are used for toilet rooms.

The first floor is entered by a flight of stone steps into a wide hall 20 x 14 feet, extending through building to south entrance. At each side of entrances are small rooms 6 feet 8 inches by 13 feet 6 inches, used as offices and janitors' rooms. There are twelve of these small rooms (4 on each floor) lighted by two windows 3 feet by 9 inches. A broad stairway at each end of the hall leads up to a landing 12 feet above, and a reverse stairway on each side off the main stair leads to the hall above. The main stair is 7 feet 6 inches wide with a wood handrail on each side, and is solid and firm. The floor of the hall is of oak, badly worn, but oiled and clean. On the right or west side is a recitation room 16 feet 6 inches by 38 feet 6 inches by 14 feet, lighted by two windows on the north, and one on the west, walls tinted neutral color, blinds to windows, blackboards are painted on the plastering. Wood wainscoting three foot high extends around room, except on south side. Heated by steam radia.ors. Floor firm and clean, but well worn. Ventilation by windows. There are five rooms of this size and description in the building, two each on first and second floor, one on third. The room adjoining is the same in every particular, *except* that there is no wainscoting on the north side of the room, and there is but *one window* in the room, and that is at the west end. This is a duplicate of the room below. There are six of these rooms, one in the basement, two on each of first and second floors, and one on the third floor. There is no ventilation except by the windows and, on a dark day, would have to use artificial light.

These rooms were made by running partitions through the north rooms of the building on the first, second and third floors, thus making two rooms of each.

The third room on the west of the hall is a large one, 37 feet 6 inches by 38 feet 6 inches by 14 feet, and is lighted by four windows, two on the west and two on the south, with blinds. The windows are 3 feet 4 inches by 9 feet, and *all* windows are fitted with boards at their base to throw the air current upward to the window casing. Blackboards on north and east sides are plaster painted with lampblack. Floors clean, but badly worn. No ventilation except by windows.

The rooms on the east side of the hall are duplicate of those on the west side, just described.

Second Floor.—The rooms on the second floor are exact duplicate of those on the first as to size, arrangement, light, heat, ventilation, condition of floors, blackboards, etc.

The superintendent's office is on this floor at the east side of the south entrance, in one of the little rooms described above.

Third Floor.—Assembly Room.—This room is 55 x 67 feet, with 22-foot ceiling. Lighted by eight windows, two on south, four on west, and two in north side, and some light from the openings to the hallways at north and south sides. All windows on this floor are 3 feet 4 inches by 10 feet. Walls are painted and the paint is cracked and scaling off. Ceiling cracked and discolored by water leaking through roof. Floor oiled and clean, but badly worn. About half the blackboards are slate, the balance painted black on the plaster. This is the best lighted room in the building, but on dark, cloudy days, they have to use artificial light in the room.

On the east side and opening into the assembly room are two small recitation rooms, 16 feet 6 inches by 38 feet 6 inches, and the library, 37 feet 6 inches by 38 feet 6 inches. The library has two windows on south and two on east side. The recitation room next to the library has one window in the east end, and the next room has two windows in the north, and one in the east end. The same description of ceilings and walls as in the assembly room applies to these rooms.

There are 19 teachers and 557 pupils enrolled; average attendance, 525.

Summary.—The building is substantial, with broad halls and stairways. There is no danger of collapse, and but little danger in case of fire, but what all the pupils could leave the building. The principal reported that there was not enough heat supplied to keep the rooms comfortable last winter; and when the windows were opened to ventilate the rooms the pupils had to put on their wraps. There are no means of ventilation, except by the windows. "The Esquimaux Method of Ventilation," is what one gentleman called it.

The lighting is bad in every room in the building, and the artificial light furnished is yellow, dim, and very hard on the eyes.

Upon sanitary grounds, I would consider the building unfit for school purposes.

I was accompanied upon my inspection by Dr. H. A. Cowing and Dr. W. J. Molloy.

After consideration of the above, the following proclamation of condemnation was adopted:

PROCLAMATION OF CONDEMNATION.

Whereas, It has been shown to the satisfaction of the State Board of Health that the high school building at Muncie, Delaware County, Ind., is insanitary, and consequently threatens the health and life of the pupils, and also interferes with their efficiency; therefore, it is

Ordered: That said high school building at Muncie, Delaware County, Ind., is condemned for school purposes, and shall not be used for said school purposes after June 1, 1910, and if any school trustee, or trustees,

any teacher or any person uses said schoolhouse for school purposes, or teaches therein, after the date above mentioned, he or she or they shall be prosecuted.

Any person mutilating or tearing down this proclamation shall be prosecuted.

Passed by the State Board of Health, May 24, 1910.

Sanitary survey of schoolhouse at Winslow, Patoka Township. Pike County, Ind., May 14. 1910, by E. S. Imel, County Health Commissioner.

Site.—As per order, I submit report of the Winslow school building as follows: In west part of town on lots 29, 30, 47 and 48, containing somewhat more than one acre. High mound in center on which building stands. Dry, sloping in all directions, well drained, but should be filled in in some places, to make better playground.

Exterior.—Frame weatherboard, in fairly good condition, all frame; brick foundation, floors about 10 inches above ground on east, and about 2 feet on west, no basement. Paths, constructed of cinders and part of boardwalk, lead to privies, but no walks only the clay leading to street. Lots are thickly covered with forest trees (far too many).

Interior.—Inside walls uneven, paper torn, plastering off in places. Floors badly worn and uneven. I enclose you exact plat of two lower rooms, with entrance vestibule, and stair steps leading upon either side of vestibule—landing at top in vestibule like lower floor. Stair steps very steep, and at half way a landing and then a half turn, entirely boxed and very dangerous.

The two upper rooms are same size as the lower floor rooms, like enclosed plat. Windows and doors same; ceiling not quite so high.

Outhouses, privies, about 35 and 40 feet from northwest corner of building, situated on side of hill or slope; 5-foot board partition separating them and about 20 feet apart. Coalhouse, northeast corner, about 15 feet from building.

Water.—Dug well on south slope about 60 feet from south side of building, about 12 feet to water, surface drains toward well.

I consider the building, and especially the stairs, very, very bad, and think this building should be removed and new modern structure take its place. The ground with a little expense to make some fills to level it up, is ideal. Most all the trees should be removed, and also a different water supply.

After consideration of the above sanitary survey, the following proclamation was adopted:

PROCLAMATION OF CONDEMNATION.

Whereas, It has been shown to the satisfaction of the State Board of Health that the schoolhouse at Winslow, Patoka Township, Pike County, Ind., is insanitary, and consequently threatens the health and life of the pupils, and also interferes with their efficiency; therefore, it is

Ordered: That said schoolhouse at Winslow, Patoka Township, Pike County, Ind., is condemned for school purposes, and shall not be used for said school purposes after June 1, 1910, and if any school trustee, or trustees, any teacher or any person uses said schoolhouse for school purposes, or teaches therein after the date above mentioned, he or she or they shall be prosecuted.

Any person mutilating or tearing down this proclamation shall be prosecuted.

Passed by the State Board of Health, May 24, 1910.

Sanitary survey of schoolhouse at Algiers, Jefferson Township, Pike County, May 19, 1910, by Dr. E. S. Imel, County Health Commissioner.

As per your order of the 17th inst., I have made a survey of schoolhouse at Algiers, Pike County, Ind., and report as follows:

Site.—House is situated in the lower side of one-half acre. West side high. Water from this side runs down towards building. As the land slopes beyond building, it mostly runs off, except one corner, which is quite swampy. Very badly situated.

Exterior of Building.—Frame, siding in very good state of preservation; brick foundation, in fairly good condition. No basement. Height from foundation to eave, about 28 or 30 feet. Lower floor, inside, about 24 x 43 feet; 6 windows in each room. Both upper and lower floors are alike, same number of windows in each, 2 x 6 feet; 12 x 36-inch glass panes in windows. Floors very rough and uneven; one brick flue for stove in each room. Ventilation through windows when lowered. Fifty seats in lower room; 45 pupils enrolled; average attendance last term of school, 32.

Upper Room.—Fifty-three seats; pupils enrolled, 35; average attendance last term, 26. Walls in very good condition, except dirty. Vestibule on west side 10 x 20 feet. From this the stairway leads to upper room, 17 steps, 18 feet from top to bottom of landing, very, very steep. About four feet wide with banisters on side.

As the rooms are the same size and same lighting, same doors, I enclose plat for lower floor. The ceiling of upper room is about 12 feet, lower room 14 feet. This is the only difference in appearance. Heated by stoves.

Outbuildings, about 100 feet from house, in low swamp of ground; 6-foot board fence protecting them from view. Fairly good condition. Mud paths lead to them when it is not water. No screens, no ventilation.

Water.—From neighbor's dug surface well. Old dug well near entrance to building, not used, but not covered as securely as it should be, and is dangerous and should be filled up. Each pupil drinks from one or the other, common tin cup or dipper.

The building is solid and in fairly good state of preservation, but badly arranged and dangerous. Stairways dangerous, both stoves in upper and lower rooms are between the pupils and the doors.

The grounds or location is very bad, no walks anywhere, gets very muddy at times. Good locations are near but very highly valued. The ground where the schoolhouse now stands is not fit for even a good "hog lot." No playgrounds to speak of.

The building certainly is not what it should be and I think dangerous in many ways (but I might add the trustee says they are so badly in debt) and would not like for my children to be compelled to attend school in it.

After consideration of the above, the following proclamation of condemnation was adopted:

PROCLAMATION OF CONDEMNATION.

Whereas, It has been shown to the satisfaction of the State Board of Health that the schoolhouse at Algiers, Jefferson Township, Pike County, Ind., is insanitary, and consequently threatens the health and life of the pupils, and also interferes with their efficiency; therefore, it is

Ordered: That said schoolhouse at Algiers, Jefferson Township, Pike County, Ind., is condemned for school purposes, and shall not be used for said school purposes after June 1, 1910, and if any school trustee, or trutees, any teacher or any person uses said schoolhouse for school purposes, or teaches therein after the date above mentioned, he or she or they shall be prosecuted.

Any person mutilating or tearing down this proclamation shall be prosecuted.

Passed by the State Board of Health, May 24, 1910.

Sanitary survey of Larch schoolhouse, District No. 8, Prairie Township, Warren County, Ind., May 5, 1910, by S. S. DeLancey, County Health Commissioner.

Have this day visited the Larch schoolhouse, in Prairie Township, southwest corner of northeast quarter section 28, township 23, north range 9 west, and find no walks to closets or screens in front. An old building 23 x 19½ x 9 feet for 25 pupils. No ventilation. Stove in middle of room, two windows on each side and in rear.

The water supply comes from an iron pump in driven well, and the drain to same in fair condition. These people should, in my opinion, have a radical change, and so advised.

After consideration of the above, the following proclamation of condemnation was adopted:

PROCLAMATION OF CONDEMNATION.

Whereas, It has been shown to the satisfaction of the State Board of Health that the schoolhouse in District No. 8, Prairie Township, Warren County, Ind., is insanitary, and consequently threatens the health and life of the pupils, and also interferes with their efficiency; therefore, it is

Ordered: That said schoolhouse in District No. 8, Prairie Township, Warren County, Ind., is condemned for school purposes, and shall not be used for said school purposes after June 1, 1910, and if any school trustee, or trustees, any teacher or any person uses said schoolhouse for school purposes, or teaches therein after the date above mentioned, he or she or they shall be prosecuted.

Any person mutilating or tearing down this proclamation shall be prosecuted.

Passed by the State Board of Health, May 24, 1910.

Inspection of the schoolhouse at Wallace, Ind., April 22, 1910, by J. R. Hicks, County Health Commissioner.

Site.—Two and one-half to three acres, square, fairly level, about one foot above the roads along the west and south sides, fairly well drained. Can be well drained into a deep ravine 100 feet south of southwest corner. Two wells, one an abandoned drilled well, the other a very shallow well, 8-foot (ordered disused by school principal), lined with tile, no sink or drain for water; should not be used. Pupils have to go to neighbors for water—very inconvenient. Ninety-five pupils at school last year and expect 20 more next year. The grounds furnish ample room for recreation, but should be leveled and tiled. A good deep well with sink and drain should be provided. The old schoolbuilding was moved to the extreme northeast corner of the lot and is used as a stable for pupil's horses. It is ramshackled and unsightly, so windshaken and poorly braced that it may blow down, hence dangerous; also filled with rubbish and manure and is a fly breeder. Should be torn down. Would furnish enough material to build a good shed for horses. The outhouses are just a few feet west of this old barn—fair buildings and kept fairly clean—are only 12 feet apart. No screens around them. Should be placed much farther apart and at least partially screened.

School Building (see plans).—Erected 15 years ago. Not painted since then. Frame (concealed work made of scraps, odds and ends), 2½ stories high; foundation 4 feet above ground, the one-half story above the second floor ceiling is much too high. This, together with the poor material in the frame-work, makes the building shake in the slightest wind. The cupola sags to the south. The swaying of the building in the wind is so great that it breaks the window glass in the east, south and west sides. All the walls are bulged outwards, and could feel the entire building reel and sway in the moderate wind that was blowing during the time I made the inspection. The foundation is of cut sandstone, sunken in many places; mortar washed out nearly every place; open along the entire north side, in a very poor condition. Shingle roof, in fair condition. Noticed over one-half dozen leaks. Basement under the north half of building, used for coal storage, open along the entire north side, hence cold floors. The open entrance to cellar is unprotected and dangerous, very damp, no drainage; outside sills of building are all dryrotting and beginning to crumble. The registers and ventilators from an old, dismantled furnace are still in the floors, lessening protection from cold, very musty smell over entire cellar and building. Eaves are in fair condition except east side, where there are several leaks. Downspouts are poor, some broken; water drains into basement and on the north side to the surface well. Window-sills rotted in nearly all the windows and no casings around the insides of any of the windows; open spaces around every window. The chimney is in very bad condition, mortar out of the cracks and ready to topple over; can see through the top of it from the ground in several places; several places below the eaves where the smoke comes through the cracks. Danger of fire very great. Trustees have made but slight yearly repairs and now declare they will spend no more money on the building.

In front of the entrance to the building (see plans) is a wide plank platform. Planks broken and warped, dangerous; entrance to the 7-foot hall is by a double door opening out. Hallway much too narrow and filled with steps and turns, very easily congested in times of danger. Doors all open into hallway. Two rooms downstairs, primary and intermediate, and are always full. Two cloakrooms. The two stairs are on each side of the hall, are much too steep, only 3 feet wide; four turns in each stair. Doors of the downstairs rooms swing out across the lower part of each stair. Floors over the entire building are hard pine, full of cracks, very uneven and full of splinters. Walls are very damp in the halls, bulged and badly cracked over the entire building. Upper hall is used as a cloakroom by the high school and grade pupils. Ceilings in every room are badly cracked and constantly falling. The two main rooms up and downstairs are each about 22 x 30 x 10 feet. The windows (glass) in all rooms are 29 inches by 7 feet 8 inches, and each room is so arranged that there is light on three sides. Every room is heated by a stove placed in the center, with no screen around it. Registers, etc., from an old dismantled furnace are still in the walls and floors. In spite of the openings around all the windows, and cracks in the walls and floors, the entire building is filled with a sickening, musty smell. The blinds in every room are of an old, thin, cracked material and afford no protection. Blackboards in every room are of slate, cloth, and pasteboard. Cannot keep floors warm because of cracks, old registers, and open basement. Thirty seats in primary, 25 in intermediate, 23 in grade, 23 in high school rooms. A small recitation room, 7 feet by 14 feet, is just off the high school room, and is much too small. Rooms are all full and overflowing. Next year will have 40 pupils in high school and can only seat 23.

Unanimous opinion that a new building is most urgently needed, but object to building it for the reason that they are not ready for it. Claim that so many new roads are building under the new road law that taxes are too high. Township indebtedness does not preclude building.

The school building is a veritable death-trap. In constant danger of blowing over or burning. The arrangement of the exits (with no other escapes) is so narrow and poor that the slightest rush would congest them. Hygienic conditions are so bad that the school term is notorious for the many sicknesses engendered.

A new and modern schoolhouse of ample capacity should be built immediately, the grounds should be leveled and drained, the old stable removed from the back of the lot, the outhouses placed farther apart and screened; a well of good drinking water provided with properly placed sink and drain, all of which the township is amply able to furnish.

After consideration of the above, the following proclamation of condemnation was adopted:

PROCLAMATION OF CONDEMNATION.

Whereas, It has been shown to the satisfaction of the State Board of Health that the schoolhouse at Wallace, Jackson Township, Fountain County, Ind., is insanitary, and consequently threatens the health and life of the pupils, and also interferes with their efficiency; therefore, it is

Ordered: That said schoolhouse at Wallace, Jackson Township, Fountain County, Ind., is condemned for school purposes, and shall not be used for said school purposes after June 1, 1910, and if any school trustee, or trustees, any teacher or any person uses said schoolhouse for school purposes, or teaches therein after the date above mentioned, he or she or they shall be prosecuted.

Any person mutilating or tearing down this proclamation shall be prosecuted.

Passed by the State Board of Health, May 24, 1910.

Sanitary survey of school lot and schoolhouse No. 1, Ward Township, Randolph County, Ind., June 27, 1910, by Grant C. Markle, M. D., County Health Commissioner.

The school lot consists of one-half acre, drained across the pike at the southwest corner by a six-inch tile. In wet weather water stands on this southwest corner. No trees on the lot. The lot is covered with grass and weeds.

The school building is a one-room, one-story brick, 24 x 34 feet. Stone foundation, and no basement.

Side and front walls cracked and have been repaired. The floor of building is good. Side walls and ceiling plastered. There are no closets or cloakrooms. The wraps and dinner buckets are hung on the wall.

The room contains 48 desks, and is heated by a box-stove in the center. Blackboard extends half way around the room as shown by drawing.

There are three outbuildings, one woodhouse and two closets. The closets are not screened, and there are no walks to either building.

I think this building and grounds insanitary and unfit for school purposes.

After consideration of the above, the following proclamation of condemnation was adopted:

PROCLAMATION OF CONDEMNATION.

Whereas, It has been shown to the satisfaction of the State Board of Health that the schoolhouse in District No. 1, Ward Township, Randolph County, Indiana, is insanitary and consequently threatens the health and life of the pupils, and also interferes with their efficiency; therefore, it is

Ordered: That said schoolhouse, District No. 1, Ward Township, Randolph County, Ind., is condemned for school purposes, and shall not be used for said school purposes after June 1, 1910, and if any school trustee, or trustees, any teacher or any person uses said schoolhouse for school purposes, or teaches therein, after the date above mentioned, he or she or they shall be prosecuted.

Any person mutilating or tearing down this proclamation shall be prosecuted.

Passed by the State Board of Health, May 24, 1910.

Sanitary survey of the South Ward Schoolhouse, Crown Point, Lake County, Ind., May 11, 1910, by Dr. G. D. Brannon, City Health Officer.

Site.—Is high and the natural drainage good. The lot fronts on one of the principal streets in residence part of the town, and has about 250 feet frontage; and is about 220 feet deep, a strip could be added to the school lot so it would front on another street. I shall recommend the town board to buy the land, as it is unimproved and could, doubtless, be bought cheap. The land can be easily drained by running a string of tile into a small brook that runs near the school building.

The school building was built in the year 1859, of common red brick, which are badly cracked and crumbling in many places. The foundation is of brick; there is no basement under the building, but an open space which retains moisture. There is no provision for ventilating this space, the partition walls are studded and lathed. The outer walls are considerably out of plumb, and are not in a straight line, the lintels over windows are in fair condition, the floors, especially the upper floor, are badly sunken, and the plastering is badly cracked and has fallen off in places. I had a civil engineer go with me, also the superintendent of the schools, and I will enclose measurements made by them, which will explain fully the size of rooms and location of doors and windows. There is no provision for ventilation of the school building. It is warmed by stoves, the water supply is from a driven well about 27 feet from the water closet, which has a deep vault. The water closet is used by all the pupils, from eighty to ninety in number. There is usually one old tin cup at the well for the children to drink from. Only one thing about the entire outfit is according to the laws in this State; the outer doors are hung so that they swing outward. As for the rest, it is about as insanitary as it is possible to imagine. I talked with both of the teachers, one of whom is a supply, the regular teacher having broken down in health this spring. Both of them say the building is, in their opinion, unfit for use and should be torn down and a new one erected.

To this report I have been asked to add my recommendation. I would most earnestly recommend that the old building be torn down, and a new one built in accordance with the rules of the State Board of Health of the State of Indiana, as contained in the report of the Superintendent of Public Instruction in 1908.

Proclamation of Condemnation.

Whereas, It has been shown to the satisfaction of the State Board of Health that the South Ward Schoolhouse, Crown Point, Lake County, Ind., is insanitary and consequently threatens the health and life of the pupils, and also interferes with their efficiency; therefore, it is

Ordered: That said South Ward Schoolhouse, Crown Point, Lake County, Ind., is condemned for school purposes, and shall not be used for said school purposes after June 1, 1910, and if any school trustee, or trustees, any teacher or any person uses said schoolhouse for school purposes, or teaches therein after the date above mentioned, he or she or they shall be prosecuted.

Any person mutilating or tearing down this proclamation shall be prosecuted.

Passed by the State Board of Health, May 24, 1910.

SPECIAL MEETING.

June 2, 1910.

Meeting called to order by President McCoy, at 1:15 p. m.

Present: Drs. McCoy, Davis, Wishard, Tucker, Hurty.

President announced the object of the meeting was to hear the bakers' objections to the "Notice to Bakers," and the order passed April 8, 1910, and to consider any other business which might be brought before the Board.

Mr. Barnard read the following brief:

CONCERNING THE WRAPPING OF BREAD.

In order to place before the Board the reasons why the recent circular letter No. 7, addressed to bakers on the subject "Protection of Bread" was, in my opinion, warranted, and why the instructions to bakers thereby expressed should be obeyed on and after July 1, 1910, I propose to set forth data and statements, showing the reasonableness and practicability of the notice, which, for the most part, have been supplied by bakers or which have been collected by the State Food Inspectors and determined at the laboratory.

At the outset it may be well to say that at all times since the establishment of the Laboratory of Hygiene, the relations between master bakers of the State and the food and drug department have been most cordial and helpful. We have found the bakers to be hearty supporters of the Pure Food Law, and that they are equally interested in all sanitary measures is shown by the fact that the Master Bakers' Association was the first association in the State to go on record as unanimously in favor of the Sanitary Law, under the provisions of which the letter relating to the protection of bread was issued. And if, at the present time, there is any disagreement between the bakers and the food department of the State Board of Health, the disagreement, I believe, is only in the methods proposed to be followed in the enforcement of the law and not in the sanitary principles or regulations of the law itself. That there is a feeling among the bakers that the suggestions in circular letter No. 7 are impractical can not, in view of the brief submitted through counsel by certain of the bakers, be denied. But that this feeling partakes in any way of animosity, either toward the inspectors of the Board or its officers, or that it had bred any feeling of positive opposition, is not apparent and I believe does not generally exist.

The Pure Food Law of 1907, and the Sanitary Food Law of 1909, define insanitary conditions as they may exist in food producing and distributing establishments and provide that all food in the process of manufacture, sale and distribution be securely protected from flies, dust and dirt. In order to secure such condition, the Sanitary Food Law is explicit in setting out the conditions of lighting, drainage, plumbing, ventilation, character of walls, ceiling and floor which shall obtain. It requires daily cleansing of all utensils, installation of suitable toilets and lavatories and the use of screens. It forbids the use of bakeshop workrooms as sleeping rooms. It provides that all employes shall be free from infectious or contagious disease and requires that operatives shall keep their hands and arms clean by washing.

The provisions of the law are not yet fully met by all the manufacturers of food stuffs in this State or by all the bakers, but the requirements are so reasonable and manifestly to the interest both of the consumer and the purchaser that we have met with no opposition, but on the contrary with much favorable comment as the work of enforcing them has been carried on. At the present time we can safely say that the baker is prepared to produce and on the whole does produce clean bread and pastries in clean bakeshops. Unfortunately, we have observed that the care exercised by the baker over his products usually ceases when his goods are taken from the oven, and that from that time until it reaches the home of the consumer the conditions of handling the bread are too frequently unsatisfactory from a sanitary standpoint. Modern methods of handling foodstuffs have decreed that the articles delivered at the kitchen door must be wrapped. It is apparent that this wrapping is in the nature of a protection against contamination. The butcher who delivered meats unwrapped, the grocer who neglected to protect his orders of dried fruits, cereals, coffee and other bulk goods, would find that no housewife would accept them. Indeed, the practice of protecting foodstuffs by wrappers, bags and cartons is practically universal as regards every product except that of the bakeshop. The baker takes his bread from the oven, places it in covered wagons either in boxes or baskets and hauls it from the bakeshop to various delivery stations, usually groceries, and transfers it from the wagon either to breadboxes or cases in the grocery store, from which it is finally taken and wrapped before it is delivered. That there is ample opportunity for bakery goods to become unclean during this handling, the details of which at this time it is unnecessary to explain more fully, is not denied even by the bakers themselves. The fact that the bread must be handled at least four times before it is finally wrapped; that during the process of loading in the delivery wagon, of unloading and of transference from the bread box to the grocery shelves, it is exposed to dust and dirt; that too frequently the baker's delivery wagon is not as clean as it should be; that the bread boxes are unwashed for months, all makes contamination to the loaf not only possible but extremely probable, and unquestionably such transportation and distribution is in violation of Section 2 of Chapter 163 of the Acts of 1909. The real question then is not *Shall the baker wrap or otherwise protect his products?* but is *Does the Sanitary Food Law require impossible and impractical things when it provides that food products shall be protected from flies, dust and dirt?*

No one, so far as has come to my knowledge, has said that the Sanitary Food Law was not both practical and possible of enforcement. In our attempts to enforce the law, we have brought 74 prosecutions in courts in every part of the State, and have yet to record a single failure to convict the offender or a single appeal from the verdict of the lower court, which of itself establishes beyond argument the fact that the law is just and right.

The position of the baker under the law is, that he cannot protect his product—

First, because of the cost of protection.

Second, because of the effect of protection upon the bread.

The wrapping of bread is the only practical way of protecting it. It may leave the bakeshop in dust-proof baskets; it may be hauled through the streets in dust-proof wagons, but it must be taken from the baskets and placed in breadboxes or carried into the grocery, there again to be handled by the grocer's clerk, who invariably places it in a suitable wrapper before delivery. The chief argument of the baker against bread wrapping is that it increases the cost of the bread. It is freely admitted that the wrapper and the labor cannot be obtained for nothing, and that the cost of bread wrapping must be paid by someone, and that that someone inevitably is the consumer. At the present time who is paying for the wrapping which each loaf bears when it is delivered at the kitchen? It is the consumer, for whatever cost is incurred by the grocer for paper, twine and labor is met finally by the man who eats the bread. Why then should the requirement that bread must be wrapped by the baker when it is clean and fresh instead of by the grocer after it has been hauled through the streets, become at once an unbearable burden? It is argued that the cost of wrapping to the baker is much greater than it is to the grocer. This argument is based upon the fact that the grocer uses a less expensive paper than the baker. Is there anything in circular letter No. 7 which requires the baker to use any different paper from what the grocer uses? Because certain peculiar papers have been devised which are eminently satisfactory for the baker's use, must it be presumed that the suggestion of the State Board of Health can only be met by the use of such paper wrappers? If the grocer can properly wrap his bread in cheap manilla paper that can be bought at 4 cents to 4½ cents per 100 sheets of the size required for a loaf of bread, cannot the baker use the same paper and obtain the same sanitary results? Counsel for the bakers has advanced the peculiar argument that the bread is wrapped by the grocer at no cost for labor. On the contrary, it costs the grocer more to wrap bread than it does the baker in the proportion that his help costs more and, because of lack of experience and skill, works less rapidly. The grocer's clerk, who is better paid than the bread wrapper, will take more than twice as long to wrap each loaf of bread, and it is folly to argue that the clerk who wraps from 100 to 200 loaves of bread per day in the grocery is performing this labor at no expense to the grocer. Every minute of his time which is used in wrapping bread is paid for. The argument that, because the help is in the store, it costs nothing to perform the labor is refuted by the daily failure of men who attempt to do business on such a theory. The only reason why the grocer wraps bread is that he wishes to deliver it to the consumer in as cleanly manner as possible.

There are other and weighty reasons why the baker should wrap or protect his bread. At the present time, under the present practice of taking up so-called stale bread, the baker is subject to a constant, considerable loss, amounting, so far as I have been able to determine by frequent inquiry, to about 5 per cent. That is, the baker delivers at the grocery stores 1,000 loaves. A day or two later he collects and takes back to the bakeshop approximately 50 loaves of bread originally good but, because of staleness, unfit for sale. This bread has been baked from good material, transferred to the grocery store and hauled back to the bakeshop, there to be sold for horse or cattle food at a price which hardly covers the original cost of the flour. It is a fact proven absolutely by the experience of hundreds of bakers that the baker who wraps his loaf will suffer no loss from stale bread, and that he can therefore afford a liberal expenditure if it cuts off this loss.

Bread at the present time is almost the only staple food which does not bear a label declaring the brand and producer. Canned goods are attractively labeled. Even butter is now wrapped in paper which indicates to the consumer the maker of the brand, but the baker has thus far neglected to make his products advertise his business except only so far as he has occasionally attached small stickers to the loaf in a manner which detracts from its appearance. The baker who wraps bread has at his command a most favorable method of advertising. Is it of no moment to the baker to know that his loaf of bread conveys to the housewife the fact that he produces other varieties of bread, cakes and pastries; that his goods can be obtained at certain stores at certain times of the day, in fact that every loaf takes home to the housewife who purchases the food supply the advertisement which at the present time is inserted at great expense in the newspapers, there to be read, if at all, in 90 cases out of a hundred, not by the housewife, but by the man of the family, who takes no thought of his food save only that it appears on his table?

At the present time the business of the baker is in its infancy. If it is to grow to large proportions, as it should, the confidence and support of the consumer must be secured. The only competitor of the baker is the housewife, and unless the housewife is convinced that the food she buys is cleanly and sanitary and in every way acceptable, is it going to be possible for the baker to compete with her oven? It has been argued that the consumer does not care whether the loaf is wrapped or not. The consumer has not cared until within the last five years whether or not his food was adulterated. Can it be said of the consumer today that he takes no interest in this important matter? The consumer is increasingly observant of his food and is paying more and more attention not only to the quality of the food but the conditions under which it is produced and distributed. The baker who can convince the consumer that his bread is not only palatable but cleanly as well, will be the successful baker. Is it not worth something to the baker to gain the confidence of the housewife?

Here, then, are three arguments why the bread should be wrapped:

1. The loss from stale bread is stopped.
2. The wrapper is a valuable advertising medium.
3. The confidence of the consumer is gained and business is increased.

The other formidable argument advanced by the counsel for the bakers is that wrapped bread is not as palatable as unwrapped bread. This argument I shall leave to the bakers to refute.

O. F. Peterson, President of the U. P. Steam Baking Company of Omaha, says: "We have wrapped millions of loaves but we never had one, not one, complaint of the consumer that the bread was injured in any way, that it had lost its flavor or anything else."

H. E. Linne of Danville, Illinois, says: "We find that wrapping bread is not detrimental to the flavor of bread, but, on the contrary, the bread is more eatable any time than an unwrapped loaf, as it keeps the crust soft and the flavor is always better."

The Juergens Baking Company of Wheeling, West Virginia, say: "We have been wrapping bread for a year, and will say that we consider it a great advantage; and as our business shows a wonderful increase—and all since we began wrapping—we feel safe in making the statement that wrapped bread is responsible. We have made a careful and exhaustive study of this wrapping proposition; and the wrapper preserves the flavor and moisture and at the same time protects the bread in the handling. The people are better pleased, and as the people are the final judges as to the quality, we know wrapping does a great part in getting the bread to the consumer in the best condition. As you know, the standard objection to baker's bread is that it is dry and tasteless, and we have overcome this by wrapping. The bread does not dry out, and the flavor is retained, and the difference between a loaf wrapped and one unwrapped at the end of twenty-four hours is very apparent to anyone, and decidedly to the credit of the wrapped loaf."

The Gartner Baking Company of Battle Creek, Michigan, say: "In reference to wrapping bread in wax wrappers, will say our experience is that wrapping has been of advantage both for sanitary conditions and for retaining moisture; and we have found that the only time when bread is injured is when it is wrapped too warm, which has a very, very bad effect."

R. D. Crawford, Emporia, Kansas, says: "I find the wrapping of bread has many advantages. Most important is the keeping of the loaf moist. And in waiting on a rush it will sell itself, as it is always ready (keep it handy). In grocery trade a clerk will hand out a wrapped loaf in preference to any other."

W. C. Busche, Livingston, Montana, says: "I have wrapped my 10-cent "Best Yet" bread ever since I came back from the National Convention at Minneapolis last summer, and as soon as I could get my waxed paper from the East. I will say that I have increased my sales on that bread from 200 to 1,000 loaves a day, and I certainly lay that to the wrapping."

Robert Bryce, of Indianapolis, one of the protestants, says: We have found no injury to the bread by wrapping it, but on the contrary, as the bread wrapped in paper is not allowed to dry out, it is salable longer than the bread that is not wrapped." The Bryce Baking Company, in advertising in the Indianapolis Star of May 4, 1910, say of their "Holsum" wrapped bread, "'Holsum' is *close-grained, substantial and satisfying.* No other bread has the *rich, delicate butter-flavor* that is so much enjoyed in 'Holsum.'" In an advertisement by this same company in the Star of March 4, this appears: "It's the *cleanest, richest-flavored, most digestible* of bread—it comes to your home with all its *oven freshness* and *delicacy* of *flavor intact*—preserved by the special 'Holsum' *wrapper.*" In the Indianapolis Star of March 25, the Bryce Baking Company say of their "Holsum" wrapped bread: "Its *rich, butter flavor* and *delicate crust* will delight you." In the Star of March 18, the Bryce Baking Company says of its "Holsum": *"It is wrapped fresh from the oven in waxed paper* that keeps in all the *delicate flavor* and comes to your table with all its *original goodness preserved.*" The advertisement of the Bryce Baking Company in the issue of June 1st, presumably expresses the present opinion of that company. That advertisement says: "The 'Holsum' Wrapper Keeps in the Freshness and Keeps Out Dirt and Dampness. The air and moisture-tight wrapper of 'Holsum' will keep it fresh, dainty and delicious for a long time. 'Holsum' a week old is far from stale." We can take no exception to these statements and we believe that they express the exact truth of the value of the wrapping of bread.

We can not find better proof of the fallacy of the argument that bread wrapping injures the quality of the bread than these statements of representative bakers. More than that, the wrapper clearly proves not only that bread wrapping has come to stay, but that it is both practicable and in accord with the public demand. One firm dealing in a wax paper wrapper sold to bakers during 1908, seventy million wrappers, in 1909 two hundred and twenty-five million wrappers, and in 1910 they estimate their sales at five hundred million wrappers. The best known bakers of the country appreciate the fact that wrapping has come to stay. As to this proposition we leave it to the bakers to speak for themselves.

George M. Haffner, one of the most progressive and successful bakers whom I know, and for several years the President of the Master Bakers' Association of Indiana, says: "Concerning the wrapping of bread by the wholesale bakers, allow me to state that the *wrapping of bread is the proper* and *sanitary way* in which the bread should be delivered and handled. In my opinion *that question is settled.*"

I again quote P. F. Peterson of Omaha: "I think the time is coming when the public will demand every loaf wrapped, and the time is not far distant when the municipality will enact laws which will make it compulsory. I predict that the time is not far distant when every loaf of bread will be wrapped at the factory before it goes on its journey towards the consumer's table."

The Nick Warisse Baking Company of Louisville say: "We confidently believe that wrapping is the proper and only sanitary way in which bread should be handled, and we believe eventually that the practice will be taken up all over the country; and, in fact, believe that municipal governments of the different cities will enact ordinances compelling the bakers to enclose their bread in a wrapper of some sort. It is a well known fact that at least 75 per cent. of bread cases and breadboxes are not fit to put bread in them, as the retail dealer does not give enough attention to the sanitary conditions in which bread ought to be handled."

The Bradford Baking Company of Los Angeles say: "We have found wrapping bread to be a great success in more ways than one. When we commenced wrapping bread in the city, it was unheard of—today 80 per cent. of the bakers are wrapping their bread."

The Bakers' Helper, one of the representative baker's journals, says of wrapping bread: "In the daily papers all over the country there are constantly appearing letters from bread consumers, pleading for the compulsory wrapping of bread by the baker, as a sanitary measure. Why should bakers wait for the enactment of laws forcing them to do what their judgment commends as a wise thing and which they know the public wants? That the wrapping of bread in the bakery will be required by law is practically certain. It is only a question of time. Bakers who go ahead of the law, and offer their bread to the public in the most cleanly fashion possible, will have the advantage over the tardy ones, and will contribute to a decided trade advance."

It has been argued that since no case of illness can be attributed to the eating of unwrapped bread, there is no occasion for enforcement of the Sanitary Law as it relates to the subject. The fallacy of such an argument is so apparent to you, gentlemen, it is not necessary to controvert it. It is sufficient to call attention to the fact that until a few years ago, no one knew how cholera was disseminated or what was the cause of the plagues which from time to time have swept all countries. When we can show, as we have done by exposing culture plates to the open air, that thousands of bacteria may be collected in five minutes on a surface not larger than the top of a loaf of bread and that many of these bacteria are disease producing, is it not reasonable to suppose that the consumer eating unprotected bread will eventually take into his body bacteria under such conditions that they will thrive and multiply to his physical detriment? It is no more necessary to point out specific instances of disease due to the eating of unprotected bread before attempting to protect the public than it is to produce an instance of infection by the tubercle bacilli due to the drinking of milk from a tuberculous cow before we prohibit the sale of such milk. There is in force an admirable order issued by the State Board of Health prohibiting the sale of such foodstuffs as baker's goods, confectionery, dried fruits, cereal and meat products, etc., unless such foods are protected from flies, dust and dirt. Seventy-two dealers in foodstuffs in this State have been prosecuted for violation of this order. In no case has the State Board of Health failed to secure conviction. In no case has the court intimated that the order was not reasonable and just. In no case has the defendant or his attorney appealed from the decision of the court. And yet, I do not know of a single case of illness which can be directly traced to the eating of food stuffs which have not been properly protected from flies, dust and dirt.

It is true that the cost of living is increasing. It is true that the consumer now willingly pays as much for 5½ ounces of crisp, fresh, protected crackers as he once paid for a full 16 ounces of soggy, dirty bulk crackers. If he did not willingly assume the increased cost of the protected goods, do you think it would have been possible for the manufacturers of these crackers to have built up an enormously successful business? Not so many years ago the people of Indianapolis pumped water from the well in their back yard and got it free of cost. At the present time they are paying from $10 to $20 a year for water. Are they not satisfied that a sanitary water supply is worth $20 a year more to them than the possibly unsafe water in their back yard?

I am convinced that the business of the baker will continue to improve in the future as it has in the past. Five years ago when we opened our laboratory the grocers of this city were wrapping bread in newspapers. They were piling it exposed on shelves and counters. The bakers were leaving it in bread boxes which sat on the sidewalk. At the present time such conditions are recognized as insanitary and illegal. Even more marked changes have been made in the bakeshops themselves and hardly a baker can be found who will not admit that his shop can not be and should not be still further improved. The problem of bread wrapping is to be worked out by the baker as these other problems have been worked out, and will, I believe, be solved just as successfully. Indeed, the condition which to my mind was the most serious, namely, that of handling small baker's goods, seems not to have given the bakers much trouble. I quote a statement of the Grocers Baking Company of Indianapolis:

"We are using folding boxes or cartons for our rolls, doughnuts and cookies. We use 2,000 or more daily. We have them made to hold two dozen each of rolls and doughnuts, and cookies fifty each. Our reason for having them made to hold two dozen is that a customer will always take a box; and by having them made to hold two dozen we always sell two dozen to a customer instead of one, and cookies likewise. Before we used these boxes we did not sell one-third of these goods that we are now selling, and this is easily explained. When we put the goods in sacks the rolls and doughnuts were always mashed and always delivered in very bad condition, and our cookies, being crisp, were more or less broken. We had to stand the loss, and the goods did not look very inviting to a customer when they were mashed or broken. Therefore, we attribute the large increase of business to the cartons, as they are now delivered in first-class condition."

Does not this statement offer convincing argument why circular letter No. 7 should continue to express the policy of the State Board of Health? In the enforcement of all sanitary laws the ideal is the thing striven for. The ideal may not be attained, but he who sets his mark below the ideal must finally fail. The counsel for the petitioners rightly says "the ideal thing from a standpoint of cleanliness is to have the bread wrapped after it is baked in a thoroughly sanitary room and passed on to the consumer without exposure to the atmosphere." I should regret very much to feel that any of the master bakers of Indiana were working to ends less ideal, and I believe that each in his own way will finally succeed in solving the problems which now appear impossible of attainment.

THE OPINION OF BAKERS AND GROCERS REPORTED BY INSPECTORS BRUNER, OWENS AND TUCKER.

J. H. Foley Company, grocers, Logansport, Indiana, say: "All breads should be wrapped and protected from flies, dust, dirt and dirty hands. You make me cover up my strawberries, prunes, meats and other foods, and I would be willing to pay more for the bread. and as to the cost, I do not count that very much."

Stuart & Bury, grocers, Logansport, Indiana, say: "We cannot have things too clean."

H. P. W. Brinkroeger, grocer, Ft. Wayne, Indiana, says: "We are *selling four times as much Perfection Bread now, than we did before they wrapped.* I would be willing to pay a fourth of a cent more for wrapped bread."

Coverdale & Archer Company, grocers, Ft. Wayne, Indiana, say: "I believe bread should be wrapped, as it is more sanitary, and would save with us. I would be willing to pay more for wrapped bread."

Felger & Wybourn, grocers, Ft. Wayne, Indiana, say: "For our part we would rather have wrapped bread. We sell about 120 loaves of wrapped bread a day to about 20 of the unwrapped."

Langard & Langard, grocers, Ft. Wayne, Indiana, say: "I'll tell you, Mr. Tucker, it's this way. If a lady comes in with a coal oil can and wants oil, we go and get it. Then she wants a loaf of bread, and if we are too busy we do not wash our hands, and if the bread is not wrapped it will taste of the oil or other filth that may be on our hands. Yes, I say wrap all breadstuff as well as other like foods."

Mr. D. O. Dunn, proprietor of the largest bakery in Seymour, says: "Will cost about $2.50 per thousand loaves. Half of trade agreed to pay cost of wrapping."

Mr. H. A. Fletcher, proprietor Home Bakery, Mitchell, Indiana, says he figures that wrapping the bread will not cost him anything—that he will get returns in the valuable advertising to more than balance the cost.

A. Haungo & Son, bakers, Bedford, Indiana, have already made arrangements with some of their wholesale trade to pay 25 cents per 100 loaves extra because of the wrapping being done in the bakery. They are not pushing that feature now, however, and will not until close to July 1st.

W. G. Salyers, French Lick, baker, says it will cost no more to wrap with waxed paper at 12½ cents per pound than it will with the ordinary paper at 5 cents or 6 cents per pound. The waxed paper costs $1.20 per 1,000 sheets 14 x 18, and the printed paper costs 15 cents per 1,000 sheets extra. The bakers at Huntingburg, Jasper, French Lick, Orleans, Mitchell, Bedford, Bloomington, and other towns in this section have already placed their orders for paper.

The bakers as a rule are pleased with the order, thinking it will prove in the end the best thing that ever happened to them. Of course, right now, some of them are "up in the air," as the druggists were at first over the re-labeling of their stocks, but generally speaking, they approve the order. (A. W. Bruner.)

Spencer, Indiana.—Two bakers will wrap the product, putting advertisement upon wrapper: "No change in size of loaf—no increase in price." Both favor the order. Grocers pleased. Health officers favorable to order.

Clay City, Indiana.—One baker will wrap. Order received favorably. No contemplated change in size of loaf or price. Grocers favor order.

Brazil, Indiana.—Three bakers will favor order with one possible exception. One dealer in bread shipped in from Terre Haute favorable to order. No contemplated change in price or size of loaf. Grocers, so far as seen, are favorable. Health officers are distributing or have distributed order.

Elnora, Indiana.—One baker will wrap. No change in size or price, favorable, grocers in line.

Bicknell, Indiana.—One baker. Order left. Grocers favor order. Health officers believe in it and are doing good work.

Sullivan, Indiana.—Grocers favorable to order. Bakers will probably wrap.

The grocers have been interviewed in about a dozen small towns receiving bread from the outside, and they are without exception in favor of the bread coming to them wrapped.

Mr. J. E. West, Brazil, Indiana, says he handles the Ideal Baking Company's bread of Terre Haute, Indiana, and has been informed by this company that they intend to wrap the bread after July 1, 1910. He thereby certifies that as a retailer of bread on the streets of Brazil he is in favor of wrapped bread, because it is cleaner and more convenient to handle. As it is he finds he must wash his hands many times along the route or wear gloves. Some of the trouble would be saved if the bread were delivered to him wrapped.

Mr. G. W. Oswatt, retail grocer, Brazil, Indiana, says: "I am in favor of wrapped bread. A grocer's hands are not always clean enough to handle the unwrapped product in a sanitary way. I ought to know about this for I have handled bread for 22 years."

M. S. Burger, Clay City, Indiana, baker, will wrap. No change in size of loaf or price. Would favor a slight increase to retailer to divide the cost of wrapping, say 25 cents per week.

A. J. Fulkerson, Clay City, Indiana, favors wrapped bread. Would be in favor of paying 15 cents per 100 loaves to have it properly wrapped.

Greenwood & Sons, Clay City, Indiana, handle wrapped bread. "Costs no more and people are better satisfied than they were with the unwrapped bread. If the price were 15 cents or 20 cents more on the hundred, we would still prefer wrapped bread. The Miller-Parrott milk bread in the oil-boiled wrapper improves with age, is as good at three days as the unwrapped is at two."

Dainert Brothers, Clay City, Indiana, say: "We get bread from Miller-Parrott, some of which is wrapped. We prefer wrapped. If the price were 15 cents or 20 cents more we would still prefer wrapped bread. We never have any lossage on day-old wrapped bread."

Louis J. Schultz, of Schultz Bakery, Brazil, Indiana, says: "We believe in the order requiring wrapped bread and propose to govern our business accordingly. It is a more sanitary way to handle the product. It gets the bread out to the customer in a more attractive form and is a good form of advertisement. It provides against being soiled or contaminated by an unclean groceryman and the blame consequently placed on the baker. Means a square deal from the seller and producer to the consumer."

A letter dated November 30, 1908, from this office to the Taggart Baking Company, Indianapolis, Indiana, states: "We regret the necessity of again calling to your attention the insanitary manner in which bread is handled by the drivers of your delivery wagons. We believe you realize the necessity for producing and delivering your products to the housewife in a cleanly manner and to this end you have provided closed wagons to be used in delivering goods. Our inspectors report, however, that frequently the front of these wagons are open so that all dust and dirt blowing from the street, the horse and the driver's clothing is deposited in the bread piled in the wagon. You must realize that such a condition is not sanitary. The practice of delivering bread in bulk, unwrapped and unprotected is of itself bad, but when coupled with the carelessness of drivers which expose it in transit to the filth of the street, makes it impossible to deliver a clean product to the consumer.

"We trust we shall not again be compelled to call to your attention this lack of observance of the Pure Food Law."

Under date of March 9, 1910, we wrote the Bryce Baking Company as follows: "This morning we saw one of your two-horse wagons driving east on East Market Street with the entire load of bread exposed. There was no protection of any kind to the piles of bread inside the cart, and all the dust and dirt kicked up by the horse's heels and blown off their backs flew past the driver on to the bread. This wagon bore on its top one of the 'Holsum' signs.

We have called to your attention before this the absolute necessity of handling the bread supply under sanitary conditions. We do not understand why this order is disregarded. We have instructed our inspectors whenever they find a baker's cart which contains unprotected bread to arrest the driver and condemn such parts of the load as is not protected."

On March 11, 1910, Robert Bryce, of the Bryce Baking Company, replied: "It has been our instruction to our men to keep the curtains, provided on the front of their wagons, closed.

"It might be that as we have not spoken about this matter for a few days they have become careless. We will take the matter up with them, and we believe that they will conform with your wishes hereafter.

"We had a few extra wagons in service which did not have the curtains on them. Today we had curtains put on these wagons, with instructions to our drivers to use them.

"Thanking you for calling our attention to the matter," etc.

Following Mr. Barnard's paper, favoring the wrapping of bread, the members visited the laboratory to witness the "bread experiment" conducted by Mr. Barnard. Over one hundred loaves of bread had been purchased, wrapped and unwrapped. The unwrapped loaves were purchased in duplicate and one of the two immediately wrapped in oiled paper. The loaves could thus be compared.

The summary was: The wrapped loves were, in many instances, soggy and more or less sour or changed in flavor and some were mouldy. The wrapped Vienna loaves had soggy crusts and it was plain that Vienna bread, wrapped as in the experiment, could not be placed on the market because of softened crust and changed flavor. The experiment sustained the claims of the bakers.

Upon consideration of all evidence, arguments and experiments, the following action was taken:

Dr. Wishard moved, seconded by Dr. Tucker—

That the order passed April 8, 1910, entitled "Notice to Bakers," and promulgated as Order No. 7, and which is found in the minutes of the meeting held April 8, 1910, be and is now suspended until January 1, 1911, and the words "July 1, 1910," in line 22 of said order are stricken out and "January 1, 1911," substituted therefor.

Unanimously carried.

Dr. Wishard moved, seconded by Dr. Tucker—

That the President shall appoint a committee of three, of which committee the State Health Commissioner shall be one, the State Food and Drug Commissioner shall be one, and a person named by the bakers shall be one; and the duty of said committee shall be to conduct experiments upon the whole question of bread wrapping and sanitary distribution of bread, particularly relating to the influence of different kinds of wrapping paper and the cost of wrapping; and said committee shall report its findings at the regular meeting of the Board to be held October 14, 1910.

Action concerning prevention of injuries and lockjaw on July 4th.

Ordered: That the county and city health officers all recommend by the use of the daily newspapers or other means, to give warning to the people of their respective jurisdictions, of the danger of the unrestricted use of firearms, cannon crackers and fireworks in general, as now practiced each Fourth of July. That the number of deaths and injuries resulting from the careless handling of fireworks each Fourth of July is appalling. That the number of fatalities is yearly increasing.

Therefore, the State Board of Health recommends to health commissioners and all health officers and mayors of the State, a "Safe and Sane Fourth of July."

Ordered: That the Secretary attend the meeting of the American Medical Association at St. Louis, June 7th-10th, to represent the Board; also that Dr. F. A. Tucker attend the meeting of the National Educators'

Association in Boston, July 1-8, to represent the Board in the Section on School Hygiene, the expenses of said delegates to be paid from the general appropriation.

ALUM IN PICKLES

Mr. E. O. Grosvenor, attorney for Alart & McGuire, New York: National Pickle and Canning Co., St. Louis; Knadler & Lucas. Louisville; Squire Dingee Co., Chicago, and Williams Bros. Co., Detroit, appeared before the Board and made an argument for the repeal of the Board's rule and instructions against the use of alum in pickles. He promised to send a brief upon the subject to each member of the Board, requesting that the subject be considered in the near future.

Mr. Sebastian Mueller, of Pittsburg, representing Heinz & Co., made an argument to show that alum was injurious and unnecessary.

Be it Resolved, That the State Board of Health in its effort to prevent disease and preserve the health of the public, do hereby

Advise, and Recommend: That the use of the common or public drinking cup, in all schools, railway and interurban passenger coaches, and all public buildings be discontinued.

Unanimously passed.

SCHOOLHOUSES CONDEMNED.

Report of inspection of schoolhouse at Castleton, Indiana, District No. 3, Lawrence Township, by J. L. Anderson, Deputy State Health Commissioner, May 20, 1910.

Site.—One-fourth mile east and north of the village, two acres in lot. Ground high and dry and sloping away from building in every direction. A cinder walk from the road to building. Dug well with iron pump back of building. Has good wooden platform and short trough to carry off waste water. Water-closets on rear line of lot in good condition, screened and tight board fence between closets. A shed for horses is in the northwest corner of lot.

Building.—One story, four roomed, brick, with slate roof; facing the east. Foundation brick. No slate or stone on foundation walls. Built in shape of Greek Cross, with two halls. Outside measurement of building 108 feet by 32 feet, north and south; 64 feet by 32 feet, east and west.

Basement.—Under center part, entered from outside the building. Size 30 feet by 30 feet by 7 feet 4 inches, and contains two large hot-air heaters which extend within one foot of the joists of floor. This is dangerous to the building and has set fire to the joists once or twice. Floor is of dirt. The walls seem to be sound but are badly water soaked near each water spout.

South Hall.—This hall is 10 feet by 32 feet by 16 feet, and extends through building. The chimney in this hall is cracked from bottom to top. Doors at each end. Is used for cloakroom. Two doors open into primary room on the left.

Primary Room.—This room is 26 feet 6 inches by 30 feet by 16 feet. There are two windows in east, south and west sides, with blinds. Wainscoted to windows. Walls papered. Ceiling not papered and plaster cracked. Blackboards painted on the plaster. Floors in good condition, oiled and clean. Heated by stove in south end of room with shield around it. Enrollment about 40, average attendance 30.

Intermediate Grade.—West center room, 30 feet by 30 feet by 16 feet. Three windows on west and one on south side. The same description applies to this room as in the primary room, except that the ceiling is papered and is water stained from the roof leaking. Enrollment 35, average attendance 35.

High School Room.—This is the east middle room. The same size and description as the intermediate. Separated from that room by folding doors, and the two rooms can be thrown into one. Enrollment 40, average attendance 35.

North Hall.—This hall is 10 feet by 30 feet by 16 feet. Doors at each end. Is used as a recitation room. No light except from the transoms over the doors. The chimney in this hall is badly cracked and crumbling and liable to fall down at a very slight jar.

North Room, Seventh and Eighth Grades.—This room is 26 feet 6 inches by 30 feet by 16 feet. The same conditions apply to this room as the primary room. This room is heated from a stove in north side of room with shield. Enrollment 50, average attendance 42. The janitor reported that he was unable to keep the rooms warm even in mild weather, and that the pupils had to wear their wraps in the schoolrooms. That several times he had the furnaces so hot he was afraid they would set fire to the building, but that he could not get any heat into the rooms, but that the heat would pour out of the basement windows at all times. There are 27 more pupils to be added to this school next fall.

Recommendation.—I would recommend that this building be condemned as insanitary and endangering the lives of the children from fire. It would be throwing money away to attempt to remodel it. I was accompanied on my inspection by the following gentlemen, viz, Mr. Mead. Mr. McGehey, J. Olvey, and F. V. Wadsworth (member of advisory board).

Proclamation of Condemnation.

Whereas, It has been shown to the satisfaction of the State Board of Health, that the schoolhouse at Castleton, District No. 3, Lawrence Township, Marion County, Ind., is insanitary, and consequently threatens the health and life of the pupils, and also interferes with their efficiency; therefore, it is

Ordered: That said schoolhouse at Castleton, District No. 3, Lawrence Township, Marion County, Ind., is condemned for school purposes, and shall not be used for said school purposes after June 10, 1910, and if any school trustee, or trustees, any teacher or any person uses said schoolhouse for school purposes, or teaches therein after the date above mentioned, he or she or they shall be prosecuted.

Any person mutilating or tearing down this proclamation shall be prosecuted.

Passed by the State Board of Health, June 2, 1910.

Sanitary survey of Acton schoolhouse, Franklin Township, Marion County, Ind., May 31, 1910, by J. N. Hurty.

Site.—One and one-half acres. Center of lot is dry. The southeast and north sides are low and wet. On the north side a short distance from the house, it is plain to be seen, at times is muddy. The site is not large enough for a schoolhouse of the size required at Acton. Besides, the building stands within 20 feet of the highway. This endangers the lives of the children, and traffic on the road certainly interferes with the school.

Building.—The building is brick, two stories, four rooms, built in 1865. Stone foundation, no basement. The walls are cracked or settled under most windows. Downspouts discharge water about 12 feet from ground and wet walls. Heated by Smith ventilating heaters.

Interior of Building.—High school room, second floor, 24 x 30 x 15 feet, contains 32 seats. Floor good; painted blackboard. Lighted from two sides. Light is sufficient.

Seventh and Eighth Grades.—Second floor, 24 x 30 x 15 feet, contains 34 seats. Floor is good, desks assorted as to quality and size. Painted blackboards; lighted from two sides. Light sufficient.

Fourth and Fifth Grades.—North room and first floor, 24 x 30 x15 feet, 40 seats. Painted blackboards. Lighted from two sides. Light sufficient. Paper skinning off from ceiling.

Primary Room.—South room, first floor, has 50 seats. Lighted from two sides. Light sufficient. Painted blackboards, walls newly finished, ugly crack over top of one window.

Windows.—Four to each room, each pane 12 x 24, 12 panes to each window.

Entrance and Hall.—The building is entered from east side through double doors, of ample size. Good stone steps. Hall is 12 x 18 feet. The stairway is boxed and leads to upper floor from directly in front of the main door, which is a good feature. The stairway has one turn, 14 steps lead to the first landing, and then 14 steps to the floor above. Steps are 5 feet 9 inches, and 6-inch tread.

Outhouses.—The outhouses are widely separated, approached with indifferent cinder paths. Both outhouses were foul and noisome.

Water.—Water is secured from a well; could not learn whether it was driven or a dug well. Water dispensed to the pupils by tin cups.

Summary and Recommendations.—The Acton schoolhouse is old, insanitary, badly arranged, wrongly lighted, not sufficiently ventilated, wrongly heated. Capacity is insufficient for present number of school children. It is badly situated and school grounds are not sufficient, and except in the high portion where the schoolhouse is situated, the site is low and wet.

I recommend this schoolhouse be condemned.

PROCLAMATION OF CONDEMNATION.

Whereas, it has been shown to the satisfaction of the State Board of Health, that the schoolhouse at Acton, Franklin Township, Marion County, Ind., is insanitary and consequently threatens the health and life of the pupils, and also interferes with their efficiency; therefore, it is

Ordered: That said schoolhouse at Acton, Franklin Township, Marion County, Ind., is condemned for school purposes, and shall not be used for said school purposes after June 1, 1911, and if any school trustee, or trustees, any teacher or any person uses said schoolhouse for school purposes, or teaches therein, after the date above mentioned, he or she or they shall be proscuted.

Any person mutilating or tearing down this proclamation shall be prosecuted.

Passed by the State Board of Health, June 2, 1910.

Report of sanitary survey of school building, District No. 6, Washington Township, Pike County, Ind., by E. S. Imel, County Health Commissioner, May 23, 1910.

Site.—One acre of ground, high, beautiful site; house in center of square, no walks to any buildings.

Exterior.—Siding boards very aged; frame structure, built on stone pillars, five to a side and one in center. North end of building, floor down almost on ground, south side about 18 inches off ground, no basement, 10½ feet to eave. Shingle roof in pretty good condition.

Interior.—Board ceiling, 9 feet high, floors rough and uneven. Stove in center of house, pipe running straight up to brick flue on joist. No screens to windows.

Outhouses bad, no walks. Water procured from farmer's dug well or a cistern, 100 yards away. Children carry it. Galvanized bucket and two tin cups to drink out of.

Seats for 44 pupils; enumeration shows 62. There are never more than 35 or 40 attend school. Average much less.

This building has been built about 35 years. However, it is pretty solid; no danger of it falling down this next school year.

But they need a new building for various reasons as given above.

I would recommend that, any way, not more than one term more of school be allowed in this building and so notified that they can arrange to build early in 1911.

After consideration of the above, the following proclamation of condemnation was adopted:

PROCLAMATION OF CONDEMNATION.

Whereas, it has been shown to the satisfaction of the State Board of Health that the schoolhouse, District No. 6, Washington Township, Pike County, Ind., is insanitary, and consequently threatens the health and life of the pupils, and also interferes with their efficiency; therefore, it is

Ordered: That said schoolhouse, District No. 6, Washington Township, Pike County, Ind., is condemned for school purposes, and shall not be used for said school purposes after June 10, 1910, and if any school trustee, or trustees, any teacher or any person uses said schoolhouse for school purposes, or teaches therein, after the date above mentioned, he or she or they shall be prosecuted.

Any person mutilating or tearing down this proclamation shall be prosecuted.

Passed by the State Board of Health, June 2, 1910.

Sanitary inspection of Mongo schoolhouse, Lagrange County, Ind., June 8, 1910, by D. W. Dryer, County Health Commissioner.

On June 7th I made a complete survey of the public school building and site of the same at Mongo, Lagrange County, Ind. Your attention had been called to this matter through petition of interested patrons and letter by myself. Relief from a situation which seemed undesirable was asked.

Survey as above shows the schoolhouse grounds to be about one acre in extent, entirely surrounded by a fine sugar-maple grove on site; the elevation while not high, yet sufficient. The soil is a clean yellow sand several feet in depth, lying above clay and gravel; is entirely dry at all times through natural drainage.

The building is some forty years old, 34 feet by 44 feet, two stories with gable roof, on stone wall of about two feet, and no basement. Is of heavy wood frame. This apparently sound except that sills in part have rotted away and been shored up at such points; the stone wall is fairly good though cracked in places and open in places under sills; the siding, cornice and other outer material except roof is in fair condition and painted white.

The roof was originally of shingles. These becoming much rotted were, without removal, covered with a fluted iron roof of medium quality and said to be now rusted through and leaking in places. Could not see from the ground.

There is a front entrance only to building into a hall about 8 feet by 10 feet. From this hall a stairway starts at front (at each side of entrance door) each side of hall, 3½ feet wide, rising some 6 feet to small landing, then rising at right angle some 6 feet more, at each inner side of building, toward center, to another small landing; a door each side about 2½ feet wide making entrance to each upper room. There are small hall space rooms at front upstairs. The ground entrance door is about four feet by eight feet, opening inward to hall as described; at each side of this lower hall are small rooms extending under stairways. There is a door at inner end of hall opening to lower room, but this has been nailed up and is not in use, the only entrance into lower main room being through door at left of main room. The space under stairway on this side has been used to store fuel, this being passed to get into main room, as it now is.

The lower assembly room is 32 feet by 33 feet, with 11 feet to ceiling; wainscoted some 3 feet; boards painted white, plastered and wall-papered above with dingy paper. All windows in building are of uniform size, old style, 12 panes to window; total glass surface of each about 26 inches by 64 inches for the window. This main room has three windows at each side and two at rear; the floor is of maple in fair state, this floor being laid over the old one. A chimney, 16 inches by 24 inches, starts on a shelf about 4 feet below ceiling at rear of building and reaches up through roof, the only outlet for one stove below and two above. This one stove of average size below is supposed to heat this main room; wood fuel used; some 30 feet of six-inch pipe.

A partition separates this room from entrance hall and sub-stairway rooms, with no light from that side. A partition separates the upstairs part into two rooms each 16 feet by 32 feet; the west room having 3 side and 2 rear windows. The east room 3 side and 1 rear window, ceilings about ten feet from floor. Floors about as below—maple laid over old floor; said to be filled in between floor and plaster below with sawdust. Similar stove to one below in each room, located near entrance corners, with some 30 feet of pipe to each, all going to only chimney; rooms papered in like quality as in lower. Blackboarding likely ample in quantity, and ranging through nearly all kinds, painted boards, cement surface, oil-cloth, pro-slate, etc. The west upper room is ventilated (if at all) by windows and a trap-door leading up to open belfry at front; the other upper, and the lower rooms by windows only. There is a general state of dilapidation from open joints, cracked walls, etc. The furniture ranges from rather old type to some that is practically new and could by repainting and varnishing be put in usable shape; some of it good enough.

The attendance of each of upper rooms is 35 or more of the lower. up to 60; prospectively, from closing other schools, will be greater next year. The air space is now below the requirement, and totally inadequate. The drinking water is supplied from a driven well in yard; seems plentiful and said to be good; tin cup at well used; dry around well.

Two old dilapidated outhouses, separated, but without dividing fence, are found at rear of lot; these are filthy and utterly improper.

Such in general is the situation of this school property. It should not be longer used for school purposes—that is the buildings. I have promised the trustee to condemn it. I wish and trust your honorable board will endorse and sustain me in this. You have the facts before you.

This old structure was doubtless creditable to the old pioneers of a half century ago, except that from manner of construction it has been always a firetrap. It is now insanitary, uncomfortable and absolutely dangerous.

It is the last town frame schoolhouse in our county, and the time is come for it to go out of use as such. Mongo is a pretty little village on Pigeon River, now having a railroad, and a progressive people. They want the best adapted to their need. Dr. A. G. Grubb, deputy health officer, is enthusiastic for it. Mr. Claud C. Smith, township trustee, is favorable and ready to act and build this summer; the leading and other citizens, so far as I could learn, are willing or favor it. It will be a good work and now is the time.

I do not hesitate to act alone, but feel your approval will help.

After consideration of the above, the following proclamation of condemnation was adopted:

PROCLAMATION OF CONDEMNATION.

Whereas, It has been shown to the satisfaction of the State Board of Health that the schoolhouse at Mongo, Springfield Township, Lagrange County, Ind., is insanitary, and consequently threatens the health and life of the pupils, and also interferes with their efficiency; therefore, it is

Ordered: That said schoolhouse at Mongo, Springfield Township, Lagrange County, Ind., is condemned for school purposes, and shall not be used for said school purposes after June 10, 1911, and if any school trustee, or trustees, any teacher, or any person uses said schoolhouse for school purposes, or teaches therein after the date above mentioned, he or she or they shall be prosecuted.

Any person mutilating or tearing down this proclamation shall be prosecuted.

Passed by the State Board of Health, June 2, 1910.

Sanitary survey of North Grove schoolhouse, known as District No. 5, Harrison Township, Miami County, Ind., by John E. Yarling, County Health Commissioner.

The trustee of Harrison Township, Mr. P. C. Steinman, and Mr. E. B. Witherow, county superintendent, were present, and together we viewed the schoolhouse and submit the following report:

We found a two-story brick schoolhouse, situated on a lot facing a street running north and south. Said lot has a frontage of 200 feet and extends back 300 feet. The lot is comparatively level, and has practically the same drainage as other lots in the vicinity. Having rained the night before, we found the lot free of any water.

To the north on said street, about one square is situated a church; also in said yard there are six maple shade trees. The coal house is north and east of said building.

The building is of brick, with a limestone rock foundation, the top of said foundation is on an average of about one foot above the surrounding lot, and the floor is about 15 inches above the rock foundation.

Said building contains four schoolrooms, two halls, and four cloakrooms. No basement.

We enter into a hall which is 10 feet long, and 8 feet wide, and leading from the hall to the west are two rooms. Room No. 1, which is to the south, is 24 feet long and 24 feet wide and 14 feet high. In said room there are two windows to the rear, two to the left, and one to the right. Said windows are 8¾ feet high and 28 inches wide. The wall paper in different parts of the room is loose and falling from the walls and ceiling. Said room has 41 seats; an enrollment of 38 pupils, with an average attendance of 34. This would give an average air space of 230 cubic feet to each pupil, using 35 as a basis of calculation.

Leading from this room is a cloakroom which is 10 feet long and 6 feet wide, lighted and ventilated by two windows to the right. Leading from the entrance hall is a room 24 feet long and 24 feet wide and 14 feet high. The paper is in bad condition, and is falling from the walls and ceiling. This room is lighted and ventilated by two windows to the rear, two to the right, and one to the left. There are 37 seats in this room, an enrollment of 40 pupils and an average attendance of 34. This would give an average air space of 230 cubic feet to each pupil, using 35 as a basis of calculation. A door to the left leads to a cloakroom 10 feet long and 6 feet wide.

From the hall lead stairways to right and left, which meet in a hall on the second floor, which is 10 feet long and 8 feet wide. From the hall to right and left, are two cloakrooms which are 10 feet long and 6 feet wide, and which are lighted and ventilated by one window in each room. The hall is lighted by two windows to the east.

From this hall to the southwest is room No. 3, which is 24 feet long and 24 feet wide and 15 feet high, and lighted and ventilated by two windows to the rear, two to the left, and one to the right. Said room contains 21 seats; has an enrollment of 13 pupils, with an average attendance of 12; this would give an average of 585 cubic feet of air space to each pupil. There are no doors from this room to the cloakroom.

From the hall we enter, to the right, into room No. 4, which is 24 feet long and 24 feet wide and 15 feet high; lighted and ventilated by two windows to the rear, two windows to the left, and one to the front. Said room contains 16 seats, has an enrollment of 19, and an average attendance of 17; this gives an average of 452 cubic feet of air space to each pupil.

All of said rooms are heated by stoves, which are not surrounded by jackets.

The walls of the halls are in fair condition.

From the building there are gravel walks leading to the outhouses, but having been used long, need a recoating of gravel. Both sexes use the same walk part way to their respective outhouses, and we recommend the outhouses for the girls be relocated, that the same walk need not be used for both sexes. The outhouses are in bad condition and need cleaning and painting. The vaults also should be cleaned.

I find the water supply is from a driven well, which is probably 100 feet deep, extending into limestone. A box should surround the well, which would prevent splashing.

We would recommend that said yard be ditched, which could be done without a great expense.

After consideration of the above, the following proclamation of condemnation was adopted:

Proclamation of Condemnation.

Whereas, It has been shown to the satisfaction of the State Board of Health, that the schoolhouse at North Grove, District No. 5, Harrison Township, Miami County, Ind., is insanitary, and consequently threatens the health and life of the pupils, and also interferes with their efficiency; therefore, it is

Ordered: That said schoolhouse at North Grove, Dictrict No. 5, Harrison Township, Miami County, Ind., is condemned for school purposes, and shall not be used for said school purposes after June 10, 1911, and if any school trustee, or trustees, any teacher or any person uses said schoolhouse for school purposes, or teaches therein after the date above mentioned, he or she or they shall be prosecuted.

Any person mutilating or tearing down this proclamation shall be prosecuted.

Passed by the State Board of Health, June 2, 1910.

Sanitary survey of Southport schoolhouse, Perry Township, Marion County, June 30, 1910, by Dr. C. A. Carter.

Site.—Is about one-half acre lot. It is located on the south side of a road or street running east and west and to the east of a public highway and the interurban railway. The east side of the ground is high, the soil is gravel mixed with clay, and at the time of inspection was perfectly dry. The ground drains toward the west. Along the highway on the west side of the ground is a low place, but it did not have the appearance of holding water at any time. The grounds are small for a school building, and they are too close to the public highway. Eight large trees are on the east side of the ground, about 20 feet from the building. Gravel walks around the building.

Building.—The building is brick with stone foundation, two stories, built in 1884. The building is a T shape. On the east wing, a crack in the wall extends the entire length between the upper and lower windows. The same condition exists in the west wing. The down spouts on the east wing are broken. On the west wing a down spout has been replaced recently, which had been leaking, the mortar being washed from between the bricks. The eaves show indication of leaking.

Interior of Building.—The building is entered from the north through double doors, the entrance being to the right, and to the left a door leads into the basement or cellar. Three steps, five feet wide, with a 9-inch tread, lead you into a 10-foot hall which separates the east and west wings and leads directly to the south wing. In the center of the hall is a large radiator, which has been used to carry heat into the hall. Foul odors come from the ventilator at this time. There is an old cellar or basement under the building, which is dark, foul and damp. At one time the building was heated by a furnace. The walls in the hall have been recently calcimined and are in fairly good condition. The floor in the hall is in very bad condition, it makes a creaking noise when you walk over it. There are six rooms to this building. Three lower and three upper rooms. The rooms are 27 x 30 x 14 feet; 14 steps, 5 feet wide, lead up the box stairway to the first landing. A turn to the left to a space of 53 inches, leads to the stairway to the second floor, which is 14 steps up. It has three rooms upstairs, one in each wing. The room in the west wing is lighted by four windows, two to the west and two to the north, two sash in each window, containing 9 glass, 12 x 24. This room contains 39 single desks in bad condition. The blackboard is painted plaster. Walls are dirty, floor bad, heated by large hot blast stove.

The room on the east wing, same size, lighted by four windows, two on east, two on north. The trees on the east side of building keep out the light. The same general conditions prevail in the east room as prevails in the west, with the exception the desks are new. The south wing upstairs contains 35 desks in bad condition, lighted by four windows, two on west and two on east. Walls water soaked in southwest corner.

East room on lower floor contains 41 desks, lighted by four windows, two on north and two on east. West room, lower floor, contains 57 desks, lighted by four windows, two on west and two on north. South wing lower floor, lighted by four windows, two on west, two on east. Could not tell how many desks belong in this room, for they have been moved around and stacked up in the corner. There is a small entrance to this room between the east and south wing, by an ordinary-sized door.

Each room has a small cloakroom. All heated by hot blast stoves.

The basement under this building is dark and damp, and a broken-down stairway leads to it.

Outbuildings.—The outbuildings for boys are located on the west side of the building, and are constructed with three compartments, with accommodations for two in each. A wooden trough used as a urinal is outside of the building. All are dirty and filthy. Building enclosed by 5-foot fence. A number of shade trees surround the ground.

The outbuilding for girls is in better condition than the one for the boys.

Water Supply.—Water is supplied from a well, which is in all probability a driven well. A large iron force pump is used to draw the water. Water supplied to the children with drinking cups.

Summary.—Building is insanitary. It is not lighted properly, and it is not in the best location for a school building. The building is also improperly heated and improperly ventilated. The site is too small for the school building. The building should be condemned for school purposes.

After consideration of the above, the following proclamation of condemnation was adopted:

Proclamation of Condemnation.

Whereas, It has been shown to the satisfaction of the State Board of Health, that the schoolhouse at Southport, Perry Township, Marion County, Ind., is insanitary, and consequently threatens the health and life of the pupils, and also interferes with their efficiency; therefore, it is

Ordered: That said schoolhouse at Southport, Perry Township, Marion County, Ind., is condemned for school purposes, and shall not be used for said school purposes after June 1, 1911, and if any school trustee, or trustees, any teacher or any person uses said schoolhouse for school purposes, or teaches therein, after the date above mentioned, he or she or they shall be prosecuted.

Any person mutilating or tearing down this proclamation shall be prosecuted.

Passed by the State Board of Health, June 2, 1910.

REGULAR QUARTERLY MEETING INDIANA STATE BOARD OF HEALTH.

JULY 8, 1910.

Called to order at 1:30 p. m., July 8, 1910, by President McCoy.

Present: Drs. McCoy, Davis, Wishard, Hurty.

President McCoy announced the meeting was for the purpose of considering and acting upon the affairs of the quarter ending June 30, 1910, and to transact any business which might properly come before the Board.

Minutes of the last regular meeting of April 8, 1910, and of the special meetings of April 13, May 24, and June 2, 1910, were read and approved in each individual item and as a whole.

REPORT OF SECRETARY FOR QUARTER ENDING JUNE 30, 1910.

The morbidity and mortality of the quarter is a little less than for the same quarter last year. Measles was epidemic in April throughout the State, every county reporting the disease extra prevalent. In April there were 80 deaths from measles, in May 82, in June 33. The consumption rate remains about stationary. For this quarter, there is no improvement over the preceding quarter.

The prominent occurrence for the quarter was the order issued by the Board concerning the wrapping of bread. This order was to go into effect July 1st, and immediately met with a fierce protest from wholesale bakers. On May 24th an appointment was made to meet the bakers and to listen to an array of facts they had to present and any argument they had to make. About fifty bakers from different parts of the State were present, and they were represented by Attorney Hornbrook. He presented a brief, which was duly made of record. An order was passed to make an investigation in the laboratory and to listen to brief in rebuttal by Mr. Barnard. The date appointed for this hearing was June 2d. Mr. Barnard's experiments and argument seemed not to establish a firm basis for the wrapping order, and, therefore, the said order was suspended until January 1, 1911, and a second order issued that a committee composed of the State Health Commissioner, the State Food and Drug Commissioner and a person appointed by the bakers, to further examine into the matter and report the experiments, conclusions and recommendations to the Board at its regular meeting, in October.

SMALLPOX COMPARISON FOR SECOND QUARTER, 1910.

DATE.	Number Cases Reported.	Number Deaths.	Number Counties Invaded.
April, 1909	74	1	18
April, 1910	81	0	18
May, 1909	88	1	13
May, 1910	89	0	14
June, 1909	103	0	41
June, 1910	75	0	23
Total, 1909	265	2	72
Total, 1910	245	0	55

TYPHOID FEVER COMPARISON FOR SECOND QUARTER, 1910.

DATE.	Number Cases Reported.	Number Deaths.	Number Counties Invaded.
April, 1909	58	33	24
April, 1910	112	32	32
May, 1909	80	35	22
May, 1910	92	26	33
June, 1909	125	34	27
June, 1910	91	27	31
Total, 1909	263	102	73
Total, 1910	295	85	96

The Secretary made the following visits:

April 10th, Sullivan; April 12th, Connersville; April 13th, Rockville; April 17th, Columbia City; April 18th, Ft. Wayne; April 19th, Huntington; April 25th, Columbus; May 20th, Tipton; May 31st, Acton; June 6th, St. Louis; June 12th, Danville; June 20th, Richmond.

Full detailed accounts of these visits are given herewith:

Sullivan, April 10th—On this date I went to Sullivan upon invitation of the Young Men's Christian Association, to deliver a lecture and also a sermon upon public health affairs. My lecture was upon the "Prevention and Cure of Tuberculosis." The sermon, delivered in the Methodist Church, was upon the work of the State Board of Health.

Connersville, April 12th—Upon this date, because of invitation of the superintendent of schools, representing the Municipal Club,

I went to Connersville to deliver a lecture upon "Disease Transmitted Through Insects." The illustrated lecture was given in the lecture room of the Carnegie Library. A large audience was present. The slides which illustrated the lecture were left with the school superintendent for further use. A resolution of thanks was passed.

Being there, I was requested by the county superintendent and the trustee of Harrison Township, Fayette County, to inspect the school known as District No. 1, Harrison Township, Fayette County. I made said inspection in company with the gentlemen named, and recommended a new building. Thereupon, the gentlemen promised that a new building would be constructed and, therefore, it was unnecessary to bring the matter before the State Board of Health.

Ft. Wayne, April 17th—This visit was made for the purpose of addressing an audience at Ft. Wayne, at Columbia City and at Huntington. All of the lectures were upon the work of the State Board of Health. Attendance in each city was good. When at Columbia City, in company with the county health officer and county superintendent, visits were made to three country schoolhouses. Upon consultation with the county superintendent and the trustees, promises were made that the schoolhouses which were visited would be promptly replaced by new ones, and this is being done at this writing.

Our tuberculosis exhibit was displayed at Columbia City for two days and one evening. The evening it was there the usual illustrated lecture upon "The Prevention and Cure of Tuberculosis" was given. At Huntington, in company with the mayor and the city health officer and the county health officer, full inspection of the town was made. Richmond is certainly the most clean and sanitary city in the State, and the second in cleanliness and sanitation is Huntington.. At this city I spoke to the high school students and also to a public audience, the subjects being the usual ones of the work of the State Board of Health and the need of public sanitation, etc.

Columbus, April 25th—On this date I went to Columbus, to deliver the usual illustrated lecture upon the "Prevention and Cure of Tuberculosis." A large audience in the Methodist Church attended the lecture and resolutions of commendation and thanks were passed.

Tipton, May 20th—The object of the visit to Tipton was to consult with the school board in regard to certain improvements to be made in the high school, and also to attend the meeting of the Ninth Councilor District Medical Society. The improvements for the schoolhouse were agreed upon and are now being installed. The medical meeting was a success. I took part in the discussions and also read my paper, entitled "The New Hygiene."

Acton, May 31st—This visit was made to inspect the schoolhouse at Acton. A report of the same has been given in detail, and presented to the Board June 2d, and schoolhouse was duly condemned.

St. Louis, June 2d—This visit was made by the direction of the Board to represent the Board in the Section on Preventive Medicine and Public Health of the American Medical Association. I had been made chairman of this Section in June, 1909. The Section meeting extended over four days. There were twenty-five papers. All of them were read and fully discussed. The meeting was a success in every particular. I feel confident I was much profited by attending this Section and hope that good will flow from it on behalf of the State.

Danville, June 12th—This visit was made to meet with the town authorities and the school authorities and to speak at the Danville Normal College. The object of the meeting with the authorities named was to help in the building of a new schoolhouse. All the phases of the situation were discussed and finally there was a unanimous agreement as to what should be done, which would be a remodeling of the schoolhouse. The plans were approved, and at this writing the said improvements are being made.

Richmond, June 20th—This visit was made to attend the annual session of the Municipal League of Indiana. I had been appointed to speak upon "Public Health and Commissioned Government and Sewerage." There was the usual good attendance at this meeting. I was cordially received and the discussions of my paper were commendatory. The Municipal League of Indiana has for its members the mayors and officers of the cities of the State.

Ordered: That the Secretary's report be received and spread of record.

Resolution offered by Dr. Davis, seconded by Dr. Wishard—

Resolved, By the State Board of Health of Indiana, that from and after this date, any bill for an act, contemplating amendments or additions to the present health laws, and food and drug laws of the State, emanating from, prepared or advocated by any member of this Board or any subordinate officer or employe, shall be presented to this Board for its consideration at a regular meeting, prior to its being submitted for legislative action. And further

Resolved, That a copy of this resolution be posted in each Department of the State Board of Health.

Unanimously carried.

STEAM CAR HYGIENE.

Judge Leo J. Hackney, general counsel C., C., C. & St. L. R. R., Cincinnati, wrote a letter to the State Board of Health, in which he entered into the importance of securing a uniform anti-spit notice from the Boards of Health in all States in which the Big Four system did business. The argument for the anti-spit notice is very plain. Judge Hackney also prepared a notice, which he thought would answer for all States, and promised, if the various State Boards of Health would pass the said notice, or rule, that the same would be posted in all of the cars of the Big Four Railroad and the company would enforce the same. The notice proposed by Judge Hackney reads as follows:

NOTICE.

Spitting Prohibited.

Penalties are prescribed by law for violating the public health laws, which forbid persons from expectorating (spitting) upon the floors, platforms, walls or furnishings of railway stations, waiting rooms and cars. This company will enforce such regulations.

After duly considering this notice, the same was adopted, in addition to the notice already passed, and which is found in the rules of the Indiana State Board of Health governing the sanitation of steam railway coaches, interurban cars, and city street cars, the same having been passed July 7, 1905. Either notice may be used.

CONDEMNATION EXTENDED.

North Grove Schoolhouse, District No. 5, Harrison Township, Miami County.

The Secretary read the following letter:

NORTH GROVE, Indiana, July 6, 1910.

State Board of Health, Indianapolis, Ind.:

Dear Sirs—Whereas, the schoolhouse at North Grove, Miami County, Ind., otherwise known as School District No. 5, has been condemned and ordered not to be used for school purposes after June 10, 1910, we, the undersigned, would ask you to extend the time for the condemnation to become effective to June 10, 1911, for the following reasons:

The time is too short from now till the beginning of school to erect a building, such as will be necessary at this place. The best architects and contractors as a rule, are employed earlier in the season.

We would be more likely to get an inferior architect and, consequently, inferior work. If given time to build until next year, we will be able to investigate more thoroughly other buildings and plans, thus enabling us to build a much better house.

We wish as much as possible to avoid mistakes in the construction of the school which might be injurious to the pupils' health in later years.

Very truly yours,

HARLEN E. PLOTNER.
SILAS GERLER.
F. GERHART.
P. C. STINEMAN, Trustee.

After consideration, the following order was adopted:

Ordered: That the date of condemnation of the North Grove schoolhouse, Miami County, be extended to June 1, 1911.

COMMITTEE REPRESENTING BUTCHERS.

A committee, representing the Indianapolis Butchers' Association, called and petitioned the Board "to repeal the order requiring that all meats shall be kept under glass cases or glass-doored refrigerators. The committee stated the city ordinance, requiring the meats to be kept as above, had been declared null and void by the court, because the city council did not have the power to make such legislation. An argument was presented to the effect that it was impracticable to handle meats in full accord with the Board's rule.

The rule referred to was Circular Letter No. 8, approved April 8, 1910. As this circular does not command that all fresh meats shall at all times be kept in refrigerators, but must be, if displayed for sale, properly protected by glass, wood, or metal cases, therefore no action was taken.

The butchers composing the committee were: William P. Cook, Charles Knarzer, Samuel Davis, John R. Schilling and Henry Dormand, all of Indianapolis.

The following schoolhouses were condemned:

Sanitary survey of schoolhouse, District No. 3, Fairview Township, Fayette County, by R. H. Elliott, County Health Commissioner, July 1, 1910.

Site.—The site is a small lot, 150 x 105 feet. Lot is fairly well drained. Stone walks lead from road to the well and to the front door. No walks to the outhouses. Outhouses within 20 feet of each other, without screens and both in bad condition.

Exterior of Building.—Frame, one story and one room, 31 feet long. 21 feet wide and 10 feet 8 inches high, inside measurements. Contains 12 single and 12 double desks, which have been in use for many years. Heated by a stove placed in the middle of the room, with some desks very close to it. Three windows on each side, each 7 x 3 feet. Blackboards made of wood and simply painted with ordinary black paint. They are very poor and rough. Floor in good condition. No hall to the building; rests on pillars, four on each side, and plenty of air space to keep the floor cool.

I recommend that the building be condemned.

After consideration of the above, the following proclamation of condemnation was adopted:

PROCLAMATION OF CONDEMNATION.

Whereas, It has been shown to the satisfaction of the State Board of Health, that the schoolhouse known as District No. 3, Fairview Township, Fayette County, Ind., is insanitary, and consequently threatens the health and life of the pupils, and also interferes with their efficiency; therefore, it is

Ordered: That said schoolhouse known as District No. 3, Fairview Township, Fayette County, Ind., is condemned for school purposes and shall not be used for said school purposes after June 1, 1911, and if any school trustee, or trustees, any teacher or any person uses said schoolhouse for school purposes, or teaches therein, after the date above mentioned, he or she or they shall be prosecuted.

Any person mutilating or tearing down this proclamation shall be prosecuted.

Passed by the State Board of Health, July 8, 1910.

Sanitary survey of schoolhouse and lot No. 9, West River Township, Randolph County, Ind. (Modoc School). by Grant C. Markle, County Health Commissioner.

Site.—The lot is 310 feet by 242 feet. High on east line, with a 20-degree slope to the west side. Natural drainage good.

Exterior of Building.—A one-story, frame building painted white, with belfry over the main entrance. The walls are in good condition. The roof leaks badly over main entrance. There is no basement.

Interior of Building.—The interior of building consists of three rooms. 2 halls and 2 cloakrooms, as shown by drawing. The walls are in good condition. Part of the ceiling in hall No. 1 and room 2 is discolored from the leak in the belfry. Blackboards are painted on the walls and extend around the rooms as shown in drawing. Single desks. Rooms ventilated by windows and transoms over doors.

Outhouses.—The outhouses are two in number, 10 feet by 6 feet situated at the north side of the lot. They are old and dilapidated, have no screens, no walks leading to them, and no fence between them.

Water Supply.—A good quality of water from a driven well supplied to the children in tin cups.

Remarks.—The building is heated by natural gas and it is impossible to keep the rooms at 70 degrees in zero weather. This building and outbuildings are undoubtedly insanitary and unfit for school purposes and I recommend that they be condemned.

After consideration of the above, the following proclamation of condemnation was adopted:

PROCLAMATION OF CONDEMNATION.

Whereas, It has been shown to the satisfaction of the State Board of Health, that the schoolhouse, District No. 9, West River Township, Randolph County, Ind., Modoc School, is insanitary, and consequently threatens the health and life of the pupils, and also interferes with their efficiency; therefore, it is

Ordered: That said schoolhouse, District No. 9, West River Township, Randolph County, Modoc School, is condemned for school purposes, and shall not be used for said school purposes after June 1, 1911, and if any school trustee, or trustees, any teacher or any person uses said schoolhouse for school purposes, or teaches therein, after the date above mentioned, he or she or they shall be prosecuted.

Any person mutilating or tearing down this proclamation shall be prosecuted.

Passed by the State Board of Health, July 8, 1910.

Sanitary inspection of schoolhouse, District No. 2, Patoka Township, Crawford County, Ind., July 27, 1910, by Dr. C. D. Luckett, County Health Commissioner.

Site.—The school grounds are flat, not properly drained. When dry, they are good, when wet they are bad. No walks to school building or from building to the closets—which are bad and unscreened, filthy, and no vaults.

Building.—The building is one story, shingle roof, 18 x 32 feet; and 56 children enumerated there for winter term. Weatherboarding is rotten in places. Three small windows on west side and three on east side. Blackboard across south end. Door in north end. You can see through the roof in places.

Stove in center of room. The ceiling is lumber, but part of it is off. Floor worn through. Bad flue. House built in 1877.

I recommend to the State Board of Health that this building be condemned.

After consideration of the above, the following proclamation of condemnation was adopted:

PROCLAMATION OF CONDEMNATION.

Whereas, It has been shown to the satisfaction of the State Board of Health that the schoolhouse known as District No. 2, Patoka Township, Crawford County, Ind., is insanitary, and consequently threatens the health and life of the pupils, and also interferes with their efficiency; therefore, it is

Ordered: That said schoolhouse known as District No. 2, Patoka Township, Crawford County, Ind., is condemned for school purposes, and shall not be used for said school purposes after June 1, 1911, and if any school trustee, or trustees, any teacher or any person uses said schoolhouse for school purposes, or teaches therein after the date above mentioned, he or she or they shall be prosecuted.

Any person mutilating or tearing down this proclamation shall be prosecuted.

Passed by the State Board of Health, July 8, 1910.

REGULAR MEETING OF THE STATE BOARD OF HEALTH.

Called to order by President McCoy at 2 p. m., October 14, 1910.

Present: Drs. McCoy, Tucker, Davis, Hurty.

The President stated the meeting was to attend to the affairs of the fourth fiscal quarter and the third statistical quarter, both ending September 30, 1910.

The President called for the reading of the minutes of the Board. The same were read and approved in each particular action and as a whole.

The President called for the reading of the Secretary's report for the last quarter.

REPORT OF SECRETARY FOR QUARTER ENDING SEPTEMBER 30, 1910.

This is the last quarter of the fiscal year. The accounts of the State Board of Health for the year ending September 30 were promptly closed and legal settlement made with the Auditor of State.

The following sums from the different departments were returned to the general fund:

From office fund	$191 72
From laboratory of hygiene fund	90 95
From food and drugs fund	46 50
From water and sewage analysis fund	79 62
Receipt for boat, bought for use of water laboratory	50 00
Laboratory	50 00
Total amount from all sources returned	$458 79

The auditor has given his quietus for the accounts to the State Board of Health. The Secretary is of the opinion that a review of expenditures will show that the moneys appropriated by the legislature for public health work have been wisely and effectively spent.

There have been no special epidemics during the last quarter. The vital statistical reports show no improvement in the health or mortality over the corresponding quarter of last year. This is a little disappointing, for, of course, we hope each year to see a marked improvement.

The appearance of acute anterior poliomyelitis in the State for the quarter is to be reported. Four deaths from this disease have been reported. The disease appeared in the following counties: Adams, Huntington, Jay, Steuben, Allen, Wayne, Vigo, Marion and St. Joseph. It may have appeared also in other counties, but has not been reported. The Secretary recommends that some action be taken in regard to this transmissible disease, which is so fatal and so fearful in its results. It seems pertinent that this disease be placed upon the reportable, if not upon the quarantine list. The Board of Health of Ft. Wayne, upon recommendation from the Allen County Medical Society, has placed acute anterior poliomyelitis among the quarantinable diseases for that city.

During the last quarter, several instances have been reported where the enforcing of the law concerning the burial of those dead of cerebro spinal meningitis within twenty-four hours after death and the keeping of such burials private, has brought considerable protest. The Quarantine Law of 1903 commands that all persons dead from cerebro spinal meningitis, as well as those dead from certain other diseases, shall have private burial, and shall be buried within twenty-four hours after death. The Secretary recommends that an order be adopted by this Board that when deaths occur from cerebro spinal meningitis, the law shall be enforced only when the disease is epidemic. Obviously it is not at all necessary to hold a strictly private funeral within twenty-four hours after death in a case of traumatic cerebro spinal meningitis, or in case of the same disease which is of tubercular origin. Surely, only the epidemic form should be considered.

The following tables show the status of smallpox and typhoid fever for the third quarter:

SMALLPOX COMPARISON FOR THIRD QUARTER, ENDING SEPTEMBER, 1910.

Date.	Number Cases Reported.	Number Deaths.	Number Counties Invaded.
July, 1909	61	2	8
July, 1910	0	0	0
August, 1909	26	0	2
August, 1910	6	0	3
September, 1909	51	0	9
September, 1910	1	0	1
Total, 1909	140	2	23
Total, 1910	7	0	4

TYPHOID FEVER COMPARISON FOR THIRD QUARTER, ENDING SEPTEMBER, 1910.

Date.	Number Cases Reported.	Number Deaths.	Number Counties Invaded.
July, 1909	267	78	60
July, 1910	246	45	47
August, 1909	464	106	69
August, 1910	446	123	74
September, 1909	757	132	81
September, 1910	800	158	83
Total, 1909	1,488	316	200
Total, 1910	1,492	326	204

VISITS.

On account of vacation and also on account of absence of demand from the people, only one visit was made by the Secretary during the quarter. The following visit was made:

September 29-30, Ft. Wayne, account of the annual meeting of the State Medical Society. As representative of the State Board, the Secretary duly presented his notice of appointment to the Secretary of the Society. The meeting lasted for three days, namely, September 28, 29, 30, although I attended the two last days only. The program was an excellent one and the meeting was an excellent success. The President, Thomas Kennedy, in his address, made complimentary mention of the work of the State Board of Health and recommended that all physicians and citizens give the Board their hearty support. This was the only point in the address that received applause from the audience, and being the only applause tendered, it is here recorded, as perhaps significant. The House of Delegates adopted resolutions recommending a liberal appropriation for the maintenance of the State Tuberculosis Hospital at Rockville. Also a resolution recommending the passage of a law for the control of ophthalmia neonatorum, also a resolution recommending a State Hospital for inebriates.

The Secretary was elected first vice-president for the coming year.

VISITS BY DR. KING.

Dr. W. F. King commenced work with the Board as Deputy State Health Commissioner, August 1st. The first month of service he spent in the different departments, in order to become familiar with their work. He also made several visits, as follows:

SPECIAL REPORT OF DR. W. F. KING.

August 4th.—Went to Frankfort, Indiana, accompanied by H. E. Bishop. Met Dr. C. A. Zinn, Clinton County Health Commissioner. Together we inspected the killing establishment of the Milner Provision Company and found the following insanitary conditions existing in violation of the law: Building, except the cooling room, old and extremely dilapidated; surroundings insanitary; building not properly screened; floors and side walls dirty and filthy; decaying animal matter, bones, entrails, sheep pelts, etc., in the killing room; hogs being fed on offal; improper and insufficient drainage; no provision for employes washing their hands or keeping themselves clean; a surface closet used by the employes, situated within twenty-five feet of the killing room, said closet being open and unscreened. It being deemed impossible to put this building in a proper sanitary condition by any amount of "cleaning up," the Milner Provision Company was ordered to cease killing in this building and advised the construction of a new slaughter house to comply with the law. Also inspected the dairy of Mr. D. F. Maish and the plant of the Atkinson Reduction Company. Both were found in good condition, with some minor suggestions made for improvement. Inspected the books and records of Dr. Zinn, County Commissioner, which were found in splendid condition.

August 9, 1910.—Ft. Wayne, Ind., accompanied by H. E. Barnard, at the request of Dr. A. P. Buchman, President Ft. Wayne Board of Health. Made a sanitary survey of the sewer system of the city, with special reference to the sewage outlet of the Institution for Feeble-Minded and the proposed improvement of the rivers in Ft. Wayne. Held a conference with the Ft. Wayne Board of Works, inspected the killing establishment of Wilkinson Brothers and the packing establishment of The Eckhart Company.

August 17, 1910.—Went to Greensburg, Ind., to investigate a complaint of a nuisance in connection with the St. John & Guthrie drug store. Made an inspection in company with Dr. Hitt, City Health Officer, and Dr. Weaver, County Commissioner. Ordered the nuisance abated by tearing down the closet building and filling the vault. Made a sanitary inspection of a Greek ice cream manufactory and the Menzies meat market, ordering some changes in both places. Inspected the books and records of Dr. Weaver, County Commissioner, which were found in most excellent shape.

August 18, 1910.—Went to Winslow, Pike County, in response to a petition from a number of citizens in regard to the proposed location of a new schoolhouse. Met the township trustee with a number of interested citizens, inspected the proposed site, which was deemed insanitary and unfit, and issued a condemnation order against it. The trustee agreed to purchase a new site, which was deemed satisfactory, and begin the construction of a new school building at once. Met the town health officer, Dr. Bethell, and made a sanitary inspection of the town with him. A number of suggestions were made which will be of benefit.

August 31, 1910.—Went to Newcastle, Ind., accompanied by Dr. Will Shimer, to investigate the typhoid situation in that city. Made a sanitary inspection of the city in company with Dr. Brubaker, County Commissioner, and Dr. Ruddel, of the City Board of Health. Reported the findings of this investigation to Dr. Simonds, of the Pathological Laboratory, for further investigation. Made a strong recommendation in regard to Bowery Creek in the city of Newcastle, which it is reported has since been acted upon. Also inspected the Jersey Creamery Company, where several conditions were found which were ordered changed.

September 11, 1910.—Went to New Harmony, Ind., to have charge, with Mr. John Owens, of the tuberculosis exhibit at the

Posey County Fair. The exhibit was in place here from September 12th to September 15th, and was visited by several thousand people, who were much interested in the descriptions and lectures given and much good was accomplished.

Secretary's report was approved and ordered spread of record in the minutes.

Motion by Dr. McCoy:

Whereas, The disease known as anterior poliomyelitis is becoming more prevalent all over the country and its contagiousness being an accepted fact; therefore, be it

Resolved, That anterior poliomyelitis shall be added to the list of diseases known as dangerous to public health and be reported to the local health officers the same as other diseases listed in Rule 10 of the Rules of the Indiana State Board of Health, and each case reported shall be carded with a warning card and discharges from patients shall be disinfected.

Unanimously adopted.

Ordered: The Secretary shall prepare a pamphlet upon acute anterior poliomyelitis and submit the same for approval to the President, and when approved the same shall be printed and distributed.

REPORT TO THE STATE BOARD OF HEALTH OF THE COMMITTEE OF THREE APPOINTED TO CONSIDER THE QUESTION OF BREAD WRAPPING AND THE SANITARY DISTRIBUTION OF BREAD.

We, your committee, after taking into consideration the aroused interest of bakers in the sanitary operation of bakeries and the distribution of baker's products, the adoption of improved and efficient methods of protecting such goods, and the impracticability of wrapping certain varieties of bread in paper wrappers because of the effect upon the distribution of moisture, recommend that the section relating to the wrapping of bread as found in lines 27 to 35 inclusive of Circular Letter No. 7, be stricken out and the following section be substituted therefor:

For the guidance of bakers it is ordered that all bakers' products be delivered to the consumer or to distributing points under the following conditions, to wit:

1. The delivery wagon shall be covered and provided with substantial protection from dirt and dust both in front and rear, and the interior shall be kept clean, brushed thoroughly before loading, and at least once each week scrubbed with a suitable cleaner and hot water.

2. The wagon shall be loaded in a room or place securely protected from flies and the dust and dirt of the street, and separate and apart from the stable, and the loaded wagon shall be drawn to the outside of the loading room before horses are attached.

3. The delivery men or employes who load the wagons shall be clothed in clean suits, and shall not pile bread against their bodies, nor shall they engage in any stable work before loading and distributing bakery products unless they change their clothing and wash their hands and arms after such work.

4. The baskets or the containers used for delivering bakery products to the consumer or distributing point shall be thoroughly clean and shall be sterilized at least once a week.

5. The delivery men shall be clothed in clean suits and shall remove driving gloves before handling bakery products. They shall be cleanly in habits and person and shall not engage in work while afflicted with any venereal or contagious disease or while any member of their family is held in quarantine.

It is the opinion of your committee that the observance of the above instructions, while not producing such ideal sanitary conditions as would be secured by the protection of the individual loaf, and although the care and control of the products after they leave the delivery wagon and while they are in the possession of the distributor is not regulated thereby, will insure the distribution of bakers' goods in a better, cleaner and more healthful condition than has been obtained in the past and that these instructions, if carefully followed, will in a measure, provide an acceptable substitute for the original order.

(Signed) A. L. TAGGART.
H. E. BARNARD.
J. N. HURTY, Chairman.

After due consideration of this report is was

Ordered: The "Notice to Bakers," passed April 8, 1910, as found in the minutes of the Board, shall be amended by striking out lines 27, 28, 29, 30, 31, 32, 33, 34, 35, the same being hereby repealed, and the following adopted in their stead.

For the guidance of bakers it is ordered that all bakers' products be delivered to the consumer or to distributing points under the following conditions, to wit:

1. The delivery wagon shall be covered and provided with substantial protection from dirt and dust both in front and rear, and the interior shall be kept clean, brushed thoroughly before loading, and at least once each week scrubbed with a suitable cleaner and hot water.

2. The wagons while being loaded shall be securely protected from flies and the dust and dirt of the street, and separate and apart from the stable.

3. The delivery men or employes who load the wagons shall be clothed in clean suits, and shall not pile bread against their bodies, nor shall they engage in any stable work before loading and distributing bakery products unless they change their clothing and wash their hands and arms after such work.

4. The baskets or the containers used for delivering bakery products to the consumer or distributing point shall be thoroughly clean and shall be sterilized at least once a week.

5. The delivery men shall be clothed in clean suits and shall remove driving gloves before handling bakery products. They shall be cleanly in habits and person and shall not engage in work while afflicted with any venereal or contagious disease, or while any member of their family is held in quarantine.

COMMUNICATION FROM MR. BARNARD.

OCTOBER 14, 1910.

Indiana State Board of Health:

Gentlemen—I beg leave to call to the attention of your honorable board the following matters which have to do with the needs and policies of the Food, Drug and Water Departments of the Laboratory of Hygiene:

1. Section 3 of the Pure Food Law of 1907 has been declared invalid by the Supreme Court and it is therefore impossible to convict proprietors who sell adulterated milk. This section should be amended by inserting in line 1, after the word "by," the word "himself."

2. It has been impossible to stop the traffic in rotten and decayed eggs because of the fact that Section 4 of the Pure Food Law was so amended at the time of its passage as to specifically regulate the sale of eggs and to declare unlawful the sale, *knowingly* of eggs unfit for food. This section should be amended by striking out the sentence, "It shall be unlawful for any person, firm or corporation to sell or offer for sale any eggs, after the same have been placed in an incubator, or to sell or offer for sale, knowingly, eggs in a rotten, decayed or decaying condition to be used for food.

3. It is apparent from the reports of inspectors that gross fraud is practiced in the sale of foods by dealers who use short weights and measures, or who, ignoring the customary standards, sell by the cup, basket or package in such a way as to make it impossible for the customer to determine the true value of his purchase. The subject of true weights and measures is commanding widespread attention and it is highly desirable that, anticipating the call for legislation along these lines, the work of the inspectors of the State Board of Health be so extended as to give them authority to seal weights and measures and prosecute those who fraudulently use them.

This can only be done by legislative act and I therefore suggest to your honorable board the careful consideration of the subject.

4. Since the resignation of Mr. Wm. D. McAbee the laboratory force has been insufficient to care for the work. This is especially true of the Water Laboratory, where it has been impossible to meet the demands for water analyses in cases of suspected typhoid infection. This condition can only be remedied by employing additional assistants, an impossibility under the present appropriations.

The work of inspection is growing rapidly in importance and in spite of the increased interest of health officers in the sanitary conditions surrounding the protection and distribution of the food supply, it is quite impossible to meet the demands for inspection work with our present force. I recommend that an additional appropriation sufficient to enable the Board to employ two more inspectors be asked of the incoming legislature.

5. Mr. Cullen Thomas has been employed at the Laboratory of Hygiene for the past 15 months at a salary of $25.00 per month. Mr. Thomas has proved himself faithful and efficient and I recommend that his salary be increased from $25.00 to $30.00 per month.

6. In view of the apparent impossibility at the present time of securing the co-operation of the baking industry in our efforts to regulate the sanitary distribution of bread by the baker and the grocer through the use of a paper wrapper, I recommend the substitution of the attached circular letter for Circular Letter No. 7, which was approved by your president and secretary April 8, 1910.

This notice obviously does not regulate the grocer's methods of handling bakers' goods nor insure the delivery of a clean loaf to the consumer, but it seems to satisfy the ideas of the bakers as to their duties in the premises, and is suggested for that purpose.

Ordered: The above recommendations adopted and authority given to the Secretary and State Food and Drug Commissioner to execute the same.

FIFTH ANNUAL REPORT

OF THE

DIVISION OF

BACTERIOLOGY AND PATHOLOGY OF THE STATE LABORATORY OF HYGIENE

FOR THE ELEVEN MONTHS ENDING SEPTEMBER 30, 1910.

J. P. SIMONDS, A. B., M. D.,
Superintendent.

WM. SHIMER, A. B., M. D.,
Assistant Superintendent.

ADA E. SCHWEITZER, M. D.,
Assistant Bacteriologist.

HERVEY M. HOOKER,
Clerk and Stenographer.

ROBERT P. JOHNSON,
Technical Assistant.

F. R. BANNON,
Assistant.

FIFTH ANNUAL REPORT OF THE DEPARTMENT OF BACTERIOLOGY AND PATHOLOGY OF THE INDIANA STATE LABORATORY OF HYGIENE.

The results of the work of the Bacteriological Laboratory during the past year have been very satisfactory in every respect. During the eleven months—November, 1909, to September, 1910, inclusive—covered by this report, 8,786 specimens were examined[1].

This number exceeds by almost 700 the largest number examined in any one whole year during the previous history of the laboratory, as is shown by Table I.

TABLE I.

SHOWING COMPARISON OF WORK OF THREE YEARS.

Nature of Specimen.	12 Months. 1908.	12 Months. 1909.	11 Months. 1910.
Sputum	3,136	3,458	3,583
Throat cultures	2,779	1,445	1,638
Widal reaction	1,270	1,508	1,404
Suspected malaria	167	194	189
Pathological tissues	165	187	309
Brains of animals for rabies	82	144	134
Suspected gonorrhea	178	349	430
Miscellaneous	310	666	1,099
Total	8,087	7,951	8,786

This table also shows that the growth has been uniform and has affected almost every department of our work. The number of specimens of blood examined for the Widal reaction is slightly less than last year, although typhoid fever has been more prevalent during the past summer than for many years. The number of throat cultures examined in 1908 exceeded by over 1,100 those examined during the past eleven months. But in that year a little less than 1,000 cultures were taken in wholesale school inspections, while less than 300 such cultures were received during the latter period. The total number of throat cultures received dur-

[1] Before this report left the Laboratory the total number of specimens examined in October, 1910, was known. This was 1,305, which makes a total of 10,091 for the twelve months, an increase of 2,004 over the largest number of any previous year.

ing the past eleven months shows a creditable increase, however. over those examined in 1909.

There has been no change in the laboratory staff during the year. Dr. Wm. Shimer and Dr. Ada E. Schweitzer continue to render excellent service, their efficiency increasing with experience. Mr. R. P. Johnson is still doing valuable service as Technical Assistant. In addition to his other duties, he has, by his efficient care of the laboratory animals, raised 118 guinea pigs, thus saving the Department more than $60.

The work of the State Bacteriological Laboratory may be conveniently classified under four heads: (1) routine, clinical examinations; (2) investigation of epidemics and other matters of public health; (3) research work of a more purely scientific nature, and (4) personal work in an effort to bring the Laboratory into closer touch with physicians and health officers.

An extended analysis of the routine, clinical examinations and reports of investigations of epidemics will be given below.

As an indication of the efforts at scientific research work by members of the laboratory staff may be mentioned the following papers which have either been published or have been accepted and will soon appear in medical journals: By Dr. Simonds, "Some Facts Concerning Diphtheria Revealed by Laboratory Examinations"[2]; "Trichinosis"[3]; "Three Years of Rabies in Indiana"[4]; "Practical Considerations on the Bacteriology of the Gastro-intestinal Tract"[5]; "Typhoid Bacilli Carriers and Their Relation to the Public Health"[6]; "Sarcoma and Tuberculosis"[7]; "Serum Diagnosis of Syphilis"[8].

Dr. Shimer has contributed the following articles: "The Tuberculin Ophthalmo-reaction, with an Analysis of the Results of 132 Tests"[9], and "Blood Cultures in Typhoid Fever"[10].

The following papers have been written by Dr. Schweitzer: "Gonorrhea in Children"[11], and "Malaria in Indiana"[12].

The work on which these papers were based was done voluntarily, often at considerable personal sacrifice of time, frequently

[2] Jour. Ind. State Med. Assn., January, 1910.
[3] Indianapolis Med. Jour., April, 1910.
[4] N. Y. Medical Record, June 4, 1910.
[5] Jour. Ind. State Med. Assn., May, 1910.
[6] Amer. Jour. of the Med. Sciences, August, 1910.
[7] Bulletin of the Johns Hopkins Hospital. (To appear soon.)
[8] Jour. Ind. State Med. Assn. (To appear soon.)
[9] Indianapolis Med. Journal.
[10] Jour. Ind. State Med. Assn. (To appear soon.)
[11] Indianapolis Med. Jour., June, 1910.
[12] Jour. Ind. State Med. Assn. (To appear soon.)

under more or less difficulties, but always with enthusiasm and perseverance. Several problems are now being investigated by members of the Laboratory staff, the results of which will probably be published during the coming year. Much more work of a similar nature but of even greater value could be done if the Laboratory had more room.

At the present rate of increase the present cramped quarters will soon be inadequate for even the routine clinical examinations. Not only are we too crowded for the most effective work, but the necessity of keeping laboratory animals in the same room where the work is done is exceedingly disagreeable. If the Laboratory is to continue to grow and to increase its usefulness to the physicians and citizens of Indiana, more commodious quarters are absolutely necessary.

In an effort to bring the work of the State Laboratory into closer touch with the physicians of the State, members of the Laboratory staff have visited county and district medical societies, in all instances being on the program either to read a paper or take part in some discussion. In this way, the physicians of about twenty county societies and of six councillor district societies have, during the year, learned at first hand something of the work of the State Laboratory. Three of the papers read at the last meeting of the Indiana State Medical Association were by members of the laboratory staff. This has been a very efficient means of extending the usefulness of the laboratory.

The forces now at work in Indiana in the interest of the public health constitute an organic whole. The highest degree of efficiency can only be secured by active and consistent co-operation between the constituent parts. Hence it has been our policy to do everything in our power to bring about more intimate and mutually helpful relations and greater co-operation between the Bacteriological Laboratory and the local and county health officers. To this end, the work of the laboratory has been explained in some detail to those attending the Annual Health Officers' School, and the lines of mutual helpfulness and more effective co-operation have been pointed out. We have also made special effort to keep health officers supplied with regulation mailing outfits for distribution among the physicians in their communities.

An analysis of the routine examinations follows:

TUBERCULOSIS.

During the past eleven months 3,583 samples of sputum were examined, an increase of 125 over the preceding twelve months. Of these, 1,059, or 29.5 per cent., were found to contain tubercle bacilli. Table II shows the number of specimens received by months.

TABLE II.

SHOWING THE NUMBER OF SPECIMENS OF SPUTUM EXAMINED BY MONTHS.

Month.	Positive.	Negative.	Totals.
November	81	209	290
December	78	183	261
January	70	203	273
February	82	247	329
March	107	351	458
April	111	240	351
May	113	266	379
June	112	251	363
July	93	190	283
August	116	209	325
September	96	175	271
Totals	1,059	2,524	3,583

As pointed out last year, the number of positive sputa was largest during the spring months and smallest in mid-winter. This is probably due to two causes: (1) The indoor life and the miserable ventilation of houses in the winter begin to show their effects at this season of the year. (2) The "common cold," looked upon as a matter-of-course during the winter months, does not disappear with the advent of spring and arouses sufficient fear of "something more serious" to send the patient to a physician.

The number of specimens of sputum received from each county is shown in Table III.

TABLE III.

SHOWING THE NUMBER OF SPECIMENS OF SPUTUM FROM EACH COUNTY.

	Pos.	Neg.	Total.		Pos.	Neg.	Total.
Adams	5	14	19	Lawrence	10	14	24
Allen	6	21	27	Madison	28	85	113
Bartholomew	23	27	50	Marion	128	375	503
Benton	8	17	25	Marshall	8	27	35
Blackford	10	14	24	Martin	14	14	28
Boone	18	30	48	Miami	18	24	42
Brown	..	1	1	Monroe	..	..	..
Carroll	5	18	23	Montgomery	10	39	49
Cass	6	13	19	Morgan	8	32	40
Clark	2	15	17	Newton	2	4	6
Clay	14	12	26	Noble	6	24	30
Clinton	15	30	45	Ohio	3	2	5
Crawford	2	4	6	Orange	1	7	8
Daviess	12	30	42	Owen	4	10	14
Dearborn	9	14	23	Parke	5	13	18
Decatur	5	16	21	Perry	2	5	7
Dekalb	10	31	41	Pike	10	19	29
Delaware	25	75	100	Porter	..	1	1
Dubois	6	16	22	Posey	5	12	17
Elkhart	18	50	68	Pulaski	7	5	12
Fayette	7	10	17	Putnam	5	15	20
Floyd	20	17	37	Randolph	17	39	56
Fountain	3	18	21	Ripley	6	16	22
Franklin	5	6	11	Rush	13	23	36
Fulton	6	11	17	Scott	1	10	11
Gibson	3	11	14	Shelby	4	13	17
Grant	30	79	109	Spencer	12	20	32
Greene	16	31	47	Starke	..	9	9
Hamilton	16	41	57	Steuben	1	4	5
Hancock	30	42	72	St. Joseph	17	29	46
Harrison	5	12	17	Sullivan	4	4	8
Hendricks	45	51	96	Switzerland	2	6	8
Henry	16	26	42	Tippecanoe	11	30	41
Howard	15	54	69	Tipton	6	14	20
Huntington	11	36	47	Union	3	1	4
Jackson	23	31	54	Vanderburgh	38	94	132
Jasper	5	8	13	Vermillion	13	27	40
Jay	15	33	48	Vigo	29	70	99
Jefferson	8	17	25	Wabash	26	42	68
Jennings	11	15	26	Warren	3	8	11
Johnson	2	12	14	Warrick	..	1	1
Knox	9	27	36	Washington	7	17	24
Kosciusko	8	29	37	Wayne	27	103	130
Lagrange	9	35	44	Wells	3	21	24
Lake	10	31	41	White	4	21	25
Laporte	4	16	20	Whitley	7	28	35
Total	531	1,147	1,678	Total	528	1,377	1,905

Total, 3,583.

For obvious reasons, the largest number of specimens of sputum have come from those counties nearest the laboratory. The number of samples from many of the counties is too small for the percentage of positive results to have any real significance. However, four counties, from each of which more than fifty specimens were received, showed more than 40 per cent. positives, the average for the entire State being 29.2 per cent. These were Hendricks, 47 per cent.; Bartholomew, 46 per cent.; Jackson, 42 per cent., and Hancock, 41 per cent. Many of the specimens from Hendricks County were from patients in the Rockwood Sanitarium near Danville. Hence, the high percentage of positive results is hardly a fair indication of conditions in the county itself. No such factor enters into the results for the other three counties.

Of the 1,049 positive specimens, 1,022 were from patients whose ages were given by the physician. The analysis of these cases by ages is shown in Table IV.

TABLE IV.

SHOWING THE AGE AND SEX OF 1,022 POSITIVE CASES.

Age.	Males.	Females.	Total.
0 to 10 years	0	1	1
11 to 15 years	3	24	27
16 to 20 years	47	68	115
21 to 30 years	192	209	401
31 to 40 years	88	114	202
41 to 50 years	63	62	125
51 to 60 years	34	23	57
61 years and up	24	29	53
Age not given	21	20	41
Totals	472	550	1,022

The above table reveals two facts: (1) That tuberculosis is somewhat more common in women (54 per cent.) than in men (46 per cent.); (2) that the disease is more common in the most active and productive period of life. This latter fact is even more convincingly shown in Table V, from which it appears that nearly two-thirds of the positive specimens were from patients between the ages of 21 and 40.

TABLE V.

SHOWING THE RELATIVE INCIDENCE OF TUBERCULOSIS IN THE VARIOUS PERIODS OF LIFE.

(Based on 1,022 Positive Examinations.)

Age.	Per cent.
0 to 20 years	14.5
21 to 40 years	61.5
41 years and up	24.0

In 917 cases the physician made a definite statement concerning possible exposure of the patient. These cases are analyzed in Table VI, in which it is shown that in almost half (47 per cent.) of the cases there was no known source of the infection. These are the patients who inhaled the tubercle bacilli in the dust of the streets, of interurban and street cars and of buildings where careless consumptives have deposited their germ-laden sputum. Of the patients who had been definitely exposed to infection, in 46 per cent. some other member of the family had tuberculosis, while 7 per cent. had been more or less closely associated with persons who were tuberculous.

TABLE VI.

SHOWING THE RELATION OF EXPOSURE TO THE DEVELOPMENT OF TUBERCULOSIS.

Extent of Exposure.	Males.	Females.	Totals.	Per cent.
Tuberculosis in patient's family	170	252	422	46
Tuberculosis in patient's assoc.	26	39	65	7
No known source of infection	214	216	430	47
Totals	410	507	917	100

In Table VII is shown the relation of the other tuberculous member of the family in the cases of 558 patients whose physicians gave definite information on this point. The same facts are shown in a graphic way in Chart I. From this it seems that when the father has tuberculosis the son and daughter have about equal chances of contracting the disease, but when the mother is consumptive the chances of the daughter's becoming tuberculous are about twice as great as the son's. The reason for this is plain. The father's relations with his children are nothing like so intimate as the mother's; nor is the son so closely associated with his mother as is the daughter. The closer association of the latter is, furthermore, usually indoors where ventilation is often none too good and conditions are more favorable to the transference of

CHART 1. SHOWING RELATIVE CHANCES OF OTHER MEMBERS OF FAMILY TAKING TUBERCULOSIS FROM TUBERCULOUS PERSONS IN THE SAME FAMILY.

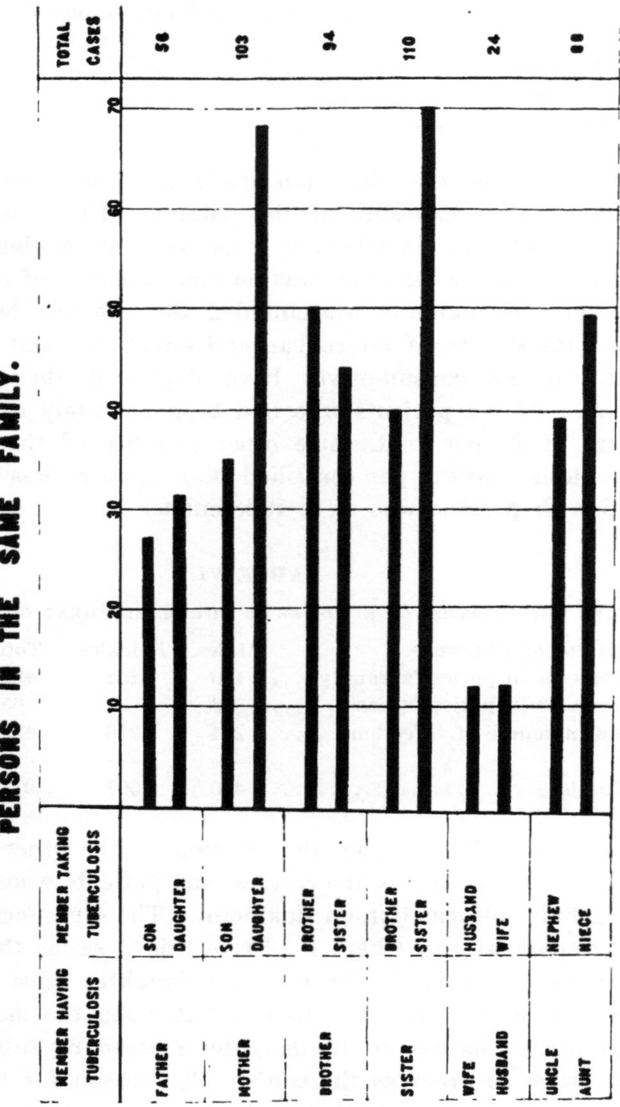

infection. When a brother has tuberculosis the chances of another brother's taking the disease are slightly larger than a sister's. But when a sister is tuberculous the chances of another sister's becoming so are nearly double a brother's. This variation is likewise explained by differences in the intimacy of association. The chances of the husband's taking the disease from his tuberculous wife are equal to the chances of the healthy wife taking it from her tuberculous husband. The chances of infection in the other instances cited in the Table and Chart are likewise proportional to the intimacy of association between the tuberculous and exposed persons.

TABLE VII.

SHOWING THE RELATION OF THE OTHER TUBERCULOSIS MEMBERS OF THE FAMILY TO THE PATIENT.

Member of family having tuberculosis.	Patients. Males.	Females.	Totals.
Father	27	29	56
Mother	35	68	103
Brother	50	44	94
Sister	40	70	110
Husband or wife	12	12	24
Uncle or aunt	39	49	88
Grandparents	13	21	34
Distant relatives	12	19	31
Children	6	12	18
Totals	234	324	558

Of the specimens of sputum examined in May, thirty-three were picked up at random on the streets. Of these, three, or 9 per cent., contained tubercle bacilli. All the positive specimens were found near the curbstone on the south side of Ohio Street just east of Illinois street. Two were found on the same day within half a block of each other. Both masses of sputum resembled each other very closely as they lay on the street and also as examined under the microscope. It is very likely that they both came from the same person. Had an attempt been made to do so, this careless disseminator of the germs of consumption could probably have been trailed for several blocks by these disgusting masses of purulent sputum. In both of these specimens the number of tubercle bacilli was enormous. This experiment is not new, but is a concrete example of the danger a careless consumptive may be to the public. It proves that there are such consumptives in Indianapolis.

DIPHTHERIA.

The total number of throat cultures examined was 1,634. Of these, 449, or 27.4 per cent., contained diphtheria bacilli. The number of cultures received each month is shown in Table VIII.

TABLE VIII.

SHOWING THE NUMBER OF THROAT CULTURES RECEIVED EACH MONTH.

Month.	Positive.	Negative.	Totals.
November	122	299	421
December	96	219	315
January	52	99	151
February	26	105	131
March	41	173	214
April	3	51	54
May	20	77	97
June	23	45	68
July	15	42	57
August	18	20	38
September	35	57	92
Totals	451	1,187	1,638

TABLE IX.

SHOWING THE NUMBER OF THROAT CULTURES RECEIVED FROM EACH COUNTY.

	Pos.	Neg.	Total.
Adams	..	..	..
Allen	..	1	1
Bartholomew ..	..	1	1
Benton	1	1	2
Blackford	..	2	2
Boone	1	..	1
Brown	..	..	..
Carroll	3	11	14
Cass	..	21	21
Clark	..	2	2
Clay	2	9	11
Clinton	..	3	3
Crawford	..	..	..
Daviess	3	4	7
Dearborn	5	2	7
Decatur	2	1	3
Dekalb	1	5	6
Delaware	17	35	52
Dubois	4	..	4
Elkhart	2	7	9
Fayette	2	5	7
Floyd	1	2	3
Fountain	..	4	4
Franklin	..	..	..
Fulton	1	2	3
Gibson	..	..	..
Grant	2	13	15
Greene	5	23	28
Hamilton	18	61	79
Hancock	5	5	10
Harrison	3	1	4
Hendricks	26	63	89
Henry	12	12	24
Howard	..	7	7
Huntington ...	..	4	4
Jackson	5	4	9
Jasper	1	3	4
Jay	..	..	..
Jefferson	5	6	11
Jennings	7	9	16
Johnson	..	4	4
Knox	17	28	45
Kosciusko	5	10	15
Lagrange	4	14	18
Lake	9	10	19
Laporte	..	2	2
Total	169	397	566

	Pos.	Neg.	Total.
Lawrence	1	..	1
Madison	71	235	306
Marion	16	111	127
Marshall	7	17	24
Martin	2	7	9
Miami	9	19	28
Monroe	..	..	..
Montgomery ...	4	5	9
Morgan	3	5	8
Newton	3	2	5
Noble	5	34	39
Ohio	..	..	..
Orange	6	3	9
Owen	5	1	6
Parke	6	2	8
Perry	..	1	1
Pike	12	14	26
Porter	11	59	70
Posey	1	2	3
Pulaski	2	1	3
Putnam	2	2	4
Randolph	15	28	43
Ripley	..	2	2
Rush	3	5	8
Scott	1	2	3
Shelby	21	68	89
Spencer	2	16	18
Starke	..	..	..
Steuben	..	..	..
St. Joseph	2	5	7
Sullivan	..	3	3
Switzerland ...	..	..	..
Tippecanoe	..	..	..
Tipton	5	7	12
Union	2	2	4
Vanderburgh ..	4	11	15
Vermillion	1	3	4
Vigo	25	28	53
Wabash	6	12	18
Warren	..	1	1
Warrick	..	..	..
Washington ...	2	1	3
Wayne	26	64	90
Wells	..	1	1
White	1	5	6
Whitley	..	6	6
Total	282	790	1,072

In Table IX, the number of cultures received from each county is shown.

Table X shows the age and sex of the patients in 251 positive first cultures. The influence of the crowding together of children in school is shown by the fact that more than 50 per cent. of these positive cases came from children between the ages of 6 and 14 years. Even more striking is the fact that 54 of these patients, i. e., 21.5 per cent., were between 6 and 8 years old. The oldest patient from whom a positive culture was received this year was 40 years.

TABLE X.

SHOWING THE AGE AND SEX IN 251 POSITIVE FIRST CULTURE CASES.

Age.	Males.	Females.	Totals.	Per cent.
Up to 5 years	33	18	51	20.4
6 to 14 years	64	64	128	51.0
15 to 20 years	11	18	29	11.5
21 to 40 years	17	26	43	17.1
Totals	125	126	251	100.0

In 983 cases the physician made some definite statement as to clinical diagnosis. The results of the comparison of the clinical and bacteriological diagnoses are shown in Tables XI and XII. From these tables it is seen that of 210 cases diagnosed diphtheria by the physician, only 116, or 55.2 per cent., proved positive.

TABLE XI.

SHOWING THE BACTERIOLOGICAL DIAGNOSIS IN 983 CASES IN WHICH THE CLINICAL DIAGNOSIS WAS STATED.

	Bacteriological Diagnosis.		
Clinical Diagnosis.	Positive.	Negative.	Totals
Diphtheria	116	94	210
Not diphtheria	98	507	605
Doubtful	44	124	168
Totals	258	725	983

TABLE XII.

SHOWING THE PERCENTAGE RELATION OF BACTERIOLOGICAL TO CLINICAL DIAGNOSIS.

	Bacteriological Diagnosis.	
Clinical Diagnosis.	Per Cent. Positive.	Per Cent. Negative.
Diphtheria	55.2	44.8
Not diphtheria	16.2	83.8
Doubtful	26.8	73.2

Of 605 cases diagnosed tonsillitis, ordinary sore throat, etc., i. e., "not diphtheria," 98, or 16.2 per cent., showed the bacilli in cultures. Out of 168 "doubtful" cases, 44, or 26.8 per cent., were found to be diphtheria. These figures furnish abundant proof of the well-known fact that it is frequently impossible to make an accurate diagnosis of diphtheria from the clinical picture alone. That the presence of a membrane or exudate is no absolute criterion in diagnosis is shown by Table XIII. From this it is seen that of 714 cases in which a membrane or exudate [13] was said to be present, only 213, or 30 per cent., were positive, while of 264 cases with no membrane or exudate, forty-two cultures, or 16 per cent., were found to contain diphtheria bacilli.

TABLE XIII.

SHOWING THE RELATION OF MEMBRANE OR EXUDATE TO BACTERIOLOGICAL FINDINGS.

Membrane or Exudate.	Bacteriological Diagnosis. Positive.	Negative.	Totals.
Present	213	501	714
Absent	42	222	264
Totals	255	723	978

Pointing out this high percentage of mistakes on the part of physicians in the diagnosis of diphtheria is not a criticism of the physicians themselves, especially not of those who for the greater safety of their patients give antitoxin when urgent clinical symptoms seem to justify its use, without waiting for a laboratory report. Such a course is to be highly commended. The facts stated above do prove, however, that a physician is not justified in depending solely on the clinical picture for final diagnosis when the results of a laboratory examination can be had within a reasonable time. This is especially important on account of the necessity of quarantine in cases of diphtheria. It is unjust to the patient and his family to place him in quarantine on a clinical diagnosis of diphtheria which, in almost 45 per cent. of the cases, is proved by bacteriological examination to be incorrect. On the other hand, it is not right to endanger the community by allowing a child to go about at will because the physician, on clinical data only, has pronounced the case not diphtheria. Such diagnoses are proved to be bacteriologically wrong in about 16 per cent. of cases.

[13] No distinction is made here between a membrane and an exudate because the statement of the physician was in so many instances so confusing that an attempt at distinction was impracticable. For instance, in many cases the physician stated that both membrane and exudate were present.

In 275 positive first culture cases the physician gave some information regarding possible exposure of the patient. The analysis of these cases is shown in Table XIV.

TABLE XIV.

SHOWING THE RELATION OF EXPOSURE TO THE DEVELOPMENT OF DIPHTHERIA.

(Based on 275 Positive First Cultures.)

Age.	Exposed.		Not Exposed.		Diphtheria in Community.	
	Number.	Per Cent.	Number.	Per Cent.	Number.	Per Cent.
Age not given	3	4.0%	2	1.8%	2	2.2%
Up to 4 years	13	17.5%	11	9.9%	14	15.5%
Five to fourteen years	36	48.6%	62	55.8%	52	57.7%
Fifteen to twenty years	8	10.8%	15	13.5%	11	12.3%
Twenty-one years and up	14	19.1%	21	19.0%	11	12.3%
Totals	74	27.1%	111	40.7%	90	32.2%

Of these 275 cases, only seventy-four, or 27.1 per cent., gave a definite history of exposure. In ninety cases, 32.2 per cent., diphtheria was known to be present in the community. In 111 cases, 40.7 per cent., there was no known exposure and no discoverable source of infection.

Epidemics or threatened epidemics of greater or less magnitude have occurred at Shelbyville, Anderson, Westfield, New Palestine, Kouts and Sandborn. Reports of these epidemics will be found in another place.

TYPHOID FEVER.

Typhoid fever has been unusually prevalent in almost all parts of the State during the past summer. Epidemics of the disease at Plainfield, New Castle, Bloomington and Thorntown have been investigated by members of the laboratory staff. The results of these investigations will be found in another place. A number of samples of water examined in this laboratory have been found at least potentially dangerous.

The number of samples of blood examined for the Widal reaction during the last eleven months was 1,404. The receipt of the specimens by months is shown in Table XV. Of these, 148, or 10.5 per cent., were positive.

TABLE XV.

SHOWING WIDAL REACTIONS BY MONTHS.

Month.	Positive.	Negative.	Total.
November	8	107	115
December	3	62	65
January	1	62	63
February	1	65	66
March	5	89	94
April	7	71	78
May	10	82	92
June	8	73	81
July	11	117	128
August	39	255	294
September	55	273	328
Totals	148	1,256	1,404

It is difficult to harmonize this small percentage of positive Widal reactions with the fact that typhoid fever is reported to have been unusually prevalent during the past summer. In order to be sure that the trouble was not in our strain of typhoid bacilli used in the test, we secured another culture through the kindness of the Surgeon-General of the Public Health and Marine Hospital. We used both strains with each sample of blood, but this did not increase our percentage of positive results.

The distribution of the specimens by counties is shown in Table XVI.

TABLE XVI.

SHOWING NUMBER OF WIDAL TESTS FROM EACH COUNTY.

	Pos.	Neg.	Total		Pos.	Neg.	Total.
Adams	..	2	2	Lawrence	1	7	8
Allen	2	17	19	Madison	8	41	49
Bartholomew ..	1		7	Marion	26	246	272
Benton	3	6	10	Marshall	1	16	17
Blackford	1		3	Martin	..	3	3
Boone	1	[illegible]	8	Miami	5	22	27
Brown	..	..	..	Monroe	..	..	..
Carroll	1	5	6	Montgomery ...	..	4	4
Cass	..	8	8	Morgan	2	9	11
Clark	..	9	9	Newton	1	10	11
Clay	..	..	..	Noble	2	18	20
Clinton	1	4	5	Ohio	..	6	6
Crawford	1	3	4	Orange	..	..	..
Daviess	..	1	1	Owen	2	3	5
Dearborn	..	5	5	Parke	..	1	1
Decatur........	1	19	20	Perry	..	4	4
Dekalb	..	5	5	Pike	1	12	13
Delaware	3	21	24	Porter	1	2	3
Dubois	..	..	..	Posey	1	4	5
Elkhart	..	8	8	Pulaski	..	2	2
Fayette	6	22	28	Putnam	..	8	8
Floyd	..	8	8	Randolph	..	16	16
Fountain	..	1	1	Ripley	..	10	10
Franklin	1	3	4	Rush	1	14	15
Fulton	..	2	2	Scott	..	..	..
Gibson	..	2	2	Shelby	..	2	2
Grant	3	26	29	Spencer	7	51	58
Greene	1	4	5	Starke	2	3	5
Hamilton	6	23	29	Steuben	..	..	..
Hancock	1	24	25	St. Joseph......	3	47	50
Harrison	..	1	1	Sullivan	..	5	5
Hendricks	16	37	53	Switzerland ...	..	..	..
Henry	6	43	49	Tippecanoe	1	29	30
Howard	..	..	..	Tipton	..	18	18
Huntington	..	8	8	Union	..	1	1
Jackson	..	6	6	Vanderburgh ..	2	41	43
Jasper	2	2	4	Vermillion	1	3	4
Jay	1	3	4	Vigo	1	24	25
Jefferson	2	18	20	Wabash	..	6	6
Jennings	1	4	5	Warren	..	2	2
Johnson	3	4	7	Warrick	..	..	..
Knox	3	11	14	Washington ...	..	7	7
Kosciusko	2	25	27	Wayne	5	67	72
Lagrange	..	21	21	Wells	..	2	2
Lake	4	16	20	White	..	15	15
Laporte	..	32	32	Whitley	1	..	1
Totals	73	475	548	Totals	75	781	856

Cultures from forty-three stools were examined for B. typhosus with negative results. All were from patients (males) who had recently had typhoid fever.

MALARIA.

Of 189 specimens of blood examined for malarial plasmodia, eleven were found to be positive. Last year seventeen positive cases were discovered. Of the eleven cases this year, six were males and five females. Five specimens were from children under 15 years of age. Four patients got their infections in this State, two in Illinois, one in Oklahoma, one in Arkansas, one indefinitely South. In one case the place of infection was not known. Tertian parasites were found in seven specimens, aestivo-autumnal in three, and the type of organism was doubtful in one. These positive specimens were received from the following counties:

Allen, 1; Elkhart, 1; Madison, 1; Marion, 3; Parke, 1; Posey, 1; Vanderburgh, 1; Vigo, 2.

VENEREAL DISEASES.

1. GONORRHEA.

Altogether 430 specimens of pus from the genital organs were examined. Of these, 144, or 33.5 per cent., were found to contain gonococci. In forty-two more cases (nearly 10 per cent.), suspicious biscuit-shaped diplococci, often Gram negative, were found, but it was not considered wise to pronounce these cases positive. Of 218 specimens from males 102, or 46.8 per cent., were positive and nineteen doubtful; while of 196 specimens from females, forty-two, or 21.4 per cent., were positive and nineteen doubtful. An analysis of these specimens is shown in Table XVII.

TABLE XVII.

SHOWING THE SEX OF PATIENTS AND RESULTS OF EXAMINATIONS OF SPECIMENS FOR GONOCOCCI.

Bacteriological Diagnosis.	Males.	Females.	Sex Not Given.	Totals.
Positive	102	42	...	144
Negative	97	135	12	244
Doubtful	19	19	4	42
Totals	218	196	16	430

In 113 cases the age of the patient was given. This number is too small to permit the drawing of definite conclusions, but sufficiently large to be suggestive. The large number of positive specimens from female patients under 12 years of age, as shown in Table XVIII, is unusual. It is due to the fact that during the year Dr. Schweitzer has made a special study of gonorrhea in female children which has resulted in the collection of an unusually large number of positive cases. A most instructive feature of the analysis is the corroboration of the well-known truth that the majority of males who have gonorrhea acquire it between the ages of 20 and 30. Thus, of eighty-one positive specimens from males, fifty-one, or 63 per cent., were from patients at that age.

TABLE XVIII.

SHOWING AGE AND SEX OF 113 POSITIVE CASES OF GONORRHEA.

Ages.	Males.	Females.	Totals.
Under 3 years	..	2	2
3 to 12 years	2	8	10
13 to 19 years	1	3	4
20 to 25 years	26	9	35
26 to 30 years	25	3	28
31 to 40 years	15	5	20
41 to 50 years	8	..	8
51 to 60 years	3	..	3
61 to 70 years	2	..	2
71 to 80 years	1	..	1
Totals	81	32	113

Table XIX shows the social status of forty-eight cases of gonorrhea or probable gonorrhea in females between the ages of 16 and 25. Many of the unmarried females were not public prostitutes. One of these specimens was from a 17-year-old girl who had come from a small country town to Indianapolis to study music, and was infected by a man from her home town who visited her here.

TABLE XIX.

SHOWING THE SOCIAL STATUS IN 48 CASES OF GONORRHEA AND PROBABLE GONORRHEA IN FEMALES BETWEEN THE AGES OF 16 AND 25.

	Diagnosis.		
Social Status.	Positive.	Doubtful.	Total
Unmarried	6	5	11
Married	11	10	21
Doubtful	12	4	16
Totals	29	19	48

The number of positive specimens from married women is comparatively large. Not a few of these were from newly married girls. In one instance a man who had had gonorrhea married against his physician's emphatic advice. The wedding occurred some three or four months after the infection began. All discharge had ceased and he thought himself well in spite of the doctor's advice. In less than three weeks he took his wife to this same doctor with an acute and very virulent gonorrheal infection. Indiana's law requiring a clean bill of health of both parties to the marriage contract does not yet work with such perfection as to thoroughly protect innocent girls from being infected with venereal diseases by husbands whose morals were previously all too lax.

Dr. Schweitzer's analysis of the cases of gonorrhea in very young girls follows:

2. GONORRHEA IN CHILDREN.

Literature by Indiana physicians on the subject of gonorrhea in children is scarce. Cursory inquiry, however, shows that this disease is much more prevalent than even physicians generally are aware. The fact that many children are infected each year should arouse not only the medical profession, but also all others who have at heart the welfare of the child.

Gonorrhea is comparatively wide-spread in the larger towns and cities where children are congregated from many sources in hospitals, asylums, day-nurseries, public bath houses, etc. Matrons, managers and caretakers very often are not aware of the presence of the disease nor of its dangers until they are horrified by an accidental revelation. In the smaller towns and rural communities cases may at times be overlooked by the physician and thus become sources of contagion.

As a case of vaginitis or urethritis many may be specific or non-specific in origin, every case presents a problem in diagnosis of the utmost importance. Upon its solution depend not only the medical treatment of the case and the future health of the child, but also not infrequently the decision of serious medico-legal questions.

The acquisition of venereal infections by children may be ascribed to (1) superstition, (2) sadism, (3) accident. Many persons infected with either gonorrhea or syphilis believe that they may get rid of their disease by infecting another, preferably an untouched virgin. A genito-urinary specialist in Indianapolis reports five cases in his practice due to this belief alone. Many cases are due to assaults by degenerates. Records show that the infection is often acquired from servants, boarders or from elder relatives with whom children sleep. Accidental infections are probably rare save in the youngest children. In addition to these causes, improper practices among the children themselves may be the means of transmitting the disease. While children are not naturally vicious they are great imitators and often innocently acquire vicious habits by imitating practices of older companions or schoolmates. Little girls are more easily infected than little boys because of the prominence of the external genitals. In every case fresh virus and a broken mucous membrane are the factors necessary to an infection.

The following cases of gonorrheal infection in very young children were studied at this laboratory:

Case 1. Female, age 2 years. Physician, Dr. J. H. Taylor. Thirteen specimens from this case were received and examined, as follows:

January 28, 1908. Smear from vaginal discharge. Enormous numbers of gonococci.

April 21, 1908. Many gonococci. Large number in one or two cells, others scattering.

April 29, 1908. (Specimen taken ninety days after exposure). Positive. Very many gonococci.

May 16, 1908. Positive, gonococci few in number.

May 28, 1908. Positive, very many gonococci; thirty in one cell. Discharge almost ceased. Genitalia normal in appearance.

June 3, 1908. Positive. Few gonococci in one cell.

June 10, 1908. Urethral smear, negative. Vaginal smear, positive. Few gonococci.

July 16, 1908. Positive; more gonococci than in the preceding specimen.

September 3, 1908. Positive; many gonococci.

October 2, 1908. Negative; no gonococci; many epithelial cells.

October 5, 1908. Smear from external genitals, positive; few gonococci. Vaginal pus, positive; one group of nine or ten in one cell, others scattered.

November 2, 1908. Negative, a few solitary cocci. Last noticeable discharge occurred October 4, 1908.

After this last date no more specimens from this case were examined at the State Laboratory. Dr. Taylor reports a complete recovery April, 1909.

The infection of this child was traced to a dirty bath towel used by a male boarder who had gonorrhea. Points of interest in this case are the manner of infection, the extreme obstinacy and the recurrences after clinical symptoms had been absent for some time.

Case 2. Female, age 3½ years. Physician, Dr. Robt. A. J. McKeand. January 21, 1910. Vaginal smear contained very many gonococci. Suspected infection indirectly from parents. The discharge from the child began about five weeks after the infection of the father, though Dr. McKeand used every precaution in his power to prevent the infection of the child. Child later reported March 16, 1910, as yielding to treatment very nicely. But this does not prove that the infection had been completely eradicated.

Case 3. Female, age 3 years. Physician, Dr. J. D. Mochelle. Vaginal smear contained very many gonococci. No later specimen received. Suspected infection from parents.

Case 4. Female, age 10 years. Physician, Dr. F. V. Martin. February 16, 1910. Smear from vagina contained very many gonococci. Dr. Martin had strong reasons to suspect that this little girl contracted gonorrhea from a woman who was visiting the family and with whom the little girl slept. This woman had a vaginal discharge and "bladder trouble" as she called it, and when informed of the suspicion of the physician left rather than submit to examination.

Dr. Martin reports this as his second case of infection of little girls through sleeping with older female "gonorrheaux." He reported on March 14, 1910, that the little girl was nearly well clinically, though a vaginal smear from this case received March 22, 1910, still contained very many gonococci.

Case 5. Male, age 9 years. Physician, Dr. Geo. B. Morris. March 28, 1910. Urethral smear contained very many gonococci. The boy contracted the disease from his bedfellow, the hired farm hand, who was 23 years of age. The infection began in the meatus. The symptoms were quite severe for some eight or ten days, after which they began gradually to subside. The boy was recovering rapidly and without complications up to April 4, 1910, when the case passed from notice. Dr. Morris reported a second case occurring three years before in which no microscopical examination was made. Boy 5 years of age and previously healthy was brought to Dr. Morris suffering from very painful micturition and marked urethral discharge. Had been sleeping with his parents. Inquiry developed the fact that the mother had gonorrhea. The father, previously suffering from the same disease, had been a patient of Dr. Morris. The disease ran a very typical course, the boy apparently recovering completely in the usual time. The case was so typical and the source of infection so definitely known that no microscopical examination was made. There were no complications.

Case 6. Male, age 1½ years. Physician, Dr. J. E. Hughes. September 23, 1910. Urethral smear contained very many gonococci. Disease began two days before. Probably indirectly infected by an aunt, aged 19, who lives at the home.

Case 7. Female, age 3 years. Physician, Dr. Arthur Guedel. September 25, 1910. Vaginal smear contained very many gonococci. Case had begun several weeks previous to the above date. History of monthly leucorrheal discharge in mother.

Case 8. Female, age 4 weeks. Physician, Dr. W. C. Haskett. September 6, 1910. Vaginal smear contained very many gonococci. Infection began about five days after the birth of the child, which occurred three months after parents' marriage. Mother had a suspicious leucorrhea of three or four months' standing at the time of the child's birth. Child also had conjunctivitis.

Case 9. Female, age 10 years. Physician, Dr. C. S. Baker. September 17, 1910. Pus from genitals contained many gonococci. Symptoms began September 10, 1910.

The above cases occurred in the practices of the physicians mentioned. Wishing to determine the prevalence of gonorrhea among children who are in some way dependent on the municipality, investigation was begun at the City Dispensary. With the co-operation of Dr. J. V. Reed, superintendent, and Dr. W. D. Hoskins and Dr. E. B. Mumford, attending physicians, sixty-seven cases were examined. Of the specimens secured, forty-two were negative, four were positive and twenty-one contained extracellular Gram negative diplococci which were not positively identified. In one of the latter, which was complicated by an ophthalmia, an examination made previous to our observation showed gonococci, so that this was really a positive case, making five in all. These are classified as follows.

Case 10. Female, age 3 years. Of Syrian parentage. September 9, 1910. Vaginal pus contained very many gonococci. The father gives an indefinite venereal history. The mother had "female trouble" seven years before, beginning one month after her marriage. The child had had "sore eyes" for one year, as has also the elder sister.

Cases 11, 12, 13 and 14 were sisters, aged 1½, 3, 6 and 10 years respectively. They were first seen in the City Dispensary and later taken to the City Hospital, where specimens were secured through the kindness of Dr. L. P. Collins, house physician. The source of infection in these cases has not yet been definitely discovered. The mother was in the hospital at the same time for a panhysterectomy, and it was thought probable that the children were infected by the parents.

These cases emphasize the following points:

(a) Latent gonorrhea in either parent may become a source of infection to the other, and later to the child. Cases 2, 3, 5, 8, 10, 11, 12 and 13.

(b) There is danger in allowing children to sleep with irresponsible older persons whose venereal history is unknown or suspicious, such as servants, visitors, boarders or older relatives. Cases 3, 4, 5 and 6.

(c) Carelessness with clothing, towels, etc., in cases of known infection is criminal. Cases 1, 2, 3, 6, 8, 9, 10, 11, 12 and 13.

(d) A case is not cured when clinical symptoms subside. Cases 1, 3 and 5 showed many gonococci when thought to be nearly well.

(e) It is very difficult for the physician to get reliable history. Cases 2, 3, 4, 6, 7, 9, 10, 11, 12 and 13.

The method used in securing specimens is a slight modification of that used by Dr. Ira Van Gieson of New York. Ordinary medicine droppers were placed in test tubes containing 5 cc. of distilled water. The tubes were plugged and sterilized in the autoclave at thirty pounds pressure for twenty minutes. Slides were prepared and numbered. After expelling the water from the pipette a specimen was secured by inserting it into the vagina and gently manipulating the bulb. If the secretion was scanty a small amount of water was left in the pipette. This was expelled into the vagina and then gently withdrawn, washing out with it the vaginal secretion. Thin smears were at once made on the glass slides and history cards with corresponding numbers were prepared. Loeffler's alkaline methylene blue and Gram's stains were used in the identification of specimens.

3. SYPHILIS.

Only twelve specimens have been examined for Spirochete pallida during the year. Three of these were found positive. In two instances the spirochetes were demonstrated with the dark-ground illuminator; in all three they were found in stained smears. This branch of our work could be made much more useful to physicians if they would learn to take smears from suspected chancres properly and send them to the laboratory.

In an attempt to work out a practical scheme for making the Wassermann test for syphilis available to the physicians of the State, we made 182 tests according to Noguchi's modification. Of these seventy-two were positive, ninety-six negative and fourteen doubtful. Some of the results were very brilliant. A man 30 years old with a suspicious sore of two weeks' duration on his lip was brought to the laboratory. His serum gave a pronounced positive reaction. Two days later he returned and we examined exudate from the sore with the dark-ground illuminator and demonstrated spirocheta pallida. On the whole, however, our experience did not seem to warrant our making the necessary preparations for doing the test as a matter of routine for the physicians of the State. Hence we now have none of the required reagents and can not make the test even if asked to do so.

. RABIES.

Of 134 brains of animals examined for evidence of rabies, sixty-eight, or 50.7 per cent., were found to be positive. In sixty-four of these positive cases Negri bodies were found, while four cases were negative on microscopical examination, but were proved positive by the biologic test. Of these four animals, two were hogs, one a cat and one a horse. They were all killed early in the disease. Altogether, thirty-five guinea pigs were used for biological tests. It is our custom to inject a guinea pig in every case in which the animal has bitten some human and the microscope fails to reveal negri bodies.

Of the sixty-eight positive cases, fifty-eight were dogs, four cows, two horses, two cats and two hogs. The number of brains examined by months is shown in Table XX.

TABLE XX.

SHOWING NUMBER OF BRAINS EXAMINED FOR RABIES EACH MONTH.

Month.	Brains Examined. Positive.	Negative.	Totals.
November	6	9	15
December	6	1	7
January	4	4	8
February	4	3	7
March	3	4	7
April	5	4	9
May	10	5	15
June	14	13	27
July	4	10	14
August	5	9	14
September	7	4	11
Totals	68	66	134

The counties from which positive heads were received are shown in Table XXI.

TABLE XXI.

SHOWING THE COUNTIES FROM WHICH POSITIVE BRAINS HAVE BEEN RECEIVED.

Northern Counties, 25 Cases.

Benton, 1; Carroll, 1; Dekalb, 1; Howard, 8; Huntington, 4; Lake, 1; Laporte, 3; Noble, 2; Porter, 1; St. Joseph, 3.

Central Counties, 36 Cases.

Clinton, 1; Decatur, 4; Delaware, 1; Hamilton, 3; Hancock, 1; Hendricks, 1; Henry, 1; Madison, 2; Marion, 3; Morgan, 4; Rush, 3; Shelby, 2; Tippecanoe, 6; Tipton, 1; Union, 1; Vigo, 1; Wayne, 1.

Southern Counties, 7 Cases.

Dearborn, 1; Greene, 1; Harrison, 1; Jackson, 1; Jennings, 1; Scott, 1; Vanderburgh, 1.

Total, 68.

During the last three years the area of greatest infection has shifted considerably. In 1908 the worst infected area extended from Marion County west through Hendricks and Parke counties. In 1909 a large number of cases occurred in Marion County, and in the northern part of the State, especially in Laporte and St. Joseph counties. The disease has now almost disappeared from Marion County. In 1908 there were fifty-two cases in this county alone; in 1909, fifteen cases, while in 1910 there have occurred only three cases. The worst infected areas in 1910 are districts which have previously been practically free from the disease. One strip of badly infected territory extends from Huntington County west through Howard, Carroll, Clinton, Tippecanoe and Benton counties, with the chief foci of infection around Kokomo and Lafayette. Another seriously involved territory extends from Wayne County southwestward, including Rush, Shelby and Decatur counties. At the present writing (November, 1910) Shelby County is the most dangerously infected district in the State.

Our records of humans and live stock bitten are very incomplete. During the year fifty-three persons were bitten by animals proved to be rabid, according to information sent to us with the heads of the animals. Six horses, thirty cows, twelve hogs and several score of dogs were said to have been bitten by those animals in whose brains negri bodies were found at the laboratory. This really gives no indication of the actual loss of live stock.

The following important losses have been reported to us:

Dr. T. Henry Davis, of Richmond, writes that thirteen cows belonging to Mr. E. L. Commons died of rabies in from twenty-three to fifty days after being bitten by a dog proved to be rabid by laboratory examination. Another cow of Mr. Commons' herd was so severely bitten that she died on the following day. Mr. Commons thus lost fourteen head of dairy cows.

From Dr. H. G. White we have received reports of the loss of seventeen head of hogs and four head of cattle in or near Kokomo.

Early this year the prospects for an abatement of the epidemic seemed promising. But the large number of positive heads received since May and the involvement of new territory renders the outlook anything but favorable.

PATHOLOGICAL TISSUES AND AUTOPSIES.

During the year 302 pathological tissues of various kinds were examined, as shown in Table XXII. The examinations are, in many ways, the most unsatisfactory part of our work. In the first place, nearly 10 per cent. of the specimens received are improperly preserved, so that satisfactory examination is impossible. Unfortunately it is frequently difficult to convince the offending—and often offended—physician that a piece of tissue the size of a pin point, or one as dry as a chip, or one placed in carbolic acid or plain water is not just as good for microscopic examination as one secured and preserved in proper manner. This has led to some unpleasant, but none the less unavoidable, misunderstandings between the laboratory and certain doctors in the State.

TABLE XXII.

CLASSIFICATION OF PATHOLOGICAL TISSUES EXAMINED.

Carcinoma	58
Sarcoma	11
Granulation tissue	18
Lipoma	6
Tuberculosis	16
Uterine curettings (non-malignant)	43
Papilloma	6
Organs from post mortems	72
Deciduoma malignum	2
Hypernephroma (?)	1
Endothelioma	1
Benign tumors of breast	6
Miscellaneous	48
Unsatisfactory	21
Total	309

In the second place, physicians often send pathological specimens for diagnosis without giving any information concerning the case. They frequently expect us to find out from what part of the body the tissue came and make the diagnosis without knowing even the age of the patient. The responsibility under such conditions of making a diagnosis that may mean a mutilating operation on the one hand or failure to operate and possible loss of life on account of the delay on the other, is, to say the least, a disquieting thought.

Finally, it is our candid opinion that such work should not be done in a State laboratory supported out of the public funds. In the first place, work of this kind has no bearing whatever on the public health; it is of value only to the patient himself. It is practically analogous to using State funds to pay the doctor's bills in cases of pneumonia, or to furnish a lawyer at State expense to defend a prisoner on a charge of assault and battery. In other words, examinations of this kind are not "exclusively and entirely for the public benefit." In the second place, it brings the State laboratory into competition with private laboratories in a field that is legitimately their own. This is not fair to those physicians who are engaged in this entirely legitimate work.

It is unfortunate that the precedent for making examinations of this kind has been set, for it is one that will be exceedingly hard to break. The question may solve itself, however, for at the present rate of growth of the laboratory, our present quarters will soon be too small for any but strictly public health work, such as examinations of sputum for tubercle bacilli, throat cultures for diphtheria, etc. We may ultimately be compelled to exclude this kind of work in order to have time and space for that which is "exclusively and entirely for the public benefit."

Of the tissues examined, sixteen showed tuberculosis. One of these specimens was from the mesentery of a sheep killed by a butcher in Albion. Three samples came from cows slaughtered for market at Vincennes, Huntington and Peru, respectively. Four specimens (intestine, pericardium, lung, costal pleura) were from a cow in a dairy herd at Muncie. Eight of the human tissues were tuberculosis, as follows: Lymph glands, 5; peritoneum, 1; spleen, 1; meninges, 1.

Cancer was found in fifty-eight specimens. The distribution by organs affected is shown in Table XXIII. As was to be expected, the largest number was from the uterus. It is interesting to note, however, that forty-three specimens of uterine curettings were found to be non-malignant.

TABLE XXIII.

SHOWING THE SOURCE OF THE TISSUES FOUND TO BE CANCEROUS.

Uterus	12
Mouth, tongue and lip	9
Stomach and intestines	6
Skin of face	3
Skin of remainder of body	7
Breast	8
Nose	2
Ovary	2
Pancreas	2
Bladder	1
Penis	1
Prostate	1
Kidney (metastatic)	1
Heart (metastatic)	1
Liver (metastatic)	1
Omentum (metastatic)	1
Unknown	1
Total	58

What was said above concerning the impropriety of the examination of pathological tissues at the State laboratory does not, of course, apply to examination of tissues from autopsies, other than medico-legal ones. Such work has a scientific value, and it is quite right that the laboratory should do its part in attempting to add to the knowledge of disease. The laboratory staff are glad of an opportunity to assist physicians by preparing and examining tissues from carefully performed post mortems. About sixty specimens of organs from post mortems were examined for physicians during the year. Many of these examinations were not satisfactory because of the bad condition in which many of them were received. In suitable cases some one from the laboratory will come to any place within reasonable distance from Indianapolis and make a post mortem examination for the physician at no expense to him or the patient's family. During the year eight autopsies have been done by members of the laboratory staff. Seven of these were done by Dr. Simonds and one by Dr. Shimer. A very brief summary of the findings at these autopsies follows:

1. Male. Age 19. Patient of Dr. C. K. Bruner, Greenfield, Ind. Died 2 p. m. October 14, 1909; autopsy 8:30 p. m. October 14, 1909.

Anatomical Diagnosis.—Verrucose endocarditis, involving mitral valve and wall of left auricle. Chronic mitral endocarditis. Marked dilatation of left auricle. Cloudy swelling of heart and liver and kidneys. Multiple infarcts in the spleen. Recent and ancient infarcts in the kidneys. Acute splenitis. Marked hypertrophy of the malpighian bodies of the spleen. Ascites. Hydropericardium. Brownish pigmentation of the lungs (brown atrophy (?)). Gangrene of the toes.

2. Male. Age 11 months. Patient of Dr. E. A. Hawk, Carrollton, Ind. Died December 22, 1909; autopsy December 23, 1909.

Anatomical Diagnosis.—Laryngeal diphtheria.

3. Male. Age 26. Patient of Dr. C. E. Stone, Shoals, Indiana. Autopsy January 13, 1910, by Dr. Shimer.

This was a very interesting case. The only pathological change of any importance was a syphilitic basic meningitis.

4. Male. Age 26. Patient of Dr. Geo. T. McCoy, Columbus, Indiana. Died 7:00 a. m. January 22, 1910; autopsy 4:00 p. m., January 22, 1910.

Anatomical Diagnosis.—Small saccular aneurysm of ascending portion of arch of the aorta. Rupture of aneurysm into pericardial cavity. Acute vegetative aortitis, chronic aortic endocarditis. Lobar pneumonia (left lower lobe, red hepatization). Acute fibrinous and chronic fibrous pleurisy.

5. Female. Age 52. Patient of Dr. E. M. Bennett, McCordsville, Indiana. Died 1:00 p. m., February 20, 1910. Autopsy 7:00 p. m., February 20, 1910.

Anatomical Diagnosis.—Scirrhous carcinoma of the left breast. Metastatic carcinoma in axillary, mediastinal, retroperitoneal and iliac glands, and in the lungs, pleura, liver, uterus and ovaries. Tuberculosis of lymph gland at hilum of lung. Fatty infiltration of the liver. Submucous fibro-myoma of the uterus.

6. Female. Age 62. Patient of Dr. W. H. White, Edinburg, Indiana. Died 1:00 p. m., March 28, 1910. Autopsy 9:00 a. m., March 29, 1910.

Anatomical Diagnosis.—Chronic interstitial nephritis (small red kidney). Simple ulcers of the duodenum, with perforation into peritoneal cavity (probably post mortem or immediately ante mortem, as there was no inflammatory reaction in the peritoneum). Calcareous gland in the hilum of the spleen.

7. Female. Age 37. Patient of Dr. D. S. Wiggins, New Castle, Indiana. Died 1:00 a. m., April 6, 1910. Autopsy 3:00 p. m., April 6, 1910.

Anatomical Diagnosis.—Tumor (ependymglioma (?)) of the fourth ventricle of the brain. Hemorrhage into the right lateral ventricle. Localized softening of the left occipital lobe. Chronic diffuse nephritis. Pulmonary tuberculosis (both apices). Chronic fibrous pleurisy. Chronic fibrous peritonitis. Fatty infiltration of the liver. Cysts of the ovary. Laparotomy scar.

8. Female. Age 40. Patient of Dr. W. C. Furney, Sharpsville, Indiana. Died May 8, 1910. Autopsy May 9, 1910.

Anatomical Diagnosis.—Chronic fibrous and acute fibrinous peritonitis. Large ovarian cyst. Healed tuberculosis of the spleen. Fatty infiltration of the liver. Edema of the lower limbs. Ulcers of the legs. Decubitus.

ANIMAL PARASITES.

Fourteen specimens of animal parasites were examined during the year. One of these was a worm from the loin of a hog. This specimen was taken from a piece of pork from a Chicago packing house. This worm was identified by Dr. George of the local branch of the United States Bureau of Animal Industry as the ordinary kidney worm of the hog, Sclerostomum pinguicola. Seven specimens of tapeworm were received, but they all consisted of one or two segments and the species could not be definitely determined. One specimen of pinworm (Oxyuris vermicularis) and one of roundworm (Ascaris lumbricoides) were received. The latter was an unusually large female, measuring 30 cm. in length.

Three specimens of supposed intestinal parasites proved to be fly larvæ.

Case 1. One of these specimens was sent to the laboratory on July 17, by Dr. C. C. Ray of Arcadia. The patient was a "man 24 years of age who had been anemic, jaundiced, and nervous, and had lost flesh for two months." There were four different types of "parasites" in this specimen. The majority of these were large "rat-tailed" maggots, two were smaller larvæ and one a pupa of the same fly. The fourth specimen was the larva of a fly, probably of the genus Homalomyia.

The bodies of the larger "rat-tailed" larvæ are cylindrical, measure 2 cm. in length, about 5 mm. in diameter and are made up of eight segments, with a distinct head. The last segment bears the tail, which varies from 1.5 to 3.5 cm. in length. Each segment is covered with fine spines, and on its ventral surface is a pair of laterally elongated tubercles which serve as prolegs. The head is distinctly differentiated. The two antennæ are short and made up of three segments, the distal one of which consists of two small tooth-like processes. On the dorsal surface of the head are two small black pedunculated processes, probably eyes.

The tails of these larvæ consist of three segments which telescope into each other. When the appendage is extended to its full length it measures 3.5 cm. in the largest larvæ. The several segments can be differentiated by the appearance of the spines on them. On the proximal segment the spines are as large and numerous as they are on the general surface of the body; on the second segment they are smaller, shorter and fewer in number.

The distal segment is quite smooth and on cross-section is quadrilobate. Its extremity is enlarged and rounded, and has four (?) openings. Between these openings are a number of hair-like processes. These larvæ live chiefly in water and their tails serve as a breathing apparatus. The telescope-like mechanism enables them to feed at varying depths below the surface. "The rosette of hairs floating on the surface of the water keeps the tip from being submerged."

The flies of which the "rat-tailed" maggots are the larvæ belong to the family Syrphidæ. The distinguishing character of the family is a spurious longitudinal vein between the third and fourth longitudinal veins on the wings. The larvæ above described belong to flies of the species Eristalis tenax, the drone fly. These flies are frequently seen hovering over flowers and resemble bees in appearance.

Case 2. These specimens were sent by Dr. J. M. Wood of Greensburg, and consisted of a number of "parasites" identified by the United States Bureau of Entomology as the larvæ of a fly of the family Homalomyia. The patient was a young woman 20 years of age. She had "suffered from anorexia; gastric disturbance; constipation; soreness and distention of the colon; nervous chills; slight fever at times and constant headache for a week. She lost weight and strength, was anemic and was troubled with insomnia." The treatment consisted of high rectal enemas of normal salt solution twice daily and the application of high frequency current to the abdomen. After the electrical treatments the enemas were followed by the discharge from the bowel of large numbers of these parasites.

The larvæ are somewhat conical in shape, being pointed anteriorly and rounded posteriorly. There are eleven segments, all of which are quite distinct. The three anterior segments have no appendages. Each of the remaining segments bears a pair of branched lateral branchiæ, or "swimerets," except the last, which has three pair. These branchiæ enable the larvæ to exist indefinitely in liquid or semiliquid media. The larvæ of the species which most frequently cause intestinal myiasis are found in vegetables, such as onions, radishes, beets, turnips, cabbage, cauliflower, etc., or in fruits; sometimes only in decaying vegetables and fruits.

The flies of this family resemble rather closely the common housefly, but are usually somewhat smaller. The family comprises a very large number of species of very diverse habits. Certain species are fairly common about the house and are often spoken of as "the lesser house fly;" others are found so frequently in privies as to be called "privy flies." Still others are common about vegetable gardens and orchards. Two varieties which have been known to cause intestinal myiasis are the onion fly (Phorbia brassicæ) and the radish fly (Anthomyia raphane). "Both these insects in the adult stage are small, light gray flies, looking rather like small house flies. The onion fly lays its eggs on the stems of onion plants, near the soil, and the hatching larvæ burrow into the underground bulb, which they soon nearly destroy. This fly appears to live on no other plant. The cabbage maggot fly lays its eggs on the stem just above or even below the ground, and the larvæ burrow into the roots. Cauliflowers as well as cabbages are attacked." The larvæ of the radish fly burrow into the roots of the radish. Infected vegetables eaten raw may easily cause intestinal myiasis.

Case 3. This case, the specimens from which were sent to the laboratory by Dr. G. F. Smith of Lawrenceburg, is of especial interest, because the same patient passed similar "parasites" in his stool during the previous summer. The patient was a male, age 26. He gave a history of having eaten raw prunes and raw dried peaches in the summer of 1909, and he, himself, thought he got the "worms" from these, especially after he claimed to have found some similar "worms" in the peaches. But he claimed not to have eaten raw dried fruit in the summer of 1910.

The "worms" passed during both summers were identical in appearance. They were white and small, measuring 2 to 3 mm. in length. The anterior end is smaller than the posterior. The segments are distinct and they are eleven (?) in number. The bodies are smooth except for the narrow grooves between the segments. Some of these larvæ were sent to the United States Bureau of Entomology for identification, and the following letter was received from Dr. Howard, Chief of the Bureau:

WASHINGTON, D. C., Sept. 30, 1910.

Dr. J. P. Simonds, Indianapolis, Ind.:

DEAR DOCTOR—Your letter of the 26th, with the accompanying specimens, duly received. Mr. Nathan Banks, of this office, has examined the larva passed by the patient this summer, and states that it is closely allied to Sarcophaga in its structure, but seems small for one of those flies. He can not place it more definitely.

Yours very truly,

L. O. HOWARD,
Chief of Bureau.

The family of Diptera, known as Sarcophaga, includes the flesh flies or bluebottles and blowflies. "These all lay their eggs or deposit living larvæ on meat, and, with some other allied species which, however, do not restrict their egg-laying to animal substances, but often deposit them on decaying vegetable matter and fruits, belong to the subfamily Sarcophaginæ, so named from the flesh-eating habits of the larvæ or maggots of the best known species." This family includes the terrible screw-worm fly (Compsomyia macellaria).

It is unfortunate that in none of these three cases was it possible to actually discover the exact source of the infection.

MENINGITIS.

In the Bulletin of the Indiana State Board of Health for December, 1909, it was stated that since epidemic meningitis had been "nearing us for a year or more from two sides" it would be no more than was to be expected if an unusually large number of cases of this disease should occur in Indiana as occurred under similar conditions in the sixties. This prediction did not prove true, however. During the year forty-two specimens of cerebrospinal fluid were examined at the State laboratory, but only four specimens from two patients contained meningococci.

Through the efforts of Dr. J. N. Hurty, the laboratory secured from the Rockefeller Institute for Medical Research a supply of Flexner's antimeningitis serum. We at once provided ourselves with a complete outfit for making lumbar puncture, injecting the serum and examining the cerebro-spinal fluid in the home of the patient. This outfit consisted of 10 cc. Luer and Burroughs-Wellcome syringes and proper needles sterilized in a Mason jar; a jar of sterile gauze; the necessary slides and stains; and a microscope. This outfit was kept ready to use at any moment it should be called for. Health officers and physicians were notified that in cases of suspected epidemic cerebro-spinal meningitis they could communicate with the superintendent of the laboratory by telephone and that he would come prepared to make the spinal puncture, examine the fluid microscopically and inject the serum if needed. About twenty trips were made during the past year in response to calls of this kind.

In the two cases of true epidemic meningitis the physicians were equipped to do their own work and the serum was sent to them for use with the understanding that they were to send proper specimens to the laboratory for examination. These two cases occurred in the practices of Dr. C. G. Beall of Ft. Wayne and Dr. R. D. Morrow of Richmond.

Dr. Beall's Case.—Male, age 6½ months. Became ill November 5, 1909, with fever, hyperesthesia, bulging of anterior fontanel, stiffness of the neck and slight convulsive movements of arms and legs. Blood count showed 19,400 leucocytes. On the next day vomiting occurred and Kernig's sign was present. Spinal puncture was made and 5 cc. of cloudy fluid withdrawn. Smears from fluid showed many polymorphonuclear leucocytes and Gram negative intra and extracellular diplococci. Cultures from fluid on blood serum and agar showed diplococci which proved to be meningococci. November 7, 1909, withdrew 12 cc. spinal fluid; injected 12 cc. serum. November 8, 1909, withdrew 12 cc. spinal fluid; injected 12 cc. serum. November 9, 1909, withdrew 12 cc. spinal fluid; injected 12 cc. serum. November 10, 1909, withdrew 12 cc. spinal fluid; injected 9 cc. serum. Smear made from the last fluid withdrawn showed a very few diplococci. Mentality remained good. November 11, 1909, withdrew 15 cc. spinal fluid. Fluid rose in glass tube ($\frac{3}{8}$-inch inside diameter) connected with needle, 10 inches above level of cord, child lying on side. November 14, withdrew 35 cc. spinal fluid; injected 22 cc. serum. Smear from spinal fluid showed a very few diplococci. November 15, 1909, withdrew 35 cc. spinal fluid; injected 20 cc. serum. At each operation anterior fontanel became less tense as the fluid was withdrawn, and as the serum was injected the tension increased a little but not to the degree present before the procedure. After the injection of November 14, tension became less and did not return. November 16, withdrew 32 cc. spinal fluid; injected 25 cc. serum. Very few organisms in smear made from this fluid. Mentality getting worse. November 19, fontanel again quite tense and bulging. November 20, withdrew 20 cc. spinal fluid. Fluid more turbid than ever before. Smear showed more organisms than on November 16. Cheyne-Stokes respiration present. This disappeared next day. November 24, 9 a. m., spinal puncture made but no fluid could be obtained, so gentle aspiration was made but nothing obtained. On withdrawing needle it was found to contain a plug of a very thick tenacious grayish-yellow substance. A smear of this shows very few pus cells and no diplococci. Anterior fontanel very tense and bulging. At 5 p. m., in consultation with Dr. M. F. Porter, it was decided to introduce a needle into the anterior fontanel and attempt to relieve the pressure. The baby was comatose, pulse very rapid. Fifty-five cc. of rather cloudy fluid was obtained and 30 cc. of serum injected. Smear made from fluid showed very few pus cells but many diplococci, majority free, some inside leucocytes. No change in baby's condition from this time until death, which occurred seven and a half hours later.

Autopsy thirty-three hours after death. On opening the spinal canal, the dura from the twelfth dorsal vertebra down to the fourth lumbar vertebra is smooth and dark blue in color. The remaining portion of the dura is somewhat injected and smooth except that from the first dorsal to the sixth dorsal vertebra there is a yellowish pink fibrinous exudate. The lower portion of the cord and cauda are found to be imbedded in a mass of very thick greenish yellow gelatinous substance. On removing the brain the same exudate was sharply defined by a complete ring of adhesions between the cerebellum and the dura, except that anteriorly a thin layer of this exudate extended forward to and included the optic commissure. On opening the lateral ventricles they were found distended with a seropurulent fluid, in which yellow gelatinous masses were floating. The other organs showed nothing noteworthy.

Dr. Morrow's Case.—Male, age 13. December 12, 1909. Patient complained of headache, soreness and stiffness along spine; some vomiting. Temperature 99.5° to 102° F.

December 18, 1909. Patient was seized with a violent attack of vomiting, seemingly projectile in character. Complained of severe headache, had several severe convulsions, in some of them assuming extreme opisthotonos. Cervical retraction remained marked. Mild delirium. Respirations rapid—35 to minute—and labored. Pulse 130, weak but regular. Tongue dry and coated, herpes on lips. Abdomen firm and decidedly "boat shaped." There are about a dozen spots upon hands, neck and face, blueish-red in color, resembling flea bites. Knee jerks, cremasteric and plantar reflexes abolished. Decided paresis of left arm. Kernig's sign positive. Pupils contracted, at times divergent strabismus. In afternoon coma became profound. Pulse 145, weak and irregular. Retraction of head persisting and occasional spastic flexion of arm. Considerable hyperesthesia upon being turned or touched. Respirations forty-five per minute and slightly irregular. Would not attempt to clear mucus from throat. Spinal puncture made and one and one-half ounces of cloudy fluid withdrawn.

December 19, 1909. Patient semi-conscious. Pulse 110, respiration 24 and temperature 102° F. Would swallow some water. In afternoon repeated spinal puncture, but unable to secure any fluid; 15 cc. of serum injected. It entered through the needle readily without use of force. On the morning of December 20 the pulse was 115, respiration 23, temperature 102° F. Mental condition clear. Neck not so stiff. Three injections of 15 cc. each were given on the three succeeding days, but the case was ultimately fatal.

Of the remaining thirty-eight specimens, eight were so contaminated that satisfactory examination was impossible; eighteen contained no bacteria of any kind; four (from three patients) contained pneumococci; three contained tubercle bacilli; and three (from one patient) contained streptococci. Some of these specimens merit more detailed mention.

Of the three specimens that contained tubercle bacilli, one was sent by Dr. J. J. Gramling of Indianapolis. The patient was a sixteen months' old male child, whose mother had tuberculosis. Another very pitiful case occurred in the practice of Dr. T. J. Shackelford of Warsaw. The patient was a bright little girl of three years. An uncle who had tuberculosis lived in the family for a few months and was very fond of the child. He died about three months before the little girl was taken sick. Forty cc. of cerebro-spinal fluid were removed by lumbar puncture. On microscopic examination tubercle bacilli in enormous numbers were found.

Three interesting cases occurred in the practices of Dr. D. C. Shaff of Clinton, Dr. Baxter Begley of Inglefield, and Dr. W. H. Foreman of Indianapolis.

Dr. Shaff's Case.—A girl seven years old began to show symptome of meningitis on May 25th. A spinal puncture was done on the following day and 40 cc. of distinctly turbid fluid was withdrawn and 30 cc. of serum injected. Smears from the fluid showed an elongated diplococcus which appeared to be capsulated. These organisms were proved by cultures to be pneumococci. No more serum was used. The patient died.

Dr. Begley's Case.—A man thirty years of age became delerious, stuporous and showed stiffness of the neck and a positive Kernig's sign on August 4th. He had suffered a slight diarrhœa on July 27th and 28th. Severe headache began July 21st, and he had a severe chill August 1st. The physician in charge removed about 20 cc. of cerebro-spinal fluid and injected 15 cc. of antimeningitis serum. Smears and cultures from the fluid showed pneumococci and no more serum was used. The case proved fatal.

Dr. Foreman's Case.—A boy five years old began to show symptoms of meningitis on April 15th, following an otitis media. The first lumbar puncture was made at 6:30 p. m., Thursday, April 21. About 35 cc. of turbid fluid was removed, and 15 cc. of Flexner's antimeningitis serum injected. Smears from the centrifugate of this fluid showed very many streptococci in chains of three to twelve organisms. The pus cells had been greatly damaged and none took the stain well. Cultures gave a very abundant growth of streptococci.

The second lumbar puncture was made at 8:00 a. m., Saturday, April 23d, a little more than thirty-six hours after the first. About 45 cc. of fluid, somewhat more turbid than that previously obtained, was withdrawn and 20 cc. of antistreptococcic serum injected into the spinal canal. Smears of this fluid without centrifugation showed more streptococci than the first specimen, but the disintegrated condition of the leucocytes was the same. Cultures were again positive.

The third puncture was made at 8:00 a. m., Sunday, April 24th, and 60 cc. of very turbid fluid containing a flocculent precipitate were withdrawn. Twenty cc. of antistreptococcic serum was injected.. Under the microscope this fluid differed very markedly from the first two specimens. There was no diminution in the number of streptococci, but the leucocytes were well preserved and many of them contained streptococci. These intracellular organisms were often swollen, stained palely and showed distinct evidence of having been killed by the phagocytes. Very many streptococci grew in cultures from this fluid.

MISCELLANEOUS.

Pus.—Of 142 specimens of pus examined four were found to contain tubercle bacilli. Twelve additional specimens of pus were from the eye. Four of these contained gonococci, two contained pneumococci, and in six no bacteria of any kind were found.

Milk.—Forty-two samples of milk were examined. Only one of these contained anything especially interesting. This sample came from Dr. T. Henry Davis of Richmond, and showed a peculiar reddish color in the cream layer. Cultures were made and a pink yeast, probably Saccharomyces rosacea, was isolated. This yeast grew well on ordinary media. On agar and Loeffler's serum there was an abundant, moist pinkish growth. No gas was produced in dextrose agar and litmis milk was rendered alkaline. The growth in broth was abundant but rapidly settled to the bottom of the tube, leaving the supervatent fluid almost clear.

Water.—Altogether seventy-six samples of water were examined in this laboratory.

Blood.—A total of eighty-nine specimens of blood were examined for diseases other than typhoid fever and malaria. Very few of the specimens of blood we receive are properly made, hence this branch of the work is not very satisfactory. Furthermore, it is liable to the same criticism as those mentioned in connection with the examination of pathological tissues. Four specimens showed the picture of pernicious anemia and three were from cases of myelogenous leukemia. Of seventeen blood cultures, three were positive. One of these contained typhoid bacilli; the other two, pneumococci.

Urine.—Altogether, 291 samples of urine were examined. Eight of these, from five patients, contained tubercle bacilli.

Puncture Fluids.—Three samples of peritoneal fluid and twenty-five of pleural fluid were examined. An analysis of the samples of cerebro-spinal fluid examined will be found in another place.

Glanders.—Cases of glanders are dealt with in this State by the State Veterinarian. Hence this laboratory receives very few specimens of this kind, having received only three during the year. All of these proved negative. One of these specimens was of especial interest. It came from the nose of a horse belonging to Mr. Frank Shellhouse of this city. The animal was said to have given a positive mallein test and had been kept in quarantine for some weeks. We were not able to isolate B. mallei from cultures made from the pus and failed to find glanders-like bacilli in stained smears. A male guinea pig was injected intraperitoneally with a small amount of pus and in three days both testicles were markedly swollen. The animal was killed and numerous pockets of pus were found in the tunica vaginalis of both sides. Smears of this pus showed pus cells and staphylococci. Cultures from the pus yielded only staphylococcus aureus. Even in the face of this decidedly positive Strauss test, we were compelled, on account of the negative microscopic examinations, and the results of cultures from the original specimen and from the pus in the tunica vaginalis of the guinea pig, to pronounce the case negative.

Feces.—Ninety-seven specimens of feces were examined during the year. Ten specimens contained large amounts of mucus. In four instances there were mucous casts of the bowel, one of them being sixteen inches long. Undigested food particles and foreign bodies in the stool often give the patient and physician some alarm. Of this kind were the following: Two specimens contained berry seeds in large numbers; one contained orange and strawberry pulp; one, the skin of a tomato; one, a small piece of lace; two, unidentified mineral matter. One of the last named specimens resembled very closely true intestinal sand.

During the year ten samples of stomach contents and two specimens of true gall-stones were examined.

EPIDEMICS.

SCHOOL INSPECTION AT SHEYBYVILLE.

For several weeks there had been almost continually one or more cases of diphtheria among the children of Shelbyville. The people of the city were becoming almost panic stricken, and it had been suggested that the schools be closed. At the request of Dr. B. G. Keeney, city health officer, and Prof. S. C. Ferrell, superintendent city schools, Dr. Simonds went to Shelbyville on November 5th, prepared to take cultures from the throats of as many school children as seemed necessary.

The work of inspection had been most admirably organized by Dr. Keeney and Professor Ferrell. Immediately after school began on the morning of November 5th, one or two physicians who had been detailed to the work went to each building and examined the throat of each child in the school. Those children whose throats were the least suspicious were temporarily isolated on one side of the room. The result of this first inspection depended largely on the standards of the physicians in charge. Several physicians isolated every child that had enlarged tonsils, redness of the throat, evidence of adenoids or any other pathological condition. In one building the inspector isolated only one child, and she had a distinct exudate on one tonsil. In others fully half the children were temporarily isolated.

As soon as the initial inspection was complete with Dr. Keeney and Professor Ferrell, Dr. Simonds re-examined the throats of those children isolated by the first inspectors and took cultures from all the worst looking throats. The inspection was made Friday morning, November 5th, and every child from whose throat a culture was taken was sent home with orders to remain out of school until permission to return was granted by the health officer. Forty-nine cultures were made. These were taken to the bacteriological laboratory of the State Board of Health and examined Saturday morning, November 6th. Not one of the cultures contained diphtheria bacilli. In this way the pupils with suspicious throats were compelled to lose only one-half day from school.

One fact impressed itself most forcibly on everyone concerned with the inspection, namely, that fully half the children in the grammar school age have more or less severe pathological conditions of the throat and teeth. Enlarged tonsils, many of them almost meeting in the middle line and obstructing respiration, speech and swallowing, and decayed teeth were the most common troubles found. Every one of these pupils had all the external marks of laggards. The officers and teachers in the schools were made to realize fully the ease and rapidity with which an epidemic of diphtheria may spread through a school when the throats of half the pupils are already pathological and, therefore, the very best kind of soil for the growth of these germs.

DIPHTHERIA AT ANDERSON.

During the latter part of October and first part of November, 1909, several cases of diphtheria occurred in the Waveland school at Anderson. On November 10, Dr. O. E. McWilliams sent cultures from forty-one pupils in this school, ten of which were found to contain diphtheria bacilli. On November 17th, he took cultures from one hundred pupils, thirty of which proved positive. Thirteen of the one hundred cultures taken on November 17th were from children from whose throats cultures had been made on November 10th. Two out of these thirteen cultures were positive at the first inspection and negative on the later one. All the remaining children gave negative results in both cultures. Omitting the thirteen duplicates, there were cultures from 128 pupils, of which forty, or 31 per cent., contained diphtheria bacilli.

After the first inspection, in which ten cases of diphtheria were found, the building was thoroughly fumigated. When thirty more cases were found on second inspection, the school was closed for a week and the building fumigated again. The epidemic was quickly stamped out by the use of proper measures.

Many of the children showed no signs of the disease and yet harbored the bacilli in their throats in large numbers. The children who were most severely affected suffered only slightly. This made this epidemic all the more dangerous because the very mildness of the symptoms prevented the children from being suspected of carrying diphtheria bacilli, and hence the opportunity of disseminating the disease very widely was greatly increased.

DIPHTHERIA AT NEW PALESTINE.

On December 23, 1909, Dr. E. A. Hawk of Carrollton brought to the bacteriological laboratory a swab from the throat of an eleven-months-old infant. The child had been ill for several days and had been given home remedies for "croup." When Dr. Hawk was called, the child was in a critical condition and he at once suspected diphtheria. The swab was taken from the throat and 3,000 units of antitoxin injected. The child was too far gone, however, for the serum to produce any effect and died within about three hours.

The swab was brought to the State Bacteriological Laboratory on the morning of the 24th. It was impossible to arrive at a satisfactory conclusion from the examination of stained smears from the swab. Dr. Simonds went to New Palestine and made a post mortem examination of the body of the child. He found the larynx and upper part of the trachea almost completely occluded with a thick dirty gray adherent membrane, which left no doubt that the case was one of laryngeal diphtheria.

Dr. L. C. Ely, health officer of New Palestine, was present at the autopsy and immediately placed the family in quarantine, ordered the school closed one day earlier than had been intended, and forbade the holding of any Christmas entertainments. On the same day cultures were taken from the throats of everyone who had been in contact with the child. Diphtheria bacilli were found in the cultures from the mother, one brother, a woman who lived next door and two members of a family who had visited the home where the infant died. The town of New Palestine was thoroughly aroused to the danger of an epidemic, and the several families in the throats of whose members diphtheria bacilli had been found submitted very gracefully to quarantine. No serious objections seem to have been raised to the forbidding of Christmas entertainments. No new positive cultures were received from any persons in New Palestine outside the families of those originally affected. Those whose cultures were positive were released only after two successive negative results of examination were obtained. The threatened epidemic was thus checked in its incipiency.

DIPHTHERIA AT THE ORPHANS' HOME OF INDIANA OF THE CHILDREN'S HOME SOCIETY.

At the request of Dr. E. C. Loehr, health officer of Hamilton County, and Dr. Z. H. Fodrea, health officer of Westfield, Dr. Shimer was sent to the Orphans' Home of the Indiana Children's Home Society on December 1, 1909, to investigate an epidemic of diphtheria. Only one child out of fifty-six was seriously sick with diphtheria; several other children, however, had sore throats. He took cultures from the throats of all the children and employes, amounting to sixty in all. Eleven children, among whom was the child with diphtheria, were sleeping in a room with only one window. In another room thirty boys slept two in a bed. The other dormitories were equally crowded. Many of the children were suffering from ringworm of the scalp, scabies and contagious impetigo. There was no running water for bathing purposes, and only six washpans for the use of all the children, and very few towels. Dr. Shimer advised the isolation of the child with diphtheria and of the children with other contagious diseases, with vigorous treatment of the same. The examination of the sixty throat cultures December 2, 1909, showed that eleven of the fifty-six children had diphtheria bacilli in their throats. This was immediately reported to Dr. Fodrea and the eleven children were isolated in the schoolhouse of the home. Dr. J. N. Hurty and Dr. Shimer visited the home December 8, 1909. They found the eleven infected children isolated in the schoolhouse without a nurse or any attendant who remained with them and did not mix with the other children. The attendants had acted on the suggestion concerning scabies and contagious impetigo and the faces and hands of the children were in a much better condition.

DIPHTHERIA AT KOUTS AND SANDBORN.

During March two small epidemics of diphtheria occurred at Kouts, Porter County, and Sandborn, Knox County, respectively.

On February 28th, we received a positive culture from the throat of a pupil in the Sandborn school. This was followed on March 11th by another case of diphtheria. A new case appeared every two to four days until March 22d, when the last positive culture from a fresh case was received. Altogether there were only seven cases of diphtheria. One of the patients was a teacher in the school, and he caused much trouble by refusing to obey quarantine. It is exceedingly unfortunate for public health work when teachers set such an example of contempt for law before their pupils, not only by refusing to co-operate with the health officer, who is conscientiously trying to do his duty, but also by placing as many obstacles as possible in the way of applying proper measures to stamp out an epidemic.

About March 6th a case of diphtheria developed in the high school at Kouts. On March 9th, Dr. Simonds went to Kouts and, with the assistance of Dr. S. J. Young, county health commissioner, and Dr. C. P. Hockett, his deputy, took cultures from the throats of two teachers and thirty-nine pupils in the room where the sick girl had been. Four of these contained diphtheria bacilli. The number of enlarged tonsils and other pathological conditions in the throats and mouths of these high school pupils was surprisingly large. The school was closed and the room thoroughly fumigated. Two new cases were found on March 16th. Owing to the effective handling of the situation by Drs. Young and Hockett, no other cases developed. The first pupil was the only one who really had the disease diphtheria; the other six were merely bacilli-carriers, and by proper treatment of their throats never showed any symptoms of the infection.

TYPHOID FEVER AT BLOOMINGTON.

On July 13th, one of the students at the summer school of Indiana University became ill with typhoid fever. Following this, a number of other students became ill and several went home. It is not certainly known how many actually had typhoid fever, as it was not possible to get accurate information concerning each student after he left the University. However, there were twelve cases of typhoid fever in Bloomington on August 4th, when an investigation into the source of the epidemic was undertaken by Dr. Simonds. Through the courtesy of Miss Zena M. Caldwell, of Lebanon; of Miss Clarice Conn, of Crawfordsville; of Mr. H. S. Gilhams, of La Grange; of Dr. Grant Goodwin, of Monticello, and of Dr. T. O. Redden, of Jolietville, information concerning six more cases was obtained.

Of the eighteen patients, thirteen were students and five residents of Bloomington. The following information was obtained concerning each case: Where patient roomed; where he took his meals; whether he drank milk; and if so, from what dairy; source of the water he drank; date of onset of illness; length of time in the city; occupation, and any other general information that could be secured.

Two of the patients were negroes in one family living in the northeastern part of the city. Little information was secured concerning them except that they drank milk, took some or all of their meals at home, used water from a cistern, that the house had no sewer connections, and that the general sanitary condition of the place was very bad. Of the sixteen other patients, thirteen were students whose homes are in various parts of the State. Of the other three, two were young women and one an unmarried man who worked and boarded in the city. All the patients roomed within an area limited to a few squares between the court house and the University, that is, just east of the center of the city. The two negroes lived a little further northeast than any of the other patients, but still within the general limits of this territory. No cases of typhoid occurred in any other part of the city.

Nine patients were habitual milk drinkers; six used it only on breakfast foods and in coffee; and one in coffee only. The milk used came from six different dairies. Not more than two patients had used milk from the same source. The cases were, therefore, not limited to any one milk route, and it does not seem at all likely that the epidemic was milk-borne. All these dairies also sold milk in other parts of the city which were free from typhoid.

Two patients, the negroes, used cistern water only. Four others used city water only. Eight students used city water at their rooms and boarding houses; two used filtered cistern water at their rooms, and all of them drank the cistern water at the University. Thus, ten of the eighteen patients had at least one common source of drinking water. Examination of the city water in the bacteriological laboratory of the University showed it to be above suspicion, while an examination of water from the University cistern proved it to be remarkably pure. The result of this analysis, together with the fact that six patients—one-third of all the cases—had not used water from the University cistern at all, is ample proof that this was not the source of the epidemic. The distribution of the cases was entirely too limited for the epidemic to have been due to city water, and too general to have been due to the University water.

It was found further that twelve and possibly thirteen of the patients had taken some or all of their meals at four restaurants located in the southwest quarter of the square immediately east of the court house. One other patient got his meals at home, which is in the southwest quarter of the next square east. Two others boarded at a club two blocks further east. Whether they ever took any meals at one of these four restaurants is not known. The remaining two patients were the negroes, who, so far as is known, got all their meals at home. The twelve patients were so distributed among the four restaurants that it was impossible to charge the epidemic to any one of them. Two had eaten at Bundy's restaurant only; three at Bundy's and the dairy lunch; one at the dairy lunch only; two at Coyle's only; and one had taken her luncheons at the Greek's restaurant, but had taken her breakfast and dinner at Mrs. Stimpson's boarding house, two or three blocks northeast; one had eaten at all four of these restaurants and one had taken a few meals at Coyle's, but boarded regularly at the boarding club two blocks east.

Bundy's restaurant and the dairy lunch are on adjoining lots. About thirty feet behind the dairy lunch, so situated that it was a little nearer the back door of Bundy's restaurant, was an open privy vault that was in an undescribably filthy condition. Although it had been cleaned out the night before, it was at the time of inspection, already full of water and refuse which had been dumped into the alley from Coyle's restaurant. Immediately behind Bundy's restaurant was another open privy vault which was not quite so bad as the first one. Flies were present in swarms in the alleys, around the privy vaults, and around the screened back doors of all four of these restaurants. It would be impossible to keep half a dozen or more flies from getting into these kitchens every time the screens were opened. It may be of some significance to note that six of the eighteen cases had taken their meals regularly at Bundy's and the dairy lunch, the two places nearest the source of the flies. Flies were exceedingly numerous about the back doors of all the buildings in this block. (See Chart I.)

About a hundred flies were caught around the vaults and around the back doors of Bundy's restaurant and the dairy lunch. An attempt was made to isolate typhoid bacilli from the bodies of these insects. Some of the flies were simply rubbed over the surface of a malachite-green-agar plate; the others were ground up in a mortar with sterile salt solution and proper dilutions of this were inoculated into plates of the same media. After thirty-six hours' incubation, the growth was washed off these plates and suspended in sterile salt solution, proper dilutions made, and replated on malachite-green-agar. After incubating for forty-eight hours, this growth was again washed off and the suspension plated out on Endo's medium. All these plates showed very great numbers of red colonies with metallic luster, which were proved by cultural tests to be colon bacilli. On many of the plates, from one-half to two-thirds of the colonies were red. Sub-cultures were made from a large number of the colorless colonies, but none of them proved to be typhoid bacilli. Several actively motile organisms were found which had the general cultural characteristics of typhoid-bacilli, uniform clouding of broth without scum formation, no gas production in dextrose agar, no liquefaction of gelatin, slight acidification of milk without coagulation, but the streak cultures on agar slants grew too luxuriantly and their edges were too uneven to justify pronouncing them typhoid bacilli. The presence of such large

CHART 1
SHOWING LOCATION OF BOARDING HOUSES

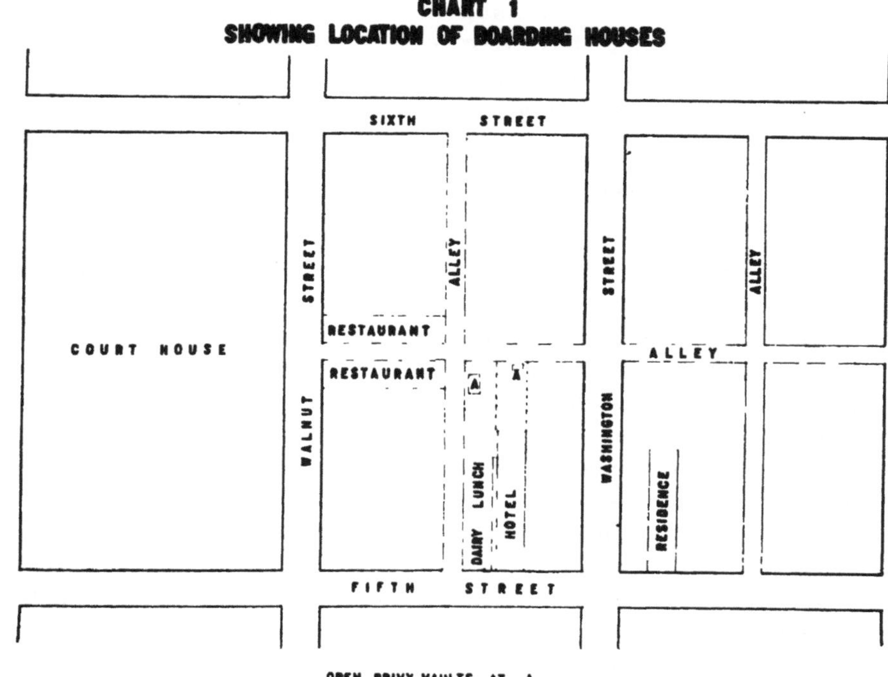

OPEN PRIVY VAULTS AT A

numbers of colon bacilli in and on the bodies of these flies is sufficient proof that they had hatched in, or fed upon, human fecal matter, the most likely place being in these open privy vaults.

In this investigation there was nothing found that would cast any suspicion whatever on milk or water—city or University—as the source of the epidemic. The only feature found common to a majority of the cases (thirteen, possibly fourteen, out of eighteen cases) was that the patients had taken their meals at places where the prevention of some contamination of food by flies was practically impossible. The greater number of these flies were undoubtedly hatched in the filthy privy vaults already mentioned, and carried with them any typhoid bacilli that may have been discharged therein by bacilli-carriers.

While the one bit of evidence necessary to prove the epidemic fly-borne, namely, the actual finding of typhoid bacilli in or on the bodies of the flies, is lacking, the circumstantial evidence is very strong that the germs of the disease were carried in food contamination by flies. The filthy, open privy vaults not only furnish the filth necessary for the growth of fly larvæ, but also infect their bodies as soon as hatched with any disease germs which happen to be present. The mere cleaning of these privies is not sufficient. They should be completely destroyed, the vaults filled up, and their owners required to connect with city sewers. If this is done, the problem of the present epidemic will no doubt be solved.

INVESTIGATION OF AN EPIDEMIC OF TYPHOID FEVER AT THORNTOWN, BOONE COUNTY, INDIANA.

This investigation was made on Saturday, August 28, 1910, to discover, if possible, the cause or causes of the typhoid epidemic said to be present in Thorntown.

With Dr. Clancy Bassett, city health officer, Dr. Shimer visited nineteen cases of supposed typhoid fever present in the town, to ascertain, if possible, the beginning, the severity and character, and the duration of the illness, the age, occupation, milk and water supply of the patients and their association with previous typhoid cases. Of these cases, twelve were probably true typhoid.

The first two persons became ill on June 6th, in the family of Bert Vaile, on Bow and Market streets. Their bowel discharges were thrown out on the ground back of the house without any attempt at disinfection. On June 29th, Mrs. Bert Vaile was taken sick with typhoid, a nurse was engaged and the bowel discharges were thereafter carefully disposed of.

The fourth case appeared on August 3d, and the patient died August 21st, the only death recorded up to the time of the investigation. The next case occurred July 3d, but it is doubtful if she had typhoid. There were no more cases until August 1st, when one case was reported, another August 2d, two on August 3d, two on August 4th, one on August 5th, one on August 6th, two on August 8th, one on August 10th, and one on August 14th, August 16th and August 18th, respectively. No new cases were reported after August 18th.

Most of the cases began in the first two weeks of August, nine cases of true typhoid having been reported during this time. This is too large a number for a town of 2,000 inhabitants.

Thorntown has no sewer system. There are only shallow privies or "dry wells" ten to twenty feet deep extending into a stratum of gravel through which the liquid portion of the sewage filters away. The wells from which drinking water is obtained are mostly driven, but are not deep, some of them extending into the same stratum of gravel which forms the bottom of the "dry wells."

The epidemic might be accounted for in several ways: First, by means of flies from the carelessly disposed of excretions from the first two cases; second, by contamination of well water; third, by contaminated ice cream; and, fourth, by a contaminated milk supply. The examination of the water from four driven wells showed them to be uniformly good.

About the middle of July there was a band concert and the ice cream was furnished by a man who gathers his milk from many farmers around Thorntown. This milk is handled under very unsanitary conditions and is not pasteurized.

Mr. O. E. Dixon supplied a large part of the milk for domestic use. His dairy barn was dark and low and the cow stable floors were in very bad condition. The milk was handled in a very small building, not over thirty feet from the barn. There was a slight attempt at screening this building, and when the visit of inspection was made the tank of the cream separator, the aerator, buckets and bottles were black with flies. The water for cleaning and washing the milk utensils came from a shallow spring which drained shallow areas about dwelling and outhouses. This spring water showed a fermentation test of 30 per cent. gas, although no colon bacilli grew on Endo's medium. The milk showed the high bacterial count on plain agar plates of 1,500,000 per cc. Fermentation test showed 40 per cent. gas. Colon bacilli overgrew everything else on plates of Endo's medium. It was also learned that this dairyman frequently filled unsterilized bottles at the wagon and that milk was sold in bottles returned from the family in which typhoid first occurred without their having been sterilized.

A summary of the survey does not indicate a definite source of the present epidemic. Thorntown has a splendid water supply from artesian wells and is abundantly able to supply everybody in the town with water. There is an ample and excellent sanitary sewer which extends to the center of the town. A survey and blue prints have been made for an extension of this sewer to every dwelling and business house within the town limits. The estimated cost of this extension is not over $25,000. This extension ought to be made and an ordinance passed to compel every property owner to destroy the privies and "dry wells" and to connect with the sanitary sewer. There ought also to be some more efficient method of garbage disposal. There should also be a town ordinance regulating the conditions for the production of milk and an adequate inspection of the dairy barns.

An analysis of the cases of typhoid fever and the results of bacteriological examination of water and milk from Thorntown are given in Tables XXIV and XXV.

TABLE XXIV.

ANALYSIS OF CASES OF TYPHOID FEVER AT THORNTOWN.

No.	NAME.	Age.	Sex.	Date of Onset.	Diagnosis	Weeks in Bed.	Number in Family.	Milk Supply.	Water Supply.
*1	M. V.	5	F	June 6	Typhoid.	4 weeks	4	Dixon	Driven well.
*2	B. V.	30	M	June 8	Typhoid.	4 weeks	4	Dixon.	Driven well.
3	Mrs. V.	29	F	June 29	Typhoid.	4 weeks	4	Dixon.	Driven well.
4	A. De St.	22	M	July 15	Typhoid.			Dixon.	Driven well.
5	B. P.	32	F	July 30				Dixon	Driven well.
6	C. A.	17	M	Aug. 1	Typhoid.			Dixon.	Driven well.
7	John O.	21	M	Aug. 2	Typhoid.	25 days		Dixon	Driven well.
8	John Mc. K.	24	M	Aug. 3	Typhoid.	26 days		?	?
9	De St.	30	M	Aug. 3	Typhoid.	Died		Dixon	Driven well.
10	Joe L.	10	M	Aug. 4	?	24 days		Dixon.	Driven well.
11	Mrs. J.	32	F	Aug. 4	Typhoid.			Dixon	Dug well.
12	R. Fe	6	M	Aug. 5	?	2 weeks	6	Dixon	Driven well.
13	C. Fe.	6	F	Aug. 6	?	6 weeks	6	Dixon.	Driven well.
14	Mrs. C.	24	F	Aug. 8	Typhoid.	21 days		Dixon.	Driven well.
15	Mrs. G.	?	M	Aug. 8	Typhoid.	21 days		Dixon	Driven well.
16	L. H.	18	M	Aug. 10	?			Dixon	Driven well.
17	Mrs. Fi.	37	F	Aug. 14	Typhoid.			Dixon	Driven well.
18	O. R.	25	F	Aug. 16	?			Dixon	Driven well.
19	W. W.	18	M	Aug. 18	?			Dixon	Driven well.

*The bowel discharges from cases 1 and 2 were thrown out on the ground back of the house without any attempt at disinfection.

TABLE XXV.

BACTERIOLOGICAL ANALYSIS OF WATER AND MILK AT THORNTOWN, INDIANA.

SOURCE OF SAMPLES.	1 to 100.	1 to 1,000.	Gas Tubes.	Red Colonies on Endo's Media.
Driven well water, Ritter's store	Very few	Very few		None.
Milk (Dixon)	Too numerous to count	1,500,000	40%	Many colon bacilli.
Spring water (Dixon)	Very few	Very few	30%	None.
Driven well water, Ritter's residence	Very few	Very few		None.
Dug well water, Johnson's residence.	2,000	20,000		Many colon bacilli.
Driven well water, Sharp's residence	Very few	Very few		None.
Driven well water, Knowl's residence	4,500	5,000		None.
Driven well water, Fink's residence	Many	Many		None.

INVESTIGATION OF AN EPIDEMIC OF TYPHOID FEVER AT THE INDIANA REFORM SCHOOL FOR BOYS.

During April and May, 1910, an extensive epidemic of typhoid fever occurred among the inmates and officers of the Indiana Reform School for Boys at Plainfield, Indiana. There were slightly less than seven hundred boys in the school at the time of the epidemic, and ninety-one of them had typhoid fever. Nine other cases occurred among the officers or their families. At least two persons who visited the institution at the beginning of the epidemic are known to have developed typhoid fever within three weeks after their visit. Among 102 cases there were only two deaths, both of them boys who were members of the school.

Dr. Ernest Cooper, attending physician to the school, very kindly furnished me with a list of all the patients, with the date of onset of the disease in each case. The first patient, the superintendent's stenographer, was taken ill April 9th. The second case appeared on April 15th, and the third on the 18th. From April 20th to May 11th, one or more cases were reported every day, with the exception of April 25th. The maximum was reached on April 29th, when twelve new cases were received into the hospital. The next highest number for one day was eight cases, on May 3d. After May 11th the number fluctuated, but averaged about one case a day until May 24th, when the last one came to the hospital. The number of cases received each day is shown in Chart II.

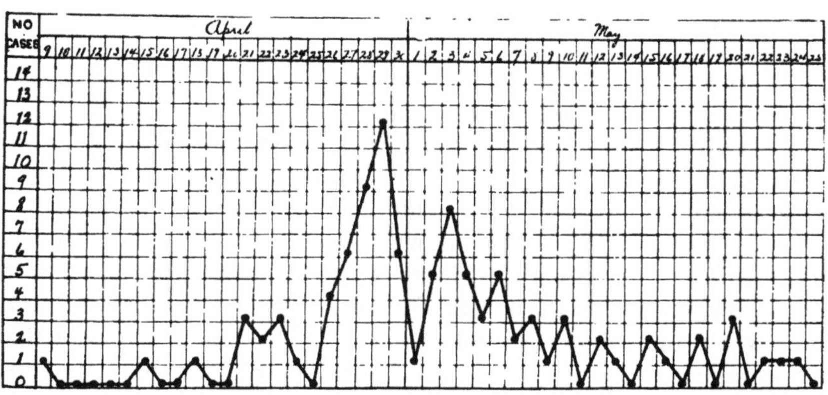

CHART II SHOWING NUMBER OF CASES REPORTED DAILY DURING THE TYPHOID EPIDEMIC AT THE REFORM SCHOOL FOR BOYS.

The boys in the school are divided into twelve companies. Each company occupies a separate building, which is used as schoolroom and dormitory. All the boys eat in a common dining room except those in Company 12. The food of these boys is prepared in the common kitchen and is carried to the dining room in the company's building. All the boys are given milk two or three times a week.

Each boy spends a certain number of hours every day in school, the remainder of the time he works at whatever task he is detailed to do. Cases of typhoid occurred in every company. Companies 1, 2 and 6 being most affected, Company 10 least so. The number of cases in each company is shown in Table XXVI.

TABLE XXVI.

SHOWING NUMBER OF CASES OF TYPHOID FEVER AMONG MEMBERS OF EACH COMPANY.

Company 1	12 cases
Company 2	13 cases
Company 3	6 cases
Company 4	3 cases
Company 5	5 cases
Company 6	12 cases
Company 7	9 cases
Company 8	8 cases
Company 9	4 cases
Company 10	2 cases
Company 11	8 cases
Company 12	9 cases
Officers and their families	9 cases
Total	100

A sanitary survey of the institution was made on May 2d. The general situation was first examined and three important facts were discovered: (1) Cases of typhoid fever occurred in the families of the officers of the school as well as among the boys. (2) The only things the boys and officers' families used in common were milk, and water from the "Big Spring," the main source of drinking water for the entire institution. (3) It was also found that cases occurred in every company in the school, but that Company 10 had escaped with only two cases. On further inquiry it was found that the boys of Company 10 used milk from the same source as the other companies, but obtained distilled water from the ice plant for drinking purposes. On questioning the two typhoid patients from this company it was found that both of the boys had been working in details away from their own company and had drunk water from various sources, including the "Big Spring."

Conditions in the dairy barn, milk house, kitchen, bakery and ice plant were found to be excellent. In the basement of each company building are a number of shower baths, the water from which comes from a large open concrete reservoir. The water of this reservoir comes from two sources; at least one-half comes through a narrow chute from a pond or small lake which is fed by numerous springs; the remainder is pumped from a creek nearly half a mile distant. The pumping station on the creek was about one hundred yards below the outlet from a septic tank into which the sewage from eleven buildings was conducted. Since that time the outlet from the septic tank has been changed and run into the creek several hundred yards below the pumping station. Water from the reservoir was examined bacteriologically a number of times. On May 2, when the creek was high as the result of a recent rain, the water in the reservoir yielded 30 per cent. gas in dextrous broth. At no other time did it yield more than 15 per cent., and once it yielded none.

The water supply of the institution had for years come from a number of natural springs. Less than two years before the epidemic occurred the largest of these springs, always designated as the "Big Spring," had been followed for some distance toward its head to the end of a series of jointed tiles put in position years before to direct the water of the spring. From the end of the line of tile an iron pipe was laid to the former outlet of the spring. (See plan of the institution.) This pipe passed immediately beneath the toilet and sewer connection of the building occupied by Company 11, but all joints were carefully leaded and there was probably no leakage. In addition to this "Big Spring," there was another in the basement of the bakehouse which furnished water for cooling the milk and much of that used in the bakery, and in the dining room and kitchen. A third spring, known as the "Old Bakehouse Spring," was in the southern half of the grounds and was not used except when some of the boys surreptitiously got water there to avoid carrying it so far.

The main sewer line runs northward near the center of the grounds. The "Bakehouse Spring" and the "Old Bakehouse Spring" are west of this main sewer line, the side from which the flow in the springs comes. One branch sewer, however, runs just south of the "Bakehouse Spring," the side from which the water

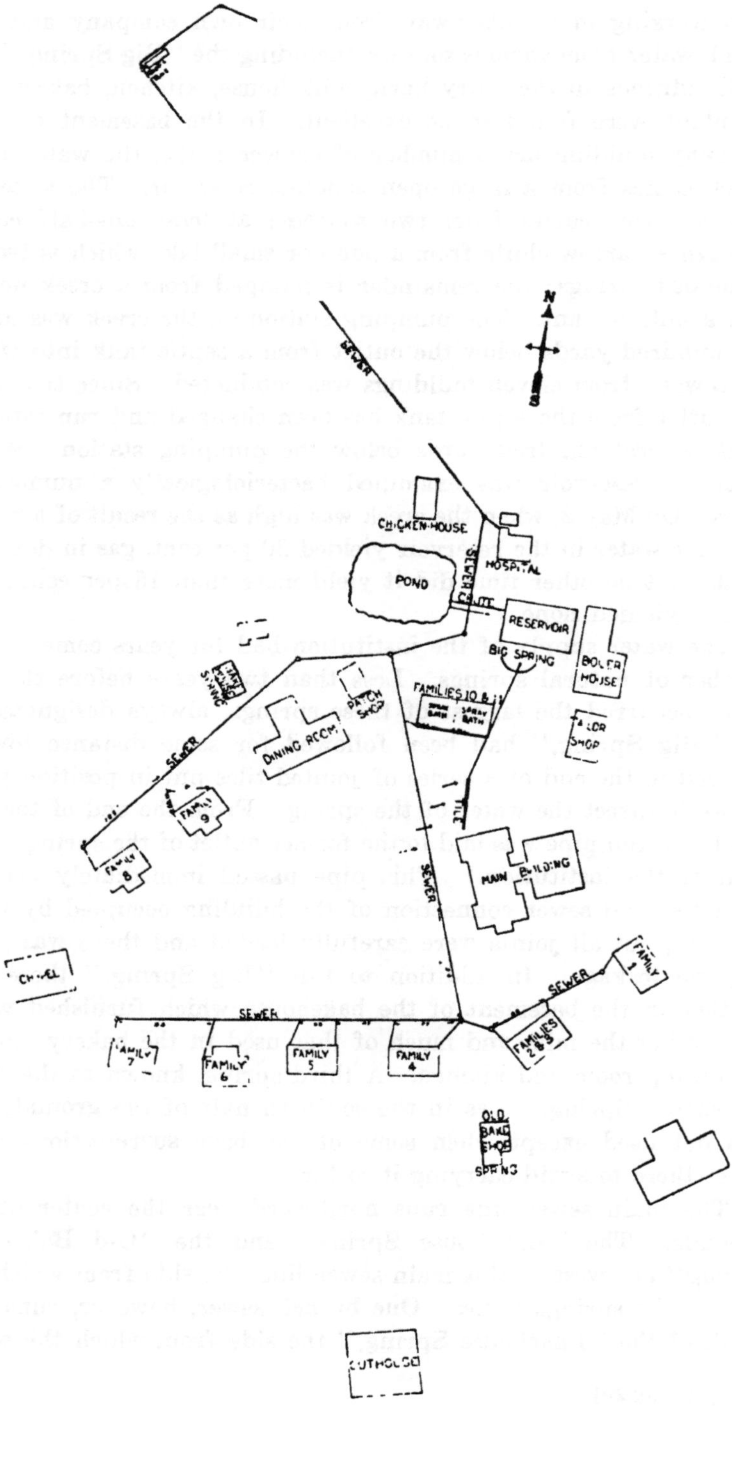

SEWER
N
S
CHICKEN HOUSE
HOSPITAL
SEWER
POND
RESERVOIR
BIG SPRING
BOILER HOUSE
FAMILIES 10 & 11
SPRAY BATH
SPRAY BATH
PATCH SHOP
DINING ROOM
TAILOR SHOP
SEWER
FAMILY 9
FAMILY 8
TILE
SEWER
MAIN BUILDING
CHAPEL
FAMILY 1
SEWER
FAMILIES 2 & 3
SEWER
FAMILY 7
FAMILY 6
FAMILY 5
FAMILY 4
OLD BAKE SHOP
SPRING

OUTHOUSE

flows to the spring. The tile which conducts the water of the "Big Spring" runs almost parallel to the main sewer line at approximately the same depth and within 15 or 20 feet of it. The upper end of the tile is probably nearer the sewer than this. After the "Big Spring" had been virtually proved to be the source of the infection, it was learned that when the sewer was laid nine years before, the engineers had great difficulty for a distance of 50 or 60 feet on account of the abundance of water in the sand in which the sewer was placed. This 50 or 60 feet was exactly opposite where the tile pipe of the "Big Spring" now is and the flow of water in the sand was noted to be toward this spring. The sewer was made of 12-inch salt-glazed tile, the joints of which were cemented. It is quite evident, then, that the water flowing from the "Big Spring" percolated around the main sewer of the institution, and that this condition of affairs had existed for nine years without any untoward results.

A systematic bacteriological examination of all the water used at the institution was undertaken. The results of the fermentation tests are shown in Table XXVII.

TABLE XXVII.

Showing Results of Fermentation Tests of Water at the Indiana Reform School for Boys.

Source of Sample.	Percentage of Gas from Samples on Different Days.									
	4-29	5-2	5-7	5-9	5-10	5-11	5-20	5-20	5-20	5-21
Big Spring	0	25%	0	30%	0	15%	0	0	0	42%
Pond	0	18%	....	....	....	....	....	....	....	....
Reservoir	0	30%	15%	....	....	....	....	....	....	....
Bake House Spring	0	0	10%	....	....	....	....	....	....	....
Inlet to reservoir (creek water)	....	15%	12%	....	....	....	....	....	....	....
Old Bake House Spring	....	....	30%	....	....	....	....	....	....	....
Old tunnel	....	..	....	....	....	....	2%	0	0	30%

Note.—Water from the "old tunnel" is from the same source as that in the "Big Spring." The sewers were flushed out on the mornings of May 2d, 10th and 20th; the samples were taken in the late afternoon of May 2d and 10th. Those examined on May 20th, were taken at 6 a. m., 12 m. and 6 p. m. respectively. The spaces left blank indicate that no specimen was taken from that source on that date.

No attempt was made to make accurate bacteriological counts after the first examination. Each specimen was first plated on Malachite-green agar. The forty-eight hour growth on this medium was washed off with sterile salt solution and suitable dilutions plated on Endo's medium. On May 2d, 11th and 21st, red colonies which were proved by cultural tests to be B. coli were isolated from the water of the "Big Spring." On May 2d, an organism having all the cultural characteristics of B. typhosus and agglutinating with serum from a typhoid patient in a dilution of 1-50 was also isolated from the same source.

That the "Big Spring" became infected from the sewer is strongly suggested, if not actually proved, by the following facts: First, about March 15th the sewers were flushed out, for the first time in several months, and considerable force was used. This was about three weeks before the first case of typhoid occurred, a period which corresponds to the incubation period of typhoid fever. Second, on April 29th, a sample of water from this spring gave no gas when inoculated into sugar broth. On the morning of May 2d, the sewers were again flushed. A sample of water taken late in the afternoon of that day gave a very suspicious gas test. Samples taken on May 20th yielded no gas. On that day the sewers were again flushed and a sample taken at 6 a. m., May 21st, gave 42 per cent. gas. Colon bacilli were actually isolated from this sample of water.

On April 21st the boys were warned not to drink water from the "Big Spring." How thoroughly this warning was obeyed is not known. About May 5th the "Big Spring" was "sealed up" so that no water could be obtained from it and the epidemic began at once to subside, the last case entering the hospital on May 24th.

The following recommendations, which have since been carried out, were made to the superintendent and board of trustees of the institution:

1. The close association of the sewer line with the source of supply of the "Big Spring" is such as to render water from that source so dangerous that it should not be used for drinking purposes under any conditions.

2. The relation of the head waters of the other springs with the sewer system is not so close, but is sufficiently so to render them dangerous as sources of supply for drinking water. The Bakehouse Spring, the water of which is used for soaking the milk pans, is especially dangerous. Any typhoid bacilli in water from this source would contaminate the milk kept in the pans. Milk is an especially good medium for typhoid bacilli to grow in. Hence a very slight contamination from this spring would cause a very marked infection of the milk—a condition which would multiply the danger of an epidemic many fold.

3. The entire present water supply of the institution is full of possible dangers and should be replaced as soon as possible by deep driven wells if the specter of another epidemic of typhoid fever is not to continue to haunt the inmates of the school.

MAILING OUTFITS.

There has been a great deal of confusion and unnecessary trouble caused at this laboratory because so many physicians send specimens to the laboratory improperly prepared and improperly wrapped. Inasmuch as the special containers sent out by the laboratory can be obtained free of charge, it is entirely unnecessary for physicians to send specimens improperly wrapped for transmission through the mails. There has been complaint from the postal authorities, and we are in receipt of the following from Mr. Bryson, postmaster at Indianapolis:

Sir—An order was issued in April by the Postmaster-General, which reads as follows:

"Complaint reaches the Department that specimens of diseased tissues are frequently sent in the mails in improper mailing cases. Postmasters will refuse to receive such matter for transmission in the mails when not put up as required by Section 495, Postal Laws and Regulations, and will under no circumstances deliver such matter to any laboratory which is not in possession of the permit required by that section."

I would suggest that you advise such doctors as do not comply with the law, that their matter will not be delivered to you unless properly wrapped.

(Signed) ROBERT H. BRYSON,
Postmaster.

The following actual occurrence shows the basis of the above complaint: In April there was received at this laboratory a very small package consisting of a small cork wrapped in a bit of paper on which was a note concerning a case of supposed tuberculosis, the whole smeared with partially dried foul-smelling sputum. The tiny vial that had contained the sputum had slipped out of the package, and in doing so had completely saturated the wrappings. It is needless to say that such practices not only endanger the health of those who had mail in the same mail bag with this little package, but they also are a very great source of danger to those who must handle these specimens in the laboratory.

This condition of affairs has been greatly improved by the efforts to bring about more active co-operation between the laboratory and the county health commissioners and their deputies. We have made an effort to keep local health officers supplied with regulation mailing outfits for distribution among the physicians in their localities. We have also urged health officers to acquaint themselves with the most approved methods of securing and preserving specimens for laboratory examination in order that they may instruct their fellow practitioners. With the outfits we have also sent circulars of information and instruction to be distributed among the local physicians. The local health officers have thus been of very great assistance to the laboratory.

Another source of trouble to the laboratory has been the failure of many physicians to pay sufficient postage on specimens. A great many packages have been received with only half enough postage on them. Our expense for excess postage has sometimes been as much as $10 or $12 a month. For some months we have been stamping each report sent out to physicians with the following:

> "Pathological and Bacteriological Specimens
> require First Class Postage, which must be paid
> in full or THEY WILL NOT BE RECEIVED."

This has brought very excellent results in reducing the amount of excess postage we have had to pay.

Table XVIII shows that 10,671 outfits have been sent out to physicians and health officers during the last eleven months.

TABLE XXVIII.

SHOWING THE NUMBER AND KIND OF OUTFITS SENT OUT EACH MONTH.

Month.	Kind of Outfits.					Totals.
	Sputum.	Diphtheria.	Widal.	Malaria.	Special.	
November	302	756	163	51	61	1,333
December	238	329	76	29	51	723
January	430	310	144	22	138	1,044
February	407	280	123	53	92	955
March	375	255	166	42	106	944
April	355	84	168	47	87	741
May	671	170	170	60	150	1,221
June	559	204	191	69	102	1,125
July	322	43	201	46	79	691
August	335	80	431	65	71	982
September	291	168	373	34	46	912
Totals	4,285	2,679	2,206	518	913	10,671

REPORT

OF THE

CHEMICAL DEPARTMENT

LABORATORY OF HYGIENE.

Year Ending September 30, 1910.

H. E. BARNARD, B. Sc.,
Chemist in Charge and State Food and Drug Commissioner.

H. E. BISHOP, B. Sc.,
Food Chemist.

I. L. MILLER, B. A.,
Drug Chemist.

J. H. BREWSTER,
Water Chemist.

WM. D. MCABEE,
Ass't Chemist.

J. P. VAN WERT,
Ass't in Water Laboratory.

J. J. HINMAN, JR.,
Ass't Chemist.

CULLEN THOMAS, Ass't Chemist.

FIFTH ANNUAL REPORT OF THE CHEMICAL DEPARTMENT OF THE LABORATORY OF HYGIENE.

H. E. BARNARD, B. Sc.

Each year presents more evidence that the conservation of health is a scientific problem to be studied in research laboratories by trained men. The State Board of Health of Indiana finds in the chemical department of its laboratory of hygiene, efficient aid in its work of protecting the water supply, securing to consumers pure food and to physicians and patients full strength and properly compounded drugs.

During the past year the work of the chemical department has been conducted along the same lines as heretofore, although the increased experience of analysts and inspectors, the more efficient co-operation of health officers and a better understanding of the laws enforced by it have all operated to secure more positive results than before.

The work of the food laboratories has been, as heretofore, in charge of Mr. H. E. Bishop, who, although he has received flattering offers to enter new fields, has preferred to serve the State in his present position.

Mr. I. L. Miller has carried forward the work of the drug laboratories and has established the value and necessity of laboratory control of the drug supply.

Mr. J. Herbert Brewster remains at the head of the water laboratories, and in that position has been of great service to water works superintendents and water companies throughout the State. He also has preferred to remain in state work to accepting positions with private companies at an increased salary.

The fact that trained men whose worth is proven by the results obtained in their laboratories and recognized by private corporations, prefer to remain in public work at nominal salaries rather than to accept increased remuneration elsewhere augurs well for the development of sanitary science and bespeaks for them and for their departments increased appreciation of their services for the public good.

Mr. W. D. McAbee, who for two years has been a most efficient analyst in the food laboratory, left the department in June to accept an appointment as chemist of the board of health of the city of Indianapolis.

Mr. J. P. Van Wert, who for a part of last year has been an assistant in the water laboratory, has resigned to accept a position as chemist in the water laboratory of the State Board of Health in Ohio.

Mr. Cullen Thomas and Mr. J. J. Hinman, Jr., have continued in their work as laboratory assistants.

Four inspectors, Mr. A. W. Bruner, Mr. F. W. Tucker, Mr. B. W. Cohn and Mr. John Owens have been kept in the field during the year and have, in the course of their work, endeavored to regulate not only the sale of foods and drugs but also the sanitary conditions of food producing and distributing establishments. That their efforts have been successful appears from the special report of the work of inspectors.

No new legislation has gone into effect nor has any part of the laws under which the laboratory is operated been rendered null by action of the courts. Much time and labor have been expended, however, in meeting the attacks brought against the pure food law by certain food manufacturing companies of New York and Michigan who, in December, 1908, went before the Federal Court with a petition for an injunction against the several members of the State Board of Health and the Pure Food and Drug Commissioners, praying that these officials be restrained from enforcing that part of the pure food law regulating the use of antiseptics, and especially urging that the business of the complainant companies was being injured by reason of the action of the State Board of Health in refusing to food manufacturers the right to use benzoate of soda. In the preparation of the defense in this case, it has been necessary for the State Food and Drug Commissioner and the State Board of Health, with their attorneys, James H. Bingham, Attorney-General, and W. H. Thompson, Assistant Attorney-General, to take the depositions of many of the complainant's witnesses in different parts of the country and, as well, in their defense to prepare and present to the court a great mass of testimony for the purpose of establishing the constitutionality of the pure food law and the right of the State Board of Health to act as it did in its enforcement. The importance of the case, as establishing the basic principle that boards of health are warranted in all reasonable efforts to protect the public and in bringing to an issue the controversy over the use of sodium benzoate which has been waged throughout the country, justifies the efforts of the State in support of the law, and the data accumulated in the more than ten thousand pages of testimony presented to the court for review, containing much scientific material which is valuable to sanitary science. Because of the prominence given the State Board of Health and the pure food law by this suit in which manufacturing interests in every part of the country are involved, the work of the department in enforcing the pure food law has been made much easier, the vigor with which the defense has been conducted without doubt deterring many manufacturers from entering the State with impure and adulterated goods. Pure food and pure drugs can never be assured so long as commercial greed and sharp competition wage war at the expense of the consumer, but wherever the unscrupulous manufacturer or dealer sees that laws are efficiently enforced and that officials are vigilant in the interest of the public, they will depart for other fields, and to that extent lessen the labor of our inspectors and chemists.

RESULTS OF ANALYSIS OF FOOD SAMPLES.

During the year 2,434 samples of food products purchased from stock by inspectors and sent in for examination by health officers, dealers or customers have been analyzed. Of this number 1,682 samples were found to be pure and properly labeled and 752 either adulterated by reason of the addition or substitution of inferior material or misbranded or mislabeled. This is equivalent to a percentage of adulteration of 30.9. In 1906 the percentage of adulteration was 42.3; in 1907, 20.8; 1908, 14.9; in 1909, 33.8.

If these figures are assigned their face value the impression will be gained that no great improvement in the food supply has followed the enactment of food laws and the work of the inspectors and food chemists. The contrary, however, is true. In 1906, the samples examined included every variety of food stuffs, while at the present time only such samples are purchased as bear on their face evidence of misbranding or probable adulteration. The percentage of adulteration is also increased markedly by the inclusion in the list of adulterated samples of all products which, while properly labeled and free from commonly used adulterants, were polluted by dirt and filth. Many samples of milk, confections and bakers' goods have been classed as adulterated for this reason and the number of adulterated samples thereby considerably increased. That under these conditions the adulteration of food samples is not higher than 30 per cent. is gratifying. It is probable that if the entire food supply were taken into consideration the amount of adulteration would be considerably below one per cent. Certain classes of food have been and always will be impure in spite of legislation. Milk, for instance, because of the very nature of its production, will be dirty. It may be possible to prevent watering and skimming, but there is no indication as yet that it will ever be possible to prevent the introduction of filth. The following summary gives in full the work of the food laboratory and classifies in proper divisions the character of the samples examined:

RESULTS OF ANALYSES OF FOOD SAMPLES.

Article Examined.	Total.	Legal.	Illegal.	Per Cent. of Adulteration
Baking Powder	5	3	2	40.0
Brandy and Wine	3	3	0	0.0
Beef—				
Corned	2	2	0	0.0
Dried	1	1	0	0.0
Potted	1	1	0	0.0
Butter	104	51	53	50.9
Carbonated drinks	256	149	107	41.8
Crushed Fruits	7	7	0	0.0
Catsups	152	34	118	77.6
Cranberries—Fresh	19	19	0	0.0
Cream	216	204	12	5.5
Extracts—				
Lemon	26	13	13	50.0
Vanilla	24	19	5	20.8
Miscellaneous Flavors	9	0	9	100.0
Fish Products	5	5	0	0.0
Flour	25	15	10	40.0
Fruit Butters and Canned Fruits	12	5	7	58.3
Fruit Ciders	109	74	35	32.1
Hamburger	34	24	10	29.4
Honey	4	4	0	0.0
Ice Cream	145	113	32	22.0
Jam	11	6	5	45.4
Jelly	11	8	3	27.2
Lard	63	36	27	42.8
Liverwurst	10	10	0	0.0
Maple Syrup	43	34	9	29.9
Maple Sugar	5	3	2	40.0
Milk	520	413	107	20.5
Condensed	3	0	3	100.0
Mother's	12	12	0	0.0
Mince Meat	8	4	4	50.0
Miscellaneous Foods	80	75	5	6.2
Mustard	17	16	1	5.9
Oysters	22	14	8	36.3
Pickles	35	13	22	62.8
Pickled Onions	11	6	5	45.4
Pigs Feet	2	2	0	0.0
Pudding-meat	2	1	1	50.0
Sausage	118	102	16	13.5
Smoked Meats—				
Bacon	2	2	0	0.0
Bologna	14	7	7	50.0
Ham	7	7	0	0.0
Meat—Miscellaneous	2	2	0	0.0
Weinerwurst	4	0	4	100.0
Spices—Miscellaneous	13	12	1	7.6
Syrups	7	5	2	28.5
Temperance Beers	135	62	73	54.0
Vinegar—				
Cider	61	36	25	41.6
Distilled—white	8	8	0	0.0
Distilled—colored	39	34	5	12.8
Whiskey	10	6	4	40.0
Total	2,434	1,682	752	30.9

PERCENTAGE OF ADULTERATION OF FOODS IN INDIANA

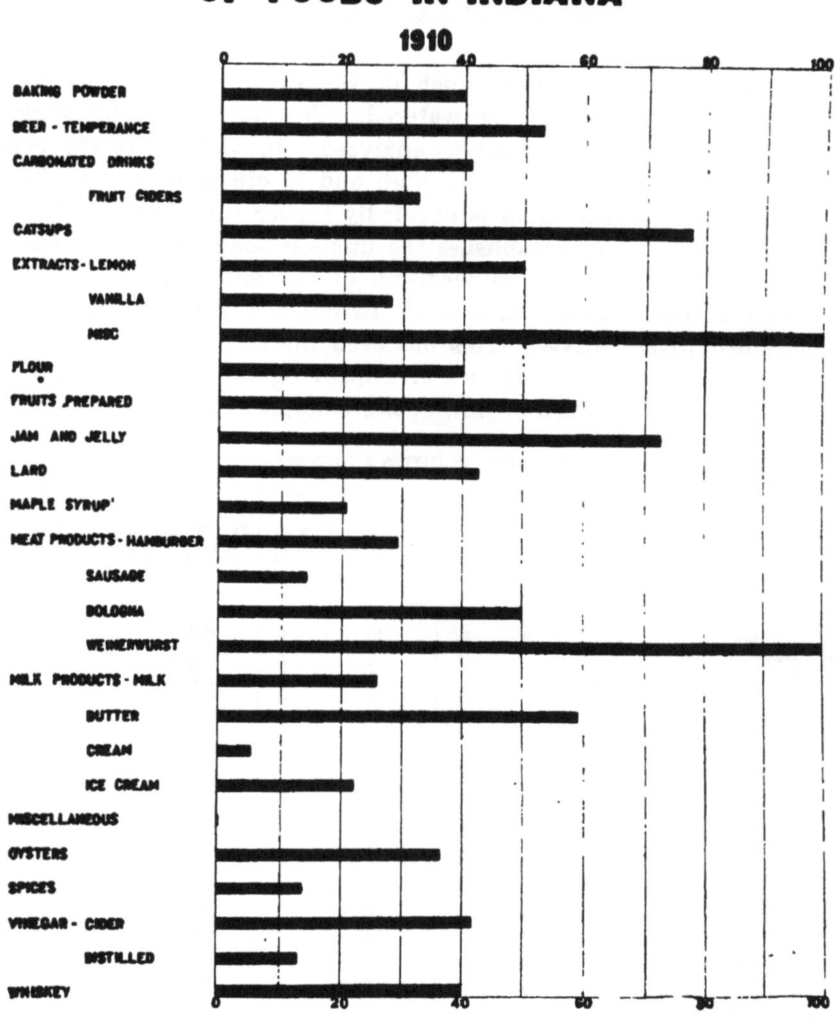

REPORT FROM FOOD LABORATORY.

DAIRY PRODUCTS.

MILK.

During the year 520 samples of milk have been analyzed, of which 107, or 20.5 per cent., were adulterated, and 413 were pure. In determining the classification samples of milk which have shown a sediment upon standing have been classed as illegal, since a dirty milk is manifestly just as much in violation of the law as milk which has been skimmed or watered. The following table shows the results of the milk samples analyzed. In some cities the percentage of adulteration is very high and in others it is low. The percentage of adulteration is decidedly higher than has been heretofore reported, and establishes the unquestionable necessity for a continued and energetic supervision of the milk supply by local officers in their cities and towns. In but few instances has milk contained preservatives. This has been the case for several years and the once common practice of improving the keeping qualities of milk by the addition of antiseptics is apparently obsolete.

MILK ANALYSES BY CITIES AND TOWNS.

LOCALITY.	Total Number Samples.	Number Above Standard.	Number Below Standard.	Per Cent. Below Standard.	Per Cent. Total Solids in Lowest Sample.	Number Containing Dirt.
Bloomington	10	10	0	0.0	....	
Bloomfield	1	0	1	100.0	11.60	
Boonville	1	1	0	0.0	....	
Columbus	4	4	0	0.0	....	
Decatur	3	3	0	0.0	....	
Evansville	42	20	22	52.3	9.55	18
French Lick	3	3	0	0.0	....	
Gary	10	9	1	10.0	11.84	
Goshen	11	10	1	9.0	....	1
Hammond	58	43	15	25.8	5.39	12
Huntington	6	6	0	0.0	....	
Indianapolis	4	4	0	0.0	....	
Jeffersonville	2	0	2	100.0	9.49	
Julietta	2	2	0	0.0	....	
Kendallville	3	3	0	0.0	....	
Knox	1	1	0	0.0	....	
LaPorte	8	8	0	0.0	....	
Lawrenceburg	9	7	2	22.2	....	[illegible]
Logansport	25	23	2	8.0	....	
Mishawaka	13	12	1	7.7	....	1
New Albany	12	12	0	0.0	....	
New Castle	3	3	0	0.0	....	
North Judson	2	2	0	0.0	....	
North Manchester	2	1	1	50.0	....	1
Peru	61	52	9	14.7	5.01	4
Plymouth	5	4	1	20.0	....	1

MILK ANALYSES BY CITIES AND TOWNS—Continued.

LOCALITY.	Total Number Samples.	Number Above Standard.	Number Below Standard.	Per Cent. Below Standard.	Per Cent. Total Solids in Lowest Sample.	Number Containing Dirt.
Princeton	5	5	0	0.0	....	
Richmond	62	44	18	29.0	9.12	8
Shelbyville	7	7	0	0.0	....	
South Bend	93	67	26	27.9	10.75	18
Spencer	1	1	0	0.0	....	
Terre Haute	26	3	3	11.5	10.30	1
Vincennes	7	6	1	14.2	11.44	
Warsaw	6	6	0	0.0	....	
West Baden	7	7	0	0.0	....	
Whiting	2	1	1	50.0	11.20	1
Winamac	3	3	0	0.0	....	
Thirty-six cities	520	413	107	20.5.	....	....

MILKS—ILLEGAL.

Lab. No.	Retailer.	Where Collected.	Total Solids.	Per Cent. Fat.	Remarks.
13389	Geo. Stemler	Jeffersonville	10.24	3.2	20% added water.
13390	John C. Stemler	Jeffersonville	9.49	2.8	23% added water.
13689	Mike Spoerner	Hammond	....	4.3	Very dirty.
13690	Mike Spoerner	Hammond	....	3.4	Very dirty.
13694	George Andres	Hammond	....	3.5	Very dirty.
13695	L. Elster	Hammond	....	3.4	Very dirty.
13698	E. Fruehling	Hammond	12.21	3.1	Below standard.
13709	A. Shneider	Gary	11.84	3.2	Below standard.
14926	E. S. Crockers	South Bend	12.07	2.5	Skimmed.
14930	W. E. Renlschlor	South Bend	11.25	2.4	Skimmed.
15097	Harry Nicodemus	Logansport	....	3.0	Below standard.
15098	W. R. Cogley	Logansport	....	3.1	Below standard.
15318	Laughlin & Coffey	Bloomfield	11.60	2.4	Below standard.
15639	Steve Senchak	Whiting	11.69	3.0	Below standard, dirty.
15642	C. Stewart	Whiting	11.20	3.1	14% added water.
16073	Sanitary Milk Co	Peru	10.59	2.5	20% added water.
16433	George McElwee	Peru	....	5.2	Dirty.
16436	P. E. Jones	Peru	....	4.7	Dirty.
16441	Peru Sanitary Milk Co	Peru	....	4.2	Dirty.
16442	Peru Sanitary Milk Co	Peru	....	4.0	Very dirty.
16444	Charles Stout	Peru	5.01	1.7	60% added water.
16782	F. W. Penny	North Manchester	....	4.2	Very dirty.
16794	B. M. Dreibelbis	Plymouth	....	4.2	Very dirty.
16877	J. F. Shine	Hammond	....	4.0	Very dirty.
17373	J. Jamieson	Hammond	10.05	2.4	7% added water.
17420	Tunk Brothers	Hammond	....	3.4	Dirty.
17422	T. Klitske	Hammond	....	3.6	Dirty.
17424	T. Klitske	Hammond	....	4.0	Very dirty.
17426	T. Klitske	Hammond	....	3.6	Dirty.
17427	George Andres	Hammond	....	4.0	Very dirty.
17434	John Pohiplats	Hammond	11.50	3.0	Skimmed, dirty.
17538	George Hitch	Evansville	....	3.2	Below standard.
17540	George Helmuth	Evansville	....	4.1	Dirty.
17541	Geo. H. Stockwell	Evansville	....	4.0	Dirty.
17544	J. Herman	Evansville	....	3.9	Dirty.
17545	George Bowler	Evansville	....	3.3	Dirty.
17546	Jos. M. Killion	Evansville	....	3.2	Dirty.
17549	J. C. Wallenmyer	Evansville	....	3.0	Below standard.
17550	Evansville Pure Milk Co	Evansville	....	4.6	Very dirty.
17551	Evansville Pure Milk Co	Evansville	....	4.0	Dirty.
17572	Carrie Conneaway	Lawrenceburg	....	3.7	Dirty.
17574	Jos. Klein	Lawrenceburg	....	4.8	Dirty.
17642	Frank Stark	South Bend	11.49	3.2	Below standard.
17645	Frank Stark	South Bend	....	3.6	Dirty.
17662	George Reaves	South Bend	11.30	3.0	Skimmed.
17750	R. Troup	South Bend	11.35	3.0	
17754	J. N. Luther	South Bend	....	4.5	Dirty.
17818	George Hitch	Evansville	....	4.4	Very dirty.

MILKS—ILLEGAL—Continued.

Lab. No.	Retailer.	Where Collected.	Total Solids.	Per Cent. Fat.	Remarks.
17819	Henry Messmeier	Evansville		4.0	Very dirty.
17821	A. D. Miller	Evansville	11.28	2.6	Below standard.
17822	Aickle Brothers	Evansville		4.0	Very dirty.
17825	J. M. Killion	Evansville		4.4	Dirt and sand.
17828	L. A. Guenther	Evansville		4.2	Very dirty.
17829	J. C. Wallenmeyer	Evansville		4.0	Very dirty.
17832	T. E. Lant & Son	Evansville		4.0	Very dirty.
17835	George H. Stockwell, Jr	Evansville		4.1	Very dirty.
17839	J. H. Baker & Son	Evansville	11.73	1.7	Skimmed.
17841	Hugo Brothers	Evansville	9.55	2.6	30% added water.
17843	Evansville Pure Milk Co	Evansville		4.2	Very dirty.
17844	Evansville Pure Milk Co	Evansville		4.0	Very dirty.
17870	Joseph Emswiler	Peru	11.53	2.8	Skimmed.
17874	Sanitary Milk Co	Peru		2.8	Below standard.
18060	Joseph Zurbriggin	Hammond		3.6	Dirty.
18430	Vincennes Milk Cond. Co	Vincennes	11.44	3.1	Below standard.
18561	Frank Gumswalt	Mishawaka		4.0	Dirty.
18632	R. P. Lankert	Richmond	9.12	3.0	16% added water.
18634	Raper Brothers	Richmond	11.35	3.2	3% added water.
18635	E. L. Command	Richmond	11.13	3.2	6% added water.
18672	J. H. Smith	Terre Haute	13.46	3.2	Below standard.
18681	J. S. Ladd	Terre Haute	10.30	1.1	Below standard.
18701	George Reaves	South Bend		2.8	Dirty.
18707	Jerome B. Sholly	South Bend		4.3	Dirty.
18736	Jacob Friedman	Hammond	5.39	2.7	70% added water.
18749	Otto Hins	South Bend	10.75	3.2	12.6 added water.
18750	E. A. Johnson	South Bend		5.0	Dirty.
18751	J. D. Shirk	South Bend		4.7	Dirty.
18752	M. P. Shelpman	South Bend		3.8	Dirty.
18757	R. Troupe	South Bend	11.42	3.1	Skimmed.
18759	Alexander Kocsis	South Bend	11.30	3.0	Sand present.
18792	——— Pitts	Richmond	12.33	3.2	Below standard.
18794	——— Sankert	R. R. 8, Richmond	10.87	3.2	7% added water.
18797	——— Huron	Richmond	12.41	3.2	Below standard.
18810	Sanitary Milk Co	Peru		2.9	Skimmed.
18825	Bert Chivington	South Bend		4.8	Very dirty.
18826	Abe Rose	South Bend		4.1	Very dirty.
18827	Abe Rose	South Bend		4.1	Very dirty.
18828	William Korn	South Bend		2.8	5% added water.
18837	Nelson Porter	South Bend		4.1	Very dirty.
18868	John Ladd	Terre Haute	10.62	1.4	Skimmed.
18949	John Tissler	Richmond	10.87	2.3	Skimmed.
18951	Oliver Meyer	Richmond	11.85	3.0	Skimmed.
18953	Jesse Gard	Richmond		4.5	Dirty.
18954	City Restaurant	Richmond	10.66	2.9	17% added water.
18956	E. L. Commoms	Richmond	12.09	3.2	Below standard.
18990	Jess Ulery	Goshen		4.5	Sand present.
19012	George Reaves	South Bend		4.1	Dirty.
19016	H. W. Nelson	South Bend		4.1	Sand present.
19019	Charles Cohn	South Bend		3.9	Sand present.
19043	J. Y. Slick	South Bend		4.2	Dirty.
19047	Bert Ray	South Bend		4.2	Dirty.
19048	South Bend Sanitary Milk Co	South Bend		4.0	Dirty.
19062	John Plocke	Richmond		3.8	Sand present.
19065	Ganes Collios	Richmond		3.5	Dirty.
19066	William Hartman	Richmond		4.5	Sand present.
19067	John Plocke	Richmond		3.9	Sand present.
19068	John Batchlor	Richmond		4.8	Dirt present.
19069	F. S. Clapp	Richmond		4.3	Sand present.
19072	C. Ratcliff	Richmond		4.7	Sand present.
19198	John Wehner	Madison	7.32	2.0	44% added water.

CREAM.

Two hundred and sixteen samples of cream were analyzed, of which 12, or 5.5 per cent., were classed as adulterated. All of the illegal samples were so classed because they contained less than 18 per cent. butter fat, their actual fat content varying from 12 to 16.8 per cent. The fat standard for cream is now apparently well established and we anticipate little difficulty in the future in keeping the cream supply up to the required 18 per cent. butter fat. In no sample of cream examined during the year was starch or thickener present. Several samples of cream were dirty, evidently because of the use of unclean bottles.

CREAMS—ILLEGAL.

Lab. No.	Retailer.	Address.	Per Cent. Fat.
15637	James McMara	Whiting	12.0
15643	C. Stewart	Whiting	15.6
16072	Sanitary Milk Co	Peru	14.0
16290	C. F. Johnson	Paoli	12.5
17371	John Pohlplatz	Hammond	14.4
17500	Sanitary Milk Co	Peru	14.4
17581	Ed F. Bender	Gary	13.6
17585	Henry Pagel	Gary	15.4
17587	Albert Schneider	Gary	12.4
*18981	Dr. C. G. Ray	Muncie	15.4
*19004	Dr. C. G. Ray	Muncie	16.8
*19006	Dr. C. G. Ray	Muncie	15.4

* Refers to samples sent in for analysis.

MOTHERS' MILK.

While the analysis of breast milk is not contemplated as part of the work of the laboratory of hygiene, occasional analyses have been made at the request of physicians. The figures obtained are interesting in showing the variation of fat contained and are set out for that purpose. The lowest fat content reported is 1.3 per cent., the highest 5 per cent.

MOTHERS' MILK.

Lab. No.	Sent in By	Per Cent. Fat.	Per Cent. Protein.
16318	W. M. Walden, M. D., Newberg	3.6	1.36
16690	C. W. Atkinson, Boswell	3.0	....
16701	Oscar Amthor, Indianapolis	1.9	....
16754	Mrs. Emma Jones, Peru	2.6	1.70
17164	Dr. A. A. Collins, Mohawk	4.1	....
17196	P. W. McCarty, Indianapolis	5.0	....
17197	P. W. McCarty, Indianapolis	2.8	....
17395	....	2.8	....
18311	T. A. Shoaf, M. D., Vedersburg	1.3	....
18665	R. H. Richards, M. D., Patricksburg	2.8	1.50
18688	Charles W. Reed, Upland	4.0	....
18908	William Tehan, Tipton	3.0	....

BUTTER.

One hundred and four samples of butter were analyzed, of which 53, or 50.9 per cent., were illegal. The illegal butter included all samples bought for butter which were oleomargarine in whole or in part, and also samples which contained more than the moisture content recognized by the Internal Revenue Department. This moisture content is 16 per cent., and 20 of the 53 illegal samples were so classed for that reason, the moisture content varying from 16.3 to 50.13 per cent. Within the past year several so-called "butter mergers" have been placed upon the market which incorporate milk with butter in approximately equal amounts. The product is sometimes sold for butter, although as a matter of fact the water content is very high and the true value of the product as determined by its butter fat content is no greater than that of the original butter used.

The sale of oleomargarine for butter is common in northern Indiana, especially in that part of the State adjacent to Chicago. In the collection of samples for analysis the inspectors endeavor to purchase from hucksters and peddlers who represent themselves to be countrymen but who are in reality cleverly disguised agents of illicit oleomargarine houses. While there can be no possible objection to oleomargarine as a food product, the large profits which can be made by selling it for butter, and especially when the seller, willing to risk detection by agents of the Internal Revenue Department, colors oleomargarine in imitation of butter and thus evades the payment of the 10-cent tax to the government, offer so great a temptation that the oleomargarine business is to no small extent conducted by "moonshiners" in quite the same way as the illegal whiskey business. The removal of the tax on colored oleomargarine would no doubt take away the incentive to fraud and tend to place the oleomargarine industry on a better business basis. There is no real reason why the coloring of oleomargarine should be practically prohibited by the Federal Government, when the coloring of butter and cheese is permitted without restriction. It is hoped that oleomargarine may sometime occupy its rightful place as a legitimate food product of undoubted merit, and that its sale for exactly what it is will be unhampered by any restrictions other than those which the Government may see fit to impose upon it for the sake of obtaining revenue. And even such a tax should, it would seem, better be levied upon articles which are not used as food and consumed for the most part by the poorer classes.

BUTTER—LEGAL.

Lab. No.	Manufacturer or Retailer.	Butyro Reading 40 C.	Reichert Meissl.	Moisture.	Spoon Test.
16145	W. A. Devault, Kendallville	43.2	26.47	7.49	Foams.
16146	W. A. Devault, Kendallville	44.2	25.97	12.68	Foams.
16184	T. H. P. M. & I. C. Company, Terre Haute	43.7	23.58	14.26	Foams.
16188	Root Dry Goods Co., Terre Haute	44.0	24.32	13.62	Foams.
16196	M. S. Burger, Clay City	44.6	24.03	11.57	Foams.
16267	Akron Creamery Co., Akron	44.0	27.54	10.60	Foams.
16267	Ideal Cafe, Mishawaka	44.6	....	....	
*16409	J. Saine & Son, Culver	43.4	26.70	12.08	Foams.
16410	H. L. Williams, Terre Haute	43.7	24.60	11.07	Foams.
16457	Warren Cohn, Rochester	41.5	25.59	12.73	Foams.
16458	J. C. Burns, Rochester	42.3	31.20	9.62	Foams.
*16465	Shaw & Jackson, Muncie	42.3	29.10	8.04	Foams.
16624	Judson Creamery Co., North Judson	43.0	23.36	10.40	Foams.
*16751	John T. Willett, South Bend	43.3	25.97	11.95	Foams.
16814	C. O. Gerard, Warsaw	41.6	25.10	11.50	Foams.
*16930	Paul J. Barcus, M.D., Crawfordsville	41.0	26.70	10.60	Foams.
*17222	Wabash Valley Creamery Co	43.0	29.50	12.06	Foams.
*17224	Mrs. W. H. Johnston, Ft. Wayne	40.5	29.10	11.05	Foams.
*17394	E. E. Locke, Indianapolis	42.4	24.94	14.83	
17412	Jerry Bremen, Hammond	42.3	26.40	26.40	
*17440	G. C. Austgen, Hammond	43.4	26.18	11.57	Foams.
17469	McCaffrey & Co., Peru	40.4	27.49	7.80	
17470	McCaffrey & Co., Peru	40.9	26.46	8.05	
17471	McCaffrey & Co., Peru	42.3	21.41	11.50	
17472	McCaffrey & Co., Peru	42.8	28.62	8.50	
17473	Glennon & Wendt, Peru	42.0	27.32	14.00	
17474	Bergman & Cumming, Peru	41.9	23.30	8.90	
17475	Bergman & Cumming, Peru	42.3	26.48	10.99	
*17487	Dr. A. G. Coyner, Kendallville	42.8	....	....	
17601	Serbion Brothers, Gary	42.8	33.23	9.80	
17612	Tittle Brothers, Gary	43.1	26.36	10.30	
17617	P. Zarabek, Gary	42.0	27.77	8.20	
17620	Garayana Tea Company, Gary	42.7	29.33	7.70	
17621	M. Hank, Gary	42.4	30.55	7.30	
17622	Rothmel, Gary	42.4	30.34	14.20	
17701	White Fruit House, Ft. Wayne	41.3	27.31	8.87	Foams.
17705	Ditto Grocery Co., Ft. Wayne	42.6	27.53	13.42	Foams.
17708	Coverdale-Archer Co., Ft. Wayne	42.5	24.05	....	Foams.
*17725	Jacob Friedman, Hammond	42.9	28.85	9.90	Foams.
*17781	G. W. Gillie, Ft. Wayde	42.0	27.49	10.06	Foams.
17955	Barrett, Indiana Harbor	43.3	26.28	15.50	Foams.
17968	Galik E. Bajar, Indiana Harbor	43.4	22.97	13.96	Foams.
*17991	John D. Hill & Co., Shelburn	42.8	23.62	10.93	Foams.
*18361	Bell Brothers, Connersville	42.1	25.00	12.15	Foams.
*18468	George M. Haffner	42.0	42.70	11.10	
18740	E. H. Day, Carmel	42.5	22.75	12.40	
*18823	J. J. Hinman, Indianapolis	41.2	29.74	8.60	
*18918	A. C. Yoder, Goshen	43.7	26.26	12.60	
*18931	R. S. Hearn, Portland	41.5	....	....	
*18977	D. Chapin, Indianapolis	41.5	....	13.80	

* Refers to samples sent to the laboratory.

BUTTER—ILLEGAL.

Lab. No.	Manufacturer or Retailer.	Butyro 40° C.	Reichert Meissl.	Moisture.	Spoon Test.
*16109	William McMasters, Indianapolis	48.1	7.16	9.06	Sputters.
*16274	Mishawaka Produce Co., Mishawaka	49.0	3.92	....	Sputters.
*16466	A. Albright, Mishawaka	49.1	1.13	15.60	Sputters.
*16467	A. Albright, Mishawaka	49.2	1.14	16.30	Sputters.
*16749	J. T. Willett, South Bend	50.8	1.05	26.08	No foam.
*16750	J. T. Willett, South Bend	49.2	1.38	16.62	No foam.
*16752	John Line, LaPorte	49.2	1.05	14.17	No foam.
16763	John Sell, North Manchester	43.5	27.25	20.55	Foams.
*16783	J. T. Willett, South Bend	48.4	1.98	11.10	No foam.
*16793	J. T. Willett, South Bend	51.8	1.64	9.38	No foam.
16812	W. W. Reed, Warsaw	48.7	7.20	8.91	Little Foam.
16815	Joe Foote, Warsaw	47.8	9.20	9.05	No foam.
16829	Lawrence H. Heiny, Ft. Wayne	52.3	2.37	18.33	No foam.
16988	T. Rowland, LaPorte	....	1.17	17.30	No foam.
16989	T. Rowland, LaPorte	49.5	1.81	21.00	No foam.
17003	Consumers Butter Co., Logansport	49.2	1.28	8.06	No foam.
17005	Consumers Butter Co., Logansport	49.2	1.30	14.40	No foam.
*17014	F. W. Smith, Indianapolis	52.3	1.23	....	No aso color.
*17015	F. W. Smith, Indianapolis	52.5	1.36	....	No aso color.
*17016	F. W. Smith, Indianapolis	48.4	2.27	....	No aso color.
17114	E. C. Schneider, Logansport	49.1	.93	16.30	No foam.
17126	E. C. Schneider, Logansport	49.1	1.45	16.60	No foam.
17392	V. J. Watson, ullivan	46.6	7.31	10.26	No foam.
17114	E. C. Schneid	49.1	.93	16.30	No foam.
17126	E. C. Schneider, Logansport	49.1	1.45	16.60	No foam.
*17393	William Herrod (no address given)	....	....	50.13	
*17456	Dr. C. C. McIntosh	43.5	23.46	21.31	
*17505	Jacob Friedman, Hammond	....	....	34.72	
*17506	Jacob Friedman, Hammond	....	....	35.56	
*17507	Jacob Friedman, Hammond	48.2	7.70	10.80	
*17527	F. W. Comeford, Gary	48.9	2.58	8.20	
17580	Max Rotterburg, East Chicago	49.1	1.58	10.60	No foam.
17598	George Hasiah, Gary	49.4	1.72	7.12	
17600	Mike Zebec, Gary	50.4	2.22	8.93	
17604	M. Scikora, Gary	49.2	1.68	7.00	
17611	S. L. Eisler, Gary	50.3	1.92	6.50	
17614	Gary Provision Co., Gary	47.9	7.75	6.50	
17675	Spiris Stratigas, Gary	46.6	12.15	....	Little foam.
17677	John Karidy, Gary	50.7	2.09	....	No foam.
17703	I. Trubarger, Ft. Wayne (short weight)	41.5	24.07	12.60	Foams.
17715	Welker Grocery Co., Ft. Wayne (short weight)	41.6	22.68	10.10	Foams.
17716	Dodame & Son, Ft. Wayne (short weight)	43.0	26.34	18.84	No foam.
17718	Heiney & Son, Ft. Wayne (short weight)	42.6	25.79	12.17	Foams.
17957	George Tiegle, Indiana Harbor	49.2	1.50	10.27	No foam.
17958	Paulsen Tea Company, Indiana Harbor	48.5	4.07	7.94	No foam.
17960	F. U. Bowser, Indiana Harbor	43.1	28.84	19.63	Foams.
17962	J. H. McAnley, Indiana Harbor	49.1	5.86	8.81	No foam.
17965	Steenberger Brothers, Indiana Harbor	49.3	1.41	10.55	No foam.
17966	F. A. Pekownik, Indiana Harbor	47.5	6.06	5.77	No foam.
17998	Ream & Son, Peru	43.8	27.79	38.29	Foams.
*18739	Blue Valley Creamery Co., Indianapolis	47.3	....	....	No foam.
*18975	D. Chapin, Indianapolis	....	....	18.30	
*18976	D. Chapin, Indianapolis	....	....	19.90	
*18978	D. Chapin, Indianapolis	....	....	22.02	
*18979	D. Chapin, Indianapolis	....	....	17.60	

* Refers to samples which were sent to the laboratory.

ICE CREAM.

One hundred and forty-five samples of ice cream were analyzed, of which 113 were legal and 32 illegal. The illegal samples for the most part are but slightly under the required standard of 8 per cent., although occasional samples are much lower. The lowest figure reported was 2.2 per cent. Ice cream manufacturers are now apparently well informed as to the formulas necessary to produce a standard product, and wherever samples have fallen below the standard it is apparent that the manufacturer has purposely used an insufficient quantity of cream.

ICE CREAM—ILLEGAL.

Lab. No.	Retailer or Manufacturer.	Address.	Per Cent. Fat.
16376	Columbus Ice & Coal Co	Columbus	7.8
17796	Chas. Giomi	South Bend	7.2
17798	J. L. Turner & Co	South Bend	5.2
17897	William H. Thompson	Huntington	5.6
17905	H. L. Conter	Decatur	6.2
17912	Sig Frank	Kokomo	7.2
18302	Furnas Ice Cream Co	Indianapolis	7.8
18303	Old Fort Ice Cream Co	Ft. Wayne	6.8
18305	Hartial Ice Cream Co	Ft. Wayne	6.6
*18371	....	Carbon	4.6
18382	Joe E. Bender	Cambridge City	6.4
18488	F. A. Green	Knox	7.6
18489	J. H. Brockhouse	Knox	3.8
18490	J. L. Turner	South Bend	6.4
18491	G. R. Howard	Culver	6.0
18505	W. B. Hollingsworth	South Bend	7.4
18506	J. W. Wittner	South Bend	7.2
18507	J. L. Turner	South Bend	5.2
18508	J. I. Noble	South Bend	6.6
18526	John Simmons	Argos	4.8
18530	Hamlett Bros	Rochester	5.4
18531	Hamlett Bros	Rochester	6.0
18532	Hamlett Bros	Rochester	6.0
18656	Hamlett Bros	Rochester	6.4
18659	Hamlett Bros	Rochester	7.0
18767	N. Schilling	South Bend	7.4
18847	Pure Milk Co	Boonville	4.2
18882	Henry Herman	Evansville	7.6
18884	Purity Ice Cream Co	Evansville	7.6
18885	George W. Cowl	Evansville	7.6
*18893	Jacob Friedman	Hammond	6.6
18944	Ike Meyer	Richmond	2.4

* Refers to sample sent in.

LARD.

Sixty-three samples of lard were analyzed, of which 36 were legal and 27, or 42.8 per cent., were illegal. The illegal list is swelled by the inclusion of 17 samples of lard compound sent in by dealers who had reason to suspect the character of the goods they were handling. One dealer sent in 12 samples for analysis which showed the presence of beef fat and cottonseed oil, although he had purchased the samples as pure lard.

LARD—LEGAL.

Lab. No.	Retailer or Manufacturer.	Butyro Reading at 40°C.
*16168	I. D. Stoops, Hymera	50.3
16380	Wm. Deaver, Columbus	51.0
16386	Fred Krause, Columbus	49.4
16417	Tare & Down, Plainville	50.6
16540	M. Wolfe, New Albany	49.0
16541	Louis Wold, New Albany	49.0
16544	Achuler & Enstings, New Albany	49.4
16545	Phil Scharfe, New Albany	49.0
16549	F. Manus & Son, New Albany	49.6
16552	Charles Umbright, New Albany	49.7
16784	I. N. Beeson, Carmel	50.6
16818	Arnold Bros., Chicago, Ill	50.0
17053	J. C. Silvers (no address)	49.7
17251	J. D. Shelly, Indianapolis	50.1
17613	Gary Provision Co., Gary	49.4
17704	I. Treiburger, Ft. Wayne	50.0
17706	Ditto Grocery Co., Ft. Wayne	50.0
17707	Fred Eckhart, Ft. Wayne	50.0
17709	Coverdale & Archer, Ft. Wayne	50.3
17710	Interurban Meat Market, Ft. Wayne	49.6
17712	Leihauf Co., Ft. Wayne	50.0
17713	E. Rosenthal, Ft. Wayne	49.0
17717	Dodame & Son, Ft. Wayne	49.7
17719	Heiney & Son, Ft. Wayne	49.8
*17742	C. G. Rea, Muncie	49.9
17845	Eckhart Packing Co., Ft. Wayne	49.7
17956	——— Barrett, Indiana Harbor	49.3
17964	Steenberger Bros., Indiana Harbor	50.1
17967	F. A. Pekownik, Indiana Harbor	50.2
18245	Bill Jones, Roan,	47.7
18849	Evansville Packing Co., Evansville	50.0
18851	Fay & Mits, Boonville	50.5
18852	National Packing Co., Chicago, Ill	50.5
18854	Klostermeyer & Kijer, Boonville	50.3
18855	Liets & Meyer, Boonville	50.4
*18973	Mrs. E. M. Bennett, McCordsville	....

LARD—ILLEGAL.

Lab. No.	Retailer or Manufacturer.	Butyro Reading at 40°C.	Cottonseed Oil Test (Halphen).	Beef Fat Crystals.
16282	Graham & Kellams, French Lick	49.25	Trace.	Present.
16383	Long & Watson, Columbus	51.10	5%	Present.
16543	H. B. Graybrook & Bros	49.30	Negative.	Present.
16547	Frank Manus, New Albany	49.00	Negative.	Present.
*16926	Geo. M. Gillie, Ft. Wayne	53.30	25%	Present.
*17155	E. J. Beardsley, Alexandria	49.30	Negative.	Present.
17477	John Kissell, Seymour	48.50	Negative.	Present.
*17520	G. W. Gillie, Ft. Wayne	54.25	30%	Present.
*17521	G. W. Gillie, Ft. Wayne	54.30	30%	Present.
17702	White Fruit House, Ft. Wayne	54.50	25%	Present.
17714	Welkers Grocery Co., Ft. Wayne	52.80	15%	Present.
17959	F. U. Bowser, Indiana Harbor	56.10	35%	Present.
17969	Galik E. Bajar, Indiana Harbor	55.50	35%	Present.
18165	H. F. Vollsner, Washington	50.30	10%	Present.
†*18257	Wm. Kahn, Madison	49.50	Negative.	Negative.
*18958	R. H. Cooper, Elwood	50.60	10%	Present.
*18959	R. H. Cooper, Elwood	50.60	10%	Present.
*18960	R. H. Cooper, Elwood	51.50	15%	Present.
*18961	R. H. Cooper, Elwood	51.40	15%	Present.
*18962	R. H. Cooper, Elwood	48.20	Negative.	Present.
*18963	R. H. Cooper, Elwood	52.80	20%	Present.
*18964	R. H. Cooper, Elwood	50.40	Negative.	Present.
*18965	R. H. Cooper, Elwood	50.80	Negative.	Present.
*18966	R. H. Cooper, Elwood	51.10	10%	Present.
*18967	R. H. Cooper, Elwood	50.50	Negative.	Present.
*18968	R. H. Cooper, Elwood	48.50	Negative.	Present.
*18969	R. H. Cooper, Elwood	49.00	5%	Present.

* Refers to samples brought to the laboratory.
† This sample contains a mould known as aspergillus niger.

FLOUR.

Twenty-five samples of flour were analyzed during the year, 15 of which were classed as legal and 10 as illegal. Several of the illegal samples were so classed because of the admixture of foreign starches or the presence of nitrites introduced in the bleaching process. By a ruling of the State Board of Health, bleaching is not prohibited in Indiana if that fact is plainly declared on the label of the package. It is apparent that flours are being sold, especially to bakers, which are not properly labeled. Several samples of straight flour have shown a protein content so high that the admixture of Durum wheat flour is strongly indicated. Such blending of flours can not be criticized, but the product must always be sold under its true name.

FLOUR—LEGAL.

Lab. No.	Classification.	Manufacturer or Retailer.	Remarks.
*16178	C. C. Fritche	C. C. Fritche, Indianapolis, Ind	No foreign ingredient present.
*17043	Wheat flour	Hermance & Dussel, Bristol, Ind	Legal.
18344	Wheat flour	Cadic Milling Co., Grandview, Ind	No nitrites present.
*18737	Wheat flour	Mrs. C. V. Ludlow, Elwood, Ind	No foreign ingredients.
18900	Wheat flour	Quaker Oats Co., Chicago, Ill	No foreign ingredients.
18929	Wheat flour	Cadic Milling Co., Grandview, Ind	No nitrites.
18930	Wheat flour	Cadic Milling Co., Grandview, Ind	No nitrites.
13579	Buckwheat	Samuel Koonts, Walkerton, Ohio	No wheat starch present.
16275	Buckwheat	Loughrey Bros., Monticello, Ind	No wheat starch present.
16308	Buckwheat	Elliottville Mlg. Co., Elliottville, N. Y	No wheat starch present.
16556	Buckwheat	W. C. Vabersdol, Greencastle, Ind	No wheat starch present.
17210	Buckwheat	E. S. Turner, Argos, Ind	No wheat starch present.
17332	Buckwheat	D. Uhl, Logansport, Ind	No wheat starch present.
17333	Buckwheat	Elliott Grocery Co., Logansport, Ind	No wheat starch present.
17334	Buckwheat	J. H. Foley, Logansport, Ind	No wheat starch present.

* Refers to "B" samples sent in for information.

FLOUR—ILLEGAL.

Lab. No.	Classification.	Manufacturer or Retailer.	Remarks.
16179	Wheat flour	Stone City Mlg. Co., Bedford, Ind	Nitrites present.
18181	Wheat flour	Wm. Luckow, Franklin, Ind	Mouldy.
18345	Wheat flour	Cadic Mlg. Co., Grandview, Ind	Nitrites present.
18346	Wheat flour	Cadic Mlg. Co., Grandview, Ind	Nitrites present.
16263	Buckwheat	Little Crow Mlg. Co., Warsaw, Ind	Wheat flour present.
16316	Buckwheat	Loughry Bros., Monticello, Ind	Wheat flour present.
16609	Buckwheat	Lathrop & Rairdin, Brazil, Ind	Wheat starch present.
17025	Buckwheat	H. A. Hank, Hamlet, Ind	About 5% wheat starch present.
17335	Buckwheat	Bishop & Co., Logansport, Ind	Slight admixture foreign starch.
17211	Pancake	L. M. Brackett & Co., Rochester, Ind	Low in weight.

CATSUP.

Catsups have been extensively studied during the past year, and a large number of complete analyses made for the purpose of determining the exact composition of various brands. In the differentiation of brands, special value has been assigned the following factors: Total soluble solids, ratio of insoluble to soluble solids, ash, sodium chloride, acidity as volatile and fixed, protein and sugar. For the purpose of comparing the formulas employed by housewives with those used by the manufacturers of well-known brands of the commercial products, 11 samples of home-made catsups were analyzed. These catsups were made during the season of 1908-1909, although one sample was prepared in 1902. In no case was any preservative used other than the condimental ingredients necessary in the formula. A study of the data shows a very great difference in composition. The total solid content, for instance, varied from 6.81 to 31.83; the ash from .85 to 5.38; the salt content from .53 to 4.00; the sugar content from 1.90 to 24.30; the total acids from .69 to 1.74; the volatile acids from .09 to .67. The variations are so wide that it is apparent that no factor, either salt, sugar or acid is of itself an essential to the keeping of tomato catsup. It is true that the catsups lowest in acidity contained considerable quantities of salt and sugar. An examination of sample 2409-D, made in the season of 1908, shows a very thin catsup prepared with a small amount of salt, almost no sugar and only a small quantity of vinegar. This catsup was, however, in perfect condition when opened and depended evidently for its keeping qualities upon proper sterilization at the time of manufacture,

COMPOSITION OF HOMEMADE NON-PRESERVED CATSUPS.

Lab. No.	Manufacturer.	Brand.	Solids.		Ash.	Salt.	Sugar.	Acids.		
			Total.	Tomato.				Total.	Volatile.	Fixed.
5013—B	Mrs. W. C. Hoffman	1908	24.56	7.51	4.31	2.87	12.74	1.74	.33	1.39
5014—B	Mrs. John Owens	1909	31.83	5.98	1.55	1.03	24.30	.87	.13	.73
2224—D	Mrs. C. E. Fithian	1909	19.73	6.61	2.68	1.62	10.44	1.23	.54	.71
5015—B	Mrs. H. S. Chamberlain	1909	11.87	4.13	1.59	.61	6.15	1.50	.67	.84
1860—C	Mrs. L. Remond	1909	20.40	6.16	.85	.53	13.39	1.11	.51	.61
2252—D	Mrs. Pearl Bennett	1909	26.64	5.46	5.38	4.00	15.80	1.29	.53	.80
5028—B	Mrs. S. C. Schutt	1909	29.75	5.69	2.61	1.66	21.45	1.26	.71	.56
2296—D	Mrs. P. S. Sullivan	1909	17.00	5.75	3.01	1.71	8.24	1.48	.34	1.14
2409—D	Mrs. F. W. Tucker	1908	6.81	3.37	1.54	.91	1.90	.91	.30	.64
1570—A—1	Mrs. L. D. Bowles	1902	23.87	5.39	3.00	2.31	15.48	.81	.51	.31
1570—A—2	Miss Ellen Dayhuff	1909	30.22	7.71	3.94	3.13	18.57	.69	.09	.57
	Average		22.06	5.79	3.36	1.85	14.40	1.17	.42	.57

It was of interest to study the various formulas used by manufacturers who, while formerly using sodium benzoate, have within the last year or so abandoned that preservative and now depend entirely upon proper sterilization and manufacturing methods to hold their product. We were successful in collecting from five companies the product which had been put up both with and without sodium benzoate. An examination of the analytical data showed no marked change in composition. The product of the Van Camp Packing Co., for instance, shows a somewhat higher total solids and a slight increase in salt, total acids and sugar. The increase in all of these factors is uniform and is evidently due to a somewhat greater concentration of the finished product. The ratio of solids to acids in the preserved catsup is .063, in the unpreserved sample .059. The catsup prepared by T. A. Snider Preserve Company, on the contrary, shows a ratio of solids to acids of .049 in the preserved catsup, .062 in the unpreserved catsup. The solid content of this brand is decidedly higher in the preserved sample because of the increase of sugar. The same is true of the Cruikshank's brand catsup prepared by Cruikshank Bros. Company. The ratio of solids to acids is .047, in the preserved sample .071. Delmonico catsup, prepared by W. D. Huffman Company, shows practically the same composition in the unpreserved and preserved sample. In fact the salt, total acid, sugar and total solid content is lower in the unpreserved sample than in the sample put up with sodium benzoate. The ratio of solids to acids is .065 in the preserved sample and .056 in the unpreserved sample. Campbell's catsup, prepared by Joseph Campbell & Co., also shows a little difference in formula in the two types of catsup, and the ratio of solids to acids is but little disturbed, being .045 in the preserved sample and .05 in the unpreserved catsup. A study of the table below demonstrates conclusively that these manufacturers did not depend for the keeping quality of their catsup upon an increased salt, sugar or acid content and, in fact, that in two instances at least, practically no change in formula was made when the use of sodium benzoate was abandoned.

TABLE SHOWING COMPOSITION OF THE SAME BRANDS OF CATSUP WITH AND WITHOUT BENZOATE.

Manufacturer and Brand.	Solids.			Ratio Insoluble to Soluble, 1 to—	Ash	NaC	Total Acids.	Protein.	Sucrose.	Ratio Solids to Acids.	Sodium Benzoate.
	Total.	Soluble.	Insoluble.								
Van Camp Packing Company..	18 98	16 86	2 12	7.9	3.52	2.31	1.20	1.20	11.72	.063	.19
"Van Camps."	23.05	19.45	3.60	5.3	4.39	2.78	1.38	2.61	13.74	.059	.00
T. A. Snider Preserve Co.....	13.25	11.69	1.56	7.4	2.41	1.60	.66	1.22	6.91	.049	.06
"Sniders."	21.14	19.26	1.88	10.2	3.90	2.94	1.32	1.70	14.45	.062	.00
Cruikshank Brothers Company.	20.07	17.02	3.05	5.8	3.64	2.78	1.44	1.97	13.05	.071	.15
"Cruikshanks."	36.57	32.22	4.35	7.4	3.77	2.05	1.71	1.83	24.89	.047	.00
W. D. Huffman Company.....	23.77	21.83	1.94	11.2	3.98	2.87	1.56	2.11	14.57	.065	.15
"Delmonico.	21.34	19.80	1.54	12.8	3.52	2.54	1.20	1.18	12.94	.056	.00
Joseph Campbell Company.....	14.19	12.72	1.47	8 6	2.81	1.94	.66	1.39	7.48	.045	.10
"Campbells."	16.80	14.38	2.42	5.9	3.17	2.11	.84	1.80	8.28	.050	.00

During the year 152 samples of catsup were analyzed, 34 of which were classed as legal and 118 as illegal. The samples rated as illegal were so classed because of the presence of benzoic acid introduced as sodium benzoate, evidently for the purpose of preventing decomposition and spoilage. These catsups in nearly every instance were misbranded. the sodium benzoate content being far in excess of that declared on the label. Certain samples of Williams Brothers' goods were labeled 1-10 and 1-12 of one per cent. sodium benzoate, but as a matter of fact, they contained .34 per cent., or four times the indicated amount.

CATSUP—LEGAL.

Lab. No.	Manufacturer.	Brand.	Acids.			Solids.		Ash.	Salt.	Sugar.
			Total.	Volatile.	Fixed.	Total.	Tomato.			
13362	Red Snapper Sauce Co., Memphis, Tenn	Red Snapper	3.60	......	......	13.54	......	2.27	1.83	......
14520	W. W. Hoyt, Chicago, Ill	......	.78	.30	.50	25.49	12.98	2.98	1.81	9.53
16220	H. J. Heinz Co., Pittsburg, Pa	Heinz	1.86	1.22	.64	35.60	7.82	3.74	2.81	25.04
16224	Beechnut Pck. Co., Canajoharie, N. Y	Beechnut	1.29	.55	.74	21.35	5.64	2.68	1.67	13.03
16228	VanCamp Pck. Co., Indianapolis, Ind	Van Camp	1.38	.40	.99	23.05	4.92	4.39	2.78	13.74
16230	J. T. Polk & Co., Greenwood, Ind	Greenwood	.96	.15	.79	18.10	5.68	2.94	1.62	9.48
16351	W. D. Huffman Co., Indianapolis, Ind	Delmonico	1.20	.26	.98	21.34	4.88	3.52	2.54	12.94
16371	Sprague Warner Co., Chicago, Ill	......	1.09	.59	.52	21.76	5.07	3.19	2.18	13.50
16984	Kothe, Wells & Bauer, Indianapolis, Ind	Koweba	1.26	.33	.95	20.02	4.72	4.25	3.11	11.05
16986	Cruikshank Bros., Indianapolis, Ind	......	1.62	.96	.74	42.60	11.61	5.58	4.21	25.41
17023	J. Campbell, Camden, Ind	Campbell's	.84	.12	.72	16.80	6.35	3.17	2.11	8.28
17029	Hirsch Bros., Louisville, Ky	Hirsch Bros	2.40	1.00	1.39	28.18	6.57	4.55	3.27	17.06
17093	W. W. Vaughn, Detroit, Mich	......	1.73	1.16	.57	23.30	5.69	3.12	1.27	16.49
17097	Home Preserving Co., Indianapolis, Ind	......	2.05	.55	1.52	26.14	15.28	2.16	1.24	8.70
17168	Jersey Pck. Co., Cincinnati, Ohio	Newport	1.24	.51	.74	23.84	11.02	2.56	1.77	10.26
17173	J. Weller, Cincinnati, Ohio	......	.99	.23	.77	20.64	5.87	3.37	2.64	11.40
17226	E. C. Hazard Co., New Jersey	......	1.11	.65	.48	16.31	3.10	3.90	3.25	9.31
17258	Sprague-Warner Co., Chicago, Ill	......	1.14	.55	.57	18.94	4.25	2.72	1.69	......
17273	A. W. Colter Can. Co., Mt. Washington, O.	Colter	1.92	1.21	.70	19.45	4.05	3.13	2.09	12.27
17315	C. S. Sullivan & Son, Denver, Ind	......	1.48	.34	1.14	17.00	5.75	3.01	1.71	8.24
17319	Fred C. Elder, Chicago, Ill	Kinzie	2.07	1.46	.58	21.87	5.73	2.77	2.30	13.37
17330	C. Callahan, LaFayette, Ind	Money Back	.99	.13	.84	22.49	5.35	4.03	2.88	13.11
17340	Kokomo Canning Co., Kokomo, Ind	......	.63	.31	.32	11.92	4.00	4.24	3.58	3.68
18067	Schnull & Co., Indianapolis, Ind	Diadem	.75	.42	.32	24.21	8.78	3.35	2.82	12.08

CATSUP—ILLEGAL.

Lab. No.	Manufacturer.	Brand.	Acidity.	Solids.	Ash.	Salt.	Sugar.	Sodium Benzoate.
14000	Lutz & Schramm, Cincinnati, Ohio		1.17	18.40	3.35	2.18	10.26	.276
14640	Williams Bros. Co., Detroit, Mich	Waldorf	1.14					.226
14651	Williams Bros. Co., Detroit, Mich	Waldorf	1.08					.207
14652	Williams Bros. Co., Detroit, Mich	Waldorf	1.14					.213
14653	Williams Bros. Co., Detroit, Mich	Waldorf	1.08					.217
14654	Williams Bros. Co., Detroit, Mich		1.02					.217
14655	Williams Bros. Co., Detroit, Mich	Waldorf	1.14					.223
14663	Curtice Bros. Co., , N. Y	Blue Label	.78					.211
14663	Curtice Bros. Co.,		.84					.208
14663	Curtice Bros. Co.,		.84					.169
14669	Williams Bros. Co.	Waldorf	.96					.179
14670		Squire	1.47					.178
14675		Fausts	1.35					.201
14679	Williams Bros. Co., Detroit, Mich	Wilco	1.08					.270
14698	Curtice Bros. Co., Rochester, N. Y	Blue Label	.72					.203
14701	Curtice Bros. Co., Rochester, N. Y	Blue Label	.84					.188
14704	Williams Bros Co., Detroit, Mich	Waldorf	1.08					.217
14705	Williams Bros. Co., Detroit, Mich	Waldorf	1.02					.210
14706	Williams Bros. Co., Detroit, Mich	Waldorf	1.08					.188
14712	National Pickling & Canning Co., St. Louis, Mo	Premium	1.17					.201
14713	National Pickling & Canning Co., St. Louis, Mo	Premium	.99					.201
14714	National Pickling & Canning Co., St. Louis, Mo	Premium	.87					.188
14715	Curtice Bros. Co., Rochester, N. Y	Blue Label	.84					.227
14718	National Pickling & Canning Co., St. Louis, Mo	Premium	1.41					.233
14622	Curtice Bros. Co., Rochester, N. Y	Blue Label	.78					.244
14723	Curtice Bros. Co., Rochester, N. Y	Blue Label	.72					.214
14753	Knadler & Lucas, Louisville, Ky	Admiral	.78					.233
14801	Williams Bros. Co., Detroit, Mich	Waldorf	1.08					.097
14802	Curtice Bros. Co., Rochester, N. Y	Blue Label	.73					.204
14803	Curtice Bros. Co., Rochester, N. Y	Blue Label	.78					.204
14804	Curtice Bros. Co., Rochester, N. Y	Blue Label	.78					.204
14805	Curtice Bros. Co., Rochester, N. Y	Blue Label	.78					.201
14806	Curtice Bros. Co., Rochester, N. Y	Blue Label	1.32					.135
14807	Curtice Bros. Co., Rochester, N. Y	Blue Label	.72					.213
14808	Curtice Bros. Co., Rochester, N. Y	Blue Label	.84					.169
14846	Curtice Bros. Co., Rochester, N. Y	Blue Label	.78					.216
14868	Williams Bros. Co., Detroit, Mich	Waldorf	.96					.217
14883	Curtice Bros. Co., Rochester, N. Y	Blue Label	.85					.164
14885	Curtice Bros. Co., Rochester, N. Y	Blue Label	.84					.160
15066	Williams Bros. Co., Detroit, Mich	Waldorf	1.20					.221
15104	Williams Bros. Co., Detroit, Mich	Waldorf	1.02					.221

5105	Williams Bros. Co., Detroit, Mich	Waldorf	.90					.168
15106	Williams Bros. Co., Detroit, Mich	Waldorf	1.08					.224
15108	Curtice Bros. Co., Rochester, N. Y	Blue Label	.84					.160
98c	Curtice rd. Co., Rochester, N. Y	Blue Label	.84					.174
1498b	uffice Bros. Co., hD, N. Y	Blue Label	.84					.129
1 99a	Curtice Bros. Co., Rochester, N. Y	Blue Label	.84					.083
1199b	Curtice Bros. Co., Rochester, N. Y	Blue Label	.84					.083
15255	Williams Bos. Co., Deit, Mich	Waldorf	1.20					.240
5256	Williams Bros. Co., Detroit, Mich	Wrf	1.08					.226
5257	Williams Bos. Co., Detroit, Mich	Wldorf	1.08					.250
15260	Williams Bros. Co., Detroit, Mich	Wldorf	1.08					.138
15261	Williams Bos. Co., Detroit, Mich	Waldorf	1.08					.138
15267	Williams Bos. Co., Detroit, Mh	Wf	1.08					.162
15268	Williams Bros. Co., Detroit, Mich	Waldorf	.72					.341
5269	Williams Bos. Co., Detroit, Mich	Waldorf	1.08					.185
15270	Williams Bos. Co., Detroit, Mich	Wrf	1.08					.244
15271	Williams Bros. Co., Dit, Mich	Waldorf	.96					.224
15271	ms Bros. Co., Detroit, Mich	Waldorf	1.08					.172
15273	Williams Bos. Co., Detroit, Mich	Waldorf	1.20					.213
15278	ms Bros. Co., Dit, Mich	Wf	1.08					.241
5279	A. H. Perfect & Co., Ft. Wayne, Ind	Perfect	.99	20.93	3.95	2.37	10.22	.408
15293	Williams Bros. Co., Droit, Mich	Waldorf	1.08					.216
5294	Williams Bs. Co., Detroit, Mich	Waldorf	.96					.177
801	Williams Bros. Co., oit, Mich	Waldorf	1.08					.213
5302	Williams Bros. Co., Droit, Mich	Waldorf	.72					.239
16147	The Horton Cato Manufacturing Co., Detroit, Mich	Royal	.84	22.76	3.23	2.60	14.25	.198
16335	Meil & Higgins, Chicago, Ill	ne Such	.88	20.01	2.78	1.74	12.38	.074
16240	bia Conserve Co., Indianapolis, Ind	Columbia						.180
16243	Kenwood Pres. Co., Chicago, Ill	Farm House	1.05	16.65	5.29	3.17	7.86	.132
16246	Schnull & Co., Indianapolis Ind	Hummer	1.44	15.54	2.04	1.28	7.22	.057
16336	Snider Pres. Co., Cincinnati, Ohio		.66	13.25	2.41	1.60	6.91	.062
16370	Elliott Grocery Co., Logansport, Ind	Index	.78	12.42	1.95	1.21	4.86	.195
16615	Acme Pres. Co		.96	17.63	2.84	2.00	11.26	.198
16757	Curtice Bros. Co., Rochester, N. Y	Blue Label	.60	16.74	3.28	2.30	8.17	.204
17020	J. Campbell, Camden, Ind		.66	14.19	1.94	2.81	7.48	.103
17094	W. W. Vaughn, Detroit, Mich							.461
17102	Faulkner-Webb Co., Indianapolis, Ind		1.45	17.32	4.09	2.99	6.75	.172
17103	J. C. Perry Co., Indianapolis, Ind		.90	10.94	2.01	1.19	3.99	.250
17104	W. D. Huffman, Indianapolis, Ind		1.08	24.14	4.38	3.03	13.94	.178
17213	Beechnut Packing Co., New York	Beechnut						.361
17228	E. C. Howard Co., New Jersey							.283
17252	Geo. A. Boyle, St. Louis, Mo		.93	10.15	3.27	2.15	3.19	.253
17256	Walsh, Lange Co., Chicago, Ill		.81	20.56	4.13	3.21	10.86	.063
17270	Franklin McVeagh Co., Chicago, Ill		.85	18.49	3.18	2.46	11.13	.149
17271	Williams Bros. Co., Detroit, Mich		.81	25.05	4.61	3.75	17.20	.152
17274	Hurs & Edler, Chicago, Ill	Kinsie	.66	16.67	4.09	3.38	8.96	.161
17277	Franklin McVeagh Co., Chicago, Ill		1.20	12.90	2.57	1.80	5.66	.095
17300	Squire-Dingee Co., Chicago, Ill	Squire	1.59	11.56	2.44	1.77	5.05	.195

CATSUP—ILLEGAL—Continued.

Lab. No.	Manufacturer.	Brand.	Acidity.	Solids.	Ash.	Salt.	Sugar.	Sodium Benzoate.
17314	E. G. Daley, Detroit, Mich	Boy	1.18	19.18	3.69	1.62	11.05	.168
17323	H. Wichert Co., Chicago, Ill		1.17	20.31	3.90	3.20	9.76	.123
17336	W. J. Quam, Chicago, Ill		1.05	18.25	3.30	2.38	9.88	.223
17342	Geo. A. Boyle, St. Louis, Mo	Boyle	.72	10.88	3.02	3.69	1.71	.227
17345	H. Wichert, Chicago, Ill		.90	21.45	6.98	5.26	12.16	Present.
17428	South Shore Catsup Co., Chicago, Ill	South Shore	.90	10.24	3.42	2.76	1.21	.207
17431	Randolph Co., Chicago, Ill	Clipper	2.11	12.12	3.34	2.87	3.83	.095
17599	National Pickling & Canning Co., St. Louis, Mo	Premium	.69	15.60	2.12	1.50	9.08	.241
17603	Union Catsup Co., Chicago, Ill	[illegible]	.99	9.00	3.16	2.62	.30	.181
17767	Kokomo Canning Co., Kokomo, Ind	Kokomo						.210
17815	Kentucky Canning Co., Owensboro, Ky	Kentucky Belle	1.08	18.61	2.45	1.67	11.28	.290
17816	Geo. Sproul Pck. Co., Harrison, Ohio	My Own	1.17	21.05	3.03	1.96	12.57	.199
4773b	Columbia Conserve Co., Indianapolis, Ind	[illegible]	.99	17.82	3.31	2.38	9.31	.112
17876	Curtice Bros. Co., Rochester, N. Y	[illegible]						.201
17884	Curtice Bros. Co., Rochester, N. Y	Blue Label						.105
17933	Williams Bros. Co., Detroit, Mich							.308
17934	Curtice Bros. Co., Rochester, N. Y							.201
17935	M. Wagner Co., Baltimore, Md							.299
17970	F. A. Pekownik, Indiana Harbor, Ind	Townsend						.204
17973	F. A. Pekownik, Indiana Harbor, Ind							.051
17975	Galik E. Babjar, Indiana Harbor, Ind							.149
17978	Dodson-Braun, St. Louis, Mo							.190
17996	Bement-Rea Co., Terre Haute, Ind	Keystone						.072
18070	W. D. Huffman, Co. Indianapolis, Ind							Present.
18098	Williams Bros. Co., Detroit, Mich	[illegible]						.138
18184	Williams Bros. Co., Detroit, Mich	Waldorf						.311
18190	Curtice Bros. Co., Rochester, N. Y	[illegible]						.187
18205	Williams Bros. Co., Detroit, Mich							.307
18306	Williams Bros. Co., Detroit, Mich	Waldorf						.135

MAPLE SYRUP.

Forty-three samples of maple syrup were analyzed, 34 of which were legal and 9 illegal. The illegal syrups were so classed because of the presence of added sugar or glucose. One sample was a very dilute syrup and, although a maple product, could not be classed as a pure maple syrup. Two of the five samples of maple sugar were not pure maple sugars since they contained added sugars not the product of the maple tree. The majority of the samples of maple syrup analyzed were not collected by inspectors, but were sent in for analysis by customers who had purchased them either from grocers or farmers and who, for some reason, suspected their purity.

MAPLE SYRUP—LEGAL.

Lab. No.	Retailer or Manufacturer.	Polarization.		Sucrose.	Total Ash.	Alk. of Ash.		Solids.
		Direct.	Invert.			Soluble.	Insoluble.	
*15797	Everson Prebster, Brownsburg	+56.6	—20.2	57.9	.824	.80	1.08	......
*16171	Kothe, Wells & Bauer, Indianapolis	......	......	......	.560	.40	.40	......
16813	W. W. Reed, Warsaw	+61.2	−14.3	58.2	.930	.28	.72	......
*17195	Kothe, Wells & Bauer, Indianapolis	+59.0	−16.9	58.0	.550	.48	.50	......
*17223	Abner Earhart, Denver	+66.8	−16.7	64.0	.578	.48	.58	......
*17267	F. W. Comeford, Gary	......	......	......	.524	.42	.50	......
*17312	V. V. Cameron, Marion	+59.6	−15.2	57.6	.510	.32	.52	60.64
*17313	V. V. Cameron, Marion	+60.8	−15.8	59.0	.720	.50	.48	68.32
*17455	H. P. Coffman, Greencastle	+65.6	−15.1	61.8	.820	.49	.54	70.57
*17631	J. C. Kashner, Thorntown	......	......	......	.61	.36	.64	65.42
17693	Kelly & Allman, Peru	+58.8	−20.4	60.6	.67	.56	.75	66.10
17694	Kelly & Allman, Peru	+48.2	−19.1	51.5	.63	.39	.33	......
17696	Wm. Doehmann, Ft. Wayne	+60.0	−20.4	61.5	.56	.44	.73	66.14
17699	Cocerdale & Archer Co., Ft. Wayne	+55.8	−20.2	......	.65	.44	1.00	68.60
*17722	C. Z. Thistlethwaite, Sheridan	+61.6	−22.0	63.9	.52	.43	.70	68.10
*17761	Mrs. Willard Hurt, Monrovia	+63.3	−13.5	58.8	.77	.54	.74	68.50
*17762	R. D. Hardman, Lafontaine	+55.8	−20.1	58.1	.78	.61	.63	69.30
*17765	Dr. D. W. Weaver, Greensburg	+61.4	−12.6	56.6	.75	.48	.77	69.60
*17766	Dr. D. W. Weaver, Greensburg	+64.6	−17.7	62.9	.60	.42	.67	69.10
*17773	R. L. Cooper, Mooresville	+59.3	−17.3	58.7	.70	.45	.62	70.10
*17774	Mike Slavin, Bluff Road	+59.4	−14.6	56.7	.75	.55	.80	66.90
*17805	Dr. John White, Terre Haute	+62.1	−14.9	58.9	.68	.39	.81	68.90
17848	J. A. Dailey, Terre Haute	+63.6	−16.6	61.4	.84	.55	.55	68.20
17852	J. W. Stern, Peru	+65.4	−16.2	62.6	.58	.48	.61	71.30
*17997	Mrs. W. H. Minnick, Angola	+62.7	−18.4	60.9	.78	.47	.60	68.10
18044	Price & Lucas, Louisville, Ky	+44.3	−13.0	44.0	.08	.10	.06	61.65
*18170	Mr. Wallace, State House, Indianapolis	+42.6	−11.2	41.0	.70	.40	1.03	68.80
*18177	J. Hunter, Elwood	+58.6	−20.4	59.8	.67	.39	.53	62.50
18250	Mrs. Nathan Myers, Wabash	+59.2	− 7.1	51.5	.62	.34	.62	65.60
*18280	F. Henry, Indianapolis	+59.2	−20.8	60.5	.65	.50	.50	68.20
*18467	Mrs. N. Meyer, Wabash	+57.6	−20.2	60.0	.61	.33	.67	65.59
*18644	Schnull & Co., Indianapolis	+60.0	−16.5	58.7	.63	.46	.54	66.54
*18645	Schnull & Co., Indianapolis	+60.2	−16.9	59.0	.49	.34	.52	61.74
*18913	W. B. Leeson, Martinsville	+60.0	− 1.5	47.2	.79	.52	.75	63.87

* Refers to samples brought to the laboratory.

MAPLE SYRUP—ILLEGAL.

Lab. No.	Retailer or Manufacturer.	Polarization.		Sucrose.	Total Ash.	Alk. of Ash.		Solids.
		Direct.	Invert.			Soluble.	Insoluble.	
14834	Reid, Murdock Co., Chicago, Ill	+55.4	−21.1	57.6	.338	.50	.38	....
15265	E. A. Charbonnaw, Detroit, Mich	+35.7	−20.6	42.5	.084	.42	.18	....
16315	Lewis Ray, Logansport	+62.6	−15.6	60.3	.020	.02	.03	....
16937	M. L. Michael, LaPorte	+60.0	−16.7	59.0	.190	.60	.20	....
*17623	F. N. Thurston, Indianapolis	+66.4	− 8.8	58.0	1.100	.36	.84	72.05
†17676	D. Stratigas, Gary	+119.2	+115.0	3.0	.210	.10	.25	....
17678	John Karidy, Gary	+58.6	−19.5	59.8	.080	.07	.14	69.00
17698	Getz, Sharp & Orr, Ft. Wayne	+55.6	−19.8	57.7	.490	.43	.58	66.30
18471	Ray O. Hoover, Akron, Ind	+30.0	−19.5	39.0	.920	.58	1.10	65.84

* Refers to samples brought to the laboratory.
† This sample is 66.4% glucose.

MAPLE SUGAR.

Lab. No.	Retailer or Manufacturer.	Polarization.		Sucrose.	Total Ash.	Alk. of Ash.		Remarks.
		Direct.	Invert.			Soluble.	Insoluble.	
17526	Clyde A. Stagg, Greensburg	+92.4	−7.48	....	1.13	.67	1.27	Legal.
17695	Kelly & Allman, Peru	....	....	....	0.99	.82	1.37	Legal.
17697	F. P. Minsch, Ft. Wayne	....	....	....	1.08	.62	1.48	Legal.
18416	J. L. Blocker, West Baden	+71.2	−6.72	50.7	1.30	.58	0.64	Not pure maple sugar.
18417	Reid, Murdock Co., Chicago, Ill.	+78.4	−1.20	61.6	0.68	.46	0.92	Not pure maple sugar.

SYRUP.

Under this heading is included samples of sorghum and molasses. Seven samples of syrup were analyzed, of which 6 were legal and 1 illegal. One sample was sold as pure sorghum, but it contained glucose, and for that reason was classed as illegal.

SYRUPS.

Lab. No.	Retailer or Manufacturer.	Brand.	Per Cent Ash.		Alkalinity of Ash.		Polarization.		Sucrose.	Remarks.
			Total.	Insoluble.	Soluble.	Insoluble.	Direct.	Invert.		
16274	Corn Product Ref. Co., New York	Magnolia	3.24	.750	1.11	.74	+63.5	+41.58	17.0	Illegal, 26.57% glucose
*16408	Morrell Simpson, Bedford	Sorghum	4.22	.570	4.40	1.20	50.0	−2.00	....	Legal.
16589	Thomas J. Trout, Bruceville	Sorghum	2.71	.510	1.10	.70	+24.8	−17.00	32.2	Legal.
16625	L. E. Mosher, North Judson	Sorghum	2.54	.620	.99	.75	+26.4	−15.40	32.2	Legal.
16843	J. C. Schnull, Peru	Sorghum	2.52	.650	1.02	.86	+32.0	−17.80	38.4	Legal.
*17194	F. L. Brown, Anderson	Sorghum	1.90	.350	1.58	.90	+52.4	+29.92	17.2	Not pure sorghum.
*17396	W. S. Easterday, Culver	Sorghum	2.44	.680	1.62	1.80	+30.4	−11.00	31.9	Legal.

* Refers to samples brought to the laboratory.

OYSTERS.

Twenty-two samples of oysters were analyzed, of which 14 were legal and 8 illegal, either because of the presence of an excess of free water or because the dealer used an illegal short measure in filling the order. The character of oysters has entirely changed in the last two years and all shucked oysters shipped into the State are now free from added ice or water.

OYSTERS—LEGAL.

Lab. No.	Retailer.	Weight (Grams).	Per Cent. Free Water.
16307	W. McCaffrey & Co., Logansport	440	6.8
16359	M. C. Shea & Co., Indianapolis	475	9.7
16360	Poultry & Oyster House, Indianapolis	509	10.8
16361	A. Booth Co., Indianapolis	1,949	14.8
16362	Frank G. Kamps, Indianapolis	1,809	10.2
16455	L. E. Downey, Rochester	485	Trace.
16456	Frank Marsh, Rochester	505	5.9
16459	R. P. True, Rochester	493	3.0
16460	E. E. Clary, Rochester	495	14.1
16461	J. T. Liston, Rochester	505	1.9
16462	O. Karn, Rochester	510	12.7
17530	Jas. M. Sowders, Indianapolis	535	14.0
17531	Nicholson & Co., Indianapolis	490	8.1
17553	Mrs. T. J. Egan, Indianapolis	460	11.5

OYSTERS—ILLEGAL.

Lab. No.	Retailer.	Weight (Grams.)	Per Cent. Free Water.	Short Measure.
16355	G. W. Nicholson, Indianapolis	467	22.1	
16368	Andrew Shorter, Winamac	575	28.8	
16479	T. G. Kamps, Indianapolis	455	24.2	
16806	M. A. Pesch, Plymouth	344	30.8	
17528	McWilliamson & Co., Indianapolis	496	18.3	
17532	Sowders Fish Co., Indianapolis	470	17.0	
17529	Earnest McCormick, Indianapolis	405	11.1	15.4%
17552	Earnest McCormick, Indianapolis	450	8.7	4.8%

SAUSAGE.

One hundred and eighteen samples of pan and pork sausage were analyzed, of which 102 were legal and 16 were illegal. The illegal samples were so classed because of the presence of sodium sulphite added as a preservative or of starch used as a binder.

SAUSAGE—ILLEGAL.

Lab. No.	Manufacturer.	Sulphites as Sodium Sulphite.	Borax.	Starch.
16345	C. L. Coppock, Jonesboro	.0569%	Absent	Absent.
16382	Long & Watson, Columbus	.0211%	Absent	Absent.
16507	Eckerts Co., Ft. Wayne		Absent	Present.
16510	Eckerts Co., Ft. Wayne		Absent	Present.
16511	G. E. Spiegel, Ft. Wayne	.0176%	Absent	Absent.
16515	Leikauf Pck. Co., Ft. Wayne		Absent	Present.
16516	Eckerts Co., Ft. Wayne		Absent	Present.
16542	H. B. Graybrook, New Albany	.3558%	Absent	Absent.
16583	Weeks Meat Co., Rushville	.0816%	Absent	Present.
16584	H. A. Kramer, Rushville	.0871%	Absent	Absent.
16710	Libby, McNeal & Libby, Chicago, Ill		Present	Absent.
16730	George Rapp, Hartford City	.0230%	Absent	Absent.
16950	Zhart Bros., LaPorte	.0220%	Absent	Absent.
16956	Tanke Bros., LaPorte	.0599%	Absent	Absent.
17616	Gary Provision Co., Gary	.0977%	Absent	Absent.
17686	F. Lassu, Mishawaka	.0498%	Absent	Absent.

PREPARED MEATS.

Under the heading "Prepared Meats" is included various types of sausage and minced meat, such as bologna, liverwurst, weinerwurst, ham, corned beef, etc. Eighty-one samples were analyzed, of which 22 were classed as illegal because of the presence of borax, sulphites or starch. In some samples both a preservative and starch was found. While the use of preservatives is decreasing, yet butchers still recognize the efficiency of sulphites in making their unsalable meats appear in good condition. The use of starch as a filler or binder is far less common than formerly and, although it is occasionally used and its presence declared on the label, yet most prepared meats are now made without it.

PREPARED MEATS—ILLEGAL.

Lab. No.	Classification.	Manufacturer.	Starch.	Borax.	Sulphites.
16732	Bloodwurst	E. E. Yeoman, Hartford City	Present	Absent	Absent.
16416	Bologna	Wallace & Carroll, Edwardsport	Present	Present	Absent.
16419	Bologna	Tare & Downs, Plainville		Present	Absent.
16669	Bologna	Anthony Stall, Brookville	Present	Present	Absent.
16682	Bologna	F. A. Maibaugh, Liberty	Present	Absent	Absent.
16720	Bologna	S. G. Spink, Dunkirk	Present	Absent	Absent.
16748	Bologna	Veit Bros., Union City	Present	Absent	Absent.
17100	Bologna	L. M. Golas, Indianapolis	Absent	Present	Absent.
16418	Hamburger	Tare & Downs, Plainville	Absent	Present	Absent.
16539	Hamburger	M. Wolfe, New Albany	Absent	Absent	Present.
16548	Hamburger	Ben Mertz & Son, New Albany	Absent	Absent	Present.
16729	Hamburger	George Rapp, Hartford City	Absent	Absent	Present.
16955	Hamburger	Fred W. Steigley, LaPorte	Absent	Absent	Present.
17101	Hamburger	L. M. Golas, Indianapolis	Absent	Absent	Present.
17106	Hamburger	Henry Dobrowitz, Indianapolis	Absent	Absent	Present.
17619	Hamburger	Tittle Bros., Gary	Absent	Absent	Present.
17684	Hamburger	A. Bucholtz, South Bend	Absent	Absent	Present.
*18231	Hamburger	Jacob Friedman, Hammond	Absent	Absent	Present.
16469	Weinerwurst	Guy Eshelman & Derr	Present	Absent	Absent.
16473	Weinerwurst	P. G. Powers, Marion	Present	Absent	Absent.
16474	Weinerwurst	Ira Emmons, Marion	Present	Absent	Absent.
16654	Weinerwurst	Ringloff & McCullen, Connersville	Present	Absent	Absent.

* Refers to samples brought to the laboratory.

The following is a list of meats, smoked, etc., analyzed and found to contain neither starch, borax, sulphites nor benzoic acid:

Classification.	Number Analyzed.
Bacon	2
Beef—	
Corned	2
Dried	1
Potted	1
Ham	7
Hamburger	24
Liverwurst	10
Meat, mixed	2
Pigs feet	2
Pudding sauce	1
Sausage—	
Bologna	7
Pan pork, etc	102
Total	161

CIDER VINEGAR.

Thirty-six of the 60 samples of cider vinegar were legal and 24 illegal. Nineteen of the illegal cider vinegars were sent in for analysis by dealers who suspected the purity of the product. It is apparent that much of the cider vinegar produced by farmers is sent to market before reaching maturity. Analyses of many samples brought to the laboratory by the producers shows the presence of alcohol, indicating that acetous fermentation is not complete. A study of the analyses of these home-made vinegars also shows that many farmers still employ vinegar formulas calling for the addition of rain water or sugar. It is unnecessary to point out that the only way to make a pure cider vinegar is to allow pure and undiluted cider to go through the several stages of fermentation required to convert all of the sugar solids of the cider into acetic acid and that the addition of any diluent, color or clarifier, or of sugar or molasses for the purpose of increasing the acidity is illegal and that the vinegar so prepared can not be sold as cider vinegar.

The fraud in the sale of vinegars continues, for the profits accruing from the sale of imitation cider vinegars are so great that the manufacturers are willing to take the chances of discovery by either Federal or State inspectors. The expert chemist of the vinegar factory is able to build up a vinegar which chemically is practically identical with a pure cider product by the use of grain vinegar, apple solids and certain chemicals, which when properly mixed meet the requirements of a standard cider vinegar.

CIDER VINEGAR—LEGAL.

Lab. No.	Retailer or Manufacturer.	Acidity.	Solid.	Ash. Total.	Ash. Alkalinity.	Lead Acetate Precipitate.	Color.	Polarization.
15853	McNarney Bros., Wabash, Indiana	4.10	2.478	.390	39.0	Heavy	Normal	— .8
16128	Harbauer Marleau Co., Toledo	4.76	2.672	.454	22.0	Heavy	Normal	— .4
16150	Williams Brothers & Co., Detroit, Michigan	4.85	3.014	.491	32.0	Medium	Nnal	— .4
16209	Hirsch Brothers, Louisville, Kentucky	4.06	3.016	.426	31.0	Medium	Nnal	—1.6
16210	Hirsch Brothers, Louisville, Kentucky	4.06	3.066	.415	31.0	Mm	Normal	—1.6
16211	Hirsch Brothers, Louisville, Kentucky	4.06	3.063	.448	31.0	Mm	dial	—1.0
16212	Hirsch Brothers, Louisville, Kentucky	4.06	3.058	.430	31.0	Mum	Normal	—1.6
16213	Hirsch Brothers, Louisville, Kentucky	4.06	3.046	.428	31.0	Medium	Normal	—1.6
16422	Price & Lucas, Louisville, Kentucky	4.04	3.431	.440	31.0	Heavy	Normal	— .8
16425	Jones Brothers Co., Louisville, Kentucky	4.31	3.011	.480	44.0	Medium	Nmal	—1.6
16426	Jones Brothers Co., Louisville, Kentucky	4.28	3.031	.407	44.0	Mum	Normal	— .8
16429	Knadler & Lucas, Louisville, Kentucky	4.06	2.946	.428	33.0	Medium	Normal	— .6
*16448	John Hortsman, Logansport, Indiana	4.28	2.244	.271	38.0	Heavy	Nnal	—1.0
16454	L. M. Brackett, Rochester	4.30	2.343	.263	24.0	Mm	Normal	— .4
16500	Hirsch Brothers, Louisville, Kentucky	4.16	3.161	.382	30.0	Mm	Normal	±0.
16595	C. M. Hill, Bruceville, Indiana	4.48	2.817	.350	26.0	Heavy	Nnal	—2.2
16613	S. F. Gurtez & Co., Brazil, Indiana	4.74	2.443	.318	28.0	Medium	Nnal	—1.6
16764	Moellerine Brothers, Fort Wayne	4.54	1.672	.247	26.0	Heavy	Normal	— .8
16850	Huntington Grocery Co., Huntington	4.27	2.564	.334	21.0	Light	Normal	±0.
*17397	W. D. Huffman, Indianapolis, Indiana	4.01	2.311	.211	24.0	Slight	Normal	— .2
*17534	Bartlett Tea Co., Indianapolis, Indiana	4.04	2.497	.214	21.0	Heavy	Normal	—1.8
*17624	R. M. Mueller, Indianapolis, Indiana	4.09	2.212	.322	30.0	Medium	Normal	— .6
*17691	Robinson Cider and Vinegar Co., Benton Harbor, Michigan	4.40	2.891	.374	28.0	Heavy	Normal	—1.2
*17700	Preussing & Co., Chicago, Illinois	4.12	2.432	.328	35.0	Heavy	Normal	—1.4
*17763	J. M. Zion, Clarks Hill, Indiana	5.28	1.627	.291	24.0	....	....	....
*17764	J. M. Zion, Clarks Hill, Indiana	5.27	1.932	.354	29.0	....	....	—1.0
17879	Baldwin & Carey, Muncie	4.22	2.893	.399	44.0	Heavy	Normal	—3.6
17952	Price & Lucas, Louisville, Kentucky	4.13	1.940	.279	23.0	Heavy	Nnal	—1.2
*18405	South Bend Grocery Co., South Bend	5.24	2.196	.280	23.0	Light	N rmal	±0.
*18503	Kothe, Wells & Bauer, Indianapolis	4.04	2.503	.342	30.0	Heavy	Normal	— .8
*18816	Levy Hamilton, Greensburg	4.76	1.525	.308	27.0	Medium	rNal	±0.
*18817	Levy Hamilton, Greensburg	4.90	1.970	.334	30.0	Medium	Normal	±0.
18848	Crutchfield & Son, Boonville	4.31	3.980	.430	42.0	Mm	Normal	—2.4
*18928	Kothe, Wells & Bauer, Indianapolis	4.19	2.283	.372	28.0	Heavy	....	—1.6
*19003	**M. F. Davis, Medora**	7.60	3.244	.479	48.0	Light	Normal	—2.8
*19097	**Kothe, Wells & Bauer, Indianapolis**	4.15	2.461	.334	32.0	Heavy	Normal	— .8

* Refers to samples brought to the laboratory.

CIDER VINEGAR—ILLEGAL.

Lab. No.	Retailer or Manufacturer.	Acidity.	Solid.	Ash. Total.	Ash. Alkalinity.	Lead Acetate Precipitate.	Color.	Polarization.
*16151	Mrs. Landes, Indianapolis	2.48	1.308	.365	34.0	Heavy	Normal	− .8
*16172	Kothe, Wells & Bauer, Indianapolis	3.80	2.032	.312	28.0	Heavy	Normal	±0.
16186	Vigo Com. Co., Terre Haute	3.74	.725	.118	20.0	Medium	Normal	−1.2
16606	O. P. Damer, Clay City	4.22	1.624	.134	14.0	Light	Normal	− .6
16765	J. Meyers, Roanoke	4.48	.741	.209	9.0	None	Normal	+1.0
*16811	LaFayette Grocery Co., LaFayette	4.38	1.078	.141	7.0	None	Normal	+3.2
*16883	Kothe, Wells & Bauer, Indianapolis	4.84	.453	.132	4.0	Light	Normal	+1.4
*17161	Cruikshank Brothers, Pittsburg, Pennsylvania	5.06	2.012	.320	26.0	Medium	Normal	−1.6
*17162	E. B. Mitchell & Co., Sinclairville, N. Y.	5.07	2.731	.217	17.0	Medium	Normal	−1.8
*17163	Kothe, Wells & Bauer, Indianapolis	3.96	2.656	.245	23.0	Very heavy	Normal	− .2
*17689	Mrs. Bringham, Indianapolis	2.10						
*17690	F. W. Law, Chicago, Illinois	4.05	1.826	.217	22.0	Light	C. W. C	− .4
*17692	Hulman & Co., Terre Haute	4.30	1.545	.232	12.0	Light	Normal	±0.
18002	National Grocery Co., South Bend	4.00	1.159	.561	16.0	Heavy		+1.6
*18008	Brought in by Dr. Bitting, LaFayette	1.93	2.350	.357	32.0	Heavy	Normal	−3.6
*18009	Brought in by Dr. Bitting, LaFayette	1.60	1.912	.351	32.0	Heavy	Normal	−2.8
*18071	Elliott Grocery Co., Logansport	4.22	1.101	.101	5.0	None		+2.0
*18365	J. B. Berterling, South Bend	4.36	1.605	.115	8.0	Light	Normal	− .4
*18432	N. A. Moore, Indianapolis	3.33	3.174	.458	26.0	Light	Normal	−1.6
*18747	Henry Deweese, Kokomo	3.615						
18818	Mr. Levy Hamilton, Greensburg	2.00	1.153	.290	20.0	Medium	Normal	±0.
18853	Pierson & Scovill, Boonville	4.64	0.620	.315	0.6	None	Normal	+0.±
*18974	G. C. Brinkmeyer, Indianapolis	2.24	1.585	.191	8.0	Light	Normal	−1.2
*19102	W. S. Frazier, Indianapolis	1.76						
*19103	W. S. Frazier, Indianapolis	2.34						

* Refers to samples brought to the laboratory.

DISTILLED VINEGAR.

Thirty-five samples of distilled vinegar were analyzed, and of these 15 were classed as illegal because of the acid content below the standard of 4 per cent. Eight uncolored distilled vinegars, all of which were legal, were analyzed.

DISTILLED VINEGAR—LEGAL.

Lab. No.	Retailer or Manufacturer.	Acidity.	Solid.	Ash.		Lead Acetate Precipitate.	Color.	Polarization.
				Total.	Alkalinity.			
16116	A. R. Ewing & Sons, Mitchell	4.30	.362	.044	4.0	None	Colored	+1.6
16191	E. C. Laughlin, Lyons, Indiana	4.02	.442	.592	13.0	None	Normal	+1.8
16194	Fred Brough, Lyons	4.19	.296	.059	5.0	None	C. W. C.	+1.2
16204	E. W. Gwartney, Linton	4.18	.286	.051	4.0	None	C. W. C.	+1.4
16205	Lawrence S. Bey, Vincennes	4.18	.295	.048	4.0	None	C. W. C.	+1.4
16206	A. L. Eberhart, Greensburg	4.18	.282	.045	4.0	None	C. W. C.	+1.4
16206	A. L. Eberhart, Greensburg	4.18	.282	.045	4.0	None	C. W. C.	+1.4
16207	Gresham & Kelldews, French Lick	4.18	.288	.049	4.0	None	C. W. C.	+1.4
16208	Davis & King, Princeton	4.18	.286	.286	4.0	None	C. W. C.	+1.4
16428	Jones Brothers Co., Louisville, Kentucky	4.30	.285	.043	2.0	None	C. W. C.	±0.
16430	Knadler & Lucas, Louisville, Kentucky	4.01	.421	.039	2.0	None	C. W. C.	+ .8
16497	Schnull & Co.	4.44	.483	.039	2.0	None	C. W. C.	+1.2
16498	Spencer Manufacturing Co., Spencer	4.14	.399	.022	2.0	None	C. W. C.	+ .8
16499	Callahan & Co., LaFayette	4.03	.141	.020	2.0	None	C. W. C.	− .8
16504	J. M. Evans, Spencer	4.20	.357	.071	4.0	None	C. W. C.	+0.
16593	Price & Lucas, Louisville, Kentucky	4.16	.267	.026	4.0	None	C. W. C.	+1.0
16605	Bement Rea, Terre Haute	3.18	.327	.026	4.0	None	C. W. C.	+2.4
16608	Price & Lucas, Louisville, Kentucky	4.14	.241	.019	2.0	None	C. W. C.	+2.0
16610	C. Ballinger & Son, Brazil	4.03	.219	.022	2.0	None	C. W. C.	+1.2
16611	Price & Lucas, Louisville, Kentucky	4.30	.249	.027	3.0	None	C. W. C.	+2.0
*16705	D. Smith, Kokomo	4.27						
16849	W. D. Huffman, Indianapolis	4.14	.274	.037	2.0	None	C. W. C.	+1.6
*17268	Henry Judy, Kokomo	4.10	.316	.036	1.0	None	C. W. C.	+ .6
17949	Schnull & Co., Indianapolis	4.72	.482	.055	1.0	None	C. W. C.	.8
*18178	Schafer Brothers, LaFayette	5.12	.882	.098	2.0	None	C. W. C.	+1.4
18462	Chas. W. Linn, Terre Haute	4.18	.269	.045	2.0	None	C. W. C.	+1.0
18590	Kothe, Wells & Bauer, Indianapolis	4.34	.257	.036	1.0	None	C. W. C.	+ .6
*18647	Greentown Canning Co., Greentown	4.22					C. W. C.	
*18663	E. H. Brubaker, New Castle	4.36	.245	.025	1.0	None	C. W. C.	+1.6
18857	Price & Lucas, Louisville, Kentucky	4.70	.356	.061	.04	Light	C. W. C.	+−0.−

* Refers to samples brought to the laboratory.

COLORED DISTILLED VINEGAR—ILLEGAL.

Lab. No.	Retailer or Manufacturer.	Acidity.	Solids.	Ash.		Lead Acetate Ppt.	Color.	Polarisation.
				Total.	Alkalinity.			
16501	Home Preserving Co., Indpls	3.63	.212	.013	2.0	None.	C.W.C.	+1.6
16761	S. Bressett, Terre Haute	2.22	.199	.019	4.0	Light.	C.W.C.	+1.0
16762	Crown Bottling Wks., Terre Haute	3.72	.230	.024	4.0	None.	C.W.C.	+2.8
*18487	D. Smith, Kokomo	3.68	......	......	......	......	......	......
16612	Decker Grocery Co., Brazil	3.93	.234	.034	2.0	None.	......	+1.2

* Refers to samples brought to the laboratory.

UNCOLORED DISTILLED VINEGAR—LEGAL.

Lab. No.	Retailer or Manufacturer.	Acidity.	Solids.	Ash.		Lead Acetate Pppt.	Polarisation.
				Total.	Alkalinity.		
16423	Price & Lucas, Louisville, Kentucky	4.22	.253	.060	3.0	None.	+ .6
16427	Jones Bros. Co., Louisville, Kentucky	4.60	.226	.036	3.05	None.	+ .8
16431	Knadler & Lucas, Louisville, Kentucky	4.02	.362	.042	3.00	None.	+ .4
16503	Heins Co., Pittsburg, Pennsylvania	5.72	.223	.032	3.05	None.	+1.4
16594	Price & Lucas, Louisville, Kentucky	4.10	.179	.023	3.00	None.	+1.0
*18648	S. V. Wilcutts, Greentown	4.32	......	......	......	......	......
18850	Hirsch Bros., Louisville, Kentucky	4.10	.508	.140	0.6	None.	±0.
18856	Bement-Seitz Co., Evansville	4.10	.295	.065	0.6	None.	±C.

* Refers to samples brought to the laboratory.

SPICES.

Before the passage of the pure food laws no one food product was more grossly adulterated than spices. At the present time, spices are rarely adulterated. During the year 2 cases of the sale of illegal spices were reported, one the sale of a prepared mustard containing benzoate of soda and the other of prepared spices for the use of sausage makers which contained 6.3 per cent. of sodium sulphite. A special study was made of the acetic acid content of prepared mustard. These goods are made more acid than almost any other food product, the amount running as high as 4.8 per cent. Including prepared mustards, 30 spices were analyzed during the year.

PREPARED MUSTARD—LEGAL.

Lab. No.	Manufacturer.	Per Cent. Acetic Acid.	Remarks.
14509	Dwinnel & Wright, Chicago, Illinois	....	Legal—labeled correctly.
14677	Natl. Pickle & Canning Co., St. Louis, Missouri	3.12	No benzoate.
14717	Williams Brothers, Detroit, Michigan	4.08	
14857	Williams Brothers, Detroit, Michigan	3.96	
14882	Charles Singler, South Bend, Indiana	....	Mixture of mustard and flour but properly labeled.
14884	Williams Brothers, Detroit, Michigan	4.08	
14904	Williams Brothers, Detroit, Michigan	3.90	
14946	Williams Brothers, Detroit, Michigan	4.08	
15083	Larkin Company, Buffalo, N. Y.	....	Legal.
15107	Williams Brothers Co., Detroit, Michigan	3.84	
15258	Williams Brothers Co., Detroit, Michigan	4.02	
15259	Williams Brothers Co., Detroit, Michigan	4.08	
15383	Williams Brothers Co., Detroit, Michigan	3.96	
15436	Williams Brothers Co., Detroit, Michigan	4.02	
15437	Williams Brothers Co., Detroit, Michigan	3.90	
16686	Home Preserving Co., Indianapolis, Indiana	....	No benzoate or salicylic acid present.

PREPARED MUSTARD—ILLEGAL.

Lab. No.	Manufacturer.	Acetic Acid, Per Cent.	Benzoate of Soda, Per Cent.	Turmeric.
14680	Alart & McGuire, New York, N. Y. (Dealer, Hulman & Co., Terre Haute)	2.64	.1526	Present.

SPICES—MISCELLANEOUS.

Lab. No.	Name and Address of Dealer.	Classification.	Remarks.
14510	J. M. Carver, Edinburg	Allspice	Legal.
14511	J. M. Carver, Edinburg	Allspice	Legal.
14512	J. M. Carver, Edinburg	Ginger	Legal.
14538	Hall & Ferguson, Owensburg	Black Pepper	Legal.
15084	Lorena Elrod, Paoli	Black Pepper	Legal.
15085	Lorena Elrod, Paoli	Ground Cloves	Legal.
15274	G. E. Bursley & Co., Ft. Wayne	Pepper	Ash content—6.14.
15614	C. Foreman, Farmersburg	Pepper	Legal.
16103	J. A. Willits, Columbia City	Black Pepper	Legal.
16266	McCaffrey & Co., Peru	Curry Powder	Legal.
16687	Ed Haywood, Rushville	Spice	Contains 6.3% sodium sulphite—Illegal.
17727	A. H. Perfect & Co., Ft. Wayne	Cinnamon	Legal.
18340	Hulman & Co., Terre Haute	Black Pepper	Legal.

PICKLED PRODUCTS.

Under this head we include sweet and sour pickled cucumbers, mixed pickles, chopped pickles, etc. A special study was made of these goods to determine their acid content and the presence or absence of sodium benzoate and alum. Of the 11 samples of pickled onions examined, 6 were classed as legal and 5 were illegal. The illegal samples were so classed because of the presence of alum, except in one instance where the label showed the use of malt vinegar when in fact distilled vinegar was employed. Of the 35 samples of various types of cucumber pickles examined, 13 were classed as legal and 22 as illegal, because of the presence of sodium benzoate or alum or both or the use of the word "malt" on the label when distilled vinegar was in fact employed. The sodium benzoate content varied from .05 to .1699. The acidity expressed in terms of acetic acid varies widely, ranging from 1.71 to 3.91. It is worthy of notice that pickles of the same brand and apparently from the same lot do not contain the same amount either of acid or sodium benzoate. One sample of Gold Medal pickles, for instance, has an acetic acid content of 2.62 with .1699 per cent sodium benzoate. Another bottle of the same brand shows acidity of 1.71 with a sodium benzoate content of .1006 per cent. The alum content is usually given on the label as one-third of one per cent. The actual amount present varies somewhat, but in two instances out of the three determinations made exceeded the amount stated.

PICKLED ONIONS—LEGAL.

Lab. No.	Manufacturer.	Acetic Acid. Per Cent.	Benzoate of Soda.	Brand.
14664	Squire Dingee Co., Chicago, Ill.	3.05	None.	Gold Medal.
14665	Squire Dingee Co., Chicago, Ill.	2.91	None.	Gold Medal.
14674	Dodson-Braun Co., St. Louis, Mo	2.98	None.	American Style.
14676	National Pickle & Canning Co., St. Louis, Mo	3.34	None.	Hot Stuff.
14678	Williams Bros. Co., Detroit, Mich	2.53	None.	Pearl.
15220	C. B. Bolinger, Shelburn	3.73	None.	

PICKLED ONIONS—ILLEGAL.

Lab. No.	Manufacturer.	Acetic Acid. Per Cent.	Benzoate.	Alum.	Brand.
14665	Dodson-Braun Co., St. Louis, Mo. *J. L. Steckler, Evansville.		None.	None.	Put up in distilled vinegar instead of malt.
15184	Williams Bros. Co., Detroit, Mich. *Petty & Huffman, Peru, Ind.		None.	Present.	Highland.
15185	Williams Bros. Co., Detroit, Mich. *Petty & Huffman, Peru, Ind.		None.	Present.	Highland.
15185	Williams Bros. Co., Detroit, Mich. *Petty & Huffman, Peru, Ind.		None.	Present.	Highland.

* Name of dealer from whom sample was purchased.

PICKLES—LEGAL.

Lab. No.	Manufacturer or Dealer.	Acetic Acid. Per Cent.	Preservatives, Benzoate or Alum.	Classification.
13237	*The C. Callahan Co., Lafayette			
13250	*Pottlizer Fancy Grocery Co., Lafayette			
14657	Squire Dingee Co., Chicago, Ill.			
14658	Squire Dingee Co., Chicago, Ill.			
14666	Dodson-Braun Co., St. Louis, Mo.			
14668	Dodson-Braun Co., St. Louis, Mo.	2.21	None.	Cupid Spiced, mixed pickles.
14672	Dodson-Braun Co., St. Louis, Mo.	2.22	None.	American Sweet.
14719	Squire Dingee Co., Chicago, Ill.			
14755	Squire Dingee Co., Chicago, Ill.			
14948	Williams Bros. Co., Detroit, Mich.			
15093	Williams Bros. Co., Detroit, Mich.		None.	Sour.
15219	*C. B. Bollinger, Shelburn	2.82	None.	
18390	*William E. Kroll, Indianapolis		None.	Sweet.

* Refers to dealers.

PICKLES—ILLEGAL.

Lab. No.	Brand.	Manufacturer.	Acetic Acid. Per Cent.	Per Cent Sodium Benzoate.	Remarks.
13249	Sweet	*Pottlizer Grocery Co., Lafayette		Present.	Alum present.
14660a	Gold Medal	Squire Dingee Co., Chicago, Ill.	2.53	.0877	
14660b	Gold Medal	Squire Dingee Co., Chicago, Ill	2.45	.0979	
14661a	Gold Medal	Squire Dingee Co., Chicago, Ill	2.64	None.	Alum present.
14661b	Gold Medal	Squire Dingee Co., Chicago, Ill	1.82	None.	Alum present.
14661c	Gold Medal	Squire Dingee Co., Chicago, Ill	2.62	.1699	
14662	Gold Medal	Squire Dingee Co., Chicago, Ill	1.71	.1006	
14667	Dodson-Braun	Dodson-Braun Co., St. Louis, Mo.			Label: "malt vinegar used." Used distilled.
14671	American Style.	Dodson-Braun Co., St. Louis, Mo.			Label: "malt vinegar used." Used distilled.
14673	American Sweet	Dodson-Braun Co., St. Louis, Mo	2.47	Present.	Label: "malt vinegar used." Used distilled.
14697	Sweet Gherkins	Williams Bros. Co., Detroit, Mich	2.12	.1267	
14721	Sweet Gherkins	Williams Bros. Co., Detroit, Mich	2.52	.1440	
14724	American Sweet	Dodson-Braun Co., St. Louis, Mo		Present.	Used distilled vinegar instead of malt.
14754	Magic City	Squire Dingee Co., Chicago, Ill.	2.56	None.	Alum.
14757	Gherkins	Williams Bros. Co., Detroit, Mich	2.84	.1166	
14758	Gherkins	Williams Bros. Co., Detroit, Mich	2.46	.1170	
15092	Sweet	Williams Bros. Co., Detroit, Mich		.0590	
15385		Williams Bros. Co., Detroit, Mich	2.40	.1123	
15386		Williams Bros. Co., Detroit, Mich	3.27	.0990	
17886	Williams	Williams Bros. Co., Detroit, Mich		.1152	.326 aluminum sulphate.
17993	Sour Spiced Gherkins	Williams Bros. Co., Detroit, Mich		None.	.414 aluminum sulphate.
17994	Sweet Gherkins.	Williams Bros. Co., Detroit, Mich		.1320	.358 aluminum sulphate.

* Refers to dealers.

BAKING POWDER.

The pure food law fixes no standard for baking powder. During the year several samples have been analyzed, usually at the request of dealers, and the results are here given:

BAKING POWDER.

Lab. No.	Brand.	Retailer or Manufacturer.	Carbon Dioxide. Per Cent.	Remarks.
16131	Primrose..........	Franklin McVeagh & Co., Chicago, Ill..........	10.50	Legal.
16133	Artic..............	Artic Mfg. Co., Grand Rapids, Mich..........	12.00	Legal.
*16712	Eddy's............	J. E. Davis, Winchester, Ind..................	7.20	Below standard.
*16713	Chapman's........	Chapman & Smith, Chicago, Ill................	3.04	Below standard.
*17391	....	W. W. Kent, Jonesboro, Ind....................	10.68	Legal.

* Refers to samples brought to the laboratory.

HONEY.

Each of the 4 samples of honey analyzed proved to be properly labeled and true to name. The addition of glucose to strained honey is largely a thing of the past, and where still practiced it is always indicated by the employment of a suitable label.

HONEY—LEGAL.

Lab. No.	Name and Address of Retailer.	Polarization.		Per Cent. Sucrose.	Invert Sugar, Per Cent.	Total Ash, Per Cent.	Remarks.
		Direct.	Invert.				
13248	Pottliser Fancy Groc. Co., Lafayette.	−14.0	−18 26	.04	69.0	.06	Labeled "Absolutely Pure." Extracted Honey.
14540	Mooney & Co., Terre Haute.........	−15.6	−18.70	.03	67.2	.07	No label.
14838	Cotton & Thalbemar, Mishawaka....	−14.3	−16.39	.02	70.8	.05	"Honey Bee Brand."
*17723	Rabbi Neustadt, Indianapolis.......	−18.0	−19.4	......	69.8	......	

* Sent in for information.

FRUIT PRODUCTS, JELLIES AND JAMS.

Twenty-two samples of fruit products were subjected to analysis during the year, of which 8 were classed as illegal. In every instance the adulterated goods were so pronounced because of the use of sodium benzoate as a preservative and not because of the employment of the sugar substitutes, the use of aniline dye, or the addition of starch and artificial flavors, as was once commonly the case with cheap goods of this character. It is interesting to note that the jams made by Curtice Bros. Co., of Rochester, N. Y., and labeled 1-10 of 1 per cent. benzoate of soda in fact contained approximately twice that amount, the actual content varying from .1844 to .2048.

JELLY—LEGAL.

Lab. No.	Classification.	Manufacturer.	Polarization. Direct 20°C.	Polarization. Invert 20°C.	Sucrose, Per Cent.	Glucose, Per Cent.
14043	Fruit Jelly........	Berry & Mayburn, Chicago, Ill........	+104.0	98.6	4.2	56.5
14966	....	Williams Bros. Co., Detroit, Mich........	+128.0	+127.6	Trace.	73.0
15262	Compound Apple..	Williams Bros. Co., Detroit, Mich........	+130.8	+130.6	Trace.	74.6
15263	Compound Apple..	Williams Bros. Co., Detroit, Mich........	+126.8	+126.5	Trace.	72.3
15384	Compound Apple..	Williams Bros. Co., Detroit, Mich........	+148.8	+135.5	10.2	79.2
16273	Plum and Apple...	Williams Bros. Co., Detroit, Mich........	....	....	....	....
18069	Jelly............	*Mrs. George M. Kreig, City............	+ 32.0	− 7.7	30.1	0.0
18232	Fruit Jelly........	The Leroux Cider Co., Toledo, O.........	− 13.2	− 18.2	3.9	0.0

* Sample was sent in for information.

JELLY—ILLEGAL.

Lab. No.	Classification.	Manufacturer.	Polarization. Direct.	Polarization. Invert.	Sucrose.	Glucose.	Benzoate of Soda.
16132	Old Virginia.......	McMechen Pres. Co., Wheeling, W.Va.	+18.8	−12.54	24.2	None.	Pres't
18233	Sunrise...........	The Leroux Cider & Vinegar Co., Toledo, Ohio....................	−18.0	−21.12	2.4	None.	Pres't
18233	Sunrise...........	The Leroux Cider & Vinegar Co., Toledo, Ohio....................	−18.6	−21.34	2.1	None.	Pres't

JAM—LEGAL.

Lab. No.	Classification.	Manufacturer.	Polarization. Direct.	Polarization. Invert.	Sucrose.	Glucose.	Benzoate of Soda.
14901	Williams..........	Williams Bros. Co., Detroit, Mich.....	+ 64.4	+ 63.8	Trace.	36.5	None.
14964	Williams..........	Williams Bros. Co., Detroit, Mich.....	....	....	......	45.8	None.
14965	Williams..........	Williams Bros. Co., Detroit, Mich.....	....	....	......	44.2	None.
14967	Williams..........	Williams Bros. Co., Detroit, Mich.....	....	....	......	48.0	None.
16273	Plum and Apple...	Webster Preserve Co., Webster, N. J..	....	....	......	......	
18577	Preserved tomatoes	*Schnull & Co., Indianapolis...........	+159.2	+128.3	3.9	77.3	None.

* Retailer.

JAM—ILLEGAL.

Lab. No.	Classification.	Manufacturer.	Benzoate of Soda.
14877	Strawberry..................	Curtice Bros. Co., Rochester, N. Y.................	0.2016
14878	Raspberry..................	Curtice Bros. Co., Rochester, N. Y.................	0.1844
14879	Red Currant.................	Curtice Bros. Co., Rochester, N. Y.................	0.1872
14880	Red Cherry.................	Curtice Bros. Co., Rochester, N. Y.................	0.2048
14881	Blackberry..................	Curtice Bros. Co., Rochester, N. Y.. ..	0.1901

FRUIT BUTTERS AND CANNED FRUITS.

Of the 12 samples of canned fruits and butters analyzed, 7 were classed as illegal, in every instance because of the presence of sodium benzoate in quantities varying from .1066 per cent. to .167 per cent. It is worthy of comment that one sample of apple butter containing .1066 per cent. of sodium benzoate was mouldy. This indicates the futility of depending upon the usual 1-10 of 1 per cent. of sodium benzoate in the preservation of food stuffs.

FRUIT BUTTERS AND CANNED FRUITS—LEGAL.

Lab. No.	Classification.	Manufacturer.	Benzoate of Soda.
17157	Blueberries	A. & R. Loggie, Canada	None.
17158	Blueberries	Sprague-Warner Co., Chicago, Ill	None.
17358	Gage Plums	Golden Gate Packing Co., California	None.
17359	Gage Plums	Golden Gate Packing Co., California	None.
17360	Gage Plums	Golden Gate Packing Co., California	None.

FRUIT BUTTERS AND CANNED FRUITS—ILLEGAL.

Lab. No.	Classification.	Manufacturer.	Benzoate of Soda.
14700	Apple Butter	Williams Bros. Co., Detroit, Mich	.1584
14902	Apple Butter	Williams Bros. Co., Detroit, Mich	.1440
14947	Apple Butter	Williams Bros. Co., Detroit, Mich	*.1066
17362	Red Raspberries	Austin-Nicholas Co., New York	Present.
17363	Red Raspberries	Austin-Nicholas Co., New York	Present.
17995	Apple Butter	Williams Bros. Co., Detroit, Mich	.1180
18253	Apple Butter	Williams Bros. Co., Detroit, Mich	.1670

* Mouldy.

SPIRITUOUS LIQUORS.

Of the 10 samples of whiskey analyzed, 6 were found to be legal and 4 illegal. The 4 illegal samples were so classed because of the presence in two instances of capsicum and in 2 others cases the product sold as whiskey contained no alcohol and was evidently nothing but sweetened water. Three brandies and wines were analyzed, all of which were found to be legal.

WHISKEY—LEGAL.

Lab. No.	Sent in by	Sp. G. 15°C.	Per Cent. Alcohol by Weight.	Per Cent. Alcohol by Volume.	Extract.
16506	T. J. Mattice, Rochester	.9325	40.99	48.42	....
17510	Wm. F. Johnson, Greensburg	.9448	37.21	44.30	.1252
17511	Wm. F. Johnson, Greensburg	.9448	37.21	44.30	.1244
17512	Wm. F. Johnson, Greensburg	.9488	35.04	41.90	.1488
17535	Farmers Home, Indianapolis	.9496	34.59	41.40	....
18003	Coonley Drug Co., South Bend	.9413	36.94	43.81	....

WHISKEY—ILLEGAL

Lab. No.	Sent in by	Sp. G. 15°C.	Per Cent. Alcohol by Weight.	Per Cent. Alcohol by Volume.	Extract.	Capsicum.
17508	Wm. F. Johnson, Greensburg............	.9547	31.67	38.10	.0860	Present.
17509	Wm. F. Johnson, Greensburg	.9551	31.45	37.85	.0968	Present.
19059	Will J. Martin, Kokomo................	*	*	*	.1148	
19060	Will J. Martin, Kokomo.................	*	*	*	.1332	

* No taste of whiskey.

BRANDY AND WINE—LEGAL.

Lab. No.	Sent in by	Sp. G. 20°C.	Per Cent. Alcohol by Weight.	Per Cent. Alcohol by Volume.	Extract.
*17504	Mrs. M. E. Brook, Brownstown..............................	....	4.27	5.37	....
†15026	Louis S. Riely, Corydon..............................	.9295	....	50.1	.0448
†18287	J. F. Danner & Son, Elnora..............................	.9400	37.60	44.5	.0190

* Wine.
† Brandy.

TEMPERANCE BEERS.

With the passage of stringent laws regulating the sale of intoxicating and malt liquors, there was created a market for nonalcoholic beverages which possess the characteristics of beer but which do not violate the liquor laws. This demand has prompted the manufacture of a great variety of so-called temperance beers, the alcohol content of which is low but which when sold properly carbonated satisfies in a measure the thirsty palate. Many of the samples examined were sent in by prosecuting attorneys, sheriffs and other State officials on the supposition that straight beers were being sold bearing temperance beer labels. One hundred thirty-six samples of so-called temperance beers were analyzed during the year, 63 of which contained less than one-half of one per cent. of alcohol and were therefore classed as legal. Seventy-three samples, on the contrary, contained more than one-half of one per cent., and could not be classed as non-alcoholic. Most of the illegal samples were, in fact, straight beers sold under the cover of a temperance beer label. Hop Cream, for instance, manufactured by Chas. Ogren of Chicago and sold generally throughout the State as a non-intoxicating beverage, contains as high as 4.41 per cent. of alcohol.

BEERS AND SO-CALLED TEMPERANCE BEERS.

Lab. No.	Manufacturer.	Brand.	Alcohol by Weight	Alcohol by Volume.	Extract.	Ash.	Protein.	Phosphoric Acid.	Maltose.	Dextrose.	Dextrine.	Immersion at 17.5°.
13800	Terre Haute Brewing Co., Terre Haute	Velveteen	.42	.52	6.072	.1672	.257	.0418				
15380	Capital City Bottling Works, Indianapolis	Taste Tells	.25	.30	6.616	.1704	.215	.0374				
15396	Home Brewing Co., Indianapolis	Homo	.00	.00	5.466	.1964	.344	.0506				
15718	Indianapolis Brewing Co., Indianapolis	Tonica	.07	.10	7.193	.2060	.357	.0550				
15719	Indianapolis Brewing Co., Indianapolis	Tonica	.11	.14	7.207	.2152	.336	.0572				
15720	Indianapolis Brewing Co., Indianapolis	Tonica	.07	.10	7.216	.3116	.339	.0572				
16117	" " " "	Tonica	.00	.00	8.097	.1904	.350	.0440	.00	1.94	4.82	
16118	" " " "	Tonica	.00	.00	8.098	.1888	.350	.0440	.00	1.94	4.82	
16169	Hoster-Columbus Assc. Brew. Co., Columbus, Ohio	Hoscola	.21	.25	6.461				1.36	.31	3.19	
16170	Max Kochlin, Brooklyn, N. Y.	Beerine	.00	.00	.966							
16173	Indianapolis Brewing Co., Indianapolis	Tonica	.00	.00	8.098	.1704	.357	.0440	.00	1.94	4.82	
16174	Indianapolis Brewing Co., Indianapolis	Tonica	.00	.00	8.098	.1704	.357	.4400	.00	1.94	4.82	
16688	Home Brewing Co., Indianapolis	Homo	.14	.17	4.751	.1368			1.03	.56	2.28	
16694	Peoples Brewing Co., Terre Haute	Y-U-N-O	.35	.44	6.880	.1860		.0260	1.83	Trace	2.32	
16695	Pabst Brewing Co., Milwaukee, Wisconsin	Pable	.00	.00	6.600	.1040		.0350	2.11	Trace	2.32	
16748	Capital City Brewing Co., Indianapolis	Dry	.21	.26								
16835	Chas. Ogren & Co., Chicago, Illinois	Blitz	.07	.09					1.40	.04	2.64	15.3
17007	Fred Miller Brewing Co., Milwaukee, Wisconsin	Vigorine	.21	.26	4.610				1.37	.02	2.43	
17008	Terre Haute Brewing Co., Terre Haute	Velveteen	.21	.26	6.058				1.94	.02	2.78	
17009	Terre Haute Brewing Co., Terre Haute	Malt Liquor	.14	.17	8.372				5.41	.07	2.03	
17010	Terre Haute Brewing Co., Terre Haute	Malt Liquor	.14	.17	8.297				5.39	.18	2.03	
17011	Terre Haute Brewing Co., Terre Haute	Malt Liquor	.14	.17	8.297				5.40	.07	2.03	
17012	Terre Haute Brewing Co., Terre Haute	Malt Liquor	.14	.17	8.297				5.40	.08	2.03	
17353	Charles Ogren & Co., Chicago, Illinois	Blits	.00	.00								
17444	Charles Ogren & Co., Chicago, Illinois		.25	.31								
17453	Charles Ogren & Co., Chicago, Illinois		.00	.00								
17503	Capital City Brewing Co., Indianapolis		.00	.00								
17554	Capital City Brewing Co., Indianapolis		.35	.44		.1280	.301	.0410	1.00	1.87	3.05	15.5
17555	Capital City Brewing Co., Indianapolis		.35	.44		.1772	.308	.0440	1.00	1.87	3.41	
17557	Capital City Brewing Co., Indianapolis		.28	.35		.1840	.315	.0410	.99	1.85	3.41	
17558	Capital City Brewing Co., Indianapolis	Dry	.28	.35		.1800	.308	.0440	1.00	1.96	3.39	
17559	Capital City Brewing Co., Indianapolis	Dry	.28	.35		.1812	.308	.0440	.98	1.98	3.39	
17560	Capital City Brewing Co., Indianapolis		.28	.35		.1800	.315	.0440	.98	1.88	3.41	
17561	Capital City Brewing Co., Indianapolis		.28	.35		.1816	.308	.0440	.98	1.88	3.41	
17562	Capital City Brewing Co., Indianapolis		.35	.44		.1880	.301	.0410	1.00	1.87	3.41	
17563	Capital City Brewing Co., Indianapolis		.28	.35		.1768	.301	.0440	.98	1.87	3.41	
17564	Capital City Brewing Co., Indianapolis		.28	.35		.1784	.301	.0440	1.00	1.87	3.41	

BEERS AND SO-CALLED TEMPERANCE BEERS—Continued

Lab No.	Manufacturer	Brand.	Alcohol by Weight	Alcohol by Volume.	Extract.	Ash	Protein	Phosphoric Acid.	Maltose	Dextrose	Dextrins.	Immersion at 17.5°.
17627	Home Brewing Co., Indianapolis	Home	.32	.40								18.4
17687	Capital City Brewing Co., Indianapolis	Dry	.42	.52								18.6
17688	Capital City Brewing Co., Indianapolis	Dry	.42	.52								18.6
17737	Charles Ogren & Co., Chicago, Illinois	Hop Cream	.46	.58	5.400							
17813	Home Brewing Co., Indianapolis	Home	.40	.61								18.7
17814	Home Brewing Co., Indianapolis	Home	.42	.61								18.6
17856	Capital City Brewing Co., Indianapolis	Dry	.28	.45								18.4
17858	Moder & Kreutzer, Peru	Home	.21	.26								18.8
17859	Moder & Kreutzer, Peru	Velvetoon	.28	.35								18.4
17860	Indianapolis Brewing Co., Indianapolis	Tonica	.00	.00								
17861	Indianapolis Brewing Co., Indianapolis	Tonica	.07	.00								18.1
17919	Capital City Brewing Co., Indianapolis	Dry	.14	.17								
17992	Charles Ogren & Co., Chicago, Illinois	Bitz	.14	.17								18.9
18480	Fred Miller Brewing Co., Milwaukee, Wisconsin	Vigorine		.44	5.450							
18481	Fred Miller Brewing Co., Milwaukee, Wisconsin	Vigorine		.45	5.450							
18482	Fred Miller Brewing Co., Milwaukee, Wisconsin	Vigorine		.44	5.450							
18496	Fred Miller Brewing Co., Milwaukee, Wisconsin		.00		7.790							
18497	Fred Miller Brewing Co., Milwaukee, Wisconsin		.00		7.790							
18512	Fred Miller Brewing Co., Milwaukee, Wisconsin	Dry	.00	.26								
18514	Fred Miller Brewing Co., Milwaukee, Wisconsin	Dry	.00	.26	6.710							
18515	Fred Miller Brewing Co., Milwaukee, Wisconsin	Tonica	.00	.00	7.740							
18662	Fred Miller Brewing Co., Milwaukee, Wisconsin	Home		.44	4.023	.1716				.41	2.17	
18717	C. L. Centlivre Brewing Co., Fort Wayne		.00	.00	4.770	.1720			1.40	.00	1.80	
18718	C. L. Centlivre Brewing Co., Fort Wayne	Tonica	.00	.00	7.718	.2416						
18719	Home Brewing Co., Indianapolis	Home	.00	.44	4.018	.1584			.40	.40	2.14	
15396	New Athens Brewing Co., E. St. Louis, Illinois	Egyptian Malt Ext	3.81	4.71	5.040	.1016	.581	.0702				
15399	New Athens Brewing Co., E. St. Louis, Illinois	Egyptian Malt Ext	3.81	4.78	5.400	.2124	.590	.0770				
16649	Charles Ogren & Co., Chicago, Illinois		3.14	3.04	4.300	.1102		.0170	1.27	.00	2.56	
16690	Home Brewing Co., Indianapolis		2.31	2.90	4.781	.0988		.0180	1.30	.13	2.24	
16691	Home Brewing Co., Indianapolis		2.43	3.05	4.550	.1008		.0180	1.21	.04	2.28	
16702	Glenwood Spring Co., Augusta, Maine		1.87	2.45						.		17.8
16792	Charles Ogren & Co., Chicago, Illinois	Hop Cream	2.13	2.66								18.8
16910	Foss Schneider Brewing Co., Cincinnati, Ohio	Nextobeer	1.87	2.37	3.998				1.11	.00	2.07	
17186	Foss Schneider Brewing Co., Cincinnati, Ohio		6.01	7.55								24.87
17232	Foss Schneider Brewing Co., Cincinnati, Ohio		5.85	7.30								24.54
17445	Foss Schneider Brewing Co., Cincinnati, Ohio		1.58	2.00								
17446	Foss Schneider Brewing Co., Cincinnati, Ohio		1.68	2.10								
17457	West Louisville Brewing Co., Louisville, Kentucky	Malt Ola	2.03	2.55								

1 458	West Louisville Brewing Co., Louisville, Kentucky	Malt Ola	2.04	2.57	......	......	......	......	......	......	......
17482	Capital City Brewing Co., Indianapolis	......	3.69	4.65	5.884	......	......	......	......	......	20.80
17483	Capital City Brewing Co., Indianapolis	......	4.75	4.71	5.480	......	......	......	......	......	20.90
17484	Home Brewing Co., Indianapolis	......	2.73	3.44	4.148	......	......	......	......	......	19.20
17485	Foss-Schneider Brewing Co., Cincinnati, Ohio	......	3 69	4.64	5.052	......	......	......	......	......	20.80
17486	Home Brewing Co., Indianapolis	......	84	1.06	5.379	......	......	......	......	......	16.20
17514	Charles gren & Co., Chicago, Illinois	Hop Cream	2.61	3.29	4.450	......	......	......	......	......	......
17515	Charles Ogren & Co., ago, I lis	......	3 78	3.09	6.209	......	......	......	......	......	......
17516	harles Ogren & Co., , llois	......	3 89	3.09	6.285	......	......	......	......	......	......
17517	Charles gren & Co., , lis	......	3.09	3.89	4.224	......	......	......	......	......	......
17518	les Ogren & Co., Chicago, Illinois	......	3.21	4.04	6.184	......	......	......	......	......	......
17519	harles Ogren & Co., Chicago, Illinois	......	4.34	3.45	5.882	......	......	......	......	......	......
17553	e Brewing Co., Indianapolis	......	2.61	3.29	3.448	......	......	......	......	......	19.00
17556	Foss-Schneider Brewing Co. nati, Ohio	......	3 82	4.80	4.876	......	......	......	......	......	21.00
17597	Foss-Schneider Brewing Co., Cincinnati, Ohio	......	3.81	4.80	5.288	......	......	......	......	......	......
17628	Co., Milwaukee, Wisconsin	Mead	1 29	1.62	......	......	......	......	......	......	16.90
17656	......	......	3.63	4.56	5.288	......	......	......	......	......	......
1 812	......	Fizz	1.97	2.49	......	......	......	......	......	......	17.95
17920	apital i rewing Co., Indianapolis	......	3.51	4.41	4.324	......	......	......	......	......	......
17921	Capital i rewing Co., Indianapolis	......	3.45	4.34	4.324	......	......	......	......	......	......
1 922	Capital i rewing Co., Indianapolis	......	3.45	4.34	4.324	......	......	......	......	......	......
18010	Capital i rewing Co., Indianapolis	......	......	4.34	4.876	......	......	......	......	......	......
18066	Charles & Co., go, lis	Hop Cream	2 61	3.29	4.450	......	......	......	......	......	......
18349	t Brewing Co., Louisville, Kentucky	Malt Ola	2 25	2.85	3.872	......	......	......	......	......	18.40
18350	West ing Co., Louisville, Kentucky	Special	1.10	1.39	4.299	......	......	......	......	......	17.60
18357	t Brewing Co., Louisville, Kentucky	......	3.81	4.80	4.751	......	......	......	......	......	......
18362	t Brewing Co., Louisville, ky	......	2 50	2.00	......	......	......	......	......	......	......
18408	West Co., Louisville, Kentucky	......	......	3.50	4.840	......	......	......	......	......	......
18436	Charles n & Co Illinois	Ogren's Pepsinated	......	3.50	4.420	......	......	......	......	......	19.30
18495	Paul ., New Albany	Maltina	2.97	3.74	6.430	......	......	......	......	......	19.60
18513	Paul ., New Albany	Dry	......	.78	6.230	......	......	......	......	......	......
18516	Paul ., New Albany	Dry	......	4.11	5.680	......	......	......	......	......	......
18517	Paul ., New Albany	......	......	3.96	5.800	......	......	......	......	......	......
18518	Paul ., New any	......	......	3.89	5.830	......	......	......	......	......	......
18519	Paul ., New ly	......	......	4.26	5.680	......	......	......	......	......	......
18529	Paul ., New any	......	......	3.89	5.850	......	......	......	......	......	......
18521	I ul ., New any	......	......	3.81	5.830	......	......	......	......	......	......
18573	Home polis	Homo	3.81	4.80	5.480	......	......	......	......	......	21.00
18573	Home ., Indianapolis	Homo	......	5.11	4.676	.1576	......	.70	.37	2.35	......
18660	Home ., Indianapolis	......	......	5.15	4.676	.1636	......	.68	.83	2.35	......
18661	Home ., Ilis	......	......	5.01	4.901	.1524	......	1.26	.11	2.14	......
18713	Home ., lis	......	......	5.07	4.701	.1624	......	......	.86	2.25	......
18714	Home ., Indianapolis	......	......	......	......	......	......	......	......	......	......
18715	Home ., Indianapolis	......	......	4.87	4.876	.1560	......	1.20	.13	2.17	......
18716	Home lis	......	......	4.87	4.901	.1572	......	1.27	.09	2 14	......
18731	les Co. o, Illinois	Hop Cream	......	3.59	5.002	......	......	......	......	......	19.40
18732	Charles Co., Chicago, Illinois	Hop Cream	......	3.74	4.826	......	......	......	......	......	19.60
18733	Charles Co., Chicago, Illinois	Hop Cream	......	3.59	5.002	......	......	......	......	......	19.40

BEERS AND SO-CALLED TEMPERANCE BEERS—Continued.

Lab. No.	Manufacturer.	Brand.	Alcohol by Weight	Alcohol by Volume.	Extract.	Ash.	Protein.	Phosphoric Acid.	Maltose.	Dextrose.	Dextrine.	Immersion at 17.5°.
17627	Home Brewing Co., Indianapolis	Homo	.32	.40								15.4
17687	Capital City Brewing Co., Indianapolis	Dry	.42	.52								15.6
17688	Capital City Brewing Co., Indianapolis	Dry	.42	.52								15.6
17737	Charles Ogren & Co., Chicago, Illinois	Hop Cream	.46	.58	5.400							
17813	Home Brewing Co., Indianapolis	Homo	.49	.61								15.7
17814	Home Brewing Co., Indianapolis	Homo	.42	.61								15.6
17856	Capital City Brewing Co., Indianapolis	Dry	.28	.35								15.4
17858	Moder & Kreutzer, Peru	Homo	.21	.26								15.3
17859	Moder & Kreutzer, Peru	Velveteen	.28	.35								15.4
17860	Indianapolis Brewing Co., Indianapolis	Tonica	.00	.00								
17861	Indianapolis Brewing Co., Indianapolis	Tonica	.07	.09								15.1
17919	Capital City Brewing Co., Indianapolis	Dry	.14	.17								
17992	Charles Ogren & Co., Chicago, Illinois	Blitz	.14	.17								15.2
18480	Fred Miller Brewing Co., Milwaukee, Wisconsin	Vigorine		.44	5.450							
18481	Fred Miller Brewing Co., Milwaukee,	Vigorine		.35	5.450							
18482	Fred Miller Brewing Co., Milwaukee, Wisconsin	Vigorine		.44	5.450							
18496	Fred Miller Brewing Co., Milwaukee, Wisconsin		.00		7.760							
18497	Fred Miller Brewing Co., Milwaukee, Wisconsin		.00		7.790							
18512	Fred Miller Brewing Co., Milwaukee, Wisconsin	Dry	.00	.26								
18514	Fred Miller Brewing Co., Milwaukee, Wisconsin	Dry	.00	.26	6.710							
18515	Fred Miller Brewing Co., Milwaukee, Wisconsin	Tonica	.00	.00	7.740							
18662	Fred Miller Brewing Co., Milwaukee, Wisconsin	Homo		.44	4.023	.1736				.31	2.17	
18717	C. L. Centlime Brewing Co., Fort Wayne		.00	.09	4.776	.1720			1.49	.00	1.89	
18718	C. L. Centlime Brewing Co., Fort Wayne	Tonica	.00	.00	7.718	.2416						
18719	Home Brewing Co., Indianapolis	Homo	.00	.44	4.048	.1584			.39	.46	2.14	
15398	New Athens Brewing Co., E. St. Louis, Illinois	Egyptian Malt Ext	3.81	4.71	5.649	.1916	.581	.0792				
15390	New Athens Brewing Co., E. St. Louis, Illionis	Egyptian Malt Ext	3.81	4.75	5.466	.2124	.560	.0770				
16689	Charles Ogren & Co., Chicago, Illinois		3.14	3.64	4.350	.1152		.0370	1.27	.00	2.56	
16690	Home Brewing Co., Indianapolis		2.31	2.90	4.783	.0988		.0380	1.20	.13	2.24	
16691	Home Brewing Co., Indianapolis		2.43	3.05	4.550	.1068		.0380	1.21	.04	2.28	
16702	Glenwood Spring Co., Augusta, Maine		1.87	2.35								17.8
16792	Charles Ogren & Co., Chicago, Illinois	Hop Cream	2.13	2.65								18.2
16916	Foss-Schneider Brewing Co., Cincinnati, Ohio	Nextobeer	1.87	2.37	3.998				1.11	.00	2.07	
17186	Foss-Schneider Brewing Co., Cincinnati, Ohio		6.01	7.55								24.87
17232	Foss-Schneider Brewing Co., Cincinnati, Ohio		5.85	7.30								24.54
17445	Foss-Schneider Brewing Co., Cincinnati, Ohio		1.58	2.00								
17446	Foss-Schneider Brewing Co., Cincinnati, Ohio		1.68	2.10								
17457	West Louisville Brewing Co., Louisville, Kentucky	Malt Ola	2.03	2.55								

17458	West Louisville Brewing Co., Louisville, Kentucky	Malt Ola	2.04	2.57								
17482	Capital City Brewing Co., Indianapolis		3.69	4.65	5.884							20.80
17483	Capital City Brewing Co., Indianapolis		4.75	4.71	5.480							20.90
17484	Home Brewing Co., Indianapolis		2.73	3.44	4.148							19.20
17485	Foss-Schneider Brewing Co., Cincinnati, Ohio		3 69	4.64	5.052							20.80
17486	Home Brewing Co., Indianapolis		.84	1.06	5.379							16.20
17514	Charles Ogren & Co., Chicago, Illinois	Hop Cream	2.61	3.29	4.450							
17515	Charles Ogren & Co., Chicago, Illinois		3.78	3.09	6.209							
17516	Charles Ogren & Co., Chicago, Illinois		3.89	3.09	6.285							
17517	Charles Ogren & Co., Chicogo, Illinois		3.09	3.89	4.224							
17518	Charles Ogren & Co., Chicago, Illinois		3.21	4.04	6.184							
17519	Charles Ogren & Co., Chicago, Illinois		4.34	3.45	5.882							
17553	Home Brewing Co., Indianapolis		2.61	3.29	3.448							19.00
17556	Foss-Schneider Brewing Co., Cincinnati, Ohio		3.82	4.80	4.876							21.00
17597	Foss-Schneider Brewing Co., Cincinnati, Ohio		3.81	4.80	5.288							
17628	Pabst Brewing Co., Milwaukee, Wisconsin	Mead	1.29	1.62								16.90
17656	Capital City Brewing Co., Indianapolis		3.63	4.56	5.288							
17812	Schlitz Brewing Co., Milwaukee, Wisconsin	Fiss	1.97	2.49								17.95
17920	Capital City Brewing Co., Indianapolis		3.51	4.41	4.324							
17921	Capital City Brewing Co., Indianapolis		3.45	4.34	4.324							
17922	Capital City Brewing Co., Indianapolis		3.45	4.34	4.324							
18010	Capital City Brewing Co., Indianapolis			4.34	4.876							
18066	Charles Ogren & Co., Chicago, Illinois	Hop Cream	2.61	3.29	4.450							
18349	West Brewing Co., Louisville, Kentucky	Malt Ola	2.25	2.85	3.872							18.40
18350	West Brewing Co., Louisville, Kentucky	Special	1.10	1.39	4.299							17.60
18357	West Brewing Co., Louisville, Kentucky		3.81	4.80	4.751							
18362	West Brewing Co., Louisville, Kentucky		2.50	2.00								
18408	West Brewing Co., Louisville, Kentucky			3.50	4.840							
18436	Charles Ogren & Co., Chicago, Illinois	Ogren's Pepsinated		3.50	4.420							19.30
18495	Paul Co., New Albany	Maltina	2.97	3.74	6.430							19.60
18513	Paul Co., New Albany	Dry		.78	6.230							
18516	Paul Co., New Albany	Dry		4.11	5.680							
18517	Paul Co., New Albany			3.96	5.800							
18518	Paul Co., New Albany			3.89	5.830							
18519	Paul Co., New Albany			4.26	5.680							
18529	Paul Co., New Albany			3.89	5.850							
18521	Paul o., New Albany			3.81	5.830							
18573	Home Co., Indianapolis	Homo	3.81	4.80	5.480							21.00
18573	Home Co., Indianapolis	Homo		5.11	4.676	.1576			.70	.37	2.35	
18660	Home Co., Indianapolis			5.15	4.676	.1636			.68	.33	2.35	
18661	Home Co., Indianapolis			5.01	4.901	.1524			1.26	.11	2.14	
18713	Home Co., Indianapolis			5.07	4.701	.1624				.86	2.25	
18714	Home Brewing Co., Indianapolis											
18715	Home Brewing Co., Indianapolis			4.87	4.876	.1560			1.20	.13	2.17	
18716	Home Brewing Co., Indianapolis			4.87	4.901	.1572			1.27	.09	2.14	
18731	Charles Ogren & Co., Chicago, Illinois	Hop Cream		3.59	5.002							19.40
18732	Charles & Co., Chicago, Illinois	Hop Cream		3.74	4.826							19.60
18733	Charles & Co., Chicago, Illinois	Hop Cream		3.59	5.002							19.40

BEERS AND SO-CALLED TEMPERANCE BEERS—Continued.

Lab. No.	Manufacturer.	Brand.	Alcohol by Weight	Alcohol by Volume.	Ex-tract.	Ash.	Pro-tein.	Phos-phoric Acid.	Malt-ose.	Dex-trose.	Dex-trine.	Immer-sion at 17.5°.
18734	Charles Ogren & Co., Chicago, Illinois			3.66	4.751							19.50
18735	Charles Ogren & Co., Chicago, Illinois			3.66	4.340							19.50
18819	Home Brewing Co., Indianapolis		3.90	4.88	4.876							
18820	Home Brewing Co., Indianapolis		3.47	4.34	4.851							
18821	Home Brewing Co., Indianapolis		4.01	5.01	4.876							
18822	Home Brewing Co., Indianapolis		3.29	4.11	4.826							
18909	Hoster-Columbus Assc. Brew. Co., Columbus, Ohio	Hos Cola		.79	6.200							
18910	Hoster-Columbus Assc. Brew. Co., Columbus, Ohio	Hos Cola		.79	6.200							
19023	Hoster-Columbus Assc. Brew. Co., Columbus, Ohio	Hop Cream		3.89	4.826							
19024	Hoster-Columbus Assc. Brew. Co., Columbus, Ohio	Cream of Hops		1.39								
19025	Charles Ogren & Co., Brewing Co., Chicago, Illinois	Hop Cream		4.41	5.077							
19057	Frank Fehr Brewing Co., Louisville, Kentucky	Fehr's Ambrosia		1.86	4.952							

CARBONATED SUMMER DRINKS.

Under this head is classified a great variety of so-called sodas made by carbonating a sweetened water to which has been added the characteristic flavors. Of the 256 samples analyzed, 149 were legal and 107 illegal. The illegal samples were usually so classed because of the presence of benzoate of soda or saccharin or both. Saccharin is still largely employed by the manufacturer of summer drinks who wishes to put out an inferior product which he can sell at a low price. A few artificially colored samples did not indicate that fact on the label, and were so classed as adulterated. The presence of a harmless color in goods of this class is not prohibited, but the use of such color must be indicated on the label.

SODAS—ILLEGAL.

Lab. No.	Manufacturer.	Brand.	Preservatives.		
			Saccharin.	Benzoate of Soda.	Salicylic Acid.
13725	Sobieski Bottling Works, Chicago, Ill	Phospho Brew	Present.	....	
13726	Sobieski Bottling Works, Chicago, Ill	Strawberry Pop	Present.	....	
15575	Lentz Bros., Ft. Wayne	Strawberry Pop	Present.	....	
15576	Lentz Bros., Ft. Wayne	Pop	Present.	....	
15581	Sam Zwig, Ft. Wayne	Iron Brew	Present.	....	
15624	H. W. Gagen, Lafayette	Orcherade	Present.	Present.	
15625	H. W. Gagen, Lafayette	Orcherade	Present.	....	
15814	Wayne Mfg. Co., Ft. Wayne	Hop Ale	....	Present.	
15815	Samuel Smith & Co., Chicago, Ill	Axo	Present.	....	Present.
15816	Phillip Burg, Auburn	Ginger Ale	Present.	....	
15820	Wayne Mfg. Co., Ft. Wayne	Cherry Phosphate	Present.	Present.	
15821	Wayne Mfg. Co.. Ft. Wayne	Orangeade	....	Present.	
15822	A. R. Champney, Elyria, Ohio	Liquid Force	Present.	Present.	
15826	R. E. Fulbertson, Kendallville	Strawberry Pop	Present.	Present.	
15827	R. E. Fulbertson, Kendallville	Ginger Ale	Present.	Present.	
15832	Barney & Allen, Columbia City	Cherrysip	Present.	Present.	
15833	Barney & Allen, Columbia City	Merry Widow High Ball	Present.	....	
15834	Barney & Allen, Columbia City	Iron Brew	Present.	Present.	
15835	Barney & Allen, Columbia City	Strawberry Pop	Present.	Present.	
15838	Wayne Mfg. Co., Ft. Wayne	Hop Ale	....	Present.	
15928	Wm. F. Zerfus, Williamsport	Pop	Present.	Present.	
15930	Wm. F. Zerfus, Williamsport	Pop	Present.	Present.	Present.
15942	Noll & Schneider, Williamsport	Ginger Ale	Present.	Present.	Present.
15950	Pitcher Bros., Williamsport	Orcherade	Present.	Present.	
16001	Gagen, H. W., Lafayette	Orcherade	Present.	Present.	
16098	Barney & Allen, Columbia City	Cherrysip	Present.	Present.	
16099	Barney & Allen, Columbia City	Strawberry Pop	Present.	....	
16136	Wayne Mfg. Co., Ft. Wayne	Cherry Phosphate	Present.	Present.	
16137	R. F. Fulbertson, Kendallville	Birch Beer	Present.	Present.	
16138	R. F. Fulbertson, Kendallville	Scotch Pop Ale	....	Present.	
16139	R. F. Fulbertson, Kendallville	Sarsaparilla	....	Present.	
16140	R. F. Fulbertson, Kendallville	Lemon Sour	Present.	Present.	
16142	R. F. Fulbertson, Kendallville	Vanilla Soda	Present.	Present.	
16143	R. F. Fulbertson, Kendallville	Jersey Creme	Present.	....	
16144	Wayne Mfg. Co., Ft. Wayne	Wayno	Present.	Present.	
16181	Litzenberger & Green, Culver	Pop	*	*	*
19190	Thuis Bottling Works, Vincennes	Strawberry	Present.	....	
16195	Red Cross Cider Co., St. Louis	White Grape	....	Present.	
16197	Red Cross Cider Co., St. Louis	Blackberry	....	Present.	
16198	Reff Cross Cider Co., St. Louis	Blackberry	....	Present.	
16199	Red Cross Cider Co., St. Louis	Juni	*	*	*
16367	Clarksville Cider Co., St. Louis	Blackberry	....	Present.	
16413	Linton Bottling Works, Linton, Ind	Apple Ade	....	Present.	
16495	Thuis Bottling Works, Vincennes	Strawberry Pop	Present.	....	
16447	Thuis Bottling Works, Vincennes	Buckeye Bounce	†	†	†

SODAS—ILLEGAL—Continued.

Lab. No.	Manufacturer.	Brand.	Preservatives.		
			Saccharin.	Benzoate of Soda.	Salicylic Acid.
16491	Thuis Bottling Works, Vincennes	Strawberry Pop	Present.	....	
16494	Thuis Bottling Works, Vincennes	Merry Widow	Present.	....	
16534	Thuis Bottling Works, Vincennes	Peach Bounce	Present.	....	
16536	City Bottling Works, New Albany	Creme Soda	Present.	....	
16616	Beechuram & Wampler, Gosport	Buckeye Bounce	Present.	Present.	
16637	Vern Hardenbrook, Walkerton	Strawberry Pop	....	....	Present.
16685	Vern Hardenbrook, Walkerton	Grape Juice	....	Present.	Present.
16692	Stivers & Draper, Sullivan	Buckeye Meade	....	Present.	Present.
16693	Stivers & Draper, Sullivan	Buckeye Bounce	Present.	Present.	
16703	R. F. Fullerton, Kendallville	Gum Foam	....	Present.	
16825	Thuis Bottling Works, Vincennes	Blood Orange	....	Present.	
16831	Bandow & Co., Milwaukee, Wis	Soda Syrup	....	....	Present.
16853	Non Intoxicating Brew. Co., Cincinnati, O	Uno Wine	....	Present.	
16917	Non Intoxicating Brew. Co., Cincinnati, O	Juni Art	....	Present.	
17032	T. B. Shaffer & Co., Sullivan	Strawberry	....	....	Present.
17304	Hardenbrook & Sons, Walkerton	Extract	....	Present.	Present.
17306	Hardenbrook & Sons, Walkerton	Extract	....	Present.	Present.
17308	Hardenbrook & Sons, Walkerton	Extract	Present.	Present.	
17311	Hardenbrook & Sons, Walkerton	Extract	....	Present.	
18030	The Liquid Carbonate Co., Chicago, Ill	Strawberry Pop	....	Present.	
18113	Indiana Bottling Co., Indianapolis	White Pop	Present.	....	
18114	Indiana Bottling Co., Indianapolis	Lemon Pop	Present.	Present.	
18115	Indiana Bottling Co., Indianapolis	Red Pop	Present.	Present.	
18116	Yuncker Bottling Works, Indianapolis	Red Pop	....	Present.	
18117	Yuncker Bottling Works, Indianapolis	Lemon Soda	Present.	Present.	
18119	Yuncker Bottling Works, Indianapolis	Red Pop	....	Present.	
18120	Yuncker Bottling Works, Indianapolis	Lemon Soda	....	Present.	
18121	Indiana Bottling Works, Indianapolis	White Pop	Present.	....	
18122	Indiana Bottling Works, Indianapolis	Lemon Pop	Present.	....	
18124	Indiana Bottling Works, Indianapolis	Red Soda	†	†	†
18141	William Laws, North Judson	Strawberry Pop	†	†	†
18202	Klee & Coleman, Indianapolis	White Soda	....	Present.	
18203	Klee & Coleman, Indianapolis	Orange Cider	....	....	
18313	James Hunter, Brazil	Strawberry Pop	Present.	....	
18439	O. M. Jeffaris, Union City	Iron Brew	Present.	....	
18440	O. M. Jeffaris, Union City	Jersey Creme	Present.	....	
18441	O. M. Jeffaris, Union City	Lemon Soda	Present.	....	
18574	William Cummings, Carbon, Ind	Mead	Present.	Present.	
18575	William Cummings, Carbon, Ind	Bounce	Present.	Present.	
18607	C. M. W. Lynn, Terre Haute	Lime Juice	....	Present.	
18653	Elbert Bros., Plymouth	Orange Cider	....	Present.	
18654	Elbert Bros , Plymouth	Strawberry	†	†	†
18721	Yuncker Bottling Works, Indianapolis	Blood Orange	†	†	†
19135	J. Vogel & Sons, Evansville	Ginger Ale	....	Present.	
19136	J. Vogel & Sons, Evansville	Rye Ola	Present.	....	
19137	J. Vogel & Sons, Evansville	Lemon Sour	Present.	....	
19138	J. Vogel & Sons, Evansville	Strawberry Pop	Present.	....	
19140	J. Vogel & Sons, Evansville	Sarsaparilla	Present.	....	
19042	David S. Crooks, Lebanon	Lime Juice	....	Present.	
19152	Mt. Valley Bottling Works, Evansville	Lemon Sour	Present.	Present.	
19153	Mt. Valley Bottling Works, Evansville	Cherry Phosphate	Present.	....	
19154	Mt. Valley Bottling Works, Evansville	Ginger Ale	Present.	Present.	
19155	Mt. Valley Bottling Works, Evansville	Lemon Sour	Present.	Present.	
19156	Mt. Valley Bottling Works, Evansville	Root Beer	Present.	Present.	
19157	Mt. Valley Bottling Works, Evansville	Sarsaparilla	Present.	....	
19159	Mt. Valley Bottling Works, Evansville	Peach Mellow	Present.	....	
19160	Mt. Valley Bottling Works, Evansville	Strawberry	Present.	....	
19161	Mt. Valley Bottling Works, Evansville	Orange Cider	Present.	....	
19162	Mt. Valley Bottling Works, Evansville	Creme Soda	Present.	....	

* Artificially colored. No label.
† Artificially flavored. No label.
‡ Artificially colored.

MISCELLANEOUS FOOD STUFFS.

Under the list of Miscellaneous Food Stuffs is classified a great variety of products, most of which were sent in for analysis by physicians or consumers who suspected that they were adulterated. Eight samples of candy suspected of containing poison were examined for the presence of arsenic, and strychnine and other alkaloids. In no instance was any indication of poison found. While persons of evil intent may add poison to candy, yet the nature of the food is such that the presence of poisonous material is not possible except when it has been placed in the candy for criminal purposes. It is true that many cases of sickness of children follow the eating of candy, but this is due not to the presence of poisons in the candy but to the ingestion by the child of a larger amount of concentrated food than his stomach can care for.

Following the report that ice cream cones were being manufactured from inferior and illegal material, an examination of some half-dozen samples was made, but in no instance was any preservative or other inhibited ingredient discovered. A number of health and so-called cereal coffees were examined for the purpose of determining whether or not the goods were true to label. Several preservatives sent in by customers or collected by inspectors were analyzed to determine their character. One sample known as "Ever Keep" contained 93.12 per cent. of boric acid. Other samples contained sodium sulphite and salicylic acid. A variety of foods, such as sauer kraut, potato salad, rhubarb pie, salted crackers, salted peanuts, etc., were analyzed to determine their salt and acetic acid content. Of the 80 samples of miscellaneous foods analyzed, 75 were classed as legal and 5 illegal.

In the illegal list was included a sample of bread-crumbs which contained arsenic, of rotten eggs, of Wheat Food, a breakfast cereal full of bugs and worms, and of horse-radish adulterated with corn meal.

MINCE MEAT.

Of the 8 samples of mince meat examined, 4 were legal and 4 illegal. These samples were all bulk mince meat, and 3 of the illegal specimens contained benzoic acid; the other sample classed as illegal was so listed because of the presence of starch.

MINCE MEAT.

Lab. No.	Manufacturer.	Benzoic Acid Salts.	Starch.	Remarks.
16305	Bessire & Co., Indianapolis	None	None	Legal.
16350	Bessire & Co., Indianapolis	None	None	Legal.
16468	Eshelman & Derr, Marion	None	Present	Adulterated.
16796	W. E. Leonard, Plymouth	None	None	Legal.
16845	J. J. Glemore, Peru	None	None	Legal.
17165	George N. Worth, Indianapolis	Present	None	Adulterated.
17166	Oscar B. Barthel, Indianapolis	Present	None	Adulterated.
17171	Miller & Hart, Chicago, Ill	Present	None	Adulterated.

FLAVORING EXTRACTS.

LEMON EXTRACT.

Of the 26 samples of lemon extract analyzed, 13 were legal and 13 illegal. These figures indicate a more serious condition of the market than is actually the case. This is due to the fact that many of the samples classed as illegal were sent in by dealers who had old stocks of goods on hand, the proper labeling of which they wished to determine. Many manufacturers of cheap lemon flavors have avoided the use of the word "extract" under the idea that if they did not call their goods "extract" they would not have to conform to any standard. As a matter of fact, lemon flavors and lemon extracts are the same thing and the same standard applies to both. Since the law went into effect but few of the extracts sold as pure goods fail to meet every requirement of the law.

VANILLA EXTRACT.

Of the 24 samples of vanilla extract analyzed, 19 were legal and 5 illegal. These samples were classed as illegal because of the use of improper labels. In two instances the product was apparently made from exhausted beans and failed to contain a sufficient amount of vanillin.

MISCELLANEOUS FLAVORS.

Of the 9 samples analyzed, all were misbranded. These products were for the most part synthetic flavors, such as banana, but they were all labeled and sold as true extracts.

VANILLA EXTRACT—LEGAL.

Lab. No.	Manufacturer or Retailer.	Vanilla.	Color.	Lead Acetate Precipitate.	Remarks.
15793	Hollowell & Ryan, Kokomo	.0975	....	Heavy...	
15794	Hollowell & Ryan, Kokomo	.0635	....	Heavy...	
16060	W. H. Dickinson, Richmond	.0944	....	Heavy...	
16808	W. L. Parish, Morristown	.1348	....	....	
16810	Colonial Mfg. Co., Detroit, Mich	.1512	....	Heavy...	Labeled "Concentrated."
17630	W. M. Bartlett, Jr., Indianapolis	....	Normal...	Fair.....	
17882	L. L. Hanley, Muncie	....	Light....	Medium..	Properly labeled.
18130	Tippecanoe Spice Mills, Indianapolis	.4068	Dark.....	Heavy...	Labeled "Vanillin Flavored."
18251	Wabash Baking Co., Wabash	....	Light....	Heavy...	
18486	J. Hungerford Smith Co., Rochester, N. Y.	.2656	Light....	V. heavy.	
18527	The Peru Grocery Co., Peru	....	Light....	Heavy...	
18536	Elliott Grocery Co., Logansport	....	Light....	Heavy...	
18538	L. M. Brackett & Co., Rochester	.1060	Dark.....	V. heavy.	
18698	W. A. Whitman, Mishawaka	.5116	Dark.....	....	Labeled "Vanillin and Coumarin Colored."
18746	Atlantic & Pacific Tea Co., Indianapolis	.1860	Light....	Medium..	
18779	Heekin Spice Co., Cincinnati, Ohio	....	Normal...	Heavy...	
18783	Indianapolis Drug Co., Indianapolis	....	Light....	Heavy...	"Pure Concentrated Cream Extract."
18787	Indianapolis Fancy Grocery Co., Indianapolis	....	Light....	Medium..	
18788	Indianapolis Fancy Grocery Co., Indianapolis	....	Light....	Heavy...	

VANILLA EXTRACT—ILLEGAL.

Lab. No.	Manufacturer or Retailer.	Vanillin.	Color.	Lead Acetate Precipitate.	Remarks.
15654	E. J. Stierwatt, Gosport	.3000	....	None....	Not genuine vanilla extract.
16649	Lewis Ashworth, Connersville	....	Brown...	Slight....	
17409	John Rushley, Hammond	....	Light....	Medium..	Made from exhausted beans.
18097	L. M. Brackett, Rochester	.6380	D. brown.	Slight ...	Labeled "Strictly Pure."
18826	McCullough Drug Co., Lawrenceburg	.3232	None....	Slight....	Labeled "Vanilla Flavoring."

EXTRACTS—MISCELLANEOUS—ILLEGAL.

Lab. No.	Manufacturer or Retailer.	Classification.	Remarks.
15276	J. A. Drake, Ft. Wayne	Pineapple......	Artificially colored. Not labeled.
15277	J. A. Drake, Ft. Wayne	Strawberry. ..	"Imitation" stamped over "Pure." Legible only by close examination.
16102	Franklin McVeagh, Chicago	Wintergreen....	18% alcohol. Odor weak and poor taste.
18262	S. A. Kuntz, Geneva	Pineapple......	Made from synthetic pineapple flavoring.
18693	W. A. Whitman, Mishawaka	Wintergreen....	1.44% oil of wintergreen.
18694	W. A. Whitman, Mishawaka	Raspberry......	Improperly labeled.
18696	W. A. Whitman, Mishawaka	Banana.........	Improperly labeled.
18780	Heekin Spice Co., Cincinnati, O.	Strawberry White Cap....	Improperly labeled.
18781	Heekin Spice Co., Cincinnati, O.	Banana White Cap..........	Improperly labeled.

FRUIT CIDERS.

Under this heading is included apple ciders, orange ciders and other fruit juices, such as raspberry juice, apricot juice, blackberry juice, etc. One hundred and nine samples of fruit ciders were analyzed, of which 74 were legal and 35 illegal. The illegal ciders are usually so classed because of the presence of benzoate of soda or benzoic acid added as a preservative. In one instance sulphites were present in a sweet cider. In several instances the ciders contained saccharin. Many of the illegal ciders were evidently wholly artificial, being made up with an apple base to which had been added characteristic flavors, artificial colors, etc.

FRUIT CIDERS—ILLEGAL.

Lab. No.	Manufacturer.	Brand.	Preservatives.			Remarks.
			Saccharin.	Sodium Benzoate.	Salicylic Acid.	
15854	Clarksville Cider Co., St. Louis	Apple Juice	None.	Pres.	None.	
16095	Chas. Hoffman, Ft. Wayne	Apple Cider	None.	Pres.	None.	
16096	Chas. Hoffman, Ft. Wayne	Apple Cider	None.	Pres.	None.	
16180	Red Cross Cider Co., St. Louis	Crab Cider	None.	Pres.	None.	
16281	R. M. Hughes & Co., Louisville, Ky.	Blackberry	None.	Pres.	None.	
16349	Clarksville Cider Co., St. Louis	Cider	None.	Pres.	None.	
16372	Henry Zeller, Winamac	Sweet Cider	None.	Pres.	None.	Sulphites present.
16411	Red Cross Cider Co., St. Louis	Crab Cider	None.	Pres.	None.	
16591	Red Cross Cider Co., St. Louis	Apricot Cider	None.	Pres.	None.	
16600	B. O. Porter, Spencer	Apple Cider	None.	Pres.	None.	
16601	B. O. Porter, Spencer	Apple Cider	None.	Pres.	None.	
16629	Chas. Hoffman, Ft. Wayne	Sweet Cider	None.	Pres.	None.	
16631	Steel & Wedel Co., Chicago	Cider	None.	Pres.	None.	
16758	George Rouch, Terre Haute	Sweet Cider	None.	Pres.	None.	
16759	Mrs. Cornelius Koll, Terre Haute	Apple Cider	None.	Pres.	None.	
16760	S. Bressett, Terre Haute	Sweet Cider	None.	Pres.	None.	
16805	Fred M. Shoemaker, Plymouth	Cider	None.	None.	Pres.	
16851	Jackson Lee Co., Toledo, Ohio	Sweet Cider	None.	Pres.	None.	
16852	Non Intoxicating Brew. Co., Cincinnati, Ohio	Sweet Cider	None.	Pres.	None.	
16854	Jackson Lee Co., Toledo, Ohio	Sweet Cider	None.	Pres.	None.	
16879	Otto E. Kollmar, Kokomo	Cherry Cider	Pres.	Pres.	None.	
17034	Quam & Co., Chicago, Ill	Sweet Cider	None.	Pres.	None.	
17035	Red Cross Cider Co., St. Louis	Crab Cider	None.	Pres.	None.	
17857	Moder & Kreutzer, Peru	Sweet Cider	Pres.	Pres.	None.	
17999	Moder & Kreutzer, Peru	Apple Cider	Pres.	Pres.	None.	
18000	Moder & Kreutzer, Peru	Apple Cider	Pres.	Pres.	None.	
18138	J. B. Lavezzoris, Chicago, Ill	Cider	None.	Pres.	Pres.	
18142	J. B. Lavezzoris, Chicago, Ill	Cider	None.	Pres.	None.	
18143	Chas. A. Hoffman, Ft. Wayne	Sweet Cider	Pres.	None.	None.	
18442	O. M. Jeffaris, Union City	Orange Cider	None.	None.	None.	Misbranded.
18443	O. M. Jeffaris, Union City	Raspberry	None.	None.	None.	Misbranded.
18449	Nick Sonntag, Dunkirk	Crab Cider	None.	None.	None.	Misbranded.
18453	Nick Sonntag, Dunkirk	Raspberry	None.	None.	None.	Misbranded.
18603	Chas. W. Lynn, Terre Haute	Apple Cider	None.	Pres.	None.	
18604	Chas. W. Lynn, Terre Haute	Apple Cider	None.	Pres.	None.	
18617	Red Cross Cider Co., St. Louis	Cherry Cider	None.	Pres.	None.	Art. colored.

REPORT FROM DRUG LABORATORY.

The same law regulates the purity of both food and drugs, and provides that the laboratories and inspectors give equal attention to these necessities of life. While food adulteration, insofar as it may affect the public health, has been nearly suppressed, the adulteration of drugs continues. This fraud must always concern the health of the consumer, and because he is usually an invalid taking drugs for the cure of disease, it is most essential that his medicines be pure. If they are not, the results of their ingestion are always disturbing and may be serious. When the food and drug law was enacted it was apparent that many of the common drugs were subject to gross adulteration. In the three years since the passage of the law we have endeavored to improve the standard of the drug supply, and without question the patient today may be far more certain of the character of his medicine than before the law went into effect. Unfortunately the improvement has not been as rapid as is desirable.

During the past year 444 drug samples have been analyzed, of which 242 were classed as legal and 202, or 45.4 per cent., as illegal. The percentage of illegal samples is by far too high, but note should be made of the fact that this list is somewhat swelled by the inclusion of mislabeled and misbranded samples. The drug law requires the statement of the alcohol and narcotic content of medicinal preparations, but in spite of the fact that special efforts have been made to bring the law to the attention of the druggists, occasional samples come into the laboratory which are not so labeled, and which must therefore be classed as adulterated.

Section 2 of the Pure Food and Drug Law of 1907 classes a drug as adulterated if, when sold under a name recognized in the U. S. P. or National Formulary, it differs from the test therein laid down for strength, quality or purity, or if its strength or purity falls below the standard or quality under which it is sold. All products of pharmaceutical houses which go into interstate trade are subject to careful scrutiny by the inspectors and chemists charged with the enforcement of the federal food law, and as a consequence of this rigid inspection such houses exercise unusual care in preparing and assaying their products. This forced control has resulted in a marked decrease in the quantity of low grade goods offered the drug trade and has spurred the highest class of pharmaceutical houses to even greater diligence and care in controlling the quality of their output.

Need for State legislation is indicated by the fact that there are in every State numbers of smaller houses which do a local business only, and whose products do not, in the usual course of trade, enter another State. Since these goods are not subject to federal supervision, they may or may not conform to U. S. P. requirements, depending upon the desire of the manufacturer to produce goods of standard quality, or of products whose only virtue is that of cheapness. And when, in the case of pharmaceuticals, an attempt is made to produce a product below normal cost, that virtue becomes a vice, since the goods so manufactured are of unknown therapeutic value and must often injure rather than aid the patient to whom they are administered.

Fortunately the food and drug law of this State exacts the same requirements of the manufacturing pharmacist as does the federal law and all goods, whether produced within the State or outside it, must conform to the requirements of the U. S. P. or National Formulary, or must meet the standards under which they are sold.

It has seemed desirable to give special attention to the character of some standard pharmaceutical preparations manufactured and sold in Indiana, and for this purpose the inspectors of the Food and Drug Department of the State Board of Health have collected drug samples which represent the product of every manufacturing pharmaceutical house which, to any considerable extent, distributes its product outside the community in which it is located. The samples collected for inspection include tinctura opii, tinctura opii deodorati, fluidum extractum hyoscyami and fluidum extractum belladonae folium. These preparations were all purchased in the original package as sent out by the manufacturer. Several of the samples were supplied by physicians, while others were taken by the inspectors who were able to procure them at drug stores. In the analyses only those factors were determined which showed the alkaloidal and alcoholic content. The amount of alcohol in each preparation was determined solely for the purpose of checking up the statement indicated on the label.

Wherever possible check analyses were made, and in summarizing the results all preparations which fell below the standard set by the U. S. P., or that declared on the label, have been classed as adulterated. In many instances this places in the illegal list goods which are very slightly below standard and which must be considered to be satisfactory pharmaceutical preparations. The results of the assays are given in full under their several headings. This work, although covering but a small portion of the field of the pharmaceutical chemist, indicates clearly the necessity for a more careful control of the manufacture of remedial agents. Since, in the manufacture of fluid extracts and tinctures, alkaloidal content of the resultant product depends upon the character of the crude product, it is obvious that no pharmaceutical house can afford, either in its own interests or that of the physician and patient, to send out preparations which have not been carefully assayed before distribution. The pharmaceutical house which does not assay both the crude drug and the finished product is not in a position to manufacture products which meet the requirement of the pharmaceutical standards under which they are sold, nor to furnish the physician with therapeutic agents which are dependable.

The sale of cocaine is regulated by special legislation and it is also required by the Pure Food and Drug Law that all products which contain it must be plainly and distinctly labeled with the amount present. In spite of the legislation which was enacted in an endeavor to control the sale of an article known to be one of the most dangerous drugs in existence, it is evident that some men who pass as druggists continually violate the law and sell cocaine in its various commercial forms to whoever may desire it and who has the money to pay for it. An instance of this nefarious practice came to light when Arthur J. Navin, a druggist of Indianapolis, was convicted of selling cocaine and fined $10 and costs. The purchase of the sample which led to the prosecution was made by an employe of the State Board of Health, who entered the store of the dependant and inquired the price of "snow." The clerk said that he had it in 25-cent and 50-cent boxes, whereupon the purchaser paid for and obtained a 25-cent box, the contents of which, upon analysis, proved to be cocaine hydrochloride. The circumstances of the sale were such that it is evident this store made a practice of selling cocaine. The practice of the defendant was first learned when officers stationed at Fort Benjamin Harrison found that many of the soldiers at the post were addicted to the use of some drug which was called "snow" by them, and that the users of the drug were known as "snow birds" to their comrades. A sample of the drug was readily obtained and submitted to the

State Laboratory for analysis, and the facts determined which later led to the purchase of the sample upon which the prosecution was based. It is a travesty upon justice and good government that a man guilty of so nefarious a crime as the selling of cocaine, possibly the most dangerous drug known, to the soldiers who constitute our national defense, could be punished in no way except by prosecution for violation of the Food and Drug Law, in not marking the package which contained the cocaine, and that his fine and costs amounted in all to but $22.00. It is to be hoped that the next Legislature will enact sufficiently rigid legislation to protect the citizens of the State from the greed of unprincipled men who are willing to cater to the craving of "dope fiends" and to indulge in the unrestrained sale of narcotic drugs. Such legislation should prohibit absolutely the sale of morphine and similar narcotics to all except to reputable physicians and other practitioners who find in the drug a legitimate use. The penalty for violation of the law should not only include a heavy fine and imprisonment, but the defendant, if he be a druggist, should be disqualified from further following his profession in the State.

During the first year after the passage of the Food and Drug Law, the inspectors gave much time to the examination of drug stores. At present they make their sanitary inspections less and less frequently, for they have learned that the greatest necessity for inspection and control lies elsewhere. This reason explains why they have visited but 1,239 drug stores during the year. The report shows that 990 of these drug stores were in good condition, and that 28 were so superior in equipment and manufacture as to merit the unusual grade of excellent. One hundred and seventy-seven drug stores were rated as in fair condition, 38 were poor and 6 were ranked as bad. It is unfortunate that many establishments operated ostensibly as drug stores are as a matter of fact but blinds behind which an illicit liquor business is conducted, and it is this class of houses which swells the number of stores rated as poor and bad. The same explanation holds as to why adulteration still is rampant among such simple preparations as spirit of camphor, tincture of iodine and tincture of iron. It is to be hoped that the pharmaceutical profession, through its associations and by appeal to the Legislature, will be able to drive from its ranks the men who debase one of the most useful professions and who violate the liquor laws of the State while posing as dispensers of relief to suffering humanity.

PERCENTAGE OF ADULTERATION OF DRUGS IN INDIANA

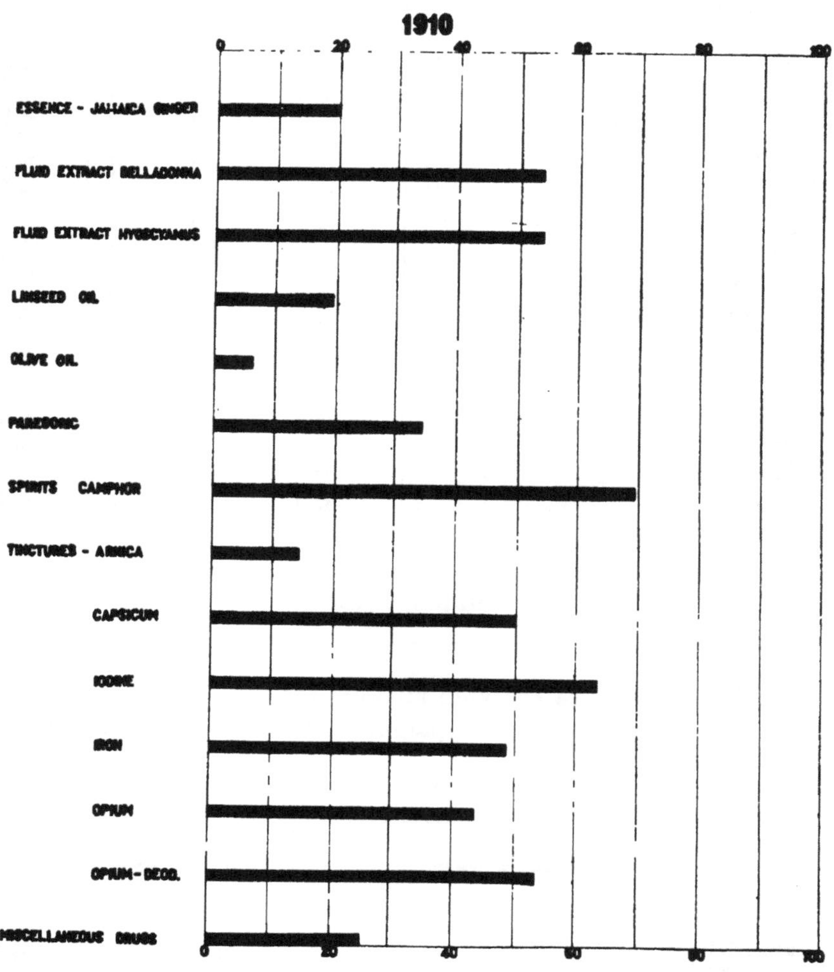

RESULT OF ANALYSIS OF DRUG SAMPLES.

Article Examined.	Legal.	Illegal.	Total.	Per Cent. of Adulteration.
Alcohol	2	0	2	0.0
Asthma Cure	1	1	2	50.0
Bay Rum	1	0	1	0.0
Beeswax, white	1	1	2	50.0
Beeswax, yellow	1	0	1	0.0
Bismuth Subnitrate	1	0	1	0.0
Carbolic Acid	1	0	1	0.0
Castor Oil	8	0	8	0.0
Cough Syrup	2	0	2	0.0
Cream Tartar	1	0	1	0.0
Essence of Jamaica Ginger	4	1	5	20.0
Essence of Peppermint	0	1	1	100.0
Fluid Extract of Belladonna	6	7	13	53.8
Fluid Extract of Hyoscyamus	5	7	12	58.3
Glycerin	2	0	2	0.0
Linseed Oil	17	4	21	19.0
Lime Water	1	0	1	0.0
Olive Oil	14	1	15	6.6
Paregoric	38	20	58	34.4
Potassium Nitrate, commercial	4	0	4	0.0
Quinine Sulphate Capsules	2	0	2	0.0
Sulphur—Flowers	3	0	3	0.0
Spirit of Camphor	28	64	92	69.5
Spirit of Turpentine	2	0	2	0.0
Sweet Spirit of Nitre	0	2	2	100.0
Tincture of Arnica	6	1	7	14.2
Tincture of Benzoin	1	0	1	0.0
Tincture of Capsicum	2	2	4	50.0
Tincture of Iodine	26	46	72	63.8
Tincture of Iron	17	16	33	48.4
Tincture of Myrrh	2	0	2	0.0
Tincture of Opium	16	13	29	44.8
Tincture of Opium Deodorized	8	9	17	52.9
Witchhazel	1	0	1	0.0
Miscellaneous Drugs	18	6	24	25.0
Total	242	202	444	45.4

OLEUM RICINI.

Castor Oil.

Of the 8 samples analyzed all were found to meet the U. S. P. requirements. This oil is apparently rarely if ever adulterated.

CASTOR OIL—LEGAL.

Lab. No.	Manufacturer or Retailer.	Sp. G., 20°C.	Refractive Index, 20°C.	Polarization, 100 mm. Tube.
13245	O. W. Pierce Co., Lafayette	.9595	1.478	13.0
14030	Billings Clapp Co., Boston	.9590	1.478	12.1
16407	Sent in from Center Point	.9610	1.478	12.1
16847	Peru Grocery Co., Peru	.9605	1.478	12.5
17348	Roosa & Ratliff, Cincinnati, Ohio	.9580	1.476	13.0
18339	Hulman & Co., Terre Haute	.9605	1.478	11.7
18457	E. L. Durkee & Co., New York	.9610	1.478	12.6
18581	W. B. Anderson, Spencer	.9610	1.478	12.5

OLEUM LINI.

Linseed Oil.

Of the 27 samples analyzed, 17 were legal and 4 illegal. The illegal samples were adulterated by the admixture of mineral oil.

LINSEED OIL—LEGAL.

Lab. No.	Source of Sample.	Sp. G., 20°C.	Refractive Index, 20°C.	Saponification Value.	Iodine Value.	Emulsion with Lime Water.	Remarks.
16059	E. R. Winters, Albany	.9312	1.4812	194.1	....	No break	
16151	G. F. Wilson, Indianapolis	.9307	1.4807	191.4	....	No break.	
16317	R. S. Tidrick, Bringhurst	.9315	1.4817	195.6	....	....	
16927	Fergers' Pharmacy, Indianapolis	.9302	1.4807	192.8	183.3	No break.	
16928	T. C. Bedford, Indianapolis	.9313	1.4815	188.3	188.6	No break.	
16929	J. N. Heims, Indianapolis	.9311	1.4817	192.1	183.3	No break.	
16930	Ed Stuckey, Indianapolis	.9315	1.4817	192.5	192.5	No break.	
16931	J. J. Keene, Indianapolis	.9302	1.4805	193.4	181.1	No break.	
16932	J. W. Hawthorne Indianapolis	.9333	1.4820	194.0	188.5	No break.	
16933	D. Mooney, Indianapolis	.9315	1.4817	194.7	191.0	No break.	
17789	Browns' Pharmacy, Lagrange	.9397	1.4812	192.7	....	No break.	

LINSEED OIL—ILLEGAL.

Lab. No.	Source of Sample.	Sp. G., 20°C.	Refractive Index, 20°C.	Saponification Value.	Iodine Value	Emulsion with Lime Water.	Remarks.
15402	*A. M. Bool Drug Store, Veedersburg.	.9260	1.4837	163.1	....	Breaks..	
16119	*Harry S. Simon, Indianapolis	.9287	1.4854	162.7	....	Breaks..	
16934	A. Burdsal Co., Indianapolis	.9293	1.4805	192.4	182.4	No break	
16935	Johnson-Woodbridge, Indianapolis	.9287	1.4797	190.7	183.1	No break.	
16936	Sargent Paint & Color Co	.9285	1.4802	191.0	179.0	No break	
16960	Stokes Bros., Indianapolis	.9293	1.4800	192.7	183.4	No break	
16961	Aldag Paint Co., Indianapolis	.9357	1.4812	187.0	184.0	No break.	
16962	Builders' Supply Co	.9270	1.4805	186.8	176.2	Breaks...	
17159	*R. L. Leeson & Sons, Elwood	.9055	1.4780	137.5	....	....	20% mineral oil.
18437	*The Great Western Oil Co., Ind'pls.	.9232	....	182.8	....	Breaks...	Part mineral oil.

* Sent in by.

OLEUM OLIVAE.

Olive Oil.

But one of the 15 samples of olive oil analyzed was adulterated. This sample contained cottonseed oil. The character of olive oil is constantly improving and it is only occasionally that an adulterated sample appears on the market.

OLIVE OIL.

Lab. No.	Source of Sample.	Sp. G., 20°C.	Refractive Index, 20°C.	Butyro Reading, 20°C.	Cotton-seed Oil.
*16177	Stromeyer & Arpe Co., New York			64.8	Negative.
16627	Robert Stevenson Co., Chicago	.9140	1.4695		Negative.
16774	C. T. Gribben, North Manchester	.9125	1.4687		Negative.
16775	J. B. Williams, North Manchester	.9130	1.4685		Negative.
16780	George Burdge, North Manchester	.9130	1.4685		Negative.
*17536	Fischer's Drug Co., Indianapolis		1.4680		Negative.
*18080	Frank Catalani, Indianapolis			69.0	75%
*18104	Montaini & Co., Indianapolis	.9135		63.8	
*18263	Frank Catalani, Indianapolis	.9143		64.4	Negative.
*18308	Jones Stevens Co., Greencastle			64.5	Negative.
*18358	Frank Catalani, Indianapolis			64.8	Negative.
18540	F. W. Fromm, South Bend	.9133	1.4687		Negative.
18743	Atlantic & Pacific Tea Co., Indianapolis		1.4672		Negative.

* Refers to samples sent to laboratory for analysis.

TINCTURA OPII CAMPHORATED.

Paregoric.

Of the 58 samples of paregoric examined, 38 were classed as legal and 20 illegal. Many of these samples were so classed because the opium content was not indicated on the label.

PAREGORIC—LEGAL.

Lab. No.	Source of Sample.	Statement on Label.	
		Alcohol, Per Cent. Volume.	Opium Gr. per fl. oz.
13801	G. W. Dalton, Coal City	47.0	1.9
14899	West End Pharmacy, Brazil	46.5	1.9
14971	Charles Coonley, South Bend	45.0	1.9
14976	Wood & Strieble, South Bend	60.0	1.9
14980	Otto C. Bastion, South Bend	46.5	1.9
14986	Nicholas Schilling, South Bend	46.5	1.9
14991	W. M. Patterson, South Bend	46.5	1.9
14995	Central Pharmacy, South Bend	47.0	1.9
15005	H. E. Freehaffer, South Bend	46.5	1.9
15015	Meyers Drug Store, South Bend	46.0	1.9
15222	H. V. Stark, Shelburn	46.5	1.9
15241	Cook & Black, Terre Haute	46.0	2.0
15288	Charles Mason, Dugger	46.5	1.9
16573	Hargrove & Mullin, Rushville	46.5	1.9
16575	F. B. Johnson, Rushville	46.5	1.9
16580	Rose & Ratliff, Cincinnati, Ohio	46.0	1.8
16642	S. O. Kennan & Son, Connersville	46.5	1.9
16645	Owl Pharmacy, Connersville	47.0	1.9
16658	M. M. Miutch, Laurel	46.5	1.9
16663	M. C. Carter, Brookville	47.0	1.9
16677	O. P. Phares, Liberty	47.0	1.9
17609	Stringfellow & Brennan, Gary	47.0	1.9
17673	H. J. Millstone, Gary	46.5	1.9
18127	Talbot & Moss, Greensburg	46.5	1.9
18145	Simon Fendig, Wheatfield	46.5	1.9
18323	Fred Boyer, Brazil	46.5	1.9
18324	Julian J. Fry, Center Point	46.5	1.9
18335	Charles E. Gillespie, Staunton	46.5	1.9
18347	John L. Wilson, Roachdale	46.5	1.9
18616	J. A. Crabbs, Ellsworth	46.5	1.9
18623	Booe & Booe, Cayuga	46.5	1.9

PAREGORIC—ILLEGAL.

Lab. No.	Source of Sample.	Statement on Label.	
		Alcohol, Per Cent. Volume.	Opium Gr. per fl. oz.
14536	Dr. Rush, Owensburg	....	*
14891	Simon Herr, Brasil	....	*
14905	J. W. Ikerd, Switz City	....	*
15010	Whites' Pharmacy, South Bend	....	*
15242	A. L. Dicken, Bloomingdale	....	*
15611	McKissick Drug Co., Hymera	....	*
16193	J. S. Simons, Lyons	....	1.84
16563	T. W. Lytle, Rushville	46.5	*
16566	F. E. Wolcott, Rushville	47.0	*
16653	L. Ashworth, Connersville	48.0	†
16661	A. J. King, Brookville	....	*
16664	K. C. Meyers, Brookville	....	*
16674	Scott Mullin, Liberty	....	*
16679	H. G. Richardson, Liberty	....	*
17606	Ralph Kahn, Gary	....	*
17667	Hall's Pharmacy, Gary	45.0	4-10 of 1%
17670	Fewer Drug Co., Gary	....	*
17939	Fred Asperger, Riley	48.0	45.6
17953	G. W. Dalton, Coal City	....	1.9
18128	St. John & Guthrie, Greensburg	45.0	1.9%
18131	L. B. Wakeman, North Judson	44.0	¼
18134	Watingers, North Judson	....	*
18571	Daniel M. Newton, Lena	....	*
18592	Jonas Winklepleck, Elnora	....	*

* Opium content not stated.
† Not more than ¼ gr. opium per fluid drachm.

SPIRITUS CAMPHORAE.

Spts. of Camphor.

Ninety-two samples of spirit of camphor were analyzed during the year, of which 28 were legal and 64 illegal. This excessively high percentage of adulteration is due to the fact that the samples still contain an insufficient quantity of camphor gum.

SPIRITS OF CAMPHOR—LEGAL.

Lab. No.	Source of Sample.	Polarization.	Per Cent. U.S.P. Str'gth.	Sp. G., 20°C.	Alc. Vol. Per Cent., 20°C.	Alc. on Label Vol. Per Cent.	Remarks.
15190	W. H. Porter Co., Logansport	12.5	104.1	.8373	79.2	86.0	
15615	Charles Parish, Farmersburg	14.5	112.5	.8333	80.7	92.0	
16014	Campbell & Kersey, Darlington	16.4	136.6	.8355	80.0	91.5	
16390	Hauser & Uplegraff, Columbus	13.1	109.1	.8293	83.6	86.0	
16392	T. E. Otto, Columbus	12.0	100.0	.8297	83.6	86.0	
16394	Stalhutt & Lowe, Columbus	12.1	100.8	.8293	82.9	86.6	
16400	C. A. Adams Co., Columbus	14.8	123.3	.8355	80.7	86.0	
16567	F. E. Wolcott, Rushville	12.8	106.6	.8206	80.4	86.0	
16577	F. B. Johnson, Rushville	12.6	105.0	.8293	81.8	86.0	
16644	S. O. Kennan & Son, Connersville	12.1	100.8	.8274	82.4	86.0	
16650	L. Ashworth, Connersville	12.4	103.3	.8299	83.6	95.0	
16657	M. M. Miutch, Laurel	12.4	103.3	.8288	83.6	86.0	
16664	M. C. Carter, Brookville	12.5	104.1	.8433	79.0	86.0	
16698	Kellars Pharmacy, Brasil	12.4	103.3	....	....	....	

SPIRITS OF CAMPHOR—LEGAL—Continued.

Lab. No.	Source of Sample.	Polarization.	Per Cent. U. S. P. Str'gth.	Sp. G., 20°C.	Alc. Vol. Per Cent., 20°C.	Alc. on Label Vol. Per Cent.	Remarks.
16897	Johnson & Hazen, Wabash	18.8	156.6	.8372	80.0	86.0	
16997	L. P. Savage, Laporte	12.0	100.0	.8300	83.6	86.0	
17006	W. L. Parish, Morristown	13.5	112.5	......	......	......	
17464	E. L. Scott, Akron	12.1	100.8	.8310	82.5	86.0	
17954	G. W. Dalton, Coal City	13.4	111.6	.8308	83.4	95.0	
18132	L. B. Wakeman, North Judson	12.9	107.5	.8298	84 6	86.0	
18154	F. E. Hart, Wolcott	12.0	100.0	.8260	87.2	86.0	
18296	H. W. Meinzen, Ft. Wayne	13.3	110.8	.8285	84.6	86.0	
18318	W. G. Moss, Spencer	16.4	136.6	.8355	81.3	93.0	
18322	Fred Boyer, Brasil	15.4	128.3	.8326	82.1	86.0	
18337	Hulman & Co., Terre Haute	6.3	52.5	.9289	45.0	50.0	"Crystal Brand." Properly labeled.

SPIRITS OF CAMPHOR—ILLEGAL.

Lab. No.	Source of Sample.	Polarization.	Per Cent. U. S. P. Strength.	Sp. G., 20°C.	Alc. Vol. Per Cent., 20°C.	Alc. on Label, Vol. Per Cent.	Remarks.
13806	Charles F. Miller, Butler	5.8	48.3	.9013	58.8	....	
15218	T. B. Shaffer Co., Sullivan	10.0	83.3	.8312	81.5	86.0	
15221	H. V. Stark, Shelburn	11.4	95.0	.8305	81.5	86.0	
15284	Arch Yasel, Elnora	1.3	10.8	.9560	30.2	....	Watered.
15613	Wint Cummins, Hymera	10.8	90.0	.8385	78.1	....	
15764	Wm. J. Walters, Battle Ground	9.0	75.0	.8256	83.6	....	
16387	A. H. Fehring, Columbus	11.2	93.3	.8295	84.9	86.0	
16388	T. J. Noblett, Columbus	10.0	83.3	.8248	85.5	86.0	
16396	H. M. Holmes, Columbus	8.2	68.3	.8286	83.6	91.5	
16402	O. H. Meuret, Columbus	10.8	90.0	.8284	84.0	86.0	
16404	Lay Bros., Columbus	7.7	97.5	.8324	81.8	86.6	
16489	Peoples Drug Store, Coalmont	11.4	95.0	.8358	80.7	....	
16490	H. F. Albert, Freelandsville	7.0	58.3	.8248	85.5	93.0	
16561	T. W. Lytle, Rushville	10.8	90.0	.8270	83.6	86.0	
16571	Hargrove & Mullin, Rushville	11.4	95.0	.8320	81.8	86.0	
16581	Rosa & Ratliff, Cincinnati	10.4	86.6	.8303	80.5	88.8	
16588	Robert Barr, Bruceville	4.4	36.6	.8795	66.8	....	Watered.
16614	Fred Hellar, Brasil	5.6	46.6	.8197	85.5	86.0	
16647	Owl Pharmacy, Connersville	9.3	77.5	.8253	86.6	86.0	
16660	A. J. King, Brookville	9.8	81.6	.8740	68.2	....	
16666	K. C. King, Brookville	10.0	83.3	.8278	84.4	....	
16675	Scott Mullin, Liberty	11.3	94.1	.8300	83.6	86.0	
16676	O. P. Phares, Liberty	11.3	94.1	.8343	82.6	86.0	
16678	H. G. Richardson, Liberty	6.0	50.0	.8830	66.1	....	
16716	Wint Cummins, Hymera	11.0	91.6	....	....	....	
16721	Keasby Drug Co., Dunkirk	9.9	82.5	.8745	68.9	....	
16807	W. L. Parish, Morristown	10.5	87.5	.8522	76.1	86.0	
16991	Red Cross Pharmacy, Laporte	11.3	94.1	.8315	82.9	86.0	
16993	E. C. Zahrt, Laporte	15.5	129.1	.8360	82.9	....	
16994	F. W. Meissner, Laporte	10.9	90.8	.8290	82.9	86.0	
17002	T. H. Boyd, Laporte	10.5	87.5	.8313	82.9	....	
17413	Kaufman & Wolf, Hammond	9.3	77.5	.8548	75.2	85.0	
17416	Edward C. Minas, Hammond	5.3	44.1	.8365	82.5	....	
17459	W. C. Hasman, Akron	10.9	90.8	.8257	84.4	86.0	
17467	Shafor & Goodwin, Mentone	10.1	84.1	.8290	83.3	86.0	
17605	Ralph Cane Co., Gary	9.1	75.8	.8287	83.3	....	
17608	Bremen & Stringfellow, Gary	9.4	78.3	.8293	83.6	86.0	
17668	Halls Pharmacy, Gary	11.6	96.6	.8315	82.5	86.0	
17669	Fewer Drug Co., Gary	10.0	83.3	.8290	83.6	....	
17674	H. J. Millstone, Gary	6.5	54.1	.8248	84.4	....	
17906	Joseph L. Graham, Riley	6.1	50.8	.8965	61.4	....	
18136	Peterson & Watts, North Judson	10.6	88.3	.8310	83.8	....	
18148	J. R. Purkey, Morocco	13.0	108.3	.8312	83.9	....	
18151	L. S. Recher, Morocco	9.7	80.8	.8280	85.7	86.0	
18153	Elmer E. Hess, Brooks	6.7	55.8	.8253	86.5	....	

SPIRITS OF CAMPHOR—ILLEGAL—Continued.

Lab. No.	Source of Sample.	polarization.	Per Cent. U. S. P. Strength.	Sp. G., 20°C.	Alc. Vol. Per Cent., 20°C.	Alc. on Label, Vol. Per Cent.	Remarks.
16156	Spencer Bros., Wolcott	9.3	77.5	.8270	84.6	86.0	
18164	Frank E. Butts, Elberfeld	29.2	243.3	.8953	55.6	80.0	
18222	C. P. Lantenschloger, Patricksburg	9.1	75.8	.8281	84.6	86.0	
18230	J. A. Callahan, Odon	11.5	95.8	.8286	83.4	85.0	
18293	C. L. Rastetter, Ft. Wayne	11.7	97.5	.8278	85.4	94.0	
18300	Dreir Bros., Ft. Wayne	12.0	100.0	.8312	82.8	....	
18316	O. E. Dun, Spencer	11.7	97.5	.8288	83.9	86.0	
18320	Julian H. Ury, Centerpoint	9.7	80.8	.8287	83.5	86.0	
18321	F. W. Schultz, Brasil	10.9	90.8	.8285	83.9	86.0	
18334	C. E. Gillaspie, Staunton	12.4	103.3	.8300	83.5	....	
18343	W. G. White Co., Louisville, Ky	10.8	90.0	.8965	58.6	....	Watered.
18348	G. W. Irwin, Roachdale	8.4	70.0	.8913	61.2	88.0	Watered.
18570	George Rohrig, Harmony	10.8	90.0	.8685	70.5	....	Watered.
18572	Daniel M. Newton, Lena	5.0	41.6	.9192	49.9	....	Watered.
18583	George L. Nelson, Quincy	12.0	100.0	.8281	84.6	....	
18585	G. W. Mayberry, Newberry	10.9	90.8	.8258	83.9	86.0	
18591	J. Winklepleck, Elnora	8.9	74.1	.8700	69.4	....	Watered.
19166	Fults & Anshier, Newberg	9.4	78.3	....	....	....	

TINCTURA ARNICAE.

Tincture of Arnica.

Of the 7 samples of tincture of arnica analyzed, 6 were legal and one illegal.

TINCTURE OF ARNICA—LEGAL.

Lab. No.	Retailer.	Sp. G., 20°C.	Alc. Vol., 20°C.	Gms. Ext. per 100 c.c.	Alc. on Label.
14501	C. E. Creelius, New Albany	.9476	45.3	2.54	46.0
14507	Taylor & Roth, Edinburg	.9472	43.7	3.25	46.0
14516	C. H. Drybread, Franklin	.9440	46.4	2.99	46.0
14779	A. F. Long, Rensselaer	.9483	40.0	1.69	46.0
16388	A. H. Fehring, Columbus	.9440	43.3	1.70	46.0
18163	Frank E. Butts, Elberfeld	.9482	44.0	1.79	45.0

TINCTURA IODI.

Tincture of Iodine.

Seventy-two samples of tincture of iodine were analyzed during the year, of which 26 were pure and 46, or 63.8 per cent., below standard. Contrary to our expectations, the character of the tincture of iodine has not improved during the last year. Carelessness in manufacture must be accepted as explanation for the excessively high percentage of adulteration.

TINCTURE OF IODINE—LEGAL.

Lab. No.	Source of Sample.	Per Cent. U. S. P. Strength.
16320	E. T. Brickley, Anderson	110.8
16321	Central Pharmacy, Anderson	102.8
16325	Cromwell & Son, Van Buren	102.3
16335	N. W. Edwards, Fairmount	107.7
16347	J. T. McPherson, Jonesboro	100.6
16565	T. W. Lytle, Rushville	100.0
16574	F. W. Johnson, Rushville	100.0
16648	Owl Pharmacy, Connersville	109.3
16662	Mrs. M. C. Carter, Brookville	101.3
16773	Charles T. Gribbin, North Manchester	103.6
16778	George Burdge, North Manchester	110.4
16893	Criswell Drug Co., Lafontaine	106.9
16899	E. Gackenhamer, Wabash	102.4
16911	R. E. Clark, Wabash	108.7
16914	Gaylord & Baumbauer, Wabash	108.7
16995	F. W. Meissner, Laporte	101.7
17000	T. H. Boyd, Laporte	109.2
17447	F. A. Rorsener, Indianapolis	101.7
17448	J. H. Stuckmeyer, Indianapolis	104.0
17451	C. D. Pearson, Indianapolis	108.2
17460	W. C. Hasman, Akron	108.9
17610	Brennan & Stringfellow	103.7
18133	L. B. Wakeman, North Judson	112.7
18157	Spencer Bros., Wolcott	100.1
18658	S. M. Newby, Rochester	142.7

TINCTURE OF IODINE—ILLEGAL.

Lab. No.	Source of Sample.	Per Cent. U. S. P. Strength.	Alcohol on Label, Vol. Per Cent.
15684	J. E. Dixon, Burrows	118.5	*
16320	E. T. Brickley, Anderson	110.8	*
16322	J. A. Rust, Anderson	86.4	*
16323	W. C. Roush, Anderson	81.6	94.9
16324	Cassell Bros., Anderson	77.5	*
16326	Fred Drake, Van Buren	....	*
16333	W. A. Beasley, Fairmount	98.7	85.0
16334	W. Hahne, Fairmount	109.5	*
16339	Peoples Drug Co., Upland	104.7	*
16340	P. R. McLeod, Summitville	93.9	85.0
16348	Rothing Louse Bros., Jonesboro	109.0	*
16643	S. O. McKennan & Son, Connersville	67.8	94.9
16656	M. M. Miutch, Laurel	84.2	94.0
16659	A. J. King, Brookville	102.1	*
16667	K. C. Meyers, Brookville	67.1	*
16699	Kellar's Pharmacy, Brazil	90.3	94.9
16714	Wint Cummins, Hymera	103.5	*
16722	Keasby Drug Co., Dunkirk	67.1	*
16776	J. B. Williams, North Manchester	84.4	94.9
16798	Fred Wensler, Plymouth	74.1	94.9
16894	G. U. Geyer, Lafontaine	87.6	94.9
16901	E. W. Swadley, Wabash	82.7	94.9
16903	Bradley Bros., Wabash	104.3	*
16990	Red Cross Pharmacy, Laporte	76.2	94.9
16992	E. C. Zahrt, Laporte	104.7	*
16998	L. P. Savage, Laporte	93.1	94.9
17415	Kaufman & Wolf, Hammond	84.8	94.9
17449	Hovey Drug Co., Indianapolis	98.9	*
17450	J. C. Clark Co., Indianapolis	94.7	94.9
17463	E. L. Scott, Akron	100.0	*
17468	Shafer & Goodwin, Mentone	78.5	94.9
17607	Ralph Kahn, Gary	76.1	*
17666	Halls' Pharmacy, Gary	94.7	96.0
17671	Fewer Drug Co., Gary	101.3	*
17672	H. J. Millstone, Gary	82.3	*
18135	Peterson & Watts, North Judson	100.9	*
18146	Simon Fendig, Wheatfield	46.8	94.9
18149	J. R. Purkey, Morocco	102.0	*
18150	L. D. Recher, Morocco	102.4	*

TINCTURE OF IODINE—ILLEGAL—Continued.

Lab. No.	Source of Sample.	Per Cent. U. S. P. Strength.	Alcohol on Label, Vol. Per Cent.
18152	Elmer E. Hess, Brooks	3	*
18155	F. E. Hart, Wolcott	.1	94.9
18292	C. L. Rostetter, Ft. Wayne	6	94.0
18297	H. W. Meinsen, Ft. Wayne	1	94.9
18298	Dreier Bros., Ft. Wayne	1 1	*
18584	G. L. Nelson, Quincy	96.8	*
18785	Mooney-Mueller Drug Co., Indianapolis	[illegible].1	94.9

* Alcohol content not stated.

TINCTURA FERRI CHLORIDI.

Tincture of Iron.

Sixteen of the 33 samples of ferric chloride analyzed did not meet the U. S. P. requirements. As is the case with tincture iodine, no improvement is noted in this well known drug and the same explanation must be made for its unsatisfactory composition.

TINCTURE OF IRON—LEGAL.

Lab. No.	Source of Sample.	Sp. G., 20°C.	Iron. Per Cent.	Alc., Vol. 20°C.	Per Cent. U. S. P. Strength.	Alc. on Label, Per Cent. Vol.
16391	Hauser & Updegraff, Columbus	1.029	5.30	57.2	117.5	62.0
16393	T. E. Otto, Columbus	1.007	4.55	59.3	100.0	60.0
16395	Stalhutt & Lowe, Columbus	1.029	6.07	60.6	132.7	62.0
16397	H. M. Holmes, Columbus	1.001	4.60	60.6	100.4	62.0
16403	O. H. Menuet, Columbus	1.023	4.95	57.4	108.1	62.0
16405	Lay Bros., Columbus	1.000	4.55	59.8	100.0	62.0
16772	C. T. Gribben, North Manchester	1.014	4.85	58.3	106.0	65.0
16777	J. B. Williams, North Manchester	1.010	4.67	57.7	103.2	63.0
16779	George Burdge, North Manchester	1.054	6.20	55.6	136.5	62.0
16900	E. Gackenheimer, Wabash	1.005	4.57	59.7	100.0	62.0
16902	E. W. Swadbey, Wabash	1.011	4.77	59.2	104.3	62.0
16912	R. E. Clark, Wabash	1.040	6.00	....	130.9	65.0
16999	L. P. Savage, Laporte	1.073	5.97	43.2	130.4	62.0
17001	T. H. Boyd, Laporte	1.025	5.12		111.8	62.0
17266	Anderson Drug Co., Anderson	....	5.15	....	110.9	
17328	Daniel Stewart Co., Indianapolis	1.005	4.62	57.0	100.9	65.0
17461	W. C. Hasman, Akron	1.033	5.12	51.6	111.8	62.0

TINCTURE OF IRON—ILLEGAL.

Lab. No.	Source of Sample.	Sp. G., 20°C.	Iron, Per Cent.	Alc., Vol. 20°C.	Per Cent. U. S. P. Strength.	Alc. on Label, Per Cent. Vol.
14659	A. A. Abraham, Veedersburg	1 029	4.25	66.0	92.9	*
16389	T. J. Noblitt, Columbus	1.947	3.37	70.1	73.8	*
16401	C. A. Adams, Columbus	1.025	4.12	50.0	90.1	62.0
16797	Fred Wenyler, Plymouth	.953	3.40	69.1	74.3	*
16892	Criswell Drug Co., Lafontaine	.984	4.25	64.3	92.9	62.0
16895	G. U. Geyer, Lafontaine	.951	3.35	77.7	73.2	62.0
16896	Johnson & Hazen, Wabash	.959	3.50	67.7	76.6	*
16904	Bradley Bros., Wabash	1.012	4.80	....	104.8	*
16913	Gaylord & Baumbauer, Wabash	1.000	4.30	58.9	93.8	62.0
16925	J. W. Danhaur, Clay City	.998	4.40	58.6	96.0	*
16996	F. W. Meissner, Laporte	1.006	4.65	57.8	101.5	*
17462	E. L. Scott, Akron	1.002	4.40	56.0	96.0	*
17466	Shafer & Goodwin, Mentone	.964	3.57	62.4	78.0	62.0
18294	C. L. Rastetter, Ft. Wayne	1.001	4.50	58.6	98.2	65.0
18295	H. W. Meinsen, Ft. Wayne	.983	4.20	61.6	91.7	62.0
18299	Dreir Bros., Ft. Wayne	.985	4.47	62.8	97.7	*

* Alcohol content not stated.

FLUIDUM EXTRACTUM BELLADONNÆ FLORIUM.

Fluid Extract of Belladonna Leaves.

No official standard is set for this preparation and in the assay we have only attempted to determine whether or not the statement on the label correctly represented the alkaloidal content. The product of different houses varied somewhat in the form of the statement of the content of mydriatic alkaloids. Some preparations indicated the presence of .30 grams mydriatic alkaloids per 100 c.c., others indicated the presence of .35 per cent. mydriatic alkaloids, 1 c.c. equaling .1 gram of the assayed drug. Still others indicated the presence of .30 per cent. mydriatic alkaloids. Thirteen samples, representing the product of nine houses, were assayed, 5 of which were of the standard stated, 5 were below the standard stated, and 3 preparations did not indicate in any way the alkaloidal content. Of these 3 samples, 2 were below .30 per cent. of mydriatic alkaloids per 100 c.c. and 1 above.

FLUID EXTRACT OF BELADONNA LEAVES.

Lab. No.	Name and Address of Manufacturer.	Mydriatic Alkaloids Grams per 100 c. c.	Mydriatic Alkaloids Declared on Label.
17078	Central Pharmacal Co., Seymour	.198	.30 Grams per 100 c. c.
17085	Eli Lilly & Co., Indianapolis	.301	.30 Grams per 100 c. c.
16964	Swan-Myers Co., Indianapolis	.238	
16973	Eli Lilly & Co., Indianapolis	.309	.30 Grams per 100 c. c.
16981	McCoy-Howe Co., Indianapolis	.252	.35%.
18020	Goshen Pharmacal Co., Goshen	.227	
17049	Eli Lilly & Co., Indianapolis	.312	.30 Grams per 100 c. c.
17058	Daniel Stewart Co., Indianapolis	.301	.30%.
17063	McCoy-Howe Co., Indianapolis	.256	.35%.
17146	Pitman-Myers Co., Indianapolis	.341	.30 Grams per 100 c. c.
17150	The Goshen Pharmacal Co., Goshen	.215	
17284	Central Pharmacal Co., Seymour	.218	.30 Grams per 100 c. c.
17291	Lafayette Pharmacal Co., Lafayette	.350	

FLUID EXTRACTUM HYOSCYAMI.

Fluid Extract of Hyoscyamus.

Twelve samples, representing the product of eight houses, were collected and analyzed. Of this number 5, or 41.66 per cent., contained the required .075 grams of mydriatic alkaloids per 100 c.c., and 7, or 58.33 per cent., contained less than the required amount. The highest alkaloidal content was .080 grams per 100 c.c., the lowest .030 grams.

FLUID EXTRACT OF HYOSCYAMUS.

Lab. No.	Name and Address of Manufacturer.	Mydriatic Alkaloids, Grams per 100 c. c.
17081	Central Pharmacal Co., Seymour	.051
17088	Eli Lilly & Co., Indianapolis	.076
16965	Swan-Myers Co., Indianapolis	.057
16974	Eli Lilly & Co., Indianapolis	.079
16983	McCoy-Howe Co., Indianapolis	.031
18019	Goshen Pharmacal Co., Goshen	.061
17051	Eli Lilly & Co., Indianapolis	.081
17061	Daniel Stewart Co., Indianapolis	.053
17069	McCoy-Howe Co., Indianapolis	.031
17140	Pitman-Myers Co., Indianapolis	.081
17151	The Goshen Pharmacal Co., Goshen	.076
17283	The Central Pharmacal Co., Seymour	.048

TINCTURA OPII.

Laudanum.

Twenty-nine samples of laudanum were analyzed during the year, of which 16 were classed as legal and 13 illegal. Twenty-nine samples of laudanum, representing seventeen houses, were examined. Sixteen, or 55.1 per cent., contained the 1.20 grams of morphine per 10 c.c. required by standard. Thirteen samples, or 44.8 per cent., did not contain the required amount of alkaloid. The sample assaying highest contained 1.429 grams of morphine per 100 c.c., while the lowest sample assayed .775 grams per 100 c.c. This last sample was so far below the required standard as to indicate either gross carelessness in manufacture or the use of too small a quantity of crude drug in the preparation of the tincture.

LAUDANUM.

Lab. No.	Name and Address of Manufacturer.	Grams Morphine per 100 c. c.
16557	Pitman-Myers Co., Indianapolis	1.34
16558	McCoy-Howe Co., Indianapolis	1.10
16559	Swan-Myers Co., Indianapolis	0.73
16560	T. W. Lytle, Rushville	1.14
16570	Hargrove & Mullin, Rushville	0.00
16578	F. B. Johnson, Rushville	1.02
16618	Pitman-Myers Co., Indianapolis	1.34
16834	Pitman-Myers Co., Indianapolis	1.32
16870	Central Pharmacal Co., Seymour	1.17
17077	Central Pharmacal Co., Seymour	1.18
17091	Chas. Leich & Co., Evansville	1.21
16966	Swan-Myers Co., Indianapolis	1.27
16975	Eli Lilly Co., Indianapolis	1.20
16977	McCoy-Howe Co., Indianapolis	1.13
17195	Ft. Wayne Drug Co., Ft. Wayne	1.19
17045	Buntin Drug Co., Terre Haute	0.87
17085	Daniel Stewart Co., Indianapolis	1.30
17089	Daniel Stewart Co., Indianapolis	1.31
17065	McCoy-Howe Co., Indianapolis	1.12

LAUDANUM—Continued.

Lab. No.	Name and Address of Manufacturer.	Grams Morphine per 100 c. c.
17070	Eli Lilly Co., Indianapolis	1.27
17071	Eli Lilly Co., Indianapolis	1.30
17143	Pitman-Myers Co., Indianapolis	1.36
17147	The Goshen Pharmacal Co., Goshen	1.30
17286	Central Pharmacal Co., Seymour	1.19
17293	The Lafayette Pharmacal Co., Lafayette	1.33
17295	The Lafayette Pharmacal Co., Lafayette	1.42
18024	The Goshen Pharmacal Co., Goshen	1.32
18162	Frank E. Butts, Elberfeld	1.11
18971	D. A. Swarter, South Whitley	1.09

TINCTURA OPII DEODORATI.

Tincture of Deodorized Opium.

Twenty-four samples, representing the product of 11 houses, were collected and analyzed. Of this number 10, or 41.6 per cent., met the required standard of 1.2 grams of crystalized morphine per 100 c.c., while 7, or 29.1 per cent. fell below the required standard. The highest alkaloidal content found was 1.346 grams morphine per 100 c.c., and the lowest .754 grams. But three samples fell below 1 gram of morphine per 100 c.c., and a number of those classed in the illegal list were but slightly below the required standard.

TINCTURE OF DEODORIZED OPIUM.

Lab. No.	Name and Address of Manufacturer.	Grams Morphine per 100 c. c.
17084	Central Pharmacal Co., Seymour	1.08
17092	Chas. Leich & Co., Evansville	1.15
16967	Swan-Myers Co., Indianapolis	0.75
16968	Eli Lilly & Co., Indianapolis	1.17
16971	Eli Lilly & Co., Indianapolis	1.16
16966	McCoy-Howe Co., Indianapolis	1.00
17177	Ft. Wayne Drug Co., Ft. Wayne	1.27
17046	Buntin Drug Co., Terre Haute	1.16
17057	Daniel Stewart Co., Indianapolis	1.26
17060	Daniel Stewart Co., Indianapolis	1.26
17067	McCoy-Howe Co., Indianapolis	0.97
17072	Eli Lilly & Co., Indianapolis	1.22
17073	Eli Lilly & Co., Indianapolis	1.21
17142	Pitman-Myers Co., Indianapolis	1.34
17294	The Lafayette Pharmacal Co., Lafayette	1.24
17287	Goshen Pharmacal Co., Goshen	1.35
18026	Goshen Pharmacal Co., Goshen	1.22

MISCELLANEOUS DRUGS.

Included in this list are 24 samples of miscellaneous drugs, for the most part sent into the laboratory for analysis by physicians who suspected their character, or who wished to determine their composition. Of the total number analyzed, 18 were pure and 6 impure. Included in the list is a sample of citric acid which upon analysis proved to be oxalic acid of 98.4 per cent. purity. This sample was undoubtedly mislabeled by the druggist who sold it.

A drug found on a sample of bread proved to be strychnin.

A rheumatism cure upon assay was found to contain 10.9 grams of sodium salicylate to a fluid ounce.

An analysis of a sample of Hay's Hair Health, prepared by The Philo Hay Specialties Co., Newark, N. J., contained much lead.

In addition to this unclassified list is included under the same heading a variety of drugs purchased in a regular way, but in each instance representing but few samples. For the sake of the analytical data which possesses considerable valuable information in showing the chemical limits of legal and illegal goods, the results of these goods are tabulated below without discussion.

MISCELLANEOUS TABLES.

ALCOHOL—LEGAL.

Lab. No.	Source of Sample.	Sp. G. 20° C.	Alcohol, Per Cent. Weight, 20° C.	Alcohol, Per Cent. Volume, 20° C.	Remarks.
14917	Sent in by Dr. W. E. Schweir, Knox, Indian..				Tested for strychnine and morphine.
15285	Carving & English, Worthington	.8185	89.7	92.5	

ASTHMA CURE.

Lab. No.	Sent in By	Remarks.
18261	C. D. Christie, Indianapolis	Caffein present. Illegal.
18466	Mrs. Ida Griffith, Van Buren	Potassium nitrate with mixture of powdered henbane and stramonium. Legal.

BAY RUM—LEGAL.

Lab. No.	Manufacturer.	Sp. G. 20° C.	Alcohol, Per Cent. Volume, 20° C.
19250	U. P. Tea Co., New York, N. Y.	.9147	54.6

BEESWAX.

Lab. No.	Source of Sample.	Butyro, 65°.C.	Saponification Value.	Melting Point, ° C.	Remarks.
13997	W. F. Peters, Madison	29.4	97.87	64.0	White wax—pure.
14001	Keffer & Co., Indianapolis	25.2	74.06	61.5	White 20% paraffin.
18271	Benjamin Douglass, Indianapolis	28.2	90.90	63.0	Yellow wax—pure.

BISMUTH SUBNITRATE—LEGAL.

Lab. No.	Sent in By	Bismuth Oxide.	Arsenic.	Remarks.
19175	J. P. Wilson, Scottsburg	79.9%	Absent.	Sample is U. S. P.

CARBOLIC ACID—LEGAL.

Lab. No.	Manufacturer.	Phenol.	Titre Point. ° C.	Remarks.
16686	The White Tar Co., New York	98.7	38.5	Sample is U. S. P. standard.

ESSENCE OF JAMAICA GINGER.

Lab. No.	Manufacturer.	Sp. G. 20° C.	Alcohol Volume, Per Cent 20° C.	Gms. Ext. per 100 c.c.	Alcohol on Label, Per Cent. Volume.	Methyl Alcohol.	Remarks.
*15856	L. H. Knoley, Gas City					None	Legal.
16058	Roosa & Ratliff, Cincinnati					None	Legal.
16562	T. W. Lytle, Rushville	.8180	88.5	0.81	93.0		Low in ext.
16646	Owl Pharmacy, Connersville	.8210	87.6	1.05	93.0		Legal.
16652	L. Ashworth, Connersville	.8262	82.2	1.93	95.0		Legal.

ESSENCE OF PEPPERMINT—ILLEGAL.

Lab. No.	Manufacturer.	Sp. G. 20° C.	Alcohol, Per Cent. Volume, 20° C.	Remarks.
16101	Franklin McVeagh, Chicago	.9670	25.8	Weak in taste and odor. No precipitation of oil.

GLYCERINE—LEGAL.

Lab. No.	Manufacturer.	Sp. G. 20° C.	Mineral Impurities.	Sulphate Radical.	Butyric Acid.	Chlorine.
15087	Larkin Co., Buffalo, N. Y.	1.255	Trace....	None....	None....	None.
18338	Hulman & Co., Terre Haute	1.250	Trace....	Trace....	Trace....	None.

LIME WATER—LEGAL.

Lab. No.	Manufacturer.	Per Cent. U. S. P.
16569	Hargrove & Mullin, Rushville	123.1

POTASSIUM NITRATE, COMMERCIAL—LEGAL.

Lab. No.	Sent in By	Per Cent. Nitrogen.	Potassium Nitrate.	Per Cent. Moisture.
17784	Walter Cogswell, Andrews	13.58	97.9	0.00
17785	Walter Cogswell, Andrews	13.69	98.7	0.00
17786	Walter Cogswell, Andrews	13.48	97.1	0.98
17787	Walter Cogswell, Andrews	13.78	99.3	0.00

QUININE SULPHATE CAPSULES.

Lab. No.	Sent in By	Remarks.
17351	George M. Coon, Marion	Responded to all tests of identity.
17357	Maude Sheets, Mt. Vernon, Indiana	Responded to all tests of identity.

SULPHUR.

Lab. No.	Of Whom Purchased.	Sulphur, Per Cent.	Remarks.
17154	A. H. Perfect & Co., Ft. Wayne	100.0	Flowers of sulphur. Legal.
	A. H. Perfect, Ft. Wayne	99.9	Precipitated sulphur. Legal.
17349	Grover Hetzner, Peru	99.9	Legal.

SWEET SPIRITS OF NITRE—ILLEGAL.

Lab. No.	Sent in By	Ethyl Nitrite.	Sp. G. 20° C.	Odor.	Remarks.
16700	Kellar's Pharmacy, Brazil	.6%	....	....	Below standard.
17481	C. A. Doede, Indianapolis	....	.8110	Ethereal oil.....	Compound spirits of ether. Illegal.

TINCTURE CAPSICUM.

Lab. No.	Source of Sample.	Sp. G. 20° C.	Alcohol, Volume.	Grams Ext. per 100 c. c.	Alcohol on Label.
14513	Muts & Lynch, Edinburg......	.8355	82.6	0.99	90.0 legal.
16568	F. E. Wolcott, Rushville.......	.8390	81.0	1.83	90.0 legal.
16572	Hargrove & Mullin, Rushville..	.8223	86.2	0 82	90.0 low in solids. Illegal.
16576	F. B. Johnson, Rusville.......	.8413	77.5	4.72	Illegal.

PROSECUTIONS.

Compliance with law does not follow enactment of statutes unless suitable machinery is provided for the enforcement of the law and a special penalty established for its violation. In the enforcement of the Pure Food, Drug and Sanitary Laws, we have found that while the great majority of dealers appreciate the necessity for the law and do all they can to comply with it, there are occasional men who, on the chance of escaping the attention of the inspectors and chemists, deal in adulterated foods and drugs, and operate their stores and factories in violation of all sanitary requirements. Wherever it is apparent that men have wilfully violated the laws under which they were operating, charges have been filed against them and actively prosecuted, not because of any desire to secure their conviction and the assessment and collection of fines, but because it seemed necessary to teach the defendant that the law was meant to be obeyed and if they would not comply with its provisions, penalties were provided to force them to do so.

During the year ending September 30, 1910, 245 prosecutions were brought for violation of the Pure Food, Drug and Sanitary Laws. The defendants were convicted in 218 cases and fines amounting to $4,358.35 assessed. In twenty-five cases the defendants were acquitted. In two cases, although found guilty, the fine was suspended. These figures do not represent the exact facts, as in nearly all of the cases where a verdict of "not guilty" was rendered, the judge assured the defendant that he was convinced of the fact that he had violated the law, but under the circumstances of the first offense he was willing to render a finding of "not guilty," establishing the further condition, however, that in the event the defendants were returned under similar charges he should not hesitate to impose the extreme penalty. In addition to the list of cases given below, it has seemed of interest to compile a table for the purpose of classifying the business of defendants and the causes for which they were convicted. From this table it appears that 48 grocers were successfully prosecuted, 32 for the sale of misbranded food, 6 for selling adulterated food, 6 for maintaining an insanitary condition in their store, 3 for selling goods containing sodium benzoate, and one for selling goods containing saccharin.

Forty-five butchers were prosecuted during the year, 19 for the sale of adulterated goods, 13 for the sale of meats preserved with sodium sulphite, 2 because of the use of borax in meats, 4 because of improper care in protecting food, 5 for maintaining insanitary conditions in the shop, and two for the sale of misbranded goods.

Fifty-two dairymen were prosecuted, 23 because of the sale of dirty milk, 20 because of the sale of skimmed and watered milk, and 9 because of unsanitary conditions at the dairy.

Of the 26 druggists prosecuted, action was brought in 16 cases for the sale of adulterated goods, in 8 cases for the failure to declare the alcohol and narcotic content, and in two cases because of the sale of misbranded drugs.

Ten of the 13 restaurant proprietors were prosecuted because of their failure properly to protect their food, and 3 because of the unsanitary condition of the restaurant.

Twenty of the 42 soft drink vendors prosecuted sold beverages preserved with benzoate of soda, 18 because of the presence of saccharin, 2 because of the use of salicylic acid, and one because of the failure to declare the presence of artificial color.

Seven of the 11 bakers prosecuted were guilty of failure to protect their goods, and four failed to maintain a proper sanitary condition in the bakeshop.

Seven ice cream manufacturers convicted sold ice cream which did not contain the required amount of butter fat.

Eight of the 10 candy manufacturers did not properly protect their candy and two maintained unsanitary conditions in the shop.

Tabulating results in another way—37 cases were brought for the sale of misbranded goods, 23 because of the use of sodium benzoate as a food preservative, 2 because of the use of salicylic acid as a food preservative, 2 for the use of borax for similar purposes, 19 for the use of saccharin as an artificial sweetening agent, 8 for the failure to declare the alcohol or narcotic content on the label, 29 for unsanitary conditions in the shop, 68 because of the sale of adulterated goods, 29 because food stuffs were not properly protected from dust or dirt, 13 because of the use of sodium sulphite in meats, and 23 for the sale of dirty milk.

TABLE SHOWING BUSINESS OF DEFENDANTS AND CAUSE FOR WHICH ACTION WAS BR OUGHT.

	Grocer.	Butcher.	Dairyman.	Druggist.	Restaurant.	Soft Drink Vender.	Baker.	Ice Cream Manufacturer.	Confectioners.	Total.
Goods misbranded	32	2	0	2	0	1	0	0	0	37
Benzoate present	3	0	0	0	0	20	0	0	0	23
Saccharin present	1	0	0	0	0	18	0	0	0	19
Alcohol or narcotic not stated	0	0	0	8	0	0	0	0	0	8
Unsanitary conditions in shop	6	5	9	0	3	0	4	0	2	29
Goods adulterated	6	19	20	16	0	0	0	7	0	68
Unprotected foods	0	4	0	0	10	0	7	0	8	29
Meat with sulphites	0	13	0	0	0	0	0	0	0	13
Dirty milk	0	0	23	0	0	0	0	0	0	23
Salicylic acid	0	0	0	0	0	2	0	0	0	2
Borax	0	2	0	0	0	0	0	0	0	2
Color artificial	0	0	0	0	0	1	0	0	0	1
Total	48	45	52	26	13	42	11	7	10	254

LIST OF PROSECUTIONS BROUGHT UNDER THE NEW FOOD AND DRUG LAW FROM OCTOBER 1, 1909, TO OCTOBER 1, 1910.

COUNTY.	Lab. No.	Name and Address of Defendant.	Why Prosecuted.	Date of Trial.	Final Disposition.
Allen	15275	J. H. Eaben, Ft. Wayne, Indiana	Selling adulterated lemon extract	Mar. 29, 1910	Fined $10 and costs.
Allen	16507	Eckert & Co., Ft. Wayne, Indiana	Selling sausage containing starch	Mar. 29, 1910	Not guilty.
Allen	16510	Eckert & Co., Ft. Wayne, Indiana	Selling sausage containing starch	Mar. 29, 1910	Not guilty.
Allen	16515	Leikauf Packing Co., Ft. Wayne, Indiana	Selling sausage containing starch	June 28, 1910	Acquitted.
Allen	16516	Eckert & Co., Ft. Wayne, Indiana	Selling sausage containing starch	Mar. 29, 1910	Not guilty.
Allen	17521	Geo. W. Giles, Ft. Wayne, Indiana	Lard containing cotton seed oil and beef fat	April 19, 1910	Fined $10 and costs.
Blackford	16730	Geo. Rapp, Hartford City, Indiana	Selling sausage containing sulphites	April 6, 1910	Fined $10 and costs.
Cass	15098	W. R. Cogley, Logansport, Indiana	Selling dirty milk	Oct. 21, 1909	Fined $10 and costs.
Cass		A. B. Maple, Logansport	Selling decayed milk	Jan. 26, 1910	Fined $10 and costs.
Cass		Louis Ludwig, Logansport	Insanitary grocery store and bakery	Jan. 7, 1910	Fined $10 and costs.
Cass		Geo. Morarity, Logansport	Insanitary grocery store and bakery	Jan. 7, 1910	Fined $10 and costs.
Cass	17003	Consumers Butter Co., Logansport	Selling oleomargarine for butter	Feb. 2, 1910	Fined $5 and costs.
Cass	17005	Consumers Butter Co., Logansport	Selling oleomargarine for butter	Feb. 2, 1910	Fined $5 and costs.
Cass	17114	E. C. Schneider, Logansport	Selling oleomargarine for butter	Feb. 2, 1910	Fined $5 and costs.
Cass	17126	E. C. Schneider, Logansport	Selling oleomargarine for butter	Feb. 2, 1910	Fined $5 and costs.
Cass		Ray Arnold, Logansport	Selling dirty cream	May 28, 1910	Fined $10 and costs.
Cass		Abraham Stern, Logansport	Insanitary slaughter house	June 29, 1910	Acquitted.
Clay		Pearl McCullough, Brazil	Selling cider containing saccharin	Oct. 22, 1910	Fined $10 and costs.
Clay		Raymond Balinger, Brazil	Insanitary store	Nov. 13, 1910	Fined $15 and costs.
Clay		Balinger & Son, Brazil	Insanitary grocery store	Nov. 13, 1909	Fined $15 and costs.
Clay		James McIntire, Brazil	Insanitary slaughter house	June 10, 1910	Fined $10 and costs.
Clay		Ed. Osman, Brazil	Selling short weight flour	June 10, 1910	Fined $25 and costs.
Clay		Walter Decker, Clay City	Selling short weight flour	June 17, 1910	Fined $10 and costs.
Clay		Daniel Morton, Knightsville	Selling spts. camphor below U. S. P. Standard	June 9, 1910	Fined $10 and costs.
Clay	16614	Fred Haller, Brazil	Selling spts. camphor below standard	Nov. 26, 1909	Fined $10 and costs.
Clay	18313	James Hunter, Brazil	Selling artificial strawberry pop containing saccharin	June 17, 1910	Fined $25 and costs.
Clay	18571	Daniel M. Newton, Lena	Selling paregoric—did not show opium content	Aug. 3, 1910	Fined $10 and costs.
Clay	18573	T. F. Harold, Carbon	Beer sold as temperance beer	Sept. 1, 1910	Fined $20 and costs.
Clay	18574	Wm. Cummings, Carbon	Mead containing benzoate of soda and saccharin	June 28, 1910	Fined $25 and costs.
Clay	18575	Wm. Cummings, Carbon	Bounce containing benzoate of soda and saccharin	June 28, 1910	Fined $10 and costs.
Daviess		Sidney Catron, Odon	Insanitary restaurant	Oct. 25, 1909	Fined $10 and costs.
Daviess	16418	Tare & Downs, Plainville	Hamburger containing starch	Nov. 9, 1909	Fined $20 and costs.
Daviess	16419	Tare & Downs, Plainville	Bologna containing starch	Nov. 9, 1909	Fined $20 and costs.
Daviess	17679	Anton Effinger, Elnora	Illegal sale of bleached flour	April 19, 1910	Fined $10 and costs.
Daviess	18591	Jonas Winklepleck, Elnora	Camphor below U. S. P. Standard	July 26, 1910	Fined $10 and costs.
Daviess	18592	Jonas Winklepleck, Elnora	Paregoric—label bore no opium content	July 29, 1910	Fined $10 and costs.
Daviess		Chas. H. Myers, Elnora	Short weight flour	July 13, 1910	Fined $10 and costs.
Dearborn		Henry Bobink, Lawrenceburg	Operating insanitary dairy	May 18, 1910	Fined $10 and costs.
Dearborn		Wm. Baker, Lawrenceburg	Operating insanitary dairy	May 18, 1910	Fined $10 and costs.
Dekalb	15814	Gust Hoffner, Butler	Hop ale containing sodium benzoate	Nov. 11, 1909	Fined $10 and costs.
Dekalb	15822	Gust Hoffner, Butler	Summer drinks containing saccharin	Nov. 18, 1909	Fined $10 and costs.

LIST OF PROSECUTIONS—Continued.

COUNTY.	Lab. No.	Name and Address of Defendant.	Why Prosecuted.	Date of Trial.	Final Disposition.
Delaware		Chas. Hinkley, Muncie	Exposed pastry	April 6, 1910	Fined $10 and costs.
Elkhart	18030	Claud Wahle, Elkhart	Pop containing benzoate of soda	July 28, 1910	Fined $10 and costs.
Fayette	16643	S. O. Kennan, Connersville	Selling tincture iodine below standard	Feb. 8, 1910	Not guilty.
Fayette	16651	L. Ashworth, Connersville	Selling lemon flavor below standard	Jan. 24, 1910	Fined $10 and costs.
Fayette	16654	Ringloff & McCullen, Connersville	Selling weinerwurst containing starch	Jan. 24, 1910	Fined $10 and costs.
Floyd	16534	Jos. Reem, New Albany	Selling peach bounce containing salicylic acid	Nov. 27, 1909	Fined $10 and costs.
Floyd	16536	City Bottling Works, New Albany	Selling soda containing saccharin	Nov. 27, 1910	Fined $10 and costs.
Floyd	16548	Ben Martz & Son, New Albany	Selling hamburger containing sulphites	Dec. 4, 1909	Fined $10 and costs.
Franklin	16667	K. C. Meyers, Brookville	Selling tincture iodine below standard	Jan. 25, 1910	Fined $10 and costs.
Franklin	16669	Anthony Stall, Brookville	Selling bologna containing borax and starch	Jan. 25, 1910	Fined $10 and costs.
Grant	16345	C. L. Cappock, Jonesboro	Selling sausage containing sulphites	Mar. 2, 1910	Not guilty.
Greene	15318	Laughlin & Coffey, Bloom	Selling milk below standard	Nov. 24, 1909	Fined $10 and costs.
Greene	16197	Joe Jackson, Jasonville	Selling cider containing benzoate of soda	Oct. 13, 1909	Fined $10 and costs.
Greene	16198		Selling blackberry cider containing sodium benzoate	Nov. 5, 1909	Fined $10 and costs.
Greene	16199	Robert Fry, Jasonville	Selling pop artificially colored	Oct. 13, 1909	Fined $10 and costs.
Grant	16345	C. L. Coppock, Jonesboro	Selling sausage containing sulphites	Mar. 22, 1910	Not guilty.
Howard		J. P. Schrupper, Kokomo	Exposed pastry	April 15, 1910	Fined $10 and costs.
Huntington	17897	Schaefer & Schaefer, Hunt	Selling ice cream below standard	May 27, 1910	Fined $10 and costs.
Jackson	17284		Fl. ex. belladonna leaves below standard in mydriatic alkaloid content	Aug. 13, 1910	Fined $10 and costs.
Jackson	17477	John Kissell, Seymour			Fined $10 and costs.
Knox	16416	Wallace & Carroll, Edwardsport		Nov. 8, 1909	Fined $10 and costs.
Knox	16415	Frank A. Thuis, Vincennes		Nov. 8, 1909	Fined $10 and costs.
Knox	16494	Frank A. Thuis, Vincennes		Nov. 28, 1909	Fined $10 and costs.
Knox	16588	Robert Barr, Bruceville		Nov. 28, 1909	Fined $10 and costs.
Kosciusko	17476	W. B. Doddridge, Mentone	improperly labeled	May 4, 1910	Fined $10 and costs.
Lake	17371	John Pohlplatz, Hammond	Selling cream below standard	Feb. 15, 1910	Fined $10 and costs.
Lake	17375	J. Jamieson, Hammond	Selling milk standard	Feb. 15, 1910	Fined $10 and costs.
Lake		James Morelli, Hammond	Unprotected stuff	Feb. 9, 1910	Fined $10 and costs.
Lake		N. Berolis, Hammond	Unprotected stuff	Feb. 9, 1910	Fined $10 and costs.
Lake		Mike Ittu, Gary	Unprotected stuff	Mar. 22, 1910	Fined $10 and costs.
Lake		M. Aronson, Gary	Selling oleomargarine for butter	Mar. 22, 1910	Fined $10 and costs.
Lake	17409	John Rushley, Hammond	Selling vanilla extract made from exhausted beans	Aug. 18, 1910	Fined $10 and costs.
Lake	17416	Edward C. Minus, Hammond	Spt. camphor below standard	Mar. 0, 1910	Fined $20 and costs.
Lake	17424	T. Klilzke, Hammond	Selling dirty milk	Mar. 9, 1910	Fined $10 and costs.
Lake	17427		Selling dirty milk	Mar. 9, 1910	Fined $10 and costs.
Lake	17434		Selling dirty milk	Mar. 9, 1910	Fined $10 and costs.
Lake			Selling exposed candy	Mar. 10, 1910	Fined $10 and costs.
Lake	17581		Cream below standard in fat content	April 6, 1910	Fined $10 and costs.
Lake	17585		Cream below standard in fat content	April 8, 1910	Fined $10 and costs.

Lake	17587	Albert Schneider, Gary	Cream below standard in fat content	April 6, 1910	Fined $10 and costs.
Lake	17598	George Hasiah, Gary	Oleomargarine sold for butter	April 7, 1910	Fined $10 and costs.
Lake	17600	Mike Zebec, Gary	Oleomargarine sold for butter	April 7, 1910	Fined $10 and costs.
Lake	17604	M. Szikora, Gary	Oleomargarine sold for butter	April 7, 1910	Fined $10 and costs.
Lake	17606	Ralph Kahn, Gary	Paregoric—alcohol and opium content not stated on label	May 27, 1910	Fined $10 and costs.
Lake	17611	S. L. Eisler, Gary	Oleomargarine sold for butter	April 20, 1910	Fined $10 and costs.
Lake	17614	S. L. Eisler, Gary	Oleomargarine sold for butter	April 20, 1910	Not guilty.
Lake	17616	S. L. Eisler, Gary	Sausage contained sulphites	April 20, 1910	Not guilty.
Lake	17619	Tittle Brothers, Gary	Hamburger contained sulphites	April 16, 1910	Fined $10 and costs.
Lake	17670	Fewer Drug Co., Gary	Selling paregoric—no alcohol content stated on label	June 22, 1910	Fined $10 and costs.
Lake	17674	H. J. Millstone, Gary	Spts. camphor—below standard	May 27, 1910	Fined $10 and costs.
Lake	17675	Spiris Stratigas, Gary	Oleomargarine sold for butter	April 7, 1910	Fined $10 and costs.
Lake	17677	John Karidy, Gary	Oleomargarine sold for butter	April 7, 1910	Fined $10 and costs.
Lake		John Konder, Gary	Dirty refrigerator	April 20, 1910	Fined $10 and costs.
Lake		Hammond Packing Co. Indiana Harbor	Transporting uncovered meat	May 25, 1910	Fined $10 and costs.
Lake	17957	Geo. Tiegle, Indiana Harbor	Selling oleomargarine for butter	May 24, 1910	Fined $10 and costs.
Lake	17958	Paulsen Tea Co., Indiana Harbor	Selling oleomargarine for butter	May 24, 1910	Fined $10 and costs.
Lake	17959	F. W. Bowser, Indiana Harbor	Selling lard containing beef fat crystals	June 24, 1910	Fined $10 and costs.
Lake	17962	J. H. McAuley, Indiana Harbor	Selling oleomargarine for butter	May 24, 1910	Fined $10 and costs.
Lake	17965	Steenberger Bros., Indiana Harbor	Selling oleomargarine for butter	May 24, 1910	Fined $10 and costs.
Lake	17966	F. A. A. Pekownik, Indiana Harbor	Selling oleomargarine for butter	May 24, 1910	Fined $10 and costs.
Lake	17969	Galik E. Bajar, Indiana Harbor	Selling lard containing beef fat crystals	June 24, 1910	Fined $10 and costs.
Lake	18060	Joe Zurbriggen, Hammond	Milk below standard and dirty	May 25, 1910	Fined $10 and costs.
Lake	18231	Sent in by Jacob Friedman, Food Inspector, Hammond	Hamburger containing sulphites	May 25, 1910	Fined $10 and costs.
Laporte	16950	Zharb Bros., Laporte	Sausage containing sulphites	Jan. 4, 1910	Fined $10 and costs.
Laporte	16951	T. Rowland, Laporte	Misbranded coffee	Dec. 22, 1909	Fined $10 and costs.
Laporte	16952	T. Rowland, Laporte	Misbranded lard	Dec. 22, 1909	Fined $10 and costs.
Laporte	16953	T. Rowland, Laporte	Misbranded butter	Dec. 22, 1909	Fined $10 and costs.
Laporte	16955	Fred W. Steigley, Laporte	Hamburger containing sulphites	Jan. 14, 1910	Fined $10 and costs.
Laporte	16956	Tauke Bros., Laporte	Sausage containing sulphites	Jan. 14, 1910	Fined $10 and costs.
Marion	16355	G. W. Nicholson, Indianapolis	Selling watered oysters	Nov. 10, 1909	Fined $10 and costs.
Marion		——— Carini, Indianapolis	Exposed candy	Dec. 22, 1909	Fined $10 and costs.
Marion	16559	Swan Meyer, Indianapolis	Tr. opium—below standard	May 11, 1910	Fined $10 and costs.
Marion	16967	Swan Meyer, Indianapolis	Tr. opium deodorized, below standard	May 11, 1910	Fined $10 and costs.
Marion	17063	McCoy-Howe Co., Indianapolis	Fl. ex. belladonna leaves—misbranded.	Aug. 13, 1910	Fined $10 and costs.
Marion	17100	L. M. Golas, Indianapolis	Selling hamburger containing sulphites	Jan. 15, 1910	Fined $10 and [illegible]
Marion	17106	Henry Dobrowitz, Indianapolis	Selling hamburger containing sulphites	Jan. 15, 1910	Fined $10 and costs.
Marion		Floyd Paine, Busy Bee Restaurant, Indianapolis	Exposed food	Jan. 12, 1910	Fined $10 and costs.
Marion		Alphonso Eberhart, Ideal Restaurant, Indianapolis	Exposed food	Jan. 12, 1910	Fined $10 and costs.
Marion	17165	Geo. W. Worth, Indianapolis	Selling mince meat containing benzoate of soda	Feb. 15, 1910	Guilty—fine suspended.
Marion	17166	Oscar B. Barthel, Indianapolis	Selling mince meat containing benzoate of soda	Feb. 15, 1910	Guilty—fine suspended.
Marion		Frank Guyetts, Thompson's Restaurant, Indianpls.	Unprotected [illegible]	Feb. 3, 1910	Fined $10 and costs.
Marion		James Solenburg, Vienna Dairy Lunch, Indianpls.	Unprotected food stuff	Feb. 3, 1910	Fined $10 and costs.
Marion		Geo. C. Asimis, Indianapolis	Unprotected rabbits	Feb. 11, 1910	Fined $10 and costs.
Marion		Oscar Beeler, Indianapolis	Unprotected rabbits	Feb. 11, 1910	Fined $10 and costs.
Marion		Oscar Adams, Indianapolis	Unprotected rabbits	Feb. 11, 1910	Fined $10 and costs.

LIST OF PROSECUTIONS—Continued.

COUNTY.	Lab. No.	Name and Address of Defendant.	Why Prosecuted.	Date of Trial.	Final Disposition.
Marion		F. Wetter, Indianapolis	Selling uncovered pastry	Mar. 3, 1910	Fined $10 and costs.
Marion		H. G. Sponsel, Indianapolis	Selling [illegible]	Mar. 3, 1910	Fined $10 and costs.
Marion		Robert Keller, Indianapolis	Selling uncovered pastry	Mar. 3, 1910	Fined $10 and costs.
Marion		Unger, Indianapolis	Selling uncovered pastry	Mar. 3, 1910	Fined $10 and costs.
Marion		Langeman, Indianapolis	Selling uncovered pastry	Mar. 3, 1910	Fined $10 and costs.
Marion		Spanos, Indianapolis	Selling uncovered food	Mar. 7, 1910	Fined $10 and costs.
Marion		C. Kresge, Indianapolis	Selling uncovered Easter candy	Mar. 15, 1910	Fined $10 and costs.
Marion		C. Kresge, Indianapolis	Selling uncovered Easter candy	Mar. 15, 1910	Fined $10 and costs.
Marion	17529	McCormick, Indianapolis	Selling short [illegible] oysters	Mar. 15, 1910	Fined $10 and costs.
[illegible]		Isaac Heims, Indianapolis	Selling adulterated maple sugar	Mar. 2, 1910	Fined $10 and costs.
Marion	17721	Arthur Navin, Indianapolis	Illegal sale of cocaine	April 16, 1910	Fined $10 and costs.
[illegible]	18113	Sector and Son, Indianapolis	Selling white pop [illegible]	July 8, 1910	Fined $10 and costs.
Marion	18114	Sector & Son, Indianapolis	Selling lemon pop containing saccharin	July 8, 1910	Fined $10 and costs.
[illegible]	18115	Sector & Son, In[illegible]	Red pop [illegible] saccharin and [illegible] of soda	July 8, 1910	Fined $10 and costs.
Marion	18120	Yuncker [illegible]	Selling lemon [illegible] benzoate	June 4, 1910	Fined $10 and costs.
Marion	18121	Lewis Sattinger, [illegible]	Selling white pop containing [illegible]	July 8, 1910	Fined $10 and costs.
Marion	18122	Lewis Sattinger, Indianapolis	Selling [illegible] pop [illegible] saccharin	July 8, 1910	Fined $10 and costs.
Marion	18203	Nee and Coleman [illegible]	Selling orange cider containing [illegible]	June 15, 1910	Fined $10 and costs.
Marshall	16794	B. M[illegible], Plymouth	Selling dirty milk	Jan. 11, 1910	Fined $10 and costs.
Marshall	16805	F. M. Shoemaker, Plymouth	Selling cider containing salicylic acid	Jan. 11, 1910	Fined $10 and costs.
Marshall	16806	M. A. [illegible], Plymouth	Selling watered [illegible]	Dec. 13, 1909	Fined $1 and costs.
Marshall	18526	John Simons, Argos	Selling ice cream below standard	July 26, 1910	Fined $10 and costs.
Marshall	18653	Elbert Bros., Plymouth	Selling orange cider [illegible] benzoate of soda	Aug. 5, 1910	Fined $10 and costs.
[illegible]	16072	Peru Sanitary Milk Co., Peru	Selling cream below standard	Nov. 6, 1909	Fined $10 and costs.
[illegible]	16444	Peru Sanitary Milk Co., Peru	Selling milk below standard	Nov. 6, 1909	Fined $10 and costs.
[illegible]		George [illegible], Peru	Uncovered push cart	Nov. 20, 1909	Fined $10 and costs.
[illegible]	16854	A. J[illegible], Peru	Selling cider containing benzoate of soda	Feb. 4, 1910	Fined $10 and costs.
[illegible]	17857	Moder & Kreutzer, Peru	Selling sweet cider [illegible]	May 28, 1910	Fined $10 and costs.
[illegible]	18810	Peru	Selling milk below standard in fat content	Sept. 12, 1910	Fined $10 and costs.
Monroe			Insanitary dairy	Feb. 7, 1910	Fined $10 and costs.
[illegible]			Operating insanitary dairy	April 15, 1910	Fined $10 and costs.
[illegible]			[illegible] insanitary dairy	May 3, 1910	Fined $10 and costs.
Monroe			Operating insanitary dairy	May 3, 1910	Fined $10 and costs.
Monroe			Operating insanitary dairy	May 3, 1910	Fined $10 and costs.
[illegible]			Operating [illegible] dairy	May 3, 1910	Fined $10 and costs.
[illegible]		Chas. Tribby, Ladoga	[illegible] dirty restaurant	Oct. 11, 1909	Fined $10 and costs.
[illegible]		Chas. Tribby, Ladoga	Exposed food stuff	Oct. 11, 1909	Fined $10 and costs.
[illegible]		Frank Stout, Crawfordsville	Operating dirty meat shop	Aug. 10, 1910	Fined $10 and costs.
Montgomery		Ansil Miller, Crawfordsville	[illegible] dirty bakery	Aug. 11, 1910	Fined $10 and costs.
Montgomery		Titus & Miller, Crawfordsville	Oyster cocktail sauce containing benzoate of soda	Aug. 25, 1910	Fined $10 and costs.

Noble	15826	R. E. Fulbertson, Kendallville	Selling pop containing saccharin	Nov. 6, 1909	Fined $10 and costs.
Orange	16281	Kinsey-Cromwell, French Lick	Selling cider containing sodium benzoate	Dec. 27, 1909	Fined $10 and costs.
Orange	16282	Graham & Kellam, French Lick	Selling lard containing beef fat	Jan. 18, 1910	Fined $10 and costs.
Orange	16290	C. F. Johnson, Paoli	Selling cream below standard	Feb. 16, 1910	Fined $10 and costs.
Owen	16112	J. R. Green, Spencer	Selling lemon extract below standard	Nov. 24, 1909	Fined $10 and costs.
Owen	16601	Benz. O. Porter, Spencer	Selling cider containing sodium benzoate	Dec. 9, 1909	Fined $25 and costs.
Owen	16616	Beechuram & Wampler, Gosport	Selling buckeye bounce containing saccharin	Nov. 24, 1909	Fined $10 and costs.
Owen		Harrison Hight, Spencer	Operating insanitary grocery	April 29, 1910	Fined $10 and costs.
Owen		Millard F. Lawson, Spencer	Operating insanitary meat shop	July 2, 1910	Fined $25 and costs.
Owen	18226	E. J. Barton, Arney	Selling vanilla extract improperly labeled	Sept. 22, 1910	Fined $10 and costs.
Owen	18458	John S. Brown, Freeman	Selling extract lemon—misbranded	Aug. 10, 1910	Fined $10 and costs.
Owen	18459	John S. Brown, Freeman	Selling lemon extract—misbranded	Aug. 10, 1910	Fined $10 and costs.
Parke		Arthur Seymour, Rockville	Uncovered confectionery	April 20, 1910	Fined $10 and costs.
Parke		Jones, Rockville		Aug. 16, 1910	Fined $10 and costs.
Parke			store	Aug. 16, 1910	Fined $10 and costs.
Pulaski	16368			Nov. 15, 1909	Fined $10 and costs.
Putnam				May 10, 1910	Fined $10 and costs.
Putnam				June 3, 1910	Fined $10 and costs.
Putnam	18348		Standard	Aug. 11, 1910	Fined $10 and costs.
Putnam	18722		Standard	July 20, 1910	Fined $25 and costs.
Randolph	18439	Oliver & Roweisser, Union City		July 4, 1910	Fined $10 and costs.
Randolph	18440	Oliver & Roweisser, Union City		July 14, 1910	Fined $10 and costs.
Starke		udson		Nov. 17, 1909	Fined $10 and costs.
Starke	16631			Jan. 17, 1910	Fined $10 and costs.
Starke	16637		containing benzoate of soda	Jan. 17, 1910	Fined $10 and costs.
Starke	18489	J. H. Brockhouse, Knox	fat content	July 6, 1910	Fined $10 and costs.
Starke	18491	John Wylie, Knox	ice cream low in fat content	July 6, 1910	Fined $10 and costs.
Sullivan		John Cain, Sullivan		Dec. 27, 1909	Fined $10 and costs.
Sullivan		Com. Martin, Sullivan		Dec. 27, 1909	Fined $10 and costs.
St. Joseph		Gurt Gianopulos, South Bend	confectionery	July 28, 1910	Fined $10 and costs.
St. Joseph		George Neidbalski, South Bend		Aug. 11, 1910	Fined $10 and costs.
St. Joseph		Steve Trembaejkiewicj, South Bend		Aug. 11, 1910	Fined $10 and costs.
St. Joseph		Mrs. Wm. Albrecht, South Bend		Aug. 11, 1910	Fined $10 and costs.
St. Joseph	18692	W. A. Whitman, Mishawaka	labeled	Sept. 1, 1910	Fined $10 and costs.
St. Joseph	18825	Bert Chivington, South Bend		Sept. 1, 1910	Fined $10 and costs.
St. Joseph	18826	Abe Rose, South Bend	milk	Sept. 2, 1910	Fined $10 and costs.
St. Joseph	18827	Abe Rose, South Bend	milk	Sept. 2, 1910	Fined $10 and costs.
St. Joseph	18828	Wm. Korn, South Bend	below standard	Sept. 2, 1910	Fined $10 and costs.
Tippecanoe	15624	H. W. Gagen, Lafayette	saccharin	Oct. 23, 1909	Fined $10 and costs.
Tippecanoe	17293	Lafayette Pharmacal Co., Lafayette	tent	Aug. 25, 1910	Fined $10 and costs.
Tippecanoe	17294	Lafayette Pharmacal Co., Lafayette	opium content	Aug. 25, 1910	Fined $10 and costs.
Union	16674	Scott Mullin, Liberty		Feb. 8, 1910	Fined $10 and costs.
Union	16679	H. G. Richardson, Liberty	label	Feb. 8, 1910	Fined $10 and costs.
Vanderburgh	17538	George Hitch, Evansville		May 13, 1910	Acquitted.
Vanderburgh	17540	George Helmuth, Evansville	dirty milk	May 13, 1910	Acquitted.
Vanderburgh	17541	George H. Stockwell, Jr., Evansville	dirty milk	May 13, 1910	Acquitted.
Vanderburgh	17546	J. M. Killion, Evansville	dirty milk	May 13, 1910	Acquitted.
Vanderburgh	17549	J. C. Wallenmeyer, Evansville	milk below standard	May 13, 1910	Fined $10 and costs.

LIST OF PROSECUTIONS—Continued.

COUNTY.	Lab. No.	Name and Address of Defendant.	Why Prosecuted.	Date of Trial.	Final Disposition.
Vanderburgh	17550	John Shafer, Evansville	Selling dirty milk	May 13, 1910	Acquitted.
Vanderburgh	17551	William Brandenburg, Evansville	Selling dirty milk	May 13, 1910	Acquitted.
Vanderburgh	17818	George Hitch, Evansville	Selling dirty milk	May 13, 1910	Acquitted.
Vanderburgh	17821	A. D. Miller, Evansville	Selling milk below standard	May 13, 1910	Fined $10 and costs.
Vanderburgh	17822	Aickle Bros., Evansville	Selling dirty milk	May 13, 1910	Fined $10 and costs.
Vanderburgh	17825	Killion, Evansville	Selling dirty milk	May 13, 1910	Acquitted.
Vanderburgh	17828	Gnenther, Evansville	Selling dirty milk	May 13, 1910	Acquitted.
Vanderburgh	17829	Wallenmayer, Evansville	Selling dirty milk	May 13, 1910	Acquitted.
Vanderburgh	17832	Laut & Son, Evansville	Selling milk below standard	May 13, 1910	Acquitted.
Vanderburgh	17835	Geo. H. Stocwell, Jr., Evansville	Selling milk below standard	May 13, 1910	Acquitted.
Vanderburgh	17839	Baker & Son, Evansville	Selling milk below standard	May 13, 1910	Fined $10 and costs.
Vanderburgh	17841	Bros., Evansville	Selling milk below standard	May 13, 1910	Acquitted.
Vanderburgh	17843		Selling dirty milk	May 13, 1910	Acquitted.
Vanderburgh	17844		Selling dirty milk	May 23, 1910	Acquitted.
Vermillion	15240		Lemon flavor—below standard	Aug. 4, 1910	Fined $10 and costs.
Vigo	16760	te	Selling cider containing benzoate of soda	April 10, 1910	Fined $10 and costs.
Vigo	17906		Spirits camphor—below standard	May 3, 1910	Fined $10 and costs.
Vigo	17945	T te	Ice cream low in fat content	April 14, 1910	Fined $10 and costs.
Vigo	17946	T te	tent	April 14, 1910	Fined $10 and costs.
Vigo		, Terre	Misbranded flour—short weight	Aug. 2, 1910	Fined $10 and costs.
Wabash	15848		Selling cider vinegar below standard		Fined $10 and costs.
Wabash	15849		Selling vinegar below standard	Mar. 7, 1910	Fined $10 and costs.
Wabash	15850		Selling vinegar below standard		Fined $10 and costs.
Wabash	16782		Selling dirty milk	Nov. 27, 1909	Fined $10 and costs.
Warrick	18847		Selling ice cream below standard in fat content	Sept. 21, 1910	Fined $10 and costs.
Wayne	18382		Selling	June 7, 1910	Fined $10 and costs.
Whitley	15832		Selling	Nov. 9, 1909	Fined $10 and costs.
Whitley	15838		Selling	Nov. 11, 1909	Fined $10 and costs.
Whitley	16095		Selling		Fined $10 and costs.
Whitley	16098		Selling	Nov. 9, 1909	Fined $10 and costs.
Whitley	16382		Selling	Dec. 14, 1909	Fined $10 and costs.

REPORT OF SANITARY INSPECTIONS.

The official regulation of sanitary conditions at food producing establishments may perhaps be looked on as an unwarranted interference with the right of the individual to conduct his business according to the dictates of his own conscience. But the absolute dependence of the majority of our population upon others for their food supply makes it necessary, in their protection, to exercise a rigid control not only over the character of food, but as well over the sanitary conditions which surround its manufacture and sale. Naturally, and fortunately, most men who engage in the production and distribution of food are careful to use good raw material and to handle it in a sanitary way, but the occasional manufacturer or dealer who is ignorant, filthy in his habits and badly equipped for his work must be regulated, and it is toward him that legislation is directed.

As the work of sanitary inspection has progressed, the value of the Sanitary Food Law enacted in 1909 has become more apparent, not only as a means of educating food manufacturers as to the sanitary essentials which they should observe, but in affording health officials a means by which careless and unclean business men may be brought to account. When the Sanitary Food Law was passed some doubt was expressed as to whether or not it would be possible to enforce its stringent provisions, but constant use of the law, both in inspection work and in the courts, has proved its positive value, and we believe established beyond doubt the reasonableness of its provisions.

Increased attention is being paid by local health officials to the sanitary conditions of their dairies, markets and restaurants, and in several cities where sanitary officers are provided the work of inspection is conducted along lines which produce most excellent results. The work of inspector John T. Willett at South Bend is especially to be commended. Mr. Willett, backed by the local board of health, has done for his city what the state inspectors are endeavoring to do for the State, and has by his efficient work secured a marked improvement in the sanitary condition of the food producing establishments of his city. If it were possible for all cities to employ a sanitary officer who could give much of his time to the enforcement of the Sanitary Food Law, an immediate change for the better would follow. It is impossible for the four state inspectors to cover their territory as it should be covered. If they can visit the larger towns in their territory once each year,

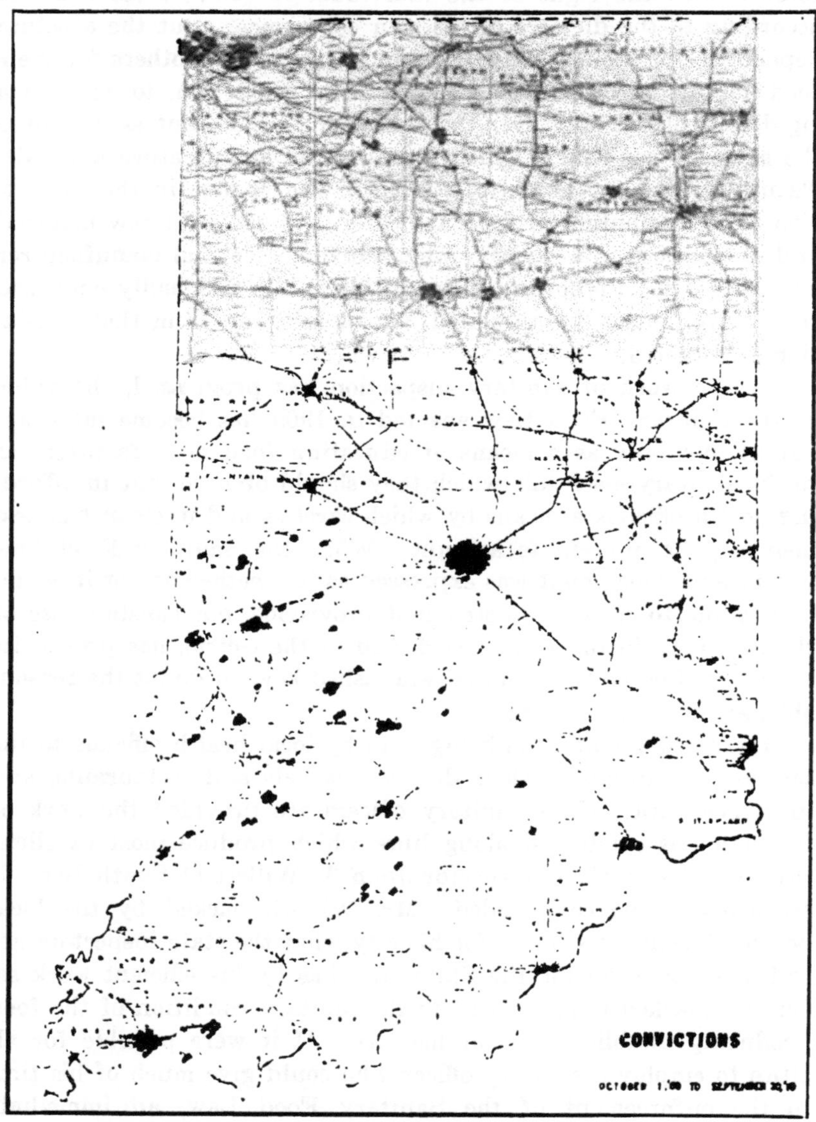

they are doing all that can be expected of them, but even such visits must be of necessity short and the work accomplished incomplete. As a matter of fact, sanitary inspections should be for the most part conducted by local officials, and the work of the state inspectors should be rather devoted to the education and training of local officials and inspectors than, as it must now be, to actual service in the field.

A special investigation was made by the inspectors during March of the weight of sacks of flour milled both in Indiana and in surrounding States and sold as fourth and eighth barrels, and in a few instances under other fractions. The examination made covered a wide range of brands sold in every part of the State under all conditions of climate and storage. The result showed an almost universal tendency toward short weight, and correspondence with many of the millers whose goods fell below the required weight indicated that a practice almost universal in its extent among Indiana millers existed of calling a 24-pound sack, $\frac{1}{8}$ barrel. The millers generally disclaimed knowledge as to what constituted the weight of a barrel of flour, although such weight has been fixed at least twice by Indiana legislators at 196 pounds net, the last legislation being enacted in 1905. Several of the millers corresponded with excused the short weight of their package by saying that they were compelled to reduce the amount of flour placed in each sack because of the competition of other millers. Such a justification of an act which is manifestly to the detriment of the purchaser and the profit of the manufacturer, is wholly inexcusable. Of 77 samples of flour weighed on tested scales in Indianapolis, every sample was short weight. In some instances the shortage exceeded $2\frac{1}{2}$ pounds to an eighth barrel, and in nearly every instance the shortage was one-half pound or over. It apparently has been the practice of the miller to weigh his sacks gross, thus selling the sack at the price of flour. Since the net weight of a barrel of flour is fixed, it is evident that the weight of a fraction of a barrel should also be taken as net. The extent of short weighting was found to be so serious that the attention of the Secretary of the State Millers' Association was called to the matter. He immediately called a meeting of the Executive Committee of the association to consider the facts and if possible to suggest a remedy for the existing unsatisfactory, if not, indeed, dishonest, trade practice. The committee went over the matter with the State Food Commissioner and expressed themselves as being fully in sympathy with the movement to regulate the weights of flour, and at once took steps to inform the milling trade of the necessity of increasing the weight of a sack of flour to meet the legal requirements. As explained to the Executive Committee, the [illegible] as an [illegible] remaining [illegible] The following table shows [illegible] offered for [illegible]

BRAND.	Maker.	Weight Given.	Billed As	Gross Weight.
	Bachman Flour Mill	24 pounds	Eighths	23¾ pounds.
	Star Roller Mills, Shelbyville, Indiana	24 pounds	Eighths	23¾ pounds.
	Pillsbury Flour Mills	24½ pounds	Eighths	24 pounds 6 ounces.
Tip-Top	Bachman Flour Mill	20 pounds	Tenths	19¾ pounds.
	Noblesville Milling Company		Eighths	23½ pounds.
Princess	Blanton Milling Co		Eighths	22½ pounds.
Diadem	Noblesville Milling Company	24 pounds	Eighths	23½ pounds.
Manna	Noblesville Milling Company	48 pounds	Fourths	47¾ pounds.
Pride of the Wabash	Charles Ferger		Eighths	23¾ pounds.
XXXX	Pillsbury Flour Mills	24½ pounds	Eighths	24 pounds 2 ounces.
XXXX	Pillsbury Flour Mills	12 pounds	Sixteenths	11 pounds 14½ ounces.
Our Pride	Haynes Milling Co., Portland, Indiana		Eighths	24 pounds.
Gold Medal	Washburn-Crosby Co		Twentieths	9 pounds 14 ounces.
Gold Medal	Washburn-Crosby Co	24½ pounds	Eighths	24 pounds 2 ounces.
H. B. XXXX	Freeport Mills Co		Eighths	23 pounds 3¾ ounces.
	Haynes Milling Co		Eighths	24 pounds 4 ounces.
Gold Medal	Washburn-Crosby	24½ pounds	Eighths	24½ pounds.
Columbia	Acme-Evans Co	24 pounds	Eighths	24 pounds.
E. Z. Bake	Acme-Evans Co	20 pounds	Tenths	19 pounds 12½ ounces.
Princess	Blanton Milling Co	24 pounds	Eighths	23 pounds 8 ounces.
Pride of Indiana	Fred Prange		Eighths	24 pounds 1 ounce.
Pride of Indiana	Fred Prange		Eighths	23 pounds 11 ounces.
Diadem	Noblesville Milling Co	24 pounds	Eighths	23 pounds 10½ ounces.
Diadem	Noblesville Milling Co	24 pounds	Eighths	24 pounds 7½ ounces.
Diadem	Noblesville Milling Co		Eighths	23 pounds 14 ounces.
Gold Medal	Washburn-Crosby	24½ pounds	Eighths	24 pounds 3 ounces.
Gold Medal	Washburn-Crosby	24½ pounds	Eighths	24 pounds 4 ounces.
H. B. XXXX	Freeport Mills Co		Eighths	22 pounds 9¾ ounces.
H. B. XXXX	Freeport Mills Co		Eighths	23 pounds 7 ounces.
H. B. XXXX	Freeport Mills Co		Eighths	23 pounds 8½ ounces.
H. B. XXXX	Freeport Mills Co		Eighths	23 pounds 8½ ounces.
H. B. XXXX	Freeport Mills Co		Eighths	23 pounds 9 ounces.
H. B. XXXX	Freeport Mills Co		Eighths	23 pounds 8¾ ounces.
H. B. XXXX	Freeport Mills Co		Eighths	23 pounds 14 ounces.
H. B. XXXX	Freeport Mills Co		Eighths	23 pounds 12½ ounces.
H. B. XXXX	Freeport Mills Co		Eighths	23 pounds 8 ounces.
H. B. XXXX	Freeport Mills Co		Eighths	23 pounds 7½ ounces.
H. B. XXXX	Freeport Mills Co		Eighths	23 pounds 4½ ounces.
H. B. XXXX	Freeport Mills Co		Eighths	23 pounds 16¾ ounces.
H. B. XXXX	Freeport Mills Co		Eighths	22 pounds 9 ounces.
Our Pride	Haynes Milling Co., Portland, Indiana		Eighths	23 pounds 14¾ ounces.
Our Pride	Haynes Milling Co., Portland, Indiana		Eighths	23 pounds 14½ ounces.

opinion of the department is that a sack of flour billed as an eighth must contain 24½ pounds net, and that any sack containing less than this amount, if sold as an eighth barrel, is misbranded and therefore in violation of the law. The following table shows the results obtained in weighing 77 samples of flour offered for sale by Indianapolis grocers:

BRAND.	Maker.	Weight Given.	Billed As	[illegible] Weight.
	Bachman Flour Mill	24 pounds	Eighths	23¾ pounds.
	Star Roller Mills, Shelbyville, Indiana	24 pounds	Eighths	23¾ pounds.
	Pillsbury Flour Mills	24½ pounds	Eighths	24 pounds 6 ounces.
Tip-Top	Bachman Flour Mill	20 pounds	Tenths	19¾ pounds.
	Noblesville Milling Company		Eighths	23½ pounds.
Princess	Blanton Milling Co		Eighths	22½ pounds.
Diadem	Noblesville Milling Company	24 pounds	Eighths	23½ pounds.
Manna	Noblesville Milling Company	48 pounds	Fourths	47¾ pounds.
Pride of the Wabash	Charles Ferger		Eighths	23¾ pounds.
XXXX	Pillsbury Flour Mills	24½ pounds	Eighths	24 pounds 2 ounces.
XXXX	Pillsbury Flour Mills	12 pounds	Sixteenths	11 pounds 14½ ounces.
Our Pride	Haynes Milling Co., Portland, Indiana		Eighths	24 pounds.
Gold Medal	Washburn-Crosby Co		Twentieths	9 pounds 14 ounces.
Gold Medal	Washburn-Crosby Co	24½ pounds	Eighths	24 pounds 2 ounces.
H. B. XXXX	Freeport Mills Co		Eighths	23 pounds 3¾ ounces.
	Haynes Milling Co		Eighths	24 pounds 4 ounces.
Gold Medal	Washburn-Crosby	24½ pounds	Eighths	24½ pounds.
Columbia	Acme-Evans Co	24 pounds	Eighths	24 pounds.
E. Z. Bake	Acme-Evans Co	20 pounds	Tenths	19 pounds 12½ ounces.
Princess	Blanton Milling Co	24 pounds	Eighths	23 pounds 8 ounces.
Pride of Indiana	Fred Prange		Eighths	24 pounds 1 ounce.
Pride of Indiana	Fred Prange		Eighths	23 pounds 11 ounces.
Diadem	Noblesville Milling Co	24 pounds	Eighths	23 pounds 10½ ounces.
Diadem	Noblesville Milling Co	24 pounds	Eighths	24 pounds 7½ ounces.
Diadem	Noblesville Milling Co		Eighths	23 pounds 14 ounces.
Gold Medal	Washburn-Crosby	24½ pounds	Eighths	24 pounds 3 ounces.
Gold Medal	Washburn-Crosby	24½ pounds	Eighths	24 pounds 4 ounces.
H. B. XXXX	Freeport Mills Co		Eighths	22 pounds 9¾ ounces.
H. B. XXXX	Freeport Mills Co.		Eighths	23 pounds 7 ounces.
H. B. XXXX	Freeport Mills Co.		Eighths	23 pounds 8½ ounces.
H. B. XXXX	Freeport Mills Co.		Eighths	23 pounds 8½ ounces.
H. B. XXXX	Freeport Mills Co.		Eighths	23 pounds 9 ounces.
H. B. XXXX	Freeport Mills Co.		Eighths	23 pounds 8¾ ounces.
H. B. XXXX	Freeport Mills Co.		Eighths	23 pounds 14 ounces.
H. B. XXXX	Freeport Mills Co.		Eighths	23 pounds 12½ ounces.
H. B. XXXX	Freeport Mills Co.		Eighths	23 pounds 8 ounces.
H. B. XXXX	Freeport Mills Co.		Eighths	23 pounds 7½ ounces.
H. B. XXXX	Freeport Mills Co.		Eighths	23 pounds 4½ ounces.
H. B. XXXX	Freeport Mills Co.		Eighths	23 pounds 16¾ ounces.
H. B. XXXX	Freeport Mills Co.		Eighths	22 pounds 9 ounces.
Our Pride	Haynes Milling Co., Portland, Indiana		Eighths	23 pounds 14¾ ounces.
Our Pride	Haynes Milling Co., Portland, Indiana		Eighths	23 pounds 14½ ounces.

BRAND.	Maker.	Weight Given.	Billed As	[illegible] Weight.
Our Pride	Haynes Ml ing Co., Portland, Indiana		Eighths	23 [illegible] 11 ounces.
Our Pride	[illegible] [illegible] Co., Portland, Indiana		Eighths	24 pounds 5½ ounces.
Our Pride	[illegible] Milling Co., Portland, Indiana		Eighths	24 pounds 4 [illegible]
Our Pride	Haynes Milling Co., Portland, [illegible]		Eighths	24 [illegible] 4 [illegible]
Our Pride	Haynes Milling Co., [illegible] [illegible]		Eighths	24 [illegible] 5 [illegible]
Our Pride	Haynes [illegible] Co., [illegible] [illegible]		Eighths	24 pounds 4 [illegible]
Our Pride	[illegible] [illegible] Co. Portland, Indiana		Eighths	23 [illegible] 14 [illegible]
Our Pride	[illegible] Milling Co. [illegible]		Eighths	24 [illegible] 14 [illegible]
Our Pride	Haynes Milling Co., Portland, I [illegible]		Eighths	24 [illegible] 1½ ounces.
Our Pride	Haynes Mi ng Co., Portland, I [illegible]		Eighths	24 pounds 5 [illegible]
[illegible] Patent	[illegible]		Eighths	23 pounds ½ ounce.
[illegible] Patent	Noblesville [illegible] Co		Eighths	23 pounds ½ [illegible]
Best Patent	[illegible] Milling Co		Eighths	23 [illegible] 5 ounces.
Best [illegible]	Noblesville [illegible] Co		Eighths	23 [illegible] 8½ ounces.
[illegible]	[illegible] Mil [illegible] Co		Eighths	23 pounds 10 [illegible]
[illegible]	[illegible] Flour Mills		Eighths	24 [illegible] 2½ ounces.
[illegible]	Pillsbury [illegible]		Eighths	24 [illegible] 3 [illegible]
[illegible]	[illegible] Flour [illegible]		Eighths	24 pounds 1½ ounces.
[illegible]	[illegible] Mills		Eighths	24 pounds 1½ ounces.
[illegible]	[illegible] Flour Mills		Eighths	24 pounds 2½ [illegible]
[illegible]	[illegible] Mills		Eighths	24 pounds 3½ [illegible]
Purena Health Flour	Purena Mills, St. Louis, Missouri	12 pounds		12 pounds 5 ounces.
[illegible] Flour	[illegible] Mills, St. Louis, [illegible]	12 pounds		11 [illegible] 8 ounces.
[illegible] Health Flour	Purena Mills, St. Louis, [illegible]	12 pounds		12 [illegible] 1 ounce.
[illegible]	Pillsbury [illegible]	12 pounds		11 [illegible] 14 [illegible]
Pillsbury	Pillsbury [illegible] Mills	12 pounds		11 pounds 14 [illegible]
Pillsbury	Pillsbury [illegible] Mills	12 pounds		11 [illegible] 14 [illegible]
[illegible]	Pillsbury [illegible] Mills	12 pounds		11 [illegible] 14 [illegible]
Pillsbury	Pillsbury [illegible]	12 pounds		11 [illegible] 15 [illegible]
Pillsbury	Pillsbury [illegible] Mills	12 pounds		11 [illegible] 12 ounces.
Gold Medal	Washburn-Crosby	10 pounds		9 [illegible] 13½ [illegible]
Gold Medal	Washburn-Crosby	10 pounds		9 [illegible] 3½ ounces.
Gold Medal	Washburn-Crosby	10 pounds		10 pounds.
Gold Medal	Washburn-Crosby	10 pounds		10 pounds.

A comparative study of the sanitary conditions in food producing and distributing establishments during the years of 1907, 1908, 1909 and 1910, shows a constant and decided improvement in all classes of establishments except the dairies. During the year 10,662 inspections were made, 320 places were graded as excellent, 5,981 as good, 3,629 as fair, 626 as poor, and 106 as bad.

Of the 205 dairies visited not a single one could be rated as excellent, and but 28 were even in good condition, 88 of the number were fair, 50 were in poor sanitary condition, and 39 were unqualifiedly bad. This data, coupled with the fact already referred to that sanitary conditions are not improving at the dairies and in fact are rather worse than in any year since the work began, is an occasion for serious thought. Without doubt advantage has been taken by the dairymen of the increased sanitary requirements to raise the price of milk, and yet the reports of our inspectors do not show that they have made any sanitary improvements in return. The one fortunate indication of the improved milk supply is that in all of the larger cities the business is falling into the hands of men who have both capital and courage, who appreciate the necessity for a pure milk supply, and who have the money and energy to supply it. Such men are building all over the State modern dairy barns, equipped with every facility for the production and distribution of sanitarily clean milk. But no matter how successful they may be the majority of our citizens must depend upon the small dairymen for food for the baby and milk and cream for the table, and it is the small dairyman who is not equipped with a properly constructed dairy barn, with tuberculin tested herds, with fly free milk houses, with pure water, and who has no conveniences for refrigeration which enable him to cool his milk and deliver it to the consumer with a minimum bacterial content. The State Dairymen's Association is to be congratulated upon its stand for the purity of the milk supply, and if the dairymen throughout the State could only bring their business up to the plane established by the rules regulating the sanitation of dairies unanimously adopted by their association the milk problem would be solved and the agitation which is now complained of as inimical to the dairy business, forever stopped.

Three thousand nine hundred and forty-three grocery stores were visited, and of this number 150 were in excellent condition, 2,381 were good, 1,215 fair, 184 poor and 13 bad. These figures show a decided improvement over other years. In 1907 but 30 per cent. of the grocery stores were good, last year 60 per cent.

were so rated. The modern grocer is rapidly coming to realize that cleanliness is his best asset, and that filth is a heavy load to carry.

Nine hundred and fifty-nine of the 1,612 meat markets visited were rated as good and 55 as excellent, 516 were fair, 78 were poor and 4 bad.

One thousand four hundred and eighty-three bakeries and confectioneries were inspected during the year. Of this number 56 were in excellent condition, 780 were good, 554 fair, 81 poor and 12 bad.

A recent inspection of bakeries in Indianapolis revealed conditions so unsanitary and seemingly impossible that a description of the shops may well be used in illustrating the necessity for sanitary laws and their most rigid enforcement.

The first bakery visited occupied a brick building in fair condition. The front shop was used chiefly for the sale of bread and other bakery goods over the counter. Its equipment was fair. Suitable show cases, bins and wall cases were available for use, but for some reason instead of being clean and filled with bread and pastries, they were dirty and full of trash, old papers and bags, and the bread which they should have held was piled on the counters. The floor was dirty and unwashed and under the counters had evidently not been washed since it was laid. Back of the salesroom the family of the baker had their kitchen and dining room. A side hall led from the salesroom to the bakeshop in the rear of the building. This bakeshop occupied a large room some 50x30 feet. Light was furnished in fair abundance by windows along one side and by a skylight. The floors were of board laid on stringers imbedded in earth. In the center of the room stood a dismantled pump which evidently was set in an abandoned well or cistern. The floor was not tight and any water thrown on the floor around the pump would readily run through to the excavation below. The ovens occupied the far end of the room and were in fair condition. The floor in front of and to each side of the ovens was covered with accumulated ashes, coal and wood. In the other end of the room the flour was stored in sacks which lay either on the floor in the dirt or on rough board platforms under which rubbish had accumulated for months. Under the windows ran the dough troughs. These troughs were coated with portions of the first dough that had ever been put in them and with additional amounts from every other batch they had contained. The covers were black with dirt, broken and worthless. The closet in which the bread was placed after being drawn from the oven was equally filthy. The racks, sides, floor and door bore a thick layer of dough, flour, ashes and mud, ground into a slimy, homogeneous mass. This condition, according to the statements of the baker, was due to the winter weather which made it impossible either to wash or sweep the floor. The doors at either end of the room opened on a narrow walk-way. Throughout the winter the ashes from the ovens were carried out one door and dumped along the walk from which they were soon tracked in and distributed on the bakeshop floor. This walk was evidently paved with brick, though the accumulated dirt made it impossible to determine the exact facts. In the rear of the bakeshop were the stable, wagon shed, fuel piles, doughnut kettles and bread baskets, each apparently striving to assert its right to the space.

It was impossible to determine where the bakeshop left off and the stable began.

The bakery contained no toilet facilities except an iron sink on one side of the room. The only water available was cold, and no soap and towels were visible. The bakeshop and its surroundings would hardly have been more unsanitary or less fitted for the production of bread.

The second bakeshop inspected revealed quite as unsanitary conditions. The front shop was cleaner, but the rest of the building was far less well adapted for bakery purposes. The bakeshop proper was located in a pit about three feet below the surface of the ground. The floor, walls, ceilings, dough troughs, closets, tables and every other part of the room of furniture was thick with accumulated dough, dirt and smoke. The tightly closed windows were almost useless so far as their original purpose of letting in light was concerned. In one corner of the room stood an indescribably filthy sink. On the opposite side of the room a black and much used towel hung on the same nail with a dirty jumper and overalls. The oven had recently been installed in a rough shed made of boards and scantling. Opening from it and practically in the same room, was an area devoted to the storage of all kinds of material, such as coal and wood. Leading off from this room was the stable, in which the bakeshop wagons and horses were kept. The floor around the wagons and leading into the bakeroom proper was thick with mud and manure from the stable. The storage room for flour was in the stable. The room itself was well built. An open transom over the door was within three feet of an unoccupied horse stall, and two windows in the rear opened into a yard in which, not 15 feet from them, was an unsanitary outhouse. The stable odor permeated the entire bakeshop.

Such descriptions as these could be given indefinitely, for the inspectors report no food manufacturing establishments as more unsanitary than the bakeshops. Their experience is but the experience of food inspectors everywhere. It is especially to be desired that the bakeshop should be a most sanitary place, since the foods there prepared come most intimately in contact with whatever of dirt or filth may be present. The bakeshop should be and under our law must be well lighted and well arranged. Its floors must be made of such impervious material that they may be thoroughly cleaned at the end of each day. Nothing but the implements of the business may be kept in the bake room proper. Fuel and ashes have no place in the bake room, neither have the clothing of employes, or toilets. All flour in barrels or sacks should be kept in a separate room, rat proof, well ventilated and so situated as not to receive objectionable odors. If a stable must be maintained on the premises, it should be so isolated from the bakeshop that no odors are noticeable and that filth cannot be carried through the rooms on the feet of employes.

It is impossible to formulate a set of rules governing the construction and operation of bakeshops, but in general it may be said that unless they are thoroughly clean, and the employes who work there cleanly and intelligent, the food there produced will not be made in a sanitary way or be hygienically fit for food.

Five hundred and fifty-eight of the 1,478 hotels and restaurants were in good condition, 14 were classed as excellent, 774 were fair, 120 poor, and 12 bad. These figures do not indicate a satisfactory sanitary condition of these important houses, and yet the work of last year showed a decided improvement over that of earlier years. But 8 per cent. of the places visited were graded as poor against 16 per cent. in 1909; but .8 per cent. were bad as against 2.2 per cent. in 1909.

Among other establishments visited were 36 creameries, 39 ice ice cream factories, 94 slaughterhouses, 93 poultry houses, 47 fish and oyster houses, 63 bottling works, 56 flour mills, 11 ice plants, 5 breweries, etc. Ten of the 94 slaughterhouses were classed as bad and 20 as poor, 2 were graded as excellent, 23 good and 39 as fair.

Two of the poultry houses were bad and 20 poor. None were rated as excellent and but 18 were in good condition; 53 were rated as fair.

COMPARATIVE STUDY OF SANITARY CONDITIONS IN 1907-1910.

INSPECTION.	Year.	Condition.				
		Excellent.	Good.	Fair.	Poor.	Bad.
		Per Cent.	Per Cent.	Per Cent.	Per Cent.	Per Cent.
Dairies	1907	5.2	16.2	43.5	19.1	15.8
	1908	1.4	14.8	44.1	26.8	12.7
	1909	1.0	20.2	39.5	30.2	8.5
	1910	0.0	13.7	42.9	24.3	19.0
Grocery stores	1907	4.2	30.9	46.5	8.8	1.4
	1908	2.8	45.5	46.1	4.9	.8
	1909	4.8	53.6	35.6	5.3	1.0
	1910	3.8	60.3	30.8	4.6	.3
Meat markets	1907	2.8	35.0	47.3	9.9	4.9
	1908	1.8	39.8	47.4	10.1	1.8
	1909	2.2	57.7	34.0	5.4	.5
	1910	3.4	58.8	32.0	4.8	.2
Drug stores	1907	8.1	58.4	30.7	3.2	0.0
	1908	5.4	74.5	15.8	1.5	0.0
	1909	3.8	72.9	18.7	3.4	.8
	1910	2.2	80.6	13.6	3.0	.4
Bakeries and confectioneries	1907	4.4	40.5	40.8	11.6	2.8
	1908	4.3	40.0	47.4	8.0	2.1
	1909	3.7	49.7	36.2	8.9	1.4
	1910	3.8	52.5	37.3	5.4	.8
Hotels and restaurants	1907	4.5	34.8	40.5	18.0	3.2
	1908	2.0	34.6	48.9	11.4	1.6
	1909	1.3	32.8	47.2	16.1	2.2
	1910	.9	37.7	52.3	8.1	.8

SUMMARY OF INSPECTIONS.

INSPECTIONS.	Number Inspected.	Number Excellent.	Number Good.	Number Fair.	Number Poor.	Number Bad.
Dairies	205	0	28	88	50	39
Wholesale grocery stores	31	3	26	2	0	0
Grocery stores	3,943	150	2,381	1,215	184	13
Meat markets	1,612	55	959	516	78	4
Drug stores	1,239	28	990	177	38	6
Bakeries and confectioneries	1 483	56	780	554	81	12
Hotels and restaurants	1,478	14	558	774	120	12
Creameries	36	0	24	11	1	0
Milk depots	19	0	6	8	5	0
Canning factories	73	1	33	33	6	0
Ice cream parlors	4	0	2	2	0	0
Ice cream factories	39	2	14	19	3	1
Slaughter houses	94	2	23	39	20	10
Poultry houses	93	0	18	53	20	2
Fish and oyster houses	47	2	21	20	4	0
Bottling works	63	3	21	28	9	2
Flour mills	56	2	45	9	0	0
Ice plants	11	0	9	2	0	0
Brewing companies	5	0	3	2	0	0
Produce companies	18	1	7	6	2	2
Fruit houses	39	1	21	16	1	0
Bread wagons	6	0	0	0	3	3
Flour and feed stores	5	0	2	3	0	0
Tea stores	3	0	3	0	0	0
Pharmaceutical companies	3	0	3	0	0	0
Chewing gum factory	1	0	1	0	0	0
Cider vinegar company	1	0	1	0	0	0
Wholesale spice company	1	0	1	0	0	0
Starch and glucose works	1	0	1	0	0	0
Lunch carts	3	0	0	2	1	0
Miscellaneous	50	0	0	50	0	0
Total inspections	10,662	320	5,981	3,629	626	106

NOTICES OF CONDEMNATION.

Section 9 of the Sanitary Food Law provides that under certain conditions the State Food and Drug Commissioner shall issue an order to the proprietors of food producing and distributing establishments where unsanitary conditions prevail requiring within a specified time the abatement of the conditions and such improvements as may be necessary. This provision of the law is most valuable, as it gives to the department power to exact sanitary improvements without resorting to prosecution, and also because the persons interested are given an opportunity to appear before the commissioner to explain the unsanitary condition. For the assistance of inspectors in reporting unsanitary conditions preparatory to the issuance of condemnation orders a report blank has been prepared which in use has proved convenient and helpful.

A sample condemnation report is here given marked by the inspector in such a way as to indicate the unsanitary conditions found at the establishment visited. The condemnation report is followed by a second blank filled in and signed by the State Food and Drug Commissioner. The first report is made a permanent record at the office of the department, the second is forwarded in duplicate to the local health or sanitary officer, one copy of which he serves upon the person to whom it is addressed, and the other filed in his office as his own record.

INSPECTORS' CONDEMNATION REPORT.

State Food and Drug Commissioner:

DEAR SIR.—On the **10th** day of **June, 1910,** I inspected the **bakery** owned, and operated by **Charles D. Brown, Argenta,** Ind., and found that the business was being conducted under unsanitary conditions and in violation of Sec. 2, Chapter 163 of the Acts of 1909, in the following respects:

Manufactories, retail stores, warehouses, hotels, restaurants, etc.	×	Building is **old**, out of repair, unsuitable for use.
	×	Ventilation, **lighting**, is **insufficient.**
		Sewage system is bad, lacking, out of repair.
	×	Floor, sidewalls, ceiling, **fixtures, are unclean.**
		Utensils used in handling food are unclean.
	×	**Screens** are not provided for **windows**, doors.
		Toilets are lacking, have bad floors, are unclean, have no ventilating flue, are in workroom, are not screened.
	×	**Washstands** not provided, unsanitary, **inaccessible.**
		Towels, not provided, dirty, not used.
		Workmen are unclean, in dress, in person.
		Cellar is damp, foul smelling, not ventilated.
		Refrigerator is unclean, mouldy, foul smelling.
	×	Workmen are allowed to sleep in workroom.
		Workmen are diseased, to-wit:
	×	**Spittoons** not cleaned daily, **contain no antiseptic.**
		Spitting on floor is allowed, practiced.
		Premises in general are unclean, untidy.
		Sidewalls, ceilings, not plastered, wainscoated, ceiled.
	×	Interior woodwork not oiled, painted, **washed.**
		Floor not impermeable, cannot be washed clean.
Dairies, milk-rooms, etc.		Buildings are old, out of repair, unsuitable for use.
		Ventilation, lighting, is insufficient.
		Horses, hens, hogs, kept in same compartment with cows.
		Stable is dirty, not whitewashed.
		Manure not removed, stored too near dairy, milkroom.
		Milkroom is not provided, dirty, unscreened, improperly built, located in house, barn, too near barn.
		Utensils are not properly washed, old, rusty, unfit.
		Water supply is inadequate, impure.
		Cattle evidently have tuberculosis, other diseases.
		Cows are unclean, not properly cleaned before milking.
		Milkmen are unclean, in person, dress, have sore hands.
		Dairyman does not know his business.
		Milk is not cooled, properly strained, refrigerated.
		Other unsanitary conditions.

In my opinion the responsible person, **Charles D. Brown,** should be given **10 days**, ... months, in which to abate the unsanitary condition and in case the order is not complied with prosecution should follow.

FRANK W. TUCKER,
State Food Inspector.

Order issued **June 12th, 1910.**

INDIANAPOLIS, IND., June 12, 1910.

Mr. Charles D. Brown, Argenta, Indiana:

DEAR SIR—State Food and Drug Inspector Frank W. Tucker, who visited your place of business June 10, 1910, reports to this office that the following unsanitary conditions exist in violation of Section 2, Chapter 163, Acts 1909, to wit:

Building is old; lighting is insufficient; fixtures are unclean; screens are not provided for windows; washstands are inaccessible; workmen are allowed to sleep in workroom; spittoons contain no antiseptic, and the interior woodwork is not washed.

Acting under the authority given me by Section 9 of the above mentioned act, you are hereby ordered to abate the unsanitary conditions or make such improvements as may be necessary to abate them before June 22, 1910. If you so desire, you may appear before me within the next five days to show cause why you should not obey this order.

Your attention is further called to Section 10 of this Act, which reads as follows:

"Any person who violates any of the provisions of this Act or who refuses to comply with any lawful orders or requirements of the State Food and Drug Commissioner, duly made in writing as provided in Section 9 of this Act, shall be guilty of a misdemeanor, and on conviction shall be punished for the first offense by a fine of not less than $10.00 nor more than $50.00; for the second offense by a fine not less than $50.00 nor more than $100.00, and for the third and subsequent offense by a fine of $200.00 and imprisonment in the county jail for not less than 30 nor more than 90 days, and each day after the expiration of the time limit for abating unsanitary conditions and completing improvements to abate such conditions as ordered by the State Food and Drug Commissioner, shall constitute a distinct and separate offense."

Yours very truly,

H. E. BARNARD,
State Food and Drug Commissioner.

During the year 383 condemnation notices were issued. It is impossible to detail the reasons for the condemnations, but a brief classification can be made by reporting them under two classes—unsanitary conditions and improper construction of building and equipment. The following table sets out a summary of the reports issued during the year.

SUMMARY OF REPORTS OF CONDEMNATIONS ISSUED DURING THE YEAR.

CLASSIFICATION.	Total.	Reasons for Condemnation.	
		Unsanitary Conditions.	Improper Construction.
Bakeries	75	52	32
Bottling works	3	3	3
Canning factories	10	8	8
Confectioneries	8	6	4
Creameries	8	3	7
Dairies	125	85	99
Drug stores	5	5	1
Groceries	24	23	3
Hotels	14	11	3
Ice cream factories	2	2	2
Meat markets	30	25	13
Miscellaneous	4	4	0
Poultry houses	7	6	3
Restaurants	38	31	13
Slaughter houses	30	25	16
Total	383	289	207

THE INFLUENCE OF THE INGESTION OF SPICES UPON THE EXCRETION OF HIPPURIC ACID.

H. E. Barnard.

Hippuric acid, benzoyl-glycocoll, is found in the urine of herbivorous animals and in small quantities in human urine, and is formed by the union of benzoic acid and glycocoll. The origin of the benzoic acid which is eliminated as hippuric acid has been attributed to the ingestion of plant foods, especially such fruits as plums, huckleberries, cranberries, etc., and aromatic food substances, such as the spices. It is also recognized that it results from a breaking down of the protein molecule which contains an aromatic nucleus.* The excretion of hippuric acid may, therefore, be expected to follow the putrefaction of protein in the intestines, even when benzoic acid as such or in simple combination may not be present in the food.

In defense of the use of sodium benzoate as a preservative in food stuffs, much stress has been laid upon the fact that the kidney excretes hippuric acid as a natural function and, by a process of inductive reasoning, it has been assumed that the benzoic acid essential to the formation of hippuric acid, was ingested as such with food. Special stress has been laid upon the fact that the common spices contain essential oils of the aromatic series, some of which theoretically are capable of oxidation to benzoic acid. For the purpose of determining whether or not such oxidation does take place in the human economy, we have recently conducted a series of experiments to determine the effect on hippuric acid excretion of the ingestion of considerable quantities of highly spiced food. The special food which was added to the usual dietary was tomato catsup, which was consumed in much larger quantities than is the usual practice. Prior to beginning the experiment, which was carried on with seven male subjects, varying in age from 21 to 35, an estimation of the hippuric acid in the urine voided was made in the case of each subject for four consecutive days. During this fore period the subjects took their ordinary food, being careful, however, not to eat catsup or to take more than the usual amount

* Novy, Physiological Chemistry, Page 156. Hammersten & Mendel, A Text Book of Physiological Chemistry, Page 588.

of spices in their foods. Following the fore period, each subject for seven days took, usually with his noon-day meal, one bottle of catsup, weighing seven ounces net. The catsup was a standard brand of good flavor, which was well but not excessively spiced and was similar in composition to the standard catsups. The urine voided was collected daily as during the fore period and the hippuric acid determined in an aliquot portion of the total amount. The analytical method employed was that of Bunge and Schmiedeberg as modified by Dakin and further modified slightly in our laboratory. The method employed in brief is as follows:

One hundred c.c. of the urine was evaporated almost to dryness on the water bath. One gram of sodium acid phosphate and 15 grams of calcium sulphate were then added and stirred with the residue until a uniform mixture was obtained. The mixture was then dried, thoroughly pulverized, placed in an "extraction thimble" and extracted with ethyl acetate in a soxhlet apparatus in the usual way. The ethyl acetate extract was then transferred to a separatory funnel and washed with four portions of 25 c.c. of saturated sodium chloride solution. The washed residue was then transferred to a Kjeldahl flask, together with 25 c.c. of distilled water, the ethyl acetate removed by distillation and the nitrogen content of the residue determined in the usual way, and from the factor obtained, the hippuric acid in the original urine calculated.

In order to determine the accuracy of the method and to eliminate the possibility of estimation as hippuric acid, of other nitrogen containing bodies, such as urea, the method was checked out by the use of known quantities of hippuric acid and of urea in control experiments.

In the first control experiment two mixtures containing 100 milligrams of hippuric acid and 2 grams of urea were added to 100 c.c. of water and the hippuric acid determined in the mixture by the method outlined above. The amount of hippuric acid recovered was 100.1 milligrams in one and 96.6 in the other. In the second control experiment two portions of urine were taken and to one was added 100 milligrams of hippuric acid. The hippuric acid was then determined in each sample and the excess in the second sample over that in the normal urine found to be 100.1 milligrams. These figures correspond almost exactly with the amounts added, and the results may be taken as a fair test of the accuracy of the method.

The appended charts, Nos. 1-7 inclusive, graphically record the hippuric acid content of the urine of the seven subjects for each day of the experiment.* It will be at once noticed that the amounts obtained are somewhat higher than the amounts usually given as the normal excretion.† This is true of the entire period, and can only be attributed to the employment of analytical methods more satisfactory than those used by the earlier investigators.

The hippuric acid excretion during the period when the tomato catsup was being taken showed no increase in quantity over that excreted during the fore period. On the contrary in no case did the average amount excreted equal the average amount excreted during the fore period. These results must be taken as indicative of the fallacy of the theory that the essential oils of spices are oxidized to benzoic acid in the course of metabolism, for if this were the case the hippuric acid excreted would, under the conditions imposed, have showed a decided rise during the seven days when the subjects were taking the spiced catsup.

The analytical work was done by Mr. I. L. Miller and Wm. D. McAbee, chemists of the State Laboratory of Hygiene, and the subjects of the experiment included all the male members of the analytical force.

*Chart No. 8 is a record of the average hippuric acid excretion during the entire experiment.

† Hammersten & Mendel, A Text Book of Physiological Chemistry, Page 585.

HIPPURIC ACID CONTENT OF URINE.

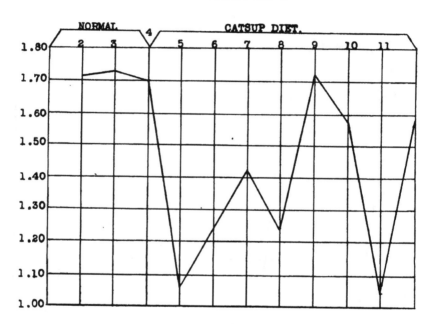

(GRAMS PER DAY)

SUBJECT NO. I

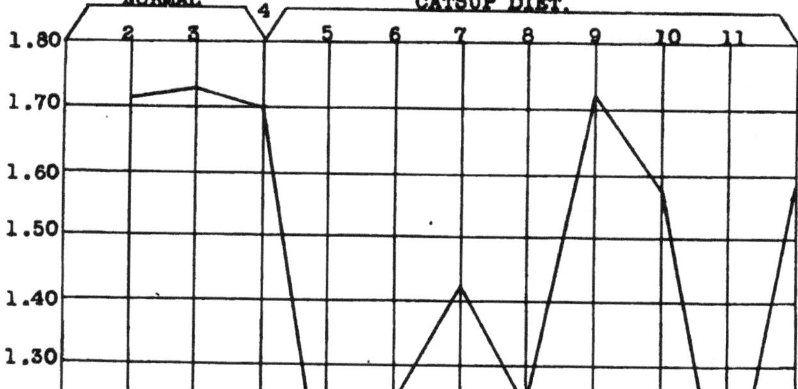

SUBJECT NO. II.

1.50

1.40

1.30

1.20

1.10

1.00

.90

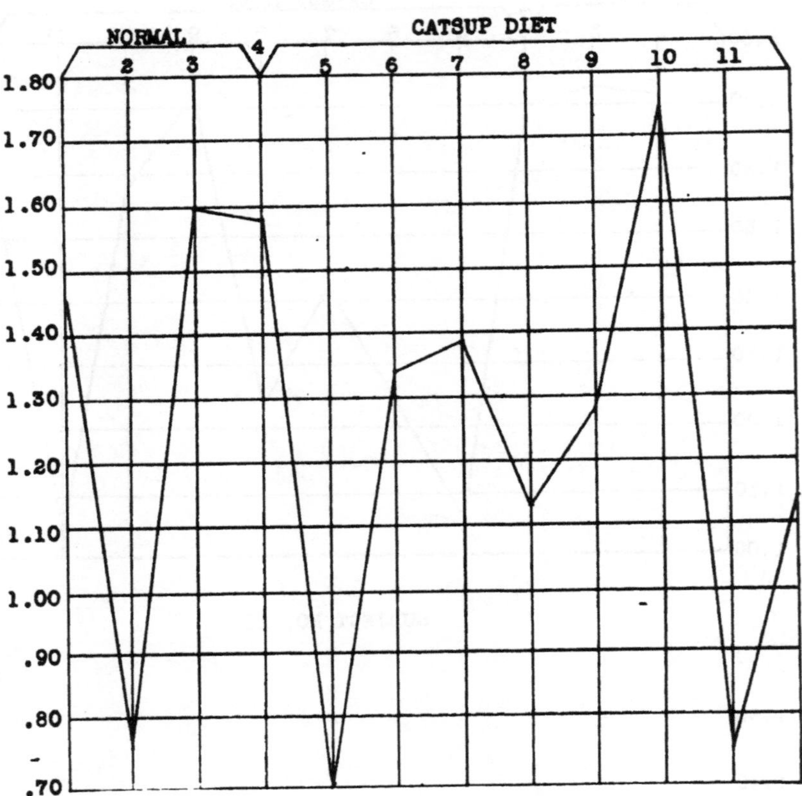
SUBJECT NO. III.
NORMAL
CATSUP DIET
2
3
4
5
6
7
8
9
10
11
1.80
1.70
1.60
1.50
1.40
1.30
1.20
1.10
1.00
.90
.80
.70

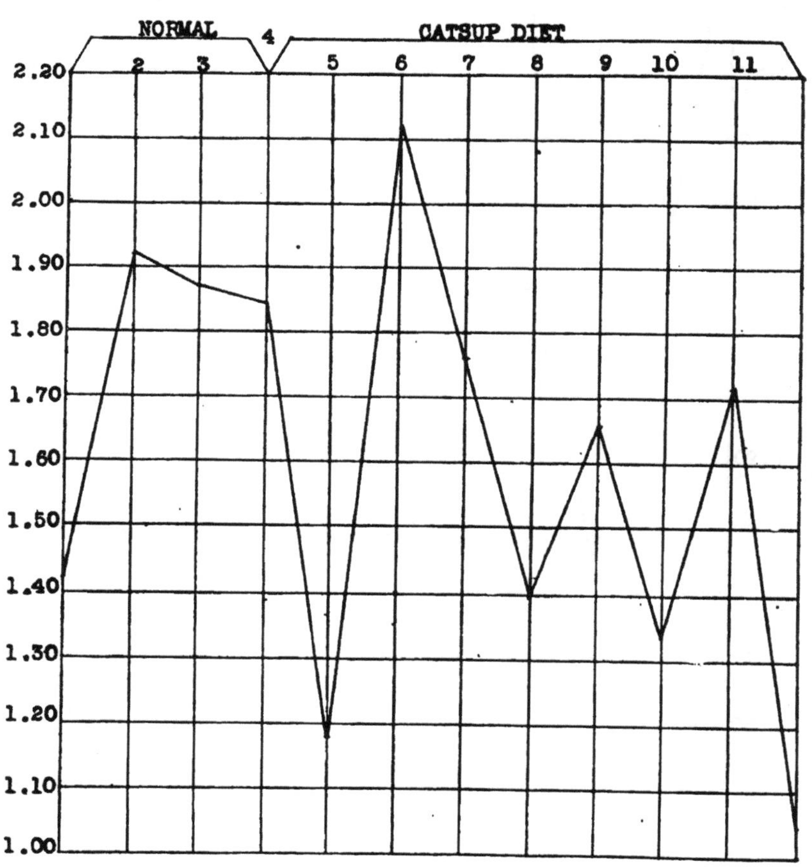
SUBJECT NO. IV.
NORMAL
CATSUP DIET
2
3
4
5
6
7
8
9
10
11
2.20
2.10
2.00
1.90
1.80
1.70
1.60
1.50
1.40
1.30
1.20
1.10
1.00

SUBJECT NO. V.

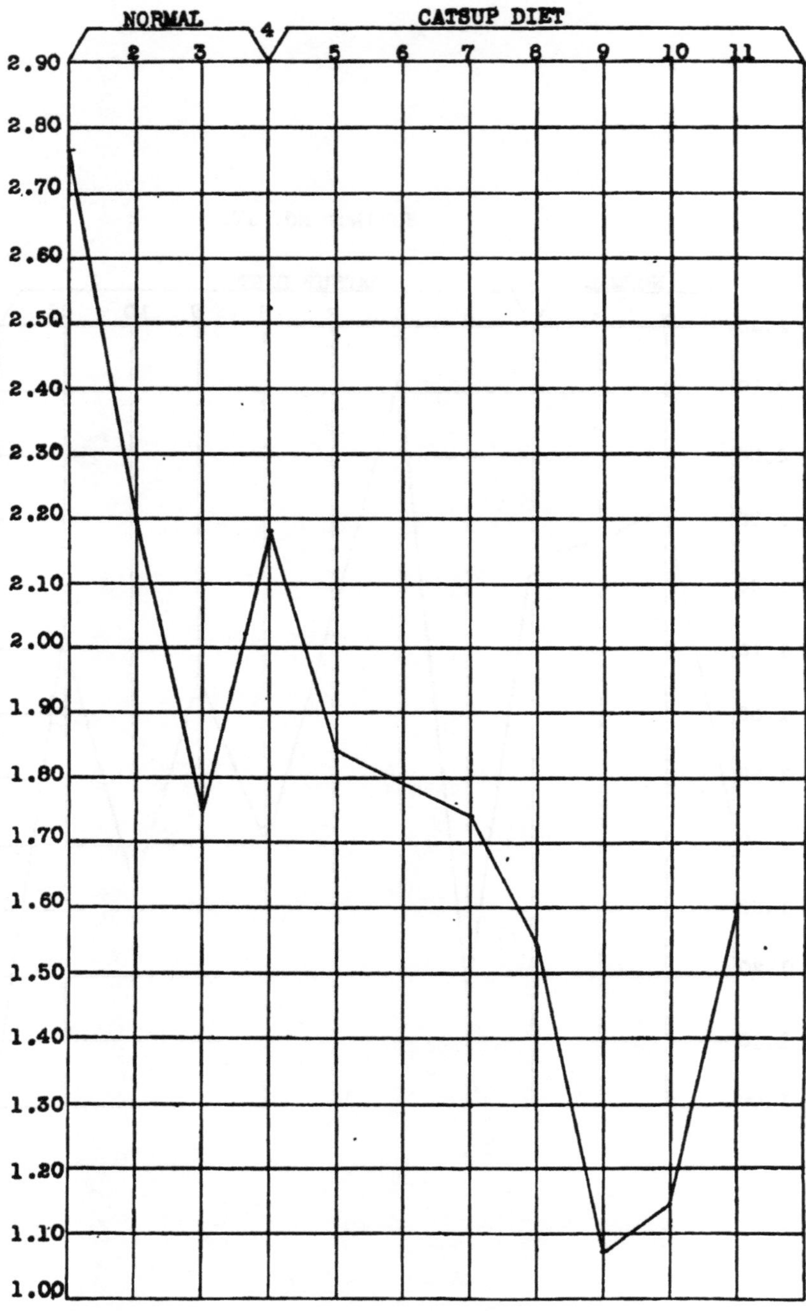

NORMAL
CATSUP DIET
2
3
4
5
6
7
8
9
10
11
2.90
2.80
2.70
2.60
2.50
2.40
2.30
2.20
2.10
2.00
1.90
1.80
1.70
1.60
1.50
1.40
1.30
1.20
1.10
1.00

SUBJECT NO. VI.

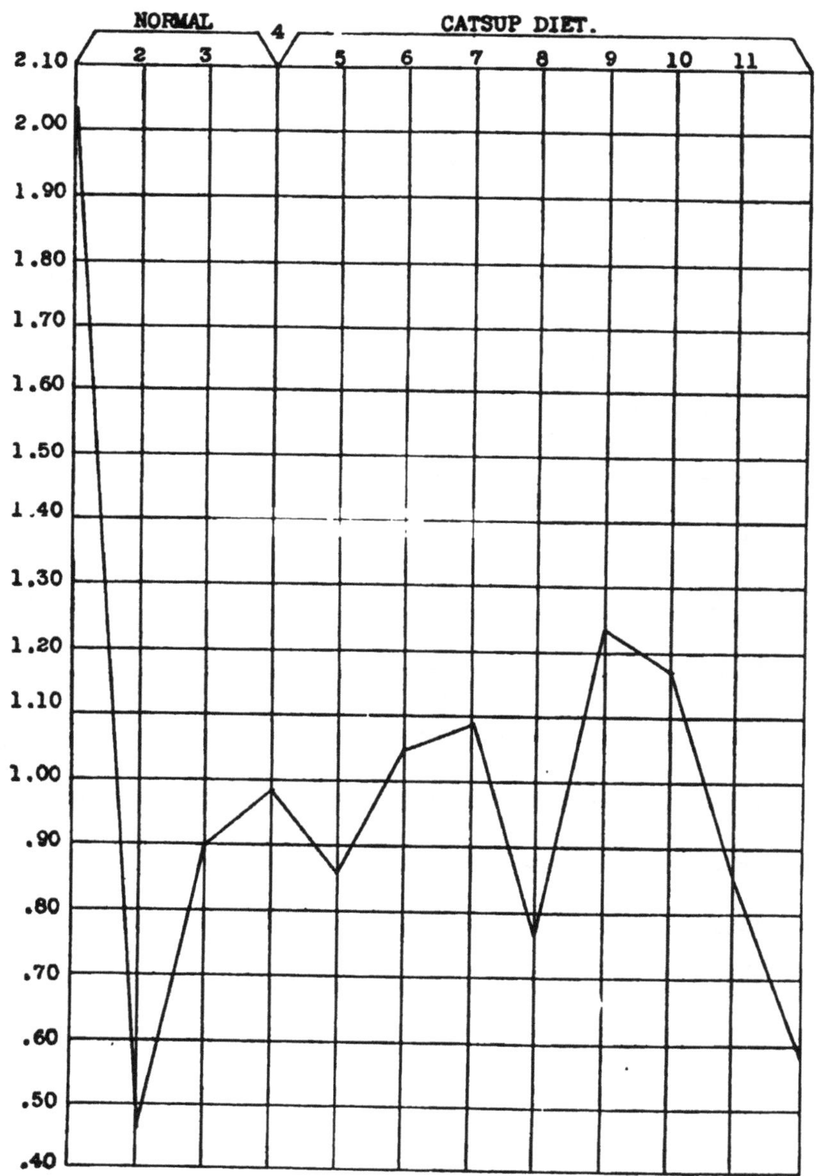

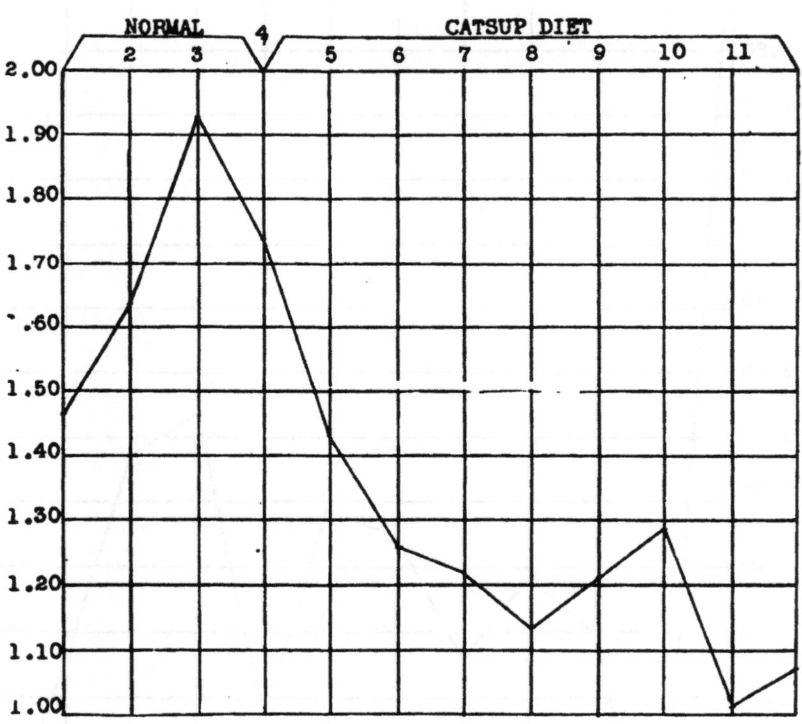
SUBJECT NO. VII.
NORMAL
CATSUP DIET
2
3
4
5
6
7
8
9
10
11
2.00
1.90
1.80
1.70
.60
1.50
1.40
1.30
1.20
1.10
1.00

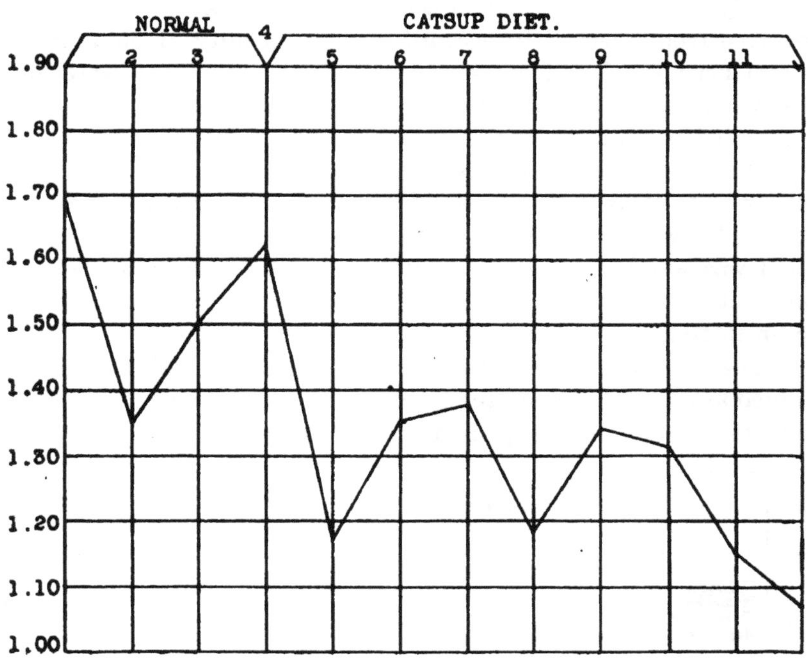
HIPPURIC ACID CONTENT OF URINE.
(GRAMS PER DAY)
NORMAL
CATSUP DIET.
2
3
4
5
6
7
8
9
10
11
1.90
1.80
1.70
1.60
1.50
1.40
1.30
1.20
1.10
1.00

SOME OBSERVATIONS ON THE MODIFIED LAWALL METHOD FOR THE DETERMINATION OF SODIUM BENZOATE IN CATSUPS.

W. D. McAbee.

It became necessary in the course of work at this laboratory to gather some proof of the accuracy of the modified LaWall method for determining sodium benzoate in catsup. Accordingly, steps were taken to check this method with four well known brands of non-preserved catsups to which known quantities of sodium benzoate had been added. These catsups were first examined qualitatively for benzoic acid and sodium benzoate, and were found to be free from them. On account of the difficulty of obtaining sodium benzoate free from water, the preservative was weighed as benzoic acid, converted into sodium benzoate by dissolving in concentrated sodium hydroxide solution and in this condition added to 50 grams of catsup which had been previously weighed out. In order to do away with all possibility of the analyst being influenced by his knowledge of the amount of preservative added, the benzoic acid was weighed by another, and the writer was unaware of the amount added, except from his analyses, until after his results had been introduced as evidence in court.

The following table gives the per cent. of sodium benzoate added as calculated from the benzoic acid used, the per cent. found, and the brands of catsup used in the experiment:

No.	Brand.	Per Cent. Added.	Per Cent. Found.
1	Columbia	.118	.118
2	Homelike	.295	.288
3	Shrewsbury	.177	.167
4	Beechnut	.236	.242

These results having proved conclusively the accuracy of the method when chemically pure preservatives were used it next became necessary to determine its accuracy when commercial benzoate was employed. The writer, in conjunction with a catsup manufacturer, then made an experimental batch of catsup containing .1124 of one per cent. commercial sodium benzoate. This catsup when analyzed showed only .095 of one per cent. of the salt, and as this was obviously too low, the purity of the benzoate used was determined by dissolving 200 milligrams of the salt in 100 c.c. of water, acidifying 50 c.c. of this and extracting with four portions of chloroform, as is done in the actual method. This extracted solution was found by analysis to contain 86.4 milligrams of absolute sodium benzoate, and the commercial salt was therefore only 86.4 per cent. pure. When calculated on this basis of purity the catsup showed by analysis .1099 per cent. sodium benzoate, which is .0025 or 2.2 per cent. less than the amount added. This loss was undoubtedly due to part of the salt passing off with the steam in the process of boiling.

Still further investigation of the method was made by using the commercial benzoate and proceeding in exactly the same manner as when the chemically pure acid was used. In this experiment also the writer did not know the amount added until after his results were inserted in the court record.

The following table gives the amount of commercial salt added, the actual amount of salt found and the amount of commercial sodium benzoate, calculated as 86.4 per cent. pure, equivalent to the actual amount found:

No.	Brand.	Per Cent. Commercial Salt Added.	Per Cent. Chemically Pure Salt Found.	Per Cent. Commercial Salt Found.
1	Columbia	.110	.097	.112
2	Columbia	.217	.187	.216

The method used was the modified LaWall and Bradshaw method, which is given as Method II, on page 70 of the 1908 proceedings of the A. O. A. C., and still further modified in this laboratory by the use of 50 grams of the sample instead of 200.

A COMPARISON OF THE KEEPING QUALITIES OF WRAPPED AND UNWRAPPED BREAD.

H. E. Barnard and H. E. Bishop.

Modern methods of handling food stuffs have decreed that the articles delivered at the kitchen door must be wrapped. It is apparent that this practice is in the nature of a protection against contamination. The butcher who delivered meats unwrapped or the grocer who neglected to protect his orders of dried fruits, cereals, coffee and other bulk goods, would find that no housewife would accept them. Indeed, the practice of protecting food stuffs by wrappers, bags and cartons is practically universal as regards every product except that of the bakeshop. The conditions surrounding the production of baker's goods, while somewhat different from those at other places where food is produced and distributed, are yet too frequently unsatisfactory, and ample opportunity for bakery goods to become unclean occurs during the process of distribution. Progressive bakers, who for years past have studied the sanitary operation of their shops, have more recently attempted to solve the problem of protecting their goods from dust and dirt after they are taken from the oven. The most feasible method of doing this yet devised has been the use of paper wrappers in which the loaf is wrapped before it leaves the bakeshop. Many bakers have adopted this method of protecting their goods, and wrapped bread may now be purchased in cities in all parts of the country, and others who do not wrap all their product cater to an exclusive trade by using the wrapper on a portion of their output.

Several objections are advanced by bakers to show why, as a sanitary measure, they should not be compelled to wrap all of their bread. They argue, first, that the cost of wrapping which primarily would fall upon them would be prohibitive unless the price of the bread to the consumer was increased. They assert that the use of the wrapper spoils the loaf by destroying the texture of the crust or allowing the bread to become soggy and finally sour or musty. These arguments are met by bakers who have successfully wrapped bread, and who assert that the cost of wrapping is more than met by the lessened number of stale loaves returned to the bakery, by the use of the bread wrapper in advertising, and by the increased business which follows the sanitary departure. A study has recently been made at the State Laboratory of Hygiene to determine, if possible, what grounds, if any, existed for the complaint that the quality of wrapped bread is injured. A number of standard varieties of bread produced by three large bakers, and including both bread sold wrapped and unwrapped, were exposed to the air for varying periods. Duplicate samples were purchased, one loaf of which was allowed to remain in its original wrapper or was wrapped in a heavy paraffin paper such as is used for the purpose, while the other loaf was either taken from its wrapper or left unwrapped. The loaves were weighed at the beginning of the study and each succeeding day until the close. The first loaves purchased on May 27th were made on the early morning of that day. Loaves were also purchased on May 28th, 30th, 31st and June 1st. The experiment was closed June 2d, at which time the first samples had been exposed seven days; the second lot six days; the third lot four days; the fourth lot three days; the fifth lot two days. A study of the weights of the loaves showed a loss of moisture in the case of the unwrapped loaves which was nearly constant from day to day, although after the fourth day the loss was slightly less rapid. At the end of seven days the first lot purchased showed a loss in weight ranging from 1.5 to 7.6 per cent. in the wrapped bread and from 13.2 to 17.3 per cent. in the unwrapped bread. The wrapped bread showing a loss of 7.6 per cent. was put up in a wrapper differing materially from the paper used on the other loaves in that it was not paraffined or waxed, and was therefore pervious to air. The average loss of moisture in the case of the wrapped loaves was 3.36 per cent. and the unwrapped loaves 14.34 per cent.

At the end of the experiment the loaves were all unwrapped and their character observed. At the end of the second day the unwrapped loaves were so dry that they could not be considered suitable for use by the average housewife, although they were still sweet and palatable. The wraped loaves of standard varieties were in as good condition as when first purchased. The wrapped loaves were also in good condition at the end of the third and fourth days, while the unwrapped loaves were hard, dry and not salable. The wrapped bread six days old in nearly every instance was soft and slightly sour. The bread opened at the end of seven days was soft but was acid to the taste and not suitable for ordinary use. The loaf wrapped in the porous paper was somewhat dry but was still palatable. One loaf of the 91 examined, after remaining in the paraffin wrapper for seven days, was mouldy. The Vienna loaves at the end of two days had a softened crust but were otherwise in good condition. The unwrapped Vienna loaf after two days was quite hard but was still in good condition. After three days the wrapped Vienna loaves had a softened and tough crust and the character of the loaf was decidedly changed. The same observation was made on the rye loaves. The wrapped Vienna and rye bread remained soft but grew tough. After the third day the unwrapped bread became hard and dry and for that reason unsalable.

In general it was observed that the paraffin wrapper kept the ordinary loaf in good condition for three, four and in some cases five days, while the unwrapped loaf became dry and stale at the end of two days. On the contrary, the loaves in the porous paper dried out more rapidly but showed less tendency to sour. The wrapped Vienna and rye loaf lost its natural characteristics rapidly as the moisture in the center of the loaf became evenly distributed throughout, thus destroying the flavor and texture of the crust, which is considered to be the most desirable characteristic of the loaf. It is evident from this study that it is not practicable to wrap either a Vienna or rye loaf in impervious paper which prevents the loss of moisture and tends to soften the crust. It is also apparent that after four or five days the ordinary wrapped loaf becomes unpalatable, due to the increase of acidity, and that such bread will eventually mould. There is noticed, however, a marked difference between the wrapped and unwrapped loaf during this time in favor of the wrapped loaf, and since the ordinary unwrapped loaf is now considered unsalable at the end of the second day, the use of the wrapper at least doubles the period during which it is merchantable.

Further studies are contemplated which will include the use of different varieties of paper, including less expensive types, porous papers, ventilated cartons and other forms of covering which will keep the loaf free from dust and the attack of flies and at the same time preserve its character and lengthen the time during which it is salable, the proper length of time which the bread should be allowed to cool before wrapping, the practicability of wrapping double loaves and the problems of a commercial nature which the baker has to meet. Studies will also be made to determine the increase in acidity of the loaf from day to day, the distribution of moisture throughout the loaf from center to crust, and such other factors as determine the palatability and wholesomeness of bread.

The table given below sets out in full the data from which the results above detailed were obtained. The daily loss of moisture is figured and the condition of each loaf at the end of the period is noted.

No.	Baker	Brand	May 27 Wt.	May 27 Loss	May 27 Per Cent Loss	May 28 Wt.	May 28 Loss	May 28 Per Cent Loss	May 29 Wt.	May 29 Loss	May 29 Per Cent Loss	May 30 Wt.	May 30 Loss	May 30 Per Cent Loss	May 31 Wt.	May 31 Loss	May 31 Per Cent Loss	June 1 Wt.	June 1 Loss	June 1 Per Cent Loss	June 2 Wt.	June 2 Loss	June 2 Per Cent Loss	Condition at End of Period
1	Taggart	Golden Cream	400			396	4	1.0	396	4	1.0	394	6	1.5	392	8	2.0	388	12	3.0	384	16	4.0	Mouldy.
2	Taggart	Golden Cream	410			392	18	4.3	375	25	8.5	362	48	11.7	355	55	18.4	345	65	15.8	339	71	17.3	Hard and dry.
3	Taggart	Snow Flake	461			458	3	0.6	456	5	1.0	453	8	1.7	449	12	2.6	446	15	3.2	440	21	4.7	Soft and slightly sour.
4	Taggart	Snow Flake	438			422	16	3.6	408	30	6.8	395	43	9.8	384	54	12.3	375	65	14.8	367	71	15.0	Hard and dry.
5	Taggart	Vienna	359			359			356	3	0.8	353	6	1.6	351	8	2.2	348	9	2.5	344	15	4.1	Crust soft, tough, otherwise edible.
6	Taggart	Vienna	392			380	12	3.0	368	24	6.1	356	36	9.2	350	43	10.2	342	50	12.7	335	57	14.6	Hard and dry.
7	Taggart	Homemade	834			833	1	0.6	831	3	0.3	829	5	0.6	826	8	0.9	824	10	1.2	821	13	1.5	Soft and slightly sour.
8	Taggart	Homemade	895	P'c	hasd	863	32	3.6	842	53	5.9	820	75	8.4	807	88	9.8	790	105	11.7	775	120	13.4	Hard and very dry.
9	Bryce	Holsum	789	Ma	y 27	779	10	1.2	769	20	2.5	767	22	2.8	749	40	5.0	732	57	7.2	729	60	7.6	Somewhat dry but edible.
10	Bryce	Holsum	825			797	28	3.4	766	59	7.1	756	66	8.0	744	81	9.8	730	95	11.4	717	108	13.0	Dry and hard.
11	Bryce	Mother's	819			819			815	4	0.4	812	7	0.8	810	9	1.1	808	11	1.3	802	17	2.0	Soft and slightly sour.
12	Bryce	Mother's	817			792	25	3.0	771	46	5.6	754	63	7.8	742	75	9.1	722	95	11.6	709	108	13.2	Hard and dry.
13	Bryce	Rye	498			496	2	0.4	496	2	0.4	495	3	0.6	493	5	1.0	491	7	1.4	491	7	1.4	Soft and tough.
14	Bryce	Rye	498			482	16	3.2	468	30	6.0	457	41	8.2	447	51	10.2	435	63	12.6	428	70	14.0	Very hard crust, inside palatable.
15	Grocers' Bk. Co.	Columbia	861			861			860	1	0.1	856	5	0.5	854	7	0.8	851	10	1.1	847	14	1.6	Soft and slightly sour.
16	Grocers' Bk. Co.	Columbia	855			822	33	3.8	800	55	6.4	780	75	8.7	764	91	10.6	747	108	12.6	732	122	14.2	Very hard.
17	Grocers' Bk. Co.	Cream				398			394	4	1.0	393	5	1.3	391	7	1.7	389	9	2.3	387	11	2.7	In fair condition.
18	Grocers' Bk. Co.	Cream				407			380	27	6.6	365	42	10.3	355	52	12.7	347	60	14.7	339	68	16.7	Hard and dry.
19	Grocers' Bk. Co.	Vienna				449			448	1	0.2	446	3	0.6	444	5	1.1	441	8	1.7	440	9	2.0	Soft and tough.
20	Grocers' Bk. Co.	Vienna				443			427	16	3.6	415	28	6.3	407	36	8.1	396	47	10.6	392	51	11.5	Hard and dry.
21	Grocers' Bk. Co.	Rye				448			445	3	0.6	443	5	1.1	441	7	1.6	441	7	1.6	437	11	2.0	Soft and tough.
22	Grocers' Bk. Co.	Rye				556			548	8	1.4	537	19	3.4	525	31	5.5	517	39	7.1	510	46	8.1	Hard crust, inside palatable.
23	Grocers' Bk. Co.	Columbia				824			823	1	0.1	821	3	0.3	820	4	0.4	816	8	0.9	814	10	1.2	Soft, in fair condition.
24	Grocers' Bk. Co.	Columbia				838			809	29	3.4	788	50	5.9	770	68	8.1	752	82	10.2	744	94	11.2	Hard and dry.
25	Bryce	Mother's				804			803	1	0.1	803	1	0.1	800	4	0.5	798	6	0.7	796	8	0.9	Soft, in fair condition.
26	Bryce	Mother's				852	P'c	hasd	825	27	3.1	804	48	5.6	785	67	7.8	770	82	9.6	758	94	11.0	Hard and dry.
27	Bryce	Holsum				827	Ma	y 28	819	8	0.9	811	16	1.9	802	25	3.0	792	35	4.2	787	40	4.8	In fair condition.
28	Bryce	Holsum				807			778	29	3.5	757	50	6.2	742	65	8.0	730	67	8.3	718	89	11.0	Hard and dry.
29	Bryce	Rye				525			525			523	2	0.3	521	4	0.7	518	7	1.3	516	9	1.7	Crust softened, in fair condition.
30	Bryce	Rye				484			468	16	3.3	454	30	6.2	442	44	9.1	432	52	10.8	424	60	12.4	Hard.
31	Taggart	Golden Cream				414			412	2	0.4	410	4	0.9	408	6	1.4	406	8	1.9	397	17	4.1	In good condition.
32	Taggart	Golden Cream				420			399	21	5.0	385	35	8.3	372	48	11.4	346	56	13.3	356	64	15.2	Hard and dry.
33	Taggart	Rye				478			476	2	0.4	476	2	0.4	474	4	0.8	471	7	1.4	459	19	3.9	Crust softened, in fair condition.
34	Taggart	Rye				488			474	14	2.8	462	26	5.3	450	38	7.7	440	48	9.8	431	57	11.7	Hardened.
35	Taggart	Snow Flake				429			426	3	4.7	424	5	1.1	421	8	1.8	421	8	1.8	416	13	3.0	Soft, in good condition.
36	Taggart	Snow Flake				441			415	26	5.9	400	41	9.3	388	53	12.0	380	61	13.8	373	68	15.4	Hard and dry.

37	Taggart	Golden Cream										394			393	1	0.2	391	3	0.8	388	8	2.0	In good condition.
38	Taggart	Golden Cream										348			332	16	4.6	325	23	6.6	302	46	13.2	Hardened.
39	Taggart	Homemade										931			927	2	0.2	927	4	0.4	926	5	0.5	Soft and slightly sour.
40	Taggart	Tiptop										1098									1025	73	6.6	In good condition.
41	Grocers' Bk. Co.	Rye										546			546			544	2	0.3	543	3	0.5	Very little change.
42	Grocers' Bk. Co.	Rye										553	P'c had		535	18	3.2	525	28	5.0	516	37	6.7	Hardened.
43	Grocers' Bk. Co.	Vienna										443	May 30		441	2	0.4	438	5	1.1	438	5	1.1	Crust softened.
44	Grocers' Bk. Co.	Vienna										455			442	13	2.9	430	25	5.5	422	38	7.2	Hardened.
45	Grocers' Bk. Co.	Cream										410			410			408	2	0.5	405	3	1.2	Soft and palatable.
46	Grocers' Bk. Co.	Cream										404			388	16	3.9	375	29	7.1	364	40	9.0	Hardened very much.
47	Grocers' Bk. Co.	Columbia										820			818	2	0.2	815	5	0.6	813	7	0.8	Soft and palatable.
48	Grocers' Bk. Co.	Columbia										845			818	87	3.2	798	47	5.5	783	62	7.3	Hardened.
49	Bryce	Honey													444			443	1	0.2	441	3	0.6	In good condition.
50	Bryce	Honey													422			400	22	5.2	389	33	7.8	Dried out.
51	Bryce	Holsum													777			767	10	13.0	758	19	2.4	In palatable condition.
52	Bryce	Holsum													765			750	15	1.9	729	36	4.7	Dry.
53	Bryce	Mother's													811			808	3	0.3	805	6	0.7	In palatable condition.
54	Bryce	Mother's													792			760	32	4.0	740	52	6.5	Dry, crumby.
55	Grocers' Bk. Co.	Columbia													850			848	2	0.2	846	4	0.4	In good condition.
56	Grocers' Bk. Co.	Columbia													829			800	29	3.5	781	48	5.7	Dry and crumby.
57	Grocers' Bk. Co.	Cream													416			416			413	3	0.7	In good condition
58	Grocers' Bk. Co.	Cream													405			383	22	5.4	372	33	8.1	Dry and crumby.
59	Grocers' Bk. Co.	Rye													558	P'c had		558			557	1	0.1	Crust softened, inside palatable.
60	Grocers' Bk. Co.	Rye													555	May 31		544	15	2.7	533	26	4.6	Hardened somewhat.
61	Grocers' Bk. Co.	Vienna													471			468	3	0.6	467	4	0.8	Crust softened, tough.
62	Grocers' Bk. Co.	Vienna													479			465	14	1.8	445	34	7.1	Hardened somewhat.
63	Taggart	Vienna													441			441			438	3	0.6	Crust softened, tough.
64	Taggart	Vienna													417			398	19	4.5	388	29	6.2	Hardened somewhat.
65	Taggart	Golden Cream													453			451	2	0.4	447	6	13.4	In good condition.
66	Taggart	Golden Cream													432			410	22	5.1	396	36	8.3	Hardened somewhat.
67	Taggart	Snow Flake													339			338	1	0.3	337	2	0.5	Soft and in good condition.
68	Taggart	Snow Flake													367			341	26	7.0	328	39	10.6	Dried out very much.
69	Taggart	Homemade													888			886	2	0.2	884	4	0.4	In good condition.
70	Taggart	Homemade													883			852	31	3.5	830	53	6.0	Somewhat dry.
71	Grocers' Bk. Co.	Rye																558			556	2	0.3	In good condition.
72	Grocers' Bk. Co.	Rye																555			537	18	3.2	In good condition.
73	Grocers' Bk. Co.	Columbia																816			811	5	0.6	In good condition.
74	Grocers' Bk. Co.	Columbia																830			800	30	3.6	In good condition.
75	Grocers' Bk. Co.	Vienna																499			497	2	0.4	Crust softened.
76	Grocers' Bk. Co.	Vienna																474			457	22	4.6	In good condition.
77	Grocers' Bk. Co.	Cream																423			422	1	0.2	In good condition.
78	Grocers' Bk. Co.	Cream																412			390	21	5.1	In good condition.
79	Bryce	Mother's																803			798	5	0.6	In good condition.
80	Bryce	Mother's																782	P'c had		756	26	3.3	In good condition.
81	Bryce	Honey																430	June 1		427	3	0.7	In good condition.
82	Bryce	Honey																408			389	18	4.1	In good condition.
83	Taggart	Golden Cream																428			424	4	0.9	In good condition.
84	Taggart	Golden Cream																425			402	20	4.7	In good condition.

No	Baker	Brand	May 27			May 28			May 29			May 30			May 31			June 1			June 2			Condition at End of Period
			Wt.	Loss	Per Cent Loss	Wt.	Loss	Per Cent Loss	Wt.	Loss	Per Cent Loss	Wt.	Loss	Per Cent Loss	Wt.	Loss	Per Cent Loss	Wt.	Loss	Per Cent Loss	Wt.	Loss	Per Cent Loss	
85	Taggart........	Vienna........	....	....	....	....	....	....	....	....	....	....	....	....	....	....	....	406	....	....	404	2	0.5	Crust softened.
86	Taggart........	Vienna........	....	....	....	....	....	....	....	....	....	....	....	....	....	....	....	395	....	....	377	18	4.6	In good condition.
87	Taggart........	Snow Flake...	....	....	....	....	....	....	....	....	....	....	....	....	....	....	....	421	....	....	420	1	0.2	In good condition.
88	Taggart........	Snow Flake...	....	....	....	....	....	....	....	....	....	....	....	....	....	....	....	425	....	....	404	21	5.0	In good condition.
89	Taggart........	Homemade...	....	....	....	....	....	....	....	....	....	....	....	....	....	....	....	877	....	....	877	....	....	In good condition.
90	Taggart........	Homemade...	....	....	....	....	....	....	....	....	....	....	....	....	....	....	....	841	....	....	813	28	3.3	In good condition.
91	Bryce..........	Holsum.......	....	....	....	....	....	....	....	....	....	....	....	....	....	....	....	749	....	....	728	21	2.8	In good condition.

INSPECTION OF CANNERIES—SEASON OF 1910.

The increasing value of land adapted for growing tomatoes, sweet corn, peas and similar vegetables which are canned extensively has naturally made it necessary for farmers to get an increased price for their products. This fact, coupled with the unusual high prices obtained for corn and hogs and other farm produce during the season of 1909 made many farmers turn to the growing of these crops rather than to those utilized by canners, and during the past season the acreage available for the canning industry was, therefore, considerably smaller than usual. Indeed, a number of canners found it impossible to secure sufficient acreage to warrant their opening, and the canneries which did operate report a diminished output. In addition to this unsatisfactory condition, heavy late frosts killed hundreds of acres of tomato plants and made replanting necessary. In many instances this was not done and the canner was still further deprived of raw material.

The quality of the pack of 1910 was excellent and the increased demand for canned goods, due possibly to a short crop and perhaps in a measure to the fact that buyers are beginning to realize that the Indiana product is of superior grade, has resulted in higher prices to the packer. This is the fourth season that the inspectors of the Food and Drug Department of the State Board of Health have visited the canneries operating throughout the State for the purpose of noting their sanitary condition and requiring a compliance in construction and operation of the plants with the Sanitary Law. During the canning season just closed the inspectors visited 84 factories located in 78 different towns. Several of these factories, however, did not operate during the season. Sixty-four of the factories visited packed tomatoes, 21 factories packed corn, 11 beans, and 30 a variety of goods such as peas, pumpkin, sauerkraut, apples, etc. Fifty-four canneries made tomato pulp. Thirty-six of these canneries used whole tomatoes in at least a part of their output. Forty-eight canners utilized trimmings of the tables, such as skins, cores, etc. The character of the pulp manufactured has on the whole been excellent. Fifty-four canners used no benzoate of soda, 40 put up pulp in barrels with salt, the remainder ran their pulp into large cans and depended upon proper sterilization to hold it in good condition. Four factories only were visited which were using benzoate of soda, and these factories used it only when so ordered for interstate trade. Two years ago it was the universal idea that benzoate of soda was as necessary to the operation of a canning factory, and especially in the manufacture of pulp, as the raw material itself. The results of the inspection of the canneries this last season destroys absolutely this contention and proves that not only is benzoate of soda unnecessary, but that canners by the selection of raw material and the use of cleanly methods in preparation can produce a better pulp than formerly. Indeed, the demand for pulp this season put up without benzoate of soda has been so great that its value has risen from $1.00 to $5.00 per barrel.

Thirty-eight of the buildings visited were in good condition. 30 were rated as fair and 40 poor. Many of the canneries are housed in old buildings, and since they are used less than two months during the year they are not as well cared for as is desirable. The factories which are in operation throughout the year are almost without exception well equipped both with buildings and improved machinery.

Sixty canners operate in frame buildings, 11 in brick buildings, while 2 have stone and cement factories. The floors of 31 factories are concrete and in 50 cases they are of wood. Fifty factories had good floors, 17 fair, and 5 factories had floors so unsatisfactory because of decay that they were rated as poor. In 32 instances the toilets were in good condition, but 40 canneries did not properly care for toilet conveniences and the premises were reported as being unclean and improperly screened. This condition was also undoubtedly due to the fact that the factory is in operation but a portion of the year.

Special attention however is being given to the installation of properly constructed and sanitary toilets, and continued improvement is noted. Thirty-eight canneries provide suitable wash rooms for their employes. Thirty-four factories do not have separate wash rooms but supply wash basins. In all save two factories the floors were cleaned daily and were in as good shape as could be expected under the conditions of operation. One factory was not provided with water under pressure, but 70 factories have an ample supply of water. Nearly all of the canneries operating are reported as apparently doing good business.

The future of the canning industry in Indiana depends first upon the ability of the packer to secure a sufficient supply of raw material within a reasonable radius. While certain crops can be hauled by rail, yet the very nature of the product makes it undesirable to subject it to shipment where delays are frequent and the character of the material impaired before delivery at the factory. The other essential to success is a receptive market and the ability to sell the season's output at a fair profit. At present the price of canned goods, especially tomato products, is largely regulated by Eastern packers. This is not as it should be, because of the fact that goods canned in Maryland and New Jersey do not on the whole compare in quality with the Indiana product nor do the canneries represent such a large investment nor are they operated under as sanitary conditions.

The Indiana packer for these reasons should be able to command a higher price for his products, and indications are that he is increasingly able to do so.

ADVANCE—

Advance Canning Company.—This company did not operate during the season of 1910. The business of the company is confined to the packing of tomatoes. The building is an old frame structure in very poor condition. The floors are of wood, and the toilets, which are outside the factory, are most unsanitary. No wash rooms are provided, and there is no adequate system for the disposal of sewage.

AMBOY—

Amboy Canning Company.—This company prepares corn, tomatoes and pumpkin. The building is of frame and in fair condition, and the floors are plank. The toilets are outside the factory and are unsatisfactory. No wash rooms are provided. The sewage is run into a nearby creek. The employes are healthy and cleanly. The factory is supplied with water under pressure but the floors are only occasionally cleaned. No tomato pulp is packed. The factory is fairly well organized and apparently successfully operated.

ANDERSON—

Anderson Canning Company.—This company packs corn, peas and tomatoes, and works tomato pulp up with salt, using the refuse and small fruit from the peeling tables. The building is of frame construction, in good condition, with good cement floors and satisfactory toilets. Wash rooms are provided for the operatives. All sewage goes into the city sewers. The factory is well organized and successfully operated. The floors are cleaned daily and the employes are healthy and cleanly in appearance and dress.

ARCADIA—

Arcadia Canning Company.—This company, which is owned by C. N. Martz, packs tomatoes and works up the refuse and small tomatoes into pulp. The building is of frame construction, in fair condition. The floors are of plank and are not sufficiently tight to allow proper washing. The toilets, which are outside the building, are in poor condition, but are properly screened. Wash rooms are provided and the operatives are apparently careful to use them, as they are cleanly in appearance and dress. The interior of the building is whitewashed and painted and presents a most creditable appearance. All machinery, carriers, buckets and tables are painted in colors. The floor of the work room is cleaned daily and sewage is carried by suitable drains to a ditch which empties some distance from the factory. The company does a good business and is a credit to the industry.

AUSTIN—

Austin Canning Company.—This company packs tomatoes, beans, apples, pumpkin, kraut and hominy. The business is conducted in a frame building in good condition with tight board floors. The toilets are in separate rooms and are in fair sanitary shape. Suitable wash rooms are provided for the use of employes, who are cleanly and healthy. All sewage is carried away by a sewer. The refuse, skins and cores of the tomato pack, as well as some of the whole fruit, is made into pulp, which is packed in barrels and preserved with salt. Water under pressure is available and is used daily to clean the work room floors. The company is well organized and is doing a good business.

Star Canning Company.—This company packs tomatoes, kraut, apples, beans and pumpkin. The factory is of frame construction, in fair condition, with tight board floors. The toilets are suitable, screened and are fairly clean. Wash rooms are provided for the employes, who appear healthy and cleanly. The waste of the factory, including wash water used daily on the work room floors, flows to a sewer. Tomato pulp made from whole, sound fruit as well as from the refuse, skins, etc., from the peeling tables, is packed in barrels with salt. The company is well organized and the business is apparently successfully operated.

BIRDSEYE—

Birdseye Canning Company.—This company packs tomatoes in a frame building in fair condition. The floors are of boards laid tight. The toilets are clean and well screened. No wash rooms are provided, but the employes are afforded an opportunity to wash. In the absence of adequate sewers all refuse is carted away from the factory. The floor of the work room is cleaned daily and, as a whole, the business is conducted in a fairly satisfactory way.

BLOOMINGDALE—

Van Camp Packing Company.—This factory, which is devoted to the canning of tomatoes, was not in operation at the time of inspection. The building is of frame construction, with plank floor, and is in fair condition. Portions of the floor are decayed and need renewing. The toilets are located outside the building and are in fair condition. No wash rooms are provided. All waste waters enter a sewer. When running the factory packs tomatoes and utilizes the refuse material in the preparation of skin pulp. The company is operated as a branch of the Van Camp Packing Company, Indianapolis, Indiana.

BROWNSBURG—

Ladoga Canning Company.—This company, which packs tomatoes only, operates in an old frame structure in very bad condition. The plank floors are full of holes and the toilets are unsanitary. No wash rooms are provided, and the factory is on the whole in poor shape to produce a clean pack.

BUNKERHILL—

Bunkerhill Canning Company.—This company packs tomatoes and pumpkin. The building, a frame building with corrugated iron siding, is old but is in fair condition. The floors are of plank. The toilets are located outside the factory and the old structures were being replaced with new buildings at the time of inspection. Wash rooms were also being installed, and the managers were doing all in their power to place the factory in good condition. In the absence of sewers all refuse is hauled away. The waste from the peeling tables is made into tomato pulp, which is packed in barrels with the addition of strong vinegar. The factory condition is improved over 1909.

CARMACK—

Carmack Canning Company.—This company packs tomatoes only. The building is of frame construction and is in poor condition. The floors are of wood. The toilets are located outside, but are in fair condition. The factory has no wash room, but basins are provided for the convenience of employes. Waste water and sewage flow to a drain and thence to a ditch. As a whole the factory is in poor condition.

CAMPBELLSBURG—

Campbellsburg Canning Factory.—This factory did not operate in the season of 1910. The condition of the plant is fair.

CHARLESTOWN—

Charlestown Canning Company.—This company packs tomatoes only, discarding the refuse. The building is of frame construction with board floors, and is in good condition. The toilets are cleanly and are well screened. There is no separate wash room, but facilities are provided employes for keeping clean. Water under pressure is available and the wash water flows to a sewer while the solid refuse is hauled away from the plant. The factory is well organized, is in good condition, and is apparently successfully operated.

CLAY CITY—

Clay City Packing Company.—This company operates its Clay City plant as a branch of the Ladoga Canning Company. The product is tomatoes, pulp, beans and kraut. The building is of frame construction, in very poor condition. A new building is badly needed and should be constructed before another season. The floor is of plank, which is decayed in places. The toilets are located outside the building and are in fair condition only. No wash rooms were provided at the opening of the 1910 season, but a second inspection in October found them in use. The sewage and waste products flow into a closed sewer. Tomato pulp is made both from whole fruit and from the refuse of the peeling table, and is packed in barrels with six pounds of salt.

CLARKS HILL—

Harmon Bradshaw Company.—This factory did not operate in 1910.

COLUMBUS—

Columbus Canning Company.—This company packs corn and tomatoes. The building is of brick and frame construction in fair condition. The floors are of board, brick and concrete. The toilets are separate, well screened, and fairly clean. A portion of the sewage flows into a sewer and the solid residues are hauled away. The tomato pulp, which is made both from whole fruit and skins and cores, is packed in barrels and preserved with salt and vinegar.

CORYDON—

Corydon Canning Company.—This company packs tomatoes and apples. The refuse from the peeling table and some whole tomatoes are worked into pulp, which is preserved with eight ounces of benzoate of soda to the barrel. The building is of frame construction with wood floors, and is in fair condition. The toilets are separate from the building and are properly screened. Facilities are provided for washing, although no wash room is maintained. The plant is in fair condition only.

CROTHERSVILLE—

Crothersville Canning Company.—This company packs tomatoes, kraut and hominy. The building is of frame construction with tight, clean, board floors and is in good condition. The toilets are separate and are well screened and in a cleanly condition. Suitable facilities are provided for washing, and the operatives are healthy and cleanly. Waste products either flow to a sewer or are hauled away. Both whole fruit and the refuse from the peeling tables are made into pulp, which is preserved by the addition of six pounds of salt to the barrel. The factory is clean and well organized.

CROTHERSVILLE—

Farmers Canning Company.—This company packs tomatoes, hominy, kraut and beans. The tomato pulp is packed in barrels, using five pounds of salt to the barrel. The floors are made of boards, which are in good condition. The toilets are separate, in good condition and properly screened. Proper facilities for washing are provided. The sewage is disposed of through a sewer. The employes are healthy and cleanly in appearance and dress. The floors of the work room are cleaned daily. Water under pressure is available. The factory is well organized and apparently successfully operated.

DALEVILLE—

J. G. Sutton.—This company packs tomatoes only. The business is conducted in a frame building of fair condition. The floors are of wood and the toilets, which are outside the building, are fairly clean. Basins are provided instead of wash rooms for the use of operatives. All sewage and waste water flows through a tile drain to a ditch. No tomato pulp is made.

DELPHI—

Great Western Canning Company.—This company packs corn and peas. The building is of stone with cement floors, and is in good condition. The toilets are outside and are not sanitary. Wash rooms are provided for the use of employes, who are clean and apparently healthy. The sewage flows through a closed sewer to the Wabash river. The factory is well organized and apparently successfully operated. The inspector ordered that the toilets be cleaned, disinfected and properly screened.

DUFF—

Duff Canning Company.—This company packs tomatoes. The business is conducted in a frame building with tight board floors in fair condition. The toilets are fairly clean and are screened. The liquid refuse is carried away by a sewer and the solid matter is hauled. Tomato pulp is made both from whole fruit and the refuse from the peeling tables. It is run into barrels and is preserved with eight pounds of salt to the barrel. The company is fairly well organized and is apparently successfully operated.

DUNREITH—

Dunreith Canning Company.—This company packs tomatoes and tomato pulp. The pulp is made from the refuse from the peeling tables and is put down with salt. The building is a frame structure with cement floors, and is in fair condition. The toilets are outside of the building and are also fairly clean. Wash rooms are provided for the use of employes, who are clean and apparently healthy. The sewage flows through a tile drain to a ditch. This factory is in good condition, the working force is well organized and the company is apparently doing a good business.

EATON—

Eaton Canning Company.—This company did not operate in 1910.

EDINBURG—

Naomi Canning Company.—This company packs corn and peas. The building is of concrete and the floors are of board and of concrete. The toilets are clean and well screened, and suitable facilities for washing are provided for employes. The sewage flows either to a sewer or is hauled away. The inspector rates this company as good.

ELNORA—

Elnora Canning Company.—This company packs tomatoes and tomato pulp. The building is of frame construction, in satisfactory condition, and the floors, which are of wood, are also good. The toilets, which are outside the building, are poor. Wash rooms are provided for employes, who are cleanly and apparently healthy. Sewage flows into an open vat from which, after settling, the solid residue is hauled away. Tomato pulp is made both from whole fruit and the refuse from the peeling tables and is packed in barrels without benzoate of soda. This plant was visited three times during the season, and on the final visit the sewage system was condemned and a new one ordered constructed before the beginning of another season.

ELWOOD—

Frazier Packing Company.—This company packs tomatoes and tomato catsup. The building is of frame and in fair condition, and the floors are of cement and wood. The toilets are located outside the building and are fair only. Basins are provided for the use of employes in lieu of wash rooms. All sewage flows to a tile drain. In the manufacture of tomato pulp both whole fruit and skins and cores are used and made up at once into catsup. The factory is well organized and apparently successfully operated.

ENGLISH—

English Canning Company.—This company packs tomatoes, and uses the skins and cores from the peeling table as well as some whole fruit in making tomato pulp, which is packed in barrels with salt. The building is of frame construction, in fair condition, and the wood floors are satisfactory. The toilets are separate from the building and are suitably screened. Proper facilities are afforded for washing hands, and the employes are healthy and cleanly in appearance and dress. The sewage flows either to a sewer or is hauled away. The floor used by the peeling force is in need of repair and instructions were given by the inspector to put it in good condition before another season.

EVANSVILLE—

Indiana Packing Company.—This company packs tomatoes and tomato pulp. The pulp is made both from whole fruit and peeling table refuse, and is put down in barrels with six pounds of salt to the barrel. The building is of frame construction, in good condition, and the floors are concrete. The toilets are in a separate building and are clean. Wash rooms are provided for the use of employes. All sewage flows to the city sewer. This factory is well equipped, is clean and is doing a good business.

FLORA—

Flora Canning Company.—This company did not operate in 1910.

FRANKFORT—

Waukesha Canning Company.—This company is in the hands of a receiver and did not operate in 1910.

GASTON—

Gaston Canning Company.—This company packs tomatoes and tomato pulp. The building is of frame construction, in fair condition, and the floors are cement. The toilets are outside the main building and are in fair condition, but no wash room is provided. The pulp is made from peeling table refuse and is preserved with acetic acid. The sewage facilities are poor. Refuse is pumped to a ditch and is not well cared for. The inspector ordered that the yard be kept clean and that a more suitable drain be built.

HENRYVILLE—

Henryville Canning Company.—This company did not operate in 1910.

HOPE—

Hope Canning Company.—This company packs corn, tomatoes and tomato pulp. The building is of frame and brick construction, and is in good condition. The floors are of concrete. The toilets are in a separate building, and are well screened and clean. The sewage is disposed of by a drain and by hauling. The pulp is made both from whole fruit and from peeling table refuse. It is put down in barrels with seven pounds of salt. The inspector gives this factory the grade of good.

HUNTINGBURG—

Huntingburg Canning Company.—This factory packs tomatoes and tomato pulp. The building is of frame construction, and is in good condition, with tight board floors. The toilets are in separate buildings and are properly screened and clean. Part of the refuse flows to a sewer, the rest is hauled away. The pulp is made both from the whole tomato and from peeling table refuse. It is put down in barrels with eight pounds of salt. This factory is given the grade of good by the inspector.

INDIANAPOLIS—

Van Camp Packing Company.—This company packs a great variety of products and operates throughout the year. An enormous business is done and the total output approximates one hundred million cans per year. The chief pack is baked beans and condensed milk, but a large business is done in canning peas, tomatoes, beans, beets, hominy, etc. The factory is of brick and is well constructed and adapted for the use to which it is put. The floors are of wood and cement. Sanitary toilets are provided and all sewage flows to the city sewer. The factory and equipment is cleaned daily. The use of benzoate of soda in catsup has been abandoned and all pulp placed in barrels is preserved with salt. The company is well organized and successfully operated.

Hagelskamp & Haverskamp Canning Factory.—This company packs tomatoes, beans, cabbage, etc., in an old frame building wholly unadapted for the use to which it is put. The floors have been reconstructed in part and such as are of cement are in good condition. The equipment is poor and old. The refuse flows to the city sewer. The toilets are unsanitary outhouses. No wash rooms are provided, and the workmen are apparently not careful to keep clean. The refuse from the peeling tables is made into tomato pulp, which is preserved with salt. Instruction was given to put in wash rooms and to make other necessary improvements. The factory is very economically operated and is doing a good business.

W. D. Huffman & Co. Canning Factory.—This company packs a variety of fruits and vegetables, but its chief output is pickles. The building used is of frame and brick, which at present is in fair condition, although it is poorly lighted and not well adapted for its use. Modern toilets have been installed during the past year and wash rooms are provided for the use of employes. While there are many points about the factory which are not satisfactory, on the whole conditions are greatly improved.

Schnull and Company.—The company operates as a branch of a wholesale grocery house and packs under the brand Topeco. It is installed in a new, modern brick building, and during the season of 1910 a frame and sheet iron building has also been used. All sewage flows to a city sewer. The toilets are also connected with the sewer and are screened and sanitary. The tomato pulp, manufactured from discarded tomatoes and waste from the peeling tables, is packed in cans. The factory is well equipped and deserves an excellent rating.

JAMESTOWN—

Jamestown Canning Company.—This factory packs pumpkin, tomatoes and tomato pulp. It operates in a frame building in good condition. The floors are also good. Toilets are located outside the building, and no wash rooms are provided for employes. The sewage flows into a branch in the rear of the factory. The tomato pulp is made from refuse from the peeling tables and is preserved in barrels by the use of ten pounds of salt. The most unsatisfactory condition observed was the lack of adequate sorting of the tomatoes before they went to the scalder.

JEFFERSONVILLE—

Jeffersonville Canning Factory.—The company packs hominy and kraut. It operates in a frame building in good condition. The floors are made of tight boards. The toilets are separate and screened, and proper sewage is provided. Wash rooms are provided and employes are cleanly in appearance and dress. The factory is successfully operated.

KEMPTON—

Kempton Canning Company.—Factory not running this year.

KENNARD—

Kennard Canning Factory.—The company packs tomatoes. The building is of frame in fair condition. The floors are made of wood, but in poor shape. Fairly good toilets are provided, which are located in the yard. Wash rooms are provided. The disposal of sewage is inadequate. Work rooms are properly screened. The employes are healthy, cleanly in appearance and dress. The tomato pulp is packed in barrels and preserved with salt. The factory is well organized and successfully operated. Orders have been given to provide better sewage disposal.

KOKOMO—

Kokomo Canning Company.—This company has packed corn only this year. They operate in a fairly good frame building. Fairly good wood and cement floors are provided. The toilets are fair and are located in the yard. Wash rooms are provided and the sewage is disposed of by means of a drain. The employes are healthy, cleanly in appearance and dress. The floor of the work room is cleaned daily. Water under pressure is available and the factory is well organized and successfully operated.

Sailor Brothers.—This company packs tomatoes, peas and corn. They operate in a brick building in good condition. The floors are of cement. Good toilets are provided, which are located in the yard. They have wash rooms, and the sewage is disposed of by means of a drain which empties into the sewer. The work rooms are properly screened. The employes are healthy and cleanly in appearance and dress. The tomato pulp is packed in barrels, using six ounces of benzoate and six pounds of salt to the barrel. The pulp is made from the refuse, skins and cores. The work room is cleaned daily. The factory is well organized and successfully operated.

LADOGA—

Ladoga Canning Company.—This company packs corn and tomatoes in a frame building in good condition. The condition of the floor is fair. Fairly good toilets and wash rooms are provided. The employes are healthy and neat in appearance. Tomato pulp is packed in barrels and made from both whole, sound fruit and refuse, skins and cores. The floor of the work room is cleaned daily. Water under pressure is available and the factory is well organized.

LAPEL—

Polk & Company.—This company packs tomatoes, using salt as a preservative. The frame building is in fair condition. The floors are of cement. Wash rooms are provided and the sewage is disposed of by means of a good drain running into a ditch. The work rooms are properly screened and the employes are healthy. The pulp, made from refuse, skins and cores, is packed in barrels. The floor of the work room is cleaned daily and the factory is well organized and successfully operated. Orders were given to whitewash and screen the toilets.

LEBANON—

Columbia Conserve Company.—This company packs catsup, condensed soup, gumbos. The company operates in a frame building in good condition. The floors are made of plank and are in good shape. Good toilets and wash rooms are provided, and the sewage is disposed of through the city sewer. The work rooms are not properly screened. The employes are apparently healthy and are cleanly and neatly dressed in uniforms. The pulp is packed partly in barrels and small cans. The pulp is made from whole, sound fruit and refuse, using no benzoate except when ordered. The floor of the work room is cleaned daily and water under pressure is available. The factory is well organized and successfully operated.

LEOTA—

Leota Canning Factory.—This factory is not running this year.

MARENGO—

Marengo Canning Company.—This company is operated in a frame building of fair condition and packs tomatoes only. Fairly good toilets are provided. No facilities for washing are provided and the sewage is hauled away. The employes are healthy and clean. The tomato pulp is packed in barrels with eight pounds of salt. The pulp is made from both whole, sound fruit and refuse, skins and cores. Water pressure is available and the floors are cleaned daily. The company is fairly well organized and operated.

MEMPHIS—

Memphis Canning Company.—Not running this year.

MUNCIE—

Thos. Best & Son.—This company packs tomatoes. The business is conducted in a frame building in good condition. The floors are of cement. The toilets are in good condition. Good wash rooms are provided and the sewage is disposed of through the city sewer. The work rooms are properly screened. The employes are healthy and cleanly in appearance and dress. The work room is cleaned daily and water pressure is available. More light and ventilation was ordered. The factory is well organized and successfully operated.

Tuhey Canning Company.—The building in which this company operates is of frame construction and is in good condition. They pack tomatoes and peas. The floors are made of cement and are in good condition. The toilets are located in the yard and are only fairly good. The sewage is disposed of through the city sewer. The work rooms are properly screened and the employes are healthy and cleanly. The tomato pulp is packed in barrels and is preserved with seven pounds of salt. The pulp is made from skins, refuse and cores. Water pressure is available and the floors are washed daily. Orders were given to provide wash basins and towels and also to screen the toilets. The factory is well organized and apparently successfully operated.

NEWBURG—

Newburg Canning Factory.—The building occupied by this company is of frame construction and is in fair condition. The floors are built of tight boards. This company packs tomatoes and apples. The toilets are only fairly clean and no wash rooms are provided. The sewage is carried off. The employes are healthy and cleanly in appearance and dress. The tomato pulp is packed in barrels, using ten pounds of salt to the barrel. The pulp is not made from whole, sound fruit, but from the refuse, skins and cores. Water under pressure is available and the floors are cleaned daily. The factory is well organized and successfully operated.

NEW CASTLE—

New Castle Canning Company.—Out of business.

NOBLESVILLE—

Noblesville Canning Factory.—This company packs corn only. The building is a frame structure, and is in poor condition. The floors are made of wood, and are in poor shape. The toilets are located outside and are only fairly clean. No wash rooms are provided. The employes are healthy and cleanly in appearance and dress. Water under pressure is available and the floors are cleaned daily. The inspector gives this factory the rate of poor.

PEKIN—

Pekin Canning Company.—This company packs tomatoes in a frame building which is in good condition. The toilets provided are good and properly screened. No wash rooms are provided, but facilities for washing are provided and the sewage is hauled away. The employes are healthy and cleanly in appearance and dress. The tomato pulp is packed in barrels, and preserved with eight pounds of salt to the barrel. The pulp is made from whole, sound fruit, refuse, skins and cores. The work room is cleaned daily with water under pressure. The factory is only fairly well organized and given the rate of fair.

PERU—

Peru Canning Factory.—This company packs peas, corn and tomatoes in a building of frame construction which is in good condition. The floors are of slats and are cemented. Ample wash rooms are provided, and the sewage is disposed of by drains or hauled away. The work rooms are properly screened and the employes are healthy and neat. The tomato pulp is packed in barrels, using no benzoate unless ordered. The pulp is made from refuse, skins and cores. Water pressure is available and the work room is cleaned daily. The factory is well organized and apparently successfully operated.

PIERCETON—

Reid Murdock Canning Company.—This company packs cabbage, pickles, catsup and chili sauce. The building is of frame construction in fair condition. The toilets are located outside the building and are only fairly clean. The sewage is either hauled or drained away. The work rooms are properly screened. The employes are healthy and clean. The tomato pulp is packed in barrels, using one-tenth of one per cent. of benzoate of soda when ordered. The pulp is made from whole, sound fruit. The work room is cleaned daily. Water under pressure is available. The factory is well organized and successfully operated.

PLAINVILLE—

Plainville Canning Company.—This company packs tomatoes and corn. They operate in a frame building, which is in good condition. The floors are of cement and in good condition. Fairly good outside toilets are provided. Wash rooms are provided and sewage is disposed of through a sewer which runs into a canal. The employes are healthy and cleanly. Pulp is made from refuse, skins and cores, and packed in barrels. The factory is well organized and operated.

PRINCETON—

Princeton Canning Company.—This company puts up tomatoes, apples and pumpkins. Tomato pulp is packed in five gallon galvanized cans, using five pounds salt to the fifty gallons. The pulp is made from whole, sound fruit. A new floor was ordered in the room where the pulp is handled. The company operates in a frame building which is in fair condition. The toilets are in fair condition and are properly screened. No wash rooms are provided. The sewage is disposed of by a sewer or hauled away. Employes are apparently healthy and neatly dressed. The work room is cleaned daily and water under pressure is available. The factory is well organized and successfully operated.

SALEM—

Canton Canning Company.—Factory not running this year. Condition of plant fair.

SCOTTSBURG—

Scottsburg Canning Company.—This company packs tomatoes, beans, hominy, kraut, pork and beans, etc. The business is conducted in a frame building in good condition. The toilets, which are separate from the factory, are clean and properly screened. Wash room facilities are provided and the sewage is disposed of by a sewer, or hauled. The work rooms are properly screened and the employes are cleanly and healthy. The tomato pulp is packed in barrels, using six pounds of salt to the barrel. The pulp is made from whole, sound fruit, refuse, skins and cores. Water pressure is available and the work room is cleaned daily. The factory is well organized and successfully operated. The inspector gave this factory the rate of good.

SELLERSBURG—

Sellersburg Canning Company.—Not running this year.

SEYMOUR—

Seymour Canning Company.—This company packs tomatoes, kraut and hominy. The factory is operated in a frame building in good condition. The toilets, which are separate from the factory, are properly screened and clean. Facilities for washing are provided. The sewage is disposed of by a sewer or hauled. The pulp is packed in barrels, and six pounds of salt is used to every forty-gallon barrel. The pulp is made from both whole, sound fruit, and refuse, skins and cores. Water pressure is available. The work room is cleaned daily. The factory is well organized and apparently successfully operated.

SHARPSVILLE—

Sharpsville Canning Company.—This company operates in a brick and frame building which is in fair condition. The company packs tomatoes. The floors of the building are cement and in good condition. The toilets, which are located in the yard, are fairly clean. Wash rooms are provided and the sewage is disposed of through a cement drain which runs to a ditch. The employes are healthy and cleanly. The tomato pulp is packed in barrels and preserved with six pounds of salt to the barrel. The pulp is made from refuse, skins and cores. The inspector rated this factory as fair.

SHELBYVILLE—

Shelbyville Canning Company.—This company packs corn only, in a frame building which is in good condition. The floors are made of cement and are in good shape. The toilets are located in the yard and are in fair condition. Ample wash rooms are provided and the sewage is disposed of through a drain which runs to a ditch. The work room is cleaned daily and the employes are apparently healthy and cleanly in appearance and dress.

SHIRLEY—

Shirley Canning Company.—This company packs tomatoes. The building is of frame construction and is in good condition. The floors are built of cement. The toilets are fairly good and are located in the yard. Wash basins are provided and the sewage is disposed of by means of a drain through the building to a ditch. Tomato pulp is packed in barrels and preserved with salt. The pulp is made from refuse, skins and cores. A tile drain to the ditch was ordered instead of the open ditch.

SPICELAND—

Spiceland Canning Company.—This company does business in a frame building which is in fair condition, having good cement floors. The toilets are located in the yard and are satisfactory. The sewage is disposed of through a good drain. The tomato pulp is packed in barrels and preserved with salt. The pulp is made from refuse, skins and cores. Proper water pressure is furnished and the factory in general is in fairly good condition.

SWAYZEE—

Swayzee Canning Company.—This company packs tomatoes and corn. The building is frame and in fairly good condition. The floors are in fair shape and are made of wood. The toilets, which are located in the yard, are fairly clean. Basins are provided for washing, and the sewage is disposed of through a drain to a ditch. Water pressure is available and the floor of the work room is cleaned daily. The factory is well organized and successfully operated.

TERRE HAUTE—

Loudon Packing Company.—This company packs tomato catsup and boullion in a frame building in good condition. The floors are made of plank and cement and are in good condition. Wash rooms are provided, and the sewage is disposed of by means of the city sewer. The pulp is made from whole, sound fruit, using no benzoate. The work room is cleaned daily and proper water pressure is available.

TIPTON—

Fame Canning Company.—This company packs tomatoes, peas and corn. The building is constructed of frame and brick and is in good condition. The floors are made of cement and are in good condition. The toilets are in fairly good condition. Ample wash rooms are provided and the sewage is disposed of through the city sewers. The pulp is packed in barrels and cans and is made from whole, sound fruit. The inspector gave the factory a good rating.

UNDERWOOD—

Hoagland Brothers.—This company operates in a frame building which has cement floors and is in good condition. The toilets are separate and are properly screened and in good condition. Facilities for washing are provided. The company packs tomatoes, beans, apples, kraut and hominy. The tomato pulp is put up in barrels, preserved with eight pounds of salt to the barrel, which is made from both whole, sound fruit and the refuse, skins and cores. Water pressure is available and the work room is cleaned daily. The factory is well organized and successfully operated.

VIENNA—

Vienna Canning Company.—This company packs tomatoes. They operate in a frame building in fairly good condition. The toilets are separate and are clean and properly screened. The sewage is disposed of by a sewer or hauled away. The employes are healthy and cleanly in appearance and dress. The tomato pulp is packed in barrels, using eight pounds of salt to the barrel. The pulp is made from both whole, sound fruit and refuse, skins and cores. The floor of the work room is cleaned daily and water under pressure is available.

WABASH—

Wabash Canning Factory.—This building is constructed of stone with cement floors in good condition. The toilets are outside and are fairly clean. The sewage is disposed of by a sewer, but the sewer in use is too small. The pulp is packed in barrels and is made from the refuse, skins and cores. The factory appears to be successfully operated.

WALKERTON—

Atwood Brothers.—The frame and brick building, which has plank floors, is in fair condition. The toilets are located outside and are in fair shape. The sewage is disposed of by a sewer or ditch. This company packs pickles, catsup and chili sauce. The pulp is packed in barrels and is made from whole, sound fruit, and refuse, skins and cores.

WARSAW—

Van Wirt Canning Company.—This company packs corn, peas and tomatoes in a good brick building. The toilets are located outside the building and are in fairly good condition. The floors are made of cement and are in good condition. Sinks are provided for washing and the sewage is drained or hauled away. The employes are apparently healthy and are neat and cleanly in appearance and dress. The work room is cleaned daily and water under pressure is available.

WESTFIELD—

Westfield Canning Company.—The frame building is in fair condition with floors of wood. There is a good drainage system, but the toilets, which are located in the yard, are only fairly satisfactory. The pulp, which is made from refuse, skins and cores, is packed in barrels and preserved with salt. The rating of this factory was fair.

WEST TERRE HAUTE—

West Terre Haute Canning Company.—This company cans tomatoes only. The building is a frame structure and the floors are made of wood and are in good condition. The toilets are located forty feet from the building and the sewage is disposed of through an open sewer into a dug well. The work rooms are not properly screened. Water under pressure is available and the work room is cleaned daily. The tomato pulp is packed in barrels and is made from both whole, sound fruit, refuse, skins and cores. Two visits were made to this factory, which seems to be operated successfully.

WINDFALL—

Jno. Shirk.—This company is operating in a frame building which is in fairly good condition. The floors are made of wood and are in good shape. The toilets, which are located in the yard, are fairly good. The sewage is disposed of through a drain running to a ditch. Basins are provided for washing. The pulp which is packed in barrels and cans is made from refuse, skins and cores. The employes are cleanly in appearance and dress, and are apparently healthy.

REPORT

FROM

WATER LABORATORY.

THE WATER SUPPLY OF INDIANA.

Each year the great problem of a pure and ample water supply receives more serious attention; each year our streams are being more heavily polluted and our ground water supply diminished, and, so far, the necessity for conservation has not appealed sufficiently to the citizens to bring about a marked reduction of these unsanitary and wasteful practices. The work of the water department of the Laboratory of Hygiene has been valuable in showing the extent to which the water supplies were already polluted and in furnishing assistance to water companies, towns and cities that were facing problems they could not meet. But little has been accomplished in the way of the enforcement of the Stream Pollution Law passed by the General Assembly, 1909. This is not due to any inherent weakness of the law but to an apparent lack of a desire of cities and communities to take advantage of its provisions in securing the protection of their streams and water supplies from pollution.

During the year a large number of water samples collected by health officers or sent in by the owners of the supplies have been analyzed to determine their potability and fitness for domestic use. The source and condition of the supplies examined is best illustrated by graphic representation and the following charts indicate clearly the results of the year's work. It is apparent from a comparative study of the charts that the public supplies are superior in character to the private supply. The work of the year has been carried on in every portion of the State and has embraced every variety of public and private water supplies. The location and type of the supplies examined and the results of the analyses are shown on the accompanying map.

WATER SUPPLIES

INDIANA

1910

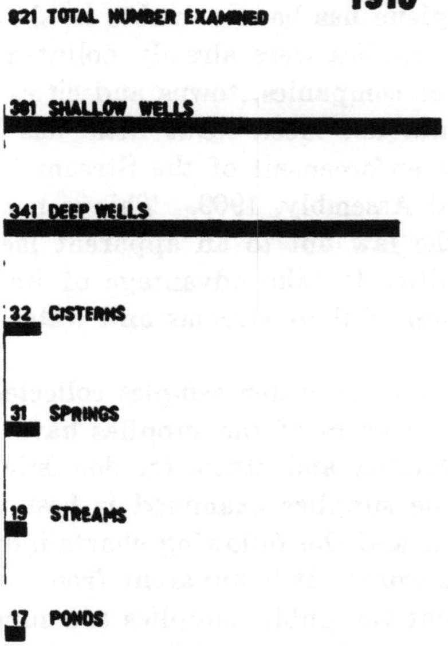

821 TOTAL NUMBER EXAMINED

381 SHALLOW WELLS

341 DEEP WELLS

32 CISTERNS

31 SPRINGS

19 STREAMS

17 PONDS

QUALITY OF SUPPLIES

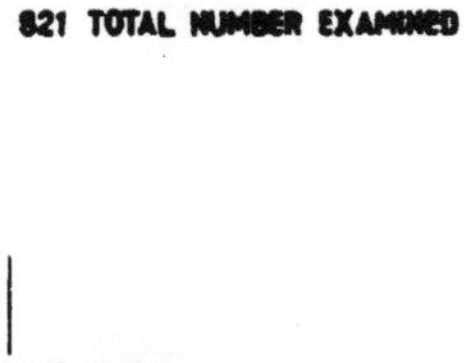

821 TOTAL NUMBER EXAMINED

195 BAD

72 DOUBTFUL

CONDITION OF PUBLIC WATER SUPPLIES IN INDIANA

1910

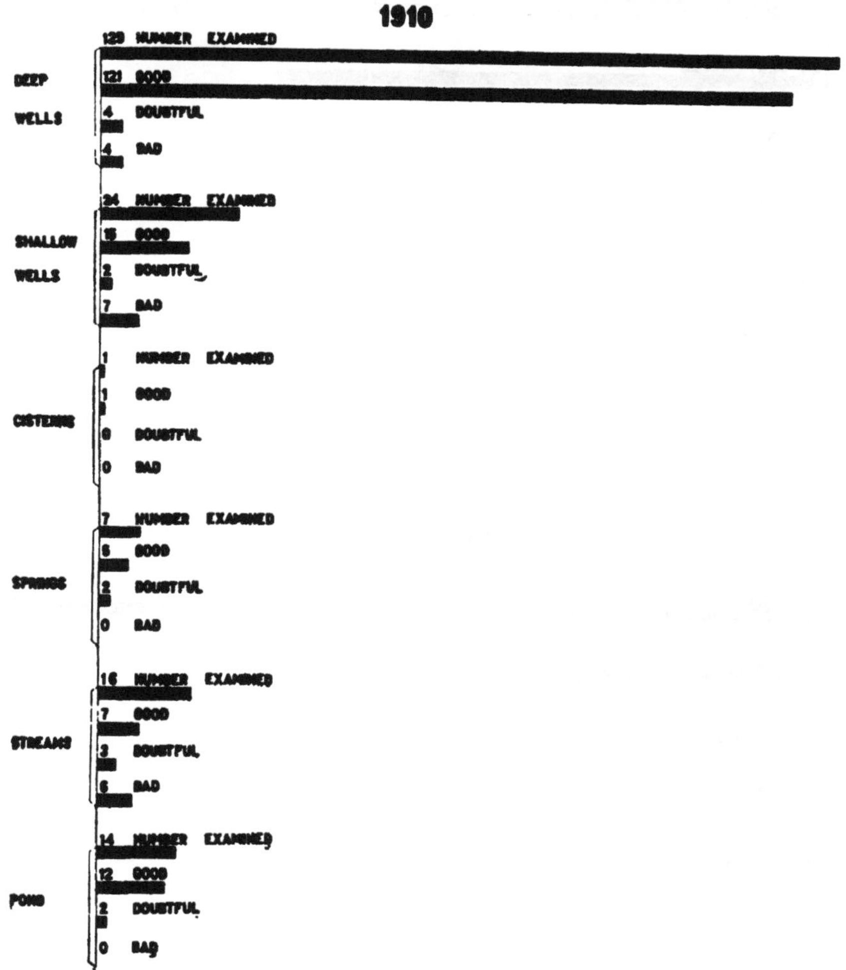

WATER SUPPLIES IN INDIANA

PUBLIC SUPPLIES

1910

191	TOTAL NUMBER EXAMINED
129	DEEP WELLS
24	SHALLOW WELLS
16	STREAMS
14	PONDS
7	SPRINGS
1	CISTERN

PRIVATE SUPPLIES

630	TOTAL NUMBER EXAMINED
357	SHALLOW WELLS
212	DEEP WELLS
31	CISTERNS
24	SPRING
3	PONDS
3	STREAMS

CONDITION OF PRIVATE WATER SUPPLIES IN INDIANA

1910

DEEP WELLS	212	NUMBER EXAMINED
	182	GOOD
	16	DOUBTFUL
	14	BAD
SHALLOW WELLS	357	NUMBER EXAMINED
	170	GOOD
	26	DOUBTFUL
	161	BAD
CISTERNS	31	NUMBER EXAMINED
	19	GOOD
	1	DOUBTFUL
	11	BAD
SPRINGS	24	NUMBER EXAMINED
	17	GOOD
	5	DOUBTFUL
	2	BAD
STREAMS	3	NUMBER EXAMINED
	3	GOOD
	0	DOUBTFUL
	0	BAD
PONDS	3	NUMBER EXAMINED
	2	GOOD
	1	DOUBTFUL
	0	BAD

Eight hundred and seventy samples of water were analyzed, of which 241 were deep well waters and waters derived from a stratum lying below clay, hard pan or rock, 378 were free shallow wells and were apparently surface waters, 17 were from streams, 22 from ponds, 31 from supplies designated as springs, but without doubt including both surface and ground waters. Thirty-two cistern waters were also analyzed. In addition to these analyses 49 miscellaneous samples were analyzed, the water being sent in from state institutions by the State Fish and Game Commissioner, and as well a number of samples from the Calumet River, where a sanitary survey was being made.

Of the deep well supplies 302 were of good quality, 18 were so polluted as to be classed as bad, and 21 were of doubtful quality; that is, they had certain chemical characteristics indicating pollution, but at the present time their condition is not so serious that they are unfit for use. Of the 378 shallow wells examined 184 were of good quality, 157 unqualifiedly bad, and 37 supplies of doubtful quality. Since a shallow well water of doubtful quality is sooner or later sure to become more seriously polluted and pass into the class of bad waters, doubtful and bad samples may be placed together. We find then that 194, or 51.3 per cent., of the drinking waters from shallow wells must be classed as unsatisfactory. Nine stream supplies were good and 6 bad, and 2 were doubtful. Twenty-two pond or lake supplies were examined. Eighteen were of good quality and four were doubtful. Of the 31 spring waters analyzed, 22 were good, 2 were bad and 7 were doubtful. It is evident that many waters sent in as spring supplies are, in fact, only surface waters, since they possess none of the characteristics of a true spring water. Of the 32 cistern waters analyzed 20 were of good quality, 11 were bad and 1 doubtful. Cistern water, which is in most instances rain water, when collected from clean roofs in water tight, clean underground tanks, should be entirely satisfactory for drinking and domestic purposes. The result of the work of the laboratory shows that 37 per cent. of the cistern waters examined were not potable. The unsatisfactory cistern supply is usually due to its location in the backyard near the privy vault, and leaking walls admitting polluted water from the outside whenever the water level in the cistern is lower than the ground water level of the soil.

Another classification may be made of the work according to the ownership of the sources of supply. One hundred and ninety-one analyses were made of water from public supplies classified as follows: 129 deep wells, 24 shallow wells, 16 streams, 14 ponds or lakes, and 7 springs. Of the deep well supplies, 121 were of good quality, 4 were bad and 4 were doubtful. The deep well waters used as public supplies are for the most part of excellent quality from a sanitary standpoint. Of the 16 streams and river supplies, 7 were of good quality, 6 bad and 3 doubtful. Several of these samples came from the Ohio River, a supply which in an unfiltered condition can never be depended upon to furnish potable water. Of the private supplies, 212 were deep wells, 357 shallow wells, 24 springs, and 31 cisterns. One hundred and eighty-two of the deep well waters were of good quality, 14 bad and 16 doubtful. But 170 of the 357 shallow well waters were potable, 151 were unquestionably bad and 36 were of doubtful quality.

An interesting classification has been made of the supplies of families whose members have contracted typhoid fever. A polluted water supply is properly suspected of being the source of typhoid infection, and it has been interesting to determine by the analyses of the water whether or not the suspicion of the users and of the family physician were well grounded. The deep well supplies, which were suspected of being the source of typhoid infection were in almost every instance potable, but 3 out of 30 samples being bad. On the contrary, the suspected shallow wells showed a much greater proportion of polluted samples than is the case with all of the shallow wells examined. Forty-four of the 79 shallow wells used by families in which a case of typhoid fever had occurred were unqualifiedly bad. This is equivalent to a percentage of 55 per cent. Eliminating from the total list of shallow well samples those from supplies suspected of causing typhoid fever the percentage of impure samples is but 38. The difference in these percentages is certainly an indication that the belief that surface water supply is a common source of typhoid infection is well founded. In this connection it is interesting to note that of the 5 cistern waters used by the typhoid patients, 4 were unqualifiedly bad.

Another comparative study has been made of the water supplies at schoolhouses. These schoolhouses are for the most part located in the country, and the supply is usually a driven well in the school yard. Nine of the supplies examined were classed as deep wells, 14 as shallow wells, and 40 springs. Eight of the deep well supplies were in good condition; one was classed as bad. Ten of the shallow wells were potable, 4 were bad. All of the so-called spring supplies were in good condition. Of the 28 samples designated as schoolhouse supplies 23 were in good condition and 5 were bad. While this proportion of bad samples is decidedly less than in the case of waters used for domestic supplies, yet the importance of the subject warrants more careful attention to the character of the public water supply. If the well is polluted the probability is that disease resulting therefrom will be distributed by the pupils to their homes, and thus polluted school supplies may become foci for the distribution of disease.

SPECIAL REPORTS OF PUBLIC WATER SUPPLIES, FILTRATION PLANTS AND SEWAGE SYSTEMS.

In addition to the routine analyses of water samples, the water department has furnished valuable assistance and advice to a number of cities. These investigations have been made at the request of health officers and superintendents of water works and sewage disposal plants. The results of the investigations follow:

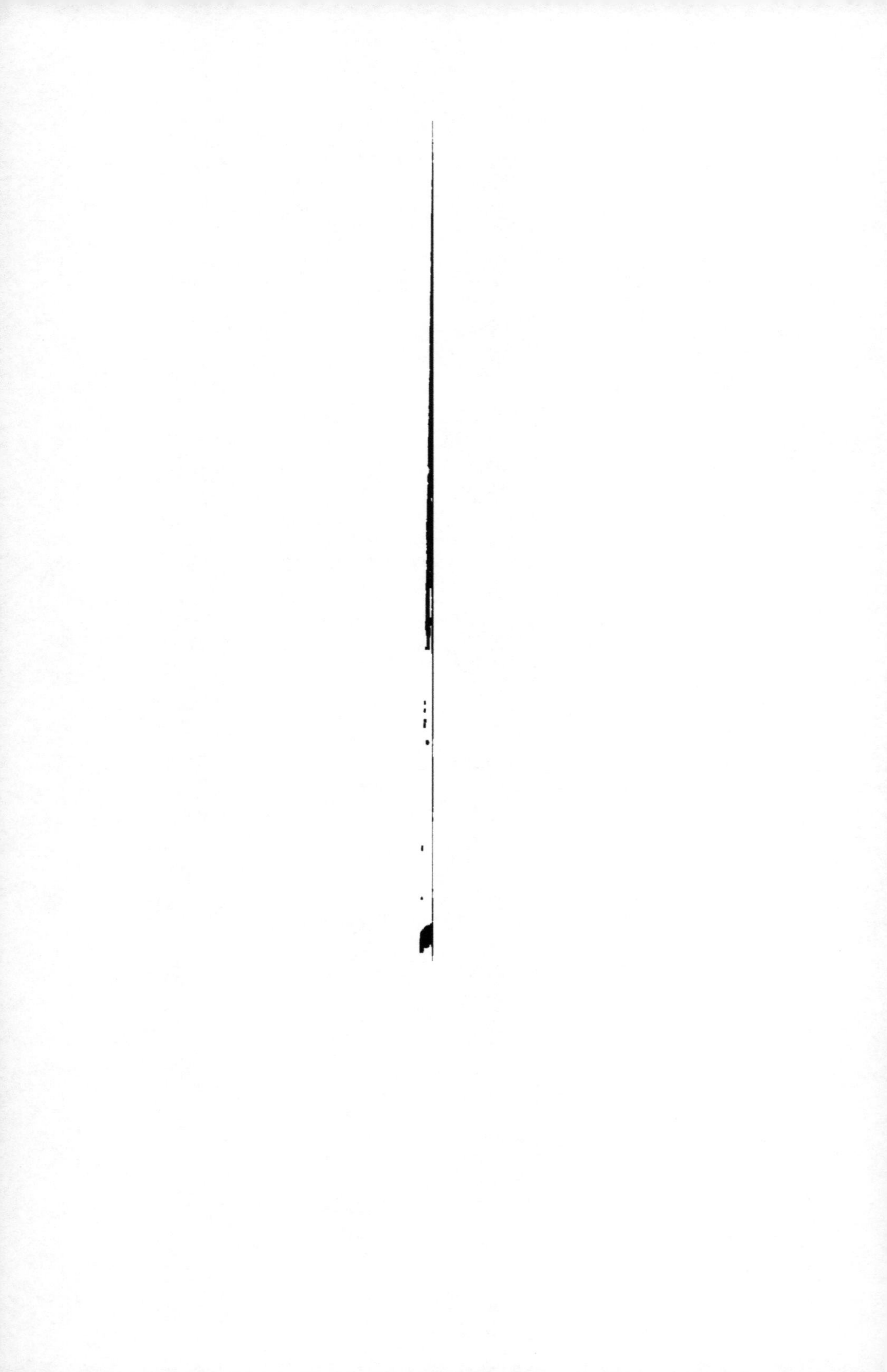

AN INVESTIGATION OF THE CALUMET RIVER DISTRICT DRAINING LAKE COUNTY, INDIANA, AND COOK COUNTY, ILLINOIS.

H. E. BARNARD AND J. H. BREWSTER.

In a study of the sanitary condition of the southern end of Lake Michigan bordering Lake County, Indiana, made in 1908 and described fully in the report of the Indiana State Board of Health of that year,* it was found that the discharge from the Grand Calumet River materially affects the potability of the water in Lake Michigan for a distance from its mouth of over ten miles in every direction, depending upon the wind and the currents in the lake. Now that the waterway connecting the Calumet River with the lake at Indiana Harbor has been opened, it is reasonable to believe that much the same conditions will be encountered in the lake at this point as are now giving trouble at South Chicago, although it is not likely that the condition will ever be as serious here as it is at South Chicago, as the chief sources of pollution near this entrance are the trunk sewer of Indiana Harbor which empties into the Calumet River, about six miles distant, and the sewer from East Chicago, about five miles distant. The length of time required for this sewage to reach the lake will give it an opportunity to become partially purified by settling. However, there will be times when some of it will reach the lake, and as the manufacturing industries are rapidly developing in this section, the trade wastes, together with this sewage, will have a far more serious effect upon the lake than is now apparent.

In the 1908 survey it was also learned that the water supplies of Whiting, Hammond, and particularly Chicago, were seriously polluted by the river discharge at South Chicago. With this knowledge at hand the State Board of Health deemed it advisable again to visit this district and determine the exact condition of the river, the amount and kind of pollution entering it from the Indiana cities, how it was disposed of, and if possible through its report to lend assistance for the final solution of the problem which faces the Indiana cities and also a part of Chicago. Since the

*See also First Report Lake Michigan Water Commission.

problem is not only interstate, but to some extent an international proposition. as yet regulated by no law or treaties, the control of the sanitary district of Chicago over that portion of the river lying in Illinois was carefully studied as preliminary to the actual investigation of conditions in the affected territory lying in Indiana.

THE CHICAGO SANITARY DISTRICT.

The Chicago Sanitary District was created under the Act of May 29, 1889, for four definite purposes: first, to divert the sewage of Chicago from Lake Michigan toward the Gulf of Mexico and so to prevent the further pollution of the waters along the city front, and to relieve the filthy, congested Chicago River and its branches; second, to protect the Chicago water supply from pollution by this sewage; third, to reclaim the "malaria preserves" along the Illinois River, to the benefit of the public health of these regions; fourth, ultimately to develop navigation between Lake Michigan and the Mississippi River. These were the primary reasons calling for the expenditure of $36,000,000 in the establishment of this district.

The Sanitary District of Chicago is divided into districts lying both within and outside the Chicago city limits. The Calumet District, which is the subdivision to be especially considered, lies south of Chicago and for drainage purposes extends from Eighty-seventh Street south to about One Hundred Fifteenth Street, and from the Indiana State line on the east to about Fortieth Avenue in the west. It lies, for the most part, very low and many acres are but one or two feet above lake level. The entire Sanitary District of Chicago contains approximately 350 square miles, 100 square miles of which is included in the Calumet District, 40 square miles of this latter area lying within the city limits.

The natural drainage of the Calumet District is into the Little Calumet and Grand Calumet rivers, discharging into Lake Michigan at the Calumet Harbor entrance. The distance from the river to the Sixty-eighth Street crib, measuring around the eastern end of the government breakwater, is about four and one-half miles. The district contains scattered centers of population, such as South Chicago, Blue Island, Riverdale, Pullman, Harvey, Dolton, West Hammond and other smaller places, the estimated population of which is now 113,000.

As before stated, the primary object of the work undertaken by the Sanitary District of Chicago was the protection of Lake

Michigan (the great reservoir from which the city of Chicago and its urban and suburban neighbors draw their drinking water) from the sewage pollution due to the discharge into it of the city of Chicago and its contiguous population. The first work undertaken was the construction of the great canal from Robey Street, Chicago, to Lockport. This work materially improved the character of the Chicago River and by turning Chicago sewage away from the lake established a protection to the city against water-borne diseases. The suburban population on the South Side was, however, afforded no relief and is still pouring its refuse indirectly into Lake Michigan.

The only available means of purifying or destroying the sewage of Chicago was by dilution, and for this purpose the Sanitary District was permitted by the governments of Canada and the United States to divert to the canal from Lake Michigan. water amounting to 10,000 cubic feet per second and the canal was designed and built to care for this amount of water. While disposal by dilution is a recognized method of sewage purification, it will fulfill its purpose satisfactorily only when held within certain limits, as sufficient dissolved oxygen must be present in the diluting water to oxidize the incoming sewage and to stimulate biological action, and the time element for action to occur is definitely fixed. It was soon discovered that the sewage from Chicago proper was sufficient to utilize this amount of water.

In 1901 it appeared through gauge readings that the capacity of the rock section of the sanitary canal was 40 per cent greater than the capacity for which it was originally intended. The canal, therefore, instead of having a capacity of only 10,000 cubic feet per second was capable of carrying 14,000 cubic feet per second. This discovery suggested the use of the additional carrying capacity of the 4,000 cubic feet per second, and it was estimated that, at the ratio of sewage dilution established by law for the sanitary canal, this excess was capable of diluting the sewage of an additional population of 1,200,000. It was then seen that as a protection to the water supply of the entire metropolitan district, an urgent necessity for sewage disposal other than what was already being provided, existed in the Calumet region.

It would seem that with this excess canal capacity it would be a relatively simple proposition to add to it the sewage of the south side. One difficulty, however, under present conditions, makes such a disposal impossible. As before stated, the 10,000 cubic feet per second flow is now caring for all the sewage it can, which means that if sewage from an additional section of the city is to be added to the present burden, a larger amount of water must be taken from Lake Michigan. But, fearing a possible lowering of the lake level, Canada will not consent to this proposition, and for this reason alone some other means of obtaining this water had to be found. It was therefore proposed, and permission was granted to the Sanitary District, to build a canal through the Sag Channel to connect the Little Calumet River at Blue Island with the main drainage canal at Sag bridge, as is shown on the accompanying chart of the Sag channel. The canal will reverse the flow of the Calumet River and intercept the sewage of that part of the Sanitary District known as the Calumet District. The capacity of this canal as designed will be 2,000 cubic feet per second. Its length will be 16¼ miles from Blue Island to the Sag bridge, and the distance from the present canal to Lake Michigan will be 27½ miles. The estimated cost will be $5,640,000, and it will be completed about 1915.

The topography and hydrography of the Calumet District admit of treatment that will secure a reversal of the current of the Calumet River and a gravity flow therefrom into the main channels of the Sanitary District through the Sag valley. Surveys have been made and a channel partially located which will accomplish this purpose. The tentative plans for this canal provide that it shall be 70 feet wide at the bottom in earth and 90 feet in rock. The summer flow of the Little and Grand Calumet rivers is quite sluggish, and the amount of water passing is entirely insufficient in quantity properly to dilute any sewage when the territory is built up, nor at low flows even the surface washings which will enter during slight rain storms. Owing to the insufficient amount of water flowing through the Little Calumet at all times, except during heavy floods, it will be necessary for the district to reverse the flow of the Grand Calumet to the extent of supplying the extra amount required.

With the completion of this canal and the diversion of all the sewage now entering the river from the Indiana line to South Chicago Harbor into this canal, the river will be much less heavily contaminated and the pollution of the lake from this source will be almost entirely eliminated. For, as will be shown later, some of the greatest sources of pollution entering the river are on the

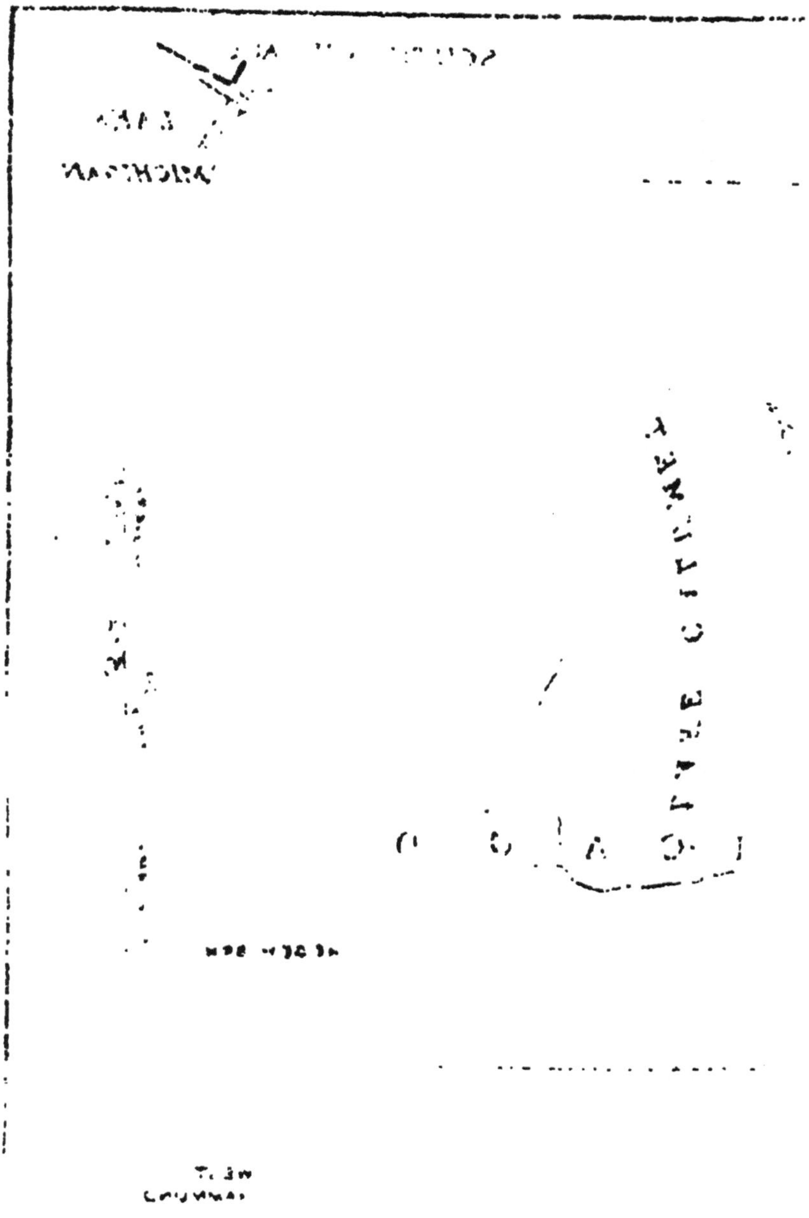

makes s
cubic fe
can, wh
the city
water m
ble lowe
proposit
taining
and pe
canal t
River a
as is sh
canal w
sewage
met Dis
cubic f
Island
to Lake
$5,640,(

The
mit of
Calume
nels of
have be
plish t
that it
in rock
ers is
insuffic
territo
which
cient a
times,
distric
supply

Wi
the sev
Chicag
contan
be
c

Illinois side of the line. It will also be shown that, except at flood periods, practically all of the sewage entering the river from the Indiana side settles out before it reaches the lake, and with the Sag canal completed, during the times of sluggish flow the Indiana sewage will be carried toward it. With the completion of this proposed scheme, it would seem that the question of sewage disposal had been practically settled for the Northern Indiana cities which now empty their sewage into the river. But there are two very important reasons why this is not so and why the proper solution should be sought in the near future; first, during the autumn the low flow of the river allows the deposition of silt from surface washings and solid particles of sewage, after which the freshets, which have been known to reach a flood stage of 13,300 cubic feet per second, would readily pick up such deposits and carry them out into the lake; second, in taking water from the Calumet River for dilution purposes, the Sanitary District wants as pure a water as is possible to be had, and if the Indiana cities do not prevent such pollution as will be shown is now taking place, the Sanitary District will compel action on the part of Indiana by legal proceedings.

THE GRAND CALUMET.

The Grand Calumet River is the name applied to a bayou of Lake Michigan, the principal use of which, other than receiving the sewage of the Indiana cities bordering it and a portion of that of South Chicago, is to afford harborage for ore, freight and produce boats navigating on the Great Lakes. This river originally had two points of entrance to the lake, one at the present city of Gary and the other at South Chicago. But as the entrance at Gary has not until recently been a harbor point, the drift of the sand practically closed the outlet and since the completion of the Gary Steel Plant it has been entirely filled with slag.

While the river was being closed at Gary, the Indiana Harbor Land Company promoted and financed the digging of a canal for harbor purposes, reaching from the lake at the harbor of the Inland Steel Company plant to the Calumet River at a point 17½ miles from the Calumet Harbor. The completion of this canal does not modify the character of the river except to shorten it about eight miles, this part of the original river now being a dead arm with no flow except that caused by the discharge from the Gary Steel Plant, which amounts to about 7,000,000 gallons a day, and the return flow of water that backs up into it when the direction of the current in the river is reversed.

The Grand Calumet River has a small drainage area, but with its tributary, the Little Calumet, drains about 806 square miles, of which 455 are in Indiana and 351 are in Illinois. Notwithstanding its name, the Grand Calumet is the smaller of the two rivers and has a drainage area of only 88 square miles. The Little Calumet, which has its headwaters in Porter County, Indiana, first flows in a general westerly direction to the Indiana State line, then northwesterly to Blue Island, Illinois, where it turns eastward and joints the Grand Calumet near Lake Calumet and finally discharges into Lake Michigan after draining an area of 718 square miles.

Lake Calumet is a shallow body of water lying in the southern portion of the Chicago city limits and covering an area of about four square miles. The lake is about six feet deep and is connected with the river by a short branch. It receives no sewage except that from the storm sewers of Pullman, Illinois. The major part of the sewage of Pullman, is collected by a separate system, pumped and delivered into the Little Calumet River at One Hundred Thirtieth Street and Indiana Avenue. This sewage, together with some trade wastes entering the river makes it at times decidedly objectionable.

The Grand Calumet River, when it has any flow at all, is a sluggish stream with the current running in either direction according to the wind and currents in Lake Michigan, but owing to the almost continual flow from the Little Calumet the prevailing current is toward South Chicago. It is about 25 miles long and has a varying width from 25 to 300 feet before reaching South Chicago Harbor, and an average depth of from six to eight feet until it reaches Lake Calumet, from which point it has an average depth of about 25 feet, which is maintained by continual dredging. The bottom up to where it has been dredged is soft muck, consisting of silt and organic deposits containing about 80% of water, which in some places is 12 to 15 feet deep. The river receives all the sewage and trade wastes from the cities and manufactories along its bank, the most important sources being the sewers of the cities of Gary, Indiana Harbor, East Chicago, Hammond, the Hammond Glue Works, the Hearst-Stein Company's

Glue Works, the West Hammond sewer, that portion of Chicago drained into the Little Calumet through the Indiana Avenue, Wentworth Avenue and Halsted Street sewers, which care for an area of about 7,000 acres, and finally, at the mouth of the river, the sewers from the Strand, a division of South Chicago, and from Ninety-second to Ninety-fifth streets, draining an area of about 6,000 acres, discharge on the north bank.

The three Indiana cities that empty their sewage into the Grand Calumet River, namely, Hammond, East Chicago and Gary, all have combined sewerage systems providing for both sanitary and storm water discharge through the same outlets. In East Chicago and Gary, the effluents consist pricipally of land run off and household wastes, as most of the manufacturing concerns have private sewers. The majority of these plants are engaged in developing the mineral industries and the principal portion of their sewage is cooling water containing no organic refuse. In Hammond for many years manufacturing plants engaged in the making of foodstuffs have deposited enormous amounts of organic sludge in the Calumet River near the sewer outlets. Some of these factories are still emptying their refuse into the river, but others are now disposing of it in other ways, which greatly improves the condition of the river.

The plant that has given the most trouble in past years is the Hammond distillery, for the reason that cattle were fattened on the distillery refuse slop, and the manure and washings from the cattle yards emptied directly into the river, but the distillery does not feed cattle at present and nothing now enters the river from this source except condensing water, as all waste materials are utilized in making by-products.

The Standard Steel Car Company is located in the southeast corner of Hammond and empties its refuse material into the Columbia Avenue sewer. This refuse contains a large amount of oil waste, which covers the surface of the water, thus injuring its appearance. A far more serious result of this oily layer is due to its preventing the air from coming in contact with the other organic matter in the river, thus retarding the process of oxidation which otherwise would constantly go on in this section of the river. Another damaging trade waste comes from the Hammond Gas Works, where the refuse tar and oil products are emptied into the river, causing the formation of a very disagreeable sludge having a strong odor.

The city of Hammond covers about 8,000 acres, but a large portion of this is unimproved property and is partially occupied by Wolf Lake and Lake George. The drainage from this unimproved section is into Lake Michigan. The residential and business section is in the south part of the city and covers about 3,600 acres. This section drains into the Calumet River through nine sewer outlets, one on each side of the river at Columbia Avenue, Calumet Avenue, Sohl Street and Hohman Street, and one coming in from the north at Sheffield Avenue. Five of these sewers are submerged below the surface of the river, the other four are open sewers. Six have a diameter of 4 feet, one of 3½ feet and the other two a diameter of 3 feet. These sewers carry both the storm water and the domestic sewage from the city of Hammond, amounting to about 5½ million gallons a day and representing the domestic waste of a population of 21,000. The extent of this sewerage system can be seen on the accompanying map of the city of Hammond.

The sewerage system of East Chicago proper drains about 2,400 acres and supplies a population of 9,500. The land is principally sand, and as few of the streets are paved there is but little surface flow or storm water entering the system. All the sewage of East Chicago is delivered to the sewage pumping station and is then pumped into the Calumet River at the foot of Magoun Avenue through a five-foot brick sewer.

Indiana Harbor, which is a subdivision of East Chicago, has its own system of sewers which covers a territory of 2,500 acres and receives the sewage of about 9,500 people. The sewers all drain to a pumping station located at One hundred Forty-eighth Street and Alder Avenue, where the sewage is pumped into an open ditch or flume way which empties into the Calumet River at Cline Avenue. The sewage of Indiana Harbor is very greatly diluted by the large quantity of water which undoubtedly comes from Lake Michigan and seeps through the sandy soil. While there are several million gallons discharged into the Calumet River through this flume way, yet the domestic waste amounts to a little over 1,500,000 gallons per day. The volume of water pumped by the East Chicago Water Company to Indiana Harbor is much greater than this, but a large portion of this pumpage is used by the mills for cooling purposes and is emptied into the canal through private sewers.

The city of Gary has a sewer system which drains an area

pe
by
p
ne
ac
se
C.
in
su
se
ot
wa
ar
dc
er
H.

2,
ci
su
of
is
A

its
an
dr
eig
an
at
dil
fr
th
Ri
a
pu
is
us
ca

of 3,700 acres, but a large portion of this at the present time is unimproved property. If the future development is as rapid as the development of the last two years, most of this area will soon be sewering into the present system, which has its main outlet into the Grand Calumet coming from Fifth Avenue. In laying out a sewer system for Gary the idea has been developed of ultimately installing a sewage purification plant from which the innocuous effluent can pass into the Little Calumet River. At such a time an overflow dam will be installed in the present Fifth Avenue sewer so that nothing will pass into the river at this point except during periods of heavy storm. If properly maintained a system of this kind will prevent the rivers from receiving befouling or deleterious matter, but at the present time the sewage entering the Grand Calumet from the five-foot trunk sewer is of the usual composition of sanitary sewage. Little effect upon the river is noticed because of the great dilution the sewage receives by the water coming from the Gary Steel Mills. When the suggested plans for the sewerage system of Gary are carried out and the proposed purification plant is constructed, it will be necessary to build a sewage pumping station at Fifteenth Avenue and Alley Twenty, for the purpose of pumping the dry weather sewage to the purification plant.

THE CALUMET RIVER.

In studying the condition of the water in the Calumet River we find that the water is comparatively of good quality from Gary to the entrance of the canal at East Chicago, but from this canal to the junction of the Little Calumet with the Grand Calumet, the river closely resembles a septic tank in appearance and action where the process of the decomposition of organic matter is continuously taking place. The septic action is always evidenced by the gas bubbles rising to the surface and in places by the large amounts of sludge which break away from the bottom and float on the surface of the water. After the inflow of the Little Calumet the water is greatly improved in appearance, although from a bacteriological standpoint it is grossly polluted from this point to the mouth of the South Chicago Harbor.

In order to determine the exact character of the water, a branch laboratory of the State Board of Health was established in the office of the East Chicago Water Company, with sufficient equipment for making the following determinations: Bacterial counts on gelatin plates, the presumptive test for B. coli as determined by the use of dextrose broth in fermentation tubes; the positive test for B. coli; putrescibility tests, and the usual chemical tests for nitrates, nitrites, chlorine, alkalinity, dissolved oxygen and oxygen consumed. The results of the presumptive tests for B. coli are given in tables from 1 to 18, inclusive, and the final summary showing the maximum, minimum and average number of bacteria, together with the per cent. of days that B. coli was present at each sampling point, is shown on table 19. The presumptive test for B. coli consisted in the inoculation of lactose broth with the water from each sampling point, and the transference of the culture thus obtained to an agar plate, from which it was isolated and transferred to gelatin tubes and fermentation tubes containing dextrose broth which were afterwards tested for indol reaction and nitrite reduction. The results of this test are shown by tables 20 to 24, inclusive. The results of the determination of nitrates, nitrites, chlorine and alkalinity, are given on tables 25 to 29, inclusive. The amount of dissolved oxygen that the water contained is shown by tables 30 to 35, inclusive, and that required to decompose the organic matter by tables 36 to 41, inclusive. In order to determine the amount of putrescible matter, samples were collected in 4-ounce glass stoppered bottles, to which was added methylene blue, after which they were placed in the incubator at 37½° C. In order that a more or less quantitative estimate might be made of the rapidity of the action, the number of hours required to destroy the color was noted. The samples were incubated for a period of 96 hours, and if the color was unchanged the test was set down negative, but if it had been destroyed the test was called positive and the hours required for this destruction noted. The results of this determination are found in tables 42 to 47, inclusive. A summary of the dissolved oxygen, oxygen consumed and putrescibility reactions is given in table 48.

Permanent sampling stations were established for the collection of samples, starting from the East Chicago Water Works intake and passing through the canal, along which five points were marked before reaching the river. The next point was established as far east in the Grand Calumet as it was possible to navigate with a motor boat, where point 7 was located, a distance of 18¼ miles from the mouth of the Calumet harbor. Points were then located about one mile apart until the outlet of the Indiana

equipment
counts on
mined by
positive te
ical tests f
gen and o
for B. coli
summary s
bacteria, t
ent at each
test for B.
water fron
ture thus
transferre
trose brotl
nitrite-red
24, inclusi
chlorine a
The amou
by tables
organic m
the amour
glass stop
which the
more or l
of the act
was noted
and if th
but if it
hours rec
determina
of the dis
tions is gi

Perma
tion of s
intake ar
were ma
tablished
navigate
of 18
the

Harbor sewer was reached where two points were located on either side close enough to determine how far this sewage traveled from its point of entrance. At the Grasselli Chemical Works, the river was sampled at the main sewer outlet, about one-fourth of a mile west and the same distance east and the same idea was followed out at the junction of the canal and the river. From this point samples were taken very close together, passing the East Chicago sewer and all sewer outlets through Hammond until the Little Calumet River was reached. In order to determine how much effect the Little Calumet had on the Grand Calumet and also to determine whether the flow of the Grand Calumet was reversed and entered the Little Calumet, three sampling points were established between the junction and Riverdale, this being the farthest point west that the motor boat could be used.

From the junction of the Little Calumet to Calumet Harbor, eight sampling points were established in order to show the variations in the river conditions and to determine what effect incoming lake water had upon it. A point was located at the outlet of Lake Calumet for the purpose of determining whether the sewage emptying in it at either Kensington or Pullman reached the river. In all, 43 sampling points covering a distance of approximately 27 miles were established. It was impossible to sample daily from all the sampling points because of the limited capacity of the laboratory, and for this reason the river was divided into two parts, one day the samples being taken from points 1 to 20 and the following day from 20 to 43. It was also impossible with the equipment and force to take daily samples for all the determinations made and this work necessarily was divided.

Samples for the putrescibility reaction, oxygen consumed and dissolved oxygen were collected from each sewer outlet as well as from each sampling point. In addition to this work, gallon samples of sewage from each of these sewers were collected and submitted to the State laboratory at Indianapolis for complete chemical and mineral analysis, the results of which are shown on table 49. After this work was completed the results were tabulated and form the basis for the construction of the accompanying chart on the variation of the composition of the Calumet River.

As shown by the tabulated results of the bacterial count, the river from Gary to South Chicago is a grossly polluted stream. The lowest average count between points 7 and 43 is 4,525 per cubic centimeter and the lowest number of times B. coli was present was 40, and this was at points between the forks and South Chicago harbor, where there was very little sewage entering the river and where the sewage from West Hammond and Hammond had been diluted by the Little Calumet River. The bacterial count between points 17 and 41 in that portion of the river which passes through East Chicago, Hammond and West Hammond, shows it to be much more heavily polluted than it is above or below these points. The average bacterial counts run from 1,000,000 to over 4,000,000 bacteria per cubic centimeter and the presumptive test for B. coli is almost invariably present. With a single exception a positive test for B. coli was found at each point, the exception being in the Little Calumet River.

The chemical analyses of water from the different sampling points are to some extent inconclusive. The nitrate contents show practically no change from point to point and are never observed except in traces. The nitrite contents, however, have some slight variations. Where the sewage in the river is dilute the nitrites increase. Where it is most concentrated, as through the Hammond district, but traces appear, and as the sampling points approach the South Chicago harbor they again increase, although in no case are they as high as might be expected. This is doubtless due to the fact that the organic matter has not been broken up and nitrification has not been sufficiently complete for the formation of nitrates and nitrites, all nitrogen still being in the form described as free or albuminoid ammonia. The chlorine content showed continual variations, but these variations were of so small a range that the only point of interest is that they were all above the normal chlorine content of Lake Michigan. The results on oxygen consumed, dissolved oxygen and the putrescibility reaction are very interesting. The oxygen consumed is the lowest in the lake water and gradually increases through the canal until the Calumet River is reached. From Gary to the canal the figures are somewhat lower, but from this point until past West Hammond the results are extremely high, reaching their maximum at the West Hammond Glue Works and then suddenly dropping off as the influx of organic matter diminishes.

In the dissolved oxygen test, the greatest amount of oxygen is shown in the water from point 1 in Lake Michigan. It gradually lessens until the Calumet River is reached, and then throughout the course of the river, with the exception of the sampling points in the Little Calumet, the oxygen content in the water is very low. The results of the putrescibility reaction parallel the others except that there is not enough putrescible matter in the water, from sampling point 1 to, and including sampling point 19, to react on the methylene blue. From this point, however, there is a quick jump, and through Hammond and West Hammond the reaction takes place almost immediately. On reaching the Little Calumet, it drops until there is almost no reaction, but the putrescible matter in the Grand Calumet does not cease to react until almost to the harbor at South Chicago.

In summing up these results, it appears that the Calumet River is, for a part of its course, a septic tank, in which the sewage entering it travels but a short distance from its point of entrance before undergoing putrefaction. But while considering this fact, the point must not be overlooked that, while a large amount of sewage is purified to some extent in the course of its flow, the purification is not complete and should not be assumed in any way to safeguard the people from a polluted lake water supply. This should be emphasized by the fact that this study of the river was made during the summer months when the river was sluggish and when there were no heavy rains to create flood conditions, which tend to flush out this section of the river and so carry the sewage many miles into the lake. Again, it must be understood that septic action is not a complete means of sewage purification, although its value in the process of purification is of great importance. It is, in fact, little more than the primary step in the production of a finished purified sewage effluent.

The chemical and mineral analyses of the sewage, taken direct from the sewer outlets in the upper part of the river and those which overflow into the canal, show an effluent which compares almost exactly with the lake water that is obtained through the water-works intake, the reason being that the water had been used principally for cooling and condensing purposes. In the ten miles of river between Gary and the canal there are but two sewers carrying domestic sewage, one of which is from the city of Gary. Its analysis is typical of such waste. The other, which is from Indiana Harbor and which, as has already been explained, carries a vast amount of seep water, is so dilute that the analytical results compare quite favorably with that of lake water and thus has little effect upon the conditions of the river except from a bacterial standpoint. The only other sewer outlets are from the Gary Steel Plant, where the water was found to be used only for cooling purposes, and from the Grasselli Chemical Works, where the same use is made of it. With this small amount of contamination and the opportunities afforded for purification by dilution and sedimentation, the reason for this improved condition is apparent. We find from the analyses that the sewer outlets through Hammond discharge typical sewage wastes and that the refuse material coming from the Hammond Glue Works is the most offensive and the most highly mineralized offal that is to be found at any point in the river. The refuse entering the river from this one point should have immediate attention, because it is not only the greatest source of contamination in the river, but the stench coming from it is so vile as to be almost nauseating. It is a condition which can be easily cared for and one that is cared for by the Hearst-Stein Glue Works, on the opposite side of the river, where large settling basins are installed and an effluent produced which contains practically no organic matter. These concentrated sewer effluents are clearly responsible for the gross contamination found through this section. The rest of the sewers between West Hammond and South Chicago discharge typical sewage effluents; but there are but five of them, and the opportunities for dilution and the time allowed for sedimentation satisfactorily explain the fact of the river along this point being found in an improved condition.

The mere fact that the Grand Calumet River passes through the principal business section of Hammond in the polluted condition above described, is a weighty reason why the people of that city should take immediate steps for its purification.

METHODS OF SEWAGE DISPOSAL.

In order to learn the manner in which to purify a river by sewage disposal, it is first of all necessary to understand what sewage is. Undoubtedly the best and most expressive definition that can be given is—dirty water. If a thousand parts of sewage are analyzed as it flows into the sewers we find that it contains approximately 998 parts of pure water, one part of mineral matter and one part of organic matter. It is the single part of organic matter or the one-thousandth part of sewage that gives all the trouble and causes all the expense which must be charged against sewage disposal. The fact that sewage is almost wholly water explains also why the utilization of this manurial content has not been found practicable. It is practically only on an irrigation proposition that any utilization can be considered, due to the necessity for a continuous application of the sewage, irrespective of rain. Special provisions must be made during wet weather, either for wasting the sewage into the rivers or for temporarily stowing it in basins. As no possibility of sewage disposal of this nature exists in northern Indiana, other methods for its destruction must be employed. Some of the available methods now being used successfully in both this country and in Europe are the treatment of sewage in settling or septic tanks followed by final treatment on intermittent sand filters, contact beds or sprinkling filters.

It is not the intent of this report to state what the solution should be, but simply to outline the conditions and leave it for further consideration, because, realizing the rapid growth now taking place through the Calumet district, and the possibilities of these cities, so closely bound together, uniting and becoming one municipality, the final solution should be one which not only answers the present needs but can fulfill any future requirements. In order that the problem may be met immediately to the satisfaction of all concerned, it would seem advisable, and it is recommended that a Sanitary District be formed to study these conditions for the purpose of reaching a final solution to take care of the entire drainage area of the Calumet River, this work to be carried on along similar lines to that of the Sanitary District of Chicago and to work with them jointly or, perhaps through proper legislation, to unite with them for the purpose of studying the conditions and solving the problem for this entire region.

KEY TO SAMPLING POINTS.

Number.	Location.
1.	East Chicago Water Intake.
2.	Canal—Inland Steel Co. Plant.
3.	Canal—Pennsylvania Railroad Bridge.
4.	Canal—Forks connecting Lake George.
5.	Canal—East Chicago Traction Bridge.
6.	Canal—Junction of Calumet River.
7.	Grand Calumet—One mile east of Wabash Railroad Bridge.
8.	Grand Calumet—Wabash Railroad Bridge at Clark.
9.	Grand Calumet—One mile west of Clark Road Bridge.
10.	Grand Calumet—Elgin, Joliet and Eastern Railroad Bridge.
11.	Grand Calumet—Indiana Harbor Sewer.
12.	Grand Calumet—One-half mile west of C., L. S. & V. S. Electric Railroad.
13.	Grand Calumet—One-half mile east of Grasselli Chemical Works.
14.	Grand Calumet—Grasselli Chemical Works Sewer.
15.	Grand Calumet—Indiana Harbor Railroad Bridge at Grasselli.
16.	Grand Calumet—One-half mile east of Canal.
17.	Grand Calumet—One-half mile west of Canal.
18.	Grand Calumet—East Chicago Sewer.
19.	Grand Calumet—One-half mile west of East Chicago Sewer.
20.	Grand Calumet—Columbia Ave. Bridge, Hammond.
21.	Grand Calumet—Calumet Ave. Bridge, Hammond.
22.	Grand Calumet—Michigan Ave. Bridge, Hammond.
23.	Grand Calumet—Hohman Ave. Bridge, Hammond.
24.	Grand Calumet—Erie Railroad Bridge, Hammond.
25.	Grand Calumet—Chicago, Hammond and Western Railroad Bridge.
26.	Grand Calumet—Hammond Glue Works.
27.	Grand Calumet—Chicago Terminal Transfer Railroad Bridge.
28.	Grand Calumet—Rand Ave. Bridge.
29.	Grand Calumet—One-half mile east of South Chicago and Southern Railroad Bridge.
30.	Grand Calumet—South Chicago and Southern Railroad Bridge.
31.	Grand Calumet—The Junction.
32.	Little Calumet—Michigan Central Railroad Bridge.

Number	Location
33.	Little Calumet—Chicago City Limits.
34.	Little Calumet—Illinois Central Railroad Bridge, Riverdale.
35.	Grand Calumet—One-half mile west of Junction.
36.	Grand Calumet—Kensington and Eastern Railroad Bridge.
37.	Grand Calumet—The Forks.
38.	Grand Calumet—South Chicago and St. Louis Railroad Bridge.
39.	Grand Calumet—Entrance to Old River Bed.
40.	Grand Calumet—106th St. Bridge, South Chicago.
41.	Grand Calumet—L. S. & M. S. Railroad Bridge, South Chicago.
42.	Grand Calumet—92d St. Bridge, South Chicago.
43.	Grand Calumet—Mouth of South Chicago Harbor.

CALUMET RIVER DISTRICT.

DEPTH OF RIVER AT SAMPLING POINTS.

Sampling Point.	Depth in Feet.	Sampling Point.	Depth in Feet.
1	23	23	6
	23	24	6½
	23	25	7
	23	26	5½
	12½	27	5
	12½	28	
	8	29	
	9½	30	6
9	9½	31	6½
10	7½	32	7½
11	8½	33	7½
12	7½	34	8¼
13	7½	35	8½
14	6	36	9½
15	5	37	7
16	7½	38	8
17	6½	39	12
18	4½	40	20
19	4	41	24
20	5	42	25
21	6½	43	27
22	5		

Soundings taken when the river was at the average mean level.

TABLE No. 1.—CALUMET RIVER DISTRICT.

NUMBER OF BACTERIA PER C.C. IN CALUMET RIVER, JUNE 29, 1910.

Laboratory Number.	Sampling Point.	Bacteria.	B. Coli Presumptive.	Sowing Diluted.	Remarks.
1700-A	6	52,500	+	1/100	
1701-A	16	48,000	+	1/000	Wind northwest to southeast.
1702-A	17	70,000	+	1/000	
1703-A	18	140,000	+	1/000	Basin medium height.
1704-A	19	200,000	Gas.	1/100	
1705-A	20	24,000	+	1/100	
1706-A	21	4,000,000	+	1/100	
1707-A	22	2,500,000	+	1/100	
1708-A	23	1,500,000	+	1/100	

TABLE No. 2—CALUMET RIVER DISTRICT.

NUMBER OF BACTERIA PER C.C. IN CALUMET RIVER, JULY 1, 1910.

Laboratory Number.	Sampling Point.	Bacteria.	B. Coli Presumptive.	Sowing Diluted.	Remarks.
1709-A	6	150,000	Gas.	1/10	Sowings made in 1/10 dilution is the cause of not being able to count plates. Wind north to south.
1710-A	16	60,000	+	1/10	
1711-A	17	85,000	+	1/10	
1712-A	18	125,000	+	1/10	
1713-A	19	200,000	+	1/00	
1714-A	21	Over growth.	+	1/10	
1715-A	22	Over growth.	+	1/10	
1716-A	23	Over growth.	+	1/10	
1717-A	24	Over growth.	+	1/10	
1718-A	25	Over growth.	+	1/10	
1719-A	26	Over growth.	+	1/10	
1720-A	27	Over growth.	+	1/10	

TABLE No. 3.—CALUMET RIVER DISTRICT.

NUMBER OF BACTERIA PER C.C. IN CALUMET RIVER, JULY 2, 1910.

Laboratory Number.	Sampling Point.	Bacteria.	B. Coli Presumptive.	Sowing Diluted.	Remarks.
1721-A	1	30,000	Suspicious.	1/10	Wind south to north.
1722-A	2	40,000	+	1/10	
1723-A	4	10,000	+	1/10	
1724-A	5	67,000	+	1/10	
1725-A	6	5,000	+	1/10	
1726-A	15	3,000	+	1/10	
1727-A	16	4,000	+	1/10	
1728-A	17	60,000	+	1/10	
1729-A	18	100,000	+	1/10	
1730-A	19	30,000	+	1/10	
1731-A	20	15,000	+	1/10	
1732-A	21	Over growth.	+	1/10	
1733-A	22	Over growth.	+	1/10	
1734-A	23	Over growth.	+	1/10	
1735-A	24	Over growth.	+	1/10	
1736-A	25	Over growth.	+	1/10	
1737-A	26	Over growth.	+	1/10	
1738-A	27	Over growth.	+	1/10	

TABLE No. 4.—CALUMET RIVER DISTRICT.

NUMBER OF BACTERIA PER C.C. IN CALUMET RIVER, JULY 7, 1910.

Laboratory Number.	Sampling Point.	Bacteria.	B. Coli Presumptive.	Sowing Diluted.	Remarks.
1739-A	7	20,000	+	1/100	Wind south to north.
1740-A	8	150,000	+	1/100	
1741-A	9	20,000	Gas.	1/100	
1742-A	10	25,000	+	1/100	
1743-A	11	75,000	+	1/100	
1744-A	12	90,000	+	1/100	
1745-A	13	60,000	+	1/100	
1746-A	14	12,500	+	1/100	
1747-A	15	7,500	+	1/100	
1748-A	16	15,000	+	1/100	
1749-A	6	30,000	+	1/100	
1750-A	5	20,000	+	1/100	

TABLE No. 5.—CALUMET RIVER DISTRICT.

NUMBER OF BACTERIA PER C.C. IN CALUMET RIVER, JULY 8, 1910.

Laboratory Number.	Sampling Point.	Bacteria.	B. Coli.Presumptive.	Sowing Diluted.	Remarks.
1751–A	1	510	Gas.	1/10	Wind south to north.
1752–A	2	1,400	+	1/10	
1753–A	3	2,000	+	1/10	
1754–A	4	2,500	+	1/10	
1755–A	5	4,000	+	1/10	
1756–A	6	7,000	+	1/100	
1757–A	17	8,000	+	1/1000	
1758–A	18	5,400,000	+	1/1000	
1759–A	19	300,000	+	1/1000	
1760–A	20	20,000	+	1/1000	
1761–A	21	10,000,000	+	1/1000	
1762–A	22	Liquified.	+	1/1000	
1763–A	23	8,000,000	+	1/1000	
1764–A	24	12,000,000	+	1/1000	
1765–A	25	7,000,000	+	1/1000	
1766–A	26	4,500,000	+	1/1000	
1767–A	27	3,250,000	+	1/1000	
1768–A	28	7,500,000	+	1/1000	
1769–A	29	5,000,000	+	1/1000	

TABLE No. 6.—CALUMET RIVER DISTRICT.

NUMBER OF BACTERIA PER C.C. IN CALUMET RIVER, JULY 11, 1910.

Laboratory Number.	Sampling Point.	Bacteria.	B. Coli Presumptive.	Sowing Diluted.	Remarks.
1770-A	30	1,485,000	+	1/1000	Wind southeast to northwest.
1771-A	31	1,000,000	+	1/1000	
1772-A	32	4,000	Gas.	1/1000	
1773-A	33	25,000	+	1/1000	Lake current southeast to northwest.
1774-A	34	560,000	+	1/1000	
1775-A	35	1,750,000	+	1/1000	River current west to east.
1776-A	36	960,000	Gas.	1/1000	Little Calumet into Grand Calumet.
1777-A	37	35,000	−	1/1000	
1778-A	38	75,000	Gas.	1/1000	
1779-A	39	14,000	Gas.	1/1000	
1780-A	40	272,000	+	1/1000	
1781-A	41	60,000	+	1/1000	
1782-A	42	115,000	+	1/1000	

TABLE No. 7.—CALUMET RIVER DISTRICT.

NUMBER OF BACTERIA PER C.C. IN CALUMET RIVER DISTRICT, JULY 12, 1910.

Laboratory Number.	Sampling Point.	Bacteria.	B. Coli Presumptive.	Sowing Diluted.	Remarks.
1783-A	1	10	–	1/10	
1784-A	2	400	–	1/10	Wind south to north.
1785-A	3	600	Gas.	1/10	
1786-A	4	5,000	+	1/10	
1787-A	5	3,600	Gas.	1/10	
1788-A	6	4,500	+	1/100	
1789-A	7	24,000	+	1/100	
1790-A	8	3,500	+	1/100	
1791-A	9	15,000	Gas.	1/100	
1792-A	10	3,600	Gas.	1/100	
1793-A	11	3,000	+	1/100	
1794-A	12	125,000	+	1/100	
1795-A	13	60,000	+	1/100	
1796-A	14	2,200	Gas.	1/100	
1797-A	15	4,000	+	1/100	
1798-A	16	7,500	+	1/100	
1799-A	17	1,700	+	1/100	

TABLE No. 8.—CALUMET RIVER DISTRICT.

NUMBER OF BACTERIA PER C.C. IN CALUMET RIVER DISTRICT, JULY 13, 1910.

Laboratory Number.	Sampling Point.	Bacteria.	B. Coli Presumptive.	Sowing Diluted.	Remarks.
1802-A	18	4,000	+	1/1000	Wind northeast to southwest.
1803-A	19	13,000	+	1/1000	
1804-A	20	33,000	+	1/1000	
1805-A	21	4,000,000	+	1/1000	Grand Calumet current east to west.
1806-A	22	2,500,000	+	1/1000	
1807-A	23	3,600,000	+	1/1000	
1808-A	24	6,000,000	+	1/1000	Little Calumet current down stream.
1809-A	25	5,400,000	+	1/1000	
1810-A	26	3,600,000	+	1/1000	
1811-A	27	4,500,000	+	1/1000	
1812-A	28	1,500,000	+	1/1000	
1813-A	29	2,100,000	+	1/1000	
1814-A	30	3,240,000	+	1/1000	
1815-A	31	3,100,000	+	1/1000	
1816-A	32	7,000	Gas.	1/1000	
1817-A	33	25,000	+	1/1000	
1818-A	34	40,000	+	1/1000	
1819-A	35	1,000,000	+	1/1000	
1820-A	37	275,000	Gas.	1/1000	

TABLE No. 9.—CALUMET RIVER DISTRICT.

NUMBER OF BACTERIA PER C.C. IN CALUMET RIVER DISTRICT, JULY 14, 1910.

Laboratory Number.	Sampling Point.	Bacteria.	B. Coli Presumptive.	Sowing Diluted.	Remarks.
1821-A	1	300	Gas.	1/10	
1822-A	2	1,750	+	1/10	Wind northeast to southwest.
1823-A	3	500	Gas.	1/10	
1824-A	4	2,500	Suspicious.	1/10	Lake current east to west.
1825-A	5	60,000	+	1/10	Grand Calumet west to east.
1826-A	6	12,500	+	1/100	
1827-A	7	30,000	+	1/100	
1828-A	8	120,000	+	1/100	
1829-A	9	6,300	+	1/100	
1830-A	10	5,000	+	1/100	
1831-A	11	500,000	+	1/100	
1832-A	12	25,000	+	1/100	
1833-A	13	60,000	+	1/100	
1834-A	14	3,500	+	1/100	
1835-A	15	3,000	Gas.	1/100	
1836-A	16	7,500	Gas.	1/100	
1837-A	17	30,000	Gas.	1/100	

TABLE No. 10.—CALUMET RIVER DISTRICT.

NUMBER OF BACTERIA PER C.C. IN CALUMET RIVER DISTRICT, JULY 15, 1910.

Laboratory Number.	Sampling Point.	Bacteria.	B. Coli Presumptive.	Sowing Diluted.	Remarks.
1838-A	18	18,000	+	1/1000	
1839-A	19	28,000	+	1/1000	Wind northeast to southwest.
1840-A	20	8,000	+	1/1000	
1841-A	21	75,000	Gas.	1/1000	Lake current east to west.
1842-A	22	2,900,000	+	1/1000	
1843-A	23	1,800,000	+	1/1000	Grand Calumet current east to west.
1844-A	24	1,400,000	+	1/1000	
1845-A	25	7,300,000	+	1/1000	Little Calumet down stream.
1846-A	27	3,750,000	+	1/1000	
1847-A	28	5,000,000	+	1/1000	
1848-A	29	2,500,000	+	1/1000	
1849-A	30	3,240,000	+	1/1000	
1850-A	31	2,160,000	+	1/1000	
1851-A	32	17,000	+	1/1000	
1852-A	33	38,000	Gas.	1/1000	
1853-A	34	740,000	+	1/1000	
1854-A	35	610,000	+	1/1000	
1855-A	36	530,000	+	1/1000	
1856-A	37	300,000	+	1/1000	
1857-A	38	37,000	Gas.	1/1000	
1858-A	39	14,000	Gas.	1/1000	
1859-A	40	40,000	+	1/1000	
1860-A	41	16,000	+	1/1000	
1861-A	42	35,000	+	1/1000	
1862-A	43	20,000	Slight gas.	1/1000	

TABLE No. 11.—CALUMET RIVER DISTRICT.

NUMBER OF BACTERIA PER C.C. IN CALUMET RIVER DISTRICT, JULY 18, 1910.

Laboratory Number.	Sampling Point.	Bacteria.	B. Coli Presumptive.	Sowing Diluted.	Remarks.
1863-A	3	940	Gas.	1/10	
1864-A	4	1,030	+	1/10	Wind north to south.
1865-A	5	3,600	+	1/10	Lake current north to south.
1866-A	6	12,000	+	1/10	
1867-A	7	600,000	+	1/100	Grand Calumet current from west to east.
1868-A	8	400,000	+	1/100	
1869-A	9	5,500	+	1/100	
1870-A	10	3,900	Suspicious.	1/100	There was a peculiarly turbid water near the chemical works during the time of sampling.
1871-A	11	24,000	+	1/100	
1872-A	12	18,000	+	1/100	
1873-A	13	....	+	1/100	
1874-A	14	....	+	1/100	
1875-A	15	2,000	Gas.	1/100	
1876-A	16	2,300	+	1/100	
1877-A	17	2,500	Suspicious.	1/100	

TABLE No. 12.—CALUMET RIVER DISTRICT.

NUMBER OF BACTERIA PER C.C. IN CALUMET RIVER DISTRICT, JULY 19, 1910.

Laboratory Number.	Sampling Point.	Bacteria.	B. Coli Presumptive.	Sowing Diluted.	Remarks.
1878-A	18	150,000	+	1/1000	
1879-A	19	60,000	+	1/1000	Wind south to west.
1880-A	20	11,000	+	1/1000	
1881-A	21	4,000,000	+	1/1000	Lake current north to south.
1882-A	22	8,100,000	+	1/1000	
1883-A	23	1,200,000	+	1/1000	Grand Calumet current west to east.
1884-A	24	840,000	+	1/1000	
1885-A	25	1,980,000	+	1/1000	Little Calumet current down stream.
1886-A	26	5,200,000	+	1/1000	
1887-A	27	4,300,000	+	1/1000	
1888-A	28	3,000,000	+	1/1000	
1889-A	29	2,400,000	+	1/1000	
1890-A	30	2,100,000	+	1/1000	
1891-A	31	1,800,000	+	1/1000	
1892-A	32	33,000	Gas.	1/1000	
1893-A	33	23,000	+	1/1000	
1894-A	34	230,000	+	1/1000	
1895-A	35	480,000	+	1/1000	
1896-A	36	55,000	Gas.	1/1000	
1897-A	37	20,000	Suspicious.	1/1000	
1898-A	38	14,000	+	1/1000	

TABLE No. 13.—CALUMET RIVER DISTRICT.

NUMBER OF BACTERIA PER C.C. IN CALUMET RIVER DISTRICT, JULY 21, 1910.

Laboratory Number.	Sampling Point.	Bacteria.	B. Coli Presumptive.	Sowing Diluted.	Remarks.
1899-A	1	50	Gas.	1/10	
1900-A	2	180	+	1/10	Wind south to north.
1901-A	3	3,600	Gas.	1/10	Lake current north to east.
1902-A	4	1,750	+	1/10	
1903-A	5	650	+	1/10	Grand Calumet current east to west.
1904-A	6	2,700	+	1/10	
1905-A	8	32,000	+	1/100	River very low.
1906-A	9	6,500	+	1/100	
1907-A	10	2,000	Gas.	1/100	
1908-A	11	1,500	Gas.	1/100	
1909-A	12	3,900	+	1/100	
1910-A	13	8,500	+	1/100	
1911-A	14	4,300	Gas.	1/100	
1912-A	15	3,500	+	1/100	
1913-A	16	2,100	+	1/100	
1914-A	17	5,000	+	1/100	
1915-A	18	30,000	+	1/100	
1916-A	19	17,500	+	1/100	

TABLE No. 14.—CALUMET RIVER DISTRICT.

NUMBER OF BACTERIA PER C.C. IN CALUMET RIVER DISTRICT, JULY 22, 1910.

Laboratory Number.	Sampling Point.	Bacteria.	B. Coli Presumptive.	Sowing Diluted.	Remarks.
1917-A	21	8,000,000	+	1/1000	
1918-A	22	10,800,000	+	1,1000	Wind south to north.
1919-A	23	240,000	+	1/1000	Lake current west to east.
1920-A	24	1,800,000	+	1/1000	Grand Calumet east to west current.
1921-A	25	540,000	+	1/1000	
1922-A	26	1,000,000	+	1/1000	Little Calumet current down stream.
1923-A	27	750,000	+	1/1000	
1924-A	28	1,600,000	+	1/1000	
1925-A	29	980,000	+	1/1000	
1926-A	30	2,200,000	+	1/1000	
1927-A	31	1,200,000	+	1/1000	
1928-A	32	35,000	+	1/1000	
1929-A	33	48,000	+	1/1000	
1930-A	34	90,000	+	1/1000	

TABLE No. 15.—CALUMET RIVER DISTRICT.

NUMBER OF BACTERIA PER C.C. IN CALUMET RIVER DISTRICT, JULY 26, 1910.

Laboratory Number.	Sampling Point.	Bacteria.	B. Coli Presumptive.	Sowing Diluted.	Remarks.
1932-A	1	60	+	1/10	
1933-A	2	840	+	1/10	Wind southeast to northwest.
1934-A	3	927	Gas.	1/10	
1935-A	4	700	+	1/10	Lake current east to west.
1936-A	5	12,000	+	1/10	
1937-A	6	3,600	+	1/10	Big Calumet east to west current.
1938-A	8	15,000	+	1/100	
1939-A	9	8,500	+	1/100	
1940-A	10	4,000	Gas.	1/100	
1941-A	11	3,800	+	1/100	
1942-A	12	30,000	+	1/100	
1943-A	13	120,000	+	1/100	
1944-A	14	35,000	+	1/100	
1945-A	15	12,000	+	1/100	
1946-A	16	24,000	+	1/100	
1947-A	17	6,000	+	1/1000	

TABLE No. 16.—CALUMET RIVER DISTRICT.

NUMBER OF BACTERIA PER C.C. IN CALUMET RIVER DISTRICT, JULY 27, 1910.

Laboratory Number.	Sampling Point.	Bacteria.	B. Coli Presumptive.	Sowing Diluted.	Remarks.
1949-A	18	14,000	+	1/1000	Wind northeast to southwest.
1950-A	19	21,000	+	1/1000	
1951-A	20	43,000	+	1/1000	
1952-A	21	1,800,000	+	1/1000	Lake current northeast to southwest.
1953-A	22	100,000	+	1/1000	
1954-A	23	800,000	+	1/1000	Grand Calumet current east to west.
1955-A	24	1,600,000	+	1/1000	
1956-A	25	1,400,000	+	1/1000	Little Calumet down stream.
1957-A	26	4,500,000	+	1/1000	
1958-A	27	3,000,000	+	1/1000	
1959-A	28	11,000,000	+	1/1000	
1960-A	29	8,600,000	Gas.	1/1000	
1961-A	30	14,000,000	+	1/1000	
1962-A	31	400,000	+	1/1000	
1963-A	32	120,000	+	1/1000	
1964-A	33	80,000	Gas.	1/1000	
1965-A	34	73,000	+	1/1000	
1966-A	35	34,000	Gas.	1/1000	
1967-A	36	146,000	+	1/1000	
1968-A	38	40,000	Gas.	1/1000	
1969-A	39	22,000	+	1/1000	
1970-A	37	85,000	+	1/1000	
1971-A	40	18,000	+	1/1000	
1972-A	41	72,000	+	1/1000	
1973-A	42	100,000	+	1/1000	
1974-A	43	60,000	+	1/1000	

TABLE No. 17.—CALUMET RIVER DISTRICT.

NUMBER OF BACTERIA PER C.C. IN CALUMET RIVER DISTRICT, JULY 29, 1910.

Laboratory Number.	Sampling Point.	Bacteria.	B. Coli Presumptive.	Sowing Diluted.	Remarks.
1975-A	1	90	–	1/10	
1976-A	2	650	+	1/10	Wind north to south.
1977-A	3	250	Gas.	1/10	Lake current east to west.
1978-A	4	1,500	+	1/10	
1979-A	5	10	–	1/10	Grand Calumet current east to west.
1980-A	6	850	+	1/10	
1981-A	8	2,100	Gas.	1/100	River low.
1982-A	9	1,400	Gas.	1/100	
1983-A	10	400	Gas.	1/100	
1984-A	11	1,500	+	1/100	
1985-A	12	4,000	+	1/100	
1986-A	13	7,600	+	1/100	
1987-A	14	9,000	+	1/100	
1988-A	15	1,200	+	1/100	
1989-A	16	2,500	+	1/100	
1990-A	17	1,300	+	1/100	
1991-A	18	48,000	+	1/100	
1992-A	19	900	Gas.	1/100	

TABLE No. 18.—CALUMET RIVER DISTRICT.

NUMBER OF BACTERIA PER C.C. IN CALUMET RIVER DISTRICT, AUGUST 1, 1910.

Laboratory Number.	Sampling Point.	Bacteria.	B. Coli Presumptive.	Sowing Diluted.	Remarks.
1994-A	19	8,000	+	1/1000	
1995-A	20	780,000	+	1/1000	Wind south to north.
1996-A	21	1,600,000	+	1/1000	
1997-A	22	900,000	+	1/1000	Lake current east to west.
1998-A	23	140,000	+	1/1000	
1999-A	24	115,000	+	1/1000	Grand Calumet current east to west.
2000-A	25	93,000	+	1/1000	
2001-A	26	1,100,000	+	1/1000	
2002-A	27	900,000	+	1/1000	Little Calumet up stream.
2003-A	28	85,000	+	1/1000	
2004-A	29	600,000	+	1/1000	
2005-A	30	400,000	+	1/1000	
2006-A	31	4,000	+	1/1000	
2007-A	32	1,000	Gas.	1/1000	
2008-A	33	55,000	+	1/1000	
2009-A	34	360,000	+	1/1000	
2010-A	35	36,000	+	1/1000	
2011-A	36	31,000	Gas.	1/1000	
2012-A	37	23,000	+	1/1000	
2013-A	38	6,000	+	1/1000	
2014-A	39	3,000	+	1/1000	
2015-A	40	5,000	+	1/1000	
2016-A	41	2,000	+	1/1000	
2017-A	42	24,000	+	1/1000	

TABLE No. 19.—CALUMET RIVER DISTRICT.

NUMBER OF BACTERIA PER C.C. IN CALUMET RIVER, JUNE 29, 1910, TO AUGUST 1, 1910.

Sampling Point.	Bacteria.			B. Coli Present During Test, Per Cent. of Days.
	Maximum.	Minimum.	Average.	
1	30,000	10	4,431	14.3
2	40,000	180	6,460	85.7
3	10,000	250	2,352	25.0
4	67,000	700	10,249	87.5
5	60,000	10	15,696	77.7
6	150,000	850	27,565	90.9
7	600,000	20,000	168,500	100.0
8	400,000	2,100	46,086	85.7
9	20,000	1,400	9,029	57.1
10	25,000	400	6,271	28.5
11	500,000	1,500	86,971	87.5
12	125,000	3,900	42,291	100.0
13	120,000	7,600	52,683	100.0
14	35,000	2,200	11,083	71.4
15	12,000	1,200	4,525	75.0
16	60,000	2,100	17,290	90.0
17	85,000	1,300	26,950	80.0
18	5,400,000	4,000	602,900	100.0
19	300,000	900	79,845	81.8
20	780,000	8,000	116,750	100.0
21	10,000,000	75,000	4,184,375	90.0
22	10,800,000	100,000	3,971,428	100.0

TABLE No. 19.—Continued

Sampling Point.	Bacteria.			B. Coli Present During Test, Per Cent. of Days.
	Maximum.	Minimum.	Average.	
23	8,100,000	140,000	1,434,286	100.0
24	12,000,000	115,000	3,170,714	100.0
25	7,000,000	98,000	2,945,500	100.0
26	7,300,000	540,000	3,820,000	100.0
27	4,500,000	90,000	2,957,143	100.0
28	11,000,000	85,000	4,119,286	100.0
29	8,600,000	600,000	3,257,143	85.7
30	14,000,000	40,000	3,783,571	100.0
31	3,100,000	4,000	1,523,286	100.0
32	1,200,000	1,000	197,429	42.8
33	80,000	23,000	40,143	71.4
34	740,000	40,000	293,000	100.0
35	1,750,000	34,000	571,429	83.3
36	960,000	31,000	332,833	40.0
37	85,000	20,000	38,333	50.0
38	75,000	6,000	20,400	40.0
39	23,000	3,000	13,250	50.0
40	272,000	5,000	83,750	100.0
41	73,000	2,000	37,500	100.0
42	115,000	24,000	68,500	100.0
43	60,000	20,000	40,000	50.0

TABLE No. 20.—CALUMET RIVER DISTRICT.

B. COLI POSITIVE TEST, AUGUST 4, 1910.

Laboratory Number.	Sampling Point.	Lactose Broth.	Agar Culture.	Gelatine Tube.	Dextrose Broth.	Indol Reaction.	Nitrite Reduction.	Results.
1	2	+	+	+	+	+	+	+
2	3	+	+	+	+	+	+	+
3	4	+	+	+	+	+	+	+
[illegible]	5	+	+	+	+	+	+	+
5	6	+	+	+	+	+	+	+
6	8	+	+	+	+	+	−	−
[illegible]	9	+	+	+	+	+	−	−
8	10	+	+	+	+	−	−	−
9	11	+	+	+	+	+	−	−
10	12	+	+	+	+	+	+	+
11	13	+	+	−	−	−	−	−
12	14	+	+	+	+	+	+	+
13	15	+	+	+	+	+	+	+
14	16	+	+	+	+	+	+	+

TABLE No. 21.—CALUMET RIVER DISTRICT.

B. COLI POSITIVE TEST, AUGUST 5, 1910.

Laboratory Number.	Sampling Point.	Lactose Broth.	Agar Culture.	Gelatine Tube.	Dextrose Broth.	Indol Reaction.	Nitrite Reduction.	Results.
15	17	+	+	+	+	+	+	+
16	18	+	+	+	+	+	−	−
17	19	+	+	+	+	+	+	+
18	20	+	+	+	+	+	+	+
19	21	+	+	+	+	+	+	+
20	22	+	+	+	+	+	+	+
21	23	+	+	+	+	+	+	+
22	24	+	+	+	+	+	+	+
23	25	+	+	+	+	+	+	+
24	26	+	+	+	+	+	+	+
25	27	+	+	+	+	+	+	+
26	28	+	+	+	+	+	+	+
27	29	+	+	+	+	+	+	+
28	30	+	+	+	+	+	+	+
29	31	+	+	+	+	+	+	+
30	32	+	+	−	+	+	+	−
31	33	+	+	+	+	+	+	+
32	34	+	+	+	+	+	+	+
33	35	+	+	+	+	+	−	−
34	36	+	+	+	+	+	+	+
35	37	+	+	+	+	+	+	+
36	38	+	+	−	+	+	−	−
37	39	+	+	+	+	+	+	+
38	40	+	+	+	+	+	+	−
39	41	+	+	−	+	+	+	−
40	42	+	+	+	+	+	+	+
41	43	+	+	+	+	+	+	+

TABLE No. 22.—CALUMET RIVER DISTRICT.

B. COLI POSITIVE TEST, AUGUST 12, 1910.

Laboratory Number.	Sampling Point.	Lactose Broth.	Agar Culture.	Gelatine Tube.	Dextrose Broth.	Indol Reaction.	Nitrite Reduction.	Results.
42	1	+	+	+	+	+	+	+
43	2	+	+	+	+	+	+	+
44	3	+	+	+	+	+	+	+
45	4	+	+	+	+	+	−	−
46	5	+	+	−	−	−	−	−
47	6	+	+	+	+	+	+	+
48	8	+	+	+	+	+	+	+
[49	9	+	+	+	+	+	+	+
50	10	+	+	+	+	+	+	+
51	11	+	+	+	+	+	+	+
52	12	+	+	+	+	+	+	+
53	13	+	+	+	+	+	+	+
54	14	+	+	+	+	+	+	+
55	15	+	+	+	+	+	+	+
56	16	+	+	+	+	+	+	+
57	17	+	+	+	+	+	+	+
58	18	+	+	+	+	+	−	−
59	19	+	+	+	+	+	+	+
60	20	+	+	+	+	+	+	+
61	21	+	+	+	+	+	+	+

TABLE No. 23.—CALUMET RIVER DISTRICT.

B. COLI POSITIVE TEST, AUGUST 15, 1910.

Laboratory Number.	Sampling Point.	Lactose Broth.	Agar Culture.	Gelatine Tube.	Dextrose Broth.	Indol Reaction.	Nitrite Reduction.	Results.
62	22	+	+	+	+	+	+	+
63	23	+	+	+	−	+	+	−
64	24	+	+	+	+	+	+	+
65	25	+	+	+	+	−	+	−
66	26	+	+	+	+	+	+	+
67	27	+	+	+	+	+	+	+
68	28	+	+	+	+	+	+	+
69	29	+	+	+	+	+	+	+
70	30	+	+	+	+	+	+	+
71	31	+	+	+	+	+	+	+
72	32	+	+	+	−	−	+	−
73	33	+	+	+	−	+	+	−
74	34	+	+	+	+	−	+	−

TABLE No. 24.—CALUMET RIVER DISTRICT.

B. COLI POSITIVE TEST, AUGUST 17, 1910.

Laboratory Number.	Sampling Point.	Lactose Broth.	Agar Culture.	Gelatine Tube.	Dextrose Broth.	Indol Reaction.	Nitrite Reduction.	Results.
75	35	+	+	+	+	+	+	+
76	36	+	+	+	+	+	+	+
77	37	+	+	+	+	+	+	+
78	38	+	+	+	−	+	−	−
79	39	+	+	+	+	+	+	+
80	40	+	+	−	+	+	+	−
81	41	+	+	+	−	+	+	−
82	42	+	+	+	+	+	+	+
83	43	+	+	−	+	−	−	−

TABLE No. 25.—CALUMET RIVER DISTRICT.

CHEMICAL ANALYSIS IN PARTS PER 100,000, AUGUST 8, 1910.

Laboratory Number.	Sampling Point.	Nitrates.	Nitrites.	Chlorine.	Alkalinity.
1	1	.0050	.0001	1.8	11.6
2	2	.0050	.0100	1.0	11.4
3	3	.0050	.1000	1.2	13.0
4	4	.0050	.2000	1.3	13.0
5	5	.0050	.2000	1.6	13.6
6	6	.0050	.1000	1.3	13.2
7	8	.0050	.0050	.9	12.6
8	9	.0050	.0070	.9	12.8
9	10	.0050	.0080	.9	12.8
10	11	.0050	.0300	.9	13.2
11	12	.0050	.0200	1.0	13.4
12	13	.0050	.0200	1.0	14.0
13	14	.0050	.0400	1.0	14.2
14	15	.0050	.2000	2.0	13.4
15	16	.0050	.2000	1.4	12.6
16	17	.0050	.2000	1.3	13.2
17	18	.0050	.2000	1.6	14.4
18	19	.0050	.2000	1.7	13.8
19	20	.0050	.1000	1.5	13.2
20	21	.0050	.0005	2.6	14.4

TABLE No. 26.—CALUMET RIVER DISTRICT.

CHEMICAL ANALYSIS IN PARTS PER 100,000, AUGUST 10, 1910.

Laboratory Number.	Sampling Point.	Nitrates.	Nitrites.	Chlorine.	Alkalinity.
21	22	.0600	.0001	1.5	19.0
22	23	.0050	.0001	3.0	17.6
23	24	.0050	.0001	3.2	15 4
24	25	.0050	.0001	3.0	14.4
25	26	.0050	.0001	4.4	15.6
26	27	.0050	.0001	3.5	16.8
27	28	.0050	.0001	3.7	16.8
28	29	.0050	.0001	3.4	16.2
29	30	.0050	.0001	4.4	18.0
30	31	.0050	.0001	3.5	17.8
31	32	.0050	.0360	2.7	22.2
32	33	.0050	.0220	2.7	22.2
33	34	.0050	.0140	2.8	22.2
34	35	.0050	.0001	3.3	19.0
35	36	.0050	.0001	3.4	21.6
36	37	.0050	.0400	3.0	21.6
37	38	.0050	.0440	3.5	19.4
38	39	.0050	.0001	3.8	19.4
39	40	.0050	.0040	3.9	20.0
40	41	.0050	.0120	3.2	18.8
41	42	.0050	.0200	1.5	13.4
42	43	.0050	.0200	1.5	10.8

TABLE No. 27.—CALUMET RIVER DISTRICT.

CHEMICAL ANALYSIS IN PARTS PER 100,000, AUGUST 12, 1910.

Laboratory Number.	Sampling Point.	Nitrates.	Nitrites.	Chlorine.	Alkalinity.
43	1	.0050	.0002	.6	11.6
44	2	.0050	.0600	1.4	11.6
45	3	.0050	.0600	1.4	11.1
46	4	.0050	.0600	1.2	13.4
47	5	.0050	.0600	1.5	13.2
48	6	.0050	.0700	1.2	13.2
49	8	.0050	.0400	1.0	12.6
50	9	.0050	.0400	.9	12.8
51	10	.0050	.0400	.9	12.6
52	11	.0050	.0400	1.0	12.6
53	12	.0050	.0440	1.1	13.0
54	13	.0050	.0600	1.0	13.4
55	14	.0050	.0600	1.1	13.8
56	15	.0050	.0700	1.3	13.8
57	16	.0050	.0760	1.4	13.6
58	17	.0050	.0760	1.3	13.0
59	18	.0050	.0700	1.2	13.6
60	19	.0050	.0600	1.3	14.0
61	20	.0050	.0500	1.4	13.8
62	21	.0050	.0002	11.0	14.8

TABLE No. 28.—CALUMET RIVER DISTRICT.

CHEMICAL ANALYSIS IN PARTS PER 100,000, AUGUST 15, 1910.

Laboratory Number.	Sampling Point.	Nitrates.	Nitrites.	Chlorine.	Alkalinity.
63	22	.0050	.0600	2.0	15.0
64	23	.0050	.0360	2.0	15.6
65	24	.0050	.0200	2.0	14.6
66	25	.0050	.0160	2.0	15.0
67	26	.0050	.0001	2.0	17.0
68	27	.0050	.0001	2.0	16.4
69	28	.0050	.0001	2.3	15.8
70	29	.0050	.0001	2.4	16.2
71	30	.0050	.0001	2.5	17.2
72	31	.0050	.0001	2.7	17.0
73	32	.0050	.0400	2.7	22.0
74	33	.0050	.0400	2.7	22.0
75	34	.0050	.0600	2.8	21.8

TABLE No. 29.—CALUMET RIVER DISTRICT.

CHEMICAL ANALYSIS IN PARTS PER 100,000, AUGUST 17, 1910.

Laboratory Number.	Sampling Point.	Nitrates.	Nitrites.	Chlorine.	Alkalinity.
76	35	.0050	.0001	3.3	19.4
77	36	.0050	.0001	3.2	18 4
78	37	.0050	.0600	3.1	18.6
79	38	.0050	.0800	2.9	18.6
80	39	.0050	.0400	3.6	19.4
81	40	.0050	.0180	3.8	19.6
82	41	.0050	.0340	4.1	20.0
83	42	.0050	.0008	3.7	19.6
84	43	.0050	.0004	2.2	14.0

TABLE No. 30.—CALUMET RÌVER DISTRICT.

DISSOLVED OXYGEN IN PARTS PER 100,000, JULY 26, 1910.

Laboratory Number.	Sampling Point.	
	1	.78
		.65
		.48
		.30
		.29
		.20
		.14
	9	.27
9	10	.40
10	11	.39
11	12	.29
12	13	.10
13	14	.25
14	15	.30
15	16	.25
16	17	.26

TABLE No. 31.—CALUMET RIVER DISTRICT.

DISSOLVED OXYGEN IN PARTS PER 100,000, JULY 29, 1910.

	Sampling Point.	Dissolved Oxyg
17	18	.43
18	19	.91
19	20	.33
20	21	.41
21	22	.28
22	23	.48
23	24	.23
24	25	.34
25	26	.27
26	27	.19
27	28	.26
28	29	.41
29	30	.02
30	31	.50
31	32	1.06
32	33	.66
33	34	.35
34	35	.21
35	36	.27
36	37	.40
37	38	.19

TABLE No. 32.—CALUMET RIVER DISTRICT.

DISSOLVED OXYGEN IN PARTS PER 100,000, JULY 29, 1910.

Laboratory Number.	Sampling Point.	Dissolved Oxygen.
38	1	.87
39	[illegible]	.57
40	[illegible]	.42
41	[illegible]	.24
42	[illegible]	.21
43	6	.17
44	8	17
45	9	.26
46	10	.36
47	11	.33
48	12	.23
49	13	.17
50	14	.36
51	15	.20
52	16	.21
53	17	.27
54	18	.26
55	19	.21

TABLE No. 33.—CALUMET RIVER DISTRICT.

DISSOLVED OXYGEN IN PARTS PER 100,000, AUGUST 1, 1910.

	Sampling Point.	
56	19	.48
57	20	.47
58	21	.19
59	22	.19
60	23	.19
61	24	.14
62	25	.13
63	26	.06
64	27	.08
65	28	.38
66	29	.34
67	30	.16
68	31	.23
69	32	.24
70	33	.33
71	34	.11
72	35	.17
73	36	.11
74	37	.50
75	38	.33
76	39	.21
77	40	.07
78	41	.11
79	42	.02

TABLE No. 34.—CALUMET RIVER DISTRICT

DISSOLVED OXYGEN IN PARTS PER 100,000, AUGUST 19, 1910.

Laboratory Number.	Sampling Point.	Dissolved Oxygen.
80	Indiana Harbor Sewer	.31
81	Gibson Sewer	.14
82	East Chicago Sewer	.02
83	Standard Steel Car Co. Sewer	Trace.
84	Calumet Ave. Sewer, North Side	.26
85	Calumet Ave. Sewer, South Side	.09
86	Hohman Ave. Sewer	.31
87	Hammond Gas Works Sewer	.00
88	Hammond Glue Works East Sewer	.00
89	Hammond Glue Works West Sewer	.00
	AUGUST 22, 1910.	
90	West Hammond Sewer	.18
91	U. S. Rolling Stock Sewer	.00
92	Lake Calumet 115th St. Sewer	.28
93	Lake Calumet 111th St. Sewer	.40
94	Hegewisch Sewer	.18
95	Glue Works East Sewer	.00
96	Hammond Glue Works Center Sewer	.00
97	Hammond Glue Works West Sewer	.00
98	Hammond Gas Works Sewer	.00
99	Hohman Ave. Sewer	.20
100	Calumet Ave. Sewer	.16

TABLE No. 35.—CALUMET RIVER DISTRICT.

DISSOLVED OXYGEN IN PARTS PER 100,000, AUGUST 24, 1910.

Laboratory Number.	Sampling Point.	Dissolved Oxygen.
101	Indiana Harbor Sewer	.25
102	Gibson Sewer	.22
103	East Chicago Sewer	.60
104	Standard Steel Car Co. Sewer	.09
105	Calumet Ave. North Sewer	.03
	AUGUST 31, 1910.	
106	Gary Steel Plant Sewer, 4 ft.	.55
107	Gary City Sewer	.00
	SEPTEMBER 2, 1910.	
108	Hammond Glue Works West Sewer	.00
109	West Hammond Sewer	.00
110	U. S. Rolling Stock Sewer	.23
111	Hegewisch Sewer	.38
	SEPTEMBER 3, 1910.	
112	Gary Steel Plant 24-Inch Sewer	.59
113	Gary Steel Plant 4-Foot Sewer	.62
114	Gary City Sewer	.00

TABLE No. 36.—CALUMET RIVER DISTRICT.

OXYGEN CONSUMED IN PARTS PER 100,000, AUGUST 2, 1910.

	Sampling Point.	
	9	.245
		.215
		.360
		.325
		.305
		.295
	9	.330
	10	.325
9	11	.345
10	12	.340
11	13	.275
12	14	.275
13	15	.335
14	16	.330
15	17	.295
16	18	.370
17	19	.320

TABLE No. 37.—CALUMET RIVER DISTRICT.

OXYGEN CONSUMED IN PARTS PER 100,000, AUGUST 3, 1910.

tory Number.	Sampling Point.	
18	20	.500
19	21	.995
20	22	.840
21	23	3.490
22	24	2.245
23	25	2.675
24	26	3.280
25	27	4.425
26	28	2.200
27	29	1.435
28	30	1.495
29	31	1.085
30	32	1.005
31	33	.960
32	34	.995
33	35	.895
34	36	1.005
35	37	.920
36	38	.875
37	39	.860
38	40	.900
39	41	.880
40	42	.735
41	43	.550

TABLE No. 38.—CALUMET RIVER DISTRICT.

OXYGEN CONSUMED IN PARTS PER 100,000, AUGUST 4, 1910.

Laboratory Number.	Sampling Point.	
42	2	.345
43		.320
44		.355
45		.370
46		.380
47		.420
48	9	.380
49	10	.410
50	11	.390
51	12	.470
52	13	.450
53	14	.500
54	15	.420
55	16	.420

TABLE . 39.—CALUMET RIVER DISTRICT.

OXYGEN CONSUMED IN PARTS PER 100,000, AUGUST 5, 1910.

	Sampling Point.	
56	17	.560
57	18	.580
58	19	.580
59	20	.660
60	21	2.940
61	22	5.690
62	23	1.000
63	24	8.420
64	25	1.520
65	26	4.730
66	27	1.400
67	28	1.640
68	29	1 350
69	30	1.380
70	31	1 222
71	32	.920
72	33	1 230
73	34	1.460
74	35	1.190
75	36	1.190
76	37	1.570
77	38	1.210
78	39	.920
79	40	1.080
80	41	1.010
81	42	1.000
82	43	.780

TABLE No. 40.—CALUMET RIVER DISTRICT.

OXYGEN CONSUMED IN PARTS PER 100,000, AUGUST 19, 1910.

Laboratory Number.	Sampling Point.	Oxygen Consumed.
83	Indiana Harbor Sewer	1.055
84	Gibson Sewer	1.415
85	East Chicago Sewer	1.535
86	Standard Steel Car Co. Sewer	1.525
87	Calumet Ave. Sewer, North Side	1.775
88	Calumet Ave. Sewer, South Side	1.945
89	Hohman Ave. Sewer	1.245
90	Hammond Gas Works Sewer	6.022
91	Hammond Glue Works East Sewer	3.375
92	Hammond Glue Works West Sewer	4.535
	AUGUST 22, 1910.	
93	West Hammond Sewer	1.975
94	U. S. Rolling Stock Sewer	1.195
95	Lake Calumet 115th St. Sewer	1.555
96	Lake Calumet 111th St. Sewer	1.635
97	Hegewisch Sewer	1.315
98	Hammond Glue Works East Sewer	19.145
99	Hammond Glue Works Center Sewer	7.185
100	Hammond Glue Works West Sewer	6.205
101	Hammond Gas Works Sewer	9.645
102	Hohman Ave. Sewer	3.055
103	Calumet Ave. Sewer	2.795

TABLE No. 41.—CALUMET RIVER DISTRICT.

OXYGEN CONSUMED, PARTS PER 100,000, AUGUST 24, 1910.

Laboratory Number.	Sampling Point.	Oxygen Consumed.
104	Indiana Harbor Sewer	1.280
105	Gibson Sewer	.850
106	East Chicago Sewer	.940
107	Standard Steel Car Co. Sewer	1.530
108	Calumet Ave. Sewer, North Side	4.300
	AUGUST 25, 1910.	
109	Gary Steel Plant 4 ft. Sewer	1.300
110	Gary City Sewer	2.640
	SEPTEMBER 2, 1910.	
111	Hammond Glue Works Center Sewer	16.870
112	West Hammond Sewer	3.340
113	U. S. Rolling Stock Sewer	1.360
114	Hegewisch Sewer	1.410
	SEPTEMBER 3, 1910.	
115	Gary Steel Plant 24 in. Sewer	.980
116	Gary Steel Plant 4 ft. Sewer	1.050
117	Gary City Sewer	2.870

TABLE No. 42.—CALUMET RIVER DISTRICT.

PUTRESCIBILITY TEST, AUGUST 2, 1910.

Laboratory Number.	Sampling Point.	Hours Incubated.	Result.
1	2	96	Negative.
		96	Negative.
		96	Negative.
		96	Negative.
		96	Negative.
		96	Negative.
	9	96	Negative.
	10	96	Negative.
9	11	96	Negative.
10	12	96	Negative.
11	13	96	Negative.
12	14	96	Negative.
13	15	96	Negative.
14	16	96	Negative.
15	17	96	Negative.
16	18	96	Negative.
17	19	96	Negative.

TABLE No. 43.—CALUMET RIVER DISTRICT.

PUTRESCIBILITY TEST, AUGUST 3, 1910.

Laboratory Number.	Sampling Point.	Hours Incubated.	Result.
18	20	96	Negative.
19	21	18	Positive.
20	22	18	Positive.
21	23	18	Positive.
22	24	18	Positive.
23	25	18	Positive.
24	26	18	Positive.
25	27	18	Positive.
26	28	18	Positive.
27	29	48	Positive.
28	30	48	Positive.
29	31	48	Positive.
30	32	60	Positive
31	33	48	Positive.
32	34	60	Positive.
33	35	60	Positive.
34	36	60	Positive.
35	37	96	Positive.
36	38	96	Negative.
37	39	96	Negative.
38	40	96	Negative.
39	41	96	Negative.
40	42	96	Negative.
41	43	96	Negative.

TABLE No. 46.—CALUMET RIVER DISTRICT.

PUTRESCIBILITY TEST, AUGUST 19, 1910.

Laboratory Number.	Sampling Point.	Hours Incubated.	Result.
84	Indiana Harbor Sewer	96	Positive.
85	Gibson Sewer	48	Positive.
86	East Chicago Sewer	18	Positive.
87	Standard Steel Car Co. Sewer	18	Positive.
88	Calumet Ave. Sewer, North Side	18	Positive.
89	Calumet Ave. Sewer, South Side	18	Positive.
90	Hohman Ave. Sewer	48	Positive.
91	Hammond Gas Works Sewer	18	Positive.
92	Hammond Glue Works East Sewer	18	Positive.
93	Hammond Glue Works Center Sewer	18	Positive.
	AUGUST 22, 1910.		
94	West Hammond Sewer	24	Positive.
95	U. S. Rolling Stock Sewer	24	Positive.
96	Lake Calumet 115th St. Sewer	48	Positive.
97	Lake Calumet 111th St. Sewer	48	Positive.
98	Hegewisch Sewer	48	Positive.
99	Hammond Glue Works East Sewer	24	Positive.
100	Hammond Glue Works Center Sewer	24	Positive.
101	Hammond Glue Works West Sewer	24	Positive.
102	Hammond Gas Works Sewer	24	Positive.
103	Hohman Ave. Sewer	24	Positive.
104	Calumet Ave. South Sewer	24	Positive.

TABLE No. 47.—CALUMET RIVER DISTRICT.

PUTRESCIBILITY TEST, AUGUST 24, 1910.

Laboratory Number.	Sampling Point.	Hours Incubated.	Result.
105	Indiana Harbor Sewer	42	Positive.
106	Gibson Sewer	42	Positive.
107	East Chicago Sewer	96	Positive.
108	Standard Steel Car Co. Sewer	42	Positive.
109	Calumet Ave. North Sewer	18	Positive.
	AUGUST 31, 1910.		
110	Gary City Sewer	18	Positive.
111	Gary Steel Plant 4 ft. Sewer	96	Negative.
	SEPTEMBER 2, 1910.		
112	Hammond Glue Works West Sewer	18	Positive.
113	West Hammond Sewer	18	Positive.
114	U. S. Rolling Stock Sewer	18	Positive.
115	Hegewisch Sewer	18	Positive.
	SEPTEMBER 3 1910.		
116	Gary Steel Plant 24 in. Sewer	96	Negative.
117	Gary Steel Plant 4 ft. Sewer	96	Negative.
118	Gary City Sewer	24	Positive.

TABLE No. 48.—VARIATIONS IN THE CALUMET RIVER WATER.

AS SHOWN BY THE AVERAGE OF OXYGEN CONSUMED, DISSOLVED OXYGEN AND PUTRESCIBILITY REACTION.

Sampling Points.	Oxygen Consumed, Parts per Million.	Dissolved Oxygen, Parts per Million.	Putrescibility Reaction. Hours Incubated.
1	No tests made.	.83	96 hours negative.
	.295	.61	96 hours negative.
	.267	.45	96 hours negative.
	.357	.27	96 hours negative.
	.348	.25	96 hours negative.
	.343	.19	96 hours negative.
7	No tests made.	No tests made.	96 hours negative.
	.358	.16	96 hours negative.
9	.355	.26	96 hours negative.
10	.368	.38	96 hours negative.
11	.368	.36	96 hours negative.
12	.405	.26	96 hours negative.
13	.363	.18	96 hours negative.
14	.388	.30	96 hours negative.
15	.378	.25	96 hours negative.
16	.375	.23	96 hours negative.
17	.428	.26	96 hours negative.
18	.475	.35	96 hours negative.
19	.450	.53	96 hours negative.
20	.575	.40	72 hours positive.
21	1.967	.30	18 hours positive.
22	4.265	.24	18 hours positive.

TABLE No. 48.—Continued.

Sampling Points.	Oxygen Consumed, Parts per Million.	Dissolved Oxygen, Parts per Million.	Putrescibility Reaction, Hours Incubated.
23	2.245	.34	18 hours positive.
24	5.333	.18	18 hours positive.
25	2.098	.24	18 hours positive.
26	4.005	.16	18 hours positive.
27	2.912	.14	18 hours positive.
28	1.920	.32	18 hours positive.
29	1.435	.37	33 hours positive.
30	1.435	.09	33 hours positive.
31	1.153	.36	33 hours positive.
32	.963	.65	96 hours positive.
33	1.105	.49	48 hours positive.
34	1.228	.23	54 hours positive.
35	1.043	.19	39 hours positive.
36	1.098	.19	39 hours positive.
37	1.245	.45	96 hours positive.
38	1.043	.26	96 hours negative.
39	.890	.21	96 hours positive.
40	.990	.07	96 hours negative.
41	.945	.11	96 hours negative.
42	.868	.02	96 hours negative.
43	.665	No tests made.	96 hours negative.

TABLE No. 49.—CALUMET RIVER DISTRICT.

CHEMICAL ANALYSIS OF SEWER OUTFALL, AUGUST 1 TO SEPTEMBER 1, 1910. RESULTS PARTS PER 100,000.

Laboratory Number	3905	3906	3907
Source of Sample	Hammond Sewer, North Side of Calumet Ave.	Indiana Harbor Sewer.	Hammond Sewer, South Side of Calumet Ave.
Free ammonia	1.4000	.4000	.7400
Albuminoid ammonia	.0900	.0500	.0800
Chlorine	98.0	1.80	.50
Nitrates	.0000	.0000	.0000
Nitrites	.0000	.0000	.0000
Iron (Fe)	.20	.28	.24
Alkalinity	21.2	25.2	20.8
Total solids	225.2	51.4	43.2
Fixed solids	193.6	40.0	28.8
Loss on ignition	31.6	11.4	14.4
Odor	Very strong sewage.	Very strong sewage.	Very strong sewage.
Turbidity	Much.	Slight.	Much.
Sediment	Much black.	Much black.	Much black.
Color	28	19	19
B. Coli	Present.	Present.	Present.
FILTERED SAMPLES ON FOLLOWING RESULTS.			
Silica	10.997	2.897	.867
Iron (Fe_2O_3) and aluminum (Al_2O_3)	1.467	.317	.412
Calcium (CaO)	9.727	13.377	10.547
Magnesium (MgO)	3.855	4.842	3.140
Sulphates (SO_4)	10.485	6.282	7.691
Carbonate alkalinity	None.	None.	None.
Bicarbonate alkalinity	21.2	25.2	20.8
Hydrate alkalinity	None.	None.	None.
Total solids	213.2	51.0	36.2
Fixed solids	193.6	45.4	30.8
Chlorine	96.4	1.8	2.8

TABLE No. 49.—Continued.

RESULTS IN PARTS PER 100,000.

Laboratory Number	3915	3916	3917
Source of Sample	Gibson Sewer.	East Chicago Sewer.	Hammond Sewer, South Side Columbia Ave.
Free ammonia	.2400	.3400	.4400
Albuminoid ammonia	.0100	.0140	.0140
Chlorine	2.00	2.50	1.00
Nitrates	.0000	.0000	.0000
Nitrites	.0010	.0100	.0001
Iron (Fe)	.28	.04	.38
Alkalinity	18.0	14.6	20.0
Total solids	66.0	37.8	57.8
Fixed solids	50.4	25.8	28.0
Loss on ignition	15.6	12.0	29.8
Odor	Very slight sewage.	Decided sewage.	Strong sewage and oil.
Turbidity	None.	None.	Marked, black and oil.
Sediment	Considerable earthy.	Much brown.	Much black.
Color	28	33	33
B. Coli	Present.	Present.	Present.
FILTERED SAMPLES ON FOLLOWING RESULTS.			
Silica	1.327	2.527	1.277
Iron (FeO_3) and aluminum (Al_2O_3)	.297	.077	.093
Calcium	19.447	8.347	10.597
Magnesium (MgO)	4.885	2.907	3.513
Sulphates (SO_4)	14.399	6.294	1.420
Carbonate alkalinity	None.	None.	None.
Bicarbonate alkalinity	18.0	14.6	20.0
Total solids	47.0	32.2	36.0
Fixed solids	42.0	25.6	32.6
Chlorine	2.0	2.5	1.0

TABLE No. 49.—Continued.

RESULTS IN PARTS PER 100,000.

Laboratory Number	3956	3957	3958
Source of Sample	Gary Steel Plant 2-Foot Sewer.	Gary Steel Plant 4-Foot Sewer.	Gary City Sewer.
Free ammonia	.2000	.1800	.7400
Albuminoid ammonia	.0040	.0040	.0400
Chlorine	.90	.70	4.00
Nitrates	.0000	.0000	.0000
Nitrites	.0004	.0003	.0000
Iron (Fe)	.24	.80	.10
Alkalinity	12.4	12.0	22.0
Total solids	26.0	25.4	49.0
Fixed solids	19.0	19.4	38.2
Loss on ignition	7.0	6.0	10.8
Odor	Distinct vegetable.	Slight earthy.	Very strong sewage.
Turbidity	None.	Very slight.	Decided.
Sediment	Much brown.	Considerable brown.	Much black.
Color	9	9	40
B. coli	Present.	Present.	Present.
Filtered Samples on Following Results.			
Silica	3.077	1.337	4.087
Iron (FeO_3) and aluminum (Al_2O_3)	None.	None.	None.
Calcium (CaO)	9.827	4.667	5.987
Magnesium (MgO)	2.19	1.824	3.544
Sulphates (SO_4)	4.254	1.882	6.632
Carbonate alkalinity	None.	None.	None.
Bicarbonate alkalinity	12.4	12.0	22.0
Total solids	19.6	20.2	38.2
Fixed solids	16.2	13.2	32.6
Chlorine	.90	7.0	4.0

TABLE No. 49.—Continued.

RESULTS IN PARTS PER 100,000.

Laboratory Number	3974	3975	3976
Source of Sample	Hammond Glue Works, West Sewer.	Hammond Glue Works, Middle Sewer.	Blast Furnace Sewer Inland Steel Co. Plant.
Free ammonia	1.4000	.6000	.1200
Albuminoid ammonia	1.4800	.4000	.0040
Chlorine	16.0	2.80	.30
Nitrates	.0000	.0000	.0000
Nitrites	.0000	.0000	.0001
Iron (Fe)	.08	.06	.14
Alkalinity	50.8	14.8	10.6
Total solids	166.2	50.0	23.6
Fixed solids	118.2	39.0	19.0
Loss on ignition	48.0	11.0	4.6
Odor	Strong foul.	Strong foul.	Distinct musty.
Turbidity	Much.	Much.	None.
Sediment	Considerable white crystaline.	Much crystaline, organic.	Considerable brown.
Color	13	13	13
B. coli	Present.	Present.	Gas formers.
FILTERED SAMPLES ON FOLLOWING RESULTS.			
Silica	8.487	2.287	3.087
Iron (FeO_3) and aluminum (Al_2O_3)	None.	None.	None.
Calcium (CaO)	4.427	9.277	5.007
Magnesium (MgO)	.716	1.112	1.894
Sulphates (SO_4)	7.534	5.128	1.214
Carbonate alkalinity	6.4	None.	None.
Bicarbonate alkalinity	44.4	14.8	10.6
Total solids	58.2	42.0	17.0
Fixed solids	40.0	33.0	14.0
Chlorine	16.0	2.80	.30

TABLE No. 49.—Continued.

RESULTS IN PARTS PER 100,000.

Laboratory Number	3977	3978	3979
Source of Sample	West Hammond Sewer.	U. S. Rolling Stock R. R. Plant Sewer.	Hegewisch Sewer.
Free ammonia	.6400	.6000	.5000
Albuminoid ammonia	.2000	.0700	.0300
Chlorine	5.80	5.40	3.80
Nitrates	.0000	.0000	.0000
Nitrites	.0000	.0000	.0040
Iron (Fe)	.20	.08	.14
Alkalinity	27.6	18.4	28.4
Total solids	64.8	60.4	69.8
Fixed solids	47.8	42.4	51.8
Loss on ignition	17.0	18.0	18.0
Odor	Strong H_2S	Strong Vegetable.	Decided Vegetable.
Turbidity	Decided.	None.	None.
Sediment	Much black.	Considerable white and organic.	Considerable brown.
Color	30	30	30
B. Coli	Present.	Present.	Present.
FILTERED SAMPLES ON FOLLOWING RESULTS.			
Silica	4.087	1.067	1.027
Iron (FeO_3) and aluminum (Al_2O_3)	None.	None.	None.
Calcium (CaO)	15.307	9.847	12.977
Magnesium (MgO)	5.561	.337	7.469
Sulphates (SO_4)	13.442	7.979	15.099
Carbonate alkalinity	None.	None.	None.
Bicarbonate alkalinity	27.6	18.4	28.4
Total solids	57.4	50.0	60.6
Fixed solids	47.4	40.8	50.0
Chlorine	5.80	5.40	3.80

TABLE No. 49.—Continued.

RESULTS IN PARTS PER 100,000.

Laboratory Number	3980	3986	3987
Source of Sample	Hearst Stein Co. Glue Works Sewer.	Inland Steel Co. Plant, South Sewer.	Hammond Gas Works Sewer.
Free ammonia	.3500	.2400	.9000
Albuminoid ammonia	.0030	.0100	.0500
Chlorine	5.80	1.30	.30
Nitrates	.0000	.0000	.0000
Nitrites	.0001	.0000	.0004
Iron (Fe)	.08	14.0	.50
Alkalinity	20.0	Acid 10.2	10.8
Total solids	69.4	117.6	41.8
Fixed solids	48.8	101.2	22.4
Loss on ignition	20.6	16.4	19.4
Odor	Slight foul.	Decided.	Distinct.
Turbidity	None.	Decided.	None.
Sediment	Much black.	Considerable black.	Much brown.
Color	30	9	30
B. Coli	Present.	Present.	Present.
Filtered Sample on Following Results.			
Silica	4.587	.597	1.717
Iron (FeO_3) and aluminum (Al_2O_3)	None.	9.817	None.
Calcium (CaO)	11.327	17.857	16.317
Magnesium (MgO)	4.009	2.529	2.604
Sulphates (SO_4)	16.623	54.811	6.183
Carbonate alkalinity	None.	None.	None.
Bicarbonate alkalinity	20.0	None.	10.8
Total solids	57.4	106.8	26.8
Fixed solids	48.4	64.4	21 0
Chlorine	5.80	1.3	.30

TABLE No. 49.—Continued.

RESULTS IN PARTS PER 100,000.

Laboratory Number	3988	3989	3990
Source of Sample	Hammond Sewer, Hohman Ave.	Inalnd Steel Co. Plant, Middle Sewer.	Interstate Mill, South Sewer.
Free ammonia	.3400	.2100	.2600
Albuminoid ammonia	.0340	.0140	.0040
Chlorine	60	.80	1.60
Nitrates	0000	.0000	.0000
Nitrites	.0000	.0000	.0080
Iron (Fe)	08	16.0	.06
Alkalinity	16.0	Acid 12.5	12.8
Total solids	37 8	134.8	38.2
Fixed solids	27.6	85.6	23.8
Loss on ignition	10 2	49 2	14.4
Odor	Strong foul.	Distinct.	Distinct.
Turbidity	None.	None.	None.
Sediment	Considerable black.	Considerable brown.	Considerable brown.
Color	19	9	13
B. Coli	Present.	Absent.	Present.
FILTERED SAMPLES ON FOLLOWING RESULTS.			
Silica	.067	2.067	1.207
Iron (FeO_3) and aluminum (Al_2O_3)	None	17.717	None.
Calcium (CaO)	13.217	6.717	14.227
Magnesium (MgO)	4.363	6 215	5.333
Sulphates (SO_4)	8.816	57.788	6.694
Carbonate alkalinity	None.	None.	None.
Bicarbonate alkalinity	16.0	None.	12.8
Total solids	31.6	122.6	29.6
Fixed solids	27.6	64.2	23.6
Chlorine	.60	.80	1.6

TABLE No. 49.—Continued.

RESULTS IN PARTS PER 100,000.

Laboratory Number	3991	3992	3993
Source of Sample	U. S. Reduction Co. Sewer.	Interstate Mills, North Sewer.	Hammond Glue Works, East Sewer.
Free ammonia	.3200	.3200	1 0600
Albuminoid ammonia	.0040	.0040	2 1000
Chlorine	3.00	1.60	18.40
Nitrates	.0100	.0100	.0000
Nitrites	.0090	.0090	.0001
Iron (Fe)	.06	.08	.20
Alkalinity	20.8	12.4	211.0
Total solids	102.4	29.4	382 4
Fixed solids	75 0	22.0	357 0
Loss on ignition	27 4	7 4	25 4
Odor	Decided.	Distinct vegetable.	Strong.
Turbidity	Slight.	None.	Slight.
Sediment	Considerable yellow.	Considerable brown.	Very much white.
Color	28	22	13
B. Coli	Present.	Present.	Present.
FILTERED SAMPLE ON FOLLOWING RESULTS.			
Silica	2.187	4 387	37.467
Iron (Fe_2O_3) and aluminum (Al_2O_3)	None.	None.	None.
Calcium (CaO)	13.227	14 827	1[illegible].644
Magnesium (MgO)	5.509	5.480	15 014
Sulphates (SO_3)	6.546	6.759	264 611
Carbonate alkalinity	None.	None.	77.6
Bicarbonate alkalinity	20.8	12.4	None.
Hydrate alkalinity	None.	None.	113.4
Total solids	88.4	28.8	3[illegible].4
Fixed solids	77.8	19.6	278.4
Chlorine	2.80	1.6	11.2

TABLE No. 49.—Continued.

RESULTS IN PARTS PER 100,000.

Laboratory Number	3994	3995
Source of Sample	Hearst Stein Co. Glue Works. Cooling Water.	Republic Mills Sewer.
Free ammonia	1.0000	.2600
Albuminoid ammonia	.0200	.0000
Chlorine	4.60	1.20
Nitrates	.0000	.0100
Nitrite	.0010	.0080
Iron (Fe)	.10	.06
Alkalinity	21.2	16.0
Total solids	46.2	27.2
Fixed solids	37.0	22.0
Loss on ignition	9.2	5.2
Odor	Strong.	Distinct.
Turbidity	Slight.	Slight.
Sediment	Much yellow.	Considerable brown.
Color	19	9
B. Coli	Present.	Present.
FILTERED SAMPLES ON FOLLOWING RESULTS.		
Silica	2.427	.567
Iron (Fe_2O_3) and aluminum (Al_2O_3)	None.	None.
Calcium (CaO)	13.847	12.447
Magnesium (MgO)	5.480	4.975
Sulphates (SO_4)	5.029	6.299
Carbonate alkalinity	None.	None.
Bicarbonate alkalinity	21.2	16.0
Total solids	44.6	24.0
Fixed solids	36.6	20.4
Chlorine	4.6	1.2

REPORT ON THE INVESTIGATION OF THE WATER SUPPLY AT FRENCH LICK, IND.

J. H. Brewster.

On September 30, 1909, a communication was received from S. F. Teaford, M. D., Health Commissioner of Orange County, stating that he had made an inspection of the water supply of the town of French Lick, Indiana, on the 14th day of September, 1909, and found it to be in very bad condition and suggesting that arrangements be made to furnish better water to the citizens of that town. The communication also stated that there had been three cases of typhoid fever reported from the physicians of Orange County during the month of September.

In accordance with this request, on November 6, 1909, the State Board of Health made an investigation of this supply for the purpose of advising such changes as might be necessary for producing a water that would meet the requirements of the law as provided by Chapter 24 of the Acts of 1909.

The supply furnishing the town of French Lick with water is owned by the French Lick Spring Company, a private company, which has a contract to furnish water for fire protection and sprinkling purposes only, although the company permits the water to be used for domestic purposes. The supply is taken from Lick Creek, which is fed by springs and the run-off from the surrounding hills. A dam has been built across this creek, so as to form a small storage reservoir from which the water is taken and passed by gravity into two brick cisterns, the larger having a capacity of 14,000 gallons and the smaller of 7,000 gallons. From these cisterns the water is pumped by an electrically driven engine of 1,440,000 gallons capacity per 24 hours into a feed line which supplies three Gould electrically driven engines of 30,000 gallons daily capacity each. These engines are located part way up the hill, and in this way divide the pumping load. These engines pump the water into a reservoir of 637,000 gallons capacity which is located on a hill, and where it goes through a water softening process. From here it passes through two iron filter tanks 14 feet in diameter and containing eight inches of crushed quartz. These filters are for the purpose of removing any precipitated solids, and no attempt is made to purify the water. The water then enters a standpipe 5½ feet in diameter and 22 feet high, from which it is distributed by gravity over the system.

As Lick Creek is located in a valley that is entirely surrounded by steep hills, it receives all the drainage from the barns and pasture lands in this section and because of the dam installed by the water company, the stream is very sluggish and at times has no apparent flow. For these reasons it becomes a stagnant body of water containing organic pollution and algæ growth that renders it wholly unsatisfactory for drinking and domestic purposes.

There are but two ways in which the law can be applied for the betterment of the public water supply. First, if the supply is filtered, the filtration must be sufficiently complete to remove all danger of disease; and second, if domestic sewage or trade wastes run into the stream, the law provides that it be stopped, or the sewage purified to render it innocuous before entering the stream, but as there is no such deleterious refuse entering this creek and no adequate filtration, the provisions of the act are in no way violated.

As a safe and wholesome water supply is always a valuable asset to a town or city, every possible means should be availed of, to obtain a potable water for French Lick. Such a supply is not only necessary for the improvement of public health conditions, but it is of great importance in enhancing the future growth of the town and as well of commercial interest to the water company itself. Improvements can be made in two ways, either by installing a purification plant in connection with the present waterworks system to filter Lick Creek water, or any surface water that may be desired, or by obtaining an underground water from flowing springs or deep wells.

A purification plant of adequate capacity in conjunction with the present system might be more cheaply installed than a deep well or a spring supply, for owing to the large quantity of mineralized water in this section, it is very probable that a large amount of money might be spent without locating a suitable water. The cost of operating such a system might be greater or less, depending entirely upon the location of such wells or springs.

The water company, realizing that the present supply is entirely unsatisfactory for drinking and domestic purposes, has made several attempts to secure water from flowing springs, but so far has been unsuccessful on account of the insufficient quantity of water obtainable. This work should be continued until a suitable water is found and, if this is not possible, the immediate installation of purification plant is recommended. It is also advised that the citizens put forth their concerted efforts in assisting the water company to obtain such a supply, as it is a mutual benefit that is to be realized.

INVESTIGATION OF THE SEWAGE CONDITION AT LAPEL.

J. H. Brewster.

The town of Lapel, with a population of about 1,000, is located on the western border of Madison County. The town has no public water supply, the water for domestic purposes being taken from private wells drilled into the limestone stratum to an average depth of 75 feet.

There is no sanitary system of sewers, but one storm sewer has been installed which drains practically all of the residential districts. It is an open joint sewer, constructed principally of unglazed farm drain tile flowing into a 30-inch open joint glazed sewer tile, which in turn flows into an open ditch at a point located at about 75 yards west of the public school building. This ditch passes through farm land for about a quarter of a mile and empties into Stony Creek, which has its origin a short distance north and which is tributary to White River.

This sewer, which was designed to take care of storm water and surface drainage only, is now receiving the domestic sewage from about 20

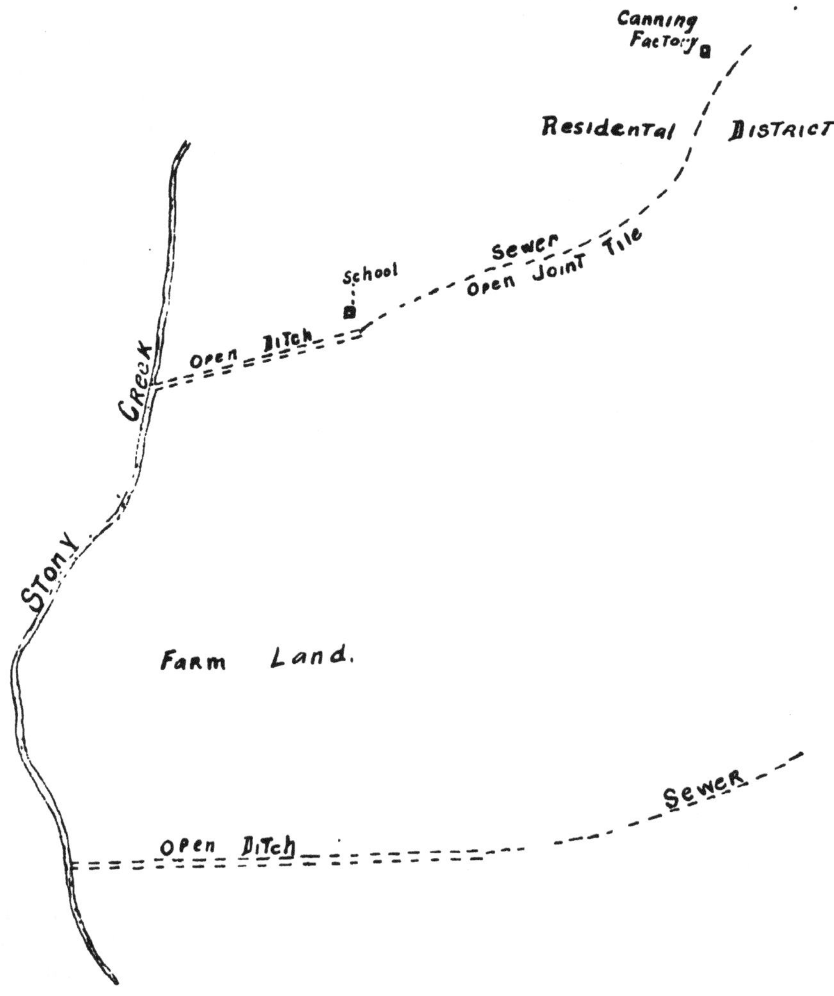

vaults and also the washing from the Lapel Canning Company, which contains a considerable amount of the seeds and peelings from tomatoes. The tomato refuse is found in sewer only during the periods of the year when the factory is in operation.

On October 8, 1909, when an investigation of this sewer was made, there had been no rain for some time previous and for this reason there was very little water flowing through the open ditch. It, however, contained a considerable amount of the refuse from the canning factory and other decomposing organic matter. The odor coming from this ditch was keenly noticed at a distance of from 40 to 50 yards on either side. The water in this ditch is used by cattle and hogs that are pastured in the fields through which it runs. Stony Creek above the entrance of this ditch is clean and unoffensive, but below its entrance the bottom and sides are completely covered with growths of algæ.

The fact that this sewer empties in the open only 75 yards from the school building is a very important reason why changes should be made immediately. It is not only a nuisance and a menace to health because of the odor that comes from it, but because it forms a breeding place for flies and mosquitoes, which are undisputed disease carriers, but it is stated by Dr. H. H. Stanford, the local health officer, that the school children frequently play in the water that passes through it. This sewer was not designed to care for domestic sewage. It is merely a drain for surface water and the emptying of other sewage into it should be immediately stopped and a suitable system for disposing of the town's waste installed.

In addition to this sewer a ten-inch tile open joint sewer that runs from the glass factory and receives some domestic sewage, also empties into an open ditch through which it is carried to Stony Creek. This sewer should be closed for all purposes except the discharge of surface water.

On January 27, 1910, Dr. Bennett V. Caffee of Terre Haute called the attention of the State Board of Health to the insanitary conditions surrounding the disposal of the refuse of the Terre Haute Paper Company. In response to his request, Mr. J. H. Brewster visited the plant of the company and made a careful study of its operation. The correspondence was between Dr. Caffee and the State Board of Health and the report of Mr. Brewster is here appended:

1333 Maple Avenue, Terre Haute, Jan. 27, 1910.

Dr. John Hurty, Sec'y State Board of Health:

Dear Sir.—I would like to call your attention to the Terre Haute Paper Company on North 19th Street, and the unsanitary conditions in connection with it. It is situated well within the city limits and is closely surrounded by residences.

The odor coming from the fermenting straw is so intense as to cause hundreds of families to tightly close their windows night and day, and even at my home, nearly one and a half miles away, I have frequently been obliged to do so and burn some deodorant.

The odor is extremely disgusting, the most sickly and nauseating I have ever experienced. I feel sure it is possible to prevent it. A slaughterhouse odor is perfume compared to it. If possible, I will be greatly obliged if you will investigate the matter.

Respectfully,

Bennett V. Caffee, M. D.

FEBRUARY 24, 1910.

Indiana State Board of Health, Indianapolis, Ind.:

GENTLEMEN.—On February 7, 1910, a communication addressed to your board by Dr. Bennett V. Caffee, 1333 Maple Avenue, Terre Haute, Indiana, was referred to this department. In accordance with instructions Mr. J. H. Brewster visited the works of the Terre Haute Paper Company on February 9th, and investigated the conditions complained of by Dr. Bennett V. Caffee. I attach herewith the original complaint signed by Dr. Caffee, and the report of the inspection signed by Mr. J. H. Brewster. It is evident that the complainant cannot avail himself of action under the Stream Pollution Law for removing the unsanitary conditions to which he refers. Without doubt, the odor from the rotaries constitutes a public nuisance and any action intended to relieve the situation should rest with the secretary of the local board of health or with other city officials, whose duty it is to regulate public nuisances. Yours very truly,

H. E. BARNARD,
Chemist to State Board of Health.

FEBRUARY 24, 1910.

Mr. H. E. Barnard, Chemist to State Board of Health, Indianapolis, Ind.:

DEAR SIR.—On February 9th, I visited the plant of the Terre Haute Paper Company, located at N. 19th Street, Terre Haute, Indiana, to investigate the complaint made to the State Board of Health under date of January 27, 1910, by Dr. Bennett V. Caffee, 1333 Maple Avenue, Terre Haute, Indiana. Upon inspection of the plant, I found that the odor complained of was due to the gases which escaped from the rotaries when they are blown off, as is necessary in the course of their operation. This odor is very disagreeable, especially when the atmosphere is heavy, thus preventing the escaping steam from rapidly diffusing through the air.

The refuse from the plant passes through a settling basin 8 feet deep, 6 feet wide and 60 feet long and having a capacity of 21,600 gallons. This settling basin is under ground and no odor comes from it. The plant uses about 2½ million gallons of water daily, all of which passes through this basin. Once each week the settlings are removed and deposited on land owned by the paper company. No appreciable odor is given off from the sediment. The refuse, after passing off through the settling basin, empties into the city sewer system and is carried to the Wabash River, two and one-half miles away. The sedimentation basin is admittedly too small to properly care for the waste, but as the refuse reaches the river as a part of the entire sewage of the city of Terre Haute, it is not clear how action can be brought against the paper company to compel them to discontinue the use of a city sewer to carry off their incompletely purified refuse until the city itself constructs a disposal plant to care for its own sewage. Since the odor complained of, which is the only feature of the operation of the plant which is held to be a nuisance, does not injure any water supply, it is evident that no remedy can be sought for the relief of the complainant under the Stream Pollution Law. Yours very truly,

J. H. BREWSTER,
Water Chemist Indiana State Board of Health.

REPORT OF THE SECOND INVESTIGATION OF THE FILTRATION PLANT OF THE SEYMOUR WATER COMPANY, SEYMOUR, INDIANA.

J. H. BREWSTER.

The first report, covering an investigation made of this plant at the request of Dr. J. H. Carter, Secretary of the Seymour City Board of Health, which contains a description of the pumping station, coagulant tanks, settling basin, filter beds, clear well, and the standpipe, was made in July, 1909. It stated that the filtration plant had not been properly operated, with the result that the filter beds were filled wih clay balls and dirt and the efficiency of the plant reduced to such an extent that a proper effluent could not be produced. It recommended that the filtration plant be thoroughly overhauled and cleaned and also that several changes be made in the method of operation.

In compliance with these recommendations, the water company dismantled the filters by removing all the sand, which was carefully washed and screened in order to separate it from the dirt and clay lumps. The tubs, which are constructed of wood, were then filled with a strong solution of lye to remove any fungous growth or bacteria that might remain around the sides or in the manifold system. After this, the sand was replaced. On account of the excessive amount of dirt that had been removed, the level of the sand beds was lowered about ten inches and as the remaining amount of sand was not sufficient for suitable operation, fresh sand was supplied until the proper level in the filter tubs was reached. In cleaning the settling basin, it was found that it was half filled with coagulant and suspended matter that had settled during the process of sedimentation, and so reduced the capacity to such an extent that the operation in this basin was materially affected. The accumulated silt was entirely removed, which allowed a much clearer water to pass to the filters, thus relieving them of a large amount of unnecessary work. The clear well and standpipe was also cleaned to remove any possibility of contamination after the water had been filtered. When this work was finished, samples of both the filtered and unfiltered water were submitted to the state laboratory for analysis. The results were as follows:

Lab. No.	Source.	Bacteria.	B. Coli.	Date.
1510A	River water	26,000	Present	Aug. 24, 1909
1511A	Settled water	16,000	Present	Aug. 24, 1909
1512A	Filter	1,200	Gas formers present	Aug. 24, 1909
1513A	Filter	800	Present	Aug. 24, 1909
1514A	Clear well	115	Absent	Aug. 24, 1909
1515A	Tap water	65	Gas formers present	Aug. 24, 1909

It is seen from these figures that the water taken from the clear well and from the tap was much better than that taken direct from the filters. This might have been due to careless operation of the plant at the time of sampling, so that the filters were not doing their best work. The plant had been operating much more effectively only a short time before, as the clear well, which is directly connected with the filter, showed better results. It was therefore suggested that more care be taken in some of the operating details, especially during the times of heavy pumpage when the filters do their greatest amount of work.

On October 2d, 12th, 13th and 14th, samples of both the filtered and unfiltered water were submitted to the state laboratory. The results of the analyses were as follows:

Date.	Source.	Bacteria.	B. Coli.	Per Cent. Efficiency.	Lab. No.
10- 2-09	Raw water	24,000	Present	....	1524A
10- 2-09	Settled water	6,850	Present	71.5	1525A
10- 2-09	Filter No. 1	200	Absent	99.2	1526A
10 -2-09	Filter No. 2	615	Present	97.4	1527A
10- 2-09	Clear well	385	Present	98.4	1528A
10- 2-09	Tap water	60	Absent	99.8	1529A
10-12-09	Raw water	20,000	Present	....	1530A
10-12-09	Settled water	7,500	Present	62.5	1531A
10-12-09	Filter No. 2	120	Absent	99.4	1532A
10-12-09	Filter No. 3	400	Present	98.0	1533A
10-12-09	Clear well	425	Present	97.9	1534A
10-12-09	Tap water	28	Gas	99.9	1535A
10-13-09	Raw water	60,000	Present	....	1537A
10-13-09	Settled water	37,000	Present	39.8	1538A
10-13-09	Filter No. 4	375	Absent	99.4	1539A
10-13-09	Filter No. 1	6C0	Absent	99.0	1540A
10-13-09	Clear well	1,250	Present	97.9	1541A
10-13-09	Tap water	70	Gas	99.9	1542A
10-14-09	Raw water	73,000	Present	....	1543A
10-14-09	Settled water	40,000	Present	45.2	1544A
10-14-09	Filter No. 3	355	Present	99.4	1545A
10-14-09	Filter No. 2	300	Absent	99.5	1546A
10-14-09	Clear well	400	Present	99.3	1547A
10-14-09	Tap water	150	Present	99.8	1548A

These figures show that the bacterial efficiency, as well as the bacterial counts, was very good, but that B. Coli, or bacteria of the colon type, were present in most of the samples. To better these conditions, it was suggested that the amount of coagulant used in the process of filtration be increased until the bacterial count in the filtered water reached 100 or less, thus probably eliminating gas-forming bacteria.

Other series of samples were submitted on October 26th, 27th and 28th and the results were as follows:

Date.	Source.	Bacteria.	B. Coli.	Lab. No.
10-26-09	Raw water	75,000	Present	1550A
10-26-09	Settled water	30,000	Present	1551A
10-26-09	Filter No. 2	3,750	Present	1552A
10-26-09	Filter No. 3	2,000	Present	1553A
10-26-09	Clear water	5,000	Present	1554A
10-26-09	Tap water	40	Absent	1555A
10-27-09	Raw water	65,000	Present	1556A
10-27-09	Settled water	40,000	Present	1557A
10-27-09	Filter No. 1	5,400	Present	1558A
10-27-09	Filter No. 4	4,100	Present	1559A
10-27-09	Filter water	6,400	Present	1560A
10-27-09	Tap water	400	Absent	1561A
10-28-09	Raw water	100,000	Present	1562A
10-28-09	Settled water	19,000	Present	1563A
10-28-09	Filter No. 2	600	Absent	1564A
10-28-09	Filter No. 3	1,100	Present	1565A
10-28-09	Clear water	1,500	Present	1566A
10-28-09	Tap water	100	Absent	1567A

From these figures it is readily noticed that the bacterial counts in the water coming from the filters and from the clear well are extremely high and that B. Coli were absent. This condition was difficult to explain, as the storage capacity is only sufficient for a 12 to 18 hour supply, not long enough to permit the natural death of the bacteria during the time between the filtration of the water and its delivery to the consumer. But as the samples collected from the plant were taken during the day run, when the pumpage is the greatest, and those taken from the tap were undoubtedly collected from water that had been filtered during the night run when the pumpage is the lightest, it seemed that the filtration must have been much more effective during the night than it was during the day. This explanation seems plausible for two reasons; first, because the slower the filtration is carried on, the more efficient will be the results; and, second, if the coagulant is not fed at a proportionate rate, as will be shown later that it was not, there will be a larger amount applied to the water during the time of light pumpage than there was during times of heavy pumpage. It was evident, however, that the operation of the plant was at fault in some way, and in view of this fact the water company requested that the State Board of Health again visit Seymour and endeavor to ascertain the cause of its trouble, and if possible, to devise some means of relief.

In accordance with this request, on November 22d, the second investigation was commenced. Samples were immediately taken for analysis and the manner of operation looked into. The plant showed that the overhauling and cleaning had been carefully and satisfactorily carried out and that most of the instruction that had been given in the previous investigation as to the methods of washing the filters and general operation was being followed. Some changes were necessary, however, for a more economical operation, one of which was the manner of feeding the coagulant. The scheme employed was to make a solution of known strength and then to arrange the tank outlet so that a certain amount of this solution would be used every hour. This caused the amount of coagulant entering the water to be constant, but by calculating the rate at which the engines were pumping and knowing the rate with which the coagulant was being fed, it was determined that the feeding, if figured in grains per gallon, was very irregular. This is shown by the accompanying table, when on November 22d, there was only 1.25 grains of the coagulant being injected into the water at the time the samples were taken, while the average for the 24 hours of that day was 2.5 grains to a gallon. On the 23d, when the samples were taken in the morning, there was 4.2 grains per gallon being used and in the evening, when the samples were again taken, 6.1 grains were being fed, while the average for the 24 hours was 6.9 grains per gallon. And again, on the 24th, 5.3 grains was being fed at the time of sampling, while the average for the day showed 8.9 grains to the gallon. From these figures it can readily be seen that during the night run, a maximum amount of coagulant is being fed, which is far in excess of that of the average amount for the 24 hours. In changing the manner of applying the solution, it was very difficult to arrange a proportionate feeding on account of the extreme irregularity with which the water was pumped, and the design of the apparatus for applying this solution was such that it was impossible automatically to control the rate by the speed of the pump. But by carefully watching the rate of pumpage and at the same time adjusting the outlet valve of the solution tank, a much more even distribution of the coagulant was produced. This is shown in the appended table, when on November 28th and 29th the amount of coagulant being injected at the time of taking the sample, was practically the same as the average for the day. If a device is installed for feeding the coagulant according to the rate of pumpage it will materially reduce the total amount used.

On account of a considerable amount of solid matter in the bottom of the coagulant tank, it was thought that for some reason the sulphate of alumina was not going in solution but remaining in a solid mass. An analysis of this sediment showed it to be 72.6 per cent. aluminum hydrate, which had been precipitated by the lime contained in the water that was used to make the solution. This waste can not readily be prevented, but it is so slight that it does not materially increase the cost of the coagulant. Other than the irregular feeding of the coagulant, the only point that was at fault in the operation was in the washing of the filter beds. On account of the large amount of dirt that had previously been found in these beds, instructions had been given the operators to wash them more thoroughly. These instructions had been interpreted to mean a much more frequent washing, and as well as the producing of a much cleaner sand than theretofore. The percentage of wash water used had never been determined, and for this reason it was not realized that the washing was far in excess of what it should be. Neither was it apparent how much money it was costing to carry on the process in this wasteful way. It was determined in the previous investigation that 1,500 gallons of water were passing through the filters each minute the wash water was turned on. On November 24th it took 88,500 gallons of water to wash the filters while the total amount of water filtered, including the wash water, was 419,300 gallons. This means that 21 per cent. of the total amount of water pumped was being used to clean the filters. As the water at this time was extremely turbid, and there had already been a great many changes in the smaller details of operation, it was not thought advisable to change the system of washing on this date, for in doing so it might confuse the local operators to such an extent as to damage the quality of the effluent. On the following day 124,500 gallons of water was used in washing the filters, while the total number of gallons filtered was 457,900, or that 27 per cent. of the total number of gallons pumped was used to clean the filters. The use of this excessive amount of water was due to the fact that the filters were being washed more frequently than necessary.

The filter plant is equipped with 4 units, each having a daily capacity of one-half million gallons. As the daily pumpage is less than one-half million gallons, the entire days' filtration could be carried on through one filter, but in order to make the process of filtration as slow as possible, thus attaining a better degree of purity than is possible with more rapid filtration, the 4 units were kept in use all of the time. If the amount of water filtered should reach the maximum of the filter capacity, it would be necessary to wash these filters about three times a day when the raw water was exceedingly turbid, as it was just at this time. But as the consumption was less than one-quarter of the plant's capacity, it was hardly necessary to wash the entire plant more than once a day. The operators did not realize that the plant was not working to its full capacity and were giving each filter three washings during the 24 hours. This means that if one filter was doing the entire work, as it was capable of doing, and was given the same amount of washing as the 4 units were receiving, it would be overhauled 12 times during the day, or once every two hours. This manner of washing the beds is very unsatisfactory, for unless an excessive amount of coagulant is used to quickly form a filter mat of sufficient thickness so as not to allow any impurities to pass beyond the sand beds, the quality of the water produced is materially injured. A filter does its poorest work when it has just been cleaned, and its best work when it has accumulated a considerable amount of coagulant in the form of a filter mat on top of the sand, providing this mat is not allowed to reach such a thickness that it cracks and so permits water to pass through the sand unfiltered. On November 26th and 27th, the washing of the filters was reduced to twice a day instead of three times. With this change the percentage of wash water dropped to 15 per cent. and 13 per cent. respectively. Since there was no evidence of the filters becoming overworked, the washing was again changed to one a day on November 28th, which resulted in the amount of wash water being reduced to 6 per cent. This is about what should be required when the turbidity of the raw water is low, as it was on this day.

Results Obtained During the Investigation.

The results of the first days' analyses showed that while a large percentage of the bacteria was being removed, yet the number of bacteria remaining after the water had passed through the filters was still very high and that B. Coli was either strongly present or indicated in every sample.

For this reason, the coagulant was increased from 2.5 grains per gallon to 6.9 grains per gallon. This change improved, to some extent, the condition of the water, as is shown in the appended table, when on November 23d the water coming from the filters had in most cases lower bacterial counts. They were still to high, however, and gas-forming bacteria were also present. Another increase in the coagulant was made on November 24th to 8.9 grains per gallon, and again, on November 25th, until it had reached a maximum of 9.6 grains per gallon. These last changes gave practically no improvement in the bacterial reductions nor in the tests for B. Coli.

The operation of the plant was now being very carefully carried on, a larger amount of coagulant being used than was needed, as well as being fed much more regularly, and the excessive washing of the filters had been stopped. There was, therefore, no reason so far as the operation was concerned, why a suitable effluent could not be produced, but the fact remained that the water was not satisfactory. It was determined from the previous investigation that the size of the settling basin was entirely too small and the design unsatisfactory. This was again shown during this investigation, as only an average of 35.8 per cent. of the bacteria was being removed before the water reached the filters. With a suitable settling basin, water containing as many bacteria as was found in the river at this time should have at least 90 per cent. removed. The lack of suitable settling basins was undoubtedly the cause of the trouble now experienced. But as the construction of a new settling basin was an expense that the water company felt could not be borne at this time, it was decided to install a sterilization plant, using hypochlorite of lime as the oxidizing agent to supplement the work of the filtration plant.

In order to show the water company that this agent would prove satisfactory, it was decided to carry on a short experiment with its use before installing a permanent feeding device. As there was no convenient appliances with which to inject the bleach into the water, one of the wooden tubs used for feeding the coagulant was utilized. In this way the applied chemical was added as the water entered the settling basin and before any of the impurities were removed. This, of course, is unadvisable, as the organic matter, as well as the bacteria, that is carried by the water is acted upon by the oxidizing agent, thus compelling the use of a larger amount of the chloride of lime than would otherwise be necessary, but as the time allowed for carrying on this experiment was limited, the appliances at hand were utilized.

In using bleach, it is advisable to have as strong a solution as possible, as the greater the strength the smaller will be the amount of solution. But as the amount of water to be treated at this plant was not over 50,000 gallons, the chloride of lime needed to sterilize it was so little that if a strong solution was made, it would be impossible to distribute it evenly through a day's run. It has been determined that a solution as weak as one half per cent. strength can be used successfully in water treatment. In most waters 5 pounds of the dry bleach to the million gallons is sufficient. Such an amount at this plant would mean that for a half per cent. solution it would take 2½ pounds of the dry powder to 60 gallons of water. The coagulant tank which was to be used while carrying on this experiment was 3 feet high and had a capacity of 850 gallons. It was impossible, therefore, to regulate a systematic feeding of a solution of one-half per cent. strength, or 60 gallons, in a tank of this size, and for this reason the solution was reduced to one twenty-eighth of one per cent. strength, which would permit of a fairly accurate rating of the feed line. The experiment was commenced by using 5 pounds of dry bleach per million gallons of water or two-tenths parts per million of available chlorine, or .045 parts per million of potential oxygen. While using the chloride of lime the coagulant was reduced from 9.7 grains per gallon to an average of 4 grains per gallon. The results from this addition of bleach and the reduced amount of alum was about the same as those previously obtained with the heavy dosing of alum and the only gain was in the saving in cost of the coagulant. It appeared probable that the inefficiency of these results was due to the weak solution that had been used, and so the strength of the solution was increased to one-half of one per cent. This necessitated the feeding of a larger quantity of the dry bleach, which amounted to 35 pounds to one million gallons of water and furnished 1.3 parts per million of available chlorine, or .3 parts per million of potential oxygen.

When the stronger solution of hypochlorite of lime had been in use about 24 hours, a very disagreeable taste, which in a short time resembled that of rotten wood, was noticed in the tap water. The solution tank, the settling basin and the filter tubs were all of wood, and as they had been in use for several years they were undoubtedly in a condition to be readily attacked by the liberated oxygen of the strong solution of bleach. The feeding of the chloride of lime through the coagulant tank was immediately stopped, and in a short time no further trouble was experienced. As is shown on the accompanying table for November 29th, the bacterial results, following the injection of this strong solution of chloride of lime, were very satisfactory; the samples from the settling basin and the filters all showing practically sterile plates with no evidence of B. Coli. The samples collected on November 28th, a short time after the usage of the stronger solution of bleach had been started, show very satisfactory results in the settling basin and the filters, but the effects had not as yet reached the clear well.

It seemed possible then that a small amount of chloride of lime properly injected into the water after it leaves the clear well would relieve the unsatisfactory condition of this supply.

Arrangements were immediately made for the installation of a suitable feeding device for adding the chemicals to the water after the filtration was complete, as it was not advisable to treat the water where it would come in contact with wood.

A house was built over the suction line of the high duty engines which takes the water from the clear well and pumps it into the standpipe. A quarter-inch tap was made in this line, through which the solution could be fed. In order to get a solution free from sediment and the right strength to be properly regulated, two galvanized iron tanks were constructed, one of which, called the dissolving tank, was two feet in diameter and 3½ feet high. It was supplied with an outlet 6 inches from the bottom, which enabled a clear solution to be drawn off after the insoluble lime had settled to the bottom. It also had a sewer outlet connected to the bottom for the purpose of cleaning out the residue. An agitating device was installed in this tank, which was operated by a half-inch water motor. The other tank, known as the feeding tank, also constructed of galvanized iron, was 4 feet 6 inches high and 1 foot 9 inches in diameter. This tank has its outlet 6 inches above the bottom, so that any precipitated solids or sediments from the dissolving tank can not enter the suction line. It also had a connection with the sewer.

The method of operation was to place enough dry powder into the dissolving tank for one dosing. After the tank had been filled with water the agitating device was started and kept in motion for about one hour, after which it was stopped and the solution allowed to settle. When it had become clear it was drawn off into the feeding tank. The outlet from this tank is connected with the quarter-inch tap into the suction main, and by properly arranging the valve, one tank full of this solution will last about 12 hours. Fortunately, this connection, which has a very small orifice into the suction line, feeds automatically with the rate of pumpage. That is, if only a small amount of water is being pumped, only a small amount of the applied chemical will be injected, but if the pumpage is heavy the suction on the feeding will be proportionately increased and a large amount of the solution will enter the water, and when the pumps are completely shut down, as often happens, especially during the night run, there will be no suction on the tank and the feeding of this solution is entirely stopped. This equipment for feeding the chloride of lime makes the operation very simple and at the same time very accurate.

On account of the small amount of available help while installing the equipment for the use of chloride of lime, it was necessary to stop the laboratory work. But as no changes were being made in the operation of the filters, no information could have been gained except that the effluent was not satisfactory, a fact already fully established.

When the treatment with calcium hypochlorite was again started, a solution of one-half per cent. strength was fed at the rate of 10 pounds to the million gallons of water treated. When this amount of hypochlorite was being used, analyses made at the water company's laboratory of the water taken from the city tap, gave the following results:

DATE.	Bacteria.	B. Coli.
December 22, 1909	58	Absent.
December 23, 1909	750	Gas formers.
December 24, 1909	60	Absent.
December 25, 1909	16	Absent.
December 26, 1909	45	Absent.
December 27, 1909	3	Absent.

It will be noticed that on December 23d the bacterial count was very high and that gas-forming bacteria were present. This is due to the fact that the feeding device, being insufficiently protected, had frozen the night before, stopping the treatment, but when it was again put into operation very satisfactory results were obtained.

The results of this investigation show that the plant as originally designed was not capable of producing the quality of water desired, but that by treating the water after it had been filtered with 10 pounds of hypochlorite of lime to the million gallons, a water of satisfactory quality could be produced.

With the operation and treatment being carried on as it is now possible, the city of Seymour should be supplied with a perfectly safe and wholesome water for drinking and domestic purposes.

SEYMOUR WATER WORKS, SEYMOUR, INDIANA.

Date.	Lab. No.	Source.	Bacteria.	Per Cent. Efficiency.	B. Coli.	Number Hours Filter in Use.
11-22-09	1570a	Raw	50,000	....	+	....
11-22-09	1571a	Settled	35,000	29.0	+	....
11-22-09	1572a	Filter No. 1	1,500	97.0	+	½
11-22-09	1573a	Filter No. 2	515	99.0	Susp.	10
11-22-09	1574a	Filter No. 3	1,100	97.8	Susp.	10
11-22-09	1575a	Filter No. 4	2,600	94.8	+	½
11-22-09	1576a	City tap	750	98.5	+	....
A. M.						
	1577a	Raw	85,000	....	+	....
11-23-09	1578a	Settled	67,500	21.0	+	....
11-23-09	1579a	Filter No. 1	1,400	98.3	Gas	½
11-23-09	1580a	Filter No. 2	650	99.2	+	7
11-23-09	1581a	Filter No. 3	500	99.4	+	7
11-23-09	1582a	Filter No. 4	1,100	98.8	Gas.	½
11-23-09	1583a	Clear well	750	99.2	Susp.	....
11-23-09	1584a	City tap	450	99.4	+	....
P. M.						
11-23-09	1585a	Raw	135,000	....	+	....
11-23-09	1586a	Filter No. 1	1,700	98.7	+	1½
11-23-09	1587a	Filter No. 2	500	99.7	Gas.	9
11-23-09	1588a	Filter No. 3	600	99.8	Gas.	9
11-23-09	1589a	Filter No. 4	700	99.6	+	1½
11-24-09	1590a	Raw	169,000	....	+	....
11-24-09	1591a	Settled	67,500	60.1	+	....
11-24-09	1592a	Filter No. 1	1,400	99.2	+	3½
11-24-09	1593a	Filter No. 2	400	99.8	+	9
11-24-09	1594a	Filter No. 3	550	99.7	+	9
11-24-09	1595a	Filter No. 4	1,875	98.9	+	3½
A. M.						
11-26-09	1596a	Raw	69,000	....	+	....
11-26-09	1597a	Settled	40,000	42.1	+	....
11-26-09	1598a	Filter No. 1	1,800	97.4	Gas.	3½
11-26-09	1599a	Filter No. 2	1,200	98.3	Gas.	11
11-26-09	1600a	Filter No. 3	900	98.7	Gas.	11
11-26-09	1601a	Filter No. 4	1,500	97.9	Gas.	3½
11-26-09	1602a	Clear well	2,400	96.6	+	....
11-26-09	1603a	City tap	400	99.5	+	....
P. M.						
11-26-09	1604a	Raw	74,000	....	+	....
11-26-09	1605a	Settled	56,000	24.3	+	....
11-26-09	1606a	Filter No. 1	1,000	98.7	−	10
11-26-09	1607a	Filter No. 2	1,700	97.7	Gas.	5
11-26-09	1608a	Filter No. 3	1,400	98.1	−	5
11-26-09	1609a	Filter No. 4	700	99.1	−	10

SEYMOUR WATER WORKS, SEYMOUR, INDIANA—Continued.

Date.	Lab. No.	Source.	Bacteria.	Per Cent. Efficiency.	B. Coli.	Number Hours Filter in Use.
11-27-09	1610a	Raw	45,000	....	+	....
11-27-09	1611a	Settled	33,000	26.7	+	....
11-27-09	1612a	Filter No. 1	1,875	95.8	+	8
11-27-09	1613a	Filter No. 2	700	98.5	Gas.	5
11-27-09	1614a	Filter No. 3	1,500	96.7	+	5
11-27-09	1615a	Filter No. 4	2,000	95.6	+	8
11-27-09	1616a	Clear well	1,400	97.0	Gas.	....
11-27-09	1617a	City tap	400	99.1	+	....
11-27-09	1618a	Creek	37,000	....	+	....
11-27-09	1619a	River above creek	50,000	....	+	....
11-28-09	1620a	Raw	33,750	....	+	....
11-28-09	1621a	Settled	10	99.9+	−	....
11-28-09	1622a	Filter No. 1	76	99.8	+	10
11-28-09	1623a	Filter No. 2	95	99.7	+	6
11-28-09	1624a	Filter No. 3	*	*	*	6
11-28-09	1625a	Filter No. 4	60	99.8	−	10
11-28-09	1626a	Clear well	230	99.3	+	....
11-28-09	1627a	City tap	500	99.8	+	....
11-28-09	1628a	Creek	4,000	....	+	....
11-28-09	1629a	River above creek	30,000	....	+	....
11-29-09	1630a	Raw	20,000	....	+	....
11-29-09	1631a	Settled	0	100	−	....
11-29-09	1632a	Filter No. 1	0	100	−	12
11-29-09	1633a	Filter No. 2	1	100	−	6
11-29-09	1634a	Filter No. 3	0	100	−	1½
11-29-09	1635a	Filter No. 4	0	100	−	9

*Sample spoiled.

DAILY OPERATION OF THE PLANT.

Date.	Grains of Coagulant Used at Time of Taking Sample.	Grains of Coagulant Used During 24 Hours.	Pounds of Coagulant Used During 24 Hours.	Gallons of Water Filtered.	Gallons of Wash Water.	Per Cent. of Wash Water.	Turbidity by Hasen's Reciprocal Rod.
11-22-09	1.25	2.5	150	419,620	−	−	.1
11-23-09 A. M.	4.2	6.9	510	520,000	−	−	.5
11-23-09 P. M.	6.1	6.9	510	520,000	−	−	1.0
11-24-09	5.3	8.9	535	419,300	88,500	21	.8
11-25-09	*	9.6	600	457,900	124,500	27	.6
11-26-09	6.8	4.8	275	420,360	64,500	15	.6
11-27-09	2.3	3.5	200	400,000	53,200	13	.3
11-28-09	2.5	2.4	150	428,780	25,500	6	.17
11-29-09	3.0	3.3	203	436,420	25,500	6	.15

*No sample taken.

REPORT OF THE INSPECTION OF THE WATER SUPPLY OF WARSAW, INDIANA.

At the request of Dr. C. W. Burkett, Health Officer of Kosciusko County, that the State Board of Health investigate the character of the water supply of the city of Warsaw, on October 8, 1909, Mr. J. H. Brewster, water chemist of the State Laboratory of Hygiene, visited Warsaw, and after making a sanitary survey of the territory and investigating the condition of the franchise, made the following report:

In 1895 a water-works system was built for the city of Warsaw which is now owned by the Winona Electric Light and Water Company. This company supplies both Winona and Warsaw, which are located about three miles apart, with water for drinking and domestic purposes and has two separate stations for doing this work. The Winona plant gets its supply from seven wells which receive spring water at a depth of 40 feet below the surface which rises to the top of the wells. This plant was built in 1905 and furnishes water to a summer population of 7,000. The water is pumped into two storage tanks of about 200,000 gallons capacity each. The summer consumption is about 750,000 gallons daily, supplied by one triplex engine of 500,000 gallons capacity and one Dean duplex engine of 250,000 gallons capacity.

The Warsaw station takes its supply from Center Lake, which is about two miles in circumference and has an average depth of 45 feet. This lake is fed principally by springs, although at the present time it receives some surface drainage. The water is taken from this lake and pumped by direct pressure, at 35 pounds, for domestic use and 60 pounds for fire protection, by two Worthington double-expansion cross-compound engines of 1,000,000 gallons daily capacity each; a standpipe of 46,875 gallons capacity is kept in reserve and is not in general use.

The company has nine miles of mains which supply about one-half of the 6,000 population with 1,000,000 gallons of water daily.

A renewal of the franchise was granted in October 1909, in which it is stated that "the company shall furnish to the city and the inhabitants thereof, water which shall be wholesome and perfectly safe for drinking and domestic purposes and shall be of such standard as shall be prescribed by the State Board of Health of the State of Indiana or by such public service commission as may hereinafter be established by the State of Indiana."

It is also stated in the franchise that the pumping station must be located within the city limits of Warsaw. With this clause inserted, the ways of obtaining a suitable quantity of water are reduced to three sources, namely: Center Lake, Pike Lake, or the drilling of a system of deep wells which might be found sufficient to furnish not only the quantity but the quality desired. This last proposal that the lake water be abandoned and a deep well system be installed is not advisable because of the possibility that such an underground supply could not be obtained. Secondly, if such a supply were possible, the cost of installation might equal or even exceed the cost for the installation of a purification plant. In several places in this State it has been found that the cost of getting the water from these wells is greater than the cost of the operation of a purification plant. In the third place a softer surface supply is much preferable to the hard well water that is usually found in this section of the country. There is also no reason why Center Lake should be abandoned and the supply taken from Pike Lake, as any necessity which will cause the purifying of Center Lake will undoubtedly be found to exist at Pike Lake. Furthermore, it is an accepted fact that surface waters and especially those lying within populated districts, are not suitable for drinking and domestic purposes until made so by proper purification.

Present Pollution of the Lake.

Numerous privy vaults and barns drain into the lake within a very short distance of the water-works intake. A drain leads out of Pike Lake and empties into Center Lake that drains a considerable portion of land that has been used for a city dumping ground. A small creek, known as

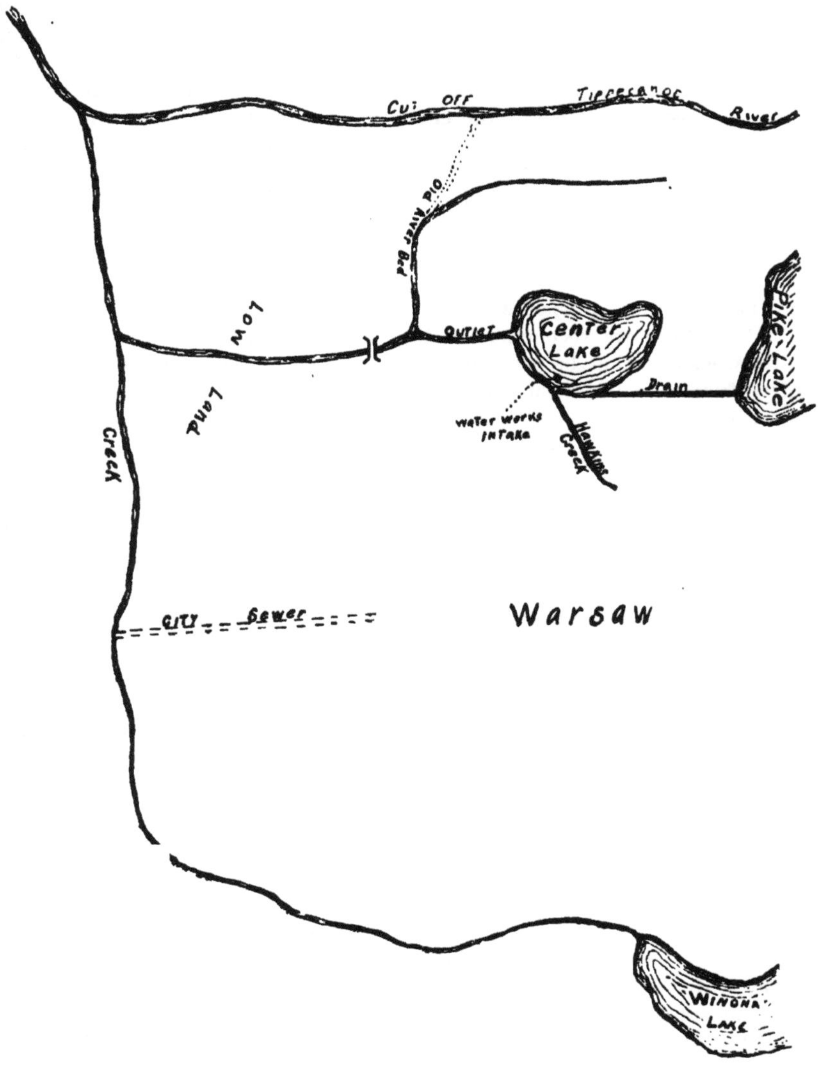

Hawkins Creek, receives some of the drainage from this dumping ground and also the drainage of several privy vaults. This creek empties into the lake within 150 feet of the water-works intake. These conditions should be removed and may be remedied by action under the stream pollution law, Chapter 24, Acts 1909. A creek leading from Winona Lake and passing within one-half mile of Center Lake, receives the city sewage at a point up stream where it receives the overflow from Center Lake. It has been stated by members of the city council that during flood periods the low lands in this section are completely under water and that because of the large amount of water coming through this creek, the current coming from Center Lake is reversed and in this way the city sewage is carried into Center Lake. This condition should be remedied as provided for by law.

At one time the bed of the Tippecanoe River came within a very short distance of Center Lake and during flood times overflowed into it. This was removed by putting in a cut-off and changing the flood of the river in another direction. Some of the citizens wish again to change the channel back to its original course for the purpose of causing a greater circulation in Center Lake. If, by doing this, no additional pollution would enter the lake this would not be objectionable, but if it would add either pollution or turbidity to the lake, it should not be permitted, because at the present time the lake acts as an impounding reservoir and also as a settling basin to remove the turbidity. It would be unwise to make it impossible to use the lake for these purposes.

It is therefore recommended that as the franchise provides that the water-works station be located within the city of Warsaw and that the water furnished be of such standard as shall be prescribed by the State Board of Health—

First, that the supply be taken from Center Lake.

Second, that the water so taken be properly purified before being pumped into the water mains.

Third, that the entrance of all sewage and polluted water into the lake be immediately stopped and that the lake shore be cleaned up and protected.

When such improvements are made the city of Warsaw will have a water supply admirably adapted for drinking and domestic purposes.

PRELIMINARY REPORT OF THE WATER SUPPLY OF ROCHESTER, INDIANA.

H. E. BARNARD.

At the request of Omar B. Smith, mayor of Rochester, on September 2, 1910, I visited that city, and in company with the mayor and J. E. Chamberlain, superintendent of the water works, made a sanitary survey of the water supply.

The supply is obtained from Lake Manitou, a shallow lake several square miles in area situated in low-lying country. It is one of a chain of three lakes originally connected but now separated by a dam which cuts off Lake Manitou and raises its level above other lakes. The lake is surrounded by farm lands and along its shores nearly one hundred summer cottages have been built, which for the most part are occupied only during the summer. At the end of the lake from which the water supply is taken is the West Side Hotel, which during the summer season is constantly filled with guests. The wash room of the hotel discharges wash water directly into the lake. The toilets are open vaults on a slough which connects with the lake some two hundred feet away. The vaults are dug in sand ten feet from the shore line. The lake is noted as a fishing ground and at least two hundred rowboats with three large and six small launches are constantly in use during the summer season. The lake is also used for swimming and bathing.

A mill-race leaves the lake near the West Side Hotel and runs toward Rochester and by the pumping station of the water supply about one-half mile from its head. At the time of my inspection the upper end of the race was filled with stagnant water, but the remainder of the distance it was dry. The bottom had recently been scraped and mud and sediment removed. The mill-race is practically an open sewer running through the city. On the left bank going toward the lake are built nine houses, each with an outhouse. Six barns are also situated on the edge of the mill-race and manure piles and hogpens lie adjacent to it and within ten feet of the bank. All the wash water from the city and adjacent land flows to the race, and following heavy rains the drainage from the street, stables, manure piles and two large barnyards runs directly to it. When the race is full the water runs from one to three feet in depth. No protection is provided at any part of its course against the inflow of sewage and no attempt is made to exclude therefrom animals or bathers.

The water supply was installed in 1894 and at the present time is in good condition. The water is taken from the mill-race and pumped to a standpipe 12 x 125 feet, of 105,000 gallons capacity. The average pumpage is 500,000 gallons per twenty-four hours. At the present time there are three hundred and fifty customers, but the water is not used for drinking and domestic purposes, as it is recognized that it is not a potable supply. During the time of cleaning the mill-race the water was taken from a creek which is dammed at the pumping station and flows into the pump well.

It is apparent that the water supply is still entirely adequate for fire protection but is not suitable for drinking and domestic purposes without purification.

The character of the water is such as admirably to fit it for purification by filtration, and the pumping station is situated sufficiently below the lake level to allow the installation of filtration systems to be operated by gravity. The installation of the system of mechanical filters will cost approximately $12,000 per unit of 500,000 gallons capacity.

The analysis of water from the driven well near the pump well shows it to be of excellent composition, relatively low in hardness and containing only a moderate amount of iron. This water is well adapted for drinking and domestic purposes, and if the supply of water at this point is sufficient for the needs of the city, I believe that an entirely satisfactory supply may be obtained by the installation of deep wells in the area adjacent to the pumping station. A study of the analysis of this water in comparison with the water from the lake shows its hardness to be six points greater than that of the lake and about ten points less than that of the average Indiana water supplies. The solid content of the ground water is six parts per 100,000 higher than that of the lake water. The iron content is .12 parts per 100,000. This quantity of iron is normal and should in no way injure the character of the water for drinking and laundry purposes. In point of palatability, color and odor, it is much superior to the lake water, although a suitable filtration of the lake water would reduce its color somewhat and also remove in part its vegetable odor. The lake water is a satisfactory surface water, and if it were not subject to constant pollution in the mill-race from the adjacent houses, outhouses and barns and at the lake, by the runoff from surrounding farms, the sewage from cottages and the hotel, and its constant use as a fishing ground, it might well continue to be utilized as a public water supply, but its condition as shown by the sanitary inspection as well as by a chemical analysis of the water is such that it is wholly unfit for drinking and domestic purposes. I suggest, therefore, that the character of the lake water be improved by the installation of a proper filtration plant, or a new supply sought in the ground water at the filtration plant.

WATER ANALYSIS OF SAMPLES FROM ROCHESTER, INDIANA.

(Parts in 100,000.)

SOURCE OF SAMPLE.	Lab. No.	Date of Collection.	Odor.	Color.	Turbidity.	Sediment.	Ammonia.		Nitrogen as		Chlorine.	Solids.		Hardness.	Iron.
							Free.	Albuminoid	Nitrates.	Nitrites.		Total.	Fixed.		
*Well, 46 ft., (owned by Marten Bros.).........	4111	10-10-10	Distinct woody.	80	V. slight...	Slight	.0010	.0160	.0000	.0000	.20	25.4	20.2	14.4	.00
†Manitou Lake..........	4112	10-10-10	Distinct woody.	80	V. slight...	Slight	.0010	.0160	.0000	.0000	.30	23.4	21.2	13.4	.00
‡Well, 20 ft., canning factory................	4114	10-10-10	None..........	4	None......	None......	.0000	.0000	.4000	.0001	2.40	54.2	48.8	25.4	.00
[1]Driven well, 42 ft., city supply..............	4115	....	None..........	20	V. much...	Much	.0024	.0004	.0000	.0000	.60	35.2	27.4	19.2	.12
[2]Creek	4116	10-10-10	None..........	20	V. much...	Much	.0030	.0020	.0000	.0000	1.00	40.0	34.4	23.4	.12
[3]Mill race...............	4122	10-10-10	Distinct woody.	80	V. slight...	Slight	.0010	.0280	.0000	.0000	.20	23.4	16.6	13.4	.00

*This is a good water.
†This water is high in organic matter and contains gas-forming bacteria.
‡This water is high in chlorine, due no doubt to the shallowness of the well and the infiltration of surface water.
[1]This is a very good water.
[2]This water is of good quality.
[3]This water contains much organic matter and gas-forming bacteria.

REPORT APPROVING THE PLANS OF HERING & FULLER FOR A SANITARY AND STORM WATER SEWAGE SYSTEM FOR VINCENNES, INDIANA.

INDIANAPOLIS, IND., June 3, 1910.

State Board of Health, Indianapolis, Ind.:

GENTLEMEN—In accordance with your directions, I have studied the plans designed by Hering & Fuller, consulting engineers and sanitary experts of New York City, for the proposed sanitary and storm sewer systems for Vincennes, Indiana, and beg to make the following report:

The proposed system is to extend through all the streets within the present city limits and will be approximately 60 miles in length and cover an area of about 1,775 acres. The system is divided into two parts, one to take care of the sanitary sewage exclusively and the other to receive only the street washings and storm water.

SANITARY SEWER SYSTEM.

The sanitary sewer system is of sufficient size, not only to take care of the present needs, but also any increase in the amount of sewage caused by the city's growth for many years to come. Provision has been made to run all the sanitary sewage to one point in the city where it may receive treatment before being emptied into the river. This is done by establishing pumping stations in those portions of the city where the sewage can not be taken care of by gravity. The plans for the disposal of the sanitary sewage at the present time are not complete, but are sufficient to meet the present needs in such a way that the effluent which will be discharged into the river will in no way be a nuisance. The proposed form of treatment consists of passing the sewage through bar screens, having a clear space of four-tenths of an inch, which will remove paper and coarse solid matters. It then passes into a basin of 30,000 gallons capacity, which is equal to a flow of about fifteen minutes at the maximum rate. This basin will serve to remove a large proportion of the coarser solids and will also provide opportunity for complete disinfection and sterilization. Appliances have been provided for the feeding of hypochlorite of lime when it is deemed advisable. This treatment will render the sewage harmless and the screening will remove most of the putrescible matter. This method is undoubtedly most advisable as an emergency treatment, and as there are no Indiana cities below Vincennes which receive water from the Wabash River, I think this treatment will be sufficient until the upstream cities have done their share toward the bettering of the general sanitary conditions in the Wabash River.

As the city of Vincennes will be at a heavy expense in installing this system of sewers, in my opinion it is not advisable to increase this expense, inasmuch as precautions have been taken to allow for emergency treatment and also to extend the system for the disposal of the sewage, when it can be installed without causing a hardship, or when Illinois provides laws which will stop the pollution of that part of the river which acts as a boundary between the two States.

Storm-Water System.

As stated by Hering & Fuller, the designing of a storm-water system was attended with several complications, due to the fact that the city is extremely level and that most of the drainage is toward the city ditch and away from the river, and also that the floods in the river interfere with free discharge of the drains, which considerably reduces their carrying capacity. This condition has been admirably met in the most part by the draining of a greater portion of the water into the city ditch and providing a pumping station for lifting the flow from the storm drains into the river at times of flood. There are several outlets that drain a small portion of the city directly into the river that will not enter into the city ditch. These have also been provided with pumps for lifting the water into the river during flood periods.

Comment.

It is noticed that of the several outlets for storm water which empty direct into the Wabash River, two discharge upstream from the water-works intake. These are the Hickman Street and St. Charles Street sewers. The Chestnut Street and Spring Garden Avenue sewers empty into Kelso Creek, which in turn drains into the river about a mile above the water-works intake. While the major portion of the storm water and all of the sanitary sewage will enter the river below the water-works intake, this portion which empties above will undoubtedly have some effect upon the quality of the water received at the water works.

While I do not think these conditions will be of material importance, as no trade waste or manufacturing refuse is to enter the storm-water sewers, yet I feel justified in making note of the fact, as it may be possible that at some future time they will require further attention.

Conclusion.

The plans as designed show that every precaution has been taken amply to provide for all parts of the city for present and future needs; that all the grades have been carefully worked out, all pumping stations completely equipped; that the material used be of the best quality; that the work is to be done under the supervision of competent engineers; and that the works must meet the requirements for which they were designed.

In my opinion the designs fully cover every detail, and I would therefore recommend their approval.

Respectfully submitted,

J. H. Brewster,
Sanitary Engineer.

INVESTIGATION OF THE WATER PURIFICATION PLANT FOR THE CITY OF VALPARAISO, INDIANA.

J. H. BREWSTER.

The water works of the city of Valparaiso is owned and operated by a private company, which takes water from Flint Lake and purifies it by means of a mechanical filtration plant before delivering it to the city.

The purification plant, which was designed and constructed by the Pittsburg Filter Manufacturing Co., was completed in the fall of 1907. At that time an official test was made, the results of which, together with a description of the plant, is embodied in the 1908 report of the State Board of Health. The results of that investigation showed that mistakes had been made in both the design and construction and until certain changes had been made the plant could not be successfully operated. Some of these corrections were made immediately by the construction company with good results, but the most important changes were not made. On account of this unsatisfactory installation, and other differences that arose between the water company and the construction company, the waterworks officials refused to accept the plant. This trouble developed into litigation, which is now pending in the federal courts, but an agreement was made that the water company might use the plant until a settlement was reached. The water company has endeavored to operate the plant under this arrangement, but up to the present time has met with little success.

Realizing the condition of the plant and desiring a more complete knowledge of the efficiency of the purification process, the superintendent, Mr. E. L. Loomis, requested the State Board of Health again to visit Valparaiso for the purpose of making a complete test of the plant and to establish a permanent laboratory and give the chief engineer, Mr. Joseph F. Bradley, such information as would enable him to do the work necessary to determine when the plant was being properly operated.

In response to the request, on June 5, 1910, the plant was visited and the establishment of the laboratory was immediately commenced. The necessary apparatus was in place and but little remained to be done except to start the work of making bacterial counts on gelatine and agar plates, the presumptive tests for B. Coli in neutral red lactose and dextrose broth, alkalinity, turbidity and color determinations and the test for alumina in the treated water.

During this time the condition of the plant was looked into, and it was found that the sandbeds contained a great many hardened spots, upon which the present apparatus for washing had no effect. It was thought that this was due to the formation of mud lumps caused by an insufficient amount of wash water, necessary because of the limited capacity of the sewer carrying off the soiled water, as described in the 1908 report.

Upon closer investigation, however, it was found that they were caused by sand getting into the system of drain pipes, which are placed six inches apart over the whole bed and empty into the clear well. The reason for these pipes becoming filled with sand was because some of the strainers, which are placed every six inches over this whole drain system, had become loosened and fallen out. This allowed the sand to enter, and consequently when the wash water was turned it could only reach such portions of the system where the sand had not entered. As a result, certain portions of the beds were not receiving any wash water at all and could not be broken up.

The water in Flint Lake is very soft and also contains a large amount of carbonic acid gas, and is particularly hard on iron pipe. For this reason the drain system, which was standard iron pipe, although the original contract called for extra heavy, was readily oxidized where the iron was exposed, as it was around the strainers, with the result that a little extra pressure at this point would cause the misplacement of a strainer. It was therefore necessary to remove all of this piping, and, in order to make the work a complete success, it was recommended that extra heavy brass pipe be used. As both filters were in the same condition it was evident that considerable time would elapse before the plant would be in shape to operate, and for this reason the work of testing the plant was discontinued until later in the summer.

The work of installing the brass pipe was completed on July 5th, and the plant again put in operation. On July 19th, a day's visit was made to the plant and it was found that the cleaning out of the drain system had improved the process of washing to a considerable extent, although it was still far from efficient. On September 12, 1910, the plant was again visited and the work of making a two weeks' test was started. During the summer months another change was made in the wash system. The line connecting the centrifugal wash pump with the filters is of 8-inch pipe, but as it enters the beds it is reduced to 6 inches. This reduction increases the friction and reduces the amount of wash water that would ordinarily reach the sand. As this six-inch pipe is set in concrete it was impossible to change it without shutting down the plant, but in order to do away with as much of this friction as possible, a 4-inch line was tapped into the 8-inch and connected with the rewash valve and when the beds were being cleaned, both the wash and the rewash lines were put in service. This change increased the amount of water entering the beds so as to produce a few inches head above the wash troughs and sewer outlet, and was of some little value in breaking up the sand, but the amount of wash water was still insufficient successfully to wash the beds. As more water can now be produced than can be cared for through the sewer, it will be of no value to pay any more attention to this part of the operation until the sewer is enlarged.

During the test care was taken to operate the plant in the best way possible under the existing conditions. The results of this test, however, were disappointing, as it was found that it was absolutely impossible to obtain continuously an effluent which was satisfactory either from a sanitary standpoint or one which would answer the requirements specified by the construction company in their original contract. The results are shown in the accompanying table under date from September 14th to September 27th. It was found that very frequently the effluent contained a larger number of bacteria than the raw water and that gas-forming bacteria, which closely resemble those of the colon type, were almost always present.

After a careful study of the plant, it seemed advisable to install apparatus for the feeding of a solution of hypochlorite of lime or bleach, to act as a sterilizing agent. This apparatus consisted of two cylindrical galvanized tanks 2 feet in diameter and 3 feet high, one to be used as a mixing tank from which the prepared solution, after settling, is decanted into the other or feeding tank, which is connected by a ½-inch pipe to the line feeding the pressure pump. This connection is so arranged that it can be used to treat the raw water if the plant should be obliged to shut down. It took several days to rate properly these tanks and to determine the amount of bleach that was necessary. During this time the results were not entirely satisfactory, but as this was simply a matter of a few days' experimenting there was no difficulty in getting the quality of the water desired. This is shown in the accompanying table under the dates of October 2d to October 8th inclusive, when the water delivered to the consumer was entirely satisfactory from a sanitary standpoint.

The reasons why the filters will not satisfactorily purify the water are as follows:

First. The plant is not of sufficient size to properly filter the water during periods of heavy pumpage such as occur through the daylight run. To filter the water at the rate of a hundred and twenty-five million gallons per acre per day, would require that six hundred eighteen thousand three hundred twenty gallons pass through each bed in 24 hours, or that if the beds filter at this rate continuously for 24 hours they would take care of 1,236,640 gallons. It was found that through this test the average amount filtered was over 800,000 gallons, or two-thirds of the amount capable of being passed at the above mentioned rate. Inasmuch as there is only a small portion of this water pumped during the night run, the rate of filtration through the day run far exceeds the 800,000 rate which is consumed, and also exceeds the 125,000,000 per acre per day rate, which is the accepted maximum rate for this type of filter. When this rate of filtration is exceeded the beds, in my opinion, can not satisfactorily purify a water such as the one to be handled at this plant, as it contains practically no turbidity, thus leaving the coagulant to form the entire mat. As a result the mat is not as firm as one formed by the coagulant with a small amount of earthy matter mixed with it, and is therefore more apt to crack, a fault which is very damaging to the process of filtration. The point of 125,000,000 rate, or 618,320 gallons for these filters, is interesting, inasmuch as the original contract calls for a maximum capacity of 1,400,000 gallons filtered in 24 hours, or 81,680 gallons more in 24 hours for each filter than the above rate, in my opinion an amount far in excess of what should be required of these beds.

To eliminate this trouble it will be necessary to equip the third bed and put it in operation, so that the filters can operate at a much lower rate than now and at the same time furnish the amount of water required.

Second. The system for washing the beds, as has been previously described, is entirely inadequate, for the reason that it is impossible to break up the beds into a liquid mass, which should be done whenever a filter is being washed. The suggestions which have been made for the installation of an air wash system will relieve this condition to some extent, but I am not positive that it will do so absolutely If it does not, the only alternative is the installation of a wash pump of larger capacity than the one now in use. The installation of this pump should be considered, as the present one is being operated at a rate of about one-fifth more than its supposed capacity.

Third. As has been previously described, the sewer outlet is too small to allow an increased wash to pass off and also too small to care for the present wash. For this reason it will be of no value to consider a better washing of the filters until arrangements have been made for carrying off the soiled water.

Fourth. It was found that during the cleaning of the settling basin the concrete trap used for passing the water directly on the beds while the basin is being emptied was cracked to such an extent that it was almost impossible to keep the proper head of water on the filters while this work was being done. These cracks should have immediate attention, as no plant should be compelled to shut down during the cleaning of any one portion of its system.

This last difficulty is in no way a cause of the poor results found in the filtered water, but the other three have a direct bearing on the results, and it is my best judgment that the plant can not be made to give a satisfactory effluent for any length of time until the above mentioned alterations are made. The installation of the bleach system will give satisfactory results until this work is completed, providing it has very careful attention.

Other points that are inconvenient in the operation are the absence of loss of head gauges and rate controllers, and as the sewer is on a hydraulic level with the top of the sand bed, it is impossible to drain the beds perfectly dry without allowing the remaining water to go into the clear well. This is a bad feature, as it is often desirous to drain a bed dry after washing, and the water in the beds at this time is quite unsuitable for use.

In conclusion, I would say that at the present time, and until such changes as have been advised can be made, the plant does not and will not answer the requirements of the original builder's contract, which states that the efficiency of the purification plant shall be such that in no case shall the average number of bacteria in the filtrate exceed 100 per cubic centimeter, except when the number of bacteria in the applied water shall exceed 3,000 per cubic centimeter, in which event the average reduction of the bacteria in the filtrate shall be at least 97 per cent. Not more than 5 per cent. of the individual samples of the filtrate shall show more than 150 bacteria per cubic centimeter or an efficiency as low as 90 per cent. No trace of decomposed coagulant shall be left in the filtrate nor shall the filtrate show acid reaction. The filtrate shall be clear, bright and practically free from color, odor, turbidity or matter in suspension, and shall be supplied at the rate of 1,400,000 gallons per twenty-four hours when the filters are operated at normal capacity.

Other than not answering the requirements of this contract the plant in itself does not produce an effluent satisfactory to the State Board of Health and must not be used as a sole means of purification without the use of hypochlorite of lime or some other satisfactory sterilizing agent until such time as the plant has been remodeled and approved by the State Board of Health.

In advising the installation of this apparatus for sterilization, which is entirely satisfactory, it is with the understanding that it is to be used for emergency purposes, such as that at hand, and should in no way take the place of the work which is required to put the plant in condition to care for the water.

With the establishment of a laboratory and the installation of a sterilization plant, the citizens of Valparaiso are furnished, and should continue to be furnished, with as satisfactory a water, from the standpoint of purity and mineral constituents, as is to be had in the State of Indiana.

TABLE 1.

CHEMICAL REPORT.

Date.	Alkalinity Raw Water.	Alkalinity Filtered.	Alum Used, Grains per Gallon.	Alum in Effluent.	Bleach Pounds per 1,000,000 Gallons.
9-14-10	24.0	13.0	1.5	Absent.	0
9-15-10	22.0	12.0	1.5	Absent.	0
9-16-10	23.0	15.0	1.5	Absent.	0
9-17-10	24.0	12.0	1.5	Absent.	0
9-18-10	23.0	12.0	1.5	Absent.	0
9-20-10	23.0	8.0	1.5	Absent.	0
9-25-10	23.0	11.0	1.5	Absent.	0
9-26-10	23.0	12.0	1.5	Absent.	0
9-27-10	23.0	10.0	1.5	Absent.	Started.
9-28-10	23.0	9.0	1.5	Absent.	6
9-29-10	23.0	8.5	1.5	Absent.	6
9-30-10	23.0	10.0	1.5	Absent.	6
10- 2-10	23.0	11.0	1.5	Absent.	5
10- 3-10	22.0	9.0	1.4	Absent.	5
10- 4-10	23.0	10.0	1.4	Absent.	5
10- 5-10	23.0	10.0	1.25	Absent.	5
10- 6-10	22.0	11.0	1.35	Absent.	5
10- 7-10	22.0	10.0	1.5	Absent.	5
10- 8-10	23.0	12.0	1.4	Absent.	5

Results in parts per million.

TABLE 2.

WATER PUMPED AND USED.

Date.	Gallons Pumped to City.	Gallons Wash Water Used.	Total Gallons Filtered.	Per Cent. Wash Water.
9-14-10	781,116	36,000	817,116	4.5
9-15-10	794,070	24,000	818,070	2.9
9-16-10	750,378	36,000	786,378	4.4
9-17-10	789,038	24,000	813,038	2.9
9-18-10	729,674	24,000	753,674	3.2
9-19-10	756,598	36,000	792,598	4.5
9-20-10	771,324	24,000	795,324	3.0
9-21-10	789,172	36,000	825,172	4.3
9-22-10	832,354	36,000	868,354	4.1
9-23-10	758,370	24,000	782,370	3.1
9-24-10	786,488	24,000	810,488	2.9
9-25-10	711,824	24,000	735,824	3.2
9-26-10	746,062	36,000	782,062	4.6
9-27-10	784,108	36,000	820,108	4.5
9-28-10	760,202	24,000	784,202	3.1
9-29-10	799,068	24,000	823,068	2.9
9-30-10	791,520	24,000	815,572	2.9
10- 2-10	710,090	24,000	734,090	3.3
10- 3-10	787,100	36,000	823,100	4.4
10- 4-10	776,458	36,000	812,458	4.4
10- 5-10	687,718	24,000	711,718	3.3
10- 6-10	762,994	24,000	786,994	3.0
10- 7-10	777,240	24,000	801,240	2.9
10- 8-10	774,180	36,000	780,180	4.6

BACTERIAL REPORT.

Date.	Lab. No.	Source.	Bacteria Per C.C.	Per Cent. Efficiency.	B. Coli. Dextrose.			B. Coli. Lactose.			Hours in Use.
9-14-10	2018-A	Lake..............	200	......	Susp.	Susp.	Susp.	......	......	......	......
9-14-10	2019-A	Raw..............	670	......	Susp.	Susp.	Susp.	......	......	......	......
9-14-10	2020-A	Filter No. 2........	590	11.9	+	Susp.	Susp.	......	......	......	......
9-14-10	2021-A	Filter No. 3........	520	22.4	+	+	+	......	......	......	......
9-14-10	2022-A	Plant tap..........	320	52.3	+	+	+	......	......	......	......
9-15-10	2023-A	Lake..............	90	......	Susp.	Susp.	+	......	......	......	......
9-15-10	2024-A	Raw..............	120	......	Susp.	Susp.	+	......	......	......	......
9-15-10	2025-A	Filter No. 2........	537	......	Susp.	Susp.	Susp.	......	......	......	......
9-15-10	2026-A	Filter No. 3........	640	......	+	+	+	......	......	......	......
9-15-10	2027-A	Plant tap..........	580	......	+	+	+	......	......	......	......
9-16-10	2028-A	Lake..............	100	......	+	+	—	+	—	—	......
9-16-10	2029-A	Raw..............	120		+	+	—	—	—	—	......
9-16-10	2030-A	Filter No. 2........	25	79.2	—	—	—	—	—	—	......
9-16-10	2031-A	Filter No. 3........	165	......	—	+	—	+	—	—	......
9-16-10	2032-A	Plant tap..........	110	8.4	—	—	—	+	+	—	......
9-17-10	2033-A	Raw..............	140	......	+	Susp.	......	—	—	......	......
9-17-10	2034-A	Filter No. 2........	550	......	—	Susp.	......	—	—	......	6
9-17-10	2035-A	Filter No. 3........	28	80.0	+	Susp.	......	—	—	......	1
9-17-10	2036-A	Plant tap..........	30	78.6	Susp.	Susp.	......	—	—	......	......
9-18-10	2037-A	Raw..............	120	......	Susp.	Susp.	......	—	—	......	......
9-18-10	2038-A	Filter No. 2........	500	......	+	+	......	—	—	......	9
9-18-10	2039-A	Filter No. 3........	400	......	+	Susp.	......	—	—	......	3
9-18-10	2040-A	Plant tap..........	375	......	+	Susp.	......	—	—	......	......
9-20-10	2041-A	Raw..............	280	......	......	......	......	......	......	......	......
9-20-10	2042-A	Filter No. 2........	300	......	......	......	......	......	......	......	12
9-20-10	2043-A	Filter No. 2........	240	14.3	......	......	......	......	......	......	1
9-20-10	2044-A	Filter No. 3........	200	28.9	......	......	......	......	......	......	7
9-20-10	2045-A	Plant tap..........	150	46.5	......	......	......	......	......	......	......
9-25-10	2046-A	Raw..............	120	......	—	—	Susp.	—	—	—	......
9-25-10	2047-A	Filter No. 3........	360	......	—	—	Gas.	—	—	—	2
9-25-10	2048-A	Filter No. 3........	250	......	—	Susp.	Susp.	—	—	—	2
9-25-10	2049-A	Plant tap..........	400	......	—	—	—	—	—	—	......
9-26-10	2050-A	Raw..............	280	......	+	Susp.	Susp.	—	—	—	......
9-26-10	2051-A	Filter No. 3........	200	28.9	......	......	......	......	......	......	20
9-26-10	2052-A	Filter No. 3........	280	......	......	......	......	......	......	......	2
9-26-10	2053-A	Plant tap..........	480	......	Susp.	Susp.	Susp.	—	—	—	......
9-27-10	2054-A	Raw..............	320	......	......	......	......	......	......	......	......
9-27-10	2055-A	Plant tap..........	340	......	......	......	......	......	......	......	......
9-28-10	2056-A	Raw..............	120	......	Gas.	......	......	—	......	......	......
9-28-10	2057-A	Filter No. 2........	440	......	+	......	......	—	......	......	8
9-28-10	2058-A	Filter No. 3........	320	......	Susp.	......	......	—	......	......	4
9-28-10	2059-A	Plant tap..........	41	65.9	Gas.	Gas.	......	—	Gas.	......	......
9-28-10	2060-A	City tap..........	650	......	—	Susp.	......	—	Gas.	......	......
9-29-10	2061-A	Raw..............	150	......	Gas.	......	......	—	......	......	......
9-29-10	2062-A	Filter No. 2........	450	—	Gas.	......	......	—	......	......	6
9-29-10	2063-A	Filter No. 3........	270	—	Gas.	......	......	—	......	......	4
9-29-10	2064-A	Plant tap..........	45	70	—	Gas.	......	Gas.	......	......	......
9-29-10	2065-A	City tap..........	67	53.4	Gas.	Gas.	......	—	......	......	......
10- 2-10	2066-A	Raw..............	*	—	+	......	......	—	......	......	......
10- 2-10	2067-A	Filter No. 2........	190	—	—	......	......	—	......	......	13
10- 2-10	2068-A	Filter No. 3........	270	—	—	......	......	—	......	......	3
10- 2-10	2069-A	Tap..............	0	100	—	—	—	—	—	—	......
10- 3-10	2070-A	Raw..............	270	—	—	......	......	—	......	......	......
10- 3-10	2071-A	Filter No. 2........	450	—	—	......	......	—	......	......	7
10- 3-10	2072-A	Filter No. 3........	690	—	—	......	......	—	......	......	1
10- 3-10	2073-A	Tap..............	16	94.1	—	—	......	—	—	......	......

*Liquified.

BACTERIAL REPORT.

Date.	Lab. No.	Source.	Bacteria Per C.C.	Per Cent. Efficiency.	B. Coli. Dextrose.			B. Coli. Lactose.			Hours in Use.
10- 4-10	2074-A	Raw	*	......	—	......	......	—	......	......	......
10- 4-10	2075-A	Filter No. 2	250	—	+	......	......	Gas.	......	......	13
10- 4-10	2076-A	Filter No. 3	420	—	—	......	......	—	......	......	5
10- 4-10	2077-A	Tap	11	—	—	—	......	—	—	......	......
10- 5-10	2078-A	Raw	190	—	—	......	......	—	......	......	......
10- 5-10	2079-A	Filter No. 2	160	15.8	—	......	......	—	......	......	3
10- 5-10	2080-A	Filter No. 3	400	—	—	......	......	—	......	......	15
10- 5-10	2081-A	Tap	0	100	—	—	......	—	—	......	......
10- 6-10	2082-A	Raw	70	—	—	......	......	—	......	......	2
10- 6-10	2083-A	Filter No. 2	10	85.7	+	......	......	—	......	......	2
10- 6-10	2084-A	Filter No. 3	10	85.7	—	......	......	—	......	......	10
10- 6-10	2085-A	Tap	0	100	—	—	......	—	—	......	......
10- 7-10	2086-A	Raw	190	—	—	......	......	—	......	......	......
10- 7-10	2087-A	Filter No. 2	200	—	—	......	......	—	......	......	6
10- 7-10	2088-A	Filter No. 3	330	—	—	......	......	—	......	......	14
10- 7-10	2089-A	Tap	0	100	—	—	......	—	—	......	......
10- 8-10	2090-A	Raw	180	—	—	......	......	—	......	......	......
10- 8-10	2091-A	Filter No. 2	150	16.7	—	......	......	—	......	......	3
10- 8-10	2092-A	Filter No. 3	290	—	—	......	......	—	......	......	20
10- 8-10	2093-A	Tap	0	100	—	—	......	—	—	......	......

*Liquified.

Results of October 2 to October 8 were submitted by Mr. Bradley.

STATISTICAL REPORT, 1910.

This report is for the calendar year 1910. The populations are those of the United States census.

In the following tables the causes of death are arranged according to the International list of Causes of Death which has been adopted by all of the registration States of the country. This international list of causes of death was used by the United States Bureau of the Census in its last statistical compilation of causes of death.

Table 1 is a classification of all deaths, with rates per 100,000 population, classified and arranged according to the international list of causes of death.

Table 2 is a classification of deaths from all causes by months, ages, color, nationality and conjugal condition.

Table 3 gives deaths from all causes by counties, months, ages, color, nationality and conjugal condition.

Table 4 gives deaths from certain diseases by geographical sections and by counties.

Table 5 gives death rates from certain important causes by counties in geographical sections.

Table 6 gives deaths in cities from important causes for the year 1910.

Table 7 gives death rates by cities from important causes for the year 1910.

Table 8 gives annual death rates for ten years, 1901 to 1911, with average of cities of 5,000 population and over, compared with rural and State rates.

Table 9 gives deaths according to occupations by months and ages.

Table 10 gives deaths from tuberculosis (all forms) with rates per 100,000 population, for certain occupations of each sex for the year 1910.

Table 11 gives deaths from poliomyelitis by counties, months, and ages for the year 1910.

Table A gives births by counties, months, color and nationality of parents. (Stillbirths excluded.)

Table B gives births by counties, number of children born to each mother, grouped ages of parents, stillbirths, plurality and illegitimate births.

Table C gives number of births, and rate per 1,000 population, by counties for year 1910.

Table D gives by counties the marriages by months, color and nationality.

Table E gives by counties the marriages by grouped ages.

BIRTHS.

The number of births reported in the State of Indiana during the year 1910 was 56,309, of which number 28,806 were males and 27,503 females. Of the total males, 28,273 were white and 533 colored. In the preceding year 54,445 births were reported; males 28,045, females 26.400. This shows an increase over the preceding year of 1,864 births, and an increase in rate of 1.5. March had the largest number of births, 5,142 and November the smallest, 4,380. March had the greatest number of deaths, 3,599 and June the lowest, 2,747. The birth (56,309) rate, 20.8, exceeds the death (36,513) rate, 13.5, per 1,000 population.

The nationality of parents appears as follows: American-born fathers, 51,123; American-born mothers, 52,017. Foreign-born fathers, 4,062; foreign-born mothers, 3,565. Nationality not reported, fathers 464; mothers 67.

Of the total number of children born to each mother, 15,815 were first, 12,249 second, 8,704 third, 6,076 fourth, 4,340 fifth, 3,016 sixth, 2,064 seventh, 1,365 eighth, 885 ninth, 608 tenth, 331 eleventh, 372 twelfth and over, 484 not reported.

As to the ages of parents, 791 fathers and 5,867 mothers were under twenty years of age. In the age period 50 and 60 there were 1,218 fathers, and 6 mothers; age period 60 to 70, 102 fathers, and between 70 and 80 there were 12 fathers.

One thousand six hundred and eighty-nine stillbirths, not in cluded in the total number of births and deaths.

The illegitimate births numbered 998, of which 522 were males and 476 females. The plural births numbered 1,317, of which 650 were males and 667 females.

MARRIAGES.

Total marriages reported 29,110. This is an increase, compared with the preceding year, of 2,654. June had the greatest number of marriages, 2,926, and May had the smallest number, 1,940.

The general statistics on marriages will be found in Tables C and D.

DEATHS.

The total number of deaths reported in 1910 was 36,513, rate 13.5. In the preceding year 36,579, rate 13.2. Males 19,292, females 17,221. White males 18,529; colored 760; white females 16,584; colored 634.

American-born, 16,785 males and 15,545 females; foreign-born, 2,234 males and 1,571 females; nationality not reported, 273 males, 105 females. Single males, 8,255; females, 6,202; married males, 7,829; females, 6,323; widowed or divorced males, 3,013; females, 4,670; conjugal condition not reported, males, 195; females, 26.

The number of deaths, with rates, for ten years, appear in the following table:

	1901.	1902.	1903.	1904.	1905.	1906.	1907.	1908.	1909.	1910.
Deaths.......	36,544	34,069	33,892	37,240	36,502	35,992	36,461	36,224	36,579	36,513
Annual rate...	14.5	13.5	13.4	14.0	13.7	13.5	13.4	13.2	13.3	13.5

Of the total number of deaths, 6,048, or 16.5 per cent. of the whole number, occurred under one year. A decrease of 4.9 per cent. over last year.

Two thousand six hundred and forty-two deaths occurred in the age period of 1 to 4, making a total loss of children under 5 years of age 8,690, or 23.7 per cent of the total deaths. Decrease of 4.1 per cent. over last year. This is 15.2 per cent. of the total births reported. Decrease of 3.4 per cent. over last year.

In the age period 5 to 19 there were 2,417 deaths or 6.6 per cent. of the total number; increase of .01 per cent. over last year. The total loss under 20 years of age is 11,107 or 30.4 per cent. of total deaths. Decrease of 4.0 per cent. over last year.

In the age period 20 to 49, practically the prime of life, there were 8,438 deaths, equal to 23.1 per cent. of the total deaths, an increase of 1.7 per cent. over preceding year.

There were 388 deaths over 90 years of age, a decrease of 32 as compared with last year.

PRINCIPAL CAUSES OF DEATH FOR THE LAST TEN YEARS, WITH AVERAGE.

The following table gives the principal causes of death in their numerical order, for the past ten years, and also the yearly average for each cause, and Chart No. 1 gives a graphic representation of the principal causes for 1910:

PRINCIPAL CAUSES OF DEATH IN INDIANA FOR THE LAST TEN YEARS, WITH AVERAGES.

		1901.	1902.	1903.	1904.	1905.	1906.	1907.	1908.	1909.	1910.	Average.
1	Organic heart disease	1,754	1,860	2,108	2,108	2,182	2,208	2,766	3,534	3,428	3,956	2,597
2	Pulmonary tuberculosis	4,169	3,952	3,915	4,436	3,998	3,854	3,888	3,825	3,706	3,853	3,959
3	Infantile diarrhœa, under 2 years	1,776	1,779	1,449	1,629	1,700	1,823	1,639	1,635	1,841	2,049	1,732
4	Accidents	1,463	1,391	1,601	1,622	1,795	1,796	1,981	2,021	2,030	1,902	1,760
5	Cerebral congestion and hemorrhage	1,264	1,272	1,346	1,435	1,351	1,496	1,599	1,695	1,932	1,885	1,527
6	Cancer	1,113	1,209	1,217	1,259	1,424	1,417	1,513	1,739	1,328	1,872	1,459
7	Bright's disease	1,066	1,133	1,164	1,296	1,423	1,549	1,644	1,420	1,616	1,847	1,415
8	Pneumonia lobar	3,384	2,758	2,634	3,487	3,124	2,800	3,258	2,574	2,752	1,823	2,686
9	Diseases of infants	1,247	1,183	1,318	1,726	1,908	1,766	1,783	1,664	1,454	1,523	1,557
10	Other circulatory diseases	574	648	596	665	637	768	837	965	1,008	1,006	770
11	Typhoid fever	1,198	1,217	1,013	1,013	928	913	933	885	875	934	960
12	Broncho pneumonia	480	417	416	472	535	576	585	676	875	917	595
13	Other forms of tuberculosis	493	440	477	542	494	602	634	702	543	857	578
14	Influenza	1,049	302	348	434	591	224	666	367	504	701	508
15	Liver diseases	513	530	527	596	578	591	561	518	599	636	564
16	Diarrhœa and enteritis, over 2 years	462	391	411	427	450	460	605	575	563	620	496
17	Stomach diseases	704	641	613	561	678	699	617	687	649	547	639
18	Other digestive diseases	662	605	519	530	498	524	491	487	536	475	432
19	Bronchitis	562	484	523	571	540	460	431	452	630	464	511
20	Measles	161	67	73	212	6	23	213	209	156	462	158
21	Whooping cough	181	164	148	94	136	157	136	416	378	459	226
22	Malformation	180	162	152	172	167	284	266	344	433	452	261
23	Suicides	254	278	254	283	338	321	361	384	404	386	337
24	Diphtheria and croup	555	424	462	314	366	402	353	315	348	381	392
25	Diabetes	204	197	197	226	231	269	252	290	201	372	252
26	Other genito-urinary diseases	243	390	437	229	194	228	266	292	318	322	291
27	Dysentery	263	277	211	184	218	235	242	245	285	304	246
28	Appendicitis	137	145	163	164	194	174	205	248	269	272	197
29	Other respiratory diseases	370	352	276	325	285	276	242	195	177	271	276
30	Rheumatism	184	209	220	266	253	274	185	174	183	247	219
31	Paralysis, without specified cause	986	762	762	935	901	777	691	399	286	241	674
32	Scarlet fever	149	150	164	192	133	101	91	95	151	205	147
33	Acute nephritis	142	150	191	207	189	230	169	234	281	174	196
34	Diseases of female genital organs	85	87	85	91	88	112	123	149	149	173	113
35	General paralysis of the insane	......	......	......	......	......	......	......	......	......	169	......
36	Skin diseases	124	181	129	140	179	170	164	177	147	167	157
37	Malaria	197	161	131	116	116	102	81	83	115	151	125
38	Simple meningitis	553	509	365	538	352	240	384	264	196	130	353
39	Homicides	48	36	62	48	85	93	122	122	100	121	84
40	Convulsions of infants	406	339	335	345	306	254	221	114	81	51	245
41	Simple peritonitis	354	366	311	375	338	265	222	99	120	38	248
42	Cerebro-spinal fever	286	187	341	347	460	481	180	154	110	22	256
43	Smallpox	21	75	195	97	35	8	8	10	5	1	45
	Total	29,965	27,880	27,909	30,981	30,404	30,092	31,608	31,933	32,259	33,507	30,636

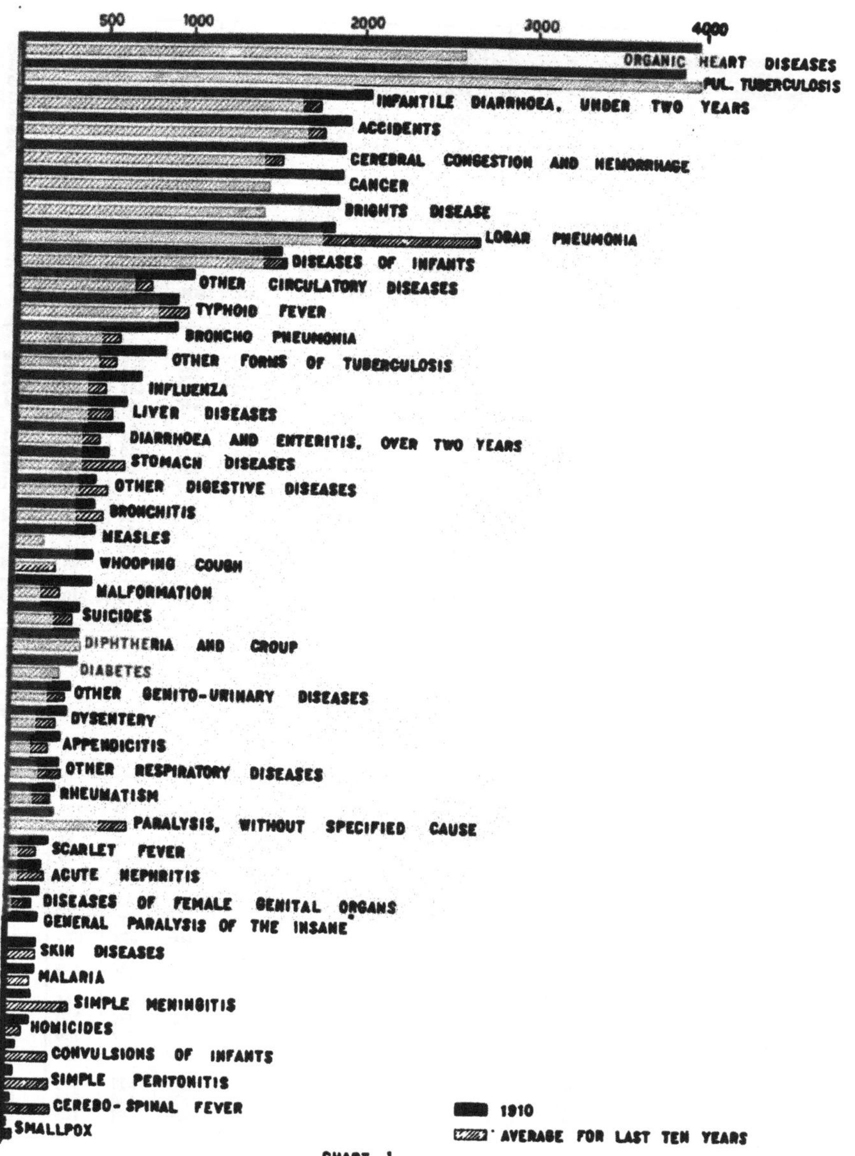
INDIANA
PRINCIPAL CAUSES OF DEATH
500
1000
2000
3000
4000
ORGANIC HEART DISEASES
PUL. TUBERCULOSIS
INFANTILE DIARRHOEA, UNDER TWO YEARS
ACCIDENTS
CEREBRAL CONGESTION AND HEMORRHAGE
CANCER
BRIGHTS DISEASE
LOBAR PNEUMONIA
DISEASES OF INFANTS
OTHER CIRCULATORY DISEASES
TYPHOID FEVER
BRONCHO PNEUMONIA
OTHER FORMS OF TUBERCULOSIS
INFLUENZA
LIVER DISEASES
DIARRHOEA AND ENTERITIS, OVER TWO YEARS
STOMACH DISEASES
OTHER DIGESTIVE DISEASES
BRONCHITIS
MEASLES
WHOOPING COUGH
MALFORMATION
SUICIDES
DIPHTHERIA AND CROUP
DIABETES
OTHER GENITO-URINARY DISEASES
DYSENTERY
APPENDICITIS
OTHER RESPIRATORY DISEASES
RHEUMATISM
PARALYSIS, WITHOUT SPECIFIED CAUSE
SCARLET FEVER
ACUTE NEPHRITIS
DISEASES OF FEMALE GENITAL ORGANS
GENERAL PARALYSIS OF THE INSANE
SKIN DISEASES
MALARIA
SIMPLE MENINGITIS
HOMICIDES
CONVULSIONS OF INFANTS
SIMPLE PERITONITIS
CEREBO-SPINAL FEVER
SMALLPOX
1910
AVERAGE FOR LAST TEN YEARS

CHART 1

TUBERCULOSIS.

HAVOC WROUGHT BY TUBERCULOSIS IN INDIANA IN 1904, 1905, 1906, 1907, 1908, 1909 AND 1910.

	1904.	1905.	1906.	1907.	1908.	1909.	1910.
Total tuberculosis deaths	4,978	4,492	4,456	4,471	4,527	4,479	4,710
Male deaths	1,807	1,745	1,675	1,964	2,085	2,112	2,191
Female deaths	3,171	2,793	2,771	2,328	2,442	2,367	2,519
Mothers, age 18 to 40, prime of life	867	987	917	826	875	1,286	1,412
Fathers, age 18 to 40, prime of life	490	315	255	343	383	994	1,040
Orphans made under 12 years of age	2,703	2,694	2,353	2,340	2,407	2,375	2,490
Homes invaded	3,396	3,307	3,283	3,849	4,022	3,866	3,909

TUBERCULOSIS, ALL FORMS.

Deaths by Months, with Average for Last Ten Years.

MONTHS.	1901.	1902.	1903.	1904.	1905.	1906.	1907.	1908.	1909.	1910.	Average.
January	389	402	368	420	419	415	373	411	389	409	399
February	440	389	350	414	407	394	428	425	374	407	402
March	433	459	445	550	461	443	449	437	451	498	462
April	449	444	411	459	426	439	455	446	449	462	444
May	420	405	388	502	391	398	384	412	418	402	411
June	348	323	363	400	361	331	356	372	410	399	366
July	3[illegible]4	320	373	397	361	329	377	357	349	373	363
August	403	331	340	390	355	367	389	314	353	368	361
September	309	353	354	347	306	307	340	341	322	354	333
October	350	305	306	365	326	344	327	330	327	359	333
November	357	320	333	352	326	346	315	344	306	311	330
December	370	345	388	582	353	343	329	338	332	368	374
Totals	4,662	4,396	4,414	5,178	4,492	4,456	4,522	4,527	4,479	4,710	4,583

TUBERCULOSIS, ALL FORMS.

Deaths by Ages, with Average for Last Ten Years.

AGES.	1901.	1902.	1903.	1904.	1905.	1906.	1907.	1908.	1909.	1910.	Average.
Under 1 year	135	113	109	144	108	126	132	152	179	184	138
1-2 years	62	68	59	99	35	62	85	36	87	102	69
2-3 years	34	31	24	42	26	38	48	30	36	39	34
3-4 years	23	17	23	25	18	31	24	21	24	29	23
4-5 years	17	12	14	13	11	24	28	15	15	22	17
5-9 years	63	51	64	68	63	64	58	55	67	60	61
10-14 years	99	98	92	126	97	106	93	100	93	92	99
15-19 years	417	401	436	501	449	411	400	400	373	370	415
20-24 years	718	672	707	725	697	681	667	609	575	653	670
25-29 years	595	593	572	614	574	577	573	532	567	590	579
30-34 years	519	464	491	509	464	464	467	432	410	484	470
35-39 years	386	346	374	436	419	375	341	356	355	350	374
40-44 years	310	311	267	316	273	242	253	312	312	300	289
45-49 years	248	235	225	286	245	260	270	259	290	238	255
50-54 years	185	224	217	232	222	221	226	227	217	276	224
55-59 years	190	181	193	206	153	171	190	225	198	213	192
60-64 years	200	153	166	189	165	170	179	200	203	195	182
65-69 years	171	155	143	152	165	162	180	202	165	188	167
70-74 years	118	124	116	136	122	122	138	162	135	161	133
75-79 years	81	76	74	75	72	96	104	92	112	99	88
80-89 years	42	38	30	47	34	35	48	48	56	54	43
90 years and over	2	1	2	3	.....	4	3	5	10	7	3

TUBERCULOSIS ALL FORMS

BY MONTHS

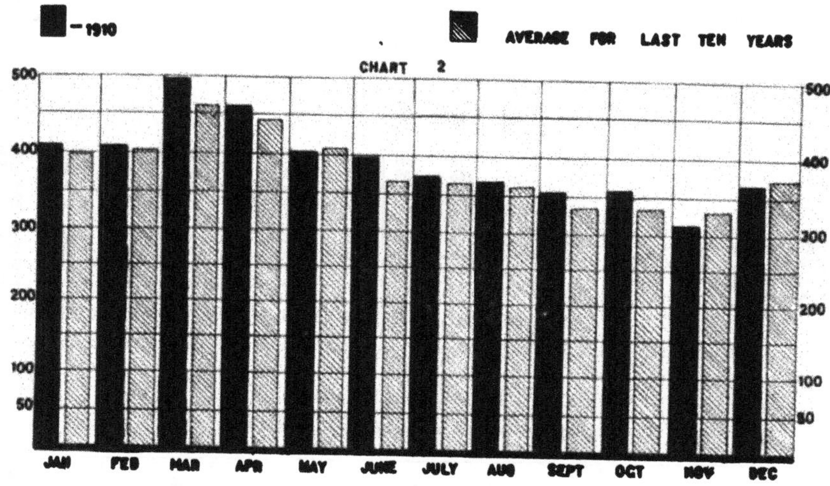

BY AGES

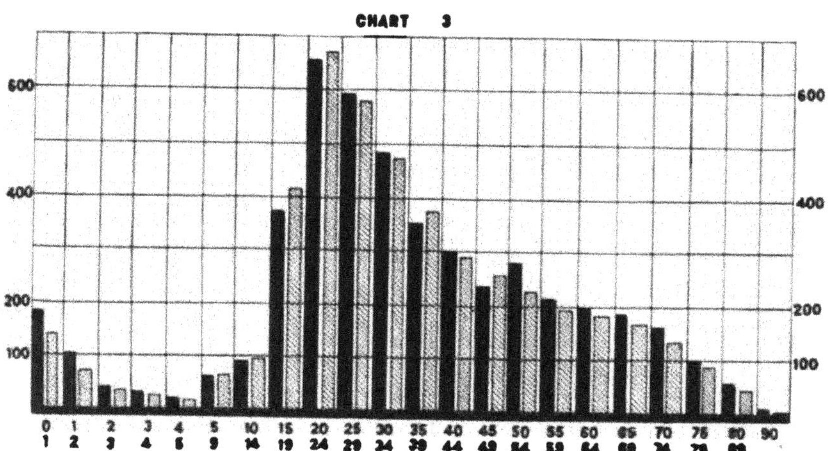

PULMONARY TUBERCULOSIS.

Deaths by Months, with Average for the Last Ten Years.

Months.	1901.	1902.	1903.	1904.	1905.	1906.	1907.	1908.	1909.	1910.	Average.
January	368	358	324	379	395	359	330	358	334	357	356
February	390	353	318	372	379	349	392	363	310	340	356
March	388	416	399	485	421	391	396	380	385	420	408
April	408	409	365	409	380	386	392	379	365	378	464
May	378	368	339	448	346	337	329	347	347	324	356
June	310	297	326	359	330	282	303	318	330	322	317
July	349	295	323	358	310	285	314	290	276	291	309
August	254	300	293	332	308	312	312	257	294	278	294
September	266	296	318	302	263	253	286	278	253	281	279
October	302	266	261	322	266	289	276	275	272	294	282
November	321	288	297	317	287	302	276	293	253	254	288
December	325	306	352	353	313	310	282	287	287	304	313
Totals	4,069	3,952	3,951	4,436	3,998	3,854	3,888	3,825	3,706	3,853	3,953

PULMONARY TUBERCULOSIS

Deaths by Ages, with Average for the Last Ten Years.

Ages.	1901.	1902.	1903.	1904.	1905.	1906.	1907.	1908.	1909.	1910.	Average.
Under 1 year	76	59	53	72	53	60	63	78	48	63	62
1–2 years	35	33	28	48	37	27	31	27	30	33	32
2–3 years	14	16	11	23	13	19	19	15	14	13	15
3–4 years	12	7	10	14	10	10	6	8	8	9	9
4–5 years	7	6	7	9	3	8	10	4	5	9	6
5–9 years	28	28	35	32	37	31	29	23	30	24	29
10–14 years	84	75	59	101	75	76	66	62	64	62	72
15–19 years	383	373	393	457	411	359	356	348	329	317	378
20–24 years	676	626	666	687	650	625	623	562	509	578	620
25–29 years	559	553	535	582	538	535	517	499	502	520	534
30–34 years	490	435	461	486	437	429	430	395	267	431	436
25–39 years	356	329	343	412	385	342	318	316	322	309	343
40–44 years	287	299	244	271	254	220	234	278	277	263	263
45–49 years	223	225	213	262	219	231	238	220	255	204	229
50–54 years	174	196	194	209	200	198	197	188	183	242	197
55–59 years	166	166	175	186	139	155	165	199	165	181	169
60–64 years	182	140	151	175	151	145	153	170	179	158	160
65–69 years	148	137	123	137	154	147	163	169	142	165	148
70–74 years	105	112	107	121	111	103	126	138	120	141	118
75–79 years	73	70	67	65	66	76	88	76	101	86	76
80–90 years	37	36	25	39	28	31	43	42	48	39	36
90 years and over	2	1	1	3	.....	4	1	3	3	6	2

PULMONARY TUBERCULOSIS

BY MONTHS

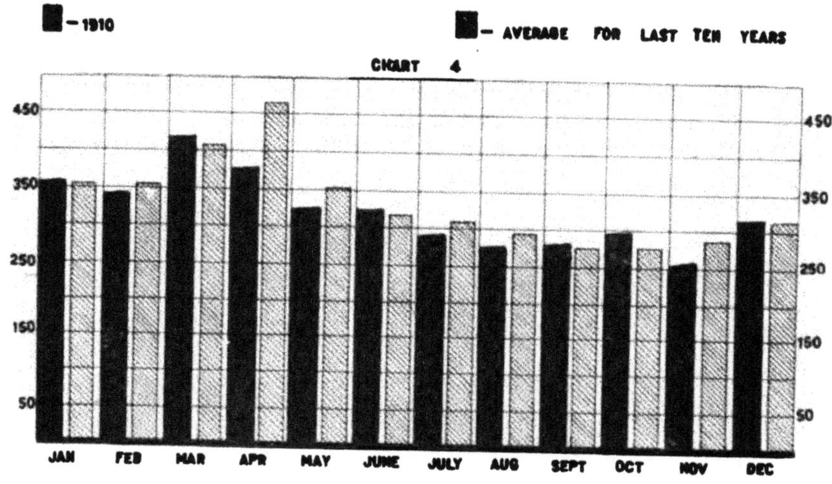

BY AGES.

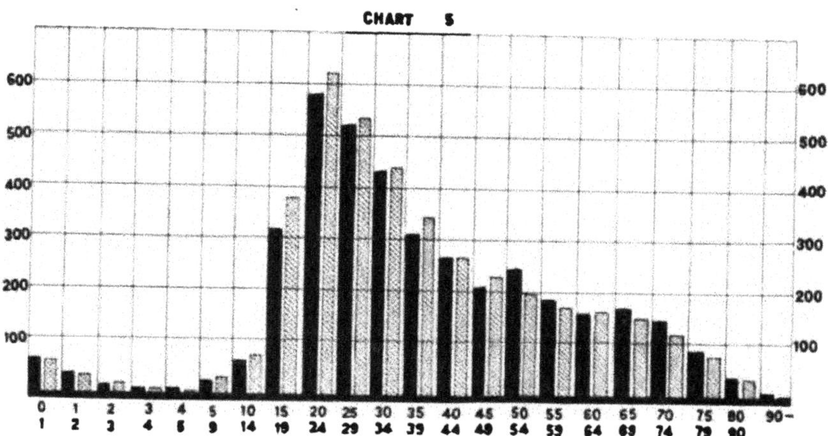

The following table, giving deaths by months, shows March had the greatest number of deaths. June had the lowest number of deaths.

Jan.	Feb.	March.	April.	May.	June.	July.	Aug.	Sept.	Oct.	Nov.	Dec.
3,039	2,972	3,599	2,967	2,757	2,747	3,064	3,406	3,010	2,892	2,932	3,128

January, February, March, April and May had the most tuberculosis deaths. December had the most pneumonia deaths. July and August were the highest in diarrhœal diseases, and September had the greatest number of typhoid deaths, 188.

TUBERCULOSIS DEATH RATES PER 100,000 BY COUNTIES FOR 1910, IN INDIANA.

State Rate, 174.4.

Counties.	Tuberculosis, All Forms.	Counties.	Tuberculosis, All Forms.
Adams	155.7	Lawrence	261.3
Allen	134.9	Madison	161.0
Bartholomew	241.9	Marion	219.3
Benton	39.4	Marshall	136.5
Blackford	170.7	Martin	223.9
Boone	182.4	Miami	139.7
Brown	17.5	Monroe	175.0
Carroll	133.5	Montgomery	160.5
Cass	165.0	Morgan	198.3
Clark	247.9	Newton	76.1
Clay	162.9	Noble	95.7
Clinton	150.0	Ohio	11.5
Crawford	348.2	Orange	215.3
Daviess	219.8	Owen	206.4
Dearborn	191.6	Parke	108.1
Decatur	191.6	Perry	177.0
Dekalb	131.7	Pike	259.2
Delaware	177.0	Porter	112.0
Dubois	211.7	Posey	212.3
Elkhart	134.7	Pulaski	112.7
Fayette	111.0	Putnam	195.0
Floyd	353.3	Randolph	175.8
Fountain	171.2	Ripley	185.1
Franklin	182.7	Rush	165.4
Fulton	142.2	Scott	14.4
Gibson	205.7	Shelby	216.4
Grant	184.6	Spencer	178.9
Greene	165.4	Starke	141.9
Hamilton	151.7	Steuben	112.1
Hancock	189.2	St. Joseph	167.2
Harrison	143.4	Sullivan	151.0
Hendricks	139.2	Switzerland	14.1
Henry	151.2	Tippecanoe	144.8
Howard	183.3	Tipton	126.0
Huntington	165.6	Union	14.3
Jackson	214.4	Vanderburgh	207.9
Jasper	69.0	Vermillion	143.1
Jay	188.3	Vigo	176.3
Jefferson	219.8	Wabash	163.4
Jennings	154.9	Warren	128.4
Johnson	171.7	Warrick	168.9
Knox	196.5	Washington	240.8
Kosciusko	92.9	Wayne	221.7
Lagrange	99.0	Wells	165.1
Lake	112.3	White	159.1
Laporte	131.0	Whitley	118.4

MONTHLY ANALYSIS OF TUBERCULOSIS.

(As Published in Monthly Bulletin.)

January, 1910.—Total number of tuberculosis deaths, all forms, 392. Pulmonary form, 347. Of the total number, 34 were males in the age period 18 to 40, and left 68 orphans. The female deaths in the same age period as above numbered 83, and left 166 orphans.

Total fathers and mothers lost in the age period of 18 to 40 were 117. Total number of orphans made, 234. Number of homes invaded, 386. Three of the tuberculosis deaths were persons over 80 years of age.

February, 1910.—Total tuberculosis deaths 387. Pulmonary form 322. Of the total number 187 were males and 173 females. Of the males 25 were married in the age period of 18 to 40 and left 50 orphans under 12 years of age. Of the females, 67 were married in the same age period and left 134 orphans. Total orphans 184. Number of homes invaded 179.

March, 1910.—Total tuberculosis deaths 478. Pulmonary form 410. Of the total number 244 were males, 234 females. Of the males 51 were married in the age period of 18 to 40, and left 102 orphans under 12 years of age. Of the females, 61 were married in the same age period as above, and left 122 orphans under 12 years of age. Total orphans 224. Total homes invaded 461. Five of the tuberculosis deaths were persons over 80 years of age.

April, 1910.—Total tuberculosis deaths 431. Of which number 194 were males, and 237 females. Of the males 30 were married in the age period 18 to 40 and left 62 orphans under 12 years of age. Of the females in the same age period 79 were married and left 160 orphans in the same age period. Total orphans made in one month by this preventable disease 220. Total number of homes invaded 397. Two hundred and sixty-four of those deaths, or 61.2 per cent. of the total, occurred in the age period of 15 to 50.

May, 1910.—Total tuberculosis deaths 384, of which 316 were of pulmonary form. Of the total deaths 35 were males, and married in the age period 18 to 40, and left 70 orphans under 12 years of age. Sixty-nine were females in the same age period and left 138 orphans in the same age period. Total lives lost in this productive age period, 104. Orphans made, 208. Homes invaded, 377.

June, 1910.—Total tuberculosis deaths 365, of which 313 were of the pulmonary form. Males deaths numbered 168, female deaths 197. Of the deaths 28 were fathers in the age period 18 to 40, and they left 57 orphans; 71 mothers in the same age period as above left 144 orphans. Total orphans made by this preventable disease, 201. Total homes invaded, 342.

July, 1910.—Total tuberculosis deaths 370, of which 305 were of the pulmonary form. Of the total number of deaths 175 were males and 195 females. Of the males, 25 were fathers in the age period 18 to 40 and left 48 orphans under 12 years of age. The mothers in the same age period numbered 70, and left 136 orphans under 12 years of age. Total number of orphans, 184. Number of homes invaded, 326.

August, 1910.—Total tuberculosis deaths 329, of which 256 were of the pulmonary form. Of the total number of deaths, 149 were fathers in the age period of 18 to 40 and they left 47 orphans under 12 years of age. One hundred and eighty young mothers in the same age period as above died and left 92 orphans. Total number of orphans, 139. Number of homes invaded, 297.

September, 1910.—Total tuberculosis deaths 334, of which 282 were the pulmonary form. The male deaths numbered 137, the female 197; of the males 20 were married in the age period of 18 to 40 and left 40 orphans under 12 years of age. Of the females, 59 were married and left 119 orphans in the same age period as above. Total orphans made by tuberculosis, 159.

October, 1910.—Total tuberculosis deaths 326, of which 266 were of the pulmonary form: males 159, females 167. Of the males in age period 18 to 40, 29 were married and left 61 orphans under 12 years of age. Of the females 55 were marred and left 111 orphans in the same age period. Total orphans made in the month, 172. Number of homes invaded, 297.

November, 1910.—Total tuberculosis deaths 296, of which 301 were of the pulmonary form. Male deaths 137, females 159. Of the males, 15 were married in the age period 18 to 40 and left 30 orphans under 12 years of age. Of the females, 60 were married in the same age period as above, and left 120 orphans, in the the same age period. Total orphans made in one month, 150. Number of homes invaded, 281.

December, 1910.—Total tuberculosis deaths 350, of which 301 were of the pulmonary form. Male deaths 161, females 189. Of the males, 33 were married in the age period of 18 to 40 and left 66 orphans under 12 years of age. Of the females, 53 were married in the same age period as above and left 106 orphans in the same age period. Total orphans made, 172. Total number of homes invaded, 328.

PNEUMONIA.

DEATHS BY MONTHS, WITH AVERAGE FOR THE LAST TEN YEARS.

Months.	1901.	1902.	1903.	1904.	1905.	1906.	1907.	1908.	1909.	1910.	Average.
January	655	473	450	579	601	490	445	425	303	349	477
February	673	535	424	750	781	439	646	454	384	327	541
March	646	497	419	761	656	541	532	414	546	417	542
April	466	371	330	576	260	404	290	277	436	223	363
May	280	207	240	326	189	232	276	166	180	193	228
June	120	104	129	115	90	119	144	74	64	127	108
July	72	70	83	101	82	88	62	45	47	59	70
August	74	97	86	69	69	82	68	52	52	79	72
September	90	113	114	86	88	98	75	69	75	87	89
October	156	169	134	135	148	189	145	103	130	154	146
November	202	196	246	251	253	300	218	195	168	299	232
December	389	307	389	353	372	410	301	243	253	426	344
Totals	3,823	3,319	3,044	4,102	3,594	3,392	3,202	2,517	2,638	2,740	3,237

DEATHS BY AGES, WITH AVERAGE FOR THE LAST TEN YEARS.

Ages.	1901.	1902.	1903.	1904.	1905.	1906.	1907.	1908.	1909.	1910.	Average.
Under 1 year	758	692	703	919	898	714	639	623	768	731	744
1–2 years	248	246	216	326	251	262	209	163	206	207	233
2–3 years	123	113	107	145	97	127	96	63	103	94	106
3–4 years	73	47	57	87	63	67	57	19	41	39	54
4–5 years	46	39	34	53	28	46	29	22	18	23	33
5–9 years	120	93	102	145	90	91	65	55	65	71	89
10–14 years	66	55	57	72	71	50	40	35	34	24	50
15–19 years	139	93	88	128	89	95	63	50	52	50	84
20–24 years	130	107	83	108	83	77	84	61	53	59	84
25–29 years	119	86	72	98	79	89	90	50	49	58	79
30–34 years	115	96	58	104	90	86	87	63	60	62	82
35–39 years	121	80	78	114	107	104	98	75	66	69	91
40–44 years	142	104	77	105	98	106	88	71	68	73	93
45–49 years	110	87	103	137	106	112	100	78	57	69	96
50–54 years	159	118	89	137	130	130	143	72	85	100	116
55–59 years	179	112	132	136	140	137	125	101	108	104	127
60–64 years	218	142	164	195	173	155	172	122	113	114	156
65–69 years	244	205	172	225	237	216	215	168	162	152	199
70–74 years	246	192	202	261	270	229	243	212	147	189	219
75–79 years	191	200	192	268	226	232	238	180	166	187	208
80–90 years	216	181	204	271	237	232	280	209	183	233	224
90 years and over	25	24	27	42	28	25	33	18	34	32	28

PNEUMONIA DEATHS

BY MONTHS

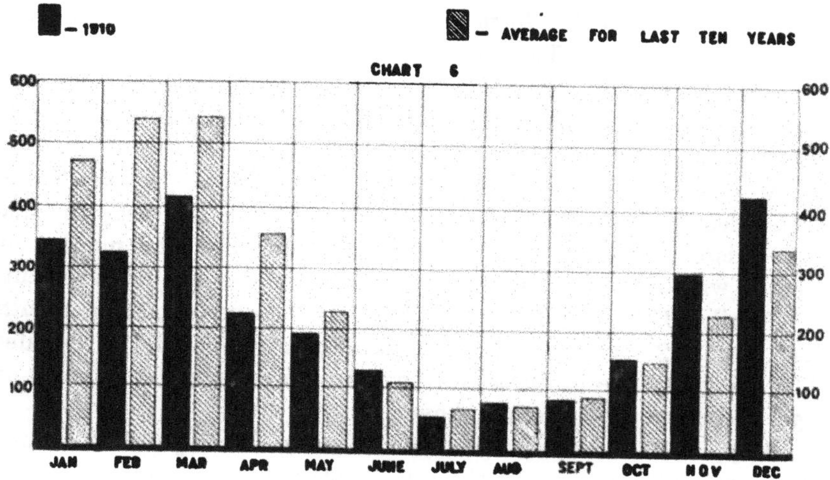

BY AGES

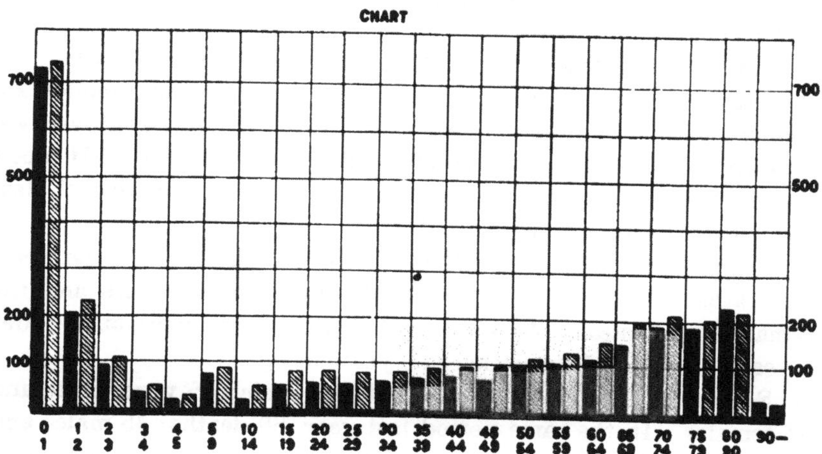

MONTHLY ANALYSIS OF PNEUMONIA DEATHS.

(As Published in Monthly Bulletin.)

January, 1910.—The disease prevailed extensively; 400 deaths. In the corresponding month last year, 367. Of the 400 deaths this month, 215 were males and 185 females. By ages they were: under 1 year of age, 70; 1 to 10, 61; 10 to 20, 16; 20 to 40, 40; 40 to 60. 64; 60 to 70, 45; 70 to 80, 58; 80 to 90, 41; 90 and over, 5.

February, 1910.—The disease existed in every county and deaths occurred in all but ten. The total deaths were 413, of which 211 were males, and 202 were females. In the same period last year, 423.

March, 1910.—The disease existed in every county of the State. Total deaths, 461. In the corresponding month last year the disease existed in every county in the State, and the total number of deaths was 574. By this comparison there was an improvement.

April, 1910.—Total deaths, 236. In the corresponding month last year, 452. The male pneumonia deaths numbered 121, females 114. Seventy-five of these deaths were children under 5 years of age, and 83 were 60 years and over.

May, 1910.—Total deaths, 183. In the corresponding month last year, 203 deaths. Of the total deaths, 112 were males and 71 females; 33 were under 1 year of age, 15 were in the age period 1 tc 5; 59 in the age period of 20 to 60; 34 were between 70 to 80, and 16 between 80 to 90.

June, 1910.—Total deaths, 120; males 60 and females 60. In the same month last year 72 deaths, males 46 and females 26. Pneumonia deaths under 1 year of age, 21; 50 years and over, 48.

July, 1910.—Total deaths, 50; males 28, females 22. It stood twenty-first in area of prevalence, and in the same month last year stood twentieth, with 61 deaths.

August, 1910.—Total deaths, 72. In the same month last year, 57 deaths. Of the 72 pneumonia deaths, 33 were males and the remainder females. There were 24 deaths from pneumonia under 1 year of age and 14 were over 60 years of age.

September, 1910.—Total deaths 82, of which 45 were males and 37 females. In the same period last year, 86 deaths; 45 males and 41 females. This disease stood eighteenth in area of prevalence. Thirty-three of the pneumonia deaths were under 1 year of age, and 14 were over 70.

October, 1910.—Total number of deaths 143, of which 76 were males and 67 females. In the same month last year 72 deaths,

33 males and 39 femals. Sixty-one deaths were under 1 year of age. Nineteen 1 to 4 and 39 were over 50 years of age.

November, 1910.—Total deaths, 296. In the same month last year, 201. Of the 296 deaths, 157 were males and 139 females. One hundred and five deaths were under 1 year of age; 45 in the age period of 1 to 4; 31 in the age period of 60 to 70; 70 to 80, 35; 80 to 90, 21; over 90, 4.

December, 1910.—Total deaths 413, of which 220 were males and 193 females. In the same month last year, 283 deaths; 252 males and 31 females. By comparison there was a decrease.

TYPHOID FEVER.

DEATHS BY MONTHS, WITH AVERAGE FOR LAST TEN YEARS.

Months.	1901.	1902.	1903.	1904.	1905.	1906.	1907.	1908.	1909.	1910.	Average.
January	74	66	61	36	511	39	72	50	40	55	53
February	50	37	53	55	35	29	57	49	21	33	41
March	49	41	55	62	34	40	48	49	38	36	45
April	41	45	45	61	26	32	38	38	34	36	39
May	35	31	39	55	33	39	42	32	36	28	37
June	27	28	42	58	48	29	30	32	37	28	36
July	81	88	64	70	57	52	58	63	80	45	65
August	148	176	120	107	121	96	145	93	119	126	125
September	198	237	193	138	203	155	141	121	144	128	175
October	222	225	165	167	154	168	133	150	162	168	172
November	185	155	104	137	101	148	84	121	110	126	127
December	88	88	72	67	65	86	75	87	54	65	74
Totals	1,198	1,217	1,013	1,013	928	913	933	885	875	934	990

DEATHS BY AGES, WITH AVERAGE FOR LAST TEN YEARS.

Ages.	1901.	1902.	1903.	1904.	1905.	1906.	1907.	1908.	1909.	1910.	Average.
Under 1 year	15	9	4	16	11	12	8	11	9	6	10
1-2 years	14	15	13	11	14	11	7	10	10	12	11
2-3 years	12	29	12	18	16	13	13	19	15	12	15
3-4 years	18	19	17	8	11	19	13	19	10	12	14
4-5 years	19	20	16	16	18	18	10	12	11	18	16
5-9 years	91	77	77	74	72	65	58	45	64	62	68
10-14 years	87	98	102	82	74	85	92	72	82	74	84
15-19 years	178	167	160	133	125	138	145	105	141	125	141
20-24 years	177	169	136	137	136	120	126	131	102	138	137
25-29 years	146	139	102	89	94	94	94	96	90	90	103
30-34 years	78	117	62	73	64	76	79	76	74	74	77
35-39 years	70	69	62	73	45	62	67	57	55	71	63
40-44 years	75	73	49	47	49	34	46	45	37	47	50
45-49 years	49	58	45	49	46	37	41	40	36	45	44
50-54 years	34	37	33	45	32	36	32	41	34	39	36
55-59 years	36	31	35	37	31	22	24	29	32	37	31
60-64 years	33	22	18	42	30	18	28	28	24	11	25
65-69 years	25	25	21	22	20	16	16	17	20	19	20
70-74 years	24	21	19	18	19	10	17	15	9	19	17
75-79 years	5	13	12	10	9	15	10	11	8	14	10
80-90 years	8	4	11	7	8	8	5	4	10	9	7
90 years and over	......	......	1	.....	......	......	......	1	2	......	......

TYPHOID FEVER DEATHS

BY MONTHS

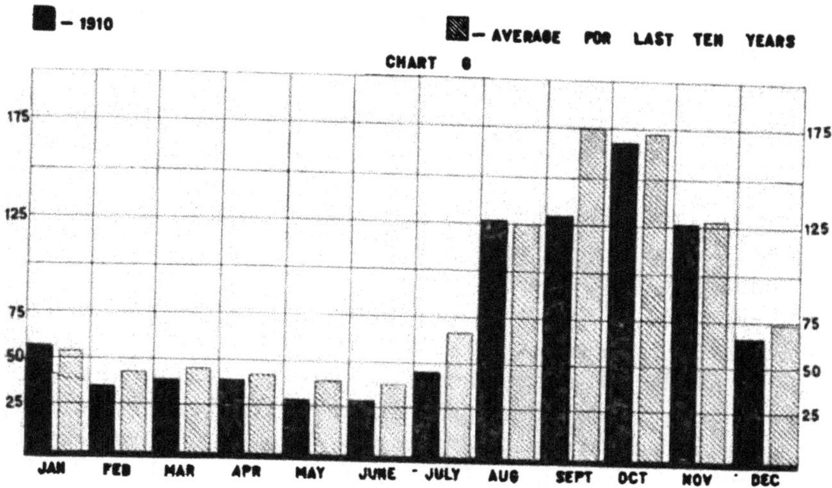

BY AGES

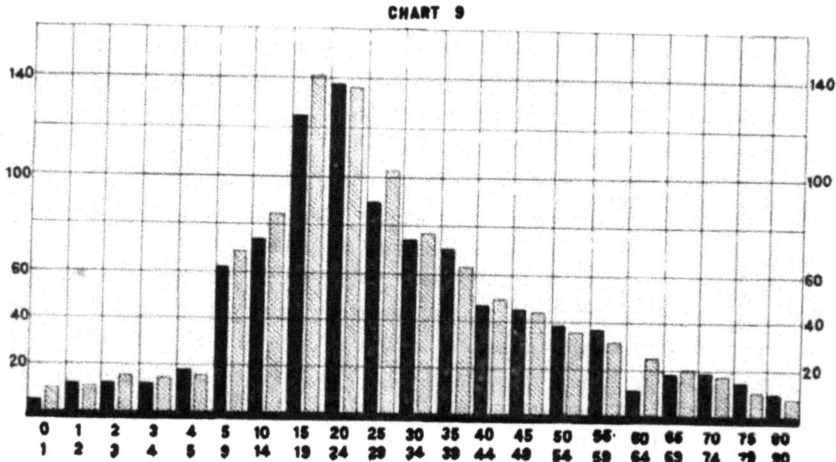

MONTHLY ANALYSIS FOR TYPHOID DEATHS.

(As Published in Monthly Bulletin.)

January, 1910.—One hundred and thirty-one cases reported from 40 counties, with 47 deaths. In the corresponding month last year 194 cases in 39 counties, with 36 deaths. It is certainly true that all cases were not reported.

February, 1910.—One hundred and ten cases in 36 counties, with 34 deaths. In the same month last year, 68 cases in 30 counties, with 19 deaths.

March, 1910.—Seventy-one cases reported in 30 counties, with 33 deaths. In the same month last year, 68 cases in 30 counties, with 31 deaths.

April, 1910.—One hundred and twelve cases in 32 counties, with 32 deaths. In the same month last year, 58 cases reported in 24 counties, with 33 deaths.

May, 1910.—Ninety-two cases reported from 33 counties, with 26 deaths. In the same period last year, 80 cases in 22 counties, with 35 deaths. This disease was reported in the following counties: Adams, 2 cases; Benton, 1; Clark, 10; Dearborn, 1; Decatur, 7; Dekalb, 2; Delaware, 1; Elkhart, 2; Gibson, 1; Hendricks, 1; Huntington, 1; Jackson, 1; Jefferson, 8; Lake, 4; Madison, 4; Marion, 13; Martin, 1; Monroe, 1; Montgomery, 1; Morgan, 1; Noble, 1; Ohio, 3; Parke, 1; Perry, 1; Putnam, 2; Rush, 1; St. Joseph, 9; Warrick, 4; Washington, 1; Wells, 3; White, 1; Whitley, 1.

June, 1910.—Niney-one cases in 31 counties, with 27 deaths. It is obvious that all cases were not reported. In the corresponding month last year, 125 cases in 27 counties, and 34 deaths. The disease was almost epidemic in Clark County, 9 cases and 2 deaths; Floyd County, 9 cases and 1 death; in Jefferson County, 8 cases and 1 death; in Washington County, 10 cases and 1 death. It will be noted that these were all southern counties.

July, 1910.—Two hundred and forty-six cases reported in 47 counties, with 45 deaths. In the same month last year, 267 cases were reported in sixty counties, with 78 deaths. The disease prevailed unusually in the following counties: Allen, 22 cases; Clark, 10; Marion, 23; Monroe, 17; Vanderburgh, 19; Washington, 25.

August, 1910.—Four hundred and forty-six cases reported in 74 counties, with 123 deaths. In the same month last year, 464 cases in 69 counties, with 106 deaths. The counties in which typhoid was epidemic were: Adams, 14 cases; Dearborn, 10; Delaware, 15; Floyd, 14; Gibson, 12; Greene, 12; Hancock, 10; Harrison, 10; Henry, 12; Jackson, 10; Lagrange, 10; Lake, 12; Madison, 15; Marion, 96; Monroe, 16; Montgomery, 13; Parke, 13; Scott, 10; Washington, 20.

September, 1910.—Eight hundred cases reported in 83 counties, with 158 deaths. In the same month last year, 757 cases in 81 counties, with 132 deaths. The disease was epidemic in the following counties: Allen County, 65 cases; Brown, 10; Clark, 11; Decatur, 13; Dekalb, 24; Delaware, 20; Elkhart, 29; Greene, 13; Hamilton, 11; Henry, 13; Kosciusko, 13; Lake, 24; Marion, 136; Montgomery, 13; Noble, 14; Owen, 12; Perry, 13; Putnam, 31; Randolph, 24; Vanderburgh, 27; Washington, 35. This record is simply awful, and it is certainly true that Indiana cannot criticize the benighted countries of Europe on account of the existence of cholera. Both are filth diseases.

October, 1910.—Seven hundred and one cases reported in 78 counties, with 159 deaths. In the same month last year, 478 cases in 75 counties, with 155 deaths.

November, 1910.—Four hundred and twenty-seven cases reported in 67 counties, with 115 deaths. In the same month last year, 301 cases with 104 deaths, in 71 counties.

December, 1910.—Three hundred and thirty-six cases reported from 47 counties, with 153 deaths. In the same month last year 131 cases reported in 50 counties, with 52 deaths

DIPHTHERIA.

DEATHS BY MONTHS, WITH AVERAGE FOR LAST TEN YEARS.

Months.	1901.	1902.	1903.	1904.	1905.	1906.	1907.	1908.	1909.	1910.	Average.
January	110	49	61	51	32	33	43	42	38	42	50
February	61	35	49	35	31	23	41	28	24	19	34
March	39	32	27	29	27	26	35	24	18	32	28
April	29	27	22	32	13	16	27	12	10	15	20
May	23	30	12	22	13	8	20	12	5	15	16
June	23	16	16	18	8	12	10	8	3	18	13
July	15	7	15	10	16	11	15	11	8	11	11
August	24	21	23	12	15	13	20	12	19	24	18
September	38	39	35	11	34	36	35	32	26	28	31
October	74	48	69	21	82	77	36	43	85	52	58
November	56	63	77	35	41	32	37	47	57	79	57
December	62	57	56	38	54	65	34	44	55	46	51
Totals	554	424	462	314	366	402	353	315	338	381	390

DEATHS BY AGES, WITH AVERAGE FOR LAST TEN YEARS.

Ages.	1901.	1902.	1903.	1904.	1905.	1906.	1907.	1908.	1909.	1910.	Average.
Under 1 year	60	51	50	28	23	26	20	21	21	28	32
1-2 years	58	36	59	47	35	45	34	43	31	44	43
2-3 years	65	61	56	33	48	51	35	54	52	43	49
3-4 years	80	39	64	46	53	47	51	36	46	42	50
4-5 years	53	45	46	22	41	58	30	23	40	43	40
5-9 years	143	122	141	99	114	124	127	90	117	119	119
10-14 years	51	46	28	26	28	35	32	23	28	35	33
15-19 years	23	14	9	5	10	10	7	9	7	14	10
20-24 years	7	1	3	1	7	1	8	3	5	4	4
25-29 years	3	1	......	1	3	......	3	3	......	4	1
30-34 years	1	1	2	1	1	......	1	4	......	1	1
35-39 years	3	......	......	1	1	1	2	3	1	1	1
40-44 years	1	1	......	......	......	2	2	......	......	1	......
45-49 years	1	......	......	......	......	......	1	......	......	......	......
50-54 years	2	......	......	1	......	1	......	......	......	1	......
55-59 years	......	......	1	......	2	......	1	1	......	......	......
60-64 years	......	1	......	......	......	......	......	1	......	1	......
65-69 years	1	......	1	......	......	......	......	......	......	......	......
70-79 years	......	......	1	......	......	......	......	......	......	......	......

DIPHTHERIA DEATHS

BY MONTHS

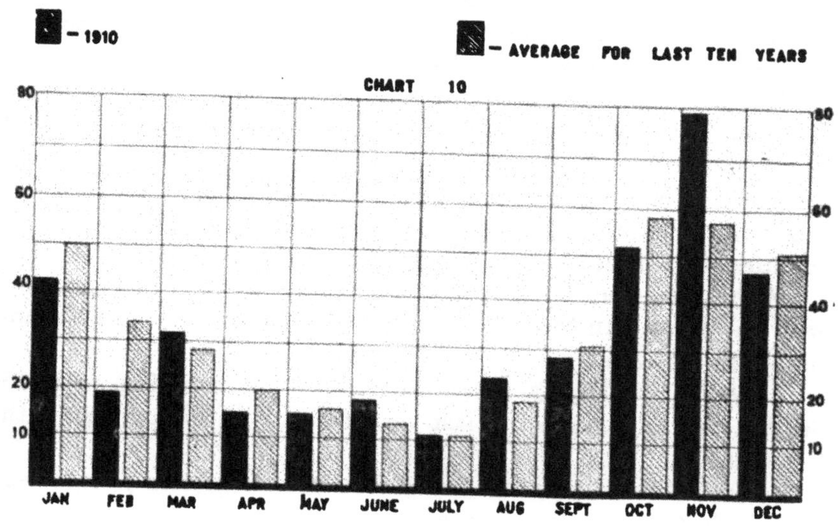

BY AGES

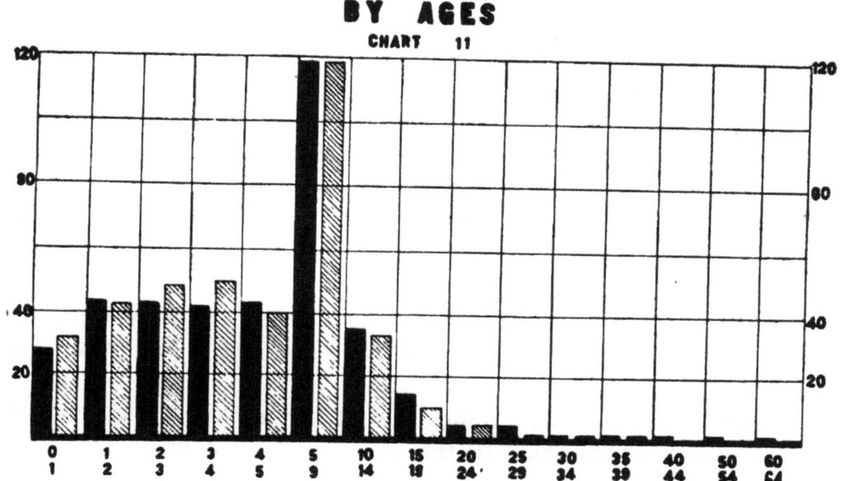

MONTHLY ANALYSIS FOR DIPHTHERIA DEATHS.

(As Published in Monthly Bulletin.)

January, 1910.—One hundred and seventy-four cases reported in 43 counties, with 40 deaths. In the same month last year, 170 cases in 45 counties, with 34 deaths.

February, 1910.—One hundred and sixty-eight cases reported in 44 counties, with 17 deaths. In the same month last year, 93 cases in 33 counties, with 18 deaths.

March, 1910.—One hundred and twenty cases in 38 counties reported, with 29 deaths. In the same month last year, 54 cases in 22 counties, with 16 deaths.

April, 1910.—One hundred and nine cases reported in 28 counties, with 13 deaths. In the same month last year, 60 cases in 21 counties, with 9 deaths.

May, 1910.—One hundred and two cases reported in 29 counties, with 14 deaths. In the same month last year, 56 cases in 21 counties, with 5 deaths.

June, 1910.—Ninety cases reported in 27 counties, with 15 deaths. In the same month last year, 54 cases in 17 counties, with 2 deaths.

July, 1910.—Eighty-two cases reported from thirty counties, with 9 deaths. In the corresponding month last year, 41 cases reported in 17 counties, with 8 deaths.

August, 1910.—One hundred and ninety-three cases in 34 counties, with 23 deaths. In the same month last year, 30 cases in 30 counties, with 17 deaths.

September, 1910.—Two hundred and thirty-one cases reported in 42 counties, with 27 deaths. In the corresponding month last year, 279 cases reported in 42 counties, with 24 deaths.

October, 1910.—Four hundred and forty-one cases reported in 52 counties, with 46 deaths. In the same month last year, 439 cases in 61 counties, with 155 deaths.

November, 1910.—Five hundred and forty-four cases reported in 65 counties, with 70 deaths. In the same month last year, 441 cases in 62 counties, with 50 deaths.

December, 1910.—One hundred and seventy-seven cases in 51 counties, with 44 deaths. In the same month last year, 320 cases in 44 counties, with 46 deaths.

SCARLET FEVER.

DEATHS BY MONTHS, WITH AVERAGE FOR LAST TEN YEARS.

Months.	1901.	1902.	1903.	1904.	1905.	1906.	1907.	1908.	1909.	1910.	Average.
January	24	22	22	24	18	11	6	13	11	16	16
February	18	19	13	24	11	9	9	17	11	33	16
March	27	18	10	33	20	12	18	10	7	26	18
April	18	11	9	22	21	7	9	15	11	21	14
May	9	5	4	15	11	7	5	5	14	21	9
June	12	3	6	9	4	10	3	5	9	13	7
July	5	6	13	4	14	7	10	4	9	11	8
August	5	6	8	6	6	3	5	1	6	11	5
September	4	8	13	7	5	6	3	6	8	8	7
October	3	19	16	12	5	8	7	4	21	11	10
November	10	24	18	17	11	14	8	5	19	21	14
December	14	9	34	19	7	7	8	10	25	13	14
Totals	149	150	166	192	133	101	91	95	151	205	143

DEATHS BY AGES, WITH AVERAGE FOR LAST TEN YEARS.

Ages.	1901.	1902.	1903.	1904.	1905.	1906.	1907.	1908.	1909.	1910.	Average.
Under 1 year	7	11	13	13	10	5	4	4	9	13	8
1–2 years	14	13	9	27	18	13	7	8	22	24	15
2–3 years	29	17	17	33	20	10	15	17	18	21	19
3–4 years	18	24	22	25	17	15	13	12	20	23	18
4–5 years	22	14	19	18	14	10	7	10	15	19	14
5–9 years	37	43	55	61	38	27	31	22	53	61	42
10–14 years	8	14	19	11	11	8	8	9	11	20	12
15–20 years	4	3	3	2	1	2	5	5	3	10	3
20–24 years	2	3	3	1	1	10	......	2	1	7	3
25–30 years	3	1	......	......	2	......	1	4	......	4	1
30–34 years	1	1	1	......	......	1	......	2	1		
35–44 years	1	......	1	......	......		......		1	......	......
45–54 years	1	......	......	1	1	......	......	......		1	......
55–90 years	......	......	1	......	......	......	......	......	......	2	......

SCARLET FEVER DEATHS

BY MONTHS

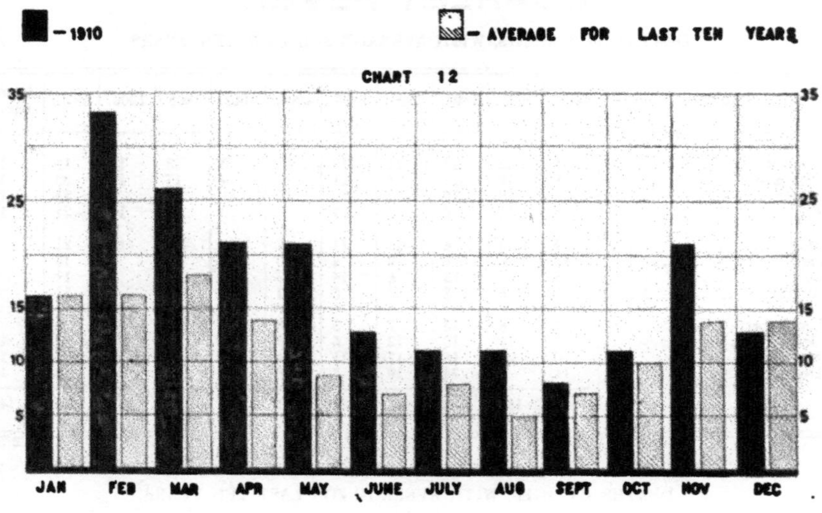

BY AGES

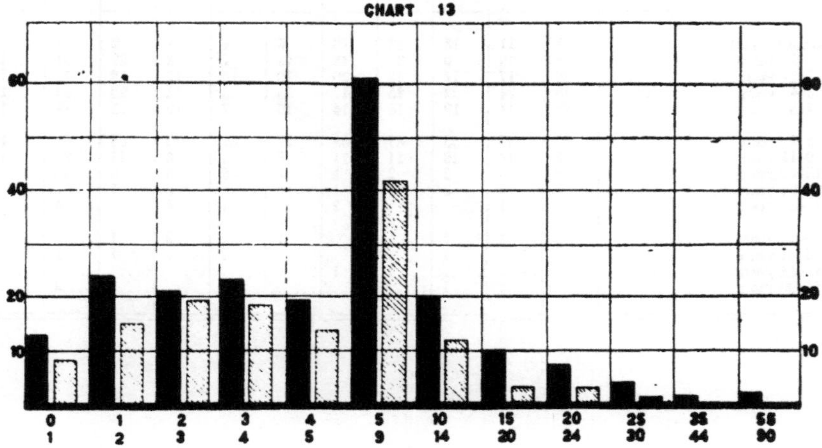

DIARRHOEAL DISEASES.

UNDER TWO YEARS OF AGE.

Deaths by Months, with Average for Last Ten Years.

Months.	1901.	1902.	1903.	1904.	1905.	1906.	1907.	1908.	1909.	1910.	Average.
January	14	15	11	29	26	28	34	39	34	45	27
February	12	14	22	30	30	25	32	33	46	30	27
March	17	14	20	33	36	29	35	34	57	39	31
April	26	21	17	24	22	39	18	48	39	45	29
May	19	29	25	29	35	42	35	39	46	63	36
June	81	116	83	54	116	71	81	89	165	128	98
July	468	455	323	307	359	321	396	322	460	491	390
August	500	569	475	498	469	484	503	420	441	528	488
September	393	337	275	344	343	447	280	292	304	356	337
October	167	130	140	204	186	232	160	204	146	203	177
November	64	56	36	49	54	66	40	83	50	72	57
December	15	23	22	28	24	39	25	32	53	49	31
Totals	1,776	1,779	1,449	1,629	1,700	1,823	1,639	1,635	1,841	2,049	1,732

TWO YEARS OF AGE AND OVER.

Deaths by Months, with Average for Last Ten Years.

Months.	1901.	1902.	1903.	1904.	1905.	1906.	1907.	1908.	1909.	1910.	Average.
January	30	25	24	30	32	26	40	38	30	36	30
February	22	23	20	38	29	36	33	26	28	20	27
March	24	28	27	37	42	35	41	35	37	28	33
April	17	28	23	28	27	41	38	28	22	24	27
May	28	30	40	33	28	30	29	43	38	29	32
June	31	25	36	30	44	29	63	57	46	34	39
July	130	129	93	73	87	78	150	116	35	99	104
August	169	170	131	110	152	119	203	165	105	146	147
September	123	86	116	104	94	130	122	143	76	83	107
October	72	59	64	63	67	92	62	88	34	62	66
November	39	39	26	32	28	39	42	50	35	28	35
December	42	27	22	33	28	40	24	28	27	31	30
Totals	727	669	622	611	658	695	847	817	563	620	682

DIARRHOEAL DISEASES

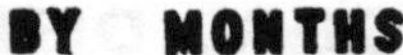

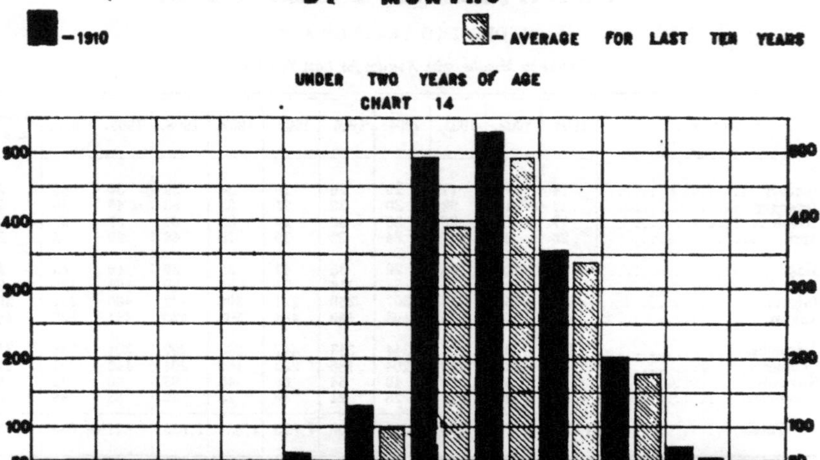

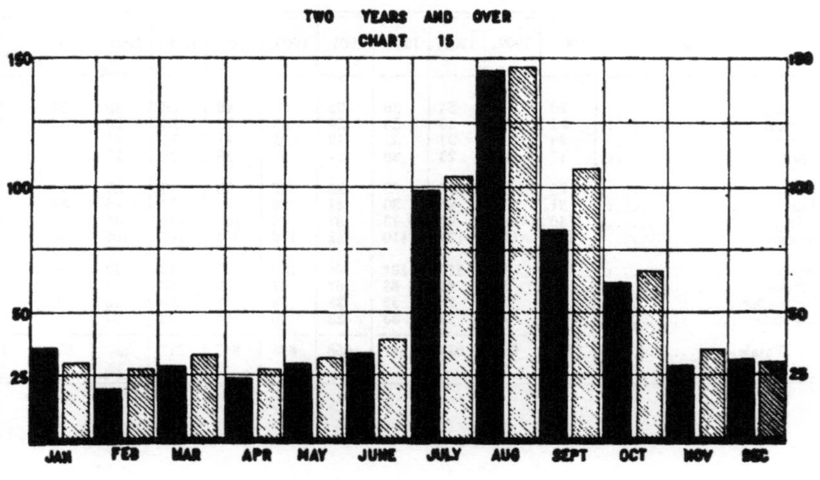

DIARRHOEAL DISEASES.

Deaths by Ages, with Average for Last Ten Years.

Ages.	1901.	1902.	1903.	1904.	1905.	1906.	1907.	1908.	1909	1910.	Average.
Under 1 year	1,118	1,070	894	1,068	1,115	1,240	1,202	1,202	1,340	1,576	1,182
1–2 years	513	533	421	384	406	417	437	433	501	473	451
2–3 years	139	140	110	112	130	116	105	126	125	140	124
3–4 years	28	34	19	40	36	31	33	34	25	37	31
4–5 years	17	13	11	21	13	20	11	16	18	13	15
5–9 years	36	23	12	31	29	17	19	16	19	22	22
10–14 years	9	8	11	13	10	6	12	6	7	9	9
15–19 years	13	7	6	4	8	8	4	3	5	9	6
20–24 years	15	14	9	15	17	12	16	14	8	8	12
25–29 years	13	15	12	13	16	21	7	14	11	8	13
30–34 years	32	12	20	14	10	10	10	11	14	7	14
35–39 years	18	28	14	15	22	17	20	13	11	10	16
40–44 years	13	14	15	19	20	19	13	12	20	11	15
45–49 years	22	20	24	19	13	14	13	19	17	15	17
50–54 years	31	30	36	33	25	30	30	20	29	18	28
55–59 years	46	57	37	37	51	37	35	46	19	16	38
60–64 years	62	60	45	57	72	59	61	45	42	37	54
65–69 years	91	73	67	68	68	90	78	78	98	50	76
70–74 years	70	80	98	88	93	99	97	81	92	61	85
75–79 years	83	98	91	88	95	107	117	103	132	66	98
80–90 years	107	102	94	89	104	124	141	132	148	66	110
90 years and over	22	11	14	12	13	18	20	22	33	17	17

DIARRHOEAL DISEASES

BY AGES.

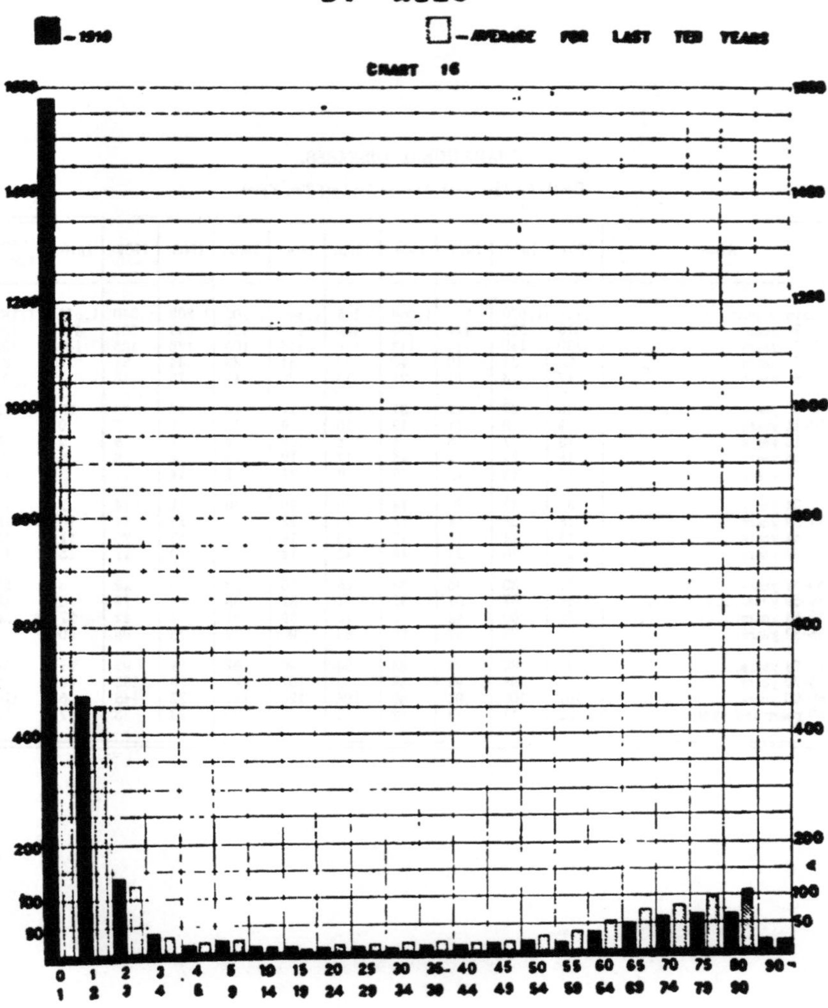

INFLUENZA.

DEATHS BY MONTHS, WITH AVERAGE FOR LAST TEN YEARS.

Months.	1901.	1902.	1903.	1904.	1905.	1906.	1907.	1908.	1909.	1910.	Average.
January	269	60	31	45	114	53	71	172	54	88	95
February	349	84	51	90	221	44	159	316	77	144	143
March	180	51	87	146	151	48	234	167	126	201	139
April	128	37	60	70	37	30	51	70	135	97	68
May	42	15	37	20	15	7	52	40	42	35	31
June	12	4	10	7	7	2	14	13	9	10	8
July	9	8	7	2	5	4	7	9	9	12	7
August	10	3	9	5	......	2	4	14	4	4	5
September	3	7	3	1	4	3	4	5	7	3	4
October	5	8	7	4	4	8	2	4	4	10	5
November	12	8	10	18	12	11	17	22	10	22	14
December	30	17	36	26	21	12	51	35	27	75	33
Totals	1,049	302	348	434	591	224	666	867	504	701	568

DEATHS BY AGES, WITH AVERAGE FOR LAST TEN YEARS.

Ages.	1901.	1902.	1903.	1904.	1905.	1906.	1907.	1908.	1909.	1910.	Average.
Under 1 year	66	47	13	32	43	14	26	32	48	46	36
1–2 years	14	7	3	4	10	3	12	11	11	18	9
2–3 years	11	4	3	1	6	5	5	10	5	14	6
3–4 years	5	4	2	4	......	......	3	6	4	3	3
4–5 years	4	4	2	......	1	2	......	1	2	4	2
5–9 years	11	9	2	3	5	2	4	10	2	9	5
10–14 years	6	4	6	7	4	3	6	10	9	6	6
15–19 years	12	3	3	6	7	4	11	16	7	9	7
20–24 years	20	4	4	3	16	3	11	13	6	13	9
25–29 years	22	2	5	8	3	......	5	11	9	16	8
30–34 years	22	2	5	7	9	2	18	15	......	16	9
35–39 years	27	6	5	7	9	4	14	24	9	15	12
40–44 years	33	1	6	6	16	3	9	21	10	22	12
45–49 years	33	6	7	13	14	10	23	30	8	23	16
50–54 years	43	12	16	9	17	13	26	37	14	26	21
55–59 years	41	14	16	19	32	6	38	34	35	38	27
60–64 years	57	5	28	22	40	11	24	50	29	34	30
65–69 years	103	35	27	37	47	24	73	86	46	69	54
70–74 years	159	35	53	73	67	31	94	115	52	87	76
75–79 years	151	39	58	61	86	31	89	131	80	96	82
80–90 years	180	51	74	94	132	43	151	182	103	122	113
90 years and over	26	7	9	15	23	8	23	21	15	19	16

INFLUENZA DEATHS

BY MONTHS

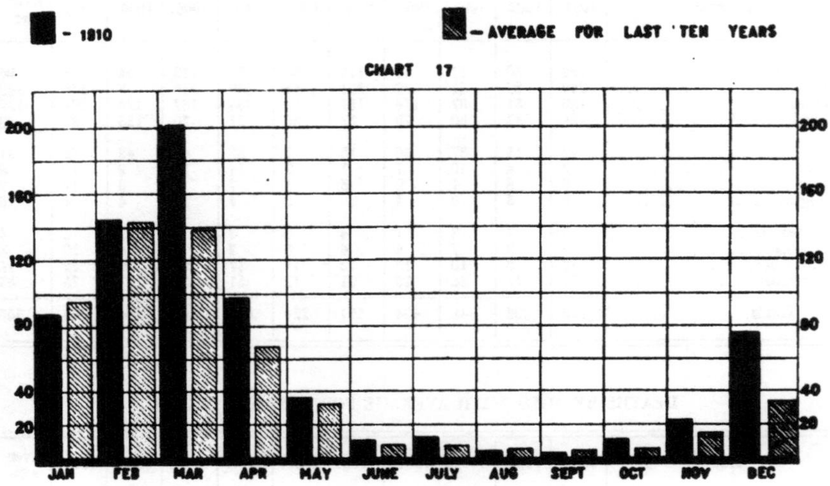

BY AGES

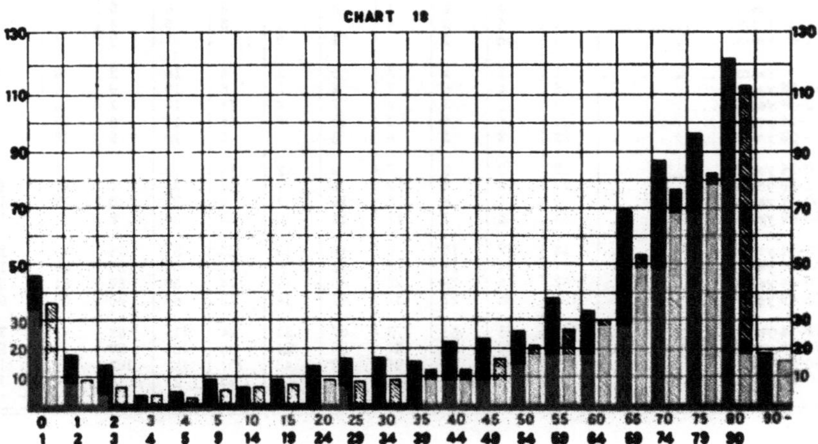

MEASLES.

DEATHS BY MONTHS, WITH AVERAGE FOR LAST TEN YEARS.

Months.	1901.	1902.	1903.	1904.	1905.	1906.	1907.	1908.	1909.	1910.	Average.
January	14	2	......	28	......	2	7	8	5	21	8
February	22	5	4	31	1	2	10	57	15	62	20
March	37	26	6	52	......	......	28	52	23	102	32
April	37	5	12	50	2	7	40	47	41	83	32
May	31	14	10	29	......	4	51	24	27	87	27
June	10	4	7	9	1	3	31	11	14	41	13
July	77	7	4	6	......	......	23	2	13	22	15
August	2	5	3	3	1	1	5	2	9	18	4
September	......	......	6	2	......	......	2	1	3	3	1
October	......	......	4	2	......	......	4	4	......	5	1
November	......	......	6	......	1	2	3	......	3	9	2
December	1	1	11	......	......	2	9	1	3	9	3
Totals	161	69	73	212	6	23	213	209	156	462	158

DEATHS BY AGES, WITH AVERAGE FOR LAST TEN YEARS.

Ages.	1901.	1902.	1903.	1904.	1905.	1906.	1907.	1908.	1909.	1910.	Average.
Under 1 year	310	28	17	65	3	5	49	50	27	73	62
1–2 years	22	11	19	27	......	9	55	29	39	116	32
2–3 years	15	6	6	26	1	1	30	13	19	69	18
3–4 years	9	2	3	7	......	......	9	14	9	32	8
4–5 years	6	3	2	10	......	1	6	8	7	17	6
5–9 years	14	5	3	13	......	1	20	26	20	49	15
10–14 years	12	......	3	10	......	......	6	9	9	24	7
15–19 years	7	3	5	9	......	1	7	16	2	10	6
20–24 years	9	2	2	6	......	1	3	5	5	10	4
25–29 years	1	1	4	1	......	1	6	8	6	9	3
30–34 years	4	3	1	5	......	2	1	4	2	14	3
35–39 years	6	......	1	11	......	1	6	7	2	10	4
40–44 years	7	2	1	7	......	......	4	5	5	7	3
45–49 years	3	1	1	6	......	......	2	3	2	7	2
50–54 years	2	2	3	2	1	......	2	5	2	1	2
55–59 years	1	......	......	......	......	......	......	......	......	8	......
60–64 years	2	......	......	1	......	......	3	......	......	2	......
65–69 years	......	4	1	1	......	......	1	1	......	1	......
70–74 years	1	1	......	1	......	......	......	3	......	2	......
75–79 years	1	......	......	2	......	......	2	1	......	2	......
80–90 years	......	......	......	2	......	......	1	......	......	......	......
90 years and over	......	1	1	......	......	......	......	......	......	......	......

MEASLES DEATHS

BY MONTHS

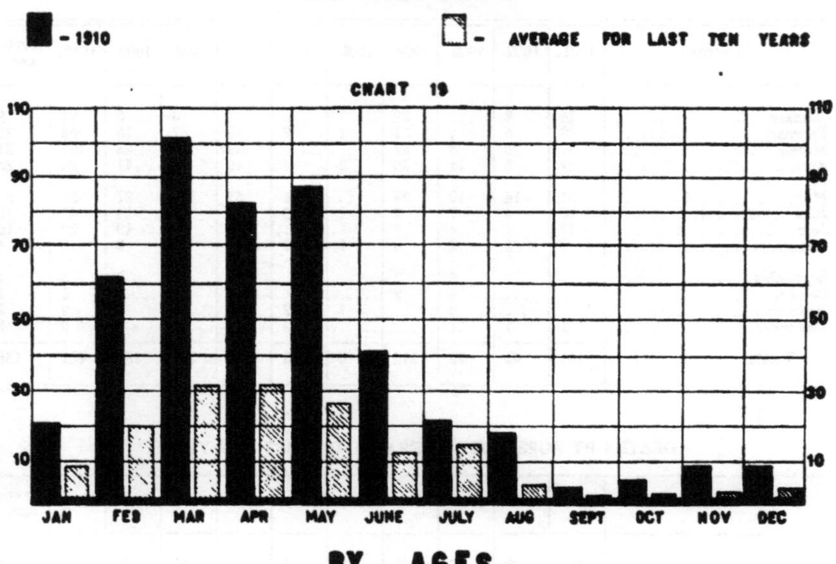

BY AGES

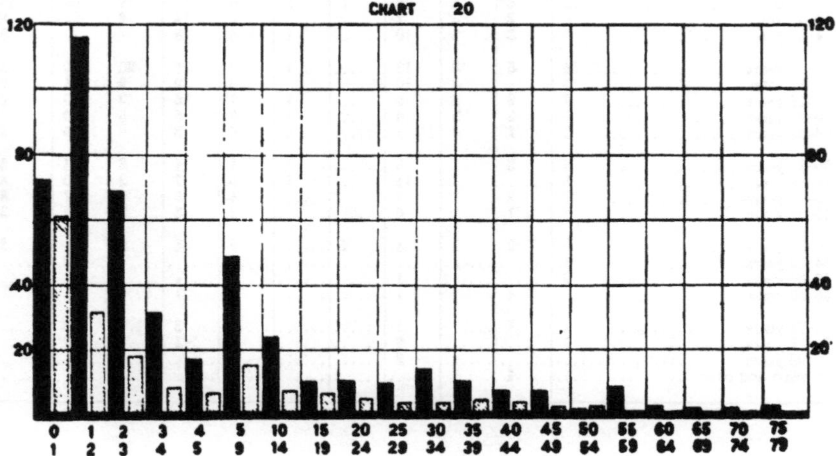

SMALLPOX.

TABLE GIVING NUMBER OF DEATHS BY MONTHS FOR LAST TEN YEARS.

Months.	1901.	1902.	1903.	1904.	1905.	1906.	1907.	1908.	1909.	1910.	Total.	Average.
January	2	4	51	8	7	......	3	......	......	......	75	7
February	2	2	55	5	11	......	2	1	......	1	79	7
March	4	3	31	3	3	......	......	2	......	......	46	4
April	1	8	21	6	3	1	1	2	1	......	44	4
May	3	1	10	7	3	......	1	......	1	......	26	2
June	3	2	3	3	4	......	1	3	......	......	19	1
July	1	15	4	6	3	1	......	......	2	......	32	3
August	......	1	14	3	......	......	......	......	......	......	18	1
September	1	7	2	17	......	2	......	......	......	......	29	2
October	2	10	......	18	......	3	......	......	......	......	33	3
November	1	4	1	13	......	......	......	......	1	......	20	2
December	1	18	3	8	1	1	......	2	......	......	34	3
Totals	21	75	195	97	35	8	8	10	5	1	455	45

MONTHLY ANALYSIS FOR SMALLPOX DEATHS.

(As Published in Monthly Bulletin.)

January, 1910.—One hundred and eighty-nine cases reported in 25 counties, with no deaths; population representing 1,169,720. In the same month last year, 148 cases in 24 counties, with no deaths; population representing 1,053,378.

February, 1910.—Eighty-three cases reported from 23 counties, with 1 death. In the corresponding month last year, 38 cases in 22 counties, with no deaths. The counties reporting smallpox were: Adams, 2; Allen, 7; Boone, 3; Clinton, 3; Crawford, 1; Daviess, 2; Decatur, 1; Dekalb, 1; Franklin, 8; Grant, 7, with 1 death. Jefferson, 2 cases; Madison, 1; Marion, 1; Marshall, 2; Miami, 1; Randolph, 1; Shelby, 16; St. Joseph, 3; Tippecanoe, 1; Vigo, 1; Wabash, 1; Warrick, 7.

March, 1910.—One hundred and seven cases reported from 21 counties with no deaths. In the same month last year, 120 cases reported from 16 counties, and no deaths. The following counties reported the disease present: Adams, 8 cases; Allen, 21; Carroll, 3; Cass, 6; Daviess, 2; Fulton, 2; Grant, 2; Greene, 2; Hamilton, 2; Howard, 2; Huntington, 2; Noble, 1; St. Joseph, 2; Tipton, 13; Vigo, 2; Warrick, 8; Wells, 1.

April, 1910.—Eighty-one cases reported from 18 counties, with no deaths. The following counties reported the disease present: Allen, 14; Clinton, 2; Daviess, 3; Delaware, 2; Gibson, 3; Grant, 2; Greene, 1; Knox, 2; Marshall, 2; Martin, 6; Miami, 5; Montgomery, 1; Orange, 22; St. Joseph, 2; Tipton, 12; Vermillion, 8; Vigo, 4; Wabash, 1.

May, 1910.—Eighty-nine cases reported in 14 counties, with no deaths. In the same month last year, 88 cases reported in 13 counties, with 1 death. The following counties reported the disease present: Allen, 6 cases; Clinton, 1; Delaware, 4; Elkhart, 1; Gibson, 1; Grant, 5; Greene, 9; Howard, 18; Marion, 5; Orange, 18; Owen, 20; St. Joseph, 3; Tipton, 1; Vigo, 6.

June, 1910.—Seventy-five cases reported from 23 counties, with no deaths. In the same month last year, 103 cases from 41 counties, with no deaths. The following counties reported the disease present: Allen, 2 cases; Carroll, 1; Clay, 1; Dekalb, 1; Grant, 8; Howard, 3; Lake, 1; Madison, 6; Marion, 1; Marshall, 1; Martin, 4; Miama, 6; Montgomery, 6; Owen, 3; Putnam, 1; St. Joseph, 7; Vigo, 22; Warren, 1; Wayne, 6.

July, 1910.—No cases reported. In the corresponding month last year, 61 cases were reported from 8 counties, and 2 deaths.

August, 1910.—Six cases reported from 3 counties, with no deaths. In the corresponding month last year, 26 cases in 2 counties, no deaths.

September, 1910.—Only 1 case reported during the month, with no deaths. Said case occurred in Marion County.

October, 1910.—Two cases reported from 2 counties, with no deaths. Counties reporting smallpox were: Dekalb, 1; Wayne, 1. In the same month last year, 6 cases reported in 3 counties, with no deaths.

November, 1910.—Fifty-three cases reported in 4 counties, with no deaths. In the same month last year, 185 cases in 13 counties, with 1 death. The following counties reported the disease present: Elkhart, 1 case; Madison, 22; Monroe, 5; Sullivan, 25.

December, 1910.—Forty-five cases reported in 7 counties, with no deaths. The cases were reported in the following counties: Dekalb, 5; Elkhart, 5; Howard, 1; Knox, 1; Madison, 32; Montgomery, 1.

VIOLENCE.

	1908.	1909.	1910.
January	212	198	197
February	172	181	179
March	174	215	263
April	186	197	200
May	242	195	188
June	223	217	243
July	234	228	273
August	251	266	251
September	244	205	241
October	209	220	207
November	196	200	214
December	184	221	234
Totals	2,527	2,543	2,690

	1908.	1909.	1910.
Accidents	2,021	2,030	1,902
Suicides	384	404	386
Homicides	122	109	121
Mob violence	...	...	...

MONTHLY RECORD OF VIOLENCE DEATHS.

(As Published in Monthly Bulletin.)

January, 1910.—Deaths from violence, 165. Males 103 and females 62. In the corresponding month last year, 158. Of the 165 deaths from violence, 3 were murders, 21 suicides, and 141 accidents. The three murders were all accomplished by gunshot. Of the suicides, gunshot caused 4, cutting throat, 3; carbolic acid, 7; arsenic and other poisons, 7. Of the accidental deaths, steam railroads caused 30; interurban, 2; street car, 1; automobile, 1; fractures (cause unspecified), 28; falls, 24; drowning, 5; burns and scalds, 14; horses and vehicles, 3; poisons of various kinds, 5, and the remainder by various means.

February, 1910.—Total number of deaths, 139, 70 of them occurring in the cities. Eight were murders, 24 suicides, and the remainder accidental. Of the murders, 6 were males and 2 females. Of the suicides, 16 were males and 8 females. The methods chosen were: gunshot, 7; hanging, 7; cutting throat, 1; carbolic acid, 7; drowning, 1; poison, 1. Of the accidental deaths, steam railroads caused 24, interurban and street cars, 3; crushing injuries, 11; machinery, 4; mines, 3; falls, 20; drowning, 6; gunshot, 1; burns and scalds, 10; horse and vehicles, 3; suffocation and asphyxia, 9; the remainder by various other causes.

March, 1910.—Total number of deaths by violence, 221. In the same month last year, 191. Of the violent deaths, there were 6 murders, 45 suicides, 170 accidental. Of the murders, females, 2; males, 4. Of the suicides, 32 males, 13 females. Methods used: Gunshot, 9; hanging, 8; drowning, 2; cutting throat, 2; jumping from four-story building, 1; striking head against iron bars, 1; carbolic acid, 7; opium and morphine, 3; strychnine, 3; chloroform, 2; other poisons, 7. Of the accidental deaths, steam railroads caused 32, interurbans, 2; street cars, 2; automobiles, 2; fracture of skull and large bones, 24; gunshot, 4; machinery, 2; mining, 3; falls, 30; burns and scalds, 31; horses and vehicles, 12; drowning, 3; tetanus, 2; the remainder by various methods.

April, 1910.—Total number of deaths from violence, 175. Murder caused 9; males, 8; females, 1. Suicide, 33; males, 25; females, 8. Accidental deaths, 133; males, 104; females, 29. Of the murders, 6 were gunshots, 1 stabbing, 2 blunt instruments. Of the suicides, 8 were gunshots, 3 by hanging, 2 drowning, 3 knife wounds, 11 carbolic acid, 2 morphine, 2 stepping in front of moving train, 2 asphyxiation. Of the accidental deaths, steam railroads, 32; interurban railroads, 3; street cars, 3; automobiles, 5; crushing injuries, 20; machinery, 3; gunshots, 4; burns and scalds, 13; drowning, 3; falls, 13; horses and vehicles, 6; and the remainder by various means.

May, 1910.—Total number of deaths, 160. In the same month last year, 172. Of the violent deaths, 6 were murders, 26 suicides and the remainder accidental. Of the murders, 3 were gunshots, 3 by cutting and stabbing. Of the suicides, 11 chose hanging, 3 gunshots, 7 carbolic acid, 4 poison, 1 by throwing self under train. Of the accidental deaths, steam railroads caused 35 deaths, street cars, 5; automobiles, 2; mining, 5; machinery, 2; crushing injuries, 2; falls, 6; horses and vehicles, 2; drowning, 12; lightning, 3, and the remainder by various means.

June, 1910.—Violent deaths numbered 212. Murders, 2; suicides, 28; accidents, 182. In the same month last year the deaths numbered 200; murder, 7; suicide, 36; accidents, 155. Of the suicides 6 were by gunshot, 2 hanging, 2 drowning, 2 asenic, 7 carbolic acid, 4 morphine. Of the accidental deaths, steam railroads caused 32; interurban, 1; street cars, 8; automobiles and vehicles, 8; fractures, 18; mining, 3; machinery, 1; crushing injuries, 4; concussion of brain, 1; falls, 18; drowning, 25; burns and scalds, 10; gunshot, 6; horses and vehicles, 7; lightning, 5; electricity, 3; and the remainder by various means.

July, 1910.—Violent deaths numbered 234. In the corresponding month last year, 196. Of the 234 deaths, 12 were murders, 36 suicides, 186 accidental deaths. Of the murders 9 males, 1 female. Killed by gunshot, 1; manner unknown, 2 males. Of the suicides, 25 were males and 11 females. The methods chosen were: Gunshots, 8; hanging, 7; railroad trains, 3; carbolic acid, 10; gas, 1; choloroform, 1; morphine, 1; strychnine, 1; arsenic, 1; unknown poison, 1; burning, 1; not reported, 1. Of the accidental deaths, steam railroads killed 39; interurban, 3; street cars, 8; automobiles, 4; motorcycle, 1; mining accidents, 8; machinery, 2; crushing injuries, 13; drowning, 40; falls, 14; burns and scalds, 10; electricity, 3; lightning, 6; horses and vehicles, 9; strychnine and other poisons, 4; gunshots, 6; struck by ball, 1; not reported, 1. Of the deaths by violence, males 190, females, 44.

August, 1910.—Deaths from violence, 237. In the same month last year, 233. The murders numbered 8, 7 being by gunshot, and one by cutting. Suicides, 35; males 22, females 13. Methods used were: Gunshots, 7; cutting throat, 3; hanging, 6; drowning, 4; burning, 1; carbolic acid, 11; morphine, 3. Accidental deaths were as follows: Steam railroads, 51; interurban trains, 4; street cars, 5; automobiles, 7; mining, 8; machinery, 3; horses and vehicles, 12; electricity, 3; lightning, 2; gunshot, 5; tetanus, 4; and the remainder by various means.

September, 1910.—Deaths from violence numbered 232. In the same month last year, 179. Of the violent deaths, 6 were murders, 28 suicides, 198 accidents. Of the suicides, 13 were women. Methods chosen were: Gunshots, 4 men; drowning, 1 man, 3 women; hanging, 2 women; jumping in front of trains, 2 men; carbolic acid, 5 men and 3 women; opium, 1 man and 3 women; other poisons, 2 men and 2 women; of the accidental deaths, 34 were caused by steam railroads: 57 by interurbans, 2 by street cars, and four by automobiles: falls, 12; mines, 11; horses and vehicles, 11; drowning, 14; electricity, 7; and the remainder by various means.

October, 1910.—Deaths from violence numbered 182, rate 76.1. In the same month last year, 190 deaths, rate 82.0. Murders numbered 8; males, 7; females, 1. Suicides 34; males 27 and females

7. Accidental deaths, 139; males, 103; females, 36. Of the suicides 12 chose gunshot, 2 artificial gas, 2 drowning, 4 hanging, 5 carbolic acid, 2 opium, 3 strychnine, 3 other poisons, 1 cutting throat. Of the accidental deaths, railroads caused 32; interurban, 5; street car, 1; automobiles, 2; horses and vehicles, 7; crushing injuries, 19; machinery, 3; mines, 3; electricity, 4; falls, 17; burns and scalds, 17; drowning, 4; gunshot, 7; suffocation, 8; and the remainder by various means.

November, 1910.—Deaths from violence, 184; rate 79.5 per 100,000. In the same month last year, 176 deaths. Murders, 16; males 13, females 3; suicides, 33; males 19, females 14. Methods chosen were: Gunshot, 8 males; drowning, 1 female; hanging, 5 males, 1 female; carbolic acid, 2 males, 7 females; poisons, 3 males; artificial gas, 1 female; wound in neck, 1 male. The accidental deaths were: Caused by steam cars, 27; interurban, 2; street cars, 4; automobiles, 2; motorcycles, 2; fractures and falls, 28; crushing injuries and machinery, 6; coal mining, 5; burns and scalds, 13; drowning, 3; gunshots, 10; horses and vehicles, 9; poisons of different kinds, 9; remainder by various causes.

December, 1910.—Deaths from violence, 217. In the same month last year, 195. The murders numbered 13, suicides, 23; remainder were accidental. All of the murdered persons were males. Of the 23 suicides, 8 males and 1 female chose gunshot; 1 female chose jumping from a high place; 1 male cutting throat; 2 males hanging; 7 males and 2 females, carbolic acid. Of the accidental deaths, 442 by steam railroads, 1 by interurban, 1 by street car, 4 by automobiles, 7 by machinery; crushing injuries, 25; burns and scalds, 20; drowning, 5; falls, 25; horses and vehicles, 8; gunshot, 13; asphyxiation and suffocation, 11. The remainder by various ways.

CANCER.

	1908.	1909.	1910.
January	117	141	145
February	134	152	133
March	120	145	165
April	162	141	167
May	153	162	162
June	140	149	157
July	171	163	154
August	150	169	165
September	155	160	157
October	171	150	159
November	137	145	152
December	129	151	156
Totals	1,739	1,828	1,872

MONTHLY ANALYSIS OF DISEASE PREVALENCE.

(As Published in Monthly Bulletin.)

January, 1910.—Tonsilitis was the most prevalent disease. This was true for November and December preceding. Pneumonia stood fourth in area of prevalence and was sixth in the preceding month. Following is the order of disease prevalence: Tonsilitis, influenza, bronchitis, pneumonia, rheumatism, measles, scarlet fever, pleuritis, typhoid fever, diphtheria and membranous croup, whooping-cough, diarrhea, chickenpox, smallpox, erysipelas, intermittent and remittent fever, inflammation of bowels, cerebro-spinal fever, puerperal fever, dysentery, cholera morbus, cholera infantum, and typho-malarial fever.

February, 1910.—There were 99 fewer deaths in February than the corresponding month last year. There was also less sickness. Influenza was the most prevalent disease, pneumonia was fifth in area of prevalence, and in February of last year it was third. The following is the order of disease prevalence: Influenza, tonsilitis, measles, bronchitis, pneumonia, rheumatism, scarlet fever, pleuritis, diphtheria and membranous croup, chickenpox, whooping-cough, typhiod fever, diarrhea, smallpox, intermittent and remittent fever, erysipelas, cerebro-spinal fever, inflammation of bowels, cholera morbus, puerperal fever, dysentery, typho-malarial fever and cholera infantum.

March, 1910.—Measles was the most prevalent disease, being reported in every county in the State. Many schools were closed on account of measles, and the disease has frequently been severe. Influenza was second in area of prevalence, rising from third place in the preceding month. Pneumonia fell to eighth in area of prevalence, being second in the preceding month. The following is in the order of prevalence: Measles, influenza, bronchitis, rheumatism, tonsilitis, pneumonia, scarlet fever, pleuritis, diphtheria and membranous croup, typhoid fever, whooping-cough, erysipelas, chickenpox, diarrhea, intermittent and remittent fever, smallpox, cerebro-spinal fever, inflammation of bowels, cholera morbus, dysentery, puerperal fever, typho-malarial fever, cholera infantum.

April, 1910.—Measles was reported the most prevalent disease. In the same month last year measles was sixth in area of prevalence. The order of prevalence is as follows: Measles, tonsilitis, bronchitis, rheumatism, influenza, tuberculosis, lobar pneumonia, bronchial pneumonia, whooping-cough, scarlet fever, typhoid fever, diarrhea, diphtheria and membranous croup, intermittent fever, erysipelas, malarial fever, chickenpox, tuberculosis all forms, smallpox, inflammation of bowels, puerperal fever, dysentery, cholera morbus, cerebro-spinal fever, and cholera infantum.

May, 1910.—Measles was reported as the most prevalent disease. In the corresponding month last year, rheumatism was so reported. The following is the order of area of prevalence: Measles, tonsilitis, rheumatism, bronchitis, pulmonary tuberculosis, influenza, whooping-cough, scarlet fever, typhoid fever, diarrhea, lobar pneumonia, bronchial pneumonia, diphtheria and membranous croup, malarial, intermittent and remittent fever, chickenpox, other forms of tuberculosis, inflammation of bowels, erysipelas, cholera morbus, smallpox, dysentery, puerperal fever, cholera infantum, cerebro-spinal fever.

June, 1910.—Measles was reported as the most prevalent disease, and this was the case in the preceding month. Rheumatism was the most prevalent in the same month last year. Following is the order of prevalence: Measles, diarrhea, rheumatism, tonsilitis, bronchitis, scarlet fever, pulmonary tuberculosis, cholera morbus, whooping-cough, dysentery, typhoid fever, malarial fever, influenza, cholera infantum, diphtheria and membranous croup, erysipelas, intermittent and remittent fever, small pox, inflammation of bowels, bronchial pneumonia, other forms of tuberculosis, lobar pneumonia, chickenpox, cerebro-spinal fever, puerperal fever.

July, 1910.—Diarrhea was reported as the most prevalent disease. This was also the case in the corresponding month last year. The number of deaths under five years of age by diarrhea was 483, and in the corresponding month last year, 454. Pneumonia falls to twenty-first place in area of prevalence. The order of disease prevalence for July is as follows: Diarrhea, cholera morbus, cholera infantum, dysentery, rheumatism, measles, typhoid fever, tonsilitis, pulmonary tuberculosis, bronchitis, malarial fever, scarlet fever, diphtheria and membranous croup, inflammation of bowels, whooping-cough, intermittent and remittent fever, other forms of tuberculosis, erysipelas, influenza, bronchial pneumonia, cerebro-spinal fever, lobar pneumonia, puerperal fever, chickenpox, smallpox.

August, 1910.—Typhoid fever was reported as the most prevalent disease, diarrhea being second. In the same month last year, diarrhea was the most prevalent and typhoid fever second. The following is the order of prevalence: Typhoid fever, diarrhea, rheumatism, dysentery, cholera morbus, cholera infantum, bronchitis, tonsilitis, pulmonary tuberculosis, scarlet fever, malarial fever, diphtheria and membranous croup, intermittent and remittent fever, measles, whooping-cough, inflammation of bowels, other forms of tuberculosis, influenza, lobar pneumonia, cerebro-spinal fever, bronchial pneumonia, erysipelas, smallpox, chickenpox, puerperal fever.

September, 1910.—Typhoid fever was reported as the most prevalent disease, rheumatism being second. Typhoid fever was the most prevalent disease in September, 1909. The following is the order of prevalence: Typhoid fever, rheumatism, tonsilitis, diarrhea, bronchitis, pulmonary tuberculosis, cholera morbus, malarial fever, cholera infantum, dysentery, intermittent and remittent fever. diphtheria and membranous croup, scarlet fever, influenza, other forms of tuberculosis, whooping-cough, inflammation of bowels, bronchial pneumonia, measles, erysipelas, lobar pneumonia, cerebro-spinal fever, puerperal fever, chickenpox, smallpox.

October, 1910.—Typhoid fever was reported as the most prevalent infectious disease—75 per cent. of observers had to deal with this disease. The following was the order of prevalence: Typhoid fever, tonsilitis, bronchitis, rheumatism, diphtheria and membranous croup, scarlet fever, pulmonary tuberculosis, influenza, diarrhea, malarial fever, bronchial pneumonia, dysentery, intermittent and remittent fever, other forms of tuberculosis, cholera morbus, measles, lobar pneumonia, cholera infantum, whooping-cough, inflammation of bowels, chickenpox, erysipelas, cerebro-spinal fever, smallpox, poliomyelitis, puerperal fever. Poliomyelitis has become almost epidemic in the State, having appeared in 16 counties. Deaths from this disease occurred in the following counties: Cass County, 2; Elkhart, 1; Grant, 1; Huntington, 1; Miami, 1; Pulaski, 1; Starke, 1; Steuben, 2; Tippecanoe, 1. One death from hydrophobia in Cass County.

November, 1910.—Bronchitis was reported as the most prevalent disease. Tonsilitis second. The following is the order of prevalence: Bronchitis, tonsilitis, typhoid fever, diphtheria and membranous croup, rheumatism, scarlet fever, influenza, bronchial pneumonia, lobar pneumonia, pulmonary tuberculosis, diarrhea, intermittent and remittent fever, malarial fever, measles, chickenpox, anterior-poliomyelitis, whooping-cough, other forms of tuberculosis, inflammation of bowels, dysentery, erysipelas, cholera morbus, cerebro-spinal fever, puerperal fever, cholera infantum, smallpox.

December, 1910.—The most prevalent disease was tonsilitis, and this was true in the corresponding month last year. The order of prevalence is as follows: Tonsilitis, bronchitis, rheumatism, influenza, lobar pneumonia, scarlet fever, diphtheria and membranous croup, typhoid fever, bronchial pneumonia, pulmonary tuberculosis, measles, diarrhea, whooping-cough, chickenpox, malarial fever, erysipelas, intermittent and remittent fever, cholera morbus, smallpox, cerebro-spinal fever, anterior-poliomyelitis, cholera infantum.

TABLES

OF

ANNUAL STATISTICAL REPORT

FOR THE YEAR 1910.

TABLE No. 1.

Deaths in Indiana During the Year Ending December 31, 1910, with Rates per 100,000 Population According to the U. S. Census of 1910.

Classification Number.	CAUSES OF DEATH.	Number of Deaths.	Death Rate per 100,000.
	I. General Diseases.—A. Epidemic Diseases.		
1	Typhoid fever	934	34.6
2	Typhus fever		
3	Relapsing fever	1	.03
4	Malaria	151	5.5
4a	Malarial cachexia		
5	Smallpox	1	.03
6	Measles	462	17.1
7	Scarlet fever	205	7.5
8	Whooping cough	459	17.0
9	Diphtheria	360	13.3
9a	Croup	21	.7
10	Influenza	701	25.9
11	Miliary fever		
12	Asiatic cholera		
13	Cholera nostras	20	.7
14	Dysentery	304	11.3
14a	Epidemic dysentery		
15	Plague		
16	Yellow fever		
17	Leprosy		
18	Erysipelas	140	5.1
19	Other epidemic diseases	9	.3
	B. Other General Diseases.		
20	Purulent infection and septicemia	58	2.1
21	Glanders	1	.03
22	Anthrax	1	.03
23	Rabies	4	1.4
24	Tetanus	47	1.7
25	Mycoses		
26	Pellagra		
27	Beriberi		
28	Tuberculosis of the lungs	3,853	142.7
29	Acute miliary tuberculosis	68	2.5

TABLE No. 1—Continued.

Classification Number.	CAUSES OF DEATH.	Number of Deaths.	Death Rate per 100,000.
30	Tuberculous meningitis	255	9.4
31	Abdominal tuberculosis	325	12.0
32	Potts' disease	31	1.1
33	White swellings	28	1.0
34	Tuberculosis of other organs	62	2.2
35	Disseminated tuberculosis	88	3.2
36	Rickets	28	1.0
37	Syphilis	158	5.8
38	Gonococcus infection	6	.2
39	Cancer and other malignant tumors of the buccal cavity	69	2.5
40	Cancer and other malignant tumors of the stomach and liver	790	29.2
41	Cancer and other malignant tumors of the peritoneum, intestines and rectum	188	6.9
42	Cancer and other malignant tumors of the female genital organs	321	10.4
43	Cancer and other malignant tumors of the breast	167	6.1
44	Cancer and other malignant tumors of the skin	119	4.4
45	Cancer and other malignant tumors of other organs and of organs not specified	218	8.0
46	Other tumors (tumors of the female genital organs excepted)	24	.8
47	Acute articular rheumatism	175	6.4
48	Chronic rheumatism and gout	72	2.6
49	Scurvy	5	.1
50	Diabetes	372	13.7
51	Exophthalmic goitre	39	1.4
52	Addison's disease	8	.2
53	Leukemia	31	1.1
54	Anemia chlorosis	126	4.6
55	Other general diseases	56	2.0
56	Alcoholism (acute or chronic)	101	3.7
57	Chronic lead poisoning	7	.2
58	Other chronic occupational poisonings	1	.03
59	Other chronic poisonings	23	.8
	II. Diseases of the Nervous System and of the Organs of Special Senses.		
60	Encephalitis	48	1.7
61	Simple meningitis	130	4.8
61a	Cerebrospinal fever	22	.8
62	Locomotor ataxia	79	2.9
63	Other diseases of the spinal cord	238	8.8
64	Cerebral hemorrhage, apoplexy	1,885	69.8
65	Softening of the brain	74	2.7
66	Paralysis without specified cause	241	8.9
67	General paralysis of the insane	169	6.0
68	Other forms of mental alienation	91	3.3
69	Epilepsy	177	6.5
70	Convulsions (non-puerperal)	2	.07
71	Convulsions of infants	51	1.8
72	Chorea	10	.3
73	Hysteria	5	.1
74a	Other diseases of the brain	63	2.3
74b	Other diseases of the nervous system	29	1.0
75	Diseases of the eyes and their annexa	5	.1
76	Diseases of the ears	42	1.5
	III. Diseases of the Circulatory System.		
77	Pericarditis	43	1.5
78	Acute endocarditis	112	4.1
79	Organic disease of the heart	3,956	146.5
80	Angina pectoris	230	8.5
81	Diseases of the arteries, atheroma, aneurism, etc	488	18.0
82	Embolism and thrombosis	98	3.6
83	Diseases of the veins, varices, hemorrhoids, phlebitis, etc	15	.5
84	Diseases of the lymphatic system (lymphangitis, etc.)	5	.1
85	Hemorrhage: other diseases of the circulatory system	15	.5

TABLE No. 1—Continued.

Classification Number.	CAUSES OF DEATH.	Number of Deaths.	Death Rate per 100,000.
	IV. DISEASES OF THE RESPIRATORY SYSTEM.		
86	Diseases of the nasal fossae	10	.3
87a	Laryngitis	25	.9
87b	Other diseases of the larynx	16	.5
88	Diseases of the thyroid body	7	.2
89	Acute bronchitis	247	9.1
90	Chronic bronchitis	217	8.0
91	Broncho-pneumonia	917	33.9
92	Lobar-pneumonia	1,823	67.5
93	Pleurisy	57	2.1
94	Pulmonary congestion, pulmonary apoplexy	24	.8
95	Gangrene of the lungs	4	.1
96	Asthma	98	3.6
97	Pulmonary emphysema	5	.1
98a	Hemorrhage of the lungs	8	.1
98b	Other diseases of the respiratory system	17	.6
	V. DISEASES OF THE DIGESTIVE SYSTEM.		
99	Diseases of the mouth and annexa	24	.8
100a	Tonsilitis	27	.9
100b	Other diseases of the pharynx	14	.5
101	Diseases of the esophagus	4	.1
102	Ulcer of the stomach	86	3.1
103a	Gastritis	252	9.3
103b	Other diseases of the stomach	209	7.7
104	Diarrhea and enteritis (under 2 years)	2,049	75.7
105	Diarrhea and enteritis (2 years and over)	620	22.9
106	Ankylostomiasis	......	......
107	Intestinal parasites	2	.07
108	Appendicitis and typhlitis	272	10.0
109a	Hernia	75	2.7
109b	Obstructions of the intestines	236	8.7
110	Other diseases of the intestines	83	3.0
111	Acute yellow atrophy of the liver	10	.03
112	Hydatid tumor of the liver	......	......
113	Cirrhosis of the liver	283	10.4
114	Biliary calculi	94	3.4
115	Other diseases of the liver	166	6.1
116	Diseases of the spleen	3	.1
117	Simple peritonitis (nonpuerperal)	38	1.4
118	Other diseases of the digestive system (cancer and tuberculosis excepted)	7	.2
	VI. NONVENEREAL DISEASES OF THE GENITO-URINARY SYSTEM AND ANNEXA.		
119	Acute nephritis	174	6.4
120	Bright's disease	1,847	68.3
121	Chyluria	5	.1
122	Other diseases of the kidneys and annexa	62	2.2
123	Calculi of the urinary passages	18	.6
124	Diseases of the bladder	95	3.5
125	Diseases of the urethra, urinary abscess, etc	7	.2
126	Diseases of the prostate	132	4.8
127	Nonvenereal diseases of the male genital organs	3	.1
128	Uterine hemorrhage (nonpuerperal)	1	.03
129	Uterine tumor (noncancerous)	50	1.8
130	Other diseases of the uterus	19	.7
131	Cysts and other tumors of the ovary	35	1.2
132a	Diseases of the tubes	61	2.2
132b	Other diseases of the female genital organs	7	.2
133	Nonpuerperal diseases of the breast (cancer excepted)	....	......

TABLE No. 1—Continued.

Classification Number.	CAUSES OF DEATH.	Number of Deaths.	Death Rate per 100,000.
	VII. The Puerperal State.		
134	Accidents of pregnancy	57	2.1
135	Puerperal hemorrhage	30	1.1
136	Other accidents of labor	16	.5
137	Puerperal septicemia	229	8.4
138	Puerperal albuminuria and convulsions	74	2.7
139	Phlegmasia alba dolens (puerperal)	3	.1
140	Other puerperal accidents	41	1.5
141	Puerperal diseases of the breast	......	....
	VIII. Diseases of the Skin and Cellular Tissue.		
142	Gangrene	114	4.2
143	Furuncle	14	.5
144	Acute abscess	11	.4
145	Other diseases of the skin and annexa	28	1.0
	IX. Diseases of the Bones and of the Organs of Locomotion.		
146	Nontuberculous diseases of the bones	67	2.4
147	Diseases of the joints (tuberculosis and cancer excepted)	7	.2
148	Amputations	......	....
149	Other diseases of the organs of locomotion	......	....
	X. Malformations.		
150a	Hydrocephalus	41	1.5
150b	Congenital malformation of the heart (cyanosis)	300	11.1
150c	Other congenital malformations	111	4.0
	XI. Diseases of Early Infancy.		
151a	Premature birth	1,123	41.4
151b	Congenital debility	223	8.2
152	Other diseases peculiar to early infancy	155	5.7
153	Lack of care	22	.8
	XII. Old Age.		
154	Senility	515	19.0
	XIII. Affections Produced by External Causes.		
155	Suicide by poison	170	6.2
156	Suicide by asphyxia	6	.2
157	Suicide by hanging or strangulation	64	2.3
158	Suicide by drowning	22	.8
159	Suicide by firearms	95	3.5
160	Suicide by cutting or piercing instruments	11	.4
161	Suicide by jumping from high places	3	.1
162	Suicide by crushing	11	.4
163	Other suicides	4	.1
164	Poisoning by food	11	.4
165	Other acute poisonings	67	2.4
166	Conflagration	14	.5
167	Burns (conflagration excepted)	169	6.2
168	Absorption of deleterious gases (conflagration excepted)	29	1.0
169	Accidental drowning	144	5.3
170	Traumatism by firearms	70	2.5
171	Traumatism by cutting or piercing instruments	8	.2
172	Traumatism by fall	414	15.3
173	Traumatism in mines and quarries	63	2.3
174	Traumatism by machines	50	2.1
175a	Railroad accidents and injuries	433	16.0
175b	Street car and interurban accidents	437	16.1
175c	Automobiles and other vehicles	82	3.0
175d	Landslides	......	....
175e	Other accidental traumatisms	87	3.2

TABLE No. 1—Continued.

Classification Number.	CAUSES OF DEATH.	Number of Deaths.	Death Rate per 100,000.
176	Injuries by animals	71	2.6
177	Starvation	.....	.....
178	Excessive cold	17	.6
179	Effects of heat	25	.9
180	Lightning	23	.8
181	Electricity (lightning excepted)	32	1.1
182	Homicide by firearms	79	2.9
183	Homicide by cutting or piercing instruments	12	.4
184	Homicide by other means	30	1.1
185	Fractures, cause not specified	9	.3
186a	Suffocation	59	2.1
186b	Injuries at birth	137	5.0
186c	Other external violence	23	.8
	XIV. Ill-Defined Diseases.		
187	Ill-defined organic diseases	1	.03
188	Sudden death	2	.07
189	Cause of death not specified or ill-defined	78	2.8
	Total deaths from all causes	36,513	1,352.0

TABLE No. 2.

Deaths from All Causes by Months, Ages, Color, Nationality and Conjugal Condition, for the Year Ending December 31, 1910. International Classification.

	Jan.	Feb.	March.	April.	May.	June.	July.	Aug.	Sept.	Oct.	Nov.	Dec.
I. GENERAL DISEASES.												
(A. Epidemic Diseases.)												
1. Typhoid fever	285	374	475	332	248	178	240	395	348	320	317	256
2. Typhus fever	55	33	36	36	28	28	45	126	188	168	126	65
3. Relapsing fever												
4. Malaria			1									
4a. Malarial cachexia	9	5	5	4	5	13	18	17	26	21	18	10
5. Smallpox		1										
6. Measles	21	62	102	83	87	41	22	18	3	5	9	9
7. Scarlet fever	16	33	26	21	21	13	11	11	8	11	21	13
8. Whooping-cough	20	56	38	49	40	42	53	63	27	28	24	19
9. Croup	5	2	3	1		1		1		4	4	
9a. Diphtheria	37	17	29	14	15	17	11	23	28	48	75	46
10. Influenza	88	144	201	97	35	10	12	4	3	10	22	75
11. Miliary fever												
12. Asiatic cholera												
13. Cholera nostras												
14. Dysentery			1			1	4	9	4	1		
14a. Epidemic dysentery	8	3	3	9	6	7	63	114	55	21	7	8
15. Plague												
16. Yellow fever												
17. Leprosy												
18. Erysipelas	24	17	28	16	10	5	1	9	6	3	11	10
19. Other epidemic diseases	2	1	2	2	1							1

[83—24829]

TABLE No. 2—Continued.

	Jan.	Feb.	March.	April.	May.	June.	July.	Aug.	Sept.	Oct.	Nov.	Dec.
(B. OTHER GENERAL DISEASES.)	677	642	781	737	683	677	631	663	611	644	563	616
20. Purulent infection and septicemia	1	2	2	3	3	9	8	10	3	6	7	4
21. Glanders						1						
22. Anthrax				1								
23. Rabies								1	1	1		1
24. Tetanus	4	4	1	3	3	4	3	9	6	6	1	3
25. Mycoses												
26. Pellagra												
27. Beriberi												
28. Tuberculosis of the lungs	257	340	420	378	324	322	291	278	281	294	254	314
29. Acute miliary tuberculosis	7	6	1	11	3	12	5	4	11	3	2	3
30. Tuberculous meningitis	13	22	26	28	21	27	23	20	20	16	15	24
31. Abdominal tuberculosis	15	17	27	30	27	26	35	50	27	26	29	16
32. Pott's disease	2	1	5		5	2	3	1	3	4	2	3
33. White swellings	4	5	2	2	2	1	2	5	1	1	3	
34. Tuberculosis of other organs	4	4	8	6	9	5	4	5	2	8	2	5
35. Disseminated tuberculosis	7	12	9	7	11	4	10	5	9	7	4	3
36. Rickets		2	4			5	3	3	2	3	2	4
37. Syphilis	17	9	20	15	10	13	10	19	10	10	15	10
38. Gonococcus infection			1	1	2				1	1		
39. Cancer and other malignant tumors of the buccal cavity	5	3	9	6	4	4	6	7	6	8	6	5
40. Cancer and other malignant tumors of the stomach and liver	60	50	63	66	78	77	59	82	63	71	54	67
41. Cancer and other malignant tumors of the peritoneum, intestines and rectum	12	14	22	15	16	13	22	12	17	11	16	18
42. Cancer and other malignant tumors of the female genital organs	28	24	31	31	24	23	27	20	30	31	21	31
43. Cancer and other malignant tumors of the breast	12	17	6	18	12	17	14	12	19	11	18	11
44. Cancer and other malignant tumors of the skin	10	5	13	12	10	4	13	13	10	9	10	10
45. Cancer and malignant tumors of other organs and of organs not specified	18	20	21	19	18	19	13	19	12	18	27	14
46. Other tumors (tumors of the female genital organs excepted)	2		3	5	2	1	2	3	1	3	2	
47. Acute articular rheumatism	9	7	14	14	24	20	16	9	19	20	8	15
48. Chronic rheumatism and gout	13	10	2	6	4	3	6	8	5	7	4	4
49. Scurvy				1				2		2		

50. Diabetes	39	46	39	25	34	32	22	28	20	29	26	32
51. Exophthalmic goitre	4	3	7	4	3	5	2	2	1	5	1	2
52. Addison's disease	1	2	2	.....	.....	.....	1	1	.....	.....	1	.....
53. Leukemia	1	1	1	4	2	4	4	4	1	4	4	1
54. Anemia chlorosis	13	10	11	10	15	10	14	12	12	8	8	3
55. Other general diseases	1	.....	.....	6	6	6	5	9	6	6	5	6
56. Alcoholism (acute or chronic)	13	4	10	7	8	5	7	8	11	9	12	7
57. Chronic lead poisoning	2	1	.....	1	.....	3	.....	.....	.....	.....	.....	.....
58. Other chronic occupation poisonings	.....	.....	.....	.....	.....	.....	.....	.....	.....	1	.....	.....
59. Other chronic poisonings	3	1	1	2	3	.....	1	2	1	5	4	.....
II. Diseases of the Nervous System and of the Organs of Special Senses.	295	296	301	268	284	253	242	270	271	285	297	299
60. Encephalitis	5	5	5	3	5	3	2	5	7	3	2	3
61. Simple meningitis	7	11	10	13	9	11	5	14	15	15	6	14
61a. Cerebrospinal fever	1	.....	1	1	.....	1	1	8	3	2	.....	4
62. Locomotor ataxia	10	4	7	7	7	3	10	8	4	4	10	5
63. Other diseases of the spinal cord	21	20	20	12	21	19	22	18	17	25	24	10
64. Cerebral hemorrhage, apoplexy	165	161	176	171	162	141	145	143	147	151	155	168
65. Softening of the brain	5	10	9	6	4	3	4	6	2	10	11	4
66. Paralysis without specified cause	35	34	17	11	15	15	15	13	17	16	25	28
67. General paralysis of the insane	8	14	12	12	11	15	8	11	19	23	17	19
68. Other forms of mental alienation	8	12	6	7	7	9	3	8	8	8	9	6
69. Epilepsy	16	14	18	12	19	17	10	16	15	13	18	9
70. Convulsions (nonpuerperal)	.....	.....	.....	.....	.....	.....	.....	.....	1	.....	1	.....
71. Convulsions of infants	5	1	7	2	6	4	5	9	4	3	2	3
72. Chorea	2	.....	2	.....	2	1	1	.....	.....	.....	.....	2
73. Hysteria	.....	1	.....	.....	1	.....	.....	.....	.....	.....	1	2
74. Other diseases of the nervous system—												
(A. Other diseases for the brain)	3	5	5	3	9	1	8	5	5	7	7	5
(B. Other diseases of the nervous system)	2	3	1	3	3	5	1	3	3	1	1	3
75. Diseases of the eye and its adnexia	.....	.....	.....	.....	1	.....	1	.....	1	1	1	.....
76. Diseases of the ear	2	1	5	5	2	5	1	3	3	3	7	5
III. Diseases of the Circulatory System	400	404	466	416	454	444	358	361	369	366	448	476
77. Pericarditis	.....	.....	3	2	6	8	2	2	5	5	7	3
78. Acute endocarditis	10	6	11	11	12	8	9	9	11	9	8	8
79. Organic disease of the heart	319	335	394	331	348	347	282	273	293	293	355	386
80. Angina pectoris	20	16	17	19	23	22	15	28	14	17	18	21
81. Diseases of the arteries, atheroma, aneurism, etc	43	34	30	44	56	50	42	37	33	27	47	45
82. Embolism and thrombosis	7	9	7	5	7	6	6	10	9	14	10	8
83. Diseases of the veins (varices, hemorrhoids, phlebitis, etc.)	.....	2	3	2	.....	1	1	.....	1	.....	1	4
84. Diseases of the lymphatic system (lymphangitis, etc.)	.....	1	.....	1	.....	.....	.....	1	1	.....	1	.....
85. Hemorrhage; other diseases of the circulatory system	1	1	1	1	2	2	1	1	2	1	1	1

TABLE No. 2—Continued.

	Jan.	Feb.	March.	April.	May.	June.	July.	Aug.	Sept.	Oct.	Nov.	Dec.
IV. Diseases of the Respiratory System.	427	407	511	282	235	174	89	115	129	203	392	511
86. Diseases of the nasal fossae	......	......	1	1	2	1	......	2	......	......	1	2
87. Diseases of the larynx—												
(A. Laryngitis)	3	1	6	3	2	2	......	......	......	1	5	2
(B. Other diseases of the larynx)	2	2	1	......	1	1	......	1	......	4	......	4
88. Diseases of the thyroid body	......	......	1	......	......	......	1	1	1	......	......	3
89. Acute bronchitis	22	25	30	21	16	13	8	9	13	21	32	37
90. Chronic bronchitis	25	28	27	16	8	9	11	12	14	10	35	22
91. Broncho-pneumonia	91	111	116	78	74	43	22	29	38	56	126	133
92. Lobar pneumonia	258	216	301	145	119	84	37	50	49	98	173	293
93. Pleurisy	10	3	10	4	3	7	4	1	3	5	5	2
94. Pulmonary congestion, pulmonary apoplexy	3	6	3	......	1	......	......	4	......	2	3	2
95. Gangrene of the lung	......	1	......	......	......	......	......	1	......	......	1	1
96. Asthma	9	11	13	10	5	10	5	4	10	5	10	6
97. Pul monary emphysema	......	......	......	......	......	1	1	1	......	......	......	2
98. Other diseases of the respiratory system—												
(A. Hemorrhage of the lungs)	1	1	2	2	......	1	......	......	......	1	......	......
(B. Other diseases of the respiratory system)	3	2	......	2	4	2	......	......	1	......	1	2
V. Diseases of the Digestive System.	242	189	253	228	214	316	758	856	612	427	247	212
99. Diseases of the mouth and adnexia	1	1	4	1	......	1	1	3	7	2	3	......
100. Diseases of the pharynx—												
(A. Tonsilitis)	2	2	4	1	3	3	1	2	5	2	1	1
(B. Other diseases of the pharynx)	1	2	1	2	2	......	1	1	......	1	3	......
101. Diseases of the esophagus	1	......	1	......	......	......	1	......	......	......	......	1
102. Ulcer of the stomach	8	7	7	7	7	10	5	8	8	8	6	5
103. Other diseases of the stomach (cancer excepted)—												
(A. Gastritis)	21	16	19	27	13	18	23	27	22	31	20	15
(B. Other diseases of the stomach)	11	9	23	11	10	15	24	25	33	12	18	1[illegible]
104 Diarrhea and enteritis (under 2 years)	45	30	39	45	63	128	491	528	356	203	72	4[illegible]

No.	Cause of death												
105.	Diarrhea and enteritis (2 years and over)	36	20	28	24	29	34	99	146	83	62	28	31
106.	Ankylotomiasis												
107.	Intestinal parasites							1			1		
108.	Appendicitis and typhlitis	22	21	24	20	19	32	31	32	22	17	20	12
109.	Hernias, intestinal obstructions—												
	(A. Hernia)	10	6	8	7	5	6	8	5	3	7	5	5
	(B. Obstructions of intestines)	14	18	24	29	16	21	21	17	20	22	14	20
110.	Other diseases of the intestines	14	6	6	5	4	11	6	5	5	7	9	5
111.	Acute yellow atrophy of the liver		4		1		1			1		3	
112.	Hydatid tumor of the liver												
113.	Cirrhosis of the liver	28	26	35	21	16	20	21	27	23	28	23	15
114.	Biliary calculi	10	9	11	9	4	3	5	9	11	12	5	6
115.	Other diseases of the liver	9	11	15	17	19	9	13	15	11	9	16	22
116.	Diseases of the spleen	1				1		1					
117.	Simple peritonitis (nonpuerperal)	8		4	1	2	3	4	6	1	3		6
118.	Other diseases of the digestive system (cancer and tuberculosis excepted)		1			1	1	1		1		1	1
VI.	**Nonvenereal Diseases of the Genito-Urinary System and Annexa.**	228	193	240	222	216	204	215	200	185	188	198	227
119.	Acute nephritis	20	13	14	14	11	14	17	8	11	21	13	18
120.	Bright's disease	169	142	180	165	162	153	142	154	128	123	157	172
121.	Chyluria		1				1	2	1				
122.	Other diseases of the kidneys and annexa	5	3	3	8	4	3	7	4	8	6	3	8
123.	Calculi of the urinary passages		1	2	1	3	2	2	3	1	1	2	
124.	Diseases of the bladder	7	4	8	8	7	7	9	9	7	7	7	15
125.	Diseases of the urethra, urinary abscess, etc	2	1	1				1		1	1		
126.	Diseases of the prostate	11	11	13	9	13	10	14	8	11	16	10	6
127.	Nonvenereal diseases of the male genital organs	1				2							
128.	Uterine hemorrhage (nonpuerperal)							1					
129.	Uterine tumor (noncancerous)	2	6	6	7	4	8	5	2	3	5		2
130.	Other diseases of the uterus	3	2	2	1			2	2	1	3	2	1
131.	Cysts and other tumors of the ovary	1	2	6	3	4	2	4	3	4	2	2	2
132.	Other diseases of the female genital organs—												
	(A. Diseases of the tubes)	4	5	5	6	6	4	9	6	9	3	2	2
	(B. Other diseases of the female genital organs)	3	2							1			1
133.	Nonpuerperal diseases of the breast (cancer excepted)												

TABLE No. 2—Continued.

	Jan.	Feb.	March.	April.	May.	June.	July.	Aug.	Sept.	Oct.	Nov.	Dec.
VII. THE PUERPERAL STATE.	51	46	45	44	36	37	41	29	21	30	32	38
134. Accidents of pregnancy	14	5	5	5	4	2	7	3	4	2	4	2
135. Puerperal hemorrhage	5	4	2		3	3	4		2	1	1	5
136. Other accidents of labor		4	1			1		3		3	1	3
137. Puerperal septicemia	19	22	21	29	19	21	17	16	11	19	19	16
138. Puerperal albuminuria and convulsions	10	7	4	6	5	7	7	6	3	4	6	9
139. Phlegmasia alba dolens (puerperal)	1				1		1					
140. Other puerperal accidents	2	4	12	4	4	3	5	1	1	1	1	3
141. Puerperal diseases of the breast												
VIII. DISEASES OF THE SKIN AND CELLULAR TISSUE.	13	14	18	15	12	15	12	11	18	11	10	18
142. Gangrene	8	11	12	11	10	8	6	8	14	7	7	12
143. Furuncle	1	1	1	1		2	1		2	1	3	1
144. Acute abscess	1		1		2	1	3		1	2		
145. Other diseases of the skin and annexa	3	2	4	3		4	2	3	1	1		5
IX. DISEASES OF THE BONES AND THE ORGANS OF LOCOMOTION.	4	13	8	7	4	8	5	8	2	5	6	4
146. Nontuberculous diseases of the bones	3	12	8	6	3	6	5	8	2	5	5	4
147. Diseases of the joints (tuberculosis and rheumatism excepted)	1	1		1	1	2					1	
148. Amputations												
149. Other diseases of the organs of locomotion												
X. MALFORMATIONS.	51	32	46	37	19	37	31	38	31	37	43	50
150. Congenital malformations (stillbirths not included)—												
(A. Hydrocephalus)	2	2	4	7	1	3	4	3	3	3	5	4
(B. Congenital malformation of the heart (cyanosis)	35	20	27	17	14	25	25	26	23	27	30	31
(C. Other congenital malformations)	14	10	15	13	4	9	2	9	5	7	8	15
XI. DISEASES OF EARLY INFANCY.	120	124	144	131	121	123	127	153	114	110	124	132
151. Congenital debility, icterus and sclerema—												
(A. Premature birth)	93	93	97	92	96	92	96	120	79	80	95	90
(B. Congenital debility)	20	12	29	24	8	14	17	23	23	12	20	21
152. Other diseases peculiar to early infancy	4	16	13	12	17	17	12	7	12	16	9	20
153. Lack of care	3	3	5	3			2	3		2		1

XII. OLD AGE.	39	53	43	42	39	33	38	42	48	49	37	52
154. Senility	39	53	43	42	39	33	38	42	48	49	37	52
XIII. AFFECTIONS PRODUCED BY EXTERNAL CAUSES.	197	179	83	200	188	243	23	31	81	97	24	234
155. Suicide by poison	14	9	22	14	12	12	16	14	15	15	17	10
156. Suicide by asphyxia			2	1			1			1	1	
157. Suicide by hanging or strangulation	1	7	8	3	8	9	7	7	2	4	6	2
158. Suicide by drowning	2	1	2	1		2	1	4	5	2	1	1
159. Suicide by firearms	4	5	10	8	8	9	7	7	6	11	10	10
160. Suicide by cutting or piercing instruments	1	1	1	3				3			1	1
161. Suicide by jumping from high place				1					1			1
162. Suicide by crushing				2	1	2	5		1			
163. Other suicides			2				1	1				
164. Poisoning by food	5	3	1			1					1	
165. Other acute poisonings	5	3	9	3	6	8	5	4	4	4	9	7
166. Conflagration	4		1		2	1				1	1	4
167. Burns (conflagration excepted)	12	13	30	14	11	9	9	13	7	17	16	18
168. Absorption of deleterious gases (conflagration excepted)	9	2	1		1	1	1		5	2	3	4
169. Accidental drowning	5	8	4	6	12	29	39	18	13	4	3	3
170. Traumatism by firearms	3	2	6	3	6	5	10	4	4	6	8	13
171. Traumatism by cutting or piercing instruments		2	2		2	1	1					
172. Traumatism by fall	41	35	61	29	22	39	20	36	27	31	30	33
173. Traumatism in mines and quarries	5	3	3		6	4	9	8	11	3	6	5
174. Traumatism by machines	4	5	1	4	4	1	4	8	7	6	3	12
175. Traumatism by other crushing—												
(A. Railroad accident and injuries)	33	24	24	27	36	36	42	57	36	36	31	41
(B. Street car and interurban)	4	6	6	7	6	9	11	10	61	7	7	3
(C. Automobiles and other vehicles)	3	2	5	4	4	15	7	11	2	10	6	13
(D. Landslides)												
(E. Other accidental traumatism)	5	9	16	13	7	7	6	2	4	3	5	7
176. Injuries by animals	2	1	4	7	8	9	11	11	5	4	6	3
177. Starvation												
178. Excessive cold	8										6	3
179. Effects of heat	1				1	10	9	3			1	
180. Lightning			1	2	3	5	9	2	1			
181. Electricity (lightning excepted)	1	1	3	5		2	4	5	6	4	1	
182. Homicide by firearms	3	5	4	5	3	3	13	9	5	9	12	8
183. Homicide by cutting or piercing instruments			1	2	3			1		1	1	3
184. Homicide by other means		3	4	5	2	1	1	2	1	3	5	3

TABLE No. 2—Continued.

	Jan.	Feb.	March.	April.	May.	June.	July.	Aug.	Sept.	Oct.	Nov.	Dec.
VII. THE PUERPERAL STATE.	51	46	45	44	36	37	41	29	21	30	32	38
134. Accidents of pregnancy	14	5	5	5	4	2	7	3	4	2	4	2
135. Puerperal hemorrhage	5	4	2		3	3	4		2	1	1	5
136. Other accidents of labor		4	1			1		3		3	1	3
137. Puerperal septicemia	19	22	21	29	19	21	17	16	11	19	19	16
138. Puerperal albuminuria and convulsions	10	7	4	6	5	7	7	6	3	4	6	9
139. Phlegmasia alba dolens (puerperal)	1				1		1					
140. Other puerperal accidents	2	4	12	4	4	3	5	1	1	1	1	3
141. Puerperal diseases of the breast												
VIII. DISEASES OF THE SKIN AND CELLULAR TISSUE.	13	14	18	15	12	15	12	11	18	11	10	18
142. Gangrene	8	11	12	11	10	8	6	8	14	7	7	12
143. Furuncle	1	1	1	1		2	1		2	1	3	1
144. Acute abscess	1		1		2	1	3		1	2		
145. Other diseases of the skin and annexa	3	2	4	3		4	2	3	1	1		5
IX. DISEASES OF THE BONES AND THE ORGANS OF LOCOMOTION.	4	13	8	7	4	8	5	8	2	5	6	4
146. Nontuberculous diseases of the bones	3	12	8	6	3	6	5	8	2	5	5	4
147. Diseases of the joints (tuberculosis and rheumatism excepted)	1	1		1	1	2					1	
148. Amputations												
149. Other diseases of the organs of locomotion												
X. MALFORMATIONS.	51	32	46	37	19	37	31	38	31	37	43	50
150. Congenital malformations (stillbirths not included)—												
(A. Hydrocephalus)	2	2	4	7	1	3	4	3	3	3	5	4
(B. Congenital malformation of the heart (cyanosis)	35	20	27	17	14	25	25	26	23	27	30	31
(C. Other congenital malformations)	14	10	15	13	4	9	2	9	5	7	8	15
XI. DISEASES OF EARLY INFANCY.	120	124	144	131	121	123	127	153	114	110	124	132
151. Congenital debility, icterus and sclerema—												
(A. Premature birth)	93	93	97	92	96	92	96	120	79	80	95	90
(B. Congenital debility)	20	12	29	24	8	14	17	23	23	12	20	21
152. Other diseases peculiar to early infancy	4	16	13	12	17	17	12	7	12	16	9	20
153. Lack of care	3	3	5	3			2	3		2		1

XII. Old Age.	39	53	43	42	39	33	38	42	48	49	37	52
154. Senility	39	53	43	42	39	33	38	42	48	49	37	52
XIII. Affections Produced by External Causes.	197	179	263	200	188	243	273	251	241	207	214	234
155. Suicide by poison	14	9	22	14	12	12	16	14	15	15	17	10
156. Suicide by asphyxia			2	1			1			1	1	
157. Suicide by hanging or strangulation	1	7	8	3	8	9	7	7	2	4	6	2
158. Suicide by drowning	2	1	2	1		2	1	4	5	2	1	1
159. Suicide by firearms	4	5	10	8	8	9	7	7	6	11	10	10
160. Suicide by cutting or piercing instruments	1	1	1	3				3			1	1
161. Suicide by jumping from high place				1					1			1
162. Suicide by crushing				2	1	2	5		1			
163. Other suicides			2				1	1				
164. Poisoning by food	5	3	1			1					1	
165. Other acute poisonings	5	3	9	3	6	8	5	4	4	4	9	7
166. Conflagration	4		1		2	1				1	1	4
167. Burns (conflagration excepted)	12	13	30	14	11	9	9	13	7	17	16	18
168. Absorption of deleterious gases (conflagration excepted)	9	2	1		1	1	1		5	2	3	4
169. Accidental drowning	5	8	4	6	12	29	39	18	13	4	3	3
170. Traumatism by firearms	3	2	6	3	6	5	10	4	4	6	8	13
171. Traumatism by cutting or piercing instruments		2	2		2	1	1					
172. Traumatism by fall	41	35	61	29	22	39	30	36	27	31	30	33
173. Traumatism in mines and quarries	5	3	3		6	4	9	8	11	3	6	5
174. Traumatism by machines	4	5	1	4	4	1	4	8	7	6	3	12
175. Traumatism by other crushing—												
(A. Railroad accident and injuries)	33	24	24	27	36	36	42	57	36	36	31	41
(B. Street car and interurban)	4	6	6	7	6	9	11	10	61	7	7	3
(C. Automobiles and other vehicles)	3	2	5	4	4	15	7	11	2	10	6	13
(D. Landslides)												
(E. Other accidental traumatism)	8	9	16	13	7	7	6	2	4	3	5	7
176. Injuries by animals	2	1	4	7	8	9	11	11	5	4	6	3
177. Starvation												
178. Excessive cold	8										6	3
179. Effects of heat	1				1	10	9	3			1	
180. Lightning			1	2	3	5	9	2	1			
181. Electricity (lightning excepted)	1	1	3	5		2	4	5	6	4	1	
182. Homicide by firearms	3	5	4	5	3	3	13	9	5	9	12	8
183. Homicide by cutting or piercing instruments			1	2	3			1		1	1	3
184. Homicide by other means		3	4	5	2	1	1	2	1	3	5	3

TABLE No. 2—Continued.

	Jan.	Feb.	March.	April.	May.	June.	July.	Aug.	Sept.	Oct	Nov.	Dec.
185. Fractures, cause not specified	1	....	2	1	....	1	....	....	1	....	2	1
186. Other external violence—												
(A. Suffocation)	6	11	6	1	3	2	5	1	3	7	2	12
(B. Injuries at birth)	12	15	19	15	9	9	9	6	8	15	10	10
(C. Other external violence)	....	3	2	4	2	1	....	4	....	1	3	3
XIV. ILL-DEFINED DISEASES.	10	6	5	6	4	5	4	14	10	10	4	3
187. Ill-defined organic disease	1	....	....	....	....	....	....	....	....	....	....	....
188. Sudden death	....	....	1	....	....	....	....	....	....	....	....	1
189. Cause of death not specified or ill defined	9	6	4	6	4	5	4	14	10	10	4	2
Total deaths from all causes	3,039	2,972	3,599	2,967	2,757	2,747	3,064	3,406	3,010	2,892	2,932	3,128

TABLE No. 2—Continued.

Deaths from All Causes by Months, Ages, Color, Nationality and Conjugal Condition, for the Year Ending December 31, 1910. International Classification

	Under 1	1	2	3	4	Total Under 5	5 to 9	10 to 14	15 to 19	20 to 24	25 to 29	30 to 34	35 to 39	40 to 44	45 to 49	50 to 54	55 to 59	60 to 64	65 to 69
I. GENERAL DISEASES—																			
(A. EPIDEMIC DISEASES.)	463	378	231	143	124	1,339	327	172	182	184	138	119	113	101	88	88	102	82	149
1. Typhoid fever	6	12	12	12	18	60	62	74	125	138	90	74	71	47	45	39	37	11	19
2. Typhus fever																			
3. Relapsing fever																			
4. Malaria	11	6	3	4	3	27	5	6	10	9	9	3	7	5	3	6	5	9	1
4a. Malarial cachexia																			8
5. Smallpox												1							
6. Measles	73	116	69	32	17	307	49	24	10	10	9	14	10	7	7	1	8	2	1
7. Scarlet fever	13	24	21	23	19	100	61	20	10	7	4		1					1	
8. Whooping-cough	241	108	50	23	15	437	18	1	1					1					
9. Croup	4	2	2	5	2	15	6												
9a. Diphtheria	24	42	41	37	41	185	113	35	14	4	4	1	1	1		1		1	
10. Influenza	46	18	14	3	4	85	9	6	9	13	16	16	15	22	23	26	36	34	67
11. Miliary fever																			
12. Asiatic cholera																			
13. Cholera nostras	1		1			2									1	2	1	3	2
14. Dysentery	9	42	17	4	5	77	3	3	2	1	3	2	4	8	4	8	8	11	35
14a. Epidemic dysentery																			
15. Plague																			
16. Yellow fever																			
17. Leprosy																			
18. Erysipelas	31	7				38	1	1	1	1	3	8	4	10	5	5	7	10	16
19. Other epidemic diseases	4	1	1			6		2		1									

TABLE No. 2—Continued.

	Jan.	Feb.	March.	April.	May.	June.	July.	Aug.	Sept.	Oct.	Nov.	Dec.
VII. THE PUERPERAL STATE.	51	46	45	44	36	37	41	29	21	30	32	38
134. Accidents of pregnancy	14	5	5	5	4	2	7	3	4	2	4	2
135. Puerperal hemorrhage	5	4	2		3	3	4		2	1	1	5
136. Other accidents of labor		4	1			1		3		3	1	3
137. Puerperal septicemia	19	22	21	29	19	21	17	16	11	19	19	16
138. Puerperal albuminuria and convulsions	10	7	4	6	5	7	7	6	3	4	6	9
139. Phlegmasia alba dolens (puerperal)	1				1		1					
140. Other puerperal accidents	2	4	12	4	4	3	5	1	1	1	1	3
141. Puerperal diseases of the breast												
VIII. DISEASES OF THE SKIN AND CELLULAR TISSUE.	13	14	18	15	12	15	12	11	18	11	10	18
142. Gangrene	8	11	12	11	10	8	6	8	14	7	7	12
143. Furuncle	1	1	1	1		2	1		2	1	3	1
144. Acute abscess	1		1		2	1	3		1	2		
145. Other diseases of the skin and annexa	3	2	4	3		4	2	3	1	1		5
IX. DISEASES OF THE BONES AND THE ORGANS OF LOCOMOTION.	4	13	8	7	4	8	5	8	2	5	6	4
146. Nontuberculous diseases of the bones	3	12	8	6	3	6	5	8	2	5	5	4
147. Diseases of the joints (tuberculosis and rheumatism excepted)	1	1		1	1	2					1	
148. Amputations												
149. Other diseases of the organs of locomotion												
X. MALFORMATIONS.	51	32	46	37	19	37	31	38	31	37	43	50
150. Congenital malformations (stillbirths not included)—												
(A. Hydrocephalus)	2	2	4	7	1	3	4	3	3	3	5	4
(B. Congenital malformation of the heart (cyanosis)	35	20	27	17	14	25	25	26	23	27	30	31
(C. Other congenital malformations)	14	10	15	13	4	9	2	9	5	7	8	15
XI. DISEASES OF EARLY INFANCY.	120	124	144	131	121	123	127	153	114	110	124	132
151. Congenital debility, icterus and sclerema—												
(A. Premature birth)	93	93	97	92	96	92	96	120	79	80	95	90
(B. Congenital debility)	20	12	29	24	8	14	17	23	23	12	20	21
152. Other diseases peculiar to early infancy	4	16	13	12	17	17	12	7	12	16	9	20
153. Lack of care	3	3	5	3			2	3		2		1

XII. Old Age.	39	53	43	42	39	33	38	42	48	49	37	52
154. Senility	39	53	43	42	39	33	38	42	48	49	37	52
XIII. Affections Produced by External Causes.	197	179	263	200	188	83	23	81	81	207	214	234
155. Suicide by poison	14	9	22	14	12	12	16	14	15	15	17	10
156. Suicide by asphyxia			2	1			1			1	1	
157. Suicide by hanging or strangulation	1	7	8	3	8	9	7	7	2	4	6	2
158. Suicide by drowning	2	1	2	1		2	1	4	5	2	1	1
159. Suicide by firearms	4	5	10	8	8	9	7	7	6	11	10	10
160. Suicide by cutting or piercing instruments	1	1	1	3				3			1	1
161. Suicide by jumping from high place				1					1			1
162. Suicide by crushing				2	1	2	5		1			
163. Other suicides			2				1	1				
164. Poisoning by food	5	3	1			1					1	
165. Other acute poisonings	5	3	9	3	6	8	5	4	4	4	9	7
166. Conflagration	4		1		2	1				1	1	4
167. Burns (conflagration excepted)	12	13	30	14	11	9	9	13	7	17	16	18
168. Absorption of deleterious gases (conflagration excepted)	9	2	1		1	1	1		5	2	3	4
169. Accidental drowning	5	8	4	6	12	29	39	18	13	4	3	3
170. Traumatism by firearms	3	2	6	3	6	5	10	4	4	6	8	13
171. Traumatism by cutting or piercing instruments		2	2		2	1	1					
172. Traumatism by fall	41	35	61	29	22	39	20	36	27	31	30	33
173. Traumatism in mines and quarries	5	3	3		6	4	9	8	11	3	6	5
174. Traumatism by machines	4	5	1	4	4	1	4	8	7	6	3	12
175. Traumatism by other crushing—												
(A. Railroad accident and injuries)	33	24	24	27	36	36	42	57	36	36	31	41
(B. Street car and interurban)	4	6	6	7	6	9	11	10	61	7	7	3
(C. Automobiles and other vehicles)	3	2	5	4	4	15	7	11	2	10	6	13
(D. Landslides)												
(E. Other accidental traumatism)	5	9	16	13	7	7	6	2	4	3	5	7
176. Injuries by animals	2	1	4	7	8	9	11	11	5	4	6	3
177. Starvation												
178. Excessive cold	8										6	3
179. Effects of heat	1				1	10	9	3			1	
180. Lightning			1	2	3	5	9	2	1			
181. Electricity (lightning excepted)	1	1	3	5		2	4	5	6	4	1	
182. Homicide by firearms	3	5	4	5	3	3	13	9	5	9	12	8
183. Homicide by cutting or piercing instruments			1	2	3			1		1	1	3
184. Homicide by other means		3	4	5	2	1	1	2	1	3	5	3

TABLE No. 2—Continued.

	Jan.	Feb.	March.	April.	May.	June.	July.	Aug.	Sept.	Oct	Nov.	Dec.
185. Fractures, cause not specified	1	....	2	1	....	1	....	....	1	....	2	1
186. Other external violence—												
(A. Suffocation)	6	11	6	1	3	2	5	1	3	7	2	12
(B. Injuries at birth)	12	15	19	15	9	9	9	6	8	15	10	10
(C. Other external violence)	....	3	2	4	2	1	....	4	....	1	3	3
XIV. Ill-Defined Diseases.	10	6	5	6	4	5	4	14	10	10	4	3
187. Ill-defined organic disease	1	....	....	....	....	....	....	....	....	....	....	....
188. Sudden death	....	....	1	....	....	....	....	....	....	....	....	1
189. Cause of death not specified or ill defined	9	6	4	6	4	5	4	14	10	10	4	2
Total deaths from all causes	3,030	2,972	3,599	2,967	2,757	2,747	3,064	3,406	3,010	2,892	2,932	3,128

TABLE No. 2—Continued.

Deaths from All Causes by Months, Ages, Color, Nationality and Conjugal Condition, for the Year Ending December 31, 1910. International Classification

	Under 1	1	2	3	4	Total Under 5	5 to 9	10 to 14	15 to 19	20 to 24	25 to 29	30 to 34	35 to 39	40 to 44	45 to 49	50 to 54	55 to 59	60 to 64	65 to 69
I. GENERAL DISEASES—																			
(A. Epidemic Diseases.)	463	378	231	143	124	1,339	327	172	182	184	138	119	113	101	88	88	102	82	149
1. Typhoid fever	6	12	12	12	18	60	62	74	125	138	90	74	71	47	45	39	37	11	19
2. Typhus fever																			
3. Relapsing fever																			
4. Malaria	11	6	3	4	3	27	5	6	10	9	9	3	7	5	3	6	5	9	1
4a. Malarial cachexia																			8
5. Smallpox												1							
6. Measles	73	116	69	32	17	307	49	24	10	10	9	14	10	7	7	1	8	2	1
7. Scarlet fever	13	24	21	23	19	100	61	20	10	7	4		1					1	
8. Whooping-cough	241	108	50	23	15	437	18	1	1					1					
9. Croup	4	2	2	5	2	15	6												
9a. Diphtheria	24	42	41	37	41	185	113	35	14	4	4	1	1	1		1		1	
10. Influenza	46	18	14	3	4	85	9	6	9	13	16	16	15	22	23	26	36	34	67
11. Miliary fever																			
12. Asiatic cholera																			
13. Cholera nostras	1		1			2									1	2	1	3	2
14. Dysentery	9	42	17	4	5	77	3	3	2	1	3	2	4	8	4	8	8	11	35
14a. Epidemic dysentery																			
15. Plague																			
16. Yellow fever																			
17. Leprosy																			
18. Erysipelas	31	7				38	1	1	1	1	3	8	4	10	5	5	7	10	16
19. Other epidemic diseases	4	1	1			6		2		1									

TABLE No. 2—Continued.

	Under 1	1	2	3	4	Total Under 5	5 to 9	10 to 14	15 to 19	20 to 24	25 to 29	30 to 34	35 to 39	40 to 44	45 to 49	50 to 54	55 to 59	60 to 64	65 to 69
(B. OTHER GENERAL DISEASES.)	322	137	52	38	35	584	97	135	423	709	644	576	483	483	518	558	533	565	552
20. Purulent infection and septicemia	7			1		8		2	3	1	3		2	3	4	2	2	8	4
21. Glanders																	1		
22. Anthrax																1			
23. Rabies				1	1	2									1		1		
24. Tetanus	24	2			1	27	6	2	1	4	1		1			1	2	1	
25. Mycosis																			
26. Pellagra																			
27. Beriberi																			
28. Tuberculosis of the lungs	63	33	13	9	9	127	24	62	317	578	520	431	309	263	204	242	181	158	165
29. Acute miliary tuberculosis	5	1	1			7	2	6	7	9	11	6	5	2	2	1	4	3	1
30. Tuberculous meningitis	69	56	19	10	10	164	20	12	11	14	2	9	4	5	3	1	4	1	1
31. Abdominal tuberculosis	26	10	3	3		42	10	6	24	33	33	23	16	18	13	22	16	23	15
32. Pott's disease	1	2	1	1		5	1		2	3	7	3	1	2	3	1	2		
33. White swellings				1	3	4	1	1	2	[illegible]	1		1	1	4	1	4	1	2
34. Tuberculosis of other organs	2	2		3		7	1	3	3	6	5	5	6	4	6	4	2	4	1
35. Disseminated tuberculosis	18	4	2			24	1	2	4	9	11	7	8	5	3	4		5	3
36. Rickets	13	7		1		21	1	2	1	1		2							
37. Syphilis	63	3	1			67	2	1	1	6	7	11	15	8	12	8	6	8	3
38. Gonococcus infection									1	3	1						1		
39. Cancer and other malignant tumors of the buccal cavity											1	1		1	1	2	8	13	8
40. Cancer and other malignant tumors of the stomach and liver			1	1		2	1	1	1		3	7	20	31	49	79	95	107	135
41. Cancer and other malignant tumors of the peritoneum, intestines and rectum											2	4	11	18	16	15	29	24	23
42. Cancer and other malignant tumors of the female genital organs									1	1	2	10	22	33	67	45	38	45	27
43. Cancer and other malignant tumors of the breast			1			1						3	6	14	29	18	19	20	20
44. Cancer and other malignant tumors of the skin									1	1		1	3	2	6	6	7	15	9

Cause																			
45. Cancer and malignant tumors of other organs and of organs not specified		2	2	2		6	2	2	3	2	6	4	4	5	22	24	17	30	
46. Other tumors (tumors of the female genital organs excepted)	1					1	1			2		1		1	3	2	5	1	4
47. Acute articular rheumatism	2	1	2	1	3	9	11	12	11	10	4	6	10	12	8	11	7	11	13
48. Chronic rheumatism and gout								2	2	2	1	3	1	3	1	4	4	7	8
49. Scurvy	2	2				4			1										
50. Diabetes	1	2	4	1	4	12	10	14	17	16	7	13	8	11	18	37	35	48	48
51. Exophthalmic goitre										3	3	4	5	5	5	3	5	2	1
52. Addison's disease										1	1			1			2	2	
53. Leukemia	1					1	1		2	2	2		2	2	5	3	5	3	2
54. Anemia chlorosis	8	3			2	13	1	3	5		1	6	5	10	12	6	17	12	17
55. Other general diseases	16	7	2	2	2	29	1	2	2	1	1	1	1	1	3	1	3	1	4
56. Alcoholism (acute or chronic)				1		1					5	12	17	19	17	10	9	8	1
57. Chronic lead poisoning											1	3	1			2			
58. Other chronic occupation poisonings																1			
59. Other chronic poisonings											2			3	1	1	2	4	2
II. DISEASES OF THE NERVOUS SYSTEM AND OF THE ORGANS OF SPECIAL SENSES.	163	38	27	24	14	66	42	27	29	38	39	71	103	111	148	219	28	318	369
60. Encephalitis	9	2	2	2		15	5	1	2	1	2	1	4	3	1	3	3	2	1
61. Simple meningitis	53	14	9	6	5	87	7	6	3		4	3	1	1	3	6	3	1	
61a. Cerebrospinal fever	5	3		2	2	12	3		1	2	2	1						1	
62. Locomotor ataxia				1		1					1	3	2	7	11	12	9	8	10
63. Other diseases of the spinal cord	13	8	7	7	4	39	13	4	4	3	1	5	6	5	10	18	11	22	18
64. Cerebral hemorrhage, apoplexy	19	2	5	1		27		5		7	8	19	37	37	66	114	30	201	36
65. Softening of the brain												2		1	2	3	3	8	6
66. Paralysis without specified cause	1			1		2						2	3	4	4	10	17	32	31
67. General paralysis of the insane										1	2	8	10	16	17	20	7	14	10
68. Other forms of mental alienation									1	3	1	3	10	11	9	9	8	10	9
69. Epilepsy	4	2	1	1	1	9	2	5	9	13	13	17	22	19	14	10	8	11	7
70. Convulsions (nonpuerperal)							2												
71. Convulsions of infants	45	4	1		1	51													
72. Chorea					1	1			3	2	1	1			1				
73. Hysteria										1			1	1	1				1
74. [illegible] of the nervous system—																			
(A. Other diseases of the brain)	3	1				4	4		4	2	3	3	4	3	5	9	4	4	5
(B. Other diseases of the nervous system)	1					1	1	2	1	1	1	3			2	2	3	3	3
75. D[illegible] eye and its adnexia	1					1								1		1			1
76. D[illegible] ear	9	2	2	3		16	5	4	1	2			3	2	2	2	2	1	1

TABLE No. 2—Continued.

	Under 1	1	2	3	4	Total Under 5	5 to 9	10 to 14	15 to 19	20 to 24	25 to 29	30 to 34	35 to 39	40 to 44	45 to 49	50 to 54	55 to 59	60 to 64	65 to 69
III. THE ULATORY SYSTEM.	40	8	9	8	6	71	28	46	56	58	65	87	124	166	215	290	352	541	656
77.			1			1	1	4	1	2	1		2		2	2	3	1	4
78.	4	1	1	4	2	12	4	1	3	5	3	6	3	7	10	14	7	6	11
79. Organic disease of heart	27	7	6	4	4	48	21	38	49	45	52	71	109	138	179	241	280	456	541
80. Angina pectoris								1	2	1	3	5	5	6	12	15	26	36	29
81. Diseases of the art atheroma, aneurism, etc	1					1			1		3	1	3	6	6	12	29	26	56
82. Embolism and thrombosis	3					3		2		4	2	2	2	4	4	5	5	12	11
83. Diseases of the veins (varices, hemorrhoids, phlebitis, etc.)							1				1	1		3	1		1	3	2
84. Diseases of the lymphatic system (lymphangitis, etc.)	1					1	1											1	2
85. Hemorrhage; other diseases of the circulatory system	4		1			5				1		1		2	1	1	1		
IV. DISEASES OF THE RESPIRATORY SYSTEM.	898	238	105	46	32	1,319	87	34	53	67	64	68	85	84	87	118	126	146	201
86. Diseases of the nasal fossae	2					2	2	3					1	1					
87. Diseases of the larynx—																			
(A. Laryngitis)	5	1	1	2	2	11	4	1	1		2	1	1	1	1				
(B. Other diseases of the larynx)	5		2	1	2	10	3	1						1	1				
88. Diseases of the thyroid body	4		1			5								1		1			
89. Acute bronchitis	135	22	6	3	3	169	6	1	1	1			2			1	2	4	6
90. Chronic bronchitis	1	2	1			4			1				2	1	2	4	8	11	18
91. Broncho-pneumonia	387	99	51	18	12	567	18	7	8	7	4	4	11	11	11	8	15	20	38
92. Lobar pneumonia	344	108	43	21	11	527	53	17	42	52	54	58	58	62	58	92	89	94	114
93. Pleurisy	3	2			2	7	1	2		4	2	1	5	4	5	3	2	7	6
94. Pulmonary congestion, pulmonary apoplexy	8	3				11		1					1		1	2		2	1
95. Gangrene of the lung	1					1											1		1
96. Asthma	1	1		1		3		1			1		4		5	5	7	5	14

97. Pulmonary emphysema										1		2							1
98. Other diseases of the respiratory system—																			
(A. Hemorrhage of the lungs)												1		1	1	1	1	1	1
(B. Other diseases of the respiratory system)	2					2				2	1	1		1	2	1	1	2	1
V. **Diseases of the Digestive System.**	1.857	512	162	53	27	2,611	81	54	73	83	72	72	94	82	97	119	138	176	201
99. Diseases of the mouth and adnexia	15	2	1		1	19			1						1			1	
100. Diseases of the pharynx—																			
(A. Tonsilitis)	2	1	1	1	3	8	6	3	2	4			1			1	2		
(B. Other diseases of the pharynx)			1	1		2	3								2	1	2		
101. Diseases of the esophagus	1					1	1												
102. Ulcer of the stomach	2					2			2	5		6	5	5	6	9	3	9	11
103. Other diseases of the stomach (cancer excepted)—																			
(A. Gastritis)	63	10	2	3		78	2		2	5	5	8	4	3	2	5	11	23	24
(B. Other diseases of the stomach)	118	14	8	4		144	1	2	2	1	1	2	4	1	1	1	2	4	12
104. Diarrhoea and enteritis (under 2 years)	1,576	473				2,049													
105. Diarrhea and enteritis (2 years and over)			140	37	13	190	22	9	9	8	8	7	10	11	15	18	16	37	50
106. Ankylotomiasis																			
107. Intestinal parasites			1			1	1												
108. Appendicitis and typhlitis	1			1	2	4	26	29	40	33	32	13	17	16	11	15	12	10	8
109. **Hernias, intestinal obstructions—**																			
(A. Hernia)	4					4					1	1		3	6	3	7	10	6
(B. Obstructions of intestines)	36	9	2	2	5	54	10	5	9	10	5	10	13	9	8	10	17	10	18
110. **Other diseases of the intestines**	18	1	2	1	1	23	3	1	1	1	3	2	3	2	3	4	5	4	8
111. **Acute yellow atrophy of the liver**												1		1		2	1		2
112. **Hydatid tumor of the liver**																			
113. **Cirrhosis of the liver**	3		1	1		5			1	1	8	8	15	20	26	26	26	41	40
114. **Biliary calculi**										2	3	2	8	4	5	11	19	5	9
115. Other diseases of the liver	12	1	3	2	2	20	4	3	2	5	2	7	7	5	10	11	14	21	12
116. Diseases of the spleen	1					1										1			1
117. Simple peritonitis (nonpuerperal)	4	1				5	2	2	2	7	3	5	5	2			1	1	
118. Other diseases of the digestive system (cancer and tuberculosis excepted.)	1					1				1	1		2		1	1			
VI. **Nonvenereal Diseases of the Genito-Urinary System and Annexa.**	35	11	2	10	5	63	8	19	25	45	57	75	87	108	133	137	194	254	253
119. **Acute nephritis**	15	7	1	4	2	29	4	7	7	4	9	8	13	13	8	3	12	10	8
120. **Bright's disease**	3	3		5	2	13	4	11	11	19	28	39	49	66	100	108	166	210	212
121. **Chyluria**					1	1							1						1
122. **Other diseases of the kidneys and annexa**	12	1				13		1				1	1	7	2	4	3	6	4
123. **Calculi of the urinary passages**	1			1		2					2	1	1			1		1	3

TABLE No. 2—Continued.

	Under 1	1	2	3	4	Total Under 5	5 to 9	10 to 14	15 to 19	20 to 24	25 to 29	30 to 34	35 to 39	40 to 44	45 to 49	50 to 54	55 to 59	60 to 64	65 to 69
124. Diseases of the bladder	3		1			4				1	1		3		1	3	5	8	8
125. Diseases of the urethra, urinary abscess, etc														2		1	1	2	
126. Diseases of the prostate															1	2	1	10	16
127. Nonvenereal diseases of the male genital organs	1					1								1					
128. Uterine hemorrhage (nonpuerperal)														1					
129. Uterine tumor (noncancerous)											2	4	3	7	12	9	2	2	1
130. Other diseases of the uterus									1	3	2	8	3	2	2	1		1	
131. Cysts and other tumors of the ovary									2	1	3	2	7	4	1	4	3	3	
132. Other diseases of the female genital Organs—																			
(A. Diseases of the tubes)									4	14	10	16	5	5	5	1	1		
(B. Other diseases of the female genital organs										3		1	1		1			1	
133. Nonpuerperal diseases of the breast (cancer excepted)																			
VII. The Puerperal State.								1	43	107	96	79	86	33	5				
134. Accidents of pregnancy								1	2	8	11	15	15	4	1				
135. Puerperal hemorrhage									3	6	8	6	4	2	1				
36. Other accidents of labor									1	1	6		8						
137. Puerperal septicemia									19	65	50	37	37	19	2				
138. Puerperal albuminuria and convulsions									13	17	11	15	13	4	1				
139. Phlegmasia alba dolens (puerperal)										1	1	1							
140. Other puerperal accidents									5	9	9	5	9	4					
141. Puerperal diseases of the breast																			
VIII. Diseases of the Skin and Cellular Tissue.	16	3	1		1	21		1	3			1	2	5	2	4	6	13	14
142. Gangrene	1		1		1	3			1			1		2		1	3	11	10
143. Furuncle	1					1								2	1	3		1	1
144. Acute abscess	2					2			1				2		1		2	1	2
145. Other diseases of the skin and annexa	12	3				15		1	1					1			1		1

IX. DISEASES OF THE BONES AND THE ORGANS OF LOCOMOTION.	13	1	3	1	......	18	11	3	3	5	4	3	3	1	3		4	3	3
146. Nontuberculous diseases of the bones	13	1	3	1	......	18	11	2	3	5	4	3	3	......	3	3	3	3	1
147. Diseases of the joints (tuberculosis and rheumatism excepted)	......	......	......	......	......	......	......												
148. Amputations	......	......	......	......	......	......	......	1	......	......	......	......	......	1	......	......	1	......	2
149. Other Diseases of the organs of locomotion	......	......	......	......	......	......	......	......	......	......	......	......	......	......	......	......	......	......	......
X. MALFORMATIONS.	435	9	4	......	......	448	4	......	......	......	......	......	......	......	......	......	......	......	......
150. Congenital malformations (still births not included)—																			
(A. Hydrocephalus)	33	3	2	......	......	38	3	......	......	......	......	......	......	......	......	......	......	......	......
(B. Congenital malformation of the heart (cyanosis))	297	1	1	......	......	299	1	......	......	......	......	......	......	......	......	......	......	......	......
(C. Other congenital malformations)	105	5	1	......	......	111	......	......	......	......	......	......	......	......	......	......	......	......	......
XI. DISEASES OF EARLY INFANCY.	1,522	1	......	......	......	1,523	......	......	......	......	......	......	......	......	......	......	......	......	......
151. Congenital debility, icterus and sclerema—																			
(A. Premature birth)	1,123	......	......	......	......	1,123	......	......	......	......	......	......	......	......	......	......	......	......	......
(B. Congenital debility)	223	......	......	......	......	223	......	......	......	......	......	......	......	......	......	......	......	......	......
152. Other diseases peculiar to early infancy	155	......	......	......	......	155	......	......	......	......	......	......	......	......	......	......	......	......	......
153. Lack of care	21	1	......	......	......	22	......	......	......	......	......	......	......	......	......	......	......	......	......
XII. OLD AGE.	......	......	......	......	......	......	......	......	......	......	......	......	......	......	......	......	......	4	21
154. Senility	......	......	......	......	......	......	......	......	......	......	......	......	......	......	......	......	......	4	21
XIII. AFFECTIONS PRODUCED BY EXTERNAL CAUSES.	233	56	37	29	19	374	92	95	162	248	218	182	169	165	175	133	129	107	91
155. Suicide by poison	......	......	......	......	......	......	......	2	15	24	28	18	17	19	9	14	6	11	3
156. Suicide by asphyxia	......	......	......	......	......	......	......	......	......	1	1	......	1	1	......	1	......	1	......
157. Suicide by hanging or strangulation	......	......	......	......	......	......	......	1	2	5	4	1	3	6	11	4	7	6	4
158. Suicide by drowning	......	......	......	......	......	......	......	......	1	2	1	2	1	1	2	5	2	1	......
159. Suicide by firearms	......	......	......	......	......	......	......	3	5	7	13	9	12	10	8	6	6	4	6
160. Suicide by cutting or piercing instruments	......	......	......	......	......	......	......	......	1	......	1	1	......	2	2	......	1	1	1
161. Suicide by jumping from high place	......	......	......	......	......	......	......	......	......	......	......	......	......	......	1	1	......	......	1
162. Suicide by crushing	......	......	......	......	......	......	......	......	......	1	......	1	1	3	1	2	1	......	......
163. Other suicides	......	......	......	......	......	......	......	......	1	1	......	......	......	......	1	......	1	......	......
164. Poisoning by food	1	1	1	......	1	4	1	......	......	1	......	......	......	1	1	......	......	1	1

TABLE No. 2—Continued*

	Under 1	1	2	3	4	Total under 5	5 to 9	10 to 14	15 to 19	20 to 24	25 to 29	30 to 34	35 to 39	40 to 44	45 to 49	50 to 54	55 to 59	60 to 64	65 to 69
165. Other acute poisonings	9	14	8	4	1	36	1			3	2	2	4	4	3	6	1	3	
166. Conflagration	1	1			2	4			1			1	3	1	1	1	1		
167. Burns (conflagration excepted)	7	21	13	14	4	59	19	11	5	7	8	8	7	5	4	7	4	6	6
168. Absorption of deleterious gases (conflagration excepted)	1					1		1	3	3	1	4	2	3		4	3		1
169. Accidental drowning	2	6	2	2		12	13	14	24	22	13	14	5	6	5	1	3	1	2
170. Traumatism by firearms			1	2	1	4	10	11	14	5	9	3	4	2	3	1		2	1
171. Traumatism by cutting or piercing instruments								1				1			1	2	1		
172. Traumatism by fall	10	4	3	3	3	23	8	15	10	14	11	9	12	18	17	17	16	20	21
173. Traumatism in mines and quarries									3	13	7	10	5	8	8	3	2	1	1
174. Traumatism by machines					1	1	1	1	6	9	6	5	4	5	5	6	5	2	1
175. Traumatism by other crushing—																			
(A. Railroad accident and injuries)					1	1	11	14	37	55	50	49	49	29	39	19	15	18	14
(B. Street car and interurban)			1			1	4		11	15	19	7	11	13	11	7	9	7	11
(C. Automobiles and other vehicles)	1	4		1	2	8	11	3	4	9	10	4	3	2	6		6	2	5
(D. Landslides)																			
(E. Other accidental traumatism)	1	1	3	1	2	8	4	6	3	9	7	3	4	5	7	7	9	6	6
176. Injuries by animals					1	1	6	5	2	6	1	4	2	4	8	6	8	4	1
177. Starvation																			
178. Excessive cold	3					3				1	2	1		1	1		4		
179. Effects of heat	2	2				4	1	1		1				1	3	3	2	3	2
180. Lightning							1	2	3		1	2	1	4		2	5	2	
181. Electricity (lightning excepted)				1		1	1	2	1	6	7	4	3	4		2	1		
182. Homicide by firearms									6	19	15	10	9	6	4	1	3	3	1
183. Homicide by cutting or piercing instruments										6		2	2		1	1			
184. Homicide by other means								1	3	2		5	1	1	7	2	3	1	2
185. Fractures cause not specified										1		1	1		3			1	
186. Other external violence—																			
(A. Suffocation)	53	1				54			1				1			1	1		
(B. Injuries at birth)	137					137													
(C. Other external violence)	5	1	5	1		12		1			1	1	1		2	1	3		

XIV. ILL-DEFINED-DISEASES.	51	2	......	......	......	53	1	......	......	1	2	1	......	1	......	1	2	1	2
187. Ill defined organic disease	......	......	......	......	......	......	......	......	......	......	......	......	......	......	......	......	......	......	......
188. Sudden death	......	......	......	......	......	......	......	......	......	......	1	......	......	......	......	......	1	......	......
189. Cause of death not specified or ill defined	51	2	......	......	......	53	1	......	......	1	1	1	......	1	......	1	1	1	2
Total deaths from all causes	6,084	1,394	633	352	263	8,690	778	587	1,052	1,545	1,399	1,334	1,349	1,340	1,471	1,670	1,814	2,210	2,512

TABLE No. 2—Continued.

Deaths from All Causes by Months, Ages, Color, Nationality and Conjugal Condition, for the Year Ending December 31, 1910. International Classification.

	70 to 74	75 to 79	80 to 84	85 to 89	90 to 94	95 and Over.	Unknown.	White.	Colored.	American.	Foreign.	Not Reported.	Single.	Married.	Widowed or Divorced.	Not Reported.	Total.
I. GENERAL DISEASES—																	
(A. EPIDEMIC DISEASES.)	172	170	152	56	24	10	......	3,662	105	3,522	220*	17	2,307	1,003	446	12	3,768
1. Typhoid fever	19	14	7	2				913	20	868	61*	5	472	404	54	4	934
2. Typhus fever																	
3. Relapsing fever								1		1					1		1
4. Malaria	16	10	6	3	1	3		143	8	131	18	2	60	61	30		151
4a. Malarial cachexia																	
5. Smallpox								1		1				1			1
6. Measles	1	2						451	11	460	2		404	49	8	1	462
7. Scarlet fever			1					200	5	203	2		197	4	3	1	205
8. Whooping cough	1							446	13	459			457	1	1		459
9. Croup								20	1	21			21				21
9a. Diphtheria								351	9	358	1	1	351	9			360
10. Influenza	87	96	89	33	13	6		678	23	606	90	5	165	306	227	3	701
11. Miliary fever																	
12. Asiatic cholera																	
13. Cholera nostras	1	6	2					20		17	2	1	4	11	5		20
14. Dysentery	39	30	40	16	9	1		298	6	264	39	1	109	102	91	2	301
14a. Epidemic dysentery																	
15. Plague																	
16. Yellow fever																	
17. Leprosy																	
18. Erysipelas	8	12	7	2	1			131	9	124	14	2	58	55	26	1	140
19. Other epidemic diseases								9		9			9				9

* Japanese

(B. Other General Diseases.)	459	347	179	58	11	4	7	7,494	430	7,151	706†	68	2,512	3,962	1,415	36	7,925
20. Purulent infection and septicemia	5	6	4	1				57	1	49	8	1	20	32	6		58
21. Glanders								1		1					1		1
22. Anthrax								1		1				1			1
23. Rabies								4		4			2	2			4
24. Tetanus			1					46	1	45	2		38	7	2		47
25. Mycoses																	
26. Pellagra																	
27. Beriberi																	
28. Tuberculosis of the Lungs	141	86	25	14	1	1	4	3,577	276	3,577	243	33	1,372	1,954	510	17	3,853
29. Acute miliary tuberculosis	2							64	4	64	2	2	36	26	5	1	68
30. Tuberculous meningitis	2	1	1					246	9	251	4		220	29	6		255
31. Abdominal tuberculosis	13	7	10		1			291	34	306	18	1	142	131	51	1	325
32. Pott's disease		1						28	3	29	2		20	7	4		31
33. White swellings	1	1	2					27	1	26	2		10	14	4		28
34. Tuberculosis of other organs	1	2	1	1				56	6	59	3		26	30	6		62
35. Disseminated tuberculosis	1	1						69	19	83	4	1	53	30	5		88
36. Rickets								23	5	28			27	1			28
37. Syphilis	1	1					1	146	11	144	7†	7	94	42	17	5	158
38. Gonococcus infection								6		6			2	4			6
39. Cancer and other malignant tumors of the buccal cavity	13	10	8	3				68	1	56	13		4	38	26	1	69
40. Cancer and other malignant tumors of the stomach and liver	107	90	44	14	4			783	7	636	152	2	51	485	252	2	790
41. Cancer and other malignant tumors of the peritoneum intestines and rectum	21	14	9	2				182	6	148	39	1	16	115	56	1	188
42. Cancer and other malignant tumors of the female genital organs	23	6					1	308	13	290	28	3	16	205	100		321
43. Cancer and other malignant tumors of the breast	8	17	8	3	1			163	4	149	17	1	17	89	61		167
44. Cancer and other malignant tumors of the skin	15	26	19	6		2		118	1	103	14	2	12	62	44	1	119
45. Cancer and malignant tumors of other organs and of organs not specified	18	17	13	6	2			215	3	189	28	1	34	132	52		218
46. Other tumors (tumors of the female genital organs excepted)	1	1		1				22	2	21	3		3	16	4	1	24
47. Acute articular rheumatism	12	13	10	5	1			171	4	154	17	4	61	78	33	3	175
48. Chronic rheumatism and gout	13	12	9					71	1	56	16		12	29	31		72
49. Scurvy								5		5			5				5

†Chinese.

TABLE No. 2—Continued.

	70 to 74	75 to 79	80 to 84	85 to 89	90 to 94	95 and Over.	Unknown.	White.	Colored.	American.	Foreign.	Not Reported.	Single.	Married.	Widowed or Divorced.	Not Reported.	Total.
50. Diabetes	42	23	10	1	1	1	......	366	6	320	47	5	90	208	74	......	372
51. Exophthalmic goitre	2	1	......	......	......	......	......	36	3	34	5	......	6	28	5	......	39
52. Addison's disease	......	1	......	......	......	......	......	8	......	7	1	......	1	5	2	......	8
53. Leukemia	1	......	......	......	......	......	......	30	1	28	3	......	9	19	3	......	31
54. Anemia chlorosis	8	7	3	......	......	......	......	125	1	116	9	1	35	73	18	......	126
55. Other general diseases	2	1	1	1	......	......	......	55	1	54	1	1	37	11	8	......	56
56. Alcoholism (acute or chronic)	1	......	......	......	......	......	1	96	5	83	16	2	37	43	19	3	101
57. Chronic lead poisoning	......	......	......	......	......	......	......	6	1	7	......	......	1	5	1	......	7
58. Other chronic occupation poisonings	......	......	......	......	......	......	......	1	......	1	......	......	......	1	......	......	1
59. Other chronic poisonings	5	2	1	......	......	......	......	23	......	21	2	......	3	11	9	......	23
II. DISEASES OF THE NERVOUS SYSTEM AND OF THE ORGANS OF SPECIAL SENSES.	441	461	277	122	44	8	......	3,274	87	2,882	449	30	656	1,608	1,079	18	3,361
60. Encephalitis	1	2	1	......	......	......	......	48	......	46	2	......	27	18	3	......	48
61. Simple meningitis	1	......	......	1	2	1	......	127	3	126	4	......	108	15	7	......	130
61a. Cerebrospinal fever	......	......	......	......	......	......	......	22	......	21	1	......	18	3	1	......	22
62. Locomotor ataxia	10	4	1	......	......	......	......	77	2	66	10	3	8	54	17	......	79
63. Other diseases of the spinal cord	29	29	18	3	......	......	......	235	3	213	24	1	76	112	50	......	238
64. Cerebral hemorrhage, apoplexy	309	315	189	99	30	6	......	1,842	43	1,560	314	11	157	952	760	16	1,885
65. Softening of the brain	16	13	13	3	4	......	......	73	1	67	7	......	1	39	34	......	74
66. Paralysis without specified cause	32	56	32	10	6	......	......	234	7	202	35	4	10	127	103	1	241
67. General paralysis of the insane	22	22	15	5	......	......	......	162	7	142	24	3	14	108	47	......	169
68. Other forms of mental alienation	7	5	4	......	1	......	......	86	5	80	10	1	16	58	16	1	91
69. Epilepsy	8	8	1	......	......	1	......	171	6	165	7	5	108	45	24	......	177
70. Convulsions (nonpuerperal)	......	......	......	......	......	......	......	2	......	2	......	......	2	......	......	......	2
71. Convulsions of infants	......	......	......	......	......	......	......	45	6	51	......	......	51	......	......	......	51
72. Chorea	......	......	1	......	......	......	......	10	......	10	......	......	5	4	1	......	10
73. Hysteria	......	......	......	......	......	......	......	4	1	5	......	......	......	5	......	......	5
74. Other diseases of the nervous system—																	
(A. Other diseases of the brain)	2	5	1	......	1	......	......	63	......	56	6	1	17	37	9	......	63
(B. Other diseases of the nervous system)	3	2	......	1	......	......	......	27	2	25	3	1	8	15	6	......	29
75. Diseases of the eye and its adnexia	......	......	1	......	......	......	......	5	......	5	......	......	2	3	......	......	5
76. Diseases of the ear	1	......	......	......	......	......	......	41	1	40	2	......	28	13	1	......	42

III. Diseases of the Circulatory System.	736	710	69	213	68	10	1	4,797	164	4,075	824‡	63	576	2,579	1,786	21	4,962
77. Pericarditis	12	4	3					37	6	31	8	4	12	22	8	1	43
78. Acute endocarditis	6	10	2	2				103	9	96	15	1	33	47	32		12
79. Organic disease of the heart	584	555	349	148	44	7	1	3,826	130	3,268	643	45	461	2,082	1,395	18	3, 86
80. Angina pectoris	44	25	11	8	1			226	4	196	32	2	15	149	66		230
81. Diseases of the arteries, atheroma, aneurism, etc.	77	103	86	53	22	3		474	13	370	109‡	9	28	213	245	2	48
82. Embolism and thrombosis	11	13	16	1	1			97	1	81	16	1	14	50	34		98
83. Diseases of the veins (varices, hemorrhoids, phlebitis, etc			1	1				15		14	1		2	9	4		15
84. Diseases of the lymphatic system (lymphangitis, etc.)								5		4		1	3	1	1		5
85. Hemorrhage; other diseases of the circulatory system	2		1					14	1	15			8	6	1		15
IV. Diseases of the Respiratory System.	281	267	220	120	37	11		3,320	155	3,019	431	25	1,720	962	83	10	3,475
86. Diseases of the nasal fossae		1						10		9	1		7	2	1		10
87. Diseases of the larynx—																	
(A. Laryngitis)	1	1						25		25			20	5			25
(B. Other diseases of the larynx)								16		16			14	2			16
88. Diseases of the thyroid body								7		7			5	1	1		7
89. Acute [illegible]	11	15	14	10	4			237	10	233	13	1	183	25	39		87
90. [illegible]	50	39	43	24	8	2		209	8	157	58	2	18	91	07	1	27
91. Broncho-pneumonia	50	60	40	25	11	2		866	51	827	86	4	629	127	60	1	97
92. [illegible]bar pneumonia	139	127	112	56	13	6		1,743	80	1,578	229	16	795	607	43	8	1, 83
93. Pleurisy	4	3	1					55	2	50	7		17	35	5		57
94. Pulmonary congestion, pulmonary apoplexy		2		1	1	1		24		21	3		12	7	5		24
95. Gangrene of the lung			1					4		4			2	2			4
96. Asthma	26	16	7	4				95	3	67	29	2	10	43	45		98
97. Pulmonary emphysema			1					5		5			1	4			5
98. Other diseases of the respiratory system—																	
(A. Hemorrhage of the lungs)			1					8		5	3		1	5	2		8
(B. Other diseases of the respiratory system)		3						16	1	15	2		6	6	5		17
V. Diseases of the Digestive System.	195	197	114	65	24	6		4,406	147	4,282	250†	22	2,997	990	553	14	4,554
99. Diseases of the mouth and adnexia					1	1		20	4	23	1		20	3	1		24
100. Diseases of the pharynx—																	
(A. Tonsilitis)								27		26	1		20	5	2		27
(B. Other diseases of the pharynx)		2	1	1				14		14			5	5	4		14
101. Diseases of the esophagus		1		1				4		3	1		2		2		4

‡ 1 Indian. † 1 Chinese.

TABLE No. 2—Continued.

	70 to 74	75 to 79	80 to 84	85 to 89	90 to 94	95 and Over.	Unknown.	White.	Colored.	American.	Foreign.	Not Reported.	Single.	Married.	Widowed or Divorced.	Not Reported.	Total.
102. Ulcer of the stomach	12	9	1		1			82	4	72	13	1	8	62	16		86
103. Other diseases of the stomach (cancer excepted)—																	
(A. Gastritis)	23	19	20	14	3	1		239	13	221	30	1	95	83	72	2	252
(B. Other diseases of the stomach)	11	6	9	4	1			203	6	201	8		153	25	31		209
104. Diarrhea and enteritis (under 2 years)								1,965	63	2,047	2†		2,049				2,049
105. Diarrhea and enteritis (2 years and over)	61	66	41	25	14	3		602	18	546	67	7	262	181	174	3	620
106. Ankylotomiasis																	
107. Intestinal parasites								2		2			2				2
108. Appendicitis and Typhlitis	2	4						264	8	254	14	4	144	111	17		272
109. Hernias, intestinal obstructions—																	
(A. Hernia)	9	12	9	2	2			73	2	57	16	2	8	38	29		75
(B. Obstructions of intestines)	20	16	9	2	1			228	8	217	17	2	92	94	49	1	236
110. Other diseases of the intestines	1	12	3	3		1		78	5	75	7	1	34	33	15	1	83
111. Acute yellow atrophy of the liver		2		1				10		8	2		2	5	3		10
112. Hydatid tumor of the liver																	
113. Cirrhosis of the liver	25	27	11	3				276	7	241	40	2	35	172	69	7	283
114. Biliary calculi	13	6	5	2				92	2	83	11		7	61	26		94
115. Other diseases of the liver	16	15	5	6	1			160	6	146	18	2	39	87	40		166
116. Diseases of the spleen								3		3			1	2			3
117. Simple peritonitis (nonpuerperal)	2			1				37	1	36	2		16	19	3		38
118. Other diseases of the digestive system (cancer and tuberculosis excepted)								7		7			3	4			7
VI. NONVENEREAL DISEASES OF THE GENITO-URINARY SYSTEM AND ANNEXA.	349	335	232	98	30	11	3	2,391	125	2,104	388	24	324	1,393	788	11	2,516
119. Acute nephritis	13	16	6	3	1			161	13	167	4	3	55	84	35		174
120. Bright's disease	282	240	183	71	24	9	2	1,756	91	1,522	310	15	193	1,017	626	11	1,847
121. Chyluria		1	1					5		4	1		1	3	1		5
122. Other diseases of the kidneys and annexa	6	6	5	1		1	1	61	1	53	8	1	18	29	15		62
123. Calculi of the urinary passages	4	2	1					18		15	2	1	4	12	2		18

† 1 Chinese.

124. Diseases of the bladder	8	24	15	11	3			86	7	71	22	2	12	44	39		95
125. Diseases of the urethra, urinary abscess, etc.			1					7		4	3		4	2	1		7
126. Diseases of the prostate	29	39	19	12	2	1		130	2	109	23		7	81	44		132
127. Nonvenereal Diseases of the male genital organs	1							3		3			2	1			3
128. Uterine hemorrhage (nonpuerperal)								1		1				1			1
129. Uterine tumor (noncancerous)	3	5						45	5	45	4	1	3	38	9		50
130. Other diseases of the uterus	1							17	2	18	1		3	13	3		19
131. Cysts and other tumors of the ovary	2	2	1					34	1	31	4		6	22	7		35
132. Other diseases of the female genital organs— (A. Diseases of the tubes)								58	3	55	5	1	15	41	5		61
(B. Other diseases of the female genital organs)								7		6	1		1	5	1		7
133. Nonpuerperal diseases of the breast (cancer excepted)																	
VII. THE PUERPERAL STATE.								441	8	414	35†	1	31	414	4	1	450
134. Accidents of pregnancy								57		54	2	1	3	54			57
135. Puerperal hemorrhage								29	1	24	6		2	27	1		30
136. Other accidents of labor								16		11	5			16			16
137. Puerperal septicemia								222	6	209	20†		22	204	3		229
138. Puerperal albuminuria and convulsions								73	1	72	2		3	70		1	74
139. Phlegmasia alba dolens (puerperal)								3		3				3			3
140. Other puerperal accidents								41		41			1	40			41
141. Puerperal diseases of the breast																	
VIII. DISEASES OF THE SKIN AND CELLULAR TISSUE.	22	28	28	14		3		158	9	139	25	3	33	63	67	4	167
142. Gangrene	18	22	26	13		3		109	5	87	24	3	10	43	58	3	114
143. Furuncle	3	1	1					14		14			2	7	4	1	14
144. Acute abscess								10	1	11			3	7	1		11
145. Other diseases of the skin and annexa	1	5	1	1				25	3	27	1		18	6	4		28
IX. DISEASES OF THE BONES AND THE ORGANS OF LOCOMOTION.		4	2	1				72	2	69	5		45	20	9		74
146. Nontuberculous diseases of the bones		3	2					65	2	63	4		44	15	8		67
147. Diseases of the joints (tuberculosis and rheumatism excepted)		1		1				7		6	1		1	5	1		7
148. Amputations																	
149. Other diseases of the organs of locomotion																	

† 1 Chinese.

TABLE No. 2—Continued.

	70 to 74	75 to 79	80 to 84	85 to 89	90 to 94	95 and Over.	Unknown.	White.	Colored.	American.	Foreign.	Not Reported.	Single.	Married.	Widowed or Divorced.	Not Reported.	Total.
X. MALFORMATIONS.	......	......	......	......	......	......	......	446	6	452	......	......	452	......	......	......	452
150. Congenital malformations (still births not included—																	
(A. Hydrocephalus)	......	......	......	......	......	......	......	40	1	41	......	......	41	......	......	......	41
(B. Congenital malformation of the heart (cyanosis)	......	......	......	......	......	......	......	295	5	300	......	......	300	......	......	......	300
(C. Other congenital malformations)	......	......	......	......	......	......	......	111	......	111	......	......	111	......	......	......	111
XI. DISEASES OF EARLY INFANCY.	......	......	......	......	......	......	......	1,467	56	1,523	......	......	1,523	......	......	......	1,523
151. Congenital debility, icterus and sclerema—																	
(A. Premature birth)	......	......	......	......	......	......	......	1,088	35	1,123	......	......	1,123	......	......	......	1,123
(B. Congenital debility)	......	......	......	......	......	......	......	211	12	223	......	......	223	......	......	......	223
152. Other diseases peculiar to early infancy	......	......	......	......	......	......	......	149	6	155	......	......	155	......	......	......	155
153. Lack of care	......	......	......	......	......	......	......	19	3	22	......	......	22	......	......	......	22
XII. OLD AGE.	44	92	167	119	54	14	......	503	11	395	110‡	10	30	112	370	3	515
154. Senility	44	92	167	119	54	14	......	503	11	395	110‡	10	30	112	370	3	515
XIII. AFFECTIONS PRODUCED BY EXTERNAL CAUSES.	94	80	86	51	15	3	21	2,604	86	2,230	346	114	1,193	1,037	370	90	2,690
155. Suicide by poison	......	2	1	1	......	......	......	159	11	154	13	3	44	97	27	2	170
156. Suicide by asphyxia	......	......	......	......	......	......	......	6	......	6	......	......	1	2	3	......	6
157. Suicide by hanging or strangulation	4	3	2	1	......	......	......	64	......	54	9	1	18	32	12	2	64
158. Suicide by drowning	......	3	1	......	......	......	......	22	......	19	2	1	5	12	5	......	22
159. Suicide by firearms	3	2	1	......	......	......	......	95	......	86	7	2	32	51	11	1	95
160. Suicide by cutting or piercing instruments	1	......	......	......	......	......	......	11	......	9	2	......	4	5	2	......	11
161. Suicide by jumping from high place	......	......	......	......	......	......	......	3	......	3	......	......	2	1	......	......	3
162. Suicide by crushing	......	......	......	......	......	......	1	11	......	7	1	3	1	5	2	3	11
163. Other suicides	......	......	......	......	......	......	......	4	......	4	......	......	2	2	......	......	4
164. Poisoning by food	......	......	......	1	......	......	......	11	......	10	1	......	6	2	3	......	11

‡ 2 Indians

165. Other acute poisonings	......	......	......	1	......	......	1	66	1	64	1	2	44	16	5	2	67
166. Conflagration	1	......	......	......	......	......	......	14	......	12	1	1	6	6	1	1	14
167. Burns (conflagration excepted)	5	4	2	2	......	......	......	163	6	149	18	2	103	42	24	......	169
168. Absorption of deleterious gases (conflagration excepted)	1	......	1	......	......	......	1	29	......	15	12	2	12	11	5	1	29
169. Accidental drowning	4	......	4	......	......	......	1	136	8	113	19	12	99	26	10	9	144
170. Traumatism by firearms		1	......	......	......	......	......	66	4	66	3	1	47	19	3	1	70
171. Traumatism by cutting or piercing instruments	......	1	1	......	......	......	......	8	......	6	2	......	1	5	2	......	8
172. Traumatism by fall	41	40	65	39	14	3	1	410	4	343	64	7	101	151	158	4	414
173. Traumatism in mines and quarries	2	......	......	......	......	......	......	62	1	47	16	......	19	39	4	1	63
174. Traumatism by machines	2	......	......	......	......	......	......	56	3	48	10	1	21	33	4	1	59
175. Traumatism by other crushing—																	
(A. Railroad accident and injuries)	9	7	1	1	1	......	14	423	10	282	94	57	171	188	21	53	433
(B. Street car and interurban)	4	3	2	1	......	......	1	133	4	115	13	9	53	60	20	4	137
(C. Automobiles and other vehicles)	3	3	1	2	......	......	......	81	1	73	9	......	41	29	11	1	82
(D. Landslides)	......	......	......	......	......	......	......	......	......	......	......	......	......	......	......	......	......
(E. Other accidental traumatism)	1	......	1	1	......	......	......	86	1	81	6	......	37	46	4	......	87
176. Injuries by animals	9	4	......	......	......	......	......	70	1	65	4	2	25	41	5	......	71
177. Starvation	......	......	......	......	......	......	......	......	......	......	......	......	......	......	......	......	......
178. Excessive cold	1	1	1	......	......	......	1	17	......	13	2	2	8	4	4	1	17
179. Effects of heat	2	1	1	......	......	......	......	24	1	24	1	......	9	14	2	......	25
180. Lightning	......	......	......	......	......	......	......	22	1	23	......	......	9	12	2	......	23
181. Electricity (lightning excepted)	......	......	......	......	......	......	......	32	......	25	7	......	16	15	1	......	32
182. Homicide by firearms	......	1	1	......	......	......	......	62	17	63	15	1	30	36	12	1	79
183. Homicide by cutting or piercing instruments	......	......	......	......	......	......	......	11	1	9	3	......	7	5	......	......	12
184. Homicide by other means	1	1	......	......	......	......	......	26	4	23	3	4	10	14	4	2	30
185. Fractures, cause not specified	......	1	......	1	......	......	......	7	2	3	5	1	3	4	2	......	9
186. Other external violence—																	
(A. Suffocation)	......	1	......	......	......	......	......	58	1	59	......	......	56	3	......	......	59
(B. Injuries at birth)	......	......	......	......	......	......	......	133	4	137	......	......	137	......	......	......	137
(C. Other external violence)	......	1	......	......	......	......	......	23	......	20	2	1	13	9	1	......	23
XIV. Ill-Defined Diseases.	6	2	3	4	......	1	......	78	3	73	7	1	58	9	13	1	81
187. Ill-defined organic disease	......	......	......	......	......	......	......	1	......	1	......	......	......	1	......	......	1
188. Sudden death	1	......	......	......	......	......	......	2	......	2	......	......	......	1	1	......	2
189. Cause of death not specified or ill defined	5	2	3	4	......	1	......	75	3	70	7	1	58	7	12	1	78
Total deaths from all causes	2,799	2,693	1,929	921	307	81	32	35,113	1,394	32,330	3,805§	378	14,457	14,152	7,683	221	36,513

§ Includes 1 Japanese, 3 Chinese, 2 Indians, total, 6.

TABLE No. 3.

Deaths in Indiana by Months, Counties, Ages, Sex, Color, Nationality and Conjugal Condition, 1910.

COUNTIES.	Sex.	Jan.	Feb.	Mar.	April.	May.	June.	July.	Aug.	Sept.	Oct.	Nov.	Dec.
Adams	Total	10	15	18	17	17	13	8	22	28	24	16	22
	Males	3	9	9	8	12	5	6	12	13	9	9	11
	Females	7	6	9	9	5	8	2	10	15	15	7	11
Allen	Total	106	83	95	99	92	83	82	114	101	93	79	92
	Males	60	42	52	49	38	46	50	56	58	48	51	48
	Females	46	41	43	50	54	37	32	58	43	45	28	44
Bartholomew	Total	32	20	38	25	23	28	18	32	22	25	31	35
	Males	17	13	19	10	12	10	12	16	13	13	18	17
	Females	15	7	19	15	11	18	6	16	9	12	13	18
Benton	Total	10	16	7	6	9	7	8	13	5	10	9	5
	Males	7	10	4	4	4	2	3	6	1	6	5	1
	Females	3	6	3	2	5	5	5	7	4	4	4	4
Blackford	Total	11	14	19	11	22	13	21	13	24	20	11	17
	Males	8	6	11	9	15	5	12	7	15	8	3	12
	Females	3	8	8	2	7	8	9	6	9	12	8	5
Boone	Total	27	24	9	32	23	18	20	29	30	27	23	24
	Males	14	9	3	16	12	9	11	19	15	13	10	9
	Females	13	15	6	16	11	9	9	10	15	14	13	15
Brown	Total	13	5	36	4	10	5	13	8	12	17	4	7
	Males	5	2	20	2	4	4	5	6	7	6	2	1
	Females	8	3	16	2	6	1	8	2	5	11	2	6
Carroll	Total	24	19	24	16	18	19	22	15	21	21	16	25
	Males	14	8	10	8	8	7	13	5	8	8	10	15
	Females	10	11	14	8	10	12	9	10	13	13	6	10
Cass	Total	52	43	53	42	50	35	43	54	53	45	49	55
	Males	25	22	31	16	24	19	26	26	32	29	24	33
	Females	27	21	22	26	26	16	17	28	21	16	25	22

Clark	Total	54	36	46	34	41	33	51	43	39	38	33	47
	Males	23	16	27	15	22	15	28	23	19	16	18	20
	Females	31	20	19	19	19	18	23	20	20	22	15	27
Clay	Total	34	42	41	38	30	26	28	39	30	36	31	28
	Males	16	24	13	20	17	9	13	15	16	18	15	18
	Females	18	18	28	18	13	17	15	24	14	18	16	10
Clinton	Total	23	26	24	20	24	25	25	24	29	29	34	20
	Males	8	13	13	7	9	16	15	9	15	20	15	13
	Females	15	13	11	13	15	9	10	15	14	9	19	7
Crawford	Total	17	14	14	17	10	9	14	9	10	17	10	10
	Males	8	6	5	9	5	6	6	5	1	12	5	5
	Females	9	8	9	8	5	3	8	4	9	5	5	5
Daviess	Total	25	27	26	30	33	19	24	34	31	34	25	29
	Males	12	9	13	17	24	5	11	19	16	18	15	19
	Females	13	18	13	13	9	14	13	15	15	16	10	10
Dearborn	Total	27	20	37	28	23	26	22	21	15	19	22	17
	Males	9	11	19	17	10	15	15	11	5	11	16	6
	Females	18	9	18	11	13	11	7	10	10	8	6	11
Decatur	Total	23	21	29	22	19	14	21	23	14	19	17	28
	Males	14	12	18	11	12	6	14	11	6	9	7	9
	Females	9	9	11	11	7	8	7	12	8	10	10	19
Dekalb	Total	24	23	28	28	28	22	25	20	34	39	25	33
	Males	9	10	11	10	13	13	13	10	19	17	14	23
	Females	15	13	17	18	15	9	12	10	15	22	11	10
Delaware	Total	40	54	57	33	41	51	59	75	64	48	56	47
	Males	22	30	28	19	17	25	28	37	29	23	29	25
	Females	18	24	29	14	24	26	31	38	35	25	27	22
Dubois	Total	20	16	21	9	13	16	14	20	12	13	14	23
	Males	9	9	12	4	8	10	10	11	3	5	5	12
	Females	11	7	9	5	5	6	4	9	9	8	9	11
Elkhart	Total	50	55	72	56	59	55	38	57	50	51	70	59
	Males	21	28	37	25	32	32	20	32	24	25	41	25
	Females	29	27	35	31	27	23	18	25	26	26	29	34
Fayette	Total	17	11	24	17	12	20	15	16	16	15	15	12
	Males	11	7	14	8	9	4	8	9	8	9	6	8
	Females	6	4	10	9	3	16	7	7	8	6	9	4

TABLE No. 3—Continued.

COUNTIES.	Sex.	Jan.	Feb.	Mar.	April.	May.	June.	July.	Aug.	Sept.	Oct.	Nov.	Dec.
Floyd	Total	44	45	45	51	41	46	39	44	37	34	59	33
	Males	21	19	20	25	18	24	16	22	16	21	28	15
	Females	23	26	25	26	23	22	23	22	21	13	29	18
Fountain	Total	31	25	25	20	20	18	20	22	19	26	24	25
	Males	16	14	7	10	12	10	9	11	13	13	15	13
	Females	15	11	18	10	8	8	11	11	6	13	9	12
Franklin	Total	13	18	19	14	15	13	16	15	19	18	12	21
	Males	6	10	12	10	9	7	9	9	10	8	6	7
	Females	7	8	7	4	6	6	7	6	9	10	6	14
Fulton	Total	19	23	23	13	15	22	14	29	17	14	21	22
	Males	12	12	13	5	5	14	9	15	12	9	8	13
	Females	7	11	10	8	10	8	5	14	5	5	13	9
Gibson	Total	40	35	48	29	26	18	42	45	22	38	27	32
	Males	28	15	25	14	8	10	20	29	15	15	18	17
	Females	12	20	23	15	18	8	22	16	7	23	9	15
Grant	Total	58	71	74	77	58	49	70	69	60	62	63	81
	Males	40	35	47	53	39	27	46	34	37	35	38	47
	Females	18	36	27	24	19	22	24	35	23	27	25	34
Greene	Total	32	42	38	38	37	36	46	49	37	40	32	42
	Males	11	20	20	21	18	17	22	29	18	23	19	21
	Females	21	22	18	17	19	19	24	20	19	17	13	21
Hamilton	Total	19	38	35	35	30	23	34	31	26	35	25	30
	Males	11	24	15	11	12	10	13	18	10	13	13	15
	Females	8	14	20	24	18	13	21	13	16	22	12	15
Hancock	Total	17	27	23	23	13	20	27	24	19	16	21	22
	Males	11	11	13	11	6	10	18	16	8	6	14	10
	Females	6	16	10	12	7	10	9	8	11	10	7	12
Harrison	Total	15	19	24	22	11	26	17	19	13	16	30	17
	Males	9	11	16	9	5	13	5	10	7	10	16	8
	Females	6	8	8	13	6	13	12	9	6	6	14	9

County													
ells	Total	12	36	25	25	27	19	23	23	16	19	22	19
	Males	7	15	16	14	18	12	12	11	12	11	14	9
	Females	5	21	9	11	9	7	11	12	4	8	8	10
Henry	till	36	36	42	37	31	26	43	57	35	25	24	35
	Males	21	17	23	19	20	12	24	25	21	14	15	21
	Females	15	19	19	18	11	14	19	32	14	11	9	14
Howard	Total	28	34	35	39	34	35	42	40	40	41	32	31
	Males	16	19	19	13	16	23	24	23	23	18	17	11
	Females	12	15	16	26	18	12	18	17	17	23	15	20
Huntington	Total	39	36	34	33	33	24	26	32	33	16	22	28
	Males	22	15	18	16	19	8	15	21	16	7	12	15
	Females	17	21	16	17	14	16	11	11	17	9	10	13
Jackson	Total	29	24	20	29	18	23	26	28	34	33	43	43
	Males	16	14	9	13	10	10	17	17	22	17	21	17
	ellles	13	10	11	16	8	13	9	11	12	16	22	26
Jasper	Total	10	11	14	11	6	9	14	12	8	6	14	5
	Males	6	7	6	3	3	6	9	4	3	4	7	2
	Females	4	4	8	8	3	3	5	8	5	2	7	3
Jay	Total	26	16	32	21	21	19	33	43	40	30	18	26
	Mles	15	8	10	16	12	10	19	22	17	19	14	14
	Females	11	8	22	5	9	9	14	21	23	11	4	12
Jefferson	Total	23	32	33	33	23	16	32	38	22	34	41	31
	Males	11	14	21	22	7	9	16	23	11	22	27	18
	Females	12	18	12	11	16	7	16	15	11	12	14	13
Jennings	till	16	8	16	14	12	12	22	13	20	9	12	28
	Males	10	1	9	5	5	4	9	8	13	3	9	13
	Females	6	7	7	9	7	8	13	5	7	6	3	15
Johnson	Total	32	27	28	21	33	16	27	22	14	21	21	25
	Males	16	17	17	12	18	11	13	14	6	12	11	9
	Females	16	10	11	9	15	5	14	8	8	9	10	16
Knox	Total	39	50	58	41	38	45	63	60	42	48	55	46
	Males	23	23	28	17	23	22	29	34	19	26	28	21
	Females	16	27	30	24	15	23	34	26	23	22	27	25
Kosciusko	Total	26	19	34	38	33	33	17	30	30	26	30	32
	Males	13	12	20	22	10	16	9	12	17	17	13	17
	Females	13	7	14	16	23	17	8	18	13	9	17	15

TABLE No. 3—Continued.

COUNTIES.	Sex.	Jan.	Feb.	Mar.	April.	May.	June.	July.	Aug.	Sept.	Oct.	Nov.	Dec.
Lagrange	Total	16	18	18	12	12	19	16	19	13	21	14	21
	Males	10	14	11	6	5	12	11	8	4	8	5	10
	Females	6	4	7	6	7	7	5	11	9	13	9	11
Lake	Total	97	85	126	93	72	88	109	122	120	88	94	114
	Males	61	53	88	57	46	59	64	73	67	56	58	72
	Females	36	32	38	36	26	29	45	49	53	32	36	42
Laporte	Total	40	62	56	38	59	57	58	58	58	44	52	62
	Males	26	40	35	24	35	39	31	36	35	23	31	37
	Females	14	22	21	14	24	18	27	22	23	21	21	25
Lawrence	Total	41	38	44	26	35	30	35	48	23	29	27	34
	Males	18	22	22	8	16	14	17	24	10	17	15	25
	Females	23	16	22	18	19	16	18	24	13	12	12	9
Madison	Total	73	69	92	62	65	62	69	105	62	65	68	74
	Males	33	36	50	34	39	24	33	52	26	28	37	36
	Females	40	33	42	28	26	38	36	53	36	37	31	38
Marion	Total	329	332	434	378	347	380	371	357	325	323	312	351
	Males	178	172	229	207	201	201	200	199	185	176	156	182
	Females	151	160	205	171	146	179	171	158	140	147	156	169
Marshall	Total	29	29	38	25	13	16	26	33	26	31	17	25
	Males	15	15	25	12	7	7	15	21	15	17	6	13
	Females	14	14	13	13	6	9	11	12	11	14	11	12
Martin	Total	19	12	17	6	11	7	15	13	7	13	8	17
	Males	8	4	6	4	7	4	7	7	4	7	1	7
	Females	11	8	11	2	4	3	8	6	3	6	7	10
Miami	Total	31	30	29	29	22	23	28	37	36	40	22	43
	Males	18	13	16	14	10	15	18	21	18	24	11	30
	Females	13	17	13	15	12	8	10	16	18	16	11	13
Monroe	Total	23	22	33	29	36	42	30	26	29	18	20	26
	Males	11	11	15	16	16	23	13	13	17	7	15	9
	Females	12	11	18	13	20	19	17	13	12	11	5	17

Montgomery	Total	34	38	50	44	32	31	32	28	24	19	29	22
	Males	15	21	31	25	20	14	17	14	9	11	14	12
	Females	19	17	19	19	12	17	15	14	15	8	15	10
Morgan	Total	24	31	32	21	25	29	30	28	23	21	23	25
	Males	12	18	16	10	14	15	20	12	16	10	12	9
	Females	12	13	16	11	11	14	10	16	7	11	11	16
Newton	Total	13	5	10	12	7	6	7	14	11	10	6	8
	Males	9	3	6	9	5	4	3	7	6	7	2	3
	Females	4	2	4	3	2	2	4	7	5	3	4	5
Noble	Total	29	20	33	26	21	18	14	26	28	18	22	12
	Males	12	11	15	14	8	8	9	15	14	7	12	5
	Females	17	9	18	12	13	10	5	11	14	11	10	7
Ohio	Total	3	2	6	5	1	3	7	4	2	3	4	5
	Males	1	1	1	2		2	4	2	1	1	2	2
	Females	2	1	5	3	1	1	3	2	1	2	2	3
Orange	Total	8	18	24	22	12	15	20	9	14	17	17	21
	Males	6	11	9	10	5	7	7	4	5	10	7	7
	Females	2	7	15	12	7	8	13	5	9	7	10	14
Owen	Total	12	17	14	14	13	11	13	17	14	11	14	9
	Males	8	7	7	4	4	7	6	9	7	8	4	3
	Females	4	10	7	10	9	4	7	8	7	3	10	6
Parke	Total	30	21	17	21	21	19	22	24	14	14	21	31
	Males	13	11	9	14	12	11	14	13	5	7	12	9
	Females	17	10	8	7	9	8	8	11	9	7	9	22
Perry	Total	22	19	23	18	19	11	16	20	13	13	24	20
	Males	11	8	9	6	10	7	10	6	9	7	12	11
	Females	11	11	14	12	9	4	6	14	4	6	12	9
Pike	Total	19	29	25	28	14	27	21	26	18	28	27	16
	Males	4	13	11	10	8	17	18	11	9	15	19	7
	Females	15	16	14	18	6	10	3	15	9	13	8	9
Porter	Total	29	19	29	18	13	13	29	12	32	25	20	27
	Males	14	10	20	10	4	6	19	4	15	15	14	16
	Females	15	9	9	8	9	7	10	8	17	10	6	11
Posey	Total	25	26	31	20	19	14	22	35	21	22	25	24
	Males	9	10	16	13	10	8	10	20	10	12	11	14
	Females	16	16	15	7	9	6	12	15	11	10	14	10

TABLE No. 3—Continued.

COUNTIES.	Sex.	Jan.	Feb.	Mar.	April.	May.	June.	July.	Aug.	Sept.	Oct.	Nov.	Dec.
Pulaski	Total	15	10	16	7	8	16	16	10	11	11	10	15
	Males	5	6	8	4	4	8	8	5	4	7	6	7
	Females	10	4	8	3	4	8	8	5	7	4	4	8
Putnam	Total	29	17	28	29	16	23	18	13	15	13	25	25
	Males	15	5	17	17	5	7	13	7	7	7	12	12
	Females	14	12	11	12	11	16	5	6	8	6	13	13
Randolph	Total	28	24	36	34	25	19	23	40	37	34	36	35
	Males	15	10	20	15	11	11	11	21	21	15	15	16
	Females	13	14	16	19	14	8	12	19	16	19	21	19
Ripley	Total	29	19	16	19	15	10	21	24	27	17	20	31
	Males	14	12	7	9	10	8	9	11	12	12	10	17
	Females	15	7	9	10	5	2	12	13	15	5	10	14
Rush	Total	18	18	28	22	22	18	25	22	17	11	11	22
	Males	10	5	14	9	10	9	15	14	10	3	5	15
	Females	8	13	14	13	12	9	10	8	7	8	6	7
Scott	Total	5	16	15	14	6	7	10	13	4	5	13	11
	Males	4	7	8	8	3	3	6	9	4	3	4	6
	Females	1	9	7	6	3	4	4	4	....	2	9	5
Shelby	Total	31	32	34	17	24	29	34	38	30	25	31	17
	Males	16	15	18	8	10	16	18	24	14	13	14	7
	Females	15	17	16	9	14	13	16	14	16	12	17	10
Spencer	Total	25	20	32	14	14	22	23	27	14	28	25	23
	Males	11	10	14	7	3	8	11	11	4	19	12	14
	Females	14	10	18	7	11	14	12	16	10	9	13	8
Starke	Total	11	14	6	13	12	13	7	13	15	6	8	10
	Males	6	8	2	7	7	7	5	7	9	3	5	6
	Females	5	6	4	6	5	6	2	6	6	3	3	4
Steuben	Total	12	8	15	16	15	8	16	17	18	18	6	11
	Males	6	4	8	8	8	5	9	11	11	9	4	6
	Females	6	4	7	8	7	3	7	6	7	9	2	5

County													
St. Joseph	Total	82	86	102	90	89	80	88	117	99	107	86	115
	Males	44	51	56	52	49	47	48	64	51	66	46	56
	Females	38	35	46	38	40	33	40	53	48	41	40	59
Sullivan	Total	31	28	28	22	37	31	48	33	34	40	33	22
	Males	21	15	11	12	20	20	26	17	17	24	22	12
	Females	10	13	17	10	17	11	22	16	17	16	11	10
Switzerland	Total	9	10	19	11	15	13	13	11	12	8	8	8
	Males	8	6	4	6	6	6	8	8	7	3	5	5
	Females	1	4	15	5	9	7	5	3	5	5	3	3
Tippecanoe	Total	61	49	65	50	48	49	37	48	35	39	50	57
	Males	35	19	40	26	19	25	23	32	15	27	21	33
	Females	26	30	25	24	29	24	14	16	20	12	29	24
Tipton	Total	14	21	20	17	14	9	18	19	24	14	21	16
	Males	5	17	14	9	6	6	13	10	16	9	11	10
	Females	9	4	6	8	8	3	5	9	8	5	10	6
Union	Total	4	9	7	8	8	4	4	8	14	5	10	4
	Males	1	3	2	4	5	4	1	5	7	3	5	1
	Females	3	6	5	4	3	....	3	3	7	2	5	3
Vanderburgh	Total	110	108	111	91	82	102	83	113	87	93	113	90
	Males	59	59	57	47	50	51	47	65	42	50	63	47
	Females	51	49	54	44	32	51	36	48	45	43	50	43
Vermillion	Total	14	15	36	18	16	17	24	17	22	20	24	32
	Males	9	7	24	9	9	5	16	4	14	9	15	15
	Females	5	8	12	9	7	12	8	13	8	11	9	17
Vigo	Total	109	84	127	103	93	113	140	113	118	88	112	109
	Males	66	47	63	50	52	61	89	60	52	48	59	64
	Females	43	37	64	53	41	52	51	53	66	40	53	45
Wabash	Total	35	26	41	33	18	20	17	28	24	32	34	27
	Males	19	17	23	16	10	10	7	14	14	17	11	15
	Females	16	9	18	17	8	10	10	14	10	15	23	12
Warren	Total	20	14	11	5	11	5	9	14	8	20	9	10
	Males	9	8	7	2	6	3	4	7	2	13	8	6
	Females	11	6	4	3	5	2	5	7	6	7	1	4
Warrick	Total	32	29	31	18	17	10	17	28	20	26	16	30
	Males	16	19	13	8	8	3	10	13	11	18	6	14
	Females	16	10	18	10	9	7	7	15	9	8	10	16

TABLE No. 3—Continued.

COUNTIES.	SEX.	Jan.	Feb.	Mar.	April.	May.	June.	July.	Aug.	Sept.	Oct.	Nov.	Dec.
Washington	Total	16	12	17	14	15	21	21	30	15	24	19	19
	Males	8	7	8	7	5	9	8	15	5	12	10	9
	Females	8	5	9	7	10	12	13	15	10	12	9	10
Wayne	Total	57	62	71	59	51	52	49	61	68	45	54	41
	Males	27	32	38	24	29	27	24	31	35	24	31	26
	Females	30	30	33	35	22	25	25	30	33	21	23	15
Wells	Total	24	15	28	28	17	21	17	25	58	18	21	22
	Males	15	8	15	18	8	10	9	12	38	6	9	10
	Females	9	7	13	10	9	11	8	13	20	12	12	12
White	Total	15	13	17	11	14	14	15	23	12	10	10	13
	Males	9	6	8	6	9	7	9	14	4	4	7	10
	Females	6	7	9	5	5	7	6	9	8	6	3	3
Whitley	Total	14	15	18	9	14	15	17	14	16	15	25	18
	Males	8	8	8	4	8	6	7	6	7	9	13	10
	Females	6	7	10	5	6	9	10	8	9	6	12	8
Total males		1,609	1,544	1,907	1,526	1,452	1,434	1,682	1,820	1,569	1,552	1,566	1,631
Total females		1,430	1,428	1,692	1,441	1,305	1,313	1,382	1,586	1,441	1,340	1,366	1,497
Grand total		3,039	2,972	3,599	2,967	2,757	2,747	3,064	3,406	3,010	2,892	2,932	3,128

TABLE No. 3—Continued.

Deaths in Indiana by Months, Counties, Ages, Sex, Color, Nationality and Conjugal Condition, 1910.

COUNTIES.	SEX.	Under 1	1	2	3	4	Under 5	5 to 9	10 to 14	15 to 19	20 to 24	25 to 29	30 to 34	35 to 39	40 to 44	45 to 49	50 to 54	55 to 59	60 to 64	65 to 69
Adams	Total	31	6	3	1	3	44	7	4	8	6	10	4	5	12	11	1	18	13	17
	Males	21	4	3	1	2	31		2	6	2	4	3	3	2	4		8	7	9
	Females	10	2			1	13	7	2	2	4	6	1	2	10	7	1	10	6	8
Allen	Total	161	31	19	6	12	229	29	31	46	54	47	43	35	48	74	53	52	61	77
	Males	98	22	7	2	5	134	17	13	18	32	25	23	15	24	40	26	26	36	47
	Females	63	9	12	4	7	95	12	18	28	22	22	20	20	24	34	27	26	25	30
Bartholomew	Total	50	15	4	3	1	73	6	5	11	15	14	15	9	7	15	15	23	21	20
	Males	29	10	3	1		43	6	2	3	9	7	8	4	2	10	8	11	10	10
	Females	21	5	1	2	1	30		3	8	6	7	7	5	5	5	7	12	11	10
Benton	Total	22	3	2	3	3	33		4	2	3	2	3	1	3	2	4	5	7	11
	Males	14			1	3	18		4	1	1				1		3	5	2	5
	Females	8	3	2	2		15			1	2	2	3	1	2	2	1		5	6
Blackford	Total	35	7	4	6	6	58	9	3	2	3	1	8	7	7	8	12	9	10	16
	Males	18	6	4	3	4	35	4		2	2		4	2	3	5	8	6	8	9
	Females	17	1		3	2	23	5	3		1	1	4	5	4	3	4	3	2	7
Boone	Total	41	8	4	2	3	58	5	3	9	13	10	9	7	6	16	10	14	14	18
	Males	27	4	2	1	1	35	4	1	7	3	8	1	2	4	7	6	6	3	4
	Females	14	4	2	1	2	23	1	2	2	10	2	8	5	2	9	4	8	11	14
Brown	Total	23	5	4	3	1	36	3	1	7	5	3		4	3	5	3	7	9	13
	Males	13	2	3	1		19	1	1	3	2	1			2	4	2	4	2	5
	Females	10	3	1	2	1	17	2		4	3	2		4	1	1	1	3	7	8
Carroll	Total	32	7	5	2	2	48	7	5	8	7	7	7	6	6	3	9	16	10	22
	Males	18	6	1		2	27	5	2	2	2	3	2	3	3	1	3	8	5	11
	Females	14	1	4	2		21	2	3	6	5	4	5	3	3	2	6	8	5	11
Cass	Total	63	12	6	4	5	90	10	14	19	30	27	16	20	29	26	42	28	43	54
	Males	29	9	3	4	1	46	6	8	14	11	12	9	13	8	18	28	14	27	28
	Females	34	3	3		4	44	4	6	5	19	15	7	7	21	8	14	14	16	26

TABLE No. 3—Continued.

COUNTIES	SEX	Under 1	1	2	3	4	Under 5	5 to 9	10 to 14	15 to 19	20 to 24	25 to 29	30 to 34	35 to 39	40 to 44	45 to 49	50 to 54	55 to 59	60 to 64	65 to 69
Clark	Total	86	22	4	8	4	118		9	10	40	21	16	15	16	20	28	20	20	41
	Males	44	12	1		2	59		1	10	31	11	8	9	7	7	11	10	11	19
	Females	42	10	3	8	2	59		8	9	9	8	8	6	9	13	17	10	10	22
Clay	Total	69	25	5	3	1	103	13	9	14	26	20	17	8	13	14	20	17	21	21
	Males	34	11	3	1	1	50	6	4	6	8	9	9	3	8	6	7	9	11	13
	Females	35	14	2	2		53	6	5	7	18	11	8	6	4	8	13	8	8	8
Clinton	Total	46	4	3	5	2	60	6	7	13	8	14	5	3	4	11	11	11	21	41
	Males	22	1	2	2	1	28	2	5	6	2	3	2			5	7	6	11	18
	Females	24	3	1	3	1	32	4	2	6	6	11	3	3	4	6	4	5	10	15
Crawford	Total	23	8	1	2	1	35	2	5	6	7	6	4	6	6	4	4	5	12	11
	Males	10	5	1	1	1	18		2	3	3		2	5	3	3	1	3	6	6
	Females	13	3		1		17	2	3	3	4	6	2	1	3	1	3	2	6	5
Daviess	Total	51	16	7	5	4	83	14	9	10	14	16	11	10	9	11	12	23	20	22
	Males	29	9	3	2		43	10	5	6	5	8	5	4	7	8	4	14	16	8
	Females	22	7	4	3	4	40	4	4	4	9	8	6	6	2	3	8	9	14	14
Dearborn	Total	22	6	4	2	2	36	4	4	7	10	12	11	4	16	12	15	19	14	22
	Males	15	3	3	1		22	1	2	5	4	6	5	1	11	7	7	10	9	12
	Females	7	3	1	1	2	14	3	2	2	6	6	6	3	5	5	8	9	5	10
Decatur	Total	30	7	6			43	2	4	7	6	6	4	4	10	8	11	19	18	20
	Males	17	3	3			23	1	1	3	1	2	1	1	4	5	6	8	9	10
	Females	13	4	3			20	1	3	4	5	4	3	3	6	3	5	8	9	10
Dekalb	Total	56	15	2		2	75	6	5	10	9	9	16	10	8	11	14	22	22	18
	Males	31	8	2		1	42	3	1	5	3	4	9	4	4	7	6	8	8	10
	Females	25	7			1	33	3	4	5	6	5	7	7	4	4	8	14	14	8
Delaware	Total	112	20	12	5	4	153	18	15	26	20	23	24	24	24	24	41	29	35	42
	Males	61	10	6	2	3	82	10	7	9	8	9	13	12	11	11	16	12	22	21
	Females	51	10	6	3	1	71	8	8	16	12	18	11	12	13	13	25	17	13	21
Dubois	Total	34	10	3	4		51	5	4	7	16	11	8	9	9	5	9	6	11	13
	Males	22	2		1		25	3		2	8	7	3	1	6	2	5	4	5	8
	Females	12	8	3	3		26	2	4	5	8	4	5	8	3	3	4	2	6	5

Elkhart	Total	90	12	13	7	1	123	11	8	22	16	27	24	27	28	32	27	42	49	50
	Males	45	7	7	4	1	64	5	3	11	6	10	15	12	13	17	13	20	24	25
	Females	45	5	6	3		59	6	5	11	10	17	9	15	15	15	14	22	25	25
Fayette	Total	45	7	4			56	4	2	1	4	5	10	7	7	9	8	10	16	16
	Males	25	4	3			32	3		1	2	2	5	4	4	4	3	5	7	9
	Females	20	3	1			24	1	2		2	3	5	3	3	5	5	5	9	7
Floyd	Total	62	15	13	3	4	97	15	4	12	34	25	18	13	17	13	22	23	29	51
	Males	38	5	6	1	1	51	10	2	3	14	14	7	8	8	10	9	9	16	26
	Females	24	10	7	2	3	46	5	2	9	20	11	11	5	9	3	13	14	13	25
Fountain	Total	38	13	7	4		62	5	5	7	9	12	6	6	11	6	15	17	19	21
	Males	21	9	4	2		36	2		4	3	6	2	4	5	6	5	9	11	12
	Females	17	4	3	2		26	3	5	3	6	6	4	2	6		10	8	8	9
Franklin	Total	25	2	3	2	2	34	3	2	4	9	2	5	8	4	4	11	10	13	13
	Males	14	2	2	1		19	3	1	3	3		4	3			6	6	10	4
	Females	11		1	1	2	15		1	1	6	2	1	5	4	4	5	4	3	9
Fulton	Total	36	6	4		3	49	5	5	5	3	9	5	5	3	6	11	13	23	19
	Males	22	3	4			29	1	2	1		2	4	1	1	1	6	5	15	13
	Females	14	3			3	20	4	3	4	3	7	1	4	2	5	5	8	8	6
Gibson	Total	67	29	8	4	1	109	15	9	15	21	18	13	15	12	15	14	18	17	29
	Males	41	22	7	3		73	8	7	5	12	9	2	2	7	5	7	8	9	15
	Females	26	7	1	1	1	36	7	2	10	9	9	11	13	5	10	7	10	8	14
Grant	Total	108	25	7	11	3	154	15	12	22	24	18	22	21	33	30	34	31	54	78
	Males	52	16	3	7	1	79	9	5	14	10	8	6	11	18	14	12	16	36	59
	Females	56	9	4	4	2	75	6	7	8	14	10	16	10	15	16	22	15	18	19
Greene	Total	110	26	9	15	7	167	14	14	15	25	17	15	18	12	15	22	11	16	25
	Males	56	14	6	7	7	90	6	6	7	12	12	5	10	5	9	10	7	10	12
	Females	54	12	3	8		77	8	8	8	13	5	10	8	7	6	12	4	6	13
Hamilton	Total	47	19	2	2	1	71	7	2	14	10	8	11	9	14	16	20	22	27	25
	Males	23	11	2		1	37	1	2	7	4	2	4	4	7	6	8	9	13	11
	Females	24	8		2		34	6		7	6	6	7	5	7	10	12	13	14	14
Hancock	Total	30	7	3		1	41	7	6	9	18	12	10	4	8	13	8	19	13	19
	Males	18	5	2		1	26	3	2	2	10	8	5	1	3	9	2	9	8	8
	Females	12	2	1			15	4	4	7	8	4	5	3	5	4	6	10	5	11
Harrison	Total	35	8	2	1	1	47	10	4	9	10	6	12	10	7	3	9	9	13	13
	Males	18	3	2	1		24	5	4	5	6	3	4	3	4	1	5	5	6	7
	Females	17	5			1	23	5		4	4	3	8	7	3	2	4	4	7	6

TABLE No. 3—Continued.

COUNTIES.	Sex.	Under 1	1	2	3	4	Under 5	5 to 9	10 to 14	15 to 19	20 to 24	25 to 29	30 to 34	35 to 39	40 to 44	45 to 49	50 to 54	55 to 59	60 to 64	65 to 69
Hendricks	Total	36	6	4	2	1	49	4	4	10	11	9	3	12	5	7	7	8	13	25
	Males	18	4	4	2	1	29	3	3	7	6	7	1	4	1	2	6	7	4	14
	Females	18	2				20	1	1	3	5	2	2	8	4	5	1	1	9	11
Henry	Total	71	17	9	4	3	104	8	4	13	23	14	13	17	7	9	13	16	27	31
	Males	36	6	7	2	2	53	3	2	9	11	7	6	10	3	4	7	12	13	17
	Females	35	11	2	2	1	51	5	2	4	12	7	7	7	4	5	6	4	14	14
Howard	Total	89	18	10	4	1	122	11	7	19	10	16	15	14	15	14	21	17	23	27
	Males	56	11	4	2		73	4	3	10	5	6	8	6	6	5	10	10	14	10
	Females	33	7	6	2	1	49	7	4	9	5	10	7	8	9	9	11	7	9	17
Huntington	Total	44	9	4	3	3	63	7	5	8	11	14	12	11	9	12	9	22	29	20
	Males	29	6	2	2	1	40	3		4	6	5	4	3	3	6	5	9	14	10
	Females	15	3	2	1	2	23	4	5	4	5	9	8	8	6	6	4	13	15	10
Jackson	Total	73	14	4	4	4	99	8	5	10	15	12	12	6	10	10	13	15	19	32
	Males	42	4	3	1	3	53	3	3	3	5	4	5	4	5	2	9	8	11	15
	Females	31	10	1	3	1	46	5	2	7	10	8	7	2	5	8	4	7	8	17
Jasper	Total	17	5	3			25	1	2	4	3	2	6	4	4	6	4	4	7	7
	Males	7	3	2			12		1	1		1	2	2	2	2	2	4	3	5
	Females	10	2	1			13	1	1	3	3	1	4	2	2	4	2		4	2
Jay	Total	51	15	4		6	76	12	9	14	19	15	10	8	12	6	13	7	19	29
	Males	27	7	3		4	41	6	4	6	12	8	5	7	6	1	9	3	8	17
	Females	24	8	1		2	35	6	5	8	7	7	5	1	6	5	4	4	11	12
Jefferson	Total	54	8	4	3	1	70	7	8	8	3	17	9	11	11	18	12	17	23	28
	Males	31	4	1	1	1	38	4	6	5	1	7	4	6	6	11	7	11	12	19
	Females	23	4	3	2		32	3	2	3	2	10	5	5	5	7	5	6	11	9
Jennings	Total	31	4	7	3		45	6	3	3	7	6	4	6	5	7	5	7	10	14
	Males	22	2	2	3		29	2	2	2	2	2	1	1	2	4	4	3	5	5
	Females	9	2	5			16	4	1	1	5	4	3	5	3	3	1	4	5	9
Johnson	Total	48	12	11	5	2	78	8	5	9	18	4	14	3	9	10	12	12	11	17
	Males	29	8	3	5		45	6	1	5	4	2	8	3	5	5	10	7	6	9
	Females	19	4	8		2	33	2	4	4	14	2	6		4	5	2	5	5	8

Knox	Total	133	43	16	11	9	212	22	4	19	27	29	26	20	17	19	20	26	22	23
	Males	70	25	8	6	6	115	9	3	10	11	13	14	8	11	10	7	9	14	5
	Females	63	18	8	5	3	97	13	1	9	16	16	12	12	6	9	13	17	8	18
Kosciusko	Total	35	9	6	6	3	59	9	4	11	13	10	9	7	5	6	17	21	26	31
	Males	21	3	1	6	1	32	5	3	6	5	4	3	4	4	1	9	9	15	16
	Females	14	6	5		2	27	4	1	5	8	6	6	3	1	5	8	12	11	15
Lagrange	Total	27	3	1		2	33	5	4	5	8	7	5	1	7	6	15	11	16	15
	Males	16	1			2	19	2	2	3	3	4	1		6	2	9	6	9	8
	Females	11	2	1			14	3	2	2	5	3	4	1	1	4	6	5	7	7
Lake	Total	373	81	29	12	7	502	30	20	28	80	67	57	64	52	54	33	45	28	33
	Males	202	42	21	7	2	274	17	12	13	59	50	44	49	37	38	24	30	18	21
	Females	171	39	8	5	5	228	13	8	15	21	17	13	15	15	16	9	15	10	12
Laporte	Total	123	14	7	5	5	154	15	7	20	20	21	29	22	27	19	27	39	29	44
	Males	74	6	5	2	2	89	9	4	11	10	14	16	15	18	14	18	14	20	28
	Females	49	8	2	3	3	65	6	3	9	10	7	13	7	9	5	9	15	9	16
Lawrence	Total	74	33	11	8	5	131	10	8	12	18	22	15	19	9	17	25	14	8	20
	Males	41	17	6	2	4	70	6	5	4	11	8	8	7	3	9	13	8	8	16
	Females	33	16	5	6	1	61	4	3	8	7	14	7	12	6	8	12	6		4
Madison	Total	178	38	19	10	5	250	24	20	25	37	36	41	23	33	31	45	43	52	37
	Males	96	19	6	6	2	129	13	10	11	13	17	18	13	16	12	22	25	29	17
	Females	82	19	13	4	3	121	11	10	14	24	19	23	10	17	19	23	18	23	20
Marion	Total	631	138	61	36	21	887	72	40	116	200	196	197	238	220	255	279	246	272	285
	Males	337	81	29	18	12	477	44	23	66	113	94	105	129	123	137	155	143	166	161
	Females	294	57	32	18	9	410	28	17	50	87	102	92	109	97	118	124	103	106	124
Marshall	Total	55	9	7	3	3	77	6	6	7	7	8	13	9	13	9	7	17	23	18
	Males	36	6	3	2	3	50	4	4	1	5	6	5	6	4	2	3	9	15	8
	Females	19	3	4	1		27	2	2	6	2	2	8	3	9	7	4	8	8	10
Martin	Total	29	9	1	2	4	45	1	2	3	5	6	9	7	4	3	6	7	8	3
	Males	14	3	1	1	1	20	1	2	1	3	1	5	3	2	2	4	5	3	
	Females	15	6		1	3	25			2	2	5	4	4	2	1	2	2	5	3
Miami	Total	44	9	5	2	2	62	6	4	10	17	19	11	13	19	14	19	19	15	31
	Males	24	6	2	2		34	3	2	5	10	8	5	10	11	8	12	11	6	17
	Females	20	3	3		2	28	3	2	5	7	11	6	3	8	6	7	8	9	14
Monroe	Total	60	21	10	4	1	96	8	8	7	13	19	10	6	11	9	10	10	22	17
	Males	37	12	9	3	1	62	3	5	1	7	10	3	4	3	5	4	6	11	10
	Females	23	9	1	1		34	5	3	6	6	9	7	2	8	4	6	4	11	7

TABLE No. 3—Continued.

COUNTIES.	Sex.	Under 1	1	2	3	4	Under 5	5 to 9	10 to 14	15 to 19	20 to 24	25 to 29	30 to 34	35 to 39	40 to 44	45 to 49	50 to 54	55 to 59	60 to 64	65 to 69
Montgomery	Total	48	15	5	2	1	71	2	8	7	20	10	5	13	11	17	17	20	34	25
	Males	28	7	3	2	....	40	2	5	4	9	3	1	2	3	9	7	16	16	14
	Females	20	8	2	....	1	31	....	3	3	11	7	4	11	8	8	10	4	18	11
Morgan	Total	44	14	2	4	1	65	3	5	5	17	11	10	12	11	8	13	21	26	28
	Males	22	6	1	4	1	34	2	4	1	5	6	8	7	6	3	5	15	14	14
	Females	22	8	1	....	....	31	1	1	4	12	5	2	5	5	5	8	6	12	14
Newton	Total	26	4	2	1	....	33	1	3	4	4	2	2	3	2	4	3	3	7	8
	Males	17	2	....	1	....	20	1	1	2	2	1	....	3	1	1	2	2	5	3
	Females	9	2	2	....	....	13	....	2	2	2	1	2	....	1	3	1	1	2	5
Noble	Total	33	4	6	2	1	46	....	....	5	11	4	7	8	6	5	10	19	21	17
	Males	15	2	5	1	....	23	....	....	1	5	....	5	5	3	4	7	8	8	9
	Females	18	2	1	1	1	23	....	....	4	6	4	2	3	3	1	3	11	13	8
Ohio	Total	3	....	1	....	....	4	1	....	1	2	....	2	1	2	....	1	3	4	10
	Males	1	....	....	....	....	1	1	....	1	1	....	1	1	1	....	....	2	1	6
	Females	2	....	1	....	....	3	....	....	....	1	....	1	....	1	....	1	1	3	4
Orange	Total	41	5	1	....	2	49	4	3	11	9	7	2	8	8	9	14	6	10	16
	Males	22	1	....	....	....	23	2	2	8	1	2	1	3	3	3	8	3	1	7
	Females	19	4	1	....	2	26	2	1	3	8	5	1	5	5	6	6	3	9	9
Owen	Total	26	6	3	1	1	37	1	6	3	3	4	6	4	9	1	4	10	14	12
	Males	13	4	1	1	1	20	1	2	....	1	....	....	....	4	1	1	7	7	6
	Females	13	2	2	....	....	17	....	4	3	2	4	6	4	5	....	3	3	7	6
Parke	Total	46	14	6	5	3	74	8	4	9	10	5	11	4	9	7	12	13	12	15
	Males	27	8	3	....	2	40	4	1	2	6	2	5	2	3	5	6	8	5	7
	Females	19	6	3	5	1	34	4	3	7	4	3	6	2	6	2	6	5	7	8
Perry	Total	47	9	7	4	1	68	8	4	4	13	5	6	8	7	7	8	8	7	12
	Males	25	5	2	1	....	33	4	3	2	4	2	3	4	1	3	4	5	5	5
	Females	22	4	5	3	1	35	4	1	2	9	3	3	4	6	4	4	3	2	7
Pike	Total	65	17	7	1	4	94	9	4	9	14	14	12	11	10	7	15	4	10	19
	Males	40	11	4	....	1	56	5	1	3	4	7	4	4	4	4	10	1	7	10
	Females	25	6	3	1	3	38	4	3	6	10	7	8	7	6	3	5	3	3	9

Porter	Total	26	8	3	4	2	43	7	5	10	11	7	10	3	9	13	11	9	25	17
	Males	14	4	1	4		23	3	3	8	6	4	8	1	5	6	7	5	12	10
	Females	12	4	2		2	20	4	2	2	5	3	2	2	4	7	4	4	13	7
Posey	Total	47	16	7	3	4	77	5	6	10	11	10	10	16	14	7	10	14	12	22
	Males	18	7	3	1		29	5	5	5	5	5	6	6	8	4	5	5	7	15
	Females	29	9	4	2	4	48		1	5	6	5	4	10	6	3	5	9	5	7
Pulaski	Total	23	6	4	1	1	35	1	6	4	5	3	7	6	3	6	8	4	7	12
	Males	15	4	3		1	23	1	4	2		1	1	2	2	3	2	3	1	4
	Females	8	2	1	1		12		2	2	5	2	6	4	1	3	6	1	6	8
Putnam	Total	30	11	4	3	2	50	6	3	5	10	8	4	13	9	12	9	19	11	18
	Males	14	10	3	1	1	29	5		2	4	3	1	3	3	5	5	14	7	10
	Females	16	1	1	2	1	21	1	3	3	6	5	3	10	6	7	4	5	4	8
Randolph	Total	53	11	6	2	2	74	6	6	11	12	12	9	16	8	13	15	21	29	37
	Males	29	6	4	1	1	41	4	4	6	4	7	2	5	5	5	11	10	11	18
	Females	24	5	2	1	1	33	2	2	5	8	5	7	11	3	8	4	11	18	19
Ripley	Total	35	12	9	1	2	59	3	4	3	9	7	11	4	7	5	8	14	16	18
	Males	19	6	5		2	32	2	2	2	4	2	5	2	1	3	4	6	9	11
	Females	16	6	4	1		27	1	2	1	5	5	6	2	6	2	4	8	7	7
Rush	Total	39	6	4			49	4	2	3	8	6	9	6	4	13	11	9	18	18
	Males	24	3	3			30	2		1	3	3	4	2	1	7	5	3	9	11
	Females	15	3	1			19	2	2	2	5	3	5	4	3	6	6	6	9	7
Scott	Total	15	7	4	1	1	28	2	3	4	5	5	3	1	2	5	6	4	8	3
	Males	7	4	3	1		15	1		2	2	1		1	2	3	4	3	5	3
	Females	8	3	1		1	13	1	3	2	3	4	3			2	2	1	3	
Shelby	Total	47	14	6	2	2	71	5	6	9	11	12	11	10	12	11	11	17	31	28
	Males	24	6	4	2	1	37	2	4	5	4	7	6	2	7	4	6	6	19	14
	Females	23	8	2		1	34	3	2	4	7	5	5	8	5	7	5	11	12	14
Spencer	Total	43	17	1	2	2	65	3	2	7	12	4	13	6	10	7	9	15	17	21
	Males	18	7	1	1	2	29	1	1	3	4	2	5	6	4	3	2	8	13	8
	Females	25	10		1		36	2	1	4	8	2	8		6	4	7	7	4	13
Starke	Total	24	3	5	2	3	37	6		2	5	5	5	3	4	2	5	7	6	8
	Males	16	2	4	1	1	24	3		1	1	2	3	1	4	1	4	5	1	4
	Females	8	1	1	1	2	13	3		1	4	3	2	2		1	1	2	5	4
Steuben	Total	24	5	1	2	1	33	4		6	7	3	5	4	2	1	8	5	11	13
	Males	13	2		1		16	2		6	6	1	1	1	2		4	2	5	8
	Females	11	3	1	1	1	17	2			1	2	4	3		1	4	3	6	5

TABLE No. 3—Continued.

COUNTIES.	Sex.	Under 1	1	2	3	4	Under 5	5 to 9	10 to 14	15 to 19	20 to 24	25 to 29	30 to 34	35 to 39	40 to 44	45 to 49	50 to 54	55 to 59	60 to 64	65 to 69
St. Joseph	Total	264	50	18	13	9	354	31	15	21	55	46	38	42	39	49	46	58	60	57
	Males	142	22	10	7	4	185	14	11	10	21	24	20	24	24	33	24	49	35	38
	Females	122	28	8	6	5	169	17	4	11	34	22	18	18	15	16	22	9	25	19
Sullivan	Total	96	24	6	3	5	134	11	5	8	18	8	12	13	10	12	14	19	18	19
	Males	48	14	.....	2	4	68	5	3	4	8	3	9	7	5	6	11	15	13	12
	Females	48	10	6	1	1	66	6	2	4	10	5	3	6	5	6	3	4	5	7
Switzerland	Total	16	8	2	1	1	28	.....	2	1	2	3	2	5	.....	5	3	6	13	13
	Males	8	6	1	.....	1	16	.....	2	.....	.....	.....	.....	4	.....	3	1	1	8	7
	Females	8	2	1	1	.....	12	.....	.....	1	2	3	2	1	.....	2	2	5	5	6
Tippecanoe	Total	64	8	6	2	1	81	7	3	11	18	20	21	18	24	29	29	32	54	44
	Males	42	4	5	2	.....	53	5	1	7	9	13	8	9	13	19	13	16	32	16
	Females	22	4	1	.....	1	28	2	2	4	9	7	13	9	11	10	16	16	22	28
Tipton	Total	43	8	3	1	2	57	2	5	4	7	8	7	8	6	10	9	11	19	19
	Males	30	5	2	1	1	39	1	2	2	4	5	4	4	6	7	6	7	7	12
	Females	13	3	1	.....	1	18	1	3	2	3	3	3	4	.....	3	3	4	12	7
Union	Total	15	1	2	1	3	22	1	3	1	2	.....	3	.....	.....	2	4	4	4	6
	Males	6	1	1	.....	1	9	.....	.....	1	1	.....	2	.....	.....	2	1	2	2	4
	Females	9	.....	1	1	2	13	1	3	.....	1	.....	1	.....	.....	.....	3	2	2	2
Vanderburgh	Total	198	32	24	13	9	276	16	14	38	53	66	58	77	63	66	53	61	74	77
	Males	112	15	11	7	5	150	5	9	19	22	37	33	39	36	34	28	35	37	51
	Females	86	17	13	6	4	126	11	5	19	31	29	25	38	27	32	25	26	37	26
Vermillion	Total	73	10	3	2	3	91	7	5	7	9	8	7	7	10	5	8	12	21	14
	Males	42	5	2	1	2	52	3	.....	4	6	6	3	4	3	5	4	5	8	9
	Females	31	5	1	1	1	39	4	5	3	3	2	4	3	7	.....	4	7	13	5
Vigo	Total	219	58	38	20	12	347	33	23	41	61	53	53	71	58	68	57	66	79	83
	Males	130	33	22	12	3	200	18	15	16	33	21	33	43	39	35	35	39	44	38
	Females	89	25	16	8	9	147	15	8	25	28	32	20	28	19	33	22	27	35	45
Wabash	Total	50	3	7	3	1	64	7	7	8	8	14	15	9	8	13	21	21	18	23
	Males	24	1	5	1	1	32	5	4	6	6	7	7	2	3	8	11	11	10	12
	Females	26	2	2	2	.....	32	2	3	2	2	7	8	7	5	5	10	10	8	11

Warren	Total	25	3	1	2		31	2	4	4	3		6	11	2	2	10	6	6	12
	Males	19	2	1	2		24	1	2	2	1		2	5	1	1	5	1	3	7
	Females	6	1				7	1	2	2	2		4	6	1	1	5	5	3	5
Warrick	Total	48	25	4	5	3	85	7	7	6	11	13	13	12	8	9	9	13	14	17
	Males	29	11		4	1	45	3	3	4	4	4	7	5	5	4	3	8	9	7
	Females	19	14	4	1	2	40	4	4	2	7	9	6	7	3	5	6	5	5	10
Washington	Total	39	12	4	4	2	61	3	4	3	9	10	8	9	9	9	10	11	8	9
	Males	20	6	1	1	1	29	1	1	1	3	3	3	2	4	1	6	6	4	3
	Females	19	6	3	3	1	32	2	3	2	6	7	5	7	5	8	4	5	4	6
Wayne	Total	62	14	9	2	5	92	12	9	19	24	21	23	32	30	33	39	38	48	56
	Males	39	5	7	1	1	53	9	6	8	13	7	12	15	18	20	24	24	24	29
	Females	23	9	2	1	4	39	3	3	11	11	14	11	17	12	13	15	14	24	27
Wells	Total	36	8	5	2	2	53	5	4	13	11	12	9	15	11	9	14	12	24	22
	Males	18	6	2	2	1	29	3	2	10	6	5	5	9	8	4	7	4	10	13
	Females	18	2	3		1	24	2	2	3	5	7	4	6	3	5	7	8	14	9
White	Total	28	6			1	35	5	3	4	10	6	4	3	1	5	6	9	9	9
	Males	20	3				23	3	1	2	5	2	2			3	3	3	4	5
	Females	8	3			1	12	2	2	2	5	4	2	3	1	2	3	6	5	4
Whitley	Total	31	9	1	1		42	4	1	4	5	1	5	7	4	3	7	7	10	21
	Males	15	3				18	4		1	3		1	3	1	2	4	6	3	10
	Females	16	6	1	1		24		1	3	2	1	4	4	3	1	3	1	7	11
Total males		3,355	753	343	189	127	4,767	418	299	522	737	673	661	675	702	777	886	1,001	1,202	1,349
Total females		2,693	641	290	163	136	3,923	360	288	530	808	726	673	674	638	694	784	813	1,008	1,163
Grand total		6,048	1,394	633	352	263	8,690	778	587	1,052	1,545	1,399	1,334	1,349	1,340	1,471	1,670	1,814	2,210	2,512

TABLE No. 3—Continued.

Deaths in Indiana by Months, Counties, Ages, Sex, Color, Nationality and Conjugal Condition, 1910

COUNTIES.	Sex.	70 to 74	75 to 79	80 to 84	85 to 89	90 to 94	95 and Over.	Unknown.	White.	Colored.	American.	Foreign.	Not Reported.	Single.	Married.	Widowed or Divorced.	Not Reported.	Total.
Adams	Total	16	19	9	5	1	....	....	210	....	174	34	2	78	84	48	....	210
	Males	9	10	4	2	....	....	....	106	....	85	19	2	46	40	20	....	106
	Females	7	9	5	3	1	....	....	104	....	89	15	....	32	44	28	....	104
Allen	Total	81	79	43	31	3	2	1	1,109	10	843	253	23	481	387	243	8	1,119
	Males	41	42	21	14	2	1	1	591	7	444	137	17	275	196	119	8	598
	Females	40	37	22	17	1	1	....	518	3	399	116	6	206	191	124	....	521
Bartholomew	Total	19	29	21	10	....	1	....	323	6	310	17	2	129	127	73	....	329
	Males	15	11	8	3	....	....	....	168	2	159	10	1	74	73	23	....	170
	Females	4	18	13	7	....	1	....	155	4	151	7	1	55	54	50	....	159
Benton	Total	6	10	6	3	....	....	....	105	....	90	14	1	48	37	20	....	105
	Males	1	6	4	2	....	....	....	53	....	49	3	1	28	17	8	....	53
	Females	5	4	2	1	....	....	....	52	....	41	11	....	20	20	12	....	52
Blackford	Total	13	17	8	5	....	....	....	195	1	186	8	2	84	84	28	....	196
	Males	5	11	3	4	....	....	....	110	1	106	3	2	48	53	10	....	111
	Females	8	6	5	1	....	....	....	85	....	80	5	....	36	31	18	....	85
Boone	Total	27	28	24	12	2	1	....	286	....	276	8	2	103	126	57	....	286
	Males	13	15	13	7	1	....	....	140	....	137	2	1	62	56	22	....	140
	Females	14	13	11	5	1	1	....	146	....	139	6	1	41	70	35	....	146
Brown	Total	8	11	11	4	1	....	....	134	....	132	2	....	52	53	29	....	134
	Males	4	6	4	3	1	....	....	64	....	62	2	....	27	24	13	....	64
	Females	4	5	7	1	....	....	....	70	....	70	....	....	25	29	16	....	70
Carroll	Total	29	25	15	8	1	1	....	240	....	222	16	2	85	99	55	1	240
	Males	15	13	5	4	....	....	....	114	....	104	10	....	45	49	19	1	114
	Females	14	12	10	4	1	1	....	126	....	118	6	2	40	50	36	....	126

County																		
Cass	Total	37	46	22	18	3			574		481	74	19	211	247	111	5	574
	Males	19	27	13	5	1			307		250	49	8	121	139	44	3	307
	Females	18	19	9	13	2			267		231	25	11	90	108	67	2	267
[illegible]k	Total	39	39	23	11	3			418	77	454	38	3	212	168	113	2	495
	Males	25	21	6	6	1			197	45	220	19	3	113	91	36	2	242
	Females	14	18	17	5	2			221	32	234	19		99	77	77		253
Clay	Total	22	29	25	13	2	1		392	11	354	45	4	175	138	89	1	403
	Males	13	15	9	6				189	5	167	26	1	89	72	33		194
	Females	9	14	16	7	2	1		203	6	187	19	3	86	66	56	1	209
[illegible]	Total	26	18	21	12	3	2		301	2	298	5		96	132	74	1	303
	Males	17	12	14	8	1	1		152	1	150	3		49	71	32	1	153
	[illegible]les	9	6	7	4	2	1		149	1	148	2		47	61	42		150
[illegible]	Total	17	9	3	5	2			150	1	147	3	1	59	63	29		151
	Males	9	3	1	1	2			72	1	71	1	1	31	32	10		73
	Females	8	6	2	4				78		76	2		28	31	19		78
Daviess	Total	21	18	16	5	4		1	335	2	318	14	5	137	139	58	3	337
	Males	11	9	8	5	1		1	178		164	10	4	80	70	25	3	178
	Females	10	9	8		3			157	2	154	4	1	57	69	33		159
Dearborn	Total	33	27	11	11	4		2	274	3	199	63	15	90	109	71	7	277
	Males	18	15	4	5	2		2	144	1	106	28	11	57	58	23	7	145
	Females	15	12	7	6	2			130	2	93	35	4	33	51	48		132
Decatur	Total	25	27	22	11	4			246	4	227	21	2	82	101	66	1	250
	Males	9	18	16	6	2			126	3	116	11	2	40	60	28	1	129
	Females	16	9	6	5	2			120	1	111	10		42	41	38		121
Dekalb	Total	29	29	25	9	4	1	1	328	1	304	22	3	114	145	67	3	329
	Males	12	18	11	4	3	1	1	161	1	147	12	3	68	68	23	3	162
	[illegible]les	17	11	14	5	1			167		157	10		46	77	44		167
Delaware	Total	49	36	34	12	4	3		603	22	598	25	2	260	245	119	1	625
	Males	28	14	20	7		1		304	8	296	14	2	135	131	45	1	312
	Females	21	22	14	5	4	2		299	14	302	11		125	114	74		313
Dubois	Total	7	10	3	6	1			190	1	158	33		96	72	24		191
	Males	5	8	2	4				98		75	23		48	37	13		98
	Females	2	2	1	2	1			92	1	83	10		47	35	11		93
Elkhart	Total	49	70	35	21	10		1	671	1	596	61	15	208	298	159	7	672
	Males	26	41	20	13	3		1	342		294	37	11	117	158	61	6	342
	[illegible]les	23	29	15	8	7			329	1	302	24	4	91	140	98	1	330

TABLE No. 3—Continued.

COUNTIES.	Sex.	70 to 74	75 to 79	80 to 84	85 to 89	90 to 94	95 and Over.	Unknown.	White.	Colored.	American.	Foreign.	Not Reported.	Single.	Married.	Widowed or Divorced.	Not Reported.	Total.
Fayette	Total	14	13	5	2	1	......	......	185	5	179	11	......	83	71	35	1	190
	Males	7	6	4	2	1	......	......	100	1	95	6	......	48	38	15	......	101
	Females	7	7	1	......	......	......	......	85	4	84	5	......	35	33	20	1	89
Floyd	Total	46	48	32	13	4	......	......	466	50	438	77	1	196	178	140	2	516
	Males	20	15	16	6	1	......	......	220	25	206	38	1	108	94	41	2	245
	Females	26	33	16	7	3	......	......	246	25	232	39	......	88	84	99	......	271
Fountain	Total	29	17	17	8	1	1	1	273	2	260	11	4	108	112	54	1	275
	Males	15	6	11	3	1	1	1	142	1	134	6	3	62	64	16	1	143
	Females	14	11	6	5	......	......	......	131	1	126	5	1	46	48	38	......	132
Franklin	Total	18	13	21	13	5	1	......	193	......	158	33	2	63	79	50	1	193
	Males	10	9	11	9	2	......	......	103	......	79	22	2	37	47	18	1	103
	Females	8	4	10	4	3	1	......	90	......	79	11	......	26	32	32	......	90
Fulton	Total	23	18	18	9	2	1	......	232	......	215	14	3	74	102	56	......	232
	Males	18	12	11	5	......	......	......	127	......	115	12	......	39	64	24	......	127
	Females	5	6	7	4	2	1	......	105	......	100	2	3	35	38	32	......	105
Gibson	Total	24	33	14	7	3	1	......	373	29	283	16	3	183	136	83	......	402
	Males	11	18	11	3	2	......	......	195	19	201	10	3	114	66	34	......	214
	Females	13	15	3	4	1	1	......	178	10	182	6	......	69	70	49	......	188
Grant	Total	94	70	54	17	7	......	2	749	43	733	45	14	268	290	224	10	792
	Males	74	54	41	10	1	......	1	448	30	431	37	10	159	164	146	9	478
	Females	20	16	13	7	6	......	4	301	13	302	8	4	109	126	78	1	314
Greene	Total	32	20	19	6	4	2	......	469	......	447	21	1	242	171	56	......	469
	Males	15	9	11	2	......	1	......	239	......	225	13	1	133	90	16	......	239
	Females	17	11	8	4	4	1	......	230	......	222	8	......	109	81	40	......	230
Hamilton	Total	33	37	22	6	6	......	1	352	9	354	5	2	120	158	83	......	361
	Males	16	20	10	3	1	......	......	161	4	160	5	......	63	73	29	......	165
	Females	17	17	12	3	5	......	1	191	5	194	......	2	57	85	54	......	196

Hancock	Total	20	19	16	8	2	....	....	248	4	245	7	....	89	117	46	....	252
	Males	10	13	9	6	....	....	....	133	1	129	5	....	53	64	17	....	134
	Females	10	6	7	2	2	....	....	115	3	116	2	....	36	53	29	....	118
Harrison	Total	18	19	21	7	2	....	....	224	5	208	19	2	91	95	43	....	229
	Males	10	10	14	2	1	....	....	118	1	107	11	1	52	47	20	....	119
	Females	8	9	7	5	1	....	....	106	4	101	8	1	39	48	23	....	110
Hendricks	Total	29	31	21	10	6	2	....	260	6	256	9	1	92	111	62	1	266
	Males	16	20	13	6	2	....	....	148	3	144	7	....	61	62	27	1	151
	Females	13	11	8	4	4	2	....	112	3	112	2	1	31	49	35	....	115
Henry	Total	38	36	26	17	9	1	1	416	11	418	8	1	163	169	91	4	427
	Males	23	26	9	9	7	....	1	224	8	227	4	1	87	102	40	3	232
	Females	15	10	17	8	2	1	....	192	3	191	4	....	76	67	51	1	195
Howard	Total	28	31	24	10	5	2	....	412	19	408	22	1	179	170	81	1	431
	Males	9	18	15	6	3	1	....	210	12	206	15	1	104	84	33	1	222
	Females	19	13	9	4	2	1	....	202	7	202	7	....	75	86	48	....	209
Huntington	Total	39	32	38	9	5	1	....	356	....	333	23	....	120	141	95	....	172
	Males	24	17	26	4	....	1	....	184	....	169	15	....	66	84	34	....	184
	Females	15	15	12	5	5	....	....	172	....	164	8	....	54	57	61	....	172
Jackson	Total	34	18	24	5	2	....	1	349	1	319	29	2	146	143	61	....	350
	Males	19	14	12	5	2	....	1	182	1	164	18	1	74	83	26	....	183
	Females	15	4	12	....	....	....	....	167	....	155	11	1	72	60	35	....	167
Jasper	Total	14	11	13	2	1	....	....	120	....	102	18	....	37	63	20	....	120
	Males	11	4	5	2	1	....	....	60	....	52	8	....	15	39	6	....	60
	Females	3	7	8	....	....	....	....	60	....	50	10	....	22	24	14	....	60
Jay	Total	24	30	11	10	1	....	....	323	2	306	18	1	135	125	65	....	325
	Males	15	15	8	4	1	....	....	176	....	162	14	....	78	71	27	....	176
	Females	9	15	3	6	....	....	....	147	2	144	4	1	57	54	38	....	149
Jefferson	Total	35	40	24	9	4	4	....	343	15	323	29	6	128	130	96	4	358
	Males	22	22	15	3	2	....	....	195	6	180	17	4	70	85	42	4	201
	Females	13	18	9	6	2	4	....	148	9	143	12	2	58	45	54	....	157
Jennings	Total	15	16	10	8	5	....	....	179	3	167	15	....	70	74	37	1	182
	Males	7	8	7	2	1	....	....	88	1	83	6	....	42	34	13	....	89
	Females	8	8	3	6	4	....	....	91	2	84	9	....	28	40	24	1	93
Johnson	Total	24	23	21	5	4	....	....	274	13	283	4	....	133	95	59	....	287
	Males	9	15	12	3	1	....	....	149	7	155	1	....	75	57	24	....	156
	Females	15	8	9	2	3	....	....	125	6	128	3	....	58	38	35	....	131

TABLE No. 3—Continued.

COUNTIES.	Sex.	70 to 74	75 to 79	80 to 84	85 to 89	90 to 94	95 and Over.	Unknown.	White.	Colored.	American.	Foreign.	Not Reported.	Single.	Married.	Widowed or Divorced.	Not Reported.	Total.
Knox	Total	23	32	29	11	2	1	1	569	16	533	48	4	303	176	103	3	585
	Males	19	17	10	6		1	1	288	5	267	22	4	160	92	38	3	293
	Females	4	15	19	5	2			281	11	266	26		143	84	65		292
Kosciusko	Total	30	40	33	13	4			346	2	328	20		107	148	93		348
	Males	13	22	17	8	2			178		166	12		64	84	30		178
	Females	17	18	16	5	2			168	2	162	8		43	64	63		170
Lagrange	Total	22	19	15	3	2			199		190	9		62	90	47		199
	Males	12	10	7	1				104		96	8		35	53	16		104
	Females	10	9	8	2	2			95		94	1		27	37	31		95
Lake	Total	33	31	20	15	6	4	6	1,194	13	796	379*	33	709	358	108	33	1,208
	Males	20	16	10	9	5	2	6	747	6	460	261*	33	438	241	42	33	754
	Females	13	15	10	6	1	2		447	7	336	118		271	117	66		454
Laporte	Total	58	55	37	21	10			630	13	430	205†	9	260	236	140	8	644
	Males	32	37	24	13	6			379	12	260	124†	8	168	156	60	8	392
	Females	26	18	13	8	4			251	1	170	81	1	92	80	80		252
Lawrence	Total	23	22	23	6	6	1	1	404	6	391	16	3	197	141	71	1	410
	Males	6	15	8	1	1		1	205	3	193	13	2	114	68	25	1	208
	Females	17	7	15	5	5	1		199	3	198	3	1	83	73	46		202
Madison	Total	51	50	43	20	5			854	12	826	37	3	369	334	163		866
	Males	27	23	20	10	3			421	7	404	22	2	198	179	51		428
	Females	24	27	23	10	2			433	5	422	15	1	171	155	112		438
Marion	Total	248	232	148	72	24	12		3,667	570	3,653	540‡	46	1,601	1,632	977	29	4,239
	Males	126	107	72	29	12	4		1,968	317	1,940	318†	28	957	911	395	23	2,286
	Females	122	125	76	43	12	8		1,699	253	1,713	222†	18	644	721	582	6	1,953
Marshall	Total	28	32	16	8	3	1		307	1	270	32	6	116	132	57	3	308
	Males	19	14	8	2	2	1		168		145	19	4	75	76	14	3	168
	Females	9	18	8	6	1			139	1	125	13	2	41	56	43		140

* One Japanese. † One Chinese. ‡ Two Chinese.

Martin	Total	9	12	6	6	2	......	1	145	......	141	1	3	66	57	22	......	145
	Males	1	3	3	4	2	......	1	66	......	63	1	2	34	26	6	......	66
	Females	8	9	3	2	......	......	......	79	......	78	......	1	32	31	16	......	79
Miami	Total	31	27	30	15	5	2	1	369	1	323	33§	14	118	164	80	8	370
	Males	23	14	13	8	5	2	1	207	1	175	22	11	71	100	30	7	208
	Females	8	13	17	7	......	......	......	161	......	148	11§	3	47	64	50	1	162
Monroe	Total	31	17	26	11	3	......	......	325	9	324	9	1	150	108	74	2	334
	Males	13	6	10	2	1	......	......	158	8	159	6	1	92	54	19	1	166
	Females	18	11	16	9	2	......	......	167	1	165	3	......	58	54	55	1	168
Montgomery	Total	38	38	23	20	2	2	......	373	10	365	18	......	123	168	92	......	383
	Males	20	27	13	10	1	1	......	197	6	190	13	......	72	96	35	......	203
	Females	18	11	10	10	1	1	......	176	4	175	5	......	51	72	57	......	180
Morgan	Total	23	32	12	7	3	......	......	311	1	299	9	4	107	142	61	2	312
	Males	11	20	5	3	1	......	......	163	1	157	5	2	55	83	24	2	164
	Females	12	12	7	4	2	......	......	148	......	142	4	2	52	59	37	......	148
Newton	Total	8	12	3	3	1	2	1	109	......	95	14	......	45	40	24	......	109
	Males	5	8	2	2	1	1	1	64	......	55	9	......	29	23	12	......	64
	Females	3	4	1	1	......	1	......	45	......	40	5	......	16	17	12	......	45
Noble	Total	27	34	23	16	6	1	1	267	......	228	33	6	69	119	79	......	267
	Males	14	14	11	9	2	1	1	130	......	107	19	4	37	69	24	......	130
	Females	13	20	12	7	4	......	......	137	......	121	14	2	32	50	55	......	137
Ohio	Total	4	2	5	2	......	1	......	42	3	39	5	1	12	22	11	......	45
	Males	1	......	1	1	......	......	......	17	2	16	2	1	6	13	......	......	19
	Females	3	2	4	1	......	1	......	25	1	23	3	......	6	9	11	......	26
Orange	Total	14	12	12	2	1	......	......	189	8	195	......	2	79	80	36	2	197
	Males	6	5	7	2	1	......	......	83	5	87	......	1	42	32	13	1	88
	Females	8	7	5	......	......	......	......	106	3	108	......	1	37	48	23	1	109
Owen	Total	11	16	12	3	3	......	......	158	1	156	2	1	58	63	37	1	159
	Males	6	9	7	1	1	......	......	74	......	71	2	1	29	33	12	......	74
	Females	*5	7	5	2	2	......	......	84	1	85	......	......	29	30	25	1	85
Parke	Total	24	17	14	5	2	......	......	252	3	240	15	......	120	90	45	......	255
	Males	13	9	6	4	2	......	......	127	3	120	10	......	64	48	18	......	130
	Females	11	8	8	1	......	......	......	125	......	120	5	......	56	42	27	......	125
Perry	Total	18	18	9	6	1	......	1	214	4	189	29	......	98	82	38	......	218
	Males	10	9	6	2	1	......	......	104	2	88	18	......	50	42	14	......	106
	Females	8	9	3	4	......	......	1	110	2	101	11	......	48	40	24	......	112

§ One Indian.

TABLE No. 3—Continued.

COUNTIES.	SEX.	70 to 74	75 to 79	80 to 84	85 to 89	90 to 94	95 and Over.	Unknown.	White.	Colored.	American.	Foreign.	Not Reported.	Single.	Married.	Widowed or Divorced.	Not Reported.	Total.
Pike	Total	14	14	9	5	3	1		278		276	2		135	101	42		278
	Males	5	8	6	1	1	1		142		140	2		78	50	14		142
	Females	9	6	3	4	2			136		136			57	51	28		136
Porter	Total	27	27	21	6	3	2		266		193	71	2	92	107	64	3	266
	Males	17	13	12	2	1	1		147		107	38	2	59	55	30	3	147
	Females	10	14	9	4	2	1		119		86	33		33	52	34		119
Posey	Total	23	12	18	6	1			260	24	257	22	5	119	108	56	1	284
	M.	12	5	12	3	1			133	10	122	17	4	54	64	25		143
	Females	11	7	6	3				127	14	135	5	1	65	44	31	1	141
Pulaski	Total	12	13	6	6	1			145		115	28	2	55	62	28		145
	Mes	6	9	2	5	1			72		56	15	1	34	27	11		72
	Females	6	4	4	1				73		59	13	1	21	35	17		73
Putnam	Total	19	29	12	8	5	1		243	8	247	4		81	114	54	2	251
	Males	11	11	6	4		1		121	3	121	3		44	65	13	2	124
	Females	8	18	6	4	5			122	5	126	1		37	49	41		127
Randolph	Total	30	34	23	12	3			369	2	358	10	3	119	166	85	1	371
	Males	11	17	12	6	2			181		175	3	3	69	76	35	1	181
	Females	19	17	11	6	1			188	2	183	7		50	90	50		190
Ripley	Total	19	17	27	13	3	1		248		193	52	3	89	96	61	2	248
	Males	10	10	16	9	1			131		113	28		48	57	25	1	131
	Females	9	7	11	4	2	1		117		90	24	3	41	39	36	1	117
Rush	Total	22	23	15	9	5			228	6	227	7		74	99	61		234
	Males	13	12	6	6	1			117	2	115	4		42	56	21		119
	Females	9	11	9	3	4			111	4	112	3		32	43	40		115
Scott	Total	14	9	11	4	1	1		119		115	4		49	43	27		119
	Males	7	5	8	3				65		63	2		24	29	12		65
	Females	7	4	3	1	1	1		54		52	2		25	14	15		54

Shelby	Total	26	31	25	11	4	.....	.....	332	10	325	16	1	127	142	72	1	342
	Males	16	15	12	6	1	.....	.....	172	1	165	7	1	68	77	27	1	173
	Females	10	16	13	5	3	.....	.....	160	9	160	9	.....	59	65	45	.....	169
Spencer	Total	25	23	18	7	2	.....	.....	252	14	242	23	1	101	107	58	.....	266
	Males	11	10	8	4	2	.....	.....	118	6	113	10	1	47	57	20	.....	124
	Females	14	13	10	3	.....	.....	.....	134	8	129	13	.....	54	50	38	.....	142
Starke	Total	13	12	6	2	.....	.....	.....	128	.....	105	23	.....	56	45	27	.....	128
	Males	7	5	6	.....	.....	.....	.....	72	.....	55	17	.....	34	26	12	.....	72
	Females	6	7	.....	2	.....	.....	.....	56	.....	50	6	.....	22	19	15	.....	56
Steuben	Total	18	26	5	6	3	.....	.....	160	.....	151	9	.....	56	60	43	1	160
	Males	11	14	3	5	2	.....	.....	89	.....	83	6	.....	32	42	14	1	89
	Females	7	12	2	1	1	.....	.....	71	.....	68	3	.....	24	18	29	.....	71
St. Joseph	Total	69	79	45	27	8	1	1	1,118	22	880	251§	10	531	397	206	7	1,141
	Males	39	38	25	12	3	.....	1	614	16	482	139	9	289	241	94	6	630
	Females	30	41	20	15	5	1	.....	504	6	398	112§	1	242	156	112	1	511
Sullivan	Total	25	25	16	11	6	1	2	383	4	361	22	4	184	132	69	2	387
	Males	14	13	9	3	6	1	2	216	1	197	17	3	98	84	33	2	217
	Females	11	12	7	8	.....	.....	.....	167	3	164	5	1	86	48	36	.....	170
Switzerland	Total	20	20	8	4	.....	2	.....	134	3	133	4	.....	34	74	29	.....	137
	Males	9	12	4	3	.....	2	.....	70	2	72	.....	.....	19	40	13	.....	72
	Females	11	8	4	1	.....	.....	.....	64	1	61	4	.....	15	34	16	.....	65
Tippecanoe	Total	72	76	30	13	4	1	1	578	10	488	92	8	173	232	179	4	588
	Males	41	37	15	4	3	.....	1	308	7	263	47	5	113	132	66	4	315
	Females	31	39	15	9	1	1	.....	270	3	225	45	3	60	100	113	.....	273
Tipton	Total	15	7	7	4	2	.....	.....	207	.....	200	5	2	82	98	27	.....	207
	Males	5	5	6	2	2	.....	.....	126	.....	120	4	2	55	59	12	.....	126
	Females	10	2	1	2	.....	.....	.....	81	.....	80	1	.....	27	39	15	.....	81
Union	Total	12	6	11	4	.....	.....	.....	84	1	80	5	.....	37	30	18	.....	85
	Males	5	3	7	2	.....	.....	.....	40	1	40	1	.....	17	18	6	.....	41
	Females	7	3	4	2	.....	.....	.....	44	.....	40	4	.....	20	12	12	.....	44
Vanderburgh	Total	73	53	38	17	7	2	1	1,049	134	977	192	14	479	442	254	8	1,183
	Males	45	26	21	7	2	.....	1	567	70	522	103	12	281	247	101	8	637
	Females	28	27	17	10	5	2	.....	482	64	455	89	2	198	195	153	.....	546
Vermillion	Total	22	10	11	1	.....	.....	.....	252	3	237	14	4	130	84	39	2	255
	Males	12	7	5	.....	.....	.....	.....	134	2	125	9	2	74	46	14	2	136
	Females	10	3	6	1	.....	.....	.....	118	1	112	5	2	56	38	25	.....	119

§ One Indian.

TABLE No. 3—Continued.

COUNTIES.	SEX.	70 to 74	75 to 79	80 to 84	85 to 89	90 to 94	95 and Over.	Unknown.	White.	Colored.	American.	Foreign.	Not Reported.	Single.	Married.	Widowed or Divorced.	Not Reported.	Total.
Vigo	Total	78	59	48	22	6	2	1	1,231	78	1,132	156	21	579	460	252	18	1,309
	Males	38	31	17	12	3	......	1	672	39	612	84	15	341	262	92	16	711
	Females	40	28	31	10	3	2	......	559	39	520	72	6	238	198	160	2	598
Wabash	Total	32	28	28	6	3	2	......	330	5	308	25	2	104	152	79	......	335
	Males	14	16	14	4	1	......	......	170	3	158	14	1	59	87	27	......	173
	Females	18	12	14	2	2	2	......	160	2	150	11	1	45	65	52	......	162
Warren	Total	16	9	12	......	......	......	......	136	......	127	9	......	48	67	21	......	136
	Males	9	4	7	......	......	......	......	75	......	72	3	......	35	33	7	......	75
	Females	7	5	5	......	......	......	......	61	......	55	6	......	13	34	14	......	61
Warrick	Total	19	17	6	6	2	......	......	270	4	256	18	......	123	103	48	......	274
	Males	12	9	2	3	2	......	......	136	3	129	10	......	66	58	15	......	139
	Females	7	8	4	3	......	......	......	134	1	127	8	......	57	45	33	......	135
Washington	Total	16	12	18	10	3	1	......	223	......	220	3	......	87	83	53	......	223
	Males	10	7	12	5	1	1	......	103	......	102	1	......	42	36	25	......	103
	Females	6	5	6	5	2	......	......	120	......	118	2	......	45	47	28	......	120
Wayne	Total	60	54	51	18	8	2	1	636	34	600	61	9	209	287	166	8	670
	Males	25	25	22	9	2	2	1	327	21	306	36	6	127	155	60	6	348
	Females	35	29	29	9	6	......	......	309	13	294	25	3	82	132	106	2	322
Wells	Total	17	26	21	11	1	4	......	294	......	283	8	3	104	134	54	2	294
	Males	12	13	12	4	......	2	......	158	......	152	3	3	63	67	27	1	158
	Females	5	13	9	7	1	2	......	136	......	131	5	......	41	67	27	1	136
White	Total	21	21	10	4	......	2	......	167	......	156	10	1	54	74	38	1	167
	Males	14	13	5	3	......	2	......	93	......	86	6	1	34	42	16	1	93
	Females	7	8	5	1	......	......	......	74	......	70	4	......	20	32	22	......	74

Whitley	Total	32	20	6	10	1	......	......	190	......	175	15	......	58	87	45	......	190
	Males	16	13	4	5	......	......	......	94	......	84	10	......	26	55	13	......	94
	Females	16	7	2	5	1	......	......	96	......	91	5	......	32	32	32	......	96
Total males		1,510	1,437	1,013	463	137	34	29	18,529	760	16,785	2,234¶	273	8,255	7,829	3,013	195	19,292
Total females		1,289	1,256	916	458	170	47	3	16,584	634	15,545	1,571‖	105	6,202	6,323	4,670	26	17,221
Grand total		2,799	2,693	1,929	921	307	81	32	35,113	1,394	32,330	3,805⊚	378	14,457	14,158	7,683	221	36,513

¶ One Japanese and two Chinese.

‖ One Chinese and two Indians.

⊚ One Japanese, three Chinese and two Indians.

TABLE No. 4.

Deaths in Indiana by Counties for the Year 1910.

STATE AND COUNTIES	Population According to U. S. Census, 1910.	Total Deaths Reported for Year 1910. (Still-births Excluded.)	Annual Death Rate Per 1,000 Population.	IMPORTANT AGES. Under 1 Year.	1 to 4 Inclusive.	5 to 9 Inclusive.	10 to 14 Inclusive.	15 to 19 Inclusive.	65 Years and Over.	DEATHS FROM IMPORTANT CAUSES. Pulmonary Tuberculosis.	Other Forms of Tuberculosis.	Typhoid Fever.	Diphtheria.	Croup.	Scarlet Fever.	Measles.	Whooping Cough.	Lobar and Broncho-Pneumonia.	Diarrhea and Enteritis. (Under 2 Years.)	Cerebro-Spinal Fever.	Poliomyelitis.	Influenza.	Puerperal Septicemia.	Cancer.	Violence.	Smallpox.
State of Indiana	2,700,876	36,513	13.5	6,048	2,642	778	587	1,052	11,274	3,853	857	934	360	21	205	462	459	2,740	2,049	22	53	701	229	1,872	2,690	1
Northern Counties	927,229	11,980	12.9	2,057	794	272	203	351	3,889	1,051	238	293	100	4	118	113	87	865	728	9	35	176	83	677	998	..
Adams	21,840	210	9.6	31	13	7	4	8	67	28	6	10	2	....	2	1	2	14	6	....	2	3	....	14	12	..
Allen	93,386	1,119	11.9	161	68	29	31	46	317	101	25	23	14	....	17	15	....	105	47	....	1	8	4	83	97	..
Benton	12,688	105	8.2	22	11	....	4	2	36	5	..	2	....	....	1	1	1	7	5	....	2	3	....	6	4	..
Blackford	15,820	196	12.3	35	23	9	3	2	59	21	6	4	1	....	1	7	1	8	9	....	....	6	....	9	17	..
Carroll	17,970	240	13.3	32	16	7	5	8	101	19	5	5	2	....	2	1	1	12	15	....	1	5	1	14	23	..
Cass	36,368	574	15.7	63	27	10	14	19	180	47	13	12	6	....	11	3	5	39	22	....	6	3	7	34	44	..
Dekalb	25,054	329	13.1	56	19	6	5	10	113	24	9	12	3	....	....	1	....	14	20	1	1	4	2	20	24	..
Elkhart	49,008	672	13.7	90	33	11	8	22	236	55	11	18	5	1	1	1	3	49	22	1	1	4	4	43	45	..
Fulton	16,879	232	13.7	36	13	5	5	5	90	21	3	4	1	....	1	3	4	13	7	....	....	14	1	16	15	..
Grant	51,426	792	15.4	108	46	15	12	22	322	86	11	15	7	....	3	13	2	56	29	....	4	9	7	38	39	1
Howard	33,177	431	12.9	89	33	11	7	19	127	45	16	15	4	....	6	3	13	34	22	....	....	6	3	28	32	..
Huntington	28,982	356	12.2	44	19	7	5	8	144	38	10	7	....	....	5	6	1	25	8	....	1	5	2	19	20	..
Jasper	13,044	120	9.2	17	8	1	2	4	48	8	1	2	2	....	2	2	....	10	10	....	....	2	1	11	5	..
Jay	24,961	325	13.0	51	25	12	9	14	105	35	12	13	5	....	2	6	5	20	17	1	1	5	....	13	25	..
Kosciusko	27,936	348	12.4	35	24	9	4	11	151	20	6	4	2	....	1	3	2	16	9	1	2	10	4	29	29	..
Lagrange	15,148	199	13.1	27	6	5	4	5	76	11	4	2	1	....	3	4	1	14	3	....	....	4	2	14	11	..
Lake	82,864	1,208	14.5	373	129	30	20	28	148	76	17	40	13	1	17	10	13	132	213	....	....	5	10	32	215	..
Laporte	45,797	644	14.0	123	31	15	7	20	225	47	13	14	6	....	7	7	7	53	38	2	1	5	1	43	54	..
Marshall	24,175	308	12.7	55	22	6	6	7	106	26	7	8	3	....	4	1	....	20	16	....	1	12	2	20	17	..

Miami	29,330	370	12.6	44	18	6	4	10	142	37	4	13	...	...	4	1	7	28	12	...	1	8	...	19	28
Newton	10,504	109	10.3	26	7	1	3	4	38	7	1	3	1	...	...	4	...	10	12	...	...	1	...	6	7
Noble	24,009	267	11.1	33	13	...	...	5	125	21	2	4	...	...	1	1	...	13	5	...	1	7	1	25	16
Porter	20,540	266	12.9	26	17	7	5	10	103	18	5	4	7	...	9	1	1	21	9	...	...	6	...	24	23
Pulaski	13,312	145	10.8	23	12	1	6	4	50	13	2	7	1	...	1	2	1	10	5	...	1	3	...	7	9
Starke	10,567	128	12.1	24	13	6	...	2	41	13	2	2	2	...	2	1	1	5	11	...	1	3	...	9	11
Steuben	14,274	160	11.2	24	9	4	...	6	71	10	6	3	1	...	1	...	1	6	6	1	3	2	1	10	6
St. Joseph	84,312	1,141	13.5	264	90	31	15	21	287	118	23	17	7	1	9	...	9	71	112	2	2	12	21	42	91
Wabash	26,926	335	12.4	50	14	7	7	8	122	27	7	7	3	1	1	2	...	20	18	...	...	9	5	20	15
Wells	22,418	294	13.1	36	17	5	4	13	102	33	4	13	...	...	1	6	1	14	9	...	...	6	3	11	45
White	17,602	167	9.4	28	7	5	3	4	67	25	3	6	...	...	1	2	1	11	6	...	1	6	1	8	6
Whitley	16,892	190	11.3	31	11	4	1	4	90	16	4	4	1	...	2	5	4	15	5	...	1	...	...	10	13
Central [illegible]	1,114,087	15,577	13.9	2,414	1,062	301	234	441	4,755	1,640	396	349	135	5	69	226	205	1,139	768	7	12	306	96	803	1,121
Bartholomew	24,813	329	13.2	50	23	6	5	11	100	47	13	12	...	...	...	11	4	20	16	...	1	5	...	18	14
Boone	24,673	286	11.5	41	17	5	3	9	112	35	10	7	1	...	...	2	2	14	14	...	...	5	1	21	11
Brown	7,975	134	16.8	23	13	3	1	7	48	10	4	7	1	...	1	5	2	15	5	1	...	5	...	1	9
Clay	32,535	403	12.4	69	34	12	9	13	113	45	8	6	4	1	4	5	14	21	23	...	1	13	3	11	30
Clinton	26,674	303	11.3	46	14	6	7	12	115	34	6	6	2	...	3	1	2	21	14	...	2	8	...	20	16
Decatur	18,793	250	13.3	30	13	2	4	7	109	33	3	6	2	...	...	1	2	15	10	...	...	6	1	14	15
Delaware	51,414	625	12.1	112	41	18	15	28	180	71	20	15	8	...	3	10	1	41	27	1	1	5	4	34	54
Fayette	14,415	190	13.2	45	11	4	2	1	51	11	5	2	2	...	...	...	4	6	21	...	...	5	...	15	10
Fountain	20,439	275	13.4	38	24	5	5	7	95	30	5	12	2	...	...	4	5	14	9	...	2	7	3	11	26
Franklin	15,335	193	12.5	25	9	3	2	4	84	21	7	5	2	...	...	1	1	21	10	...	...	4	1	15	10
Hamilton	27,026	361	13.3	47	24	7	2	14	130	33	8	15	5	...	4	7	3	13	20	...	...	12	1	18	19
Hancock	19,030	252	13.2	30	11	7	6	9	84	32	4	8	2	...	1	4	4	11	13	...	...	8	2	13	18
Hendricks	20,840	266	12.7	36	13	4	4	10	124	25	4	10	1	...	...	5	2	15	13	...	...	7	...	12	15
Henry	29,758	427	14.3	71	33	8	4	13	159	36	9	7	5	...	2	8	6	25	31	1	...	5	6	15	36
Johnson	20,394	287	14.0	48	30	8	5	9	94	27	8	8	2	...	3	4	8	27	15	1	...	6	2	5	14
Madison	65,224	866	13.2	178	72	24	20	25	206	85	20	27	15	2	3	28	3	77	63	1	...	19	11	32	56
Marion	263,661	4,239	16.0	631	256	72	40	116	1,021	449	129	74	17	...	11	48	66	243	193	1	1	73	26	199	310
Monroe	23,426	334	14.2	60	36	8	8	7	105	35	6	10	...	...	4	9	13	35	12	...	...	6	2	24	23
Montgomery	29,296	383	13.0	48	23	2	8	7	148	38	9	6	...	...	...	6	2	29	14	...	...	9	3	83	20
Morgan	21,182	312	14.7	44	21	3	5	5	105	36	9	9	...	...	...	1	7	21	12	...	...	8	3	16	23
Owen	14,063	159	11.3	26	11	1	6	3	57	23	6	2	...	...	1	1	2	9	4	...	...	2	...	9	6
Parke	22,214	255	11.4	46	28	8	4	9	77	21	3	6	7	1	1	4	1	17	17	1	...	5	2	12	28
Putnam	20,520	251	12.2	30	20	6	3	5	92	31	9	1	2	...	...	8	7	27	6	...	...	5	1	16	16
Randolph	29,013	371	12.7	53	21	6	6	11	139	36	15	6	2	...	...	8	3	30	9	...	...	2	4	28	23
Rush	19,349	234	12.1	39	10	4	2	3	92	25	7	4	1	...	...	...	...	13	12	...	...	7	...	18	23

TABLE No. 4—Continued.

STATE AND COUNTIES.	Population According to U. S. Census, 1910.	Total Deaths Reported for Year 1910. (Still-births Excluded.)	Annual Death Rate Per 1,000 Population.	Important Ages. Under 1 Year.	1 to 4 Inclusive.	5 to 9 Inclusive.	10 to 14 Inclusive.	15 to 19 Inclusive.	65 Years and Over.	Deaths from Important Causes. Pulmonary Tuberculosis.	Other Forms of Tuberculosis.	Typhoid Fever.	Diphtheria.	Croup.	Scarlet Fever.	Measles.	Whooping Cough.	Lobar and Broncho-Pneumonia.	Diarrhea and Enteritis. (Under 2 Years.)	Cerebro-Spinal Fever.	Poliomyelitis.	Influenza.	Puerperal Septicemia.	Cancer.	Violence.	Smallpox.
Shelby	26,802	342	12.7	47	24	5	6	9	125	53	5	9	2	1	1	4	1	25	14	....	...	8	3	11	19	..
Tippecanoe	40,063	588	14 6	64	17	7	3	11	241	51	7	12	3	....	....	5	2	38	20	....	2	11	3	41	48	..
Tipton	17,459	207	18.8	43	14	2	5	4	54	20	2	4	1	....	5	5	2	9	11	....	....	1	2	13	19	..
Union	6,260	85	13.5	15	7	1	3	1	39	5	4	1	1	....	1	....	1	3	2	....	....	6	....	4	6	..
Vermillion	18,865	255	13.5	73	18	7	5	7	58	22	5	5	3	....	2	3	7	19	24	....	1	4	1	11	24	..
Vigo	87,930	1,309	14.8	219	128	33	23	41	299	125	30	37	29	....	14	21	23	103	91	....	1	16	10	67	131	..
Warren	10,899	136	12.4	25	6	2	4	4	49	11	3	2	....	....	....	1	2	6	7	....	....	2	....	6	12	..
Wayne	43,757	670	15.3	62	30	12	9	19	250	84	13	8	13	....	5	6	3	56	16	....	....	21	1	38	47	..
Southern Counties	659,560	8,956	13.5	1,577	796	205	150	260	2,630	1,162	223	292	125	12	18	123	167	736	553	6	6	219	50	392	571	..
Clark	30,260	495	16 3	86	32	...	9	19	156	44	31	13	2	1	...	9	10	40	30	....	....	12	1	25	31	..
Crawford	12,057	151	12 5	23	12	2	5	6	47	36	6	8	1	....	....	1	4	8	5	....	....	8	....	4	4	..
Daviess	27,747	337	12 1	51	32	14	9	10	87	51	10	7	10	....	4	2	9	27	18	....	....	5	....	14	20	..
Dearborn	21,396	277	12 9	22	14	4	4	7	110	35	6	6	1	1	....	2	4	32	7	....	....	5	1	14	29	..
Dubois	19,843	191	9.6	34	17	5	4	7	40	39	3	11	2	....	....	....	7	22	11	....	1	4	....	4	12	..
Floyd	30,293	516	17.0	62	35	15	4	12	194	90	17	5	13	2	1	8	6	26	24	....	....	15	2	30	20	..
Gibson	30,137	402	13.3	67	42	15	9	15	111	52	10	19	7	....	3	8	....	26	27	2	....	11	4	15	24	..
Greene	36,873	469	12.7	110	57	14	14	15	108	52	9	15	14	....	2	16	11	45	46	....	1	13	3	9	37	..
Harrison	20,232	229	11.3	35	12	10	4	9	80	26	3	12	2	....	1	3	1	12	5	....	....	4	1	15	16	..
Jackson	24,727	350	14.1	73	26	8	5	10	116	49	4	21	4	3	1	3	10	27	20	....	....	7	1	17	20	..
Jefferson	20,483	358	17.8	54	16	7	8	8	144	33	12	6	2	....	....	3	11	29	15	....	2	4	....	18	25	..
Jennings	14,203	182	12.8	31	14	6	3	3	68	20	2	1	1	....	....	6	2	14	14	....	....	6	....	9	12	..
Knox	39,183	585	14.9	133	79	22	4	19	122	73	4	16	19	1	2	11	16	50	50	....	1	11	4	22	44	..
Lawrence	30,625	410	13.3	74	57	10	8	12	102	58	22	22	2	....	1	11	9	32	33	....	....	9	3	10	23	..
Martin	12,950	145	11.1	29	16	1	2	3	39	24	5	8	3	....	....	....	4	7	11	....	....	6	1	6	8	..

Ohio	4,329	45	10.3	3	1	1	....	1	24	5	....	....	....	....	....	....	....	3	2	....	....	1	....	6	3	..
Orange	17,192	197	11.4	41	8	4	3	11	57	30	7	8	3	....	....	1	5	11	9	....	....	7	2	8	10	..
Perry	18,078	218	12.0	47	21	8	4	4	65	25	7	6	6	3	....	....	5	23	12	....	1	5	3	5	12	..
Pike	19,684	278	14.1	65	29	9	4	9	65	39	12	14	9	....	....	....	8	18	22	2	....	11	2	10	15	..
Posey	21,670	284	13.1	47	30	5	6	10	82	41	5	7	4	....	1	8	....	27	20	....	....	11	2	13	16	..
Ripley	19,452	248	12.7	35	24	3	4	3	98	32	4	8	1	....	....	2	2	29	12	1	....	6	3	7	12	..
Scott	8,323	119	14.3	15	13	2	3	4	43	12	....	4	2	....	....	....	1	10	5	....	....	4	....	5	11	..
Spencer	20,676	266	12.8	43	22	3	2	7	96	33	4	11	2	....	....	1	....	26	17	....	....	7	2	8	13	..
Sullivan	32,439	387	11.9	96	38	11	5	8	105	40	9	10	4	....	....	4	17	22	38	....	....	12	1	18	45	..
Switzerland	9,914	137	13.8	16	12	....	2	1	67	12	2	1	1	....	....	....	5	8	4	....	....	4	1	7	5	..
Vanderburgh	77,438	1,183	15.2	198	78	16	14	38	268	145	16	31	6	1	2	11	8	112	71	1	....	17	10	71	88	..
Warrick	21,911	274	12.5	48	37	7	7	6	67	29	8	15	4	....	....	5	10	34	18	....	....	11	2	10	8	..
Washington	17,445	223	12.7	39	22	3	4	3	69	37	5	7	....	....	....	8	2	16	7	....	....	3	2	12	8	..

TABLE No. 5.

Death Rate by Counties for the Year 1910.

STATE AND COUNTIES.	Population According to U. S. Census 1910.	Total Deaths Reported for 1910. (Stillbirths Excluded).	Annual Death Rate Per 1,000 Population.	Deaths from Important Causes per 100,000 Population. Pulmonary Tuberculosis.	Other Forms of Tuberculosis.	Typhoid Fever.	Diphtheria.	Croup.	Scarlet Fever.	Measles.	Whooping Cough.	Lobar and Broncho-Pneumonia.	Diarrhea and Enteritis. (Under 2 Years.)	Cerebro-Spinal Fever.	Poliomyelitis.	Influenza.	Puerperal Septicemia.	Cancer.	Violence.	Smallpox.
State of Indiana	2,700,876	36,513	13.5	142.7	31 7	34.5	13.3	.7	7.5	17.1	17.0	101.5	75.8	.8	1.9	25.9	8.4	69.3	99.6	.03
Northern Counties	97 ,29	11,90	29.	34 .	36	36	107.	.4	12.7	12.1	9.3	93.2	78.5	.9	3.7	18.9	8.9	73.0	107.6	....
Adams	21,840	210	9.6	128.2	27.4	45.7	9 1	....	9.1	4.5	9.1	64.0	27.4	....	9.1	13.7	....	64.0	54.9	....
Allen	93,386	1,119	11.9	108.1	26 7	24 6	14 9	....	18.2	16.0	....	112.4	50.3	....	1.0	8.5	4.2	88.8	103.9	....
Benton	12,688	105	8.2	39.4	....	15.7	....	....	7.8	7.8	7.8	55.1	39.4	....	15.7	23.6	....	47.2	31.5	....
Blackford	15,820	196	12.3	132.8	37 9	25.2	6 3	....	6.3	44.2	6.3	50.5	56.8	....	....	37.9	....	56.8	107.4	....
Carroll	17,970	240	13.3	105.7	27.8	27.8	11 1	....	11.1	5.5	5.5	66.7	83.4	....	5.5	27.8	5.5	77.9	128.0	....
Cass	36,368	574	15.7	129.2	34.1	33 0	16.5	....	30.2	8.2	13.7	107.2	60.4	....	16.5	8.2	19.2	93.5	121.0	....
Dekalb	25,054	329	13.1	95.8	35 9	47.9	11.9	....	....	3.9	....	55.8	79 8	3.9	3.9	15.9	7.9	79.8	95.8	....
Elkhart	49,008	672	13.7	112.2	22.4	36.7	10 2	2.0	2.0	2.0	6.1	99.9	44.8	2.0	2.0	8.1	8.1	87.7	91.8	....
Fulton	16,879	232	13.7	124.4	17 7	23.7	5.9	....	5.9	17.7	23.7	77.0	41.4	....	....	82.9	5.9	94.7	88.8	....
Grant	51,426	792	15.4	167.2	21 3	29.1	13 6	....	5.8	25.2	3.8	108.9	59.3	....	7.7	17.5	13.6	73.9	75.8	1.9
Howard	33,177	431	12.9	135.6	48.2	45.2	12.0	....	18.0	9.0	39.1	102.5	66.3	....	....	18.0	9.0	84.4	96.4	....
Huntington	28,982	356	12.2	134.2	34 5	24.1	....	....	17.2	20.7	3.4	86.2	27.6	....	3.4	17.2	6.9	65.5	69.0	....
Jasper	13,044	120	9.2	61.3	7 7	15.3	15.3	....	15.3	15.3	....	77.6	77.6	....	....	15.3	7.7	84.3	38.3	....
Jay	24,961	325	13.0	140.3	48.0	52.0	20.0	....	8.0	24.0	20.0	80.1	68.1	4.0	4.0	20.0	....	52.0	100.2	....
Kosciusko	27,936	348	12.4	71.5	21 4	14 3	7.1	....	3.5	10.7	7.1	57.2	82.1	3.5	7.1	35.7	14.3	103.7	103.7	....
Lagrange	15,148	199	13.1	72.6	26 4	13 2	6 6	....	19.8	26.4	6.6	92.4	19.8	....	....	26.4	13.2	92.4	72.6	....
Lake	82,864	1,208	14.5	91.7	20 5	48 2	15.6	1.2	20.5	12.0	15.6	159.3	257.1	....	....	6.0	12.0	38.6	259.5	....
Laporte	45,797	644	14.0	102.6	38 3	30 5	13.1	....	15.2	15.2	15.2	115.7	82.9	4.3	2.1	10 9	2.1	93.9	117.9	....
Marshall	24,175	308	12 7	107 6	28 9	33 0	12 4	....	16.5	41 3	....	82 7	66.1	....	4.1	49.6	8 2	82.7	70.3	....

Miami	29,350	370	12.6	126.1	13.6	44.2			13.6	3.4	23.8	95.4	40.8		3.4	27.2		64.7	95.4	
Newton	10,504	109	10 3	66.6	9.5	27.9	95			38.1		95.2	114.3			9.5		57.1	66.6	
Noble	24,009	267	11 1	87.4	8.3	16.6			4.1	4.1		54.0	20.8		4.1	29.1	4.1	103.9	66.6	
Porter	20,540	266	12 9	87.6	24.3	19.4	34.0		43.8	4.8	48	102.2	43.8			29.2		116.9	112.0	
Pulaski	13,32	145	10 8	97.4	15.0	52.5	7.5		7.5	15.0	7.5	75.1	37.5		7.5	22.5		52.5	67.6	
Starke	10,67	128	12.1	123.0	18.9	18.9	18.9		18.9	9.4	9.4	47.3	104.1		9.4	28.4		85.1	104.1	
Steuben	14,24	160	11.2	70.0	42.0	21.0	7.0		7.0		7.0	42.0	42.0	7.0	21.0	14.0	7.0	70.0	42.0	
St. Joseph	84,312	1,141	13.5	140.0	27.2	20.1	8.3	1.1	10.6		10.6	84.2	132.8	2.3	2.3	14.2	24.3	49.8	106.0	
Wabash	26,926	335	12.4	100.2	25.9	25.9	11.1	3.7	3.7	7.4		74.2	66.8			26.5	18.5	74.2	55.6	
Wells	2818	294	13.1	147.3	17.8	58.0			4.4	26.7	4.4	62.4	40.1			26.7	13.3	49.0	200.8	
White	17,602	167	9.4	142.2	17.0	34.1			5.6	11.3	5.6	62.5	34.1		5.6	34.1	5.6	45.5	34.1	
Whitley	16,892	190	11.3	94.7	23.6	23.6	5.9		11.8	29.6	23.6	88.8	29.6		5.9			59.2	76.9	
Central Counties	1,114,087	15,577	13.9	83	35.	33.	12.1	.4	61	202	184	102.	689	.6	10	27.4	8.6	70.	100.6	
Bartholomew	24,813	329	13.2	189.5	52.4	48.3				44.3	16 1	80.6	64.4		4.0	20.1		72.5	56.4	
Boone	24,673	286	11.5	141.9	40.5	28.3	4.0			8.1	8.1	56.7	56.7			20.2	4.0	85.1	44.5	
Brown	7,975	134	16.8	125.4	50.1	87.7	12.5		12.5	62.7	25.0	188.1	62.7	12.5		62.7		12.5	112.8	
Clay	32,535	403	12.4	138.3	24.5	18.4	12.2	3.0	12.2	15.3	43.0	64.5	70.6		3.1	39.9	9.2	33.8	92.2	
Clinton	26,674	303	11.3	127.5	22.5	22.5	7.4		11.2	3.7	7.4	78.7	52.4		7.4	30.0		74.9	59.9	
Decatur	18,793	250	13.3	175.6	15.9	31.9	10.6			5.3	10.6	79.8	53.2			31.9	5.3	74.5	79.8	
Delaware	51,44	625	12.1	138.1	38.9	29.1	13.5		5.0	16.4	1.6	69.4	45.7	1.6	1.6	9.7	7.7	57.6	91.5	
Fayette	14,45	190	13.2	76.3	34.7	13.8	13.8				27.7	41.6	145.7			34.7		104.1	69.3	
Fountain	20,439	275	13.4	146.8	24.4	58.7	9.7			19.5	24.4	68.4	44.0		9.7	34.2	14.6	53.8	127.2	
Franklin	1835	193	12.5	137.0	45.6	32.6	13.0			6.5	6.5	137.0	65.2			26.0	6 5	97.8	65.2	
Hamilton	27,026	361	13.3	122.1	29.6	55.5	18.5		14.8	25.9	10.1	48.1	75.7			44.4	3.7	66.6	70.3	
Hancock	19,030	252	13.2	168.2	21.0	42.0	10.5		5 2	21.0	21.0	57.8	68.3			42.0	10.5	68.3	94.6	
Hendricks	20,840	266	12.7	120.0	19.2	47.9	4.7			24.0	9.5	71.9	62.3			33.5		57.5	71.9	
Henry	29,758	427	14.3	121.0	30.2	23.5	16.8		6.7	26.8	20.1	84.0	104.2	3.3		16.8	20.1	50.4	121.0	
Johnson	20,394	287	14.0	132.4	39.2	39.2	9.8		14.7	19.6	39.2	132.4	73.5	4.9		29.4	9.8	24.5	68.6	
Madison	65,224	866	13.2	130.3	30.6	41.4	23.0	3.0	4.5	42.9	4.5	118.1	96.5	1.5		29·1	16.8	49.0	85.8	
Marion	263,661	4,239	16.0	170.3	48.9	28.0	6.4		4.1	18.2	25.0	130.1	73.2	.3	.3	27.6	9.8	75.5	117.6	
Monroe	23,426	334	14.2	149.4	25.6	42.6			17.0	38.4	55.4	149.4	51.2			25.6	8.5	102.4	98.1	
Montgomery	29,296	383	13.0	129.8	30.7	20.4				20.4	6.8	99.C	47.8			30.7	10.2	112.7	68 2	
Morgan	21,182	312	14.7	170.0	42.4	42.4				4.7	33.0	99.1	56.6			37.7	14.1	75.5	108.6	
Owen	14,053	159	11.3	163.7	42.7	14.2			·7.1	7.1	14.2	64.0	28.4			14.2		28.4	42.7	
Parke	22,214	255	11.4	94.5	13.5	27.0	31.5	4.5	4.5	18.0	4.5	76.5	76.5	4.5		22.5	9.0	54.0	126.1	
Putnam	20,520	251	12.2	151.1	43.8	4.8	9.7			38.9	34.1	131.6	29.2			24.3	4.8	77.9	77.9	
Randolph	29,013	371	12.7	124.1	51.7	20.6	6.8			27.5	10.1	101.0	31.0			6.8	13.7	96.5	79.3	
Rush	19,349	234	12.1	129.2	36.1	20.6	5.1					67.1	62 0			36.1		98.0	67.1	

TABLE No. 5—Continued.

STATE AND COUNTIES.	Population According to U. S. Census 1910.	Total Deaths Reported for 1910. (Stillbirths Excluded.)	Annual Death Rate Per 1,000 Population.	Deaths from Important Causes per 100,000 Population.																
				Pulmonary Tuberculosis.	Other Forms of Tuberculosis.	Typhoid Fever.	Diphtheria.	Croup.	Scarlet Fever.	Measles.	Whooping Cough.	Lobar and Broncho-Pneumonia.	Diarrhea and Enteritis. (Under 2 Years.)	Cerebro-Spinal Fever.	Poliomyelitis.	Influenza.	Puerperal Septicemia.	Cancer.	Violence.	Smallpox.
Shelby	26,802	342	12.7	197.8	18.6	33.5	7.4	3.7	3.7	14.9	3.7	93.2	52.2	......	......	29.8	11.2	41.0	70.9	....
Tippecanoe	40,063	588	14 6	127.3	17 4	29.9	7.4	......	......	12.4	4.9	94.8	49.9	......	4.9	27.4	7.4	102.4	119.8	....
Tipton	17,459	207	18.8	114.6	11.4	22.9	5.7	......	28.6	28.6	11.4	51.5	63.0	......	......	57.2	11.4	74.4	108.9	....
Union	6,260	85	13.5	79.8	63.9	15.9	15.9	......	15.9	......	15.9	47.9	31.9	......	......	95.8	......	63.9	95.8	....
Vermillion	18,85	255	13.5	116.6	26.5	26.5	15.9	......	10.6	15.9	37.0	100.7	127.2	......	5.2	21.2	5.2	58.2	127.2	....
Vigo	87,80	1,309	14 8	142.2	34.1	42.0	32.9	......	15.9	23.8	26.1	117.1	101.1	......	1.1	18 2	11.3	76.2	145.6	....
Warren	10.89	136	12.4	100.9	27.5	18.3	......	......	......	9.1	18.3	55.0	64.2	......	......	18.3	......	55.0	110.1	....
Wayne	43,57	670	15.3	191.9	29.7	18.2	29.7	......	11.4	13.7	6.8	128.0	36.5	......	......	47.9	2.2	86.8	107.4	....
Southern Counties	69 ,50	8,956	13.5	61 .	38.	44.2	16.4	1.5	2.3	16.2	22.0	97.1	72.9	.7	.7	28.8	7.5	51.7	75.3	....
Clark	30,260	495	16.3	145.4	102.4	42.9	6.6	3.3	......	29.7	33.0	132.2	99.1	......	......	39.6	3.3	82.6	102.4	....
Crawford	12,057	151	12.5	298.5	49.7	67.8	8.2	......	......	8.2	33.1	67.8	41.4	......	......	67.8	......	33.1	33.1	....
Daviess	27,747	337	12 1	183.8	36.0	25.2	36.0	......	14.4	7.2	32.4	97.3	64.8	......	......	18.0	......	50.4	72.0	....
Dearborn	21,396	277	12.9	163.6	28.0	28.0	4.6	4.6	......	9.3	18.7	149.5	82.7	......	......	23.3	4.6	65.4	135.5	....
Dubois	19,843	191	9.6	196.6	15 1	55.4	10.0	......	......	......	35.2	110.9	55.4	......	5.0	20.1	......	20.1	60.4	....
Floyd	30,293	516	17.0	297 1	56.1	16.5	42.9	6.6	3.3	26.4	19.8	85.8	79.2	......	......	49.5	6.6	99.0	66.0	....
Gibson	30,137	402	13.3	172.5	33.1	63.0	23.2	......	9.9	26.5	......	86.2	89.6	6.6	......	36.5	13.2	49.7	79.6	....
Greene	36,873	469	12.7	141.0	24.4	40.6	37.9	......	5.4	43.3	29.8	122.0	124.8	......	2.7	35.2	8.1	24.4	100.3	....
Harrison	20,232	229	11.3	128.5	14.8	59.3	9.8	......	4.9	14.8	4.9	59.3	24.7	......	......	19.7	4.9	74.1	79.0	....
Jackson	24,727	350	14.1	193.6	16.1	84.9	16.1	12.1	4.0	12.1	40.4	109.2	80.8	......	......	28.3	4.0	68.7	80.8	....
Jefferson	20,483	38	17.8	61 .1	58.6	29.3	9.7	......	......	14.6	53.7	141.6	73.2	......	9.7	19.5	......	87.9	122.1	....
Jennings	14,203	82	12.8	40 .8	14.0	7.0	7.0	......	......	42.2	14.0	98.5	98.5	......	......	42 2	......	63.3	84.5	....
Knox	39,183	85	4. 9	83 .	10.2	40.8	48.5	2.5	5.1	28.0	40.8	127.6	127.6	......	2.5	28.0	10.2	56.1	112.3	....
Lawrence	30,625	40	13.3	89 .4	71.8	71.8	6.6	......	3.2	35.8	29.3	104.5	107.8	......	......	29.3	9.7	32.6	75.1	....
Martin	12,950	45	11.1	85 .3	38.6	61.7	23.1	......	......	......	30.8	54.0	84.9	......	......	46 3	7.7	46.3	61.7	....

NORTHERN SA

Total population ....
Total deaths........
Death rate per 1,000.
Pulmonary tubercul
100,000 ....
Typhoid, rate per 10
Diphtheria, rate per
Scarlet fever, rate pe
Diarrheal diseases, r

CENTRAL SAN

Total population....
Total deaths.......
Death rate per 1,000
Pulmonary tubercul
100,000 ....
Typhoid, rate per 1
Diphtheria, rate per
Scarlet fever, rate p
Diarrheal diseases, r

SOUTHERN
SECTIO

Total population...
Total deaths ......
Death rate per 1,000
Pulmonary tuberculo
per 100,000......
Typhoid, rate per 1
Diptheria, rate per
Scarlet fever, rate pe
Diarrheal diseases,
100,000..........

Ohio	4,329	45	10.3	115.5	......	......	......	......	......	......	......	69.3	46.2	......	......	23.1	......	138.6	69.3	....
Orange	17,192	197	11.4	174.5	40.7	46.5	17.4	......	......	5.8	29.0	63.9	52.3	......	......	40.7	11.6	46.5	58.1	....
Perry	18,078	218	12.0	138.3	38.7	33.1	33.1	16.5	......	......	27.6	127.2	66.0	......	5.5	27.6	16.5	27.6	66.0	....
Pike	19,684	278	14.1	198.2	60.9	71.1	45.7	......	......	......	40.6	91.4	111.8	10.1	......	55.9	10.1	50.8	76.2	....
Posey	21,670	284	13.1	189.2	23.0	32.8	18.4	......	4.6	36.9	......	124.6	92.2	......	......	50.7	9.2	59.9	73.8	....
Ripley	19,452	248	12.7	164.5	20.5	41.1	5.1	......	......	10.2	10.2	149.1	61.7	5.1	......	30.8	10.2	35.9	61.7	....
Scott	8,323	119	14.3	144.2	......	48.0	24.0	......	......	......	12.0	120.1	60.0	......	......	48.0	......	60.0	132.2	....
Spencer	20,676	266	12.8	159.6	19.3	53.1	9.6	......	......	4.8	......	125.7	82.1	......	......	33.8	9.6	38.6	62.8	....
Sullivan	32,439	387	11.9	123.3	27.7	30.8	12.3	......	......	12.3	52.4	67.8	117.1	......	......	36.9	3.0	55.4	138.7	....
Switzerland	9,914	137	13.8	121.0	20.1	10.0	10.0	......	......	......	50.4	80.6	40.3	......	......	40.3	10.0	70.6	50.4	....
Vanderburgh	77,438	1,183	15.2	187.3	20.6	40.0	7.7	1.2	2.5	14.2	10.1	144.6	91.7	1.2	......	21.9	12.9	91.7	113.6	....
Warrick	21,911	274	12.5	132.4	36.5	68.4	18.2	......	......	22.8	45.6	155.2	82.1	......	......	50.2	9.1	45.6	36.5	....
Washington	17.445	223	12.7	212.2	28.6	40.1	......	......	......	45.8	11.4	91.7	40.1	......	......	17.2	11.4	68.8	45.8	....

TABLE No. 6.

Deaths in Indiana, by Cities for Year 1910.

CITIES.	Population According to U. S. Census 1910.	Total Deaths Reported for the Year 1910. (Still-births excluded.)	Annual Death Rate Per 1,000 Population.	IMPORTANT AGES. Under 1 Year.	1 to 4 inclusive.	5 to 9 inclusive.	10 to 14 inclusive.	15 to 19 inclusive.	65 Years and Over.	DEATHS FROM IMPORTANT CAUSES PER 100,000 POPULATION. Pulmonary Tuberculosis.	Other Forms of Tuberculosis.	Typhoid Fever.	Diphtheria.	Croup.	Scarlet Fever.	Measles.	Whooping Cough.	Lobar and Broncho-Pneumonia.	Diarrhea and Enteritis. (Under 2 Years.)	Cerebro-Spinal Fever.	Poliomyelitis.	Influenza.	Puerperal Septicemia.	Cancer.	Violence.	Smallpox.
Cities of First Class. Pation 100,000 and over	233,650	3,831	16.4	564	235	*69	39	104	876	410	101	82	16	...	10	44	57	314	165	....	1	66	20	166	288	..
I pidlis	233,650	3,831	16.4	564	235	69	39	104	876	410	101	82	16	...	10	44	57	314	165	....	1	66	20	166	288	..
Cities of Sand Class. Ration 5,000 to 100,000	245,421	3,476	14.2	603	234	76	62	114	787	373	68	69	33	1	31	34	24	284	187	....	3	34	30	211	298	..
Evansville	69,647	938	13.4	172	59	14	10	37	191	123	12	23	4	...	....	9	7	86	61	....	....	14	9	60	75	..
Fort Wayne	63,933	831	13.0	93	36	22	27	33	231	79	23	17	9	...	12	11	....	77	48	....	1	5	3	65	74	..
Terre Haute	58,157	946	16.2	149	81	19	12	33	214	87	17	20	16	...	12	14	14	75	62	....	....	8	7	51	91	..
South Bend	53,684	761	14.1	189	58	21	13	11	151	84	16	9	4	1	7	....	3	46	156	....	2	7	11	35	58	..
Cities of Third Class. Population 20,000 to 45,000	130,440	2,026	15.5	328	127	60	33	58	598	244	41	48	35	1	13	31	14	156	122	....	1	32	10	111	182	..
Muncie	24,005	368	15.3	64	25	12	7	14	148	44	9	9	4	...	2	4	1	27	15	....	1	2	....	22	30	..
Anderson	22,476	330	14.6	60	26	9	11	10	62	31	4	13	6	...	....	14	....	30	27	....	....	....	6	9	31	..
Richmond	22,324	310	13.9	46	16	10	2	9	105	42	8	2	9	...	3	4	....	31	11	....	....	11	....	20	17	..
Hammond	20,925	307	14.6	74	23	12	6	8	34	22	7	11	2	...	7	1	7	34	30	....	....	2	2	13	61	..
New Albany	20,629	376	182	46	29	11	4	10	129	71	9	3	12	1	1	5	6	20	21	...	....	12	2	26	9	..
Lafayette	20,081	335	16 6	38	8	6	3	7	120	34	4	10	2	. .	....	3	...	14	18	.	....	5	.	21	34	..

Cities of Fourth Class. Population 10,000 to 20,000	209,566	3,240	15.4	713	268	66	40	100	846	283	69	94	34	...	26	41	44	285	285	1	4	30	30	161	346	..
Marion	19,359	243	12.5	51	21	7	2	12	109	28	5	8	3	...	....	4	....	20	15	....	1	5	3	15	21	..
Elkhart	19,282	268	13.9	31	12	5	6	8	82	15	4	3	1	...	....	1	1	25	3	....	....	2	4	18	21	..
East Chicago	19,098	293	15.3	133	49	7	1	5	15	16	4	5	2	...	6	7	1	56	70	....	....	1	....	3	77	..
Logansport	19,050	304	15.9	38	15	3	8	10	92	27	6	9	4	...	6	2	1	19	12	....	2	2	7	23	27	..
Michigan City	19,027	281	14.7	68	20	9	2	11	71	31	6	10	3	...	2	5	5	32	26	1	1	1	1	21	16	..
Kokomo	17,010	257	15.1	51	26	7	2	14	65	27	8	13	3	...	3	1	10	21	15	....	....	3	2	18	19	..
Gary	16,802	273	16.2	97	36	5	5	7	7	11	2	17	7	...	....	1	3	26	68	....	....	....	4	3	74	..
Vincennes	14,895	286	19.2	60	30	7	...	12	54	41	7	2	5	...	....	7	8	27	21	....	....	5	2	8	30	..
Mishawaka	11,886	138	11.6	30	13	7	1	1	33	6	2	2	2	...	1	....	6	11	8	....	....	2	4	5	8	..
Elwood	11,028	173	15.6	51	19	3	3	1	40	15	5	6	1	...	....	8	1	12	18	....	....	3	2	4	7	..
Peru	10,910	145	13.3	15	8	1	2	5	39	19	2	7	....	...	1	....	1	10	3	....	....	2	....	8	12	..
Laporte	10,525	188	17.8	32	4	3	2	6	70	8	5	3	2	...	5	1	1	7	5	....	....	....	....	15	18	..
Jeffersonville	10,412	200	19.2	40	11	....	3	7	57	22	9	7	1	...	....	3	6	13	15	....	....	2	....	11	13	..
Huntington	10,272	191	18.6	16	4	2	3	1	49	17	4	2	....	...	2	1	....	6	6	....	....	2	1	9	3	..
Cities of Fifth Class. Population under 10,000	328,210	4,755	14.4	788	356	103	74	122	1,554	561	124	108	48	1	25	56	64	326	280	3	5	102	29	265	321	1
Brazil	9,540	111	11.6	17	12	3	3	6	38	18	1	3	1	....	....	1	5	7	6	....	....	8	1	8	13	..
Shelbyville	9,500	129	13.5	14	10	3	1	4	47	20	3	1	1	1	1	....	....	12	3	....	....	5	1	7	9	..
Newcastle	9,446	141	14.9	32	21	4	1	1	30	8	5	5	3	....	....	3	4	9	18	1	....	1	4	6	14	..
Crawfordsville	9,371	141	15.0	19	6	....	3	2	54	17	3	1	....	....	....	....	....	9	5	....	....	5	....	13	6	..
Bloomington	8,838	165	18.6	28	17	7	4	3	51	14	3	5	....	....	3	4	7	18	7	....	....	3	1	9	11	..
Columbus	8,813	152	17.2	18	11	2	3	5	42	24	6	10	....	....	....	6	1	7	8	....	....	3	....	8	6	..
Bedford	8,716	138	15.8	20	25	4	2	2	30	15	4	6	2	....	1	7	....	11	13	....	....	2	1	2	8	..
Wabash	8,687	112	12.8	21	4	1	....	....	37	6	2	2	....	....	....	....	....	5	9	....	....	7	1	4	5	..
Frankfort	8,634	90	10.4	18	5	....	2	4	36	13	1	1	2	....	....	....	1	7	4	....	....	1	....	4	6	..
Goshen	8,514	113	13.2	18	5	1	1	3	50	7	1	2	....	....	....	....	....	7	1	1	....	....	....	5	8	..
Washington	7,854	101	12.8	10	10	1	....	....	16	21	2	1	2	....	1	1	....	8	3	....	....	2	....	7	9	..
Connersville	7,738	103	13.3	23	7	3	1	1	22	8	3	1	2	....	....	....	2	2	13	....	....	2	....	8	5	..
Valparaiso	6,987	89	12.7	8	3	2	1	2	36	9	1	1	1	....	4	....	....	13	2	....	....	2	....	11	6	..
Madison	6,934	145	20.9	17	9	1	6	4	59	14	7	2	1	....	....	....	4	11	5	....	....	2	....	11	11	..
Whiting	6,587	88	13.3	36	14	1	....	2	9	5	1	4	1	....	2	....	....	5	21	....	....	....	....	2	5	..
Princeton	6,448	104	16.1	10	10	4	1	5	27	17	1	4	....	....	2	1	....	12	4	....	....	....	1	5	7	..
Seymour	6,305	74	11.7	15	5	2	1	4	24	13	....	4	1	....	....	1	1	5	6	....	....	3	....	3	6	..
Clinton	6,229	86	13.8	39	7	3	2	1	9	8	1	1	2	....	1	1	2	6	17	....	1	1	....	1	8	..
Hartford City	6,187	94	15 2	15	14	5	1	1	30	10	2	1	....	....	....	4	....	4	3	....	....	2	....	4	8	..
Linton	5,906	85	14.3	30	12	7	1	1	10	5	....	....	7	....	1	2	5	12	13	....	....	3	1	1	5	..

TABLE No. 6—Continued.

CITIES.	Population According to U. S. Census, 1910.	Total Deaths Reported for the Year 1910. (Still-births excluded.)	Annual Death Rate Per 1,000 Population.	Important Ages.						Deaths from Important Causes per 100,000 Population.																
				Under 1 Year.	1 to 4 inclusive.	5 to 9 inclusive.	10 to 14 inclusive.	15 to 19 inclusive.	65 Years and Over.	Pulmonary Tuberculosis.	Other Forms of Tuberculosis.	Typhoid Fever.	Diphtheria.	Croup.	Scarlet Fever.	Measles.	Whooping Cough.	Lobar and Broncho-Pneumonia.	Diarrhea and Enteritis. (Under 2 Years.)	Cerebro-Spinal Fever.	Poliomyelitis.	Influenza.	Puerperal Septicemia.	Cancer.	Violence.	Smallpox.
Mt. Vernon	5,563	85	15.2	14	6		4	5	29	14	2	2				2		9	3			1		4	10	
Lebanon	5,474	91	16.6	16	2	1	1	3	44	12	2	1	1				1	4	5			1		5	5	
Greensburg	5,420	80	14.7	10	3	1	2	1	46	11	2	2				1		3	4			1		5	6	
Portland	5,130	84	16.3	9	6	6	1	5	22	11	2	2	2			1	2	8	5	1		2		2	9	
Alexandria	5,096	57	11.1	13	5	5	2		12	6	1	2	6				1	6					1	2	2	
Noblesville	5,073	64	12.6	11	3	3		6	15	4	1	2	3			2		2	5					6	3	
Bluffton	4,987	76	15.2	10	6	3	1	3	28	9	3	5				4		7	4			3	1	4	6	
Kendallville	4,981	47	9.4	8	2				16	3	1							5	3			1		4	4	
Rushville	4,925	80	16.2	14	2	1	1	2	36	7	3							4	2			2		6	4	
Martinsville	4,529	98	21.6	10	9		1	1	26	12	2	1				1	2	6	3			5	1	5	3	
Franklin	4,502	68	15.1	7	4	3	3	3	26	8	3		1		3	1		2	2			2	1	3		
Decatur	4,471	50	11.1	9	4	2	3		14	6	1	2					2	4	1		2	1		4	3	
Greenfield	4,448	61	13.7	8	4		1	2	19	13	1	1					2	2	5			3		3	3	
Warsaw	4,430	75	16.9	5	2	2	1	3	29	6	2	1	1				1	3				2	2	7	8	
Aurora	4,410	85	19.2	8	2	2	1	2	30	11	2	3	1				2	8	3					1	9	
Winchester	4,266	60	14.0	7	4				30	8	3					2		3	1			1		7	2	
Garrett	4,149	60	14.4	14	1		2	2	15	5	3	5						2	4					2	5	
Sullivan	4,115	58	14.1	17	2			1	21	8	2					2	1	2	6			1		5	7	
Tipton	4,075	47	11.5	12	4		1	1	12	7		1			1	2	1	3	2				2	4	4	
Boonville	3,934	58	14.7	4	12	1		1	13	7	3	1	1				4	5	5			3		3	3	
Lawrenceburg	3,930	56	14.2	3	2		2	3	18	7								11				2	1	4	9	
Auburn	3,919	38	9.6	7	2	3		2	18	5		5						1	4			3		5	4	
Plymouth	3,838	63	16.4	13	4	1	1	1	21	7	1		1		3			1	6		1	1		4	3	
Greencastle	3,790	51	13 4	5	3		1	3	16	9	6	1				2		2	2			1	1	3	1	
Columbia City	3,448	42	12.1	4	1	2		2	26	7	1		1		1			5	1					2	3	

Mitchell	3,438	61	17.7	15	8	1	...	3	16	10	9	...	...	...	...	...	3	3	4	...	...	...	2	1	3	...
Tell City	3,369	40	11.8	6	1	1	...	...	14	7	2	...	1	...	...	...	...	3	2	...	...	1	2	...	2	...
Rochester	3,364	53	15.7	8	3	...	1	...	24	7	1	1	...	...	...	...	2	...	2	...	...	1	...	3	1	...
Attica	3,335	34	10.2	12	1	...	...	1	16	5	1	1	...	...	...	...	1	4	2	...	...	1	1	2	3	...
Gas City	3,224	48	14.8	11	4	1	2	2	6	7	...	...	...	...	...	3	1	2	3	...	...	1	1	3	3	1
Union City	3,209	54	16.8	6	6	1	1	2	17	5	3	1	...	...	...	...	...	7	...	...	...	...	1	6	8	...
Dunkirk	3,031	35	11.5	9	4	1	2	1	12	7	3	1	...	...	...	...	...	1	1	...	...	1	...	2	5	...
North Vernon	2,915	36	12.3	7	...	3	...	1	11	4	...	...	...	...	...	...	...	3	3	...	...	1	...	...	1	...
Montpelier	2,786	33	11.8	10	4	1	1	...	7	5	1	...	...	...	1	2	1	2	3	...	...	1	...	...	...	...
Rockport	2,736	46	16.8	4	2	...	...	1	18	8	...	1	...	...	...	...	...	6	3	...	...	...	...	...	2	...
Angola	2,610	41	15.7	9	4	...	...	1	16	5	2	...	...	...	...	...	...	1	1	...	...	...	...	2	2	...
Huntingburg	2,464	31	12.5	5	...	1	...	2	6	4	...	2	...	...	...	...	3	3	...	...	1	1	...	2	5	...
Rensselaer	2,393	36	15.0	3	2	...	...	...	19	3	...	...	...	...	...	...	...	2	1	...	...	...	...	3	4	...
Ligonier	2,173	34	15.6	2	...	...	...	...	17	2	...	2	...	...	...	...	...	...	...	...	...	2	...	3	2	...
Monticello	2,168	19	8.7	3	...	...	...	...	10	4	...	...	...	...	...	...	...	1	2	...	...	1	...	1	...	...
Delphi	2,161	43	19.9	3	3	1	...	1	27	...	1	1	...	...	...	...	...	2	1	...	...	...	...	2	...	...
Loogootee	2,154	31	14.4	5	4	...	1	1	8	7	1	1	2	...	...	...	2	...	3	...	...	...	...	1	1	...
Cannelton	2,130	24	11.2	3	1	...	...	1	9	3	2	...	...	...	...	...	...	1	2	...	...	...	...	1	2	...
Covington	2,069	35	16.9	4	1	1	1	1	14	5	...	2	...	...	...	...	...	...	1	...	...	1	...	4	1	...
Butler City	1,818	33	18.1	8	2	...	1	1	10	2	1	...	1	...	...	...	...	3	5	...	...	...	...	2	...	...
Veedersburg	1,757	25	14.2	5	...	...	1	...	8	2	1	1	...	...	...	...	...	...	...	...	...	1	...	2	4	...
Rising Sun	1,513	29	19.1	3	1	1	...	...	17	3	...	...	...	...	...	...	...	3	2	...	...	1	...	3	...	...
Vevay	1,256	27	21.5	1	3	...	...	...	13	1	2	2	...	...	...	...	...	1	2	...	...	...	1	3	...	...
Total Urban Population	1,147,277	17,328	15.1	2,996	1,229	374	248	498	4,661	1,871	403	401	166	3	105	206	203	1,365	1,039	4	14	264	119	864	1,435	1
Total Rural Population	1,553,579	19,185	12.?	3,052	1,429	401	339	1,554	6,613	1,982	454	533	194	18	100	256	256	1,375	1,010	18	39	437	110	1,008	1,255	...

TABLE No. 7.

Death Rates by Cities for the Year 1910.

CITIES.	Population, According to U. S. Census, 1910.	Total Deaths Reported for the Year 1910. (Still-births Excluded.)	Annual Death Rate Per 1,000 Population.	Deaths from Important Causes pe 100,000 Population.																
				Pulmonary Tuberculosis.	Other Forms of Tuberculosis.	Typhoid Fever.	Diphtheria.	Croup.	Scarlet Fever.	Measles.	Whooping Cough.	Lobar and Broncho-Pneumonia.	Diarrhea and Enteritis. (Under 2 Years.)	Cerebro-Spinal Fever.	Poliomyelitis.	Influenza.	Puerperal Septicemia.	Cancer.	Violence.	Smallpox.
Cities of First Class. Population 100,000 and over.........	233,650	3,831	16.4	175.5	43.2	35.0	6.8	......	4.2	18.8	24.3	134.4	70.6	......	.4	28.2	8.5	71.0	123.2	......
Indianapolis........	233,650	3,831	16.4	175.5	43.2	35.0	6.8	......	4.2	18.8	24.3	134.4	70.6	......	.4	28.2	8.5	71.0	123.2	......
Cities of Second Class. Population 45,000 to 100,000.......	245,421	3,476	14.2	152.0	27.8	28.1	13.4	.4	12.6	13.8	9.7	115.7	76.1	......	1.2	13.8	12.2	85.9	121.4	......
Evansville..........	69,647	938	13.4	176.6	17.2	33.0	5.7	......	......	12.9	10.0	123.5	87.5	......	......	20.1	......	86.1	107.7	......
Fort Wayne.........	63,933	831	13.0	123.5	35.9	26.5	14.0	......	18.7	17.2	......	120.5	75.0	......	1.5	7.8	4.6	101.7	115.7	......
Terre Haute.........	58,157	946	16.2	149.6	29.2	34.3	27.5	......	20.6	24.0	24.0	129.0	106.6	......	......	13.7	12.1	87.7	156.5	......
South Bend.........	53,684	761	14.1	156.5	29.8	16.7	7.4	1.8	13.0	......	5.5	85.7	290.6	......	3.8	13.0	20.4	65.2	108.0	......
Cities of Third Class. Population 20,000 to 45,000.........	130,440	2,026	15.5	187.1	31.4	36.8	26.8	.7	9.9	23.7	10.7	119.6	93.5	......	.7	24.5	7.6	85.1	139.5	......
Muncie............	24,005	368	15.3	183.3	37.4	37.4	16.6	......	8.3	16.6	4.1	112.5	62.4	......	4.1	8.3	......	91.6	125.0	......
Anderson..........	22,476	330	14.6	137.9	17.8	57.8	26.7	......	......	62.2	......	133.5	120.1	......	......	......	26 7	40.0	137.9	......
Richmond..........	22,324	310	13.9	188.2	35.8	8.9	40.3	......	13.4	17.9	......	138.9	49.2	......	......	49.2	......	89.6	76.1	......
Hammond.........	20,925	307	14.6	105.1	33.4	52.5	9.5	......	33.4	4.7	33.4	162.5	143.4	......	......	9.5	9.5	63.1	291.5	......
New Albany........	20,629	376	18.2	344.2	43.6	14.5	58.1	4.8	4.8	24.2	29.0	96.9	101.8	......	......	58.1	9.6	126.0	43.6	......
Lafayette..........	20,081	335	16 6	169.3	19.9	49.8	9.9	......	......	14.6	......	69.7	89.6	......	......	24.9	......	104.6	169.3	......

Cities of Fourth Class Population 10,000 to 20,0.	69 ,56	3,240	54.	31 .	39.	42.	.	......	12.4	95.	21.0	135.8	38 .	.4	1.9	33.	.	58.	61 .	......
Marion............	19,39	33	12.5	144.6	25.8	41.3	15.5	......	......	20.6	......	103.3	77.4	......	5.1	25.8	15.5	77.4	108.5	......
Elkhart............	19,32	88	13.9	77.8	20.7	15.5	5.1	......	......	5.1	5.1	129.7	15.5	......	......	10.3	20.7	93.3	108.9	......
East Chicago.......	19,08	93	15.3	83.7	20.9	26.1	10.4	......	31.4	36.6	5.2	293.2	366.5	......	......	5.2	......	15.5	399.4	......
Logansport.........	19,60	64	15.9	141.7	31.5	47.2	21.0	......	31.5	10.5	5.2	99.7	63.0	......	10.5	10.5	36.7	120.7	141.7	......
Michigan City......	19,07	81	14.7	162.9	31.5	52.5	15.7	......	10.5	26.2	26.2	168.1	136.6	5.2	5.2	5.2	5.2	110.3	84.0	......
Kokomo............	17,00	87	51.	58 .7	47.0	76.4	17.6	......	76.	5.7	57.4	123.5	88.1	......	......	17.6	11.7	105.8	111.7	......
Gary...............	16,92	23	62.	65.4	11.9	101.2	41.6	......	......	5.9	17.8	154.8	404.8	......	......	......	23.8	17.8	440.5	......
Vincennes..........	14,95	26	92.	25 .2	46.9	13.4	33.5	......	......	46.9	53.6	181.2	140.9	......	......	33.5	13.4	53.6	201.3	......
Mishawaka..........	11,86	38	16.	50.4	16.8	16.8	16.8	......	8.4	......	50.4	92.5	67.2	......	......	16.8	33.6	42.0	67.2	......
Elwood............	11,08	73	56.	36 .0	45.3	54.5	9.0	......	......	25.	9.0	108.8	163.2	......	......	27.2	18.1	33.2	63.4	......
Peru..............	10,910	45	33.	74 .2	18.3	64.1	......	......	9.1	......	9.1	91.6	27.3	......	......	33.	......	73.3	110.0	......
Laporte............	10,525	88	78.	76.0	47.5	28.5	19.0	......	47.5	9.5	9.5	66.4	47.5	......	......	......	......	142.5	171.0	......
Jeffersonville......	10,412	90	92.	21 .4	86.5	67.2	9.6	......	......	28.8	57.6	122.1	147.5	......	......	19.2	......	101.0	122.1	......
Huntington	10,272	91	86.	65 .5	38.9	19.4	......	......	19.4	9.7	......	58.4	58.4	......	......	19.4	9.7	87.6	29.2	......
Cities of Fifth Class. Population under 10,000........	328,210	4,755	44.	70 .	37.	39.	14.9	.3	7.6	70.	95.	93.	33.	.9	1.5	30.	88	97.	98.	.3
Brazil............	9,540	111	11.6	188.7	10.4	31.4	10.4	......	......	10.4	52.4	73.3	62.9	......	......	83.8	10.4	88.8	136.3	......
Shelbyville.	9,500	129	13.5	210.5	31.5	10.5	10.5	10.5	10.5	......	......	126.3	31.5	......	......	51.4	10.5	73.6	94.7	......
Newcastle..........	9,446	141	14.9	84.7	52.9	52.9	31.7	......	......	31.7	42.3	95.2	190.6	10.5	......	10.5	42.3	63.5	148.2	......
Crawfordsville......	9,371	141	15.0	181.4	32.0	10.6	......	......	......	......	......	96.0	53.3	......	......	53.3	......	138.7	64.0	......
Bloomington.	8,838	165	18.6	158.4	33.9	56.5	......	......	33.9	45.2	79.1	203.6	79.1	......	......	33.9	11.3	101.8	124.4	......
Columbus..........	8,813	152	17.2	272.3	68.1	113.5	......	......	......	68.1	13.	79.4	90.7	......	......	34.0	......	90.7	68.1	......
Bedford............	8,716	138	15.8	172.1	45.9	68.8	22.9	......	11.4	93.	......	126.2	149.1	......	......	22.9	11.4	22.9	91.8	......
Wabash............	8,687	112	12,8	69.0	23.0	23.0	......	......	......	......	......	760.1	103.6	......	......	80.5	11.5	46.0	57.5	......
Frankfort..........	8,634	90	10.4	150.6	11.5	11.5	23.1	......	......	......	11.5	81.0	46.3	......	......	11.5	......	46.3	69.5	......
Goshen............	8,514	113	13.2	82.2	11.7	23.4	......	......	......	......	......	82.2	11.7	11.7	......	......	......	58.7	93.9	......
Washington...	7,854	101	12.8	267.3	25.4	12.7	25.4	......	27.	12.7	......	101.8	38.1	......	......	25.4	......	89.1	114.6	......
Connersville.......	7,738	103	13.3	103.4	38.7	12.9	25.8	......	......	......	25.8	25.8	168.0	......	......	25.8	......	108.4	64.6	......
Valparaiso.........	6,987	89	12.7	128.8	14.3	14.3	14.3	......	32.	......	......	186.0	28.6	......	......	28.6	......	157.4	85.8	......
Madison...........	6,934	145	20.9	201.9	100.9	28.8	14.4	......	......	......	57.6	158.6	72.1	......	......	28.8	......	158.6	158.6	......
Whiting............	6,587	88	13.3	75.9	15.1	60.7	15.1	......	30.3	......	......	75.9	318.8	......	......	......	......	30.3	75.9	......
Princeton..........	6,448	104	16.1	263.6	15.5	62.0	......	......	31.0	15.5	......	186.1	62.0	......	......	......	15.5	77.5	108.6	......
Seymour...........	6,306	74	11.7	206.1	......	63.4	15.8	......	......	15.8	15.8	79.3	95.1	......	......	47.5	......	47.5	95.1	......
Clinton............	6,229	86	13.8	128.4	16.0	16.0	40.4	......	16.0	16.0	40.4	96.3	272.9	......	16.0	16.0	......	16.0	128.4	......
Hartford City.......	6,187	94	15.2	161.6	32.3	16.1	......	......	......	64.6	......	64.6	48.4	......	......	32.3	......	64.6	129.3	......
Linton.............	5,906	85	14.3	84.6	......	......	118.5	......	16.9	33.8	84.6	203.2	220.1	......	......	50.7	16.9	16.9	84.6	......

TABLE No. 7—Continued.

CITIES.	Population, According to U. S. Census, 1910.	Total Deaths Reported for the Year 1910. (Still-births Excluded.)	Annual Death Rate Per 1,000 Population.	DEATHS FROM IMPORTANT CAUSES PER 100,000 POPULATION.																
				Pulmonary Tuberculosis.	Other Forms of Tuberculosis.	Typhoid Fever.	Diphtheria.	Croup.	Scarlet Fever.	Measles.	Whooping Cough.	Lobar and Broncho-Pneumonia.	Diarrhea and Enteritis. (Under 2 Years.)	Cerebro-Spinal Fever.	Poliomyelitis.	Influenza.	Puerperal Septicemia.	Cancer.	Violence.	Smallpox.
Mt. Vernon	5,563	85	15.2	251.6	35.9	35.9				35.9		161.7	53.9			17.9		71.9	179.8	
Lebanon	5,474	91	16.6	219.2	36.5	18.2	18.2				18.2	73.0	91.3			18.2		91.3	91.3	
Greensburg	5,420	80	14.7	202.9	36.9	36.9				18.4		55.3	73.8			18.4		92.2	110.7	
Portland	5,130	84	16.3	170.3	38.9	38.9	89.			19.4	38.9	156.0	97.4	19.4		38.9		38.9	175.4	
Alexandria	5,096	57	11.1	117.8	19.6	39.2	178.				19.6	117.8					19.6	39.2	39.2	
Noblesville	5,073	64	12 6	78.8	19.7	39.4	91.			39.4		39.4	98.5					118.3	59.1	
Bluffton	4,987	76	15.2	180 5	60.1	100.3				80.2		140.4	80.2			60.1	20.0	80.2	120.3	
Kendallville	4,981	47	9.4	60.2	20.0							100.4	60.2			20.0		80.3	80.3	
Rushville	4,925	80	16 2	142.1	60.9							81.2	40.6			40.6		121.8	81.2	
Martinsville	4,529	98	21.6	265.0	44.1	22.0				22.0	44.1	132.5	66.2			110.4	22.0	110.4	66.2	
Franklin	4,502	68	15.1	177.7	66.6		22.0		66.6	22.0		44.4	44.4			44.4	22.0	66.6		
Decatur	4,471	50	11.1	134.2	22.3	44.7					44.7	89.4	22.3		44.7	22.0		89.4	67.1	
Greenfield	4,448	61	13.7	292 2	22.4	22.4					44.9	44.9	112.4			67.5		67.5	67.5	
Warsaw	4,430	75	16.9	135.5	45.1	22.5	22 5				22.5	67.7				45.1	45.1	155.5	180.6	
Aurora	4,410	85	19 2	249.4	45.3	68.0	22.6				45.3	181.4	68.0					22.6	204.1	
Winchester	4,266	60	14.0	187.5	70.3					46.8		70.3	23.4			23.4		164.1	46.8	
Garrett	4,149	60	14.4	120.5	72.3	120.5						48.2	98.6					48.2	120.5	
Sullivan	4,115	58	14.1	194.4	48.6					48.6	24.3	48.6	139.3			24.3		121.5	170.1	
Tipton	4,075	47	11.5	171.8		24.5			24.5	49.0	24.5	73.6	49.0				49 0	98.1	98.1	
Boonville	3,934	58	14.7	178.0	76.2	25.4	25.4				101.7	127.1	127.1			76.2		76.2	76.2	
Lawrenceburg	3,930	56	14.2	178.1								279.9				50.8	25.4	101.8	229.0	
Auburn	3,919	38	9.6	178.6	25.5		25.5		76.5			25.5	153.1		25.5	25.5		102.1	76.5	
Plymouth	3,838	63	16.4	234.5	156.3	26.0				52.1		52.1	52.1			26.0	26 0	78.1	26.0	
Greencastle	3,790	51	13.4	237.5	158.3	26 3				52.7		52.7	52.7			26 3	26.3	79.1	26.3	
Columbia City	3,448	42	12.1	203.0	29.0		29.0		29.0			145.0	29.0					58.0	69.0	

iMhell	3,438	61	17.7	290.9	261.7	......	......	......	......	......	87.2	87.2	116.3	......	......	......	58.1	29.0	87.2	......
Tell City	3,369	40	11.8	207.8	59.3	......	29.6	......	......	......	......	89.0	59.3	......	......	29.6	59.3	......	59.3	......
Roch ter	3,364	53	15.7	208.1	29.7	29.7	......	......	......	......	59.4	......	59.4	......	......	29.7	......	89.1	29.7	......
Attica	3,335	34	10.2	150.0	29.9	29.9	......	......	......	......	29.9	120.0	59.9	......	......	29.9	29.9	59.9	89.9	......
Gas City	3,224	48	14.8	217.1	......	......	......	......	......	93.0	31.0	62.0	93.0	......	......	31.0	31.0	93.0	93.0	31.0
Union City	3,209	54	16.8	155.9	93.5	31.1	......	......	......	......	......	218.2	......	......	......	......	31.1	187.1	249.4	......
[illegible]rk	3,031	35	11.5	231.0	99.0	33.0	......	......	......	......	......	33.0	33.0	......	......	33.0	......	65.8	165.0	......
North [illegible]on	2,915	36	12.3	137.2	102.9	102.9	......	......	......	......	......	......	......	......	......	34.3	......	......	34.3	......
Montpelier	2,786	33	11.8	179.5	35.9	......	......	......	35.9	71.8	35.9	71.8	107.7	......	......	35.9	......	......	......	......
Rockport	2,736	46	16.8	292.3	......	36.5	......	......	......	......	......	219.3	109.6	......	......	......	......	......	73.0	......
[illegible]ola	2,610	41	15.7	[illegible]1.6	76.6	......	......	......	......	......	......	38.3	38.3	......	......	......	......	76.6	76.6	......
[illegible]g	2,464	31	12.5	162.4	......	81.1	......	......	......	......	121.8	121.8	......	......	40.5	40.5	......	81.1	202.9	......
Rensselaer	2,393	36	15.0	125.4	......	......	......	......	......	......	......	83.5	41.7	......	......	......	......	135.4	167.2	......
Ligonier	2,173	34	15.6	92.0	......	92.0	......	......	......	......	......	......	......	......	......	92.0	......	138.0	92.0	......
[illegible]lo	2,168	19	8.7	184.5	......	......	......	......	......	......	......	46.1	92.2	......	......	46.1	......	46.1	......	......
Delphi	2,161	43	19.9	......	46.2	46.2	......	......	......	......	......	92.5	46.2	......	......	......	......	92.5	......	......
Loogootee	2,154	31	14.4	325.0	46.4	46.4	92.8	......	......	......	92.8	......	139.3	......	......	......	......	46.4	46.4	......
Cannelton	2,130	24	11.2	140.8	93.8	......	......	......	......	......	......	46.9	93.8	......	......	......	......	46.9	93.8	......
Covington	2,069	35	16.9	241.6	......	96.6	......	......	......	......	......	......	48.3	......	......	48.3	......	193.3	48.3	......
Butler [illegible]	1,818	33	18.1	110.0	55.0	......	55.0	......	......	......	......	165.0	275.1	......	......	......	......	110.0	......	......
Veedersburg	1,757	25	14.2	113.8	56.9	56.9	......	......	......	......	......	......	......	......	......	56.9	......	113.8	227.6	......
Rising Sun	1,513	29	19.1	198.3	......	......	......	......	......	......	......	198.3	132.2	......	......	66.1	......	198.3	......	......
Vevay	1,256	27	215	79.6	159.2	159.2	......	......	......	......	......	79.6	159.2	......	......	......	......	79.6	238.8	......
Total Urban Population	1,147,277	17,328	15.1	163.0	35.1	34.9	14.4	.2	9.1	17.9	17.7	119.0	90.5	.3	.1	23.0	10.3	75.3	124.9	.08
Total Rural Population	1,553,599	19,185	12.3	127.6	29.2	34.3	12.4	1.1	6.4	16.4	16.4	88.5	65.0	1.1	2.5	28.1	7.0	64.9	80.7	......

TABLE No. 8.

Annual Death Rates for Ten Years, 1901 to 1910 Inclusive, With Average of Cities of 5,000 (Estimated) Population and Over, Compared With Rural and State Rates.

	1901	1902	1903	1904	1905	1906	1907	1908	1909	1910, State Population, 2,700,876	Rate 13.5	Average 13.2
										Population.		
CITIES—												
Indianapolis	16.9	16.2	18.1	17.4	16.0	16.4	16.4	14.3	14.8	233,650	16.4	16.2
Evansville	14.5	11.2	14.7	14.9	14.4	15.1	13.8	14.4	15.0	69,647	13.4	14.1
Fort Wayne	14.8	14.1	14.8	14.0	13.9	16.3	15.7	14.6	13.7	69,933	13.0	14.4
Terre Haute	19.1	20.6	18.3	23.1	21.0	22.5	17.6	17.2	18.0	55,157	16.2	19.3
South Bend	15.0	14.6	19.2	15.9	17.1	16.8	16.1	16.3	17.3	53,684	14.1	16.2
Muncie	16.0	16.7	18.1	17.8	16.0	14.8	15.7	15.9	15.1	24,005	15.3	16.1
Anderson	17.5	16.7	14.6	15.5	12.1	13.3	13.1	11.2	14.5	22,476	14.6	14.3
Richmond	16.6	18.3	14.0	15.8	14.0	16.1	15.2	15.6	16.8	22,324	13.9	15.6
Hammond	14.8	18.1	19.1	15.4	15.2	17.9	17.2	14.6	13.8	20,925	14.6	16.0
New Albany	18.0	17.4	16.6	18.1	18.1	16.1	17.6	15.8	14.2	20,629	18.2	17.0
Lafayette	16.8	17.9	18.4	21.5	21.6	18.6	16.0	17.7	19.4	20,081	16.6	18.4
Marion	15.8	15.5	17.5	16.6	14.0	13.6	11.5	9.6	11.0	19,359	12.5	13.7
Elkhart	13.2	12.5	14.3	15.4	13.6	14.0	14.2	13.4	14.2	19,282	13.9	13.8
East Chicago	6.5	10.1	9.3	12.4	14.5	18.5	32.2	26.5	29.0	19,098	15.3	17.4
Logansport	17.5	15.1	15.9	17.6	17.1	16.0	14.8	18.4	16.6	19,050	15.9	16.4
Michigan City	14.7	14.5	18.6	14.7	14.1	14.3	15.4	12.1	11.5	19,027	14.7	14.4
Kokomo	16.0	16.1	20.8	18.5	18.7	20.0	18.1	19.7	17.3	17,010	15.1	18.0
Gary	.....	.....	.....	.....	.....	.....	.....	.....	.....	16,802	16.2	.....
Vincennes	19.2	17.8	15.1	22.2	20.7	20.0	18.5	18.6	15.4	14,895	19.2	19.9
Mishawaka	10.5	13.8	17.0	19.2	24.3	21.4	21.9	13.0	13.5	11,886	11.6	16.6
Elwood	15.1	14.0	14.7	13.4	11.6	8.4	8.6	9.4	10.1	11,028	15.6	12.0
Peru	13.0	13.4	12.1	13.3	11.2	13.8	13.5	12.0	15.4	10,910	13.3	13.1
Laporte	15.4	13.7	17.3	18.2	17.5	20.7	19.8	15.0	15.9	10,525	17.8	17.1
Jeffersonville	22.3	19.5	21.7	20.3	17.3	19.7	20.2	13.1	15.0	10,412	19.2	18.8
Huntington	13.4	13.2	16.5	17.1	12.7	13.4	12.2	14.0	14.6	10,272	18.6	14.3
Brasil	10.0	14.1	8.0	20.0	12.5	12.8	16.9	1 .3	13.0	9,540	11.6	13.2
Shelbyville	14.2	13.7	14.7	16.5	16.5	16.4	14.0	12.7	14.3	9,500	13.5	14.5
New Castle	.....	.....	.....	.....	.....	.....	.....	.....	.....	9,446	14.9	.....
Crawfordsville	16.4	17.4	13.9	20.5	20.0	20.3	22.1	1 .7	22.4	9,371	15.0	18.7
Bloomington	11.8	17.3	14.8	16.9	18.9	19.7	14.7	1[illegible] 9	17.2	8,836	18.6	16.2
Columbus	16.3	15.8	15.8	18.5	14.8	17.1	15.1	17.7	14.8	8,813	17.2	16.3
Bedford	10.9	12.4	11.3	19.5	18.1	18.0	19.2	16.8	14.8	8,716	15.8	15.6
Wabash	11.0	13.8	9.8	14.3	12.7	13.0	12.0	14.6	13.5	8,687	12.8	12.7
Frankfort	15.5	14.1	17.0	15.1	20.0	18.7	17.6	17.2	14.8	8,634	10.4	16.0
Goshen	10.6	11.8	11.1	12.5	14.0	18.1	16.3	15.3	13.0	8,514	13.2	13.5
Washington	16.5	14.6	15.5	15.9	14.2	16.5	11.5	13.2	11.0	7,854	12.8	14.1
Connersville	16.0	13.2	13.9	17.6	14.8	15.3	15.3	18 6	16.6	7,738	13.3	15.4
Valparaiso	11.9	10.9	13.9	15.6	11.5	12.4	11.2	13.3	12 3	6,987	12.7	12.5
Madison	16.3	18.0	18.1	17.7	15.0	18.4	19.8	19.7	19.0	6,934	20.9	18.2
Whiting	.....	.....	.....	11.4	10.3	14.1	14.7	13.5	14.0	6,587	13.3	13.0
Princeton	11.0	10.9	9.6	15.3	17.2	13.9	14.5	19.2	18.9	6,448	16.1	14.6
Seymour	13.9	12.9	13.0	16.1	15.8	15.6	16.6	21.6	20.0	6,305	11.7	15.7
Clinton	.....	.....	.....	.....	.....	.....	.....	.....	.....	6,229	13.8	.....
Hartford City	12.2	12.0	11.1	13.0	12.0	8.8	11.9	9.8	11.2	6,187	15.2	11.7
Linton	.....	8.6	9.7	12.5	11.8	11.7	10.4	10.6	11.2	5,906	14.3	10.0
Mt. Vernon	21.6	22.4	16.0	17.9	18.4	17.9	18.8	15.1	11.5	5,563	15.2	17.4
Lebanon	.....	.....	.....	.....	.....	.....	.....	.....	.....	5,474	16.6	.....
Greensburg	20.3	17.6	16.9	18.5	16.2	21 2	14.7	17.5	20.0	5,420	14.7	17.7
Portland	.....	.....	.....	.....	.....	.....	.....	.....	.....	5,130	16.3	.....
Alexandria	16.1	13.9	14.1	11.4	4.4	6.9	7.9	9.9	12.1	5,096	11.1	10.7
Noblesville	.....	.....	.....	.....	.....	.....	.....	10 9	11.3	5,073	12.6	.....
Average	15 3	15 3	15 4	16.8	15 8	16 4	15 6	13.4	15.1	1,147,277	15.1	15.4
STATE	13 8	12 8	12 2	13 5	13 7	13 5	13.4	12 5	13.3	2,700,876	13.5	13.2
RURAL	14.9	13.3	12.9	14.2	13.9	13.3	11.6	11 6	11.1	1,553,599	12.3	12 9

TABLE No. 9.

Deaths by Occupations, Months and Ages for the Year Ending December 31, 1910.

OCCUPATIONS.	Sex.	Jan.	Feb.	Mar.	Apr.	May.	June.	July.	Aug.	Sept.	Oct.	Nov.	Dec.
Actors and actresses	Males	1	1		1	1	2		1				
	Females			1									
Aeronauts and aviators	Males						1		1				
Architects	Males				1	1		1					
Artists and authors	Males				1	1	1					1	3
	Females				1								
Athletes	Males			1	1			1					
Bakers and confectioners	Males	4		3	1	2	2	1	4		5	5	2
Bankers, brokers and officials of companies	Males	7	5	5	5		6		4	4	4	9	2
Barbers	Males	9	10	9	9	8	2	4	1	8	5	7	3
Bartenders	Males	16	1	4	7	6	7	8	7	16	11	9	11
	Females		1								1		
Basket makers	Males	1					1		1		1		
Blacksmiths	Males	8	10	15	13	7	11	8	12	7	9	9	7
Bookbinders	Males	1								1			
Bookkeepers, clerks and copyists	Males	9	7	10	13	9	7	8	5	7	8	10	7
	Females	1		1	2			1	2	3	1	1	5
Brewers, distillers, etc	Males	2	1			1		1	2			1	2
Brickmakers	Males		2	1							1		
Builders and contractors	Males	8	7	6	10	10	11	5	3	4	6	8	5
Butchers	Males	8	4	3	4	7	8	4	5	5	6	4	5

TABLE No. 9—Continued.

OCCUPATIONS.	Sex.	Jan.	Feb	Mar.	Apr.	May.	June.	July.	Aug.	Sept.	Oct.	Nov.	Dec.
Cabinet makers	Males	4	5	3	1	5	1	5	6	2	3	3	4
Carpenters	Males	33	26	50	45	30	39	27	31	38	39	48	48
Carriage and wagon makers	Males	2	3	4	2			2	3	4	1	2	7
Cashiers	Males								1				
Chauffeurs	Males	1	1	2		1		1	1				1
Chemists and druggists	Males	6	6	7	3	7		6	5	4	4	6	1
Chiropodists	Males										1		
Cigar makers	Males	1	1		1	3	4	1		4	3	1	3
	Females	2			1								1
Cleaners and dyers	Males							1					
Clergymen	Males	5	8	8	10	9	5	10	7	7	7		6
	Females												1
Collectors, agents and auctioneers	Males	12	8	10	10	5	8	7	9	8	8	7	10
	Females									1			
Commercial travelers	Males	8	1	4	4	4	6	5	3	6	5	6	2
Compositors, printers and pressmen	Males	5	4	5	3	1	1	4	6	3	5	5	2
	Females					1							
Cooks and caterers	Males	2	8	3	4	4	2	4	2	1	2		3
	Females		1			1		1	2	1	2		2
Coopers	Males	4	6	3	3	3	1	3	4		1	6	4
Dairymen	Males	1	1			1					1	2	1
Dentists	Males	2	3	1	1	3		3	3	2	1	1	2
Draftsmen	Males		2	1								2	
Electricians	Males	3	1	5		1	1	2	3	3	3	4	3

Electric railway employes	Males	1	2	2	1	2	2	1	......	4	3	3	1
Elevator operators	Males	1											
Engineers and firemen (railway)	Males	12	15	14	12	10	8	17	10	14	13	20	11
Engineers and firemen (stationary)	Males	3	1	7	1	1	3	2	2	1	2	5	3
Engravers	Males						1	1			2		
Factory employes	Males	10	9	5	7	5	6	3	7	6	11	7	5
	Females	2			1	1	1	1		2	2	2	1
Farmers	Males	427	428	498	377	392	361	354	367	340	371	334	397
Firemen (city)	Males	1		1	1	2	1	1		1	1	2	2
Furriers	Males												
Gardeners, florists and nurserymen	Males	5	3		5	6	8	4	3	2	6	2	6
	Females		1										
Glassworkers	Males	4	6	10	4	6	5	8	2	2	4	6	2
Government employes	Males			1	2			1					
Government officials	Males							1					
Hairdressers, manicurists and masseurs	Females				1	1					1		
Harness makers and saddlers	Males	5	1	3	2	2	2	5		1	2	1	3
Hotel and boarding house keepers	Males	2		3	4	1	1	3	3	2	4	4	4
	Females	1		1					2	1		1	
Housework (general)	Females	756	776	880	790	711	694	693	671	690	713	712	824
Hunters and fishermen	Males			1	1		1	1	1				
Inspectors	Males		2	1	1	1	1	3	4	3		3	
Janitors and janitresses	Males	3	1	1	4		1	1	2	3	1	5	
	Females		1										
Journalists and publishers	Males	2	1				3	1			2		
Laborers	Males	179	167	207	178	165	182	155	171	168	174	176	216
Launderers and laundresses	Males	1				3	1			1			
	Females		2	1	2	1	1	1	2	2			1

TABLE No. 9—Continued.

OCCUPATIONS.	Sex.	Jan.	Feb.	Mar.	Apr.	May.	June.	July.	Aug.	Sept.	Oct.	Nov.	Dec.
Lawyers	Males	7	5	5	6	8	3	2	4	6	6	5	5
Librarians	Males	......	......	......	......	......	......	......	......	......	......	......	......
Liverymen	Males	1	6	3	1	3	3	2	5	......	4	3	4
Lumbermen	Males	1	2	1	2	......	1	2	1	2	1	1	......
Machinists	Males	14	9	25	14	10	11	13	18	15	13	13	17
Mail service	Males	3	1	2	2	2	......	2	4	......	2	2	3
Managers and superintendents	Males	4	4	8	6	1	3	3	7	9	3	......	5
	Females	1	1	......	......	......	......	......	......	1	......	......	3
Manufacturers	Males	6	3	7	3	1	7	3	1	6	3	2	4
Marble and stone cutters	Males	......	1	3	......	2	......	1	......	3	2	2	1
Masons	Males	5	6	9	10	8	11	7	4	4	6	11	12
Mechanics	Males	3	5	5	2	1	12	7	11	7	1	12	8
Merchants and dealers	Males	39	43	45	29	32	30	31	24	37	35	40	33
	Females	1	......	1	1	......	1	......	1	......	......	1	1
Messengers and porters	Males	3	2	7	2	11	3	2	6	3	6	1	......
Millers	Males	5	5	2	2	2	1	1	......	......	2	3	7
Milliners and seamstresses	Females	10	5	6	12	14	8	3	5	9	10	7	11
Miners and quarrymen	Males	22	20	18	17	17	10	17	30	18	15	29	17
Molders, iron and steel workers	Males	6	10	5	10	5	8	5	8	7	7	10	12
Musicians	Males	1	3	4	2	3	2	5	1	1	......	2	2
	Females	2	2	2	2	2	1	......	1	3	......	1	1

Nuns	Females	3	3	1	1	1	3	3	4	5		1	3
Nurses	Males			2			1				1		2
	Females	3	2	2	1	1		3		5		2	3
Oculists and opticians	Males						1						
Oil workers	Males	2		1	2	2	2	2	1	4	3	1	2
Osteopaths	Males												
Packers	Males	1					2	1	1				
Painters, glaziers and varnishers	Males	12	14	13	15	10	15	16	10	10	18	13	11
Paper hangers, decorators and window dressers	Males	1	3	2	2		2	2	7		1		3
Peddlers	Males	1	2	1	1	2		1	1	1	1	2	1
Photographers	Males	3		4	1	1		1	2	3			1
Physicians and surgeons	Males	8	10	13	10	9	6	7	4	14	8	11	9
Plasterers and lathers	Males	2	4	7	2	6	2	6	3	7	2	1	1
Plumbers	Males	3	3	3	2	2		6	1	2	1	2	1
Policemen, detectives and watchmen	Males	4	5	5	4	6	4	5	6	3	3	3	2
Potters	Males	1		1	1	1	1					3	1
Professors and teachers	Males	3	3	3	2	4	2	3	3	5	4	6	2
	Females	7	5	4	8	8	7	2	5	6	3	4	4
Public officials	Males	5	6	7	3	1	1	1	3	3	2	4	3
Sailors	Males	1		5	1	1	2	4	4	4	3	2	1
Salesmen and saleswomen	Males	20	7	23	16	15	14	14	12	14	17	16	11
	Females		2	3	4	2	4	2	3	1		3	4
Scientists	Males							1					
Servants, caretakers and attendants	Males	5	4	6	3	1	2		3	2	4	2	1
	Females	18	29	12	14	15	20	15	24	14	12	9	4

TABLE No. 9—Continued.

OCCUPATIONS.	SEX.	Jan.	Feb.	Mar.	Apr.	May.	June.	July.	Aug.	Sept.	Oct.	Nov.	Dec.
Shoemakers	Males	6	......	5	7	4	3	5	5	4	4	5	7
Steam railway employes	Males	28	12	28	14	9	19	18	15	20	17	18	21
Stenographers and secretaries	Males	1	1	......	3	1	1	2	......	......	......	1	......
	Females	3	2	......	3	......	2	3	2	1	1	2	1
Stock dealers	Males	7	4	3	2	3	3	1	4	1	2	3	2
Students	Males	10	6	10	8	9	8	9	12	7	6	7	3
	Females	5	5	6	9	2	6	5	10	8	4	4	9
Surveyors and civil engineers	Males	1	......	1	1	......	1	3	......	......	1	......	1
Tailors	Males	2	4	6	4	4	2	6	4	2	4	3	7
	Females	......	1	......	1	......	......	1	......	1	1	1	1
Tanners and curriers	Males	......	......	......	1	1	1	2	1	......	1	......	1
Teamsters and drivers	Males	7	14	17	11	8	10	12	12	6	5	15	14
Telegraph and telephone operators	Males	2	2	3	1	2	2	1	2	......	......	4	3
	Females	1	1	2	1	1	2	......	......	3	1	......	......
Tinners	Males	3	4	2	1	......	4	4	4	2	3	2	......
Undertakers	Males	......	2	......	2	......	1	2	2	......	......	2	1
Upholsterers	Males	......	......	2	2	......	......	......	1	......	......	......	......
Veterinary surgeons	Males	1	......	......	......	......	......	......	1	1	1	1	2
Volunteer soldiers and pensioners	Males	4	2	9	3	3	3	4	7	5	2	2	7
Watchmakers, jewelers and lapidaries	Males	1	......	5	......	2	2	1	1	3	1	3	1
	Females	1	......	......	......	......	......	......	......	......	......	......	......

Weavers	Males	1						1	1				
	Females			1		1	1			1			1
No occupation reported	Males	163	141	195	165	156	141	147	170	145	119	150	135
	Females	296	272	361	247	269	251	181	247	240	190	255	248
Totals	Males	1,248	1,146	1,448	1,156	1,095	1,077	1,075	1,129	1,068	1,076	1,142	1,182
	Females	1,113	1,112	1,285	1,102	1,032	1,002	915	981	998	942	1,006	1,128
Total, 15 years and over													
Under 15 years													
Grand total													

TABLE No. 9—Continued.

Deaths by Occupations, Months and Ages, for the Year Ending December 31, 1910.

OCCUPATIONS.	SEX.	15 to 19	20 to 24	25 to 29	30 to 34	35 to 39	40 to 44	45 to 49	50 to 54	55 to 59	60 to 64	65 to 69	70 to 74	75 to 79	80 to 90	90 and over.	Un-known	TOTALS. Males.	TOTALS. Females.
Actors and actresses	Males	1	1		1	2	1			1								7	
	Females								1										1
Aeronauts and aviators	Males		1			1												2	
Architects	Males			1		1							1					3	
Artists and authors	Males			1				1	1		2	1		1				7	
	Females					1													1
Athletes	Males			1		1				1								3	
Bakers and confectioners	Males	1	3	3	3	3	2	2	3	3	3		2	1				29	
Bankers, brokers and officials of Companies	Males		1	2	1	4	6	2	2	3	8	10	4	4	3	1		51	
Barbers	Males	1	7	12	8	7	11	9	7	3	2	3	2	1	2			75	
Bartenders	Males			8	15	20	12	10	13	11	8	1	4		1			103	
	Females		1									1							2
Basket makers	Males		1							1	1		1					4	
Blacksmiths	Males		3	3	4	7	6	4	4	10	15	15	12	18	14	1		116	
Bookbinders	Males		1					1										2	
Bookkeepers, clerks and copyists	Males	5	12	12	9	12	3	8	6	4	7	9	5	6	2			100	
	Females	3	4	4	2	1	1	1	1										17
Brewers, distillers, etc	Males	1			1		1	2	2		1	1		1				10	
Brickmakers	Males						1	1				1	1					4	

Builders and contractors	Males		1	1	1	6	8	3	7	8	11	11	10	5	11			83	
Butchers	Males	1	7	2	6	4	7	4		8	7	8	1	1	7			63	
Cabinet makers	Males	3		1		1	2	1	5	3	4	2	3	2	14	1		42	
Carpenters	Males	2	9	16	13	15	24	25	38	52	39	54	56	48	58	5		454	
Carriage and wagon makers	Males		1				1	1		2	6	4	4	2	8	1		30	
Cashiers	Males			1														1	
Chauffeurs	Males		4	2				1	1									8	
Chemists and druggists	Males	1	2	4	2	3	3	6	6	3	5	7	3	1	9			55	
Chiropodists	Males				1													1	
Cigar makers	Males	1		4	3		1	1	6		1	1	1		3			22	
	Females	1	2			1													4
Cleaners and dyers	Males						1											1	
Clergymen	Males		2	1		1	4	6	3	5	9	6	18	12	12	3		82	
	Females								1										1
Collectors, agents and auctioneers	Males		2	6	5	5	7	9	8	11	16	14	9	6	4			102	
	Females			1															1
Commercial travelers	Males		3	1	2	4	5	9	4	9	6	2	5	4				54	
Compositors, printers and pressmen	Males	4	4	3	3	3	6	4	2	3	4	2	3	2	1			44	
	Females	1																	1
Cooks and caterers	Males	1	2	2	1	2	3	5	4	1	2	3	2	3	3	1		35	
	Females			2	1		2		2	2			1						10
Coopers	Males		1		2		1	1	3	2	4		5	9	9	1		38	
Dairymen	Males			1			2		2				1		1			7	
Dentists	Males			3	3	1	2	3		2	1	4	2	1				22	
Draftsmen	Males	1	1		1	1							1					5	
Electricians	Males		9	8	3	2	4	4	3	1								34	
Electric railway employes	Males	3	4	4	4	2	2	1	2									22	
Elevator operators	Males		1															1	

TABLE No. 9—Continued.

OCCUPATIONS.	Sex.	15 to 19	20 to 24	25 to 29	30 to 34	35 to 39	40 to 44	45 to 49	50 to 54	55 to 59	60 to 64	65 to 69	70 to 74	75 to 79	80 to 90	90 and over.	Un-known	Totals. Males.	Totals. Females.
Engineers and firemen (railway)....	Males....	......	7	19	7	11	17	15	11	20	11	16	6	5	10	1	......	156	......
Engineers and firemen (stationary).	Males....	2	......	2	......	3	2	2	4	3	5	2	4	2	......	......	......	31	......
Engravers....................	Males....	......	......	1	1	......	......	......	......	2	......	......	......	......	......	......	......	4	......
Factory employes..............	Males....	6	10	9	8	9	5	4	3	5	9	3	6	4	......	......	......	81	......
	Females..	3	6	2	2	......	......	......	......	......	......	......	......	......	......	......	......	......	13
Farmers......................	Males....	104	138	123	97	115	136	176	245	315	444	560	705	683	727	78	......	4,646	......
Firemen (city)................	Males....	......	1	......	1	1	1	1	3	2	2	......	......	......	1	......	......	13	......
Furriers.....................	Males....	......	......	......	......	......	......	......	......	......	......	......	......	......	......	......	......	......	......
Gardeners, florists and nurserymen.	Males....	1	......	......	2	2	1	2	2	3	4	5	14	9	5	......	......	50	......
	Females..	......	......	......	......	......	......	......	......	1	......	......	......	......	......	......	......	......	1
Glassworkers..................	Males....	4	10	6	9	5	4	6	1	2	3	1	5	3	......	......	......	59	......
Government employes...........	Males....	......	......	......	1	2	......	......	......	......	1	......	......	......	......	......	......	4	......
Government officials...........	Males....	......	1	......	......	......	......	......	......	......	......	......	......	......	......	......	......	1	......
Hairdressers, manicurists and masseurs......................	Females..	......	1	......	......	......	......	2	......	......	......	......	......	......	......	......	......	......	3
Harness makers and saddlers.......	Males....	......	1	......	1	3	1	4	1	3	2	2	1	2	6	......	......	27	......
Hotel and boarding house keepers..	Males....	......	1	......	......	5	2	2	5	4	3	3	3	2	......	1	......	31	......
	Females..	......	......	......	......	......	1	......	......	1	2	......	......	1	1	......	......	......	6
Housework (general).............	Females..	156	532	582	556	568	550	590	684	674	769	823	897	728	702	96	3	......	8,910
Hunters and fishermen...........	Males....	......	1	......	......	......	1	1	......	......	......	1	......	1	......	......	......	5	......
Inspectors....................	Males....	1	......	1	1	1	2	3	1	2	3	3	......	......	1	......	......	19	......

Janitors and janitresses	Males	......	......	1	2	2	3	3	4	2	2	1	1	1	......	......	......	22	......
	Females	......	......	......	......	......	......	......	......	......	......	......	......	1	......	......	......	......	1
Journalists and publishers	Males	......	......	......	......	5	......	2	......	......	1	......	......	1	......	......	......	9	......
Laborers	Males	112	195	152	163	144	151	169	175	166	169	166	151	130	88	3	4	2,138	......
Launderers and laundresses	Males	......	2	......	......	......	......	......	1	1	1	1	......	......	1	......	......	7	......
	Females	2	......	1	2	1	4	......	......	1	1	......	......	......	......	......	......	......	12
Lawyers	Males	......	......	2	4	......	2	1	7	9	9	6	10	6	4	2	......	62	......
Librarians	Males	......	......	......	......	......	......	......	......	......	......	......	......	......	......	......	......	......	......
Liverymen	Males	1	......	1	3	4	3	3	4	6	6	3	......	......	1	......	......	35	......
Lumbermen	Males	......	......	2	1	1	......	1	1	1	1	2	3	1	......	......	......	14	......
Machinists	Males	13	11	20	12	15	16	14	10	14	12	8	13	6	6	1	1	172	......
Mail service	Males	......	......	2	3	1	3	3	3	......	......	7	1	......	......	......	......	23	......
Managers and superintendents	Males	1	1	1	2	7	8	15	5	2	5	1	2	1	2	......	......	53	......
	Females	......	......	......	......	......	......	......	2	1	2	1	......	......	......	......	......	......	6
Manufacturers	Males	......	1	1	1	4	......	4	4	6	5	3	5	6	6	......	......	46	......
Marble and stone cutters	Males	......	2	2	......	1	......	1	3	2	1	1	......	1	1	......	......	15	......
Masons	Males	1	......	2	4	5	9	6	6	7	8	14	10	11	9	1	......	93	......
Mechanics	Males	2	4	2	7	9	4	4	2	8	5	6	5	8	7	1	......	74	......
Merchants and dealers	Males	......	8	11	21	23	25	22	43	44	41	43	56	40	37	4	......	418	......
	Females	......	......	1	......	......	1	......	......	1	2	1	......	......	......	1	......	......	7
Messengers and porters	Males	8	9	6	6	5	4	1	4	1	2	......	......	......	......	......	......	46	......
Millers	Males	......	......	1	1	......	......	......	......	2	4	5	7	5	4	1	......	30	......
Milliners and seamstresses	Females	3	11	11	8	6	5	13	11	7	11	5	5	1	3	......	......	......	100
Miners and quarrymen	Males	13	22	19	21	25	18	17	19	19	17	11	11	13	2	1	2	230	......
Molders, iron and steel workers	Males	1	7	16	7	9	10	11	4	6	5	8	3	......	6	......	......	93	......
Musicians	Males	1	......	3	3	2	......	3	1	1	4	1	2	2	1	2	......	26	......
	Females	5	2	3	2	1	1	......	......	......	1	1	1	......	......	......	......	......	17

TABLE No. 9—Continued.

OCCUPATIONS.	Sex.	15 to 19	20 to 24	25 to 29	30 to 34	35 to 39	40 to 44	45 to 49	50 to 54	55 to 59	60 to 64	65 to 69	70 to 74	75 to 79	80 to 90	90 and over.	Unknown	Totals. Males.	Totals. Females.
Nuns	Females	2	5	1	1	2	1	3	2	1	5	1	1	......	3	......	......	......	28
Nurses	Males	......	......	2	......	......	1	......	2	1	......	......	......	......	......	......	......	6	......
	Females	2	2	3	2	2	1	2	1	......	1	1	4	1	......	......	......	......	22
Oculists and opticians	Males	......	......	......	......	......	......	......	......	......	......	......	......	1	......	......	......	1	......
Oil workers	Males	......	2	......	5	1	3	1	3	2	......	2	1	2	......	......	......	22	......
Osteopaths	Males	......	......	......	......	......	......	......	......	......	......	......	......	......	......	......	......	......	......
Packers	Males	......	1	......	......	1	......	......	......	1	1	1	......	......	......	......	......	5	......
Painters, glaziers and varnishers	Males	4	14	8	15	9	13	14	9	14	18	14	15	5	5	......	......	157	......
Paper hangers, decorators and window dressers	Males	......	2	1	2	6	2	2	4	1	2	1	......	......	......	......	......	23	......
Peddlers	Males	......	......	......	1	......	4	2	1	1	2	......	1	1	......	1	......	14	......
Photographers	Males	......	1	1	......	2	1	3	1	4	......	1	1	......	1	......	......	16	......
Physicians and surgeons	Males	......	......	4	4	6	2	4	12	9	13	10	16	13	13	3	......	109	......
Plasterers and lathers	Males	......	......	5	2	4	1	3	8	1	5	2	3	3	6	......	......	43	......
Plumbers	Males	1	2	2	4	4	4	1	3	......	......	1	1	2	1	......	......	26	......
Policemen, detectives and watchmen	Males	......	......	3	1	......	1	9	8	10	9	7	2	1	3	1	......	50	......
Potters	Males	......	3	......	1	1	......	2	......	......	1	......	......	......	1	......	......	9	......
Professors and teachers	Males	1	6	3	2	3	4	3	......	4	3	2	1	4	4	......	......	40	......
	Females	1	19	11	8	6	1	5	2	......	5	2	1	2	......	......	......	......	63
Public officials	Males	......	......	1	1	......	......	4	4	4	2	7	4	9	2	1	......	39	......

Sailors	Males	......	7	4	3	......	......	......	1	......	1	......	1	3	6	1	1	28	......
Salesmen and saleswomen	Males	20	25	19	12	12	11	13	13	16	20	6	7	4	1	......	......	179	......
	Females	7	6	5	7	1	......	1	1	......	......	......	......	......	......	......	......	......	28
Scientists	Males	......	......	......	......	......	......	......	......	......	......	......	1	......	......	......	......	1	......
Servants, caretakers and attendants	Males	2	7	4	2	1	4	3	4	2	......	1	2	......	......	1	......	33	......
	Females	31	41	14	18	8	18	12	10	11	8	7	3	3	2	......	......	......	187
Shoemakers	Males	1	1	......	......	......	......	2	1	4	8	8	7	11	10	2	......	55	......
Steam railway employes	Males	10	24	27	28	24	13	15	11	16	19	15	9	4	4	......	......	219	......
Stenographers and secretaries	Males	1	3	3	......	......	1	......	......	......	1	1	......	......	......	......	......	10	......
	Females	3	7	5	4	......	......	1	......	......	......	......	......	......	......	......	......	......	20
Stock dealers	Males	......	1	......	1	2	3	7	3	3	4	2	8	......	1	......	......	35	......
Students	Males	70	20	3	2	......	......	......	......	......	......	......	......	......	......	......	......	95	......
	Females	66	5	2	......	......	......	......	......	......	......	......	......	......	......	......	......	......	73
Surveyors and civil engineers	Males	......	......	......	......	1	1	......	......	......	......	......	2	3	2	......	......	9	......
Tailors	Males	......	2	2	......	2	3	3	5	4	1	5	4	7	7	3	......	48	......
	Females	......	......	2	1	1	2	......	......	......	......	......	......	......	1	......	......	......	7
Tanners and curriers	Males	......	1	......	......	......	......	......	......	1	......	......	2	1	3	......	......	8	......
Teamsters and drivers	Males	4	8	10	17	6	9	10	6	13	17	12	10	2	7	......	......	131	......
Telegraph and telephone operators	Males	1	6	2	1	......	4	2	3	......	1	1	1	......	......	......	......	22	......
	Females	2	5	4	......	1	......	......	......	......	......	......	......	......	......	......	......	......	12
Tinners	Males	......	3	1	1	3	5	2	......	2	5	4	2	......	1	......	......	29	......
Undertakers	Males	......	2	1	......	1	......	......	2	1	2	2	......	1	......	......	......	12	......
Upholsterers	Males	......	......	1	1	......	1	......	......	......	......	......	1	1	......	......	......	5	......
Veterinary surgeons	Males	......	......	1	......	......	......	......	......	......	1	1	2	......	2	......	......	7	......
Volunteer soldiers and pensioners	Males	1	3	1	......	2	1	......	1	1	6	10	11	8	5	1	......	51	......
Watchmakers, jewelers and lapidaries	Males	......	......	2	......	3	1	1	1	1	2	2	3	2	2	......	......	20	......
	Females	1	......	......	......	......	......	......	......	......	......	......	......	......	......	......	......	......	1

TABLE No. 9—Continued.

OCCUPATIONS.	SEX.	15 to 19	20 to 24	25 to 29	30 to 34	35 to 39	40 to 44	45 to 49	50 to 54	55 to 59	60 to 64	65 to 69	70 to 74	75 to 79	80 to 90	90 and over.	Un-known	TOTALS.	
																		Males.	Fe-males.
Weavers	Males			1									1	1				3	
	Females					1	1			1				1	1				5
No occupation reported	Males	122	69	52	67	53	60	67	81	91	149	181	249	272	259	47	8	1,827	
	Females	231	169	73	66	72	44	47	67	99	163	328	338	523	704	120	13		3,057
[illegible]ls	Males	532	727	672	654	676	707	794	885	1,014	1,240	1,341	1,548	1,432	1,433	171	16	13,842	
	Females	520	818	727	680	673	633	677	785	800	970	1,171	1,251	1,261	1,417	217	16		12,616
Total, 15 years and over																			26,458
Under 15 years																			10,055
Grand total																			36,513

TABLE No. 10.

Deaths from Tuberculosis, all Forms, with Rates per 100,000 Population, for Certain Occupations of Each Sex, for Year 1910.

	OCCUPATIONS.	Number of Deaths 15 Years of Age and Over.	Death Rates per 100,000.
	MALES.		
1.	Farmers	486	17.9
2.	Laborers	409	15.1
3.	No occupations reported	243	8.9
4.	Carpenters	62	2.2
5.	Salesmen	49	1.8
6.	Merchants and dealers	38	1.4
7.	Machinists	31	1.1
8.	Barbers	28	1.0
9.	Students	25	.9
10.	Bookkeepers, clerks and copyists	23	.8
11.	Factory employes	22	.8
12.	Steam railway employes	22	.8
13.	Teamsters and drivers	22	.8
14.	Painters, glaziers and varnishers	21	.7
15.	Miners and quarrymen	20	.7
16.	Messengers and porters	18	.6
17.	Moulders, iron and steel workers	17	.6
18.	Engineers and firemen (railway)	16	.5
19.	Glassworkers	16	.5
20.	Blacksmiths	15	.5
21.	Mechanics	14	.5
22.	Butchers	13	.4
23.	Compositors, printers and pressmen	12	.4
24.	Collectors, agents and auctioneers	11	.4
25.	Bartenders	10	.3
26.	Masons	10	.3
27.	Plasterers and lathers	10	.3
28.	Bakers and confectioners	9	.3
29.	Chemists and druggists	8	.2
30.	Cigar makers	8	.2
31.	Professors and teachers	8	.2
32.	Builders and contractors	7	.2
33.	Liverymen	7	.2
34.	Physicians and surgeons	7	.2
35.	Plumbers	7	.2
36.	Commercial travelers	6	.2
37.	Dentists	6	.2
38.	Stock dealers	6	.2
39.	Volunteer soldiers and pensioners	6	.2
40.	Cooks and caterers	5	.1
41.	Coopers	5	.1
42.	Musicians	5	.1
43.	Telegraph and telephone operators	5	.1
44.	Actors	4	.1
45.	Bankers, brokers and officials of companies	4	.1
46.	Carriage and wagon makers	4	.1
47.	Clergymen	4	.1
48.	Electricians	4	.1
49.	Electric railway employes	4	.1
50.	Hotel and boarding house keepers	4	.1
51.	Managers and superintendents	4	.1
52.	Paper hangers, decorators and window dressers	4	.1
53.	Sailors	4	.1
54.	Servants, caretakers and attendants	4	.1
55.	Brewers, distillers, etc	3	.1

TABLE No. 10—Continued.

	OCCUPATIONS.	Number of Deaths 15 Years of Age and Over.	Death Rates per 100,000.
56.	Cabinet makers	3	.1
57.	Engineers and firemen (stationary)	3	.1
58.	Gardeners florists and nurserymen	3	.1
59.	Harness makers and saddlers	3	.1
60.	Lawyers	3	.1
61.	Mail service	3	.1
62.	Marble and stone cutters	3	.1
63.	Oil workers	3	.1
64.	Photographers	3	.1
65.	Potters	3	.1
66.	Shoemakers	3	.1
67.	Secretaries and stenographers	3	.1
68.	Undertakers	3	.1
69.	Upholsterers	3	.1
70.	Watchmakers, jewelers and lapidaries	3	.1
71.	Architects	2	.07
72.	Basket makers	2	.07
73.	Brick makers	2	.07
74.	Cashiers	2	.07
75.	Draftsmen	2	.07
76.	Inspectors	2	.07
77.	Janitors	2	.07
78.	Journalists and publishers	2	.07
79.	Launderers	2	.07
80.	Manufacturers	2	.07
81.	Millers	2	.07
82.	Policemen, detectives and watchmen	2	.07
83.	Public officials	2	.07
84.	Tailors	2	.07
85.	Athletes	1	.03
86.	Bookbinders	1	.03
87.	Chauffeurs	1	.03
88.	Engravers	1	.03
89.	Government employes	1	.03
90.	Hunters and fishermen	1	.03
91.	Lumbermen	1	.03
92.	Packers	1	.03
93.	Peddlers	1	.03
94.	Veterinary surgeons	1	.03
	FEMALES.		
1.	General housework	1,540	57.0
2.	No occupations reported	431	15.9
3.	Servants, caretakers and attendants	53	1.9
4.	Students	34	1.2
5.	Professors and teachers	26	.9
6.	Milliners and seamstresses	22	.8
7.	Saleswomen	17	.6
8.	Secretaries and stenographers	12	.4
9.	Bookkeepers, clerks and copyists	9	.3
10.	Telegraph and telephone operators	8	.3
11.	Factory employes	7	.2
12.	Laundresses	7	.2
13.	Musicians	6	.2
14.	Nurses	6	.2
15.	Cooks and cateresses	4	.1
16.	Compositors and printers	2	.07
17.	Nuns	2	.07
18.	Tailoresses	2	.07
19.	Bakers and confectioners	1	.03
20.	Cigar makers	1	.03
21.	Clergywomen	1	.03
22.	Agents	1	.03
	Total males	1,891	70.0
	Total females	2,193	81.1
	Total all occupations	4,084	151.2

TABLE No. 11.

Poliomyelitis by Months, Ages and Counties, for the Year Ending December 31, 1910.

MONTHS.

January	2	July	5
February	3	August	4
March	2	September	2
April	1	October	12
May	2	November	14
June	....	December	6

AGES.

Under 1 year	13	Twenty to twenty-four years	2
One to two years	9	Twenty-five to thirty years	....
Two to five years	16	Thirty to thirty-four years	....
Five to nine years	10	Thirty-five to forty years	....
Ten to fourteen years	2	Forty to forty-four years	....
Fifteen to twenty years	....	Forty-five to fifty years	....
		Fifty years and over	1

COUNTIES.

Adams	2	Knox	1
Allen	1	Kosciusko	2
Bartholomew	1	Laporte	1
Benton	2	Marion	1
Carroll	1	Marshall	1
Cass	6	Miami	1
Clay	1	Noble	1
Clinton	2	Perry	1
Dekalb	1	Pulaski	1
Delaware	1	Steuben	3
Dubois	1	St. Joseph	2
Elkhart	1	Starke	1
Fountain	2	Tippecanoe	2
Grant	4	Vermillion	1
Greene	1	Vigo	1
Huntington	1	White	1
Jefferson	2	Whitley	1
Jay	1		

Total males	33
Total females	20
Total	53

TABLE C.

Number of Births and Rates per 1,000 Population by Counties, for Year 1910.

	Number.	Rate.
NORTHERN COUNTIES—		
Adams	508	23.2
Allen	1,517	16.2
Benton	227	17.8
Blackford	380	24.0
Carroll	383	21.3
Cass	718	19.7
Dekalb	499	19.9
Elkhart	988	20.1
Fulton	340	20.1
Grant	1,034	20.1
Howard	710	21.4
Huntington	642	22.1
Jasper	259	19.8
Jay	583	23.3
Kosciusko	542	19.3
Lagrange	334	22.0
Lake	1,726	20.8
Laporte	942	20.5
Marshall	495	20.4
Miami	584	19.9
Newton	247	23.5
Noble	460	19.1
Porter	381	18.5
Pulaski	173	13.0
Starke	200	18.9
Steuben	202	14.1
St. Joseph	2,288	27.1
Wabash	496	18.4
Wells	462	20.6
White	395	22.4
Whitley	284	16.8
CENTRAL COUNTIES—		
Bartholomew	491	19.7
Boone	509	20.6
Brown	172	21.5
Clay	729	22.4
Clinton	500	18.7
Decatur	374	19.9
Delaware	1,138	22.1
Fayette	282	19.5
Fountain	406	19.8
Franklin	279	18.2
Hamilton	546	20.2
Hancock	328	17.2
Hendricks	380	18.2
Henry	671	22.5
CENTRAL COUNTIES—Cont.		
Johnson	391	19.1
Madison	1,535	23.5
Marion	5,208	19.7
Monroe	580	24.7
Montgomery	597	20.3
Morgan	485	22.9
Owen	259	18.4
Parke	381	17.1
Putnam	417	20.3
Randolph	620	21.3
Rush	362	18.7
Shelby	509	18.9
Tippecanoe	640	15 1
Tipton	456	26.1
Union	119	19.0
Vermillion	490	25.9
Vigo	1,756	19.9
Warren	257	23.5
Wayne	763	17.4
SOUTHERN COUNTIES—		
Clark	557	18.4
Crawford	224	18.5
Daviess	760	27.3
Dearborn	336	15.7
Dubois	543	27.3
Floyd	519	17.1
Gibson	682	22.6
Greene	956	25.9
Harrison	441	21.7
Jackson	693	28.0
Jefferson	422	20.6
Jennings	348	24.5
Knox	1,053	26.8
Lawrence	808	26.3
Martin	301	23.2
Ohio	67	15.4
Orange	402	23.3
Perry	419	23.1
Pike	490	24.9
Posey	431	19.8
Ripley	381	19.5
Scott	199	23.9
Spencer	427	20.6
Sullivan	856	26.3
Switzerland	195	19.6
Vanderburgh	1,390	17.9
Warrick	447	20.4
Washington	333	19.0
STATE	56,309	20.8
NORTHERN COUNTIES	18,999	20 4
CENTRAL COUNTIES	22,630	20.3
SOUTHERN COUNTIES	14,680	22 2
HIGHEST RATE—		
Jackson County		28.0
LOWEST RATE—		
Pulaski County		13.0

TABLE A.

Births by Months, Color, Nationality of Parents, for the Year Ending December 31, 1910. (Stillbirths Excluded.)

COUNTIES.	1910.												Sex.			Color.				Nationality of Parents.					
																White.		Colored.		American.		Foreign.		Not Reported.	
	January.	February.	March.	April.	May.	June.	July.	August.	September.	October.	November.	December.	Males.	Females.	Total.	Males.	Females.	Males.	Females.	Fathers.	Mothers.	Fathers.	Mothers.	Fathers.	Mothers.
Adams	46	58	51	40	43	26	48	30	48	39	41	38	255	253	508	255	253	....	....	478	485	21	15	2	1
Allen	113	120	157	110	112	134	126	131	128	137	110	139	801	716	517	797	714	4	2	1,320	1,356	174	144	12	6
Bartholomew	46	34	48	36	37	39	43	39	45	50	33	41	255	236	491	251	234	4	2	473	482	9	2	2	....
Beton	24	10	20	29	13	18	23	22	16	21	18	13	112	115	227	112	115	....	....	211	215	10	7	1	....
Blackford	37	35	37	25	28	30	28	29	34	38	34	25	191	189	380	190	189	1	....	356	360	9	9	7	3
Boone	32	31	48	36	43	39	47	61	45	46	26	55	270	239	509	270	239	....	....	498	503	3	1	3	....
Brown	9	22	11	15	12	13	15	16	16	11	13	19	94	78	172	94	78	....	....	169	170	2	1	1	1
Carroll	32	37	31	30	26	24	41	42	22	42	31	25	212	171	383	212	171	....	....	378	381	1	....	2	....
Cass	62	48	69	55	48	58	76	55	56	78	64	49	357	361	718	357	360	....	1	675	689	31	21	5	1
Clark	45	45	41	45	31	54	42	49	71	38	44	52	286	271	557	262	254	24	17	531	538	8	3	4	2
Clay	51	73	63	54	59	61	64	85	62	50	47	60	393	336	729	391	331	2	5	673	692	42	27	5	1
Clinton	42	36	46	48	47	39	44	47	36	40	39	36	245	255	500	244	255	1	....	490	492	3	1	1	1
Crawford	16	13	25	21	9	7	18	27	24	25	19	20	117	107	224	117	107	....	....	215	217	....	....	2	....
Daviess	52	66	58	67	49	65	70	66	77	71	65	54	381	379	760	379	377	2	2	744	748	3	4	5	....
Dearborn	31	24	33	20	37	33	31	24	28	14	31	30	170	166	336	169	165	1	1	318	322	6	4	11	9
Decatur	23	33	24	46	22	29	30	36	37	30	33	31	185	189	374	182	188	3	1	364	366	3	4	4	1
Dekalb	40	33	44	39	36	33	43	51	47	46	46	41	241	258	499	241	258	....	....	472	466	18	24	1	1
Delaware	88	72	123	95	87	101	102	95	97	96	106	76	561	577	1,138	544	564	17	13	1,102	1,102	23	27	4	....
Dubois	44	49	44	50	52	37	35	42	65	41	46	38	277	266	543	277	266	....	....	525	531	6	2	4	2
Elkhart	81	88	94	73	82	79	101	96	73	79	70	72	519	469	988	518	469	1	....	920	935	51	40	5	1
Fayette	16	25	29	25	37	20	21	22	22	18	26	21	136	146	282	129	145	7	1	275	278	4	2	1	....
Floyd	46	52	46	35	32	51	42	47	44	39	33	52	264	255	519	257	241	7	14	499	500	9	10	2	....
Fountain	39	29	44	40	22	27	31	33	47	36	28	30	191	215	406	191	215	....	....	392	394	8	7	1	....
Franklin	25	27	28	21	29	26	19	20	22	28	17	17	147	132	279	147	132	....	....	267	270	6	4	3	2
Fulton	26	34	34	43	21	28	20	38	14	27	25	30	176	164	340	176	164	....	....	334	335	1	1	1	....

TABLE A—Continued.

COUNTIES.	1910.												Sex.			Color.				Nationality of Parents.					
																White.		Colored.		American.		Foreign.		Not Reported.	
	January.	February.	March.	April.	May.	June.	July.	August.	September.	October.	November.	December.	Males.	Females.	Total.	Males.	Females.	Males.	Females.	Fathers.	Mothers.	Fathers.	Mothers.	Fathers.	Mothers.
Gibson	63	53	71	45	49	43	51	61	64	60	47	75	356	326	682	344	317	12	9	658	668	5	3	8	....
Grant	85	82	81	81	92	83	76	83	99	93	86	93	497	537	1,034	492	532	5	5	993	995	24	26	4	....
Greene	95	98	77	82	68	54	91	84	80	86	55	86	480	476	956	479	475	1	1	871	890	67	54	6	....
Hamilton	46	31	51	41	50	46	63	49	51	48	32	38	276	270	546	269	267	7	3	531	525	2	2	5	1
Hancock	23	33	28	26	29	18	28	28	31	28	32	24	160	168	328	158	167	2	1	319	323	4	4	4	....
Harrison	29	42	42	35	36	35	32	42	38	43	31	36	210	231	441	210	230	....	1	433	436	3	1	1	....
Hendricks	20	30	36	37	32	37	35	29	35	35	25	29	208	172	380	207	172	1	....	370	374	1	....	4	1
Henry	46	55	63	69	63	48	53	61	55	61	44	53	313	358	671	307	353	6	5	643	647	16.	16	4	....
Howard	63	53	58	52	62	69	61	58	67	51	58	58	377	333	710	373	327	4	6	677	687	19	15	7	1
Huntington	47	50	69	61	53	43	53	64	43	56	49	54	319	323	642	319	323	....	....	619	627	10	6	4	....
Jackson	53	54	53	45	57	52	60	61	82	74	47	55	361	332	693	360	330	1	2	668	675	7	4	4	....
Jasper	22	12	13	23	26	21	24	24	33	20	14	27	133	126	259	133	126	....	....	233	242	18	11	4	2
Jay	50	26	57	55	37	55	52	58	48	49	54	42	299	284	583	299	283	....	1	564	571	6	5	8	2
Jefferson	30	32	36	36	37	37	45	36	44	35	26	28	224	198	422	218	190	6	8	409	413	5	2	1	....
Jennings	28	24	36	26	28	26	35	31	38	28	22	26	180	168	348	172	162	8	6	332	338	5	4	5	....
Johnson	43	34	23	22	29	33	33	36	32	30	33	43	223	168	391	219	165	4	3	382	385	3	1	1	....
Knox	103	90	82	101	75	76	89	80	104	86	77	90	522	531	1,053	519	525	3	6	979	1,004	46	31	10	....
Kosciusko	49	39	59	42	41	41	52	50	45	49	36	39	305	237	542	304	237	1	....	529	534	7	5	3	....
Lagrange	25	17	35	25	33	33	24	23	33	34	22	30	181	153	334	181	153	....	....	322	325	5	3	1	....
Lake	173	120	156	106	140	128	161	147	163	163	118	152	883	843	1,726	882	843	1	....	897	959	797	747	14	2
Laporte	68	83	75	74	65	72	89	108	93	76	81	63	499	443	942	497	443	2	....	691	711	228	214	8	2
Lawrence	65	65	60	72	58	54	74	78	73	68	69	72	417	391	808	417	388	....	3	772	778	21	23	4	1
Madison	128	144	140	139	134	116	132	152	121	110	120	99	792	743	1,535	788	736	4	7	1,415	1,442	97	79	9	....
Marion	472	441	465	459	374	420	442	455	421	444	413	402	2,677	2,531	5,208	2,454	2,329	223	202	4,553	4,692	533	464	75	5
Marshall	43	37	57	34	39	34	39	45	42	41	47	37	243	252	495	243	252	....	....	480	485	6	3	3	1
Martin	35	23	28	21	19	30	21	20	33	28	29	19	164	187	351	164	187	....	....	292	296	2	....	2	....
Miami	44	45	52	44	42	45	56	47	60	54	43	52	297	287	584	296	287	1	....	552	560	19	16	5	....
Monroe	45	43	43	47	53	48	52	49	61	57	29	53	305	275	580	303	271	2	4	555	563	8	7	8	1
Montgomery	48	39	56	46	55	45	49	63	54	56	50	36	299	298	597	296	295	3	3	591	592	3	3	1	....
Morgan	45	43	40	31	35	43	48	44	37	47	40	32	261	224	485	258	223	3	1	470	476	2	2	6	....

Newton	19	21	21	19	25	15	22	24	16	23	17	25	137	110	247	126	110	1	....	234	235	7	7	3	2
Noble	35	35	41	43	28	[illegible]	43	21	38	44	38	35	230	230	460	230	230	....	....	444	450	11	7	2	....
Ohio	6	7	8	6	5	6	6	9	4	1	2	7	37	30	67	37	29	....	1	65	66	....	....	1	....
Orange	31	39	36	38	38	36	31	25	33	31	28	38	196	206	402	195	204	1	2	392	396	3	....	1	....
Owen	15	24	22	23	25	27	17	16	25	27	22	16	130	129	259	127	129	3	....	250	251	....	1	2	....
Parke	32	28	36	29	33	32	29	39	37	25	27	34	192	189	381	191	188	1	1	367	368	10	9	1	1
Perry	36	38	34	23	39	26	41	43	39	30	27	43	225	194	419	221	191	4	3	406	413	6	2	3	....
Pike	39	40	54	27	28	42	42	43	54	49	35	37	234	256	490	234	255	....	1	475	482	2	1	6	....
Porter	40	40	27	36	30	29	33	29	25	34	28	30	212	169	381	212	169	....	....	319	330	55	46	2	....
Posey	38	49	37	27	28	36	45	38	44	34	28	27	213	218	431	208	214	5	4	422	427	1	....	4	....
Pulaski	14	11	20	10	17	7	12	16	21	14	14	17	96	77	173	96	77	....	....	160	164	9	7	2	....
Putnam	27	37	29	33	34	34	35	51	41	40	25	31	211	206	417	209	205	2	1	409	412	1	....	2	....
Randolph	59	51	53	50	60	47	49	61	46	52	54	38	328	292	620	324	289	4	3	606	610	....	1	5	....
Ripley	43	28	39	26	23	23	34	37	34	23	35	36	186	195	381	186	195	....	....	361	369	11	6	3	....
Rush	28	33	29	21	30	33	27	29	33	38	31	30	205	157	362	202	154	3	3	346	348	1	2	4	1
Scott	18	12	17	17	16	16	14	11	19	20	27	12	92	107	199	92	107	....	....	195	196	....	....	1	....
Shelby	57	37	50	51	38	28	42	39	46	42	45	34	260	249	509	257	242	3	7	495	499	5	5	4	....
Spencer	26	33	39	27	29	43	41	46	38	34	41	30	224	203	427	216	195	8	8	420	421	1	2	2	....
Starke	19	21	17	18	17	23	16	16	10	10	12	21	89	111	200	89	111	....	....	162	170	33	28	3	....
Steuben	17	15	19	10	15	16	18	27	22	14	19	10	109	93	202	109	93	....	....	197	199	3	1	1	1
St. Joseph	216	174	217	188	199	171	204	186	203	188	177	165	1,173	1,115	2,288	1,170	1,110	3	5	1,306	1,383	956	889	12	2
Sullivan	80	77	84	64	56	56	64	73	75	73	76	78	437	419	856	437	417	....	2	760	782	77	63	10	2
Switzerland	24	19	11	15	5	12	15	19	28	16	16	15	88	107	195	88	107	....	....	194	194	1	1	....	....
Tippecanoe	45	57	62	53	57	65	69	53	47	36	48	49	328	312	640	326	308	2	4	567	589	57	43	12	4
Tipton	41	30	38	49	31	41	41	46	34	34	33	38	238	218	456	238	218	....	....	445	450	....	1	6	....
Union	7	13	17	9	4	12	9	14	11	10	8	5	61	58	119	59	55	2	3	115	114	2	3	....	....
Vanderburgh	97	122	137	93	94	102	135	132	138	118	114	108	713	677	1,390	657	629	56	48	1,294	1,321	52	44	20	1
Vermillion	35	36	48	44	53	42	41	36	37	32	42	44	233	257	490	229	255	4	2	345	357	136	129	5	....
Vigo	146	138	167	114	143	129	153	164	163	146	135	158	931	825	1,756	900	791	31	34	1,590	1,628	133	110	15	....
Wabash	44	51	42	40	38	51	38	33	40	38	51	30	257	239	496	255	237	2	2	473	484	14	8	5	....
Warren	25	19	24	31	16	20	18	22	22	13	26	21	147	110	257	147	109	....	1	248	249	1	1	1	....
Warrick	35	38	46	35	40	37	38	43	34	32	32	37	225	222	447	221	221	4	1	442	442	1	1	....	....
Washington	22	21	28	18	20	39	30	34	35	25	29	32	166	167	333	166	167	....	....	329	329	....	....	....	....
Wayne	67	45	82	54	71	64	61	71	73	50	76	49	410	353	763	391	341	19	12	723	736	30	22	5	....
Wells	34	37	53	27	35	40	47	40	43	33	31	42	215	247	462	215	247	....	....	445	449	8	7	3	....
White	28	31	33	26	25	25	32	34	42	44	38	37	198	197	395	198	197	....	....	373	386	14	6	5	....
Whitley	27	17	35	18	27	22	28	15	28	25	19	23	133	151	284	132	151	1	....	270	273	1	1	5	2
Grand total	4,724	4,556	5,142	4,484	4,397	4,452	4,900	5,009	5,034	4,743	4,380	4,488	28,806	27,503	56,309	28,273	27,019	533	484	51,123	52,017	4,062	3,565	464	67

TABLE B.

Births, Number of Children Born to Each Mother, Grouped Ages of Parents, Still, Plurality and Illegitimate Births, for Year Ending December 31, 1910.

COUNTIES.	Total Births.	Number of Children Born to Each Mother.												
		First.	Second.	Third.	Fourth.	Fifth.	Sixth.	Seventh.	Eighth.	Ninth.	Tenth.	Eleventh.	Twelfth and Over.	Not Reported.
Adams	508	129	93	80	72	41	30	20	15	5	9	9	5	......
Allen	1,517	451	344	234	150	120	83	32	30	23	22	11	10	7
Bartholomew	491	127	116	65	66	36	23	20	15	9	3	2	2	7
Benton	227	60	50	37	23	16	12	10	4	4	3	1	2	5
Blackford	380	105	78	66	42	24	19	16	11	7	4	3	1	4
Boone	500	150	112	78	55	45	24	17	11	7	3	......	3	4
Brown	172	40	32	15	26	16	13	9	9	6	3	1	1	1
Carroll	383	108	82	59	41	21	21	13	18	8	4	2	2	4
Cass	718	230	154	116	77	58	33	16	13	11	3	2	1	4
Clark	557	159	131	72	60	35	41	23	15	9	2	3	4	3
Clay	729	193	135	129	67	59	42	28	25	15	15	2	7	12
Clinton	500	144	123	58	51	47	27	13	9	8	8	5	2	5
Crawford	224	61	45	37	29	18	10	8	5	1	2	2	2	4
Daviess	760	193	148	109	75	77	51	35	29	13	9	6	11	4
Dearborn	336	93	80	57	28	23	20	12	5	1	7	1	4	5
Decatur	374	119	73	60	38	21	24	19	9	2	......	3	2	4
Dekalb	499	141	93	87	62	42	28	21	7	6	5	1	1	5
Delaware	1,138	335	257	198	100	82	59	37	18	23	9	4	7	9
Dubois	543	121	108	83	64	46	46	26	19	12	8	2	2	6
Elkhart	988	291	232	175	81	69	45	37	29	13	8	5	3	......
Fayette	282	77	74	48	27	13	8	15	6	2	1	1	2	8
Floyd	519	153	126	72	50	38	22	18	19	8	4	2	6	1
Fountain	406	127	94	55	48	34	15	10	6	7	3	4	2	1
Franklin	279	57	65	42	36	18	16	10	8	6	5	3	4	9
Fulton	340	97	69	56	42	30	18	6	6	7	2	2	4	1

Gibson	682	179	145	117	79	51	29	29	19	10	12	3	5	4
Grant	1,034	285	232	155	104	74	55	34	20	24	9	9	8	25
Greene	956	248	197	163	116	77	46	39	30	16	8	4	4	8
Hamilton	546	151	120	68	73	44	24	18	13	12	7	5	5	6
[illegible]k	328	104	67	57	28	28	18	10	4	2	4		4	2
Harrison	141	112	66	67	53	51	29	18	14	10	8	2	6	5
Hendricks	380	94	90	60	44	39	22	13	8	5	2	1	2	
Henry	671	222	159	115	57	34	24	21	13	8	2	4	5	7
Howard	710	224	158	95	67	56	47	21	12	11	8	4	1	6
Huntington	642	176	128	101	92	52	31	24	21	6	2	3	3	3
Jackson	693	170	134	104	82	66	44	30	22	8	10	6	3	14
Jasper	259	65	53	37	33	19	14	8	11	4	5	3	2	5
Jay	583	154	123	79	66	49	39	15	21	13	5	5	5	9
Jefferson	422	115	96	64	43	33	17	17	9	8	7	6	2	5
[illegible]	348	68	63	59	41	46	26	15	12	8	2	3	4	1
Johnson	391	114	87	56	37	31	32	15	7	5	4	1	1	1
Knox	1,053	275	221	160	111	84	70	35	31	20	13	6	9	18
Kosciusko	542	162	127	77	56	45	27	20	9	7	6			6
Lagrange	334	88	72	53	39	32	17	11	3	6	5	2	4	2
Lake	1,726	466	400	281	193	124	83	58	38	21	21	11	13	17
Laporte	942	258	219	148	111	55	57	27	22	12	11	10	9	3
Lawrence	808	200	145	124	108	78	42	42	21	14	11	7	6	10
Madison	1,535	431	330	238	177	119	90	45	34	19	24	5	9	14
Marion	5,208	1,816	1,221	799	493	313	203	142	82	61	32	16	22	8
Marshall	495	123	106	71	64	42	26	29	13	4	5	2	4	6
Martin	301	70	58	46	33	28	14	21	11	5	4	4	5	2
Miami	584	171	142	80	64	41	32	20	12	9	5	1	1	6
[illegible]oe	580	147	120	92	70	52	26	25	13	13	7	5	3	7
Montgomery	597	187	122	96	76	34	30	19	12	2	8	6	2	3
Morgan	485	133	100	66	60	40	28	19	14	4	8	3	2	8
Newton	247	64	43	49	27	16	20	10	4	3	6	1	1	3
Noble	460	132	111	63	53	32	20	16	16	4	5	2	3	3
Ohio	67	17	16	15	2	7	2	1	3	3		1		
[illegible]ge	402	104	95	59	37	29	20	25	11	8	8	2	1	3
[illegible]en	259	51	57	47	25	26	15	12	9	6	3	2		6
Parke	381	103	76	55	39	34	25	19	15	6	4	1	1	3
Perry	419	101	88	61	49	37	27	20	10	15	4	6		1
Pike	190	121	88	70	59	47	29	28	16	15	5	2	10	
Porter	381	88	79	60	45	28	26	16	16	5	6	2	3	7
Posey	431	108	94	71	48	33	30	19	8	8	2	4	3	3

TABLE B—Continued.

COUNTIES.	Total Births.	Number of Children Born to Each Mother.												
		First.	Second.	Third.	Fourth.	Fifth.	Sixth.	Seventh.	Eighth.	Ninth.	Tenth.	Eleventh.	Twelfth and Over.	Not Reported.
Pulaski	173	39	35	27	28	11	9	8	3	3	5	3	1	1
Putnam	417	119	102	60	42	27	24	10	14	7	5	1	2	4
Randolph	620	171	119	105	58	62	33	24	18	12	6	3	3	6
Ripley	381	113	79	47	43	23	21	20	7	7	5	3	3	10
Rush	362	104	79	63	30	19	24	14	8	7	6		2	6
Scott	199	47	41	33	27	14	15	8	6	3	1	1	3	
Shelby	509	129	130	89	53	42	19	17	7	5	4	4	4	6
Spencer	427	116	88	65	50	41	23	21	8	4	3	4	1	3
Starke	200	45	37	22	27	25	17	9	7	5	1	2	2	1
Steuben	202	71	47	27	19	15	10	3	5	2				3
St. Joseph	2,288	577	506	361	263	189	127	90	56	42	36	12	23	6
Sullivan	856	220	180	124	84	74	60	41	23	28	8	7	9	3
Switzerland	195	54	38	35	22	7	12	14	5	4	3		1	
Tippecanoe	640	176	139	106	67	55	26	26	8	12	10	5	2	8
Tipton	456	139	77	90	42	35	24	17	11	4	9	1	2	5
Union	119	22	30	19	14	12	4	2	2	3		1		
Vanderburgh	1,390	447	324	217	123	86	73	40	29	24	9	9	9	
Vermillion	490	111	98	72	63	43	42	24	16	7	2	4	7	1
Vigo	1,756	495	394	257	187	130	86	60	50	32	17	11	10	27
Wabash	496	142	108	79	58	28	27	14	9	6	6	5	4	10
Warren	257	71	46	42	22	28	14	14	7	2	3	3	1	4
Warrick	447	104	86	67	54	46	24	26	9	6	2	2	5	6
Washington	333	90	70	41	38	31	11	12	13	8	5	4	5	5
Wayne	763	240	181	123	85	41	28	22	14	8	9	3	4	5
Wells	462	121	102	69	49	41	28	19	11	6	5	4	3	4
White	395	107	87	51	30	38	24	22	13	6	5	1	3	2
Whitley	284	77	64	47	28	22	15	10	6	4	3	1	2	5
Grand Total	56,309	15,815	12 249	9,704	6,076	4,340	3,016	2,064	1,365	885	608	331	372	484

TABLE B—Continued.

Births, Number of Children Born to Each Mother, Grouped Ages of Parents, Still, Plurality and Illegimate Births, for Year Ending December 31, 1910.

COUNTIES.	Grouped Ages of Parents.														Still-births.		Plurality Births.		Illegitimate Births.	
	Under 20.		20 to 30.		30 to 40.		40 to 50.		50 to 60.		60 to 70.	70 to 80.	Not Reported.							
	Fathers.	Mothers.	Fathers.	Mothers.	Fathers.	Mothers.	Fathers.	Mothers.	Fathers.	Mothers.	Fathers.	Fathers.	Fathers.	Mothers.	Males.	Females.	Males.	Females.	Males.	Females.
Adams	3	47	220	265	187	157	73	27	12	......	1	......	5	5	8	8	7	7	1	1
Allen	7	91	666	874	582	461	195	71	36	......	2	......	18	9	32	26	8	14	8	8
Bartholomew	12	48	200	281	204	138	55	16	9	......	......	......	4	1	7	12	5	9	1	3
Benton	......	15	92	130	92	66	33	10	4	......	......	......	1	1	2	2	5	5	1	1
Blackford	5	54	185	201	115	89	49	18	5	......	......	......	13	10	......	5	11	5	2	3
Boone	11	54	228	285	181	133	70	29	9	......	1	......	4	3	3	7	5	5	3	2
Brown	3	23	63	76	68	65	26	8	11	......	1	......	......	......	2	3	......	......	2	4
Carroll	4	39	183	210	127	113	52	18	11	......	1	......	3	1	3	2	2	2	1	4
Cass	9	70	338	415	247	195	94	24	14	......	1	......	8	7	17	15	7	7	4	7
Clark	8	48	243	308	201	164	66	21	18	......	......	......	7	2	12	11	17	11	5	5
Clay	5	60	333	397	248	214	100	40	18	......	1	......	15	9	12	8	9	9	8	5
Clinton	14	65	253	288	148	113	68	23	6	......	......	......	5	5	5	11	9	3	1	2
Crawford	1	23	93	121	78	66	35	5	5	......	......	......	5	2	2	......	8	6	1	4
Daviess	14	86	327	394	265	223	117	46	16	......	4	......	9	3	14	14	6	10	5	7
Dearborn	3	30	139	184	123	98	53	14	5	......	......	......	12	9	8	3	1	1	3	2
Decatur	4	35	153	208	152	111	43	17	10	......	1	1	7	......	......	6	2	4	2	4
Dekalb	11	49	201	261	185	152	77	23	9	......	......	......	8	6	6	12	6	10	4	4
Delaware	20	139	554	621	388	315	139	48	19	......	3	......	6	6	19	17	9	9	13	1
Dubois	5	31	214	280	212	190	92	31	8	......	......	......	4	3	4	5	5	11	3	2
Elkhart	11	90	452	572	382	268	111	42	10	......	2	......	8	4	17	8	10	14	10	7

TABLE B—Continued.

COUNTIES.	Grouped Ages of Parents. Under 20. Fathers.	Under 20. Mothers.	20 to 30. Fathers.	20 to 30. Mothers.	30 to 40. Fathers.	30 to 40. Mothers.	40 to 50. Fathers.	40 to 50. Mothers.	50 to 60. Fathers.	50 to 60. Mothers.	60 to 70. Fathers.	70 to 80. Fathers.	Not Reported. Fathers.	Not Reported. Mothers.	Still-births. Males.	Still-births. Females.	Plurality Births. Males.	Plurality Births. Females.	Illegitimate Births. Males.	Illegitimate Births. Females.
Fayette	3	29	134	146	92	85	38	17	8	.....	2	.....	3	3	3	5	2	2	1	1
Floyd	11	67	215	263	206	155	60	24	10	.....	1	.....	7	1	10	8	12	6	6	7
Fountain	9	60	186	211	124	116	75	14	6	.....	1	.....	.....	.....	5	6	6	4	3	4
Franklin	2	14	86	145	128	99	49	16	7	.....	.....	.....	4	2	3	1	4	2	.....	3
Fulton	2	43	166	182	121	92	39	17	5	.....	.....	.....	3	2	2	2	1	7	2	2
Gibson	15	81	294	373	248	177	85	36	16	.....	.....	.....	13	4	10	12	8	14	14	8
Grant	24	123	456	539	351	295	157	54	20	1	3	.....	10	9	16	13	14	12	5	5
Greene	18	132	455	530	326	245	119	33	13	.....	4	.....	9	4	18	13	12	12	6	3
Hamilton	10	66	246	289	170	153	92	27	11	.....	.....	.....	9	3	13	10	3	10	7	4
Hancock	2	33	153	187	114	89	42	15	9	1	1	.....	6	2	6	6	2	.....	2	4
Harrison	4	39	174	218	160	147	79	29	13	.....	.....	.....	7	4	5	6	4	4	2	2
Hendricks	6	32	151	195	153	129	53	17	7	.....	1	.....	4	2	7	1	6	4	2	3
Henry	5	75	341	383	218	176	75	26	14	.....	1	.....	9	3	12	9	9	7	3	5
Howard	13	80	322	412	257	187	91	21	13	.....	1	.....	6	3	12	10	6	8	4	6
Huntington	6	37	278	379	252	191	78	25	11	.....	1	.....	7	1	9	2	12	6	7	2
Jackson	9	60	280	363	254	214	101	37	22	.....	2	.....	11	5	10	16	12	16	1	5
Jasper	4	25	98	126	96	83	38	15	9	.....	2	.....	8	6	5	5	3	5	2	2
Jay	8	91	267	301	211	151	71	28	9	.....	2	.....	10	7	9	7	4	6	5	5
Jefferson	10	47	169	219	152	129	65	18	14	.....	.....	1	4	2	6	7	8	6	.....	3
Jennings	3	30	103	158	153	129	65	25	13	.....	.....	.....	5	.....	4	5	8	4	6	2
Johnson	7	43	178	203	129	121	57	17	11	1	1	.....	3	1	3	5	3	7	2	4
Knox	22	127	415	534	388	320	165	53	29	.....	1	.....	15	1	16	15	16	17	10	9
Kosciusko	8	62	260	313	180	133	77	26	8	.....	1	.....	5	5	5	6	6	.....	4	3
Lagrange	2	29	150	184	128	100	42	15	5	.....	.....	.....	1	.....	8	2	5	7	1	1
Lake	6	116	743	1,038	729	435	192	59	13	.....	2	.....	23	10	30	23	21	15	7	9

Laporte	6	82	418	537	357	269	118	33	11	......	4	......	13	6	21	18	17	10	4	5
Lawrence	10	114	369	417	282	220	108	37	16	......	1	......	11	9	20	11	12	10	9	7
Madison	26	187	740	898	523	365	196	63	21	......	1	1	13	8	34	26	12	16	11	9
Marion	94	589	2,417	2,954	1,929	1,435	588	171	69	......	7	1	56	12	105	88	39	55	103	99
Marshall	8	43	213	275	178	149	72	22	13	......	2	......	3	......	12	4	6	6	......	2
Martin	3	26	125	162	104	87	55	20	5	1	1	......	3	......	7	4	5	5	2	3
Miami	8	68	259	317	215	165	76	26	11	......	2	......	5	......	8	......	6	10	4	4
Monroe	10	72	254	311	201	151	79	31	11	......	2	......	14	6	8	6	9	9	4	10
Montgomery	7	68	282	336	206	163	82	27	14	......	2	......	2	1	10	8	3	1	6	2
Morgan	8	51	196	270	172	127	68	18	13	......	2	......	19	12	7	2	10	4	4	7
Newton	2	25	103	127	97	77	35	11	4	......	......	......	3	4	1	......	3	3	5	......
Noble	6	38	192	267	165	130	82	20	8	......	2	......	2	2	6	9	2	4	2	4
Ohio	1	6	20	31	33	22	9	5	......	......	1	......	2	2	2	1	......	2	......	......
Orange	5	52	173	212	134	104	72	24	9	......	......	......	3	4	4	3	6	6	3	2
Owen	3	33	95	119	103	82	41	16	5	......	......	1	4	2	6	1	5	9	3	1
Parke	1	47	178	216	120	99	62	14	13	......	......	1	3	2	8	5	2	4	1	......
Perry	5	34	160	228	169	127	66	25	12	......	......	......	3	1	2	5	5	3	1	3
Pike	14	63	204	257	172	136	71	22	12	......	......	......	10	5	7	7	8	6	6	10
Porter	......	25	154	204	137	125	76	21	7	......	......	......	2	1	6	1	4	6	5	1
Posey	6	43	171	229	149	126	79	20	8	......	2	......	12	9	5	9	6	2	4	4
Pulaski	4	21	73	92	55	48	31	8	5	1	......	......	3	1	4	1	2	2	4	2
Putnam	11	50	196	227	140	115	44	17	14	......	1	......	6	3	1	3	5	5	3	......
Randolph	12	75	270	311	219	200	85	21	14	......	1	......	10	4	10	8	6	12	10	4
Ripley	1	26	144	211	157	114	49	20	11	......	3	1	9	4	5	3	4	5	6	3
Rush	2	33	150	210	133	86	46	19	10	......	......	......	10	3	2	6	10	9	2	5
Scott	3	21	76	93	81	71	28	11	6	......	1	......	1	......	3	3	......	6	4	......
Shelby	7	50	240	282	185	149	52	20	10	......	1	......	9	3	5	8	6	4	3	3
Spencer	1	42	184	224	148	125	65	27	16	......	......	1	8	5	4	4	4	4	2	5
Starke	2	24	73	93	81	68	36	12	3	......	......	......	3	1	1	2	1	3	1	4
Steuben	5	18	103	122	66	53	22	7	3	......	......	......	2	1	1	3	......	2	1	1
St. Joseph	25	169	1,012	1,332	898	673	296	97	32	1	......	......	11	2	45	31	16	12	9	8
Sullivan	12	115	383	455	300	231	126	40	13	......	2	......	11	6	14	9	12	6	11	9
Switzerland	1	20	71	87	74	68	43	18	4	......	1	......	1	2	2	4	......	......	1	4
Tippecanoe	6	58	263	347	236	188	102	40	16	......	1	......	12	3	7	9	3	5	8	5
Tipton	14	55	211	253	146	117	63	22	9	......	......	......	8	4	9	5	5	5	6	4
Union	1	9	49	69	48	33	13	5	4	......	......	1	1	1	4	1	3	1	1	......
Vanderburgh	20	172	652	749	452	370	193	72	30	......	2	......	17	3	26	22	21	27	26	21
Vermillion	7	58	191	259	193	146	72	20	13	......	1	......	9	3	8	3	5	3	5	3
Vigo	26	204	804	999	613	452	240	75	36	......	1	......	18	8	42	27	21	15	23	15

TABLE B—Continued.

COUNTIES.	Grouped Ages of Parents.														Still-births.		Plurality Births.		Illegitimate Births.	
	Under 20.		20 to 30.		30 to 40.		40 to 50.		50 to 60.		60 to 70.	70 to 80.	Not Reported.							
	Fathers.	Mothers.	Fathers.	Mothers.	Fathers.	Mothers.	Fathers.	Mothers.	Fathers.	Mothers.	Fathers.	Fathers.	Fathers.	Mothers.	Males.	Females.	Males.	Females.	Males.	Females.
Fayette	3	29	134	146	92	85	38	17	8	......	2	......	3	3	3	5	2	2	1	1
Floyd	11	67	215	263	206	155	60	24	10	......	1	......	7	1	10	8	12	6	6	7
Fountain	9	60	186	211	124	116	75	14	6	......	1	......	......	......	5	6	6	4	3	4
Franklin	2	14	86	145	128	99	49	16	7	......	......	......	4	2	3	1	4	2	......	3
Fulton	2	43	166	182	121	92	39	17	5	......	......	......	3	2	2	2	1	7	2	2
Gibson	15	81	294	373	248	177	85	36	16	......	......	......	13	4	10	12	8	14	14	8
Grant	24	123	456	539	351	295	157	54	20	1	3	......	10	9	16	13	14	12	5	5
Greene	18	132	455	530	326	245	119	33	13	......	4	......	9	4	18	13	12	12	6	3
Hamilton	10	66	246	289	170	153	92	27	11	......	......	......	9	3	13	10	3	10	7	4
Hancock	2	33	153	187	114	89	42	15	9	1	1	......	6	2	6	6	2	......	2	4
Harrison	4	39	174	218	160	147	79	29	13	......	......	......	7	4	5	6	4	4	2	2
Hendricks	6	32	151	195	153	129	53	17	7	......	1	......	4	2	7	1	6	4	2	3
Henry	5	75	341	383	218	176	75	26	14	......	1	......	9	3	12	9	9	7	3	5
Howard	13	80	322	412	257	187	91	21	13	......	1	......	6	3	12	10	6	8	4	6
Huntington	6	37	278	379	252	191	78	25	11	......	1	......	7	1	9	2	12	6	7	2
Jackson	9	60	280	363	254	214	101	37	22	......	2	......	11	5	10	16	12	16	1	5
Jasper	4	25	98	126	96	83	38	15	9	......	2	......	8	6	5	5	3	5	2	2
Jay	8	91	267	301	211	151	71	28	9	......	2	......	10	7	9	7	4	6	5	5
Jefferson	10	47	169	219	152	129	65	18	14	......	......	1	4	2	6	7	8	6	......	3
Jennings	3	30	103	158	153	129	65	25	13	......	......	......	5	......	4	5	8	4	6	2
Johnson	7	43	178	203	129	121	57	17	11	1	1	......	3	1	3	5	3	7	2	4
Knox	22	127	415	534	388	320	165	53	29	......	1	......	15	1	16	15	16	17	10	9
Kosciusko	8	62	260	313	180	133	77	26	8	......	1	......	5	5	5	6	6	......	4	3
Lagrange	2	29	150	184	128	100	42	15	5	......	......	......	1	......	8	2	5	7	1	1
Lake	6	116	743	1,038	729	495	192	59	13	......	2	......	23	10	30	23	21	15	7	9

County																				
Laporte	6	82	418	537	357	269	118	33	11	—	4	—	13	6	21	18	17	10	4	5
Lawrence	10	114	369	417	282	220	108	37	16	—	1	—	11	9	20	11	12	10	9	7
Madison	26	187	740	898	523	365	196	63	21	—	1	1	13	8	34	26	12	16	11	9
Marion	94	589	2,417	2,954	1,929	1,435	588	171	69	—	7	1	56	12	105	88	39	55	103	99
Marshall	8	43	213	275	178	149	72	22	13	—	2	—	3	—	12	4	6	6	—	2
Martin	3	26	125	162	104	87	55	20	5	1	1	—	3	—	7	4	5	5	2	3
Miami	8	68	259	317	215	165	76	26	11	—	2	—	5	—	8	—	6	10	4	4
Monroe	10	72	254	311	201	151	79	31	11	—	2	—	14	6	8	6	9	9	4	10
Montgomery	7	68	282	336	206	163	82	27	14	—	2	—	2	1	10	8	3	1	6	2
Morgan	8	51	196	270	172	127	68	18	13	—	2	—	19	12	7	2	10	4	4	7
Newton	2	25	103	127	97	77	35	11	4	—	—	—	3	4	1	—	3	3	5	—
Noble	6	38	192	267	165	130	82	20	8	—	2	—	2	2	6	9	2	4	2	4
Ohio	1	6	20	31	33	22	9	5	—	—	1	—	2	2	2	1	—	2	—	—
Orange	5	52	173	212	134	104	72	24	9	—	—	—	3	4	4	3	6	6	3	2
Owen	3	33	95	119	103	82	41	16	5	—	—	1	4	2	6	1	5	9	3	1
Parke	1	47	178	216	120	99	62	14	13	—	—	1	3	2	8	5	2	4	1	—
Perry	5	34	160	228	169	127	66	25	12	—	—	—	3	1	2	5	5	3	1	3
Pike	14	63	204	257	172	136	71	22	12	—	—	—	10	5	7	7	8	6	6	10
Porter	—	25	154	204	137	125	76	21	7	—	—	—	2	1	6	1	4	6	5	1
Posey	6	43	171	229	149	126	79	20	8	—	2	—	12	9	5	9	6	2	4	4
Pulaski	4	21	73	92	55	48	31	8	5	1	—	—	3	1	4	1	2	2	4	2
Putnam	11	50	196	227	140	115	44	17	14	—	1	—	6	3	1	3	5	5	3	—
Randolph	12	75	270	311	219	200	85	21	14	—	1	—	10	4	10	8	6	12	10	4
Ripley	1	26	144	211	157	114	49	20	11	—	3	1	9	4	5	3	4	5	6	3
Rush	2	33	150	210	133	86	46	19	10	—	—	—	10	3	2	6	10	9	2	5
Scott	3	21	76	93	81	71	28	11	6	—	1	—	1	—	3	3	—	6	4	—
Shelby	7	50	240	282	185	149	52	20	10	—	1	—	9	3	5	8	6	4	3	3
Spencer	1	42	184	224	148	125	65	27	16	—	—	1	8	5	4	4	4	4	2	5
Starke	2	24	73	93	81	68	36	12	3	—	—	—	3	1	1	2	1	3	1	4
Steuben	5	18	103	122	66	53	22	7	3	—	—	—	2	1	1	3	—	2	1	1
St. Joseph	25	169	1,012	1,332	898	673	296	97	32	1	—	—	11	2	45	31	16	12	9	8
Sullivan	12	115	383	455	300	231	126	40	13	—	2	—	11	6	14	9	12	6	11	9
Switzerland	1	20	71	87	74	68	43	18	4	—	1	—	1	2	2	4	—	—	1	4
Tippecanoe	6	58	263	347	236	188	102	40	16	—	1	—	12	3	7	9	3	5	8	5
Tipton	14	55	211	253	146	117	63	22	9	—	—	—	8	4	9	5	5	5	6	4
Union	1	9	49	69	48	33	13	5	4	—	—	1	1	1	4	1	3	1	1	—
Vanderburgh	20	172	652	749	452	370	193	72	30	—	2	—	17	3	26	22	21	27	26	21
Vermillion	7	58	191	259	193	146	72	20	13	—	1	—	9	3	8	3	5	3	5	3
Vigo	26	204	804	999	613	452	240	75	36	—	1	—	18	8	42	27	21	15	23	15

TABLE B—Continued.

COUNTIES.	Grouped Ages of Parents.														Still-births.		Plurality Births.		Illegitimate Births.	
	Under 20.		20 to 30.		30 to 40.		40 to 50.		50 to 60.		60 to 70.	70 to 80.	Not Reported.							
	Fathers.	Mothers.	Fathers.	Mothers.	Fathers.	Mothers.	Fathers.	Mothers.	Fathers.	Mothers.	Fathers.	Fathers.	Fathers.	Mothers.	Males.	Females.	Males.	Females.	Males.	Females.
Wabash	8	56	234	278	167	125	60	27	10	.....	4	......	9	6	7	8	5	3	5	4
Warren	2	28	108	144	99	57	20	15	9	.....	.....	......	2	6	5	4	5	9	1	3
Warrick	5	43	188	221	162	151	66	23	14	.....	1	......	7	5	9	5	3	5	.....	4
Washington	6	26	132	176	117	93	54	26	9	.....	3	1	7	8	6	2	5	3	4	3
Wayne	8	70	370	443	271	199	88	41	12	.....	1	......	8	5	12	9	6	4	10	5
Wells	11	50	210	246	145	129	68	29	11	.....	2	2	7	2	3	5	6	6	2	5
White	5	41	160	221	152	113	59	16	4	.....	1	......	11	1	7	3	.....	6	2	3
Whitley	4	29	110	138	107	88	41	17	5	.....	1	......	8	4	2	.....	7	9	2	2
Grand total	791	5,867	24,837	30,911	20,416	15,953	7,660	2,566	1,116	6	102	12	715	346	923	766	650	667	522	476

TABLE D.

Marriages by Months, Color and Nationality, for Year Ending December 31, 1910.

COUNTIES.	1910.												Color.		Nationality.						Total.
															American.		Foreign.		Not Reported.		
	January.	February.	March.	April.	May.	June.	July.	August.	September.	October.	November.	December.	White.	Colored.	Grooms.	Brides.	Grooms.	Brides.	Grooms.	Brides.	
Adams	12	13	13	11	18	12	5	18	20	30	18	21	191		156	160	23	21	12	10	191
Allen	83	31	47	82	81	110	44	65	88	135	45	77	880	8	825	843	62	43	1	2	888
Bartholomew	23	13	19	11	15	20	20	17	32	24	20	26	240		237	234	3	6			240
Benton	11	14	12	3	10	8	10	10	8	4	5	7	101	1	99	99	3	3			102
Blackford	13	18	19	19	14	9	8	15	11	16	14	20	175	1	172	173	4	2		1	176
Boone	13	12	24	13	13	19	20	15	22	20	18	15	204		180	180			24	24	204
Brown	5	5	5	5	5	4	6	6	5	9	6	11	72		72	72					72
Carroll	19	20	14	11	3	16	9	13	15	17	18	13	168		168	167		1			168
Cass	39	32	19	35	33	46	23	27	32	54	31	28	393	6	330	333	49	47	20	19	399
Clark	67	67	76	93	126	161	150	139	119	108	134	78	1,105	213	1,297	1,302	17	11	4	5	1,318
Clay	32	15	18	25	24	19	31	16	18	29	26	25	276	2	267	272	11	6			278
Clinton	25	22	16	16	13	20	13	17	26	29	19	31	246	1	244	246	3	1			247
Crawford	6	8	10	13	5	8	8	10	9	3	4	8	92		54	67	23	15	15	10	92
Daviess	19	22	12	22	18	14	13	17	24	19	45	17	242		242	242					242
Dearborn	15	17	13	22	16	24	9	13	21	17	14	20	200	1	200	198	1	3			201
Decatur	11	9	10	12	12	16	4	6	16	10	13	18	137		135	136	2	1			137
Dekalb	24	15	17	23	11	29	19	8	17	24	24	19	230		224	226	6	4			230
Delaware	79	35	42	46	38	54	49	48	49	54	36	53	558	25	544	547	22	18	17	18	583
Dubois	5	7	12	22	13	16	7	12	24	11	18	16	163		163	163					163
Elkhart	27	31	49	33	36	45	30	42	33	40	49	49	462	2	308	295	45	32	111	137	464

TABLE D—Continued.

COUNTIES.	1910.												Color.		Nationality.						Total.
															American.		Foreign.		Not Reported.		
	January.	February.	March.	April.	May.	June.	July.	August.	September.	October.	November	December.	White.	Colored.	Grooms.	Brides.	Grooms.	Brides.	Grooms.	Brides.	
Fayette	5	5	2	6	7	7	5	13	12	14	6	10	87	5	92	92	......	......	......	......	92
Floyd	16	20	23	29	20	30	18	19	39	35	41	33	303	20	313	318	5	......	5	5	323
Fountain	15	13	15	8	9	15	8	8	25	15	21	21	173	......	168	171	5	1	......	1	173
Franklin	6	8	4	4	3	13	14	9	10	12	13	11	107	......	107	107	......	......	......	......	107
Fulton	11	13	13	9	17	12	6	19	12	16	14	18	160	......	159	160	1	......	......	......	160
Gibson	16	18	12	15	11	10	25	28	18	24	33	25	213	22	234	234	1	1	......	......	235
Grant	36	39	44	37	37	55	36	39	39	55	36	61	486	28	505	510	9	4	......	......	514
Greene	25	21	39	18	26	27	24	30	34	26	31	41	342	......	323	332	19	10	......	......	342
Hamilton	14	15	22	18	15	23	17	23	33	46	30	21	257	20	276	277	1	......	......	......	277
Hancock	10	5	17	13	5	13	9	12	14	9	19	19	142	3	144	144	1	1	......	......	145
Harrison	6	10	12	15	14	5	8	6	21	9	12	19	135	2	137	137	......	......	......	......	137
Hendricks	8	9	9	7	6	18	5	14	9	18	11	16	127	3	129	130	1	......	......	......	130
Henry	21	9	31	19	14	14	26	41	54	22	27	35	306	7	313	313	......	......	......	......	313
Howard	18	29	35	32	25	34	22	26	29	31	39	40	356	4	353	352	7	8	......	......	360
Huntington	19	29	24	27	22	25	9	29	28	29	39	27	307	......	306	305	1	2	......	......	307
Jackson	17	10	19	26	14	23	10	20	16	21	13	25	213	1	212	213	1	1	1	......	214
Jasper	8	14	7	11	10	11	7	3	3	7	9	11	101	......	97	98	4	3	......	......	101
Jay	16	14	33	20	23	11	15	22	21	27	22	30	252	2	251	250	3	3	......	1	254
Jefferson	21	27	25	20	12	23	10	19	22	26	27	22	250	4	254	253	......	1	......	......	254
Jennings	7	7	10	12	8	13	13	12	9	13	10	14	125	3	128	128	......	......	......	......	128
Johnson	13	12	20	8	8	20	9	11	18	17	11	10	150	7	157	157	......	......	......	......	157
Knox	46	36	46	40	26	49	37	46	57	50	65	61	552	7	540	552	19	7	......	......	559
Kosciusko	17	21	23	19	14	19	15	13	24	31	25	25	246	......	246	246	......	......	......	......	246
Lagrange	6	10	10	9	18	19	9	10	12	14	16	21	154	......	154	154	......	......	......	......	154
Lake	175	126	90	145	143	171	145	141	151	158	182	174	1,749	52	1,304	1,345	497	456	......	......	1,801

Lake	24	30	28	54	32	69	43	48	45	53	56	29	508	3	411	444	99	67	1		511
Lawrence	20	22	17	25	17	22	26	18	21	26	31	32	275	2	277	277					277
Madison	58	51	58	60	45	79	49	53	47	64	60	72	682	14	662	672	34	24			696
Marion	214	195	166	227	214	406	243	255	253	398	300	269	2,770	370	2,423	2,958	211	174	6	8	3,140
Marshall	11	12	22	14	13	15	17	13	22	25	17	32	214		213	213	1	1			214
Martin	9	7	5	21	4	7	8	11	10	6	9	13	110		110	110					110
Miami	16	31	30	27	14	28	19	22	20	19	42	33	293	8	291	294	10	7			301
Monroe	23	21	20	12	15	33	25	16	16	36	24	19	251	9	258	258	2			2	260
Montgomery	23	20	16	18	14	31	24	25	19	19	35	26	267	3	270	270					270
Morgan	16	14	21	15	9	15	13	17	15	15	10	22	182		182	182					182
Newton	9	9	3	5	4	3	3	5	6	6	9	6	68		65	67	3	1			68
Noble	15	21	14	13	16	23	16	10	15	20	21	27	211		202	207	9	4			211
Ohio	1	10	1	3		3	2	2	4	5	6	1	37	1	38	37				1	38
Orange	8	10	16	16	12	20	11	11	16	13	16	11	152	8	160	160					160
Owen	3	7	7	2	9	8	6	9	14	16	6	6	91	2	93	93					93
Parke	11	6	20	11	14	16	13	21	18	15	12	17	170	4	170	172	3	2	1		174
Perry	1	10	8	18	8	12	10	11	20	16	22	5	137	4	141	141					141
Pike	10	15	12	18	12	14	15	16	8	30	15	29	193	1	190	189	1	1	3	4	194
Porter	13	16	17	14	10	23	12	16	20	22	21	18	202		176	187	25	12	1	3	202
Posey	25	14	19	31	22	15	21	33	23	23	25	29	269	11	280	280					280
Pulaski	8	11	7	16	6	17	3	5	11	8	9	14	115		113	114	2	1			115
Putnam	26	8	12	15	11	20	20	20	20	14	14	21	197	4	201	201					201
Randolph	15	20	26	20	15	26	19	19	11	24	21	37	251	2	251	253	2				253
Ripley	14	7	12	13	8	8	18	5	8	11	7	13	124		124	124					124
Rush	7	12	9	12	10	15	5	14	12	11	11	8	122	4	126	126					126
Scott	5	8	7	2	8	3	2	7	6	8	8	8	72		71	72	1				72
Shelby	26	26	12	25	13	19	23	19	28	33	24	18	259	7	260	266	6				266
Spencer	18	17	25	26	20	16	17	33	36	25	31	25	266	23	289	289					289
Starke	7	4	9	7	8	7	4	6	4	9	8	6	79		52	58	27	21			79
Steuben	13	10	8	6	7	18	9	6	13	22	17	13	142		140	142	2				142
St. Joseph	55	62	51	71	60	127	105	59	68	91	88	87	914	10	685	718	239	206			924
Sullivan	34	17	27	39	10	24	16	25	29	23	46	37	327		310	318	17	9			327
Switzerland	5	6	5	7	3	8	5	3	3	4	4	7	60		60	60					60
Tippecanoe	26	35	22	30	17	62	16	23	42	40	39	30	380	2	363	376	19	6			382
Tipton	18	16	15	16	3	10	9	22	11	18	21	28	187		186	187	1				187
Union	3	4	3	1	3	5	2	2	2	8	7	6	44	2	46	46					46
Vanderburgh	79	57	86	82	80	95	110	91	89	139	112	94	995	119	1,001	1,014	113	100			1,114
Vermillion	16	17	8	9	7	9	10	7	17	15	15	21	149	2	124	127	27	24			151
Vigo	83	89	80	93	69	136	102	114	123	113	125	129	1,214	42	1,150	1,199	89	41	17	16	1,25

TABLE D—Continued.

COUNTIES.	1910.												Color.		Nationality.						Total.
															American.		Foreign.		Not Reported.		
	January.	February.	March.	April.	May.	June.	July.	August.	September.	October.	November.	December.	White.	Colored.	Grooms.	Brides.	Grooms.	Brides.	Grooms.	Brides.	
Wabash	18	22	23	17	11	24	5	24	19	16	34	20	232	1	231	230	1	2	1	1	233
Warren	5	11	10	6	3	4	8	4	8	3	11	16	89	.....	87	87	2	2	.....	.....	89
Warrick	15	15	16	8	14	18	23	17	22	17	22	21	206	2	208	208	.....	.....	.....	.....	208
Washington	11	9	16	7	3	16	4	10	16	14	18	29	153	.....	153	153	.....	.....	.....	.....	153
Wayne	27	23	26	32	27	41	31	35	42	45	50	44	394	29	415	413	8	6	.....	4	423
Wells	17	17	17	23	10	22	13	23	14	20	24	10	210	.....	209	210	1	.....	.....	.....	210
White	13	27	14	15	10	13	8	11	9	8	10	13	151	.....	150	150	1	1	.....	.....	151
Whitley	11	5	9	10	9	11	6	8	12	16	19	13	129	.....	129	129	.....	.....	.....	.....	129
Grand Total	2,165	2,002	2,087	2,296	1,940	2,926	2,149	2,351	2,587	2,960	2,841	2,806	27,971	1,139	27,065	27,414	1,805	1,424	240	272	29,110

TABLE E.

Marriages, Grouped Ages, for the Year Ending December 31, 1910.

COUNTIES.	Under 20.		20 to 30.		30 to 40.		40 to 50.		50 to 60.		60 to 70.		70 to 80.		80 and Over.		Not Reported.		Total.
	Grooms.	Brides.	Grooms.	Brides.	Grooms.	Brides.	Grooms.	Brides.	Grooms.	Brides.	Grooms.	Brides.	Grooms.	Brides.	Grooms.	Brides.	Grooms.	Brides.	
Adams	7	37	135	127	39	23	8	3	1				1	1					191
Allen	7	140	621	579	169	111	46	36	22	14	15	5	4	1	1		3	2	888
Bartholomew	7	55	159	135	36	25	17	13	10	7	6	4	5	1					240
Benton	1	21	82	70	15	9	4	1										1	102
Blackford	12	74	105	71	29	14	9	6	4	2	1		1				15	9	176
Boone	7	57	135	112	41	19	12	9	1	1	4	5	3	1	1				204
Brown	4	32	52	27	14	4	2	1										8	72
Carroll	5	40	124	109	24	11	8	5	3	1	1	2	3						168
Cass	3	83	285	245	76	53	24	12	7	4	3		1	1				1	399
Clark	22	549	997	800	194	116	68	39	20	8	9	2	3				5	4	1,318
Clay	6	78	198	154	43	21	13	12	9	8	5	3	1	1	1		2	1	278
Clinton	19	80	160	125	34	27	15	8	11	5	4	1	2				2	1	247
Crawford	43	44	22	23	10	11	11	9	5	4	1	1							92
Daviess	12	69	163	131	36	22	15	10	11	7	4	3	1						242
Dearborn	2	26	113	129	61	31	12	9	7	5	4		1	1			1		201
Decatur	5	37	94	81	21	9	7	3	3	5	5	1	1	1			1		137
Dekalb	6	62	158	133	43	14	9	13	7	5	5	3	2						230
Delaware	17	162	403	311	84	71	44	24	24	8	8	6	2				1	1	583
Dubois	6	52	118	87	24	10	3	7	5	4	7	3							163
Elkhart	7	93	309	277	74	45	21	19	26	22	15	3	2	1	1		9	4	464
Fayette	4	24	62	55	19	10	4	1	3	1								1	92
Floyd	5	83	204	160	53	54	38	14	9	4	5	2	4	1			5	5	323
Fountain	6	44	113	97	34	20	12	8	6	2			2	1				1	173
Franklin	1	17	77	74	19	11	6	2	3	3	1								107
Fulton	2	37	110	93	26	16	8	3	7	7	5			1	2	1		2	160

TABLE E—Continued.

COUNTIES.	Under 20.		20 to 30.		30 to 40.		40 to 50.		50 to 60.		60 to 70.		70 to 80.		80 and Over.		Not Reported.		Total.
	Grooms.	Brides.	Grooms.	Brides.	Grooms.	Brides.	Grooms.	Brides.	Grooms.	Brides.	Grooms.	Brides.	Grooms.	Brides.	Grooms.	Brides.	Grooms.	Brides.	
[illegible]	3	63	174	145	43	16	6	6	6	3	2	2	1	......	......	......	......	......	235
[illegible]	15	121	371	306	63	46	23	23	15	12	14	5	4	1	......	......	3	......	514
Grant	16	136	253	171	48	22	13	7	9	2	1	1	1	......	......	......	1	3	342
Hamilton	11	71	193	158	36	19	19	13	10	9	3	2	3	3	2	......	......	2	277
[illegible]	6	42	99	80	30	15	5	6	4	1	1	......	......	1	......	......	......	......	145
Harrison	5	29	86	83	25	11	9	4	6	7	6	2	......	......	......	......	......	1	137
Hendricks	2	30	74	71	38	22	11	6	1	......	4	......	......	1	......	......	......	......	130
Henry	8	83	206	160	56	37	17	16	11	11	7	4	5	2	......	......	3	......	313
Howard	9	89	245	187	48	41	28	25	16	13	8	4	5	1	1	......	......	......	360
[illegible]	6	63	204	190	59	28	16	9	10	9	8	7	4	1	......	......	......	......	307
[illegible]	4	71	160	118	28	13	10	6	5	2	3	2	3	2	1	......	......	......	214
Jasper	3	20	72	60	19	8	6	1	......	1	1	......	......	......	......	......	......	2	101
Jay	6	77	181	138	42	19	11	8	5	6	6	4	......	......	......	......	3	2	254
Jefferson	14	99	164	120	49	22	14	9	11	4	2	......	......	......	......	......	......	......	254
Jennings	6	39	81	67	24	15	10	4	5	1	......	......	1	......	......	......	1	2	128
Johnson	5	52	123	85	16	11	6	5	5	3	2	......	......	......	......	......	......	1	157
Knox	26	186	356	276	110	60	44	23	16	11	4	......	1	......	......	......	2	3	559
Kosciusko	21	85	165	126	32	15	11	9	7	5	7	5	3	1	......	......	......	......	246
Lagrange	5	41	114	93	18	14	12	4	3	1	1	1	1	......	......	......	......	......	154
Lake	7	283	1,011	994	460	339	242	146	55	25	24	10	......	......	......	......	2	4	1,801
Laporte	7	90	317	292	120	84	40	36	22	6	5	3	......	......	......	......	......	......	511
[illegible]	11	95	185	129	43	33	25	15	8	4	3	......	2	1	......	......	......	......	277
[illegible]	22	180	432	352	136	80	45	47	32	21	21	7	3	3	......	......	5	6	696
Marion	78	629	2,056	1,868	633	417	220	151	98	52	40	15	11	......	......	......	4	8	3,140
Marshall	7	54	143	118	32	24	15	8	9	5	2	......	......	......	......	......	6	5	214
Martin	7	42	79	56	13	6	3	2	3	4	2	......	3	......	......	......	......	......	110
Miami	27	91	187	160	50	24	18	18	12	5	2	......	2	3	2	......	1	......	301
[illegible]	17	106	159	110	42	22	17	11	10	7	8	2	6	1	......	......	1	1	260
Mntgomery	4	63	181	154	49	35	20	11	11	4	4	1	......	......	......	......	1	2	270
Morgan	18	80	121	82	30	11	7	4	4	1	1	......	......	......	......	......	1	4	182

Newton	4	17	48	45	11	3	3	1	1	1	1	1	......	......	......	......	......	......	68
Noble	14	70	145	112	32	13	14	7	3	5	2	1	1	......	......	......	......	3	211
Ohio	1	8	25	27	9	3	2	......	1	......	......	......	......	......	......	......	......	......	38
Orange	4	27	103	96	25	22	13	7	10	6	3	2	2	......	......	......	......	......	160
Owen	3	23	65	53	5	3	7	5	5	4	3	1	2	1	......	......	3	3	93
Parke	3	55	129	97	19	10	10	7	6	3	6	1	1	1	......	......	......	......	174
Perry	3	24	88	87	29	19	6	4	5	1	2	2	2	......	1	......	5	4	141
Pike	22	70	120	93	23	14	12	11	11	5	5	......	......	......	......	......	1	1	194
Porter	1	23	128	135	46	29	17	7	5	4	3	3	1	......	......	......	1	1	202
Posey	5	95	204	141	48	30	9	6	11	6	1	......	......	......	......	......	2	2	280
Pulaski	......	21	85	76	14	8	8	7	3	2	2	1	1	......	......	......	2	......	115
Putnam	13	54	131	114	31	17	15	9	7	1	2	1	1	......	......	......	1	5	201
Randolph	12	73	185	145	33	21	9	9	7	3	6	2	......	......	1	......	......	......	253
Ripley	3	30	78	63	22	21	12	5	5	3	2	1	2	1	......	......	......	......	124
Rush	5	34	87	70	21	13	4	6	7	3	2	......	......	......	......	......	......	......	126
Scott	1	16	45	38	19	12	4	3	1	3	2	......	......	......	......	......	......	......	72
Shelby	9	60	182	159	46	28	18	14	6	2	3	3	2	......	......	......	......	......	266
Spencer	8	83	205	140	47	29	15	11	11	5	......	......	2	......	......	......	1	1	289
Starke	2	25	57	39	16	11	1	3	1	1	2	......	......	......	......	......	......	......	79
Steuben	3	21	94	94	21	12	16	6	3	5	5	2	......	......	......	......	......	2	142
St. Joseph	13	166	643	581	175	110	50	42	23	12	10	8	6	3	1	1	3	1	924
Sullivan	18	133	231	150	46	22	19	14	6	4	5	3	2	1	......	......	......	......	327
Switzerland	......	8	38	39	12	7	5	3	4	3	1	......	......	......	......	......	......	......	60
Tippecanoe	7	70	236	228	82	48	25	20	16	10	12	2	3	2	......	......	1	2	382
Tipton	17	64	136	102	23	13	5	3	2	3	1	2	3	......	......	......	......	......	187
Union	1	13	33	23	6	5	2	2	2	1	2	1	......	......	......	......	......	1	46
Vanderburgh	22	240	777	676	186	120	72	51	35	17	8	1	8	......	......	......	6	9	1,114
Vermillion	6	59	116	67	18	19	8	5	3	......	......	1	......	......	......	......	......	......	151
Vigo	77	391	811	625	217	144	100	60	24	15	9	7	8	2	......	......	10	12	1,256
Wabash	5	41	151	144	41	26	13	9	8	5	8	4	3	1	......	......	4	3	233
Warren	7	37	61	39	12	5	2	5	5	2	2	1	......	......	......	......	......	......	89
Warrick	9	59	134	113	40	21	8	4	5	3	6	2	2	......	......	......	4	6	208
Washington	16	72	91	61	31	11	8	6	3	1	4	2	......	......	......	......	......	......	153
Wayne	5	93	292	242	75	53	32	23	9	9	7	2	2	......	......	......	1	1	423
Wells	19	58	136	125	36	12	8	7	4	7	6	1	......	......	......	......	1	......	210
White	4	46	109	88	24	10	8	4	4	1	1	1	1	1	......	......	......	......	151
Whitley	4	27	101	76	18	17	5	3	1	2	......	......	......	......	......	......	......	4	129
Grand total	938	7,512	9,491	6,186	5,175	3,227	1,904	1,289	876	520	434	180	153	46	15	2	124	148	29,110

INDEX.

A.

Page
djourned Meeting of State Board of Health.......................... 36
dulteration of Food in Indiana by Percentage for 1910—
Dairy Products—
Butter 226
Legal 227
Illegal 228
Cream 224
Illegal 225
Milk 222
Milk Analysis by Cities and Towns...................... 222
Illegal 223
Baking Powder 254
Catsup 232
Composition of Home-made Non-preserved Catsup............ 233
Table Showing Composition of Same Brands with and without Benzoate 235
Legal 237
Illegal 237
Carbonated Summer Drinks................................. 263
Sodas 263
Illegal 263
Cider Vinegar 246
Legal 247
Illegal 248
Distilled Vinegar 249
Legal 250
Illegal 251
Uncolored Distilled Vinegar—Legal....................... 251
Flour 231
Legal 231
Illegal 231
Flavoring Extracts 266
Fruit Ciders 268
Illegal 268
Lemon Extract 266
Vanilla Extract 266
Legal 267
Illegal 267
Miscellaneous Flavors 266
Illegal 267

Adulteration of Food in Indiana by Percentage for 1910—Cont'd. Page

Fruit Products 255
Jelly 256
Legal 256
Illegal 256
Jam 256
Legal 256
Illegal 256
Fruit Butters and Canned Fruits 257
Legal 257
Illegal 257
Honey 255
Ice Cream 229
Legal 229
Lard 229
Legal 230
Illegal 231
Maple Sugar 242
Maple Syrup 241
Legal 241
Illegal 242
Miscellaneous 252
Mothers' Milk 225
Pickled Products 252
Pickles 254
Legal 254
Illegal 254
Pickled Onions 253
Legal 253
Illegal 253
Miscellaneous Food Stuffs 265
Mince Meat 266
Prepared Meats 245
Illegal 245
Classification 245
Prepared Mustard 252
Legal 252
Illegal 252
Oysters 244
Legal 244
Illegal 244
Sausage 244
Illegal 245
Spices 251
Spirituous Liquors 257
Whisky 257
Legal 257
Illegal 257

Adulteration of Food in Indiana by Percentage for 1910—Cont'd. Page
Temperance Beers 258
Legal 258
Illegal 258
Syrup 258
Alum in Pickles 244
..... 127

B.

Bruce Lake 70

C.

Condemnation Extended 43
District No. 1—Hensley Township, Johnson County 43
Conference with Bakers 97
Brief of Mr. Hornbrook, Attorney for Bakers 97
Conference of State Board of Health Officers—Annual 105
Program 105
Committee Representing Butchers 142
Communication from Mr. Barnard 152
Contents of Report of State Board of Health 6

D.

Doings and Investigations of State Board of Health 6

E.

Employes of State Board of Health 5
Epidemics 8
Examination of Health Officers 46
Examination Papers—Action Taken 41
Expense of State Board of Health 22
Expense of Pure Food and Drugs 32

F.

Financial Statement 16
State Board of Health, October 1, 1909–September 30, 1910 16
Recapitulation 22
Appropriation 22
Expense 22
Laboratory of Hygiene, October 1, 1909–September 30, 1910 23
Pure Food and Drug Laboratory 28
Recapitulation 28
Expense 28
Water Laboratory 33

H.

Page

Health Law 12
Hygiene in Public Schools.. 10
Hygiene—On Steam Cars 141

I.

Indiana State Board of Health—
Contents of Report 5
Doings and Investigations 6
Employes 5
Epidemics 8
Health Law 12
Letter of Transmittal 4
Organization 5
Pollution of Streams, Water Supplies and Sewers.. 11
Prevention of Blindness 12
Pure Food and Drug Law.. 14
Rabies 13
Recommendations 10
Sanitary Schoolhouses, Examination of School Children and Teaching Hygiene in Public Schools.. 10
Sanitary Work 7
State Laboratory of Hygiene.. 9
Vital Statistics 6
Weights and Measures 14
Inspection of Public School Houses—
Acton, Franklin Township, Marion County.. 129
Algiers, Jefferson Township, Pike County.. 108
Covington 72
Crawfordsville High School 92
Daleville 84
District No. 3, Castleton, Lawrence Township, Marion County... 127
District No. 9, Center Township, Gibson County.. 88
District No. 2, Decker Township, Knox County.. 75
District No. 5, Harrison Township, Miami County.. 133
District No. 3, Fairview Township, Fayette County.. 142
District No. 2, Hortonville, Washington Township, Hamilton Co.. 78
District No. 1, Jefferson Township, Jay County.. 81
District No. 2, Jefferson Township, Putnam County.. 82
District No. 9, Center Township, Vigo County.. 89
District No. 2, Patoka Township, Crawford County.. 144
District No. 4, Pierson Township, Vigo County.. 87
District No. 8, Prairie Township, Warren County.. 110
District No. 6, Washington Township, Pike County.. 130
District No. 1, Ward Township, Randolph County.. 113
District No. 9, West River Township, Randolph County.. 143
Emison District No. 8, Busseron Township, Knox County.. 74
Howe 59

Inspection of Public School Houses—Continued. Page
Middleburg, Harrison Township, Clay County.................... 86
Mongo, Lagrange County 143
Monroe City, Harrison Township, Knox County................. 76
Mt. Vernon 62
Muncie High School 105
New Bethel, Franklin Township, Marion County................ 73
Prairie Creek, Vigo County................................. 91
School No. 15, Pipe Creek Township, Madison County.......... 77
No. 1, District No. 4, Wayne Township, Henry County......... 71
Southport, Perry Township, Marion County.................... 135
South Ward Schoolhouse, Crown Point, Lake County............ 114
Urbana 80
Wallace 111
Winslow, Patoka Township, Pike County...................... 108

L.

Law of Health 12
Law of Pure Food and Drugs................................. 28
Letter from Markle—
Extension of Proclamation of Schoolhouse.................... 71
Letter from North Grove—
Proclamation of Condemnation Asked for and Granted for District No. 5.. 141
Letter of Transmittal to Governor Marshall.................. 4

M.

Medical Examination of School Children...................... 10
Meeting (Joint) of the Ohio River Sanitary Commission at Columbus, Ohio 53
Meetings of the Board—
Regular Meeting, Quarter ending September 30, 1909 38
Regular Meeting, Quarter ending December 31, 1909 46
Regular Meeting, Quarter ending March 31, 1910 63
Regular Meeting, Quarter ending June 30, 1910 137
Regular Meeting, Quarter ending September 30, 1910.......... 145
Special Meeting 44
Special Meeting 45
Special Meeting 59
Special Meeting 61
Special Meeting 96
Special Meeting 97
Special Meeting 115

N.

Notice to Bakers 94
Notice to Butchers and Meat Shop Proprietors................ 94

O.

Page

Opinion of Bakers and Grocers—Wrapping of Bread—Inspectors Bruner, Owen and Tucker....123
Organization of State Board of Health.... 5
Owen Bill 70

P.

Pollution of Streams, Water Supplies and Sewers.... 11
Prevention of Blindness 12
Proclamation of Condemnation of Schoolhouses—
Acton, Franklin Township, Marion County.... 130
Algiers, Jefferson Township, Pike County.... 108
Central School Building, Mt. Vernon, Posey County.... 62
Covington, Franklin County 93
Daleville, Delaware County 86
District No. 3, Castleton, Lawrence Township, Marion County.... 128
District No. 2, Decker Township, Knox County.... 75
District No. 3, Fairview Township, Fayette County.... 143
District No. 5, Harrison Township, Miami County.... 134
District No. 2, Hortonville, Washington Township, Hamilton County 80
District No. 1, Jefferson Township, Jay County 82
District No. 2, Jefferson Township, Putnam County 83
District Nos. 1 and 2, Medina Township, Warren County.... 90
District No. 2, Patoka Township, Crawford County.... 145
District No. 4, Pierson Township, Vigo County.... 88
District No. 8, Prairie Township, Warren County.... 110
District No. 7, Ward Township, Randolph County.... 113
District No. 6, Washington Township, Pike County.... 130
District No. 9, West River Township, Randolph County.... 144
Emison District No. 8, Busseron Township, Knox County.... 75
Francisco District No. 9, Center Township, Gibson County.... 89
Galveston, Cass County 94
Monroe City, Harrison Township, Clay County.... 87
Mongo, Springfield Township, Lagrange County.... 133
Muncie High School 107
No. 15, Pipe Creek Township, Madison County.... 78
No. 1, District No. 4, Wayne Township, Henry County.... 72
Orleans, Orange County 93
Prairie Creek, Prairie Creek Township, Vigo County.... 92
Southport, Perry Township, Marion County....136
South Ward Schoolhouse, Crown Point, Lake County.... 115
Urbana, Wabash County 81
Winslow, Patoka Township, Pike County.... 108
Pure Food and Drug Law.... 28

R.

	Page
Rabies	13
Recapitulation of State Board of Health—	
Appropriations	22
Expense	22
Recapitulation of Pure Food and Drugs—	
Expense	32
Recommendations	10
Recommendations	55
Regular Meeting, Quarter ending September 30, 1909	38
Regular Meeting, Quarter ending December 31, 1909	46
Regular Meeting, Quarter ending March 31, 1910	63
Regular Meeting, Quarter ending June 30, 1910	137
Regular Meeting, Quarter ending September 30, 1910	145
Report of Secretary for Each Quarter	
Report of Dr. W. F. King—Special	148
Report of State Board of Health on Bread Wrapping and Distribution	150

S.

Sanitary Schoolhouses	10
Sanitary Work	7
Schools Condemned	71
Schools Condemned	105
Schools Condemned	127
Smallpox Comparison—For Third Quarter, 1909	40
Smallpox Comparison—For Fourth Quarter, 1909	53
Smallpox Comparison—For First Quarter, 1910	69
Smallpox Comparison—For Second Quarter, 1910	138
Smallpox Comparison—For Third Quarter, 1910	147
Special Meeting of Board of Health	44
Special Meeting of Board of Health	45
Special Meeting of Board of Health	59
Program	60
Conference with County Health Commissioners—	
Object—To Confer Together Concerning the Public Health Work.	60
Special Meeting	61
Special Meeting	96
Special Meeting	97
Special Meeting	115
State Laboratory of Hygiene	9
Tuberculosis Hospital—State	69
Typhoid Fever—Comparisons—	
For Third Quarter, 1909	40
For Fourth Quarter, 1909	53
For First Quarter, 1910	69
For Second Quarter, 1910	138
For Third Quarter, 1910	147

V.

Page
Visits by the Secretary...... 48
Visits by the Secretary..... 138
Visits by the Secretary..... 147
Visits by Dr. King..... 148
Vital Statistics 6

W.

Weights and Measures..... 14
Wrapping of Bread..... 115

CHEMICAL DEPARTMENT OF HYGIENE.

A.

Adulteration of Drugs by Percentage for 1910..... 269
Result of Analysis of Drug Samples..... 274
Fluid Extraction Hyoscyami—Fluid Extract of Hyoscyamus. 282
Fluidum Extractum Belladonae Florium—Fluid Extract of Belladonna leaves 282
Miscellaneous Drugs 285
Alcohol—Legal 285
Asthma Cure 285
Bay Rum 286
Beeswax 286
Bismuth Subnitrate—Legal 286
Carbolic Acid—Legal 286
Essence of Jamaica Ginger..... 286
Essence of Peppermint—Illegal..... 286
Glycerine—Legal 287
Lime Water—Legal 287
Potassium Nitrate—Commercial—Legal 287
Quinine Sulphate Capsules..... 287
Sweet Spirits of Nitrate—Illegal..... 287
Oleum Lini—Linseed Oil..... 275
Legal 275
Illegal 275
Oleum Olivae—Olive Oil..... 275
Oleum Ricini—Castor Oil..... 274
Legal 274
Spirits Camphorae—Spirits of Camphor..... 277
Legal 277
Illegal 278
Tinctura Arnicae—Tincture of Arnica..... 279
Legal 279

Adulteration of Drugs by Percentage for 1910—Continued. Page
Tinctura Ferri Ghloridi—Tincture of Iron.................. 281
Legal 281
Illegal 281
Tinctura Iodia—Tincture of Iodine.......................... 279
Legal 280
Illegal 280
Tinctura Opii Deodirati—Tincture of Deodorized Opium..... 284
Tinctura Opii—Laudanum 283
Tinctura Opii Camphorated—Paregoric 276
Legal 276
Illegal 277
Animal Parasites 187

B.

Baking Powder—Analysis 255
Beers—Temperance—Analysis 258
Bread—Comparison of Keeping Qualities of Wrapped and Unwrapped 324
Butter Analysis 226

C.

Calumet River 365
Calumet River District 374
Tables Nos. 1-49.....................................474-430
Cancer Deaths 504
Chart 1... 164
Hereditary Tuberculosis 164
Chart 1... 203
Showing Location of Boarding Houses at Bloomington............ 203
Chicago Sanitary District..................................... 358
Comparison of Keeping Qualities of Wrapped and Unwrapped Bread.. 324
Deaths—
Principal Causes for Last Ten Years—with Average.............. 466
Cancer—
Monthly Analysis for Disease's Prevalence............. 904
Diarrhœal Diseases—
Chart 14—By Months 490
Chart 15—Two Years and Over.......................... 490
Chart 16—By Ages 492
Diphtheria—
Chart 10—By Months 485
Chart 11—By Ages 485
Monthly Analysis for Diphtheria Deaths................ 486
Influenza—
Chart 17—By Months 494
Chart 18—By Ages 494
Measles—
Chart 19—By Months 495
Chart 20—By Ages 495

Deaths—Continued. Page

Pneumonia—

Chart 6—By Months 477

Chart 7—By Ages 477

Pulmonary Tuberculosis—

Chart 4—By Months 471

Chart 5—By Ages 471

Tuberculosis—

Chart 1........ 467

Chart 2—By Months 469

Chart 3—By Ages 469

Scarlet Fever—

Chart 12—By Months 488

Chart 13—By Ages 488

Smallpox—

Monthly Analysis for Smallpox Deaths........ 498

Typhoid Fever—

Chart 8—By Months 481

Chart 9—By Ages 481

Monthly Analysis for Typhoid Deaths........ 482

Violence—

Monthly Analysis for Violence Deaths........ 500

Diphtheria 166

At Anderson 197

At Kouts and Sandborn........ 199

At New Palestine........ 198

At Orphans' Home—Children's Home Society........ 199

Drugs—Miscellaneous—Analysis 285

E.

Epidemics—

School Inspection at Shelbyville........ 196

Diphtheria at Anderson 197

Diphtheria at Kouts and Sandborn........ 199

Diphtheria at New Palestine 198

Diphtheria at Orphans' Home—Children's Home Society........ 199

Typhoid Fever at Bloomington........ 200

Chart 1—Showing Location of Boarding Houses........ 203

Typhoid Fever at Thorntown, Boone County........ 204

Investigation 204

Typhoid Fever at Indiana Reform School for Boys........ 207

Investigation 207

Chart 2—Showing Number of Cases Reported Daily During Epidemic ....

Table 26—Showing Number of Cases of Fever Among Members of Each Company........ 208

Diagram of Grounds........ 210

Table 27—Showing Results of Fermentation Tests of Water.. 211

F.

Page
Flavoring Extracts—Analysis 266
Flour—Analysis 231
Fluid Extractum Hyoscyami—Analysis 282
Fluidum Extractum Belladonnae Florium—Analysis 282
Food Stuffs—Miscellaneous—Analysis 265
Fruit Butters and Canned Fruits—Analysis 257
Fruit Ciders—Analysis 268
Fruit Products—Jellies, Jams—Analysis 256

G.

Gonorrhea 173
Gonorrhea in Children 175
Grand Calumet 361

H.

Hippurii Acid Contents of Urine 315
Subjects 1–8 315–321
Honey—Analysis 255
Ice Cream—Analysis 329
Influence of Ingestion of Spices Upon the Excretion of Hippurii Acid. 312
Subjects 1–8—
Grams per Day—Catsup Diet 315–321
Influenza—Deaths 403
Inspection of Canneries by Cities for 1910—
Advance 333
Amboy 333
Anderson 333
Arcadia 333
Austin 334
Birdseye 334
Bloomington 334
Brownsburg 335
Bunker Hill 335
Carmack 335
Campbellsburg 335
Charlestown 335
Clay City 335
Clarks Hill 336
Columbus 336
Corydon 336
Crothersville 336
Daleville 336
Delphi 337
Duff 337
Dunreith 337
Eaton 337
Edinburg 337

Inspection of Canneries by Cities for 1910—Continued. Page

Elnora 337
Elwood 338
English 338
Evansville 338
Flora 338
Frankfort 338
Gaston 338
Henryville 338
Hope 338
Huntingburg 339
Indianapolis 339
Jamestown 340
Jeffersonville 340
Kempton 340
Kennard 340
Kokomo 340
Ladoga 341
Lapel 341
Lebanon 341
Leota 341
Marengo 341
Memphis 341
Muncie 341
Newburg 342
New Castle 342
Noblesville 342
Pekin 342
Peru 342
Pierceton 343
Plainville 343
Princeton 343
Salem 343
Scottsburg 343
Sellersburg 344
Seymour 344
Sharpsville 344
Shelbyville 344
Shirley 344
Spiceland 344
Swayzee 345
Terre Haute 345
Underwood 345
Vienna 345
Walkerton 346
Warsaw 346
Westfield 346
West Terre Haute 346
Windfall 346
Inspectors' Condemnation Report.... 309

Page
Investigation of Calumet River District 357
Chicago Sanitary District 358
Grand Calumet 361
Calumet River 365
Methods of Sewage Disposal 370
Investigation of Sewage Condition at Lapel 432
Investigation of Water Purification Plant for Valparaiso 454
Table 1—Chemical Report 459
Table 2—Water Pumped and Used 459
Bacterial Report 460
Investigation of Typhoid Fever Epidemic—Indiana Reform School for Boys 207
Investigation of Typhiod Fever Epidemic—Thorntown, Boone County. 204

K.

Key to Sampling Points of Grand Calumet Location 372

L.

Lard Analysis 229
Letter from Indianapolis—
Mr. H. E. Barnard, State Food and Drug Commissioner 310
Letter from Terre Haute—
Unsanitary Condition of Terre Haute Paper Company 434
Liquors, Spiritous—Analysis 257
List of Prosecutions Under New Food and Drugs Law, from October 1, 1909, to October 1, 1910 291

M.

Malaria 173
Maple Syrup—Analysis 241
Mailing Outfits—
Complaint Against Specimens of Diseased Tissues Being Sent in the Mails in Improper Mailing Cases 213
Measles—Deaths 495
Meningitis 190
Methods of Sewage Disposal 370
Milk—Analysis by Cities and Towns 222
Miscellaneous Specimens 144
Mothers' Milk 225

N.

Notice of Condemnations—
Inspectors' Condemnation Report 309
Summary of Reports Issued During the Year 311

O.

Page
Observation on Lawful Methods for Determination of Sodium Benzoate in Catsups 322
Oleum Lini—Linseed Oil 275
Oleum Olivate—Olive Oil 275
Oleum Ricini—Castor Oil—Analysis 274
Oysters—Analysis 244

P.

Pathological Tissues and Autopsies 182
Pickled Products—Analysis 252
Pneumonia—
Deaths 476
Monthly Analysis 478
Private Water Supplies in Indiana 352
Condition 353
Prosecutions 288
Table Showing Business of Defendant and Cause for which Action was Brought 290
List of Prosecutions Brought Under New Food and Drugs Law from October 1, 1909, to October 1, 1910 291
Public Water Supplies in Indiana 351
Condition 351
Pulmonary Tuberculosis—Deaths 470

R

Rabies 180
Report—Fifth Annual—Department of Bacteriology and Pathology ... 157
Report of Chemical Department of Laboratory of Hygiene 217
Report from Drug Laboratory 270
Report from Food Laboratory 222
Report of Investigation of Water Supply at French Lick 431
Report of Inspection of Water Supply of Warsaw, Indiana 445
Present Pollution of the Lake 447
Report of Sanitary and Storm Water Sewage System for Vincennes, Indiana 452
Sanitary Sewer System 452
Storm Water System 453
Comment—Conclusion 453
Report of Second Investigation of Filtration Plant of Seymour Water Company, Seymour 436
Results Obtained During Investigation 440
Report on Statistics for 1910 462
Births 463
Marriages 463
Deaths 464
Report of Public Water Supplies 356
Report from Water Laboratory 349
Result of Analysis of Drug Samples 274
Result of Analysis of Food Samples 219

S

Page

Sanitary Conditions 372
Sausage—Analysis 245
Scarlet Fever—Deaths 487
Sewage Disposal—Methods 370
Spices—Analysis 252
Spirituus Camphoræ—Analysis 277
Smallpox—Deaths 497
Seymour Water Works, Seymour, Indiana 444
Daily Operation of the Plant 445
Statistical Report of Laboratory of Hygiene for 1910—
Births 463
Marriages 463
Deaths 464
Table 1—Causes of Death 508
Table 2—Deaths—International Classification 513
Table 3—Deaths by Ages, Sex, Nationality 538
Table 4—Deaths by Counties 566
Table 5—Death Rate by Counties 570
Table 6—Deaths by Cities 574
Table 7—Death Rate by Cities 578
Table 8—Annual Death Rates 582
Table 9—Deaths by Occupation 583
Table 10—Deaths from Tuberculosis 597
Table 11—Poliomyelitis by Months, Ages and Counties 599
Table A—Births by Months, Nationality of Parents 601
Table B—Numuber of Children Born to Each Mother 604
Table C—Marriages by Months, Nationality 611
Table E—Marriages—Grouped Ages 615
Syrups—Analysis 243

T

Table 1—Comparison of Work for Last Three Years 157
Table 2—Specimens of Sputum Examined by Months 160
Table 3—Specimens of Sputum from Each Counuty 161
Table 4—Age and Sex of Cases 162
Table 5—Tuberculosis in Various Periods of Life 163
Table 6—Relation of Exposure to Tuberculosis 163
Table 7—Relation of Tuberculosis Members of Family to Patient... 165
Table 8—Number of Throat Culture Received Each Month 166
Table 9—Number of Throat Culture from Each County 167
Table 10—Age and Sex of First Culture Cases 168
Table 11—Bacteriological Diagnosis 168
Table 12—Percentage Relation of Bacteriological to Clinical Diagnosis 168
Table 13—Relation of Membrane to Bacteriological Findings 169
Table 14—Relation of Exposure to Development of Diphtheria 170
Table 15—Widal Reaction by Months 171
Table 16—Number of Widal Tests from Counties 172

Lightning Source UK Ltd.
Milton Keynes UK
UKHW012035070119
335138UK00011B/551/P